TimeOut

Barcelona

timeout.com/barcelona

Penguin Books

PENGUIN BOOKS

Published by the Penguin Group
Penguin Books Ltd, 80 Strand, London WC2R ORL, England
Penguin Group (USA) Inc., 375 Hudson Street, New York, New York 10014, USA
Penguin Books Australia Ltd, 250 Camberwell Road, Camberwell, Victoria 3124, Australia
Penguin Books Canada Ltd, 10 Alcorn Avenue, Toronto, Ontario, Canada M4V 3B2
Penguin Books (NZ) Ltd, cnr Rosedale and Airborne Roads, Albany, Auckland, New Zealand

Penguin Books Ltd, Registered Offices: Harmondsworth, Middlesex, England

First published 1996
Second edition 1998
Third edition 2000
Fourth edition 2001
Fifth edition 2002

Sixth edition 2003
10 9 8 7 6 5 4 3 2 1

Copyright © Time Out Group Ltd 1996, 1998, 2000, 2001, 2002, 2003
All rights reserved

Colour reprographics by Icon, Crowne House, 56-58 Southwark Street, London SE1 1UN
Printed and bound by Cayfosa-Quebecor, Ctra. de Caldes, Km 3 08 130 Sta, Perpètua de Mogoda, Barcelona, Spain

Edited and designed by
Time Out Guides Limited
Universal House
251 Tottenham Court Road
London W1T 7AB
Tel + 44 (0)20 7813 3000
Fax + 44 (0)20 7813 6001
Email guides@timeout.com
www.timeout.com

Editorial

Editor Sally Davies
Deputy Editor Christi Daugherty
Listings Editors Belinda Walberg, Nuria
  Rodriguez, Cecily Doyle
Copy Editor Lily Dunn
Proofreaders Tamsin Shelton, Ros Sales
Indexer Jackie Brind

Editorial Director Peter Fiennes
Series Editor Ruth Jarvis
Deputy Series Editor Jonathan Cox
Guides Co-ordinator Anna Norman

Design

Group Art Director John Oakey
Art Director Mandy Martin
Art Editor Scott Moore
Senior Designer Tracey Ridgewell
Designers Astrid Kogler, Sam Lands
Digital Imaging Dan Conway
Ad Make-up Glen Impey
Picture Editor Kerri Littlefield
Acting Picture Editor Kit Burnet
Acting Deputy Picture Editor Martha Houghton
Picture Desk Trainee Bella Wood

Advertising

Group Commercial Director Lesley Gill
Sales Director Mark Phillips
International Sales Manager Ross Canadé
Advertisement Sales (Barcelona) Creative Media Group
Advertising Assistant Sabrina Ancilleri

Administration

Chairman Tony Elliott
Chief Operating Officer Kevin Ellis
Managing Director Mike Hardwick
Group Financial Director Richard Waterlow
Group Marketing Director Christine Cort
Marketing Manager Mandy Martinez
US Publicity & Marketing Associate Rosella Albanese
Group General Manager Nichola Coulthard
Guides Production Director Mark Lamond
Production Controller Samantha Furniss
Accountant Sarah Bostock

Features in this guide were written and researched by

Introduction Sally Davies. **History** Nick Rider (*The serenos* Nadia Feddo). **Barcelona Today** William Truini (*Talking a dying language* Matthew Tree; *Barcelona by numbers* Sally Davies). **Architecture** Nick Rider. **Modernisme** Nick Rider (*On the tiles* Jeffrey Swartz). **Accommodation** Amber Ockrassa, Juliet King. **Sightseeing: Introduction** Sally Davies. **Barri Gòtic** Sally Davies (*How to: Dance the Sardana* Nadia Feddo). **Raval** Jeffrey Swartz (*How to: hold on to your wallet* Sally Davies). **Sant Pere & the Born** Sally Davies (*1714 and all that* Jonathan Bennett). **Barceloneta & the Ports** Jonathan Bennett (*Colonic denigration* Daniel Campi). **Montjuïc** Jeffrey Swartz. **The Eixample** Daniel Campi (*The last great temple* Jeffrey Swartz). **Gràcia & Other Districts** Sally Davies (*The man with the plan* Adam de Havenon; *Top ten works of street art* Jeffrey Swartz). **Restaurants** Sally Davies (*Treading a fine wine* Richard Neill; *Eating by design* Jeffrey Swartz). **Cafés & Bars** Sally Davies (*Dens of yore* Adam de Havenon). **Shops & Services** Nadia Feddo (*I should cocoa* Adam de Havenon). **Festivals & Events** Nadia Feddo. **Children** Nadia Feddo. **Film** Jonathan Bennett (*It's the reel thing* Rob Stone). **Galleries** Jeffrey Swartz. **Gay & Lesbian** Simon Chappell. **Music** *Classical & Opera* Jonathan Bennett; *Rock, Roots & Jazz* Kirsten Foster. **Nightlife** Tara Stevens, Nick Chapman. **Sport & Fitness** Robert Southon (*How to: be a Barça fan* Daniel Campi). **Theatre & Dance** *Theatre* Jeffrey Swartz; *Dance* Nuria Rodriguez. **Trips Out of Town: Getting Started** Sally Davies. **Around Barcelona** Sarah Andrews. **Tarragona & the Costa Daurada** Sally Davies (*The Wine Country* Sarah Andrews). **Girona & the Costa Brava** Sally Davies. **Vic to the Pyrenees** Sally Davies (*Besalú & Olot* Sarah Andrews; *Berga & Puigcerdà* Tara Stevens). **Directory** Nuria Rodriguez, Amber Ockrassa, Adam de Havenon, Sally Davies.

The Editor would like to thank: Agustí Argelich, Albert Folch, Alfonso Blanco, Andrew Dillon, Antoni Espanya, Cath Phillips, Dante Battistella, DJ Xocoa, Esther Jones, Inés Martinez, John O'Donovan, Jordi Falgas, Maria Mena, Marti Guixé, Montse Planas, Montse Pozo, Nati Paloma, Nick Rider, Roca Pujol, Steven Guest, Tara Stevens, Verònica Mas, William Truini.

Maps by Mapworld, 71 Blandy Road, Henley on Thames, Oxon RG9 1QB, and JS Graphics (john@jsgraphics.co.uk).

Photography by Alys Tomlinson except: pages 7, 15 and 16 AKG London; page 26 AFP; pages 75, 211, 215 and 217 Oriol Tarridas; page 138 Heloise Bergman; page 149 Xavier Cervera; pages 39, 98, 213, 294 and 295 Sally Davies; page 280 Art Directors and TRIP; page 255 Jordi Roses; page 288 Manuel Segura; page 291 Corbis; pages 297 and 298 Jonathan Cox.

The following images were provided by the featured establishments/artists: pages 10, 18, 23, 24, 25, 220, 273, 292.

Contents

Introduction   2

In Context   5

History   7
Barcelona Today   29
Architecture   33
Modernisme   39

Accommodation   45

Accommodation   46

Sightseeing   71

Introduction   72
Barri Gòtic   75
Raval   86
Sant Pere & the Born   92
Barceloneta & the Ports   99
Montjuïc   104
The Eixample   111
Gràcia & Other Districts   119

Eat, Drink, Shop   133

Restaurants   134
Cafés & Bars   165
Shops & Services   181

Arts & Entertainment   209

Festivals & Events   210
Children   219
Film   223
Galleries   227
Gay & Lesbian   231
Music   238
Nightlife   247
Sport & Fitness   263
Theatre & Dance   269

Directory   301

Getting Around   302
Resources A-Z   307
Catalan Vocabulary   321
Spanish Vocabulary   322
Further Reference   323
Index   324

Trips Out of Town   275

Getting Started   276
Around Barcelona   277
Tarragona & the Costa Daurada   282
Map: Tarragona   283
Girona & the Costa Brava   289
Map: Girona   289
Vic to the Pyrenees   296

Maps   331

Trips Out of Town   332
Around Barcelona   333
Street Index   334
Street Maps   337
RENFE Local Trains   346
Metro   347
Barcelona Areas   348

Introduction

Among all the hoary old clichés trotted out by guidebook writers when adequate words escape them, you will hear that Barcelona (not to mention Madrid, Berlin, London, Rome and indeed most others) is 'a city of contradictions'. The discerning reader will recognise this hackneyed twaddle for what it is.

No, Barcelona's just a regular city, like any other. A regular, ardently Europhile, forward-thinking and progressive city, which falls over itself to impress blue-chip companies with its business acumen... not to mention its peculiar language, parades of giants, gingerbread houses, scatological Christmas customs, *sardana* dancing, Lenten sardine-burying and human castles.

Really a very ordinary city, whose citizens have an unbounded zeal for new technology, and most especially mobile phones and the internet, but are utterly reluctant to deal with strangers any other way but face to face. Ordinary Catholic citizens with the second lowest birth-rate in the world, who are, incidentally, devoutly loyal to their patron saint (St George, after whom they name their sons) but only really fascinated by his dragon, whose tiled, carved, bejewelled and wrought-iron incarnations are found all over town.

A perfectly normal if proud and flashy city, keen to hold the world in thrall with its designer nous and immaculate grooming, whose astounding monuments are allowed to be trampled on, lived in and taken for granted as part of the urban fabric. Ragged merry drunks are free to regale passers-by from the feet of Gaudí's lamp-posts; kids swarm over his benches; concerts take place almost nightly within the fantastical, delirious Palau de la Música and skateboarders get to claim Richard Rogers' MACBA forecourt as their own. Many of the *really* fabulous buildings become the property of the old and the sick, like the spectacular Hospital de Sant Pau, the Hospital del Mar taking up prime real estate on the beach and the elaborate Modernista old people's homes and *farmàcias* everywhere. And why shouldn't they?

City of contradictions. Pah.

ABOUT THE TIME OUT CITY GUIDES

The *Time Out Barcelona Guide* is one of an expanding series of Time Out City Guides produced by the people behind London and New York's successful listings magazines. Our guides are all written and updated by resident experts who have striven to provide you with all the most up-to-date information you'll need to explore the city, whether you're a local or first-time visitor.

THE LOWDOWN ON THE LISTINGS

Above all, we've tried to make this book as useful as possible. Addresses, telephone numbers, websites, transport information, opening times, admission prices and credit card details are all included in our listings. And, as far as possible, we've given details of facilities, services and events, all checked and correct at the time we went to press. However, owners and managers can change their arrangements at any time, and often do. Many small shops and businesses in Barcelona do not keep precise opening hours and may close earlier or later than stated here. Similarly, arts programmes are often finalised very late, and liable to change. Before you go out of your way, we would advise you whenever possible to phone and check opening times, ticket prices and other particulars. While every effort has been made to ensure the accuracy of the information contained here, the publishers cannot accept responsibility for any errors it may contain.

PRICES AND PAYMENT

Prices throughout this guide are given in euros. The prices we've supplied should be treated as guidelines, not gospel. If they vary wildly from those we've quoted, please write and let us know. We aim to give the best and most up-to-date advice, so we always want to know if you've been badly treated or overcharged. Wherever possible we have factored in the sales tax (IVA), which many restaurants and hotels leave out of their advertised rates.

We have noted whether venues take credit cards but have only listed the major cards – American Express (**AmEx**), Diners Club (**DC**), MasterCard (**MC**) and Visa (**V**).

There is an online version of this guide, as well as weekly events listings for over 35 international cities, at **www.timeout.com**.

Many business will also accept other cards, including **JCB**. Some shops, restaurants and attractions take travellers' cheques.

THE LIE OF THE LAND
We have divided the city into areas – simplified, for convenience, from the full complexity of Barcelona's geography – and the relevant area name is given with each venue listed in this guide. For a map showing the different city areas and how they relate to our sightseeing chapters, *see p348*. Wherever possible, a map reference is provided for every venue listed, indicating the page and grid reference at which it can be found on the street maps.

TELEPHONE NUMBERS
It is necessary to dial provincial area codes with all numbers in Spain, even for local calls. Hence all normal Barcelona numbers begin 93, whether you're calling from inside or outside the city. From abroad, you must dial 34 (the international dialling code for Spain) followed by the number given in the book – which includes the initial 93. For more information on telephones and codes, *see p317*.

ESSENTIAL INFORMATION
For all the practical information you'll need for visiting the city – including emergency phone numbers, visa and customs information, advice on facilities for the disabled, emergency telephone numbers, a list of useful websites and the lowdown on the local transport network – turn to the **Directory** chapter at the back of this guide. It starts on page 302.

LANGUAGE
Barcelona is a bilingual city; street signs, tourist information and menus can be in either Catalan or Spanish, and this is reflected in the guide. We have tried to use whichever is more commonly used or appropriate in each case.

MAPS
The map section at the book includes some overviews of the greater Barcelona area and its neighbourhoods; detailed street maps of the Eixample, the Raval, Gràcia and other districts, and a scale map of the Old City, with a comprehensive street index; a large regional page map for planning trips out of town and maps of the local rail and metro networks. The maps start on page 333.

LET US KNOW WHAT YOU THINK
We hope you enjoy the *Time Out Barcelona Guide*, and we'd like to know what you think of it. We welcome tips for places that you consider we should include in future editions and take notice of your criticism of our choices. There's a reader's reply card at the back of this book – or you can email us at guides@timeout.com.

Advertisers

In Context

History 7
Barcelona Today 29
Architecture 33
Modernisme 39

Features

Hero worship 8
Sleazy does it 10
Protest city 18
The serenos 23
Key events 27
Barcelona by numbers 31
Talking a dying language 32
All that glitters 36
On the tiles 40
Don't miss Modernisme 42

Barcelona
Bus Turístic

Discover the most captivating Mediterranean city on board the Barcelona Bus Turístic.

✓ 2 sightseeing routes for the price of one.

✓ 25 stops at points of interest.

✓ Get on and off the Bus as you please! Combine both routes by changing buses at any of these 3 connecting stops: Plaça de Catalunya, Passeig de Gràcia - La Pedrera and Francesc Macià - Diagonal.

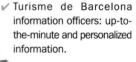

Route North
Red

Route South
Blue

✓ Turisme de Barcelona information officers: up-to-the-minute and personalized information.

✓ A comprehensive guide with detailed information about the sights and each of the stops.

AND THAT'S NOT ALL!

✓ A discount voucher booklet with savings of over 90 € on your visits.

On the Barcelona Bus Turístic you will find assistance, comfort and countless advantages.

ⓘ 010   **www.barcelonaturisme.com**   **www.tmb.net**

History

From counts and kings to Franco's fascism – you can say this for Barcelona: it's never been boring.

Life in Barcelona has never been a smooth and serene process. The city's tale is not a straightforward story of steady growth from small beginnings to wealth and status. Instead, it is a an epic in which the city has struggled from boom to disaster and back again to such an extent that the ebb and flow of its fortunes surely would have worn out a less stubborn town. This in part reflects Barcelona's peculiar status as the capital of a country, Catalonia, that has never been too steady in terms of its own existence. Catalonia, too, can recall both its time as a major European power and its years as nothing more than a disgruntled subdivision of a larger entity. Looking at just its first 1,000 years, you see that Barcelona seesawed between relative growth and severe decline, and faced repeated invasions from both the north and the south. This long and unstable beginning

affected its residents; leaving them with traditions and characteristics distinct from those elsewhere on the Iberian peninsula.

The Romans founded Barcelona in about 15 BC, on the Mons Taber, a small hill between two streams that provided a good view of the Mediterranean, and which today is crowned by the cathedral. The plain around it was sparsely inhabited by the Laetani, an agrarian Iberian people known for producing grain and honey and for gathering oysters. Named Barcino, the town was much smaller than Tarraco (Tarragona), the capital of the Roman province of Hispania Citerior, but had the only harbour, albeit a poor one, between there and Narbonne.

Like virtually every other Roman new town in Europe, Barcino was a fortified rectangle with a crossroads at its centre (where the Plaça Sant Jaume is today). It was an unimportant

Hero worship

Every country, for good or bad, has its warrior heroes. Standing out from the crowd in Catalonia's medieval golden age are two fierce commanders both called Roger: Roger de Llúria and Roger de Flor. Both were actually Italian by birth. Their Catalan connections came through the infinitely tangled struggle over southern Italy between the Crown of Aragon and the Angevin dynasty (headed by the Count of Anjou, a younger brother of the King of France).

ROGER DE LLURIA

Roger de Llúria (or Ruggiero di Loria, to Italians) was born in Basilicata, east of Naples, in about 1250. His mother was lady-in-waiting to Constanza, daughter of King Manfred of Sicily, and went with her to Catalonia, taking the 12-year-old Roger along, for the princess's wedding to Pere II of Aragon in 1262. Soon afterwards Manfred's kingdom was seized by Charles of Anjou, and the Catalan court became a refuge of sorts for Sicilian aristocrats. Roger de Llúria soon became a great friend of Pere II, who gave him enormous estates in Valencia. There he practised his military skills in a series of skirmishes with Muslim Granada. A few years later, in 1282, Pere II took advantage of an anti-French revolt in Sicily to attempt to reclaim his wife's kingdom. This move set off a ferocious war that ultimately pitted the

Crown of Aragon against the Angevins, France itself, some Italian states and even the Catholic Church.

De Llúria went with him, and discovered his talents as an admiral. His genius was in his ability to make a virtue of the weaknesses of the Catalan fleet: the Catalans were nearly always outnumbered, but rather than hide the fact he repeatedly ordered that they should attack at the riskiest point with the maximum ferocity, so that his opponents would panic and scatter – a tactic so reckless that hero-status was all but guaranteed. What's more, the ploy worked, and Roger won spectacular naval victories at Malta, Naples and, in his greatest exploit, off Roses in 1285, stopping single-handedly a full-scale French invasion.

Now equipped with a fearsome reputation, De Llúria carried on fighting, battering a variety of Christians as well as a few cities in North Africa until his death in 1305. Now officially a hero, he was buried amid the royal tombs at Santes Creus.

ROGER DE FLOR

Roger de Flor was less used to regal company, and never actually set foot in Catalonia. He was born a poverty-stricken minor aristocrat in Brindisi in 1268, and signed up aged 15 with the fleet of the Knights Templar, which fought to protect Christians against the Turks. Roger made

provincial town, but the rich plain provided it with a produce garden, and the sea gave it an incipient maritime trade. It acquired a Jewish community very soon after its foundation, and was associated with some Christian martyrs, notably Barcelona's first patron saint, Santa Eulàlia. She was supposedly executed at the end of the third century via a series of revolting tortures, including being rolled naked inside a sealed barrel full of glass shards down the alley now called Baixada (descent) de Santa Eulàlia.

Barcino did accept Christianity a short while afterwards, in AD 312, together with the rest of the Roman Empire, which by then was under growing threat of invasion. To that end, in the fourth century, the town's somewhat rough defences were replaced with massive stone walls, many sections of which can still be seen today. These ramparts ensured the city's continuity, by making it a stronghold much desired by later warlords. (For more on the relics of Roman Barcelona, *see chapter* **Barri Gòtic**.)

Nonetheless, its formidable defences could not prevent the empire's disintegration. In 415, Barcelona briefly became capital of the kingdom of the Visigoths, under their chieftain Ataülf. He brought with him as a prisoner Gala Placidia, the 20-year-old daughter of a Roman emperor, whom he forced into marriage. She is famous as a woman of strong character, and is credited with helping to convert the barbarian king to Christianity. She was, perhaps, fortunate in that Ataülf died shortly afterwards, and she left, married Emperor Constantius I, and became the most powerful figure in the court of Byzantium.

The Visigoths soon moved southwards from Barcelona to extend their control over the whole Iberian peninsula. For the next 400 years the town was a neglected backwater. It was in a shambles when the Muslims swept across the peninsula after 711, easily crushing Goth resistance. They made little attempt to settle Catalonia, but much of the Christian population retreated into the Pyrenees anyway.

a name for himself as a fighter, but he was accused of siphoning off booty destined for the Church, and so a papal order for his arrest was issued, and he fled. After making a living as a pirate, he arrived in Sicily in 1291, where he met up with the Almogàvers. These were his kindred spirits indeed – self-governing bands of Catalan soldiers who had gone to the island with Pere II in 1282. Roger soon fought his way to the top of their ladder, such as it was, and became their leader. With him in charge, in 1301 they won a major victory at Messina, which for a time forced the Pope to recognise the Catalan hold on Sicily and brought the wars to an end.

This, though, left the Almogàvers with nothing to do, and opened up the awkward possibility that the Church could pursue its old demand for Roger de Flor to be given up as a prisoner. To get the Almogàvers out of his way, Frederic, brother of Jaume II of Aragon and ruler of Sicily, suggested Roger and his men should offer their services to the Byzantine Emperor to fight the Turks, thus embarking them on the greatest legend of the Catalan Middle Ages – the Almogàvers' Greek adventure. Known as the Companyia Catalana or 'Catalan Company', they arrived in Constantinople in 1302, and in an epic two-year march around Asia Minor, although vastly outnumbered, they defeated the Turks

in battles that delayed for years further Muslim encroachments on Byzantium. They then returned to Constantinople expecting to be paid for their efforts. However, the unruly army was regarded with great suspicion (they had always combined some handy piracy and pilfering with their fighting), and negotiations dragged on until Roger de Flor was brutally assassinated at a banquet held in his honour by the Byzantine crown prince in 1305. Enraged at this treachery, the Almogàvers launched the *Venjança Catalana,* the 'Catalan Vengeance', pillaging European Turkey before marching south into Greece. They took Athens, and then carved out two independent duchies at Athens and Neopatria that would remain under Catalan rule until the 1390s.

Every hero needs a PR agent, and the two Rogers' foremost mouthpiece was Ramon Muntaner, who served under both of them and recounted their deeds in his *Chronicle of the 1320s* in such dramatic terms that they seemed to counterbalance De Llúria's frequent brutality and De Flor's greedy thieving. They and their lieutenants could then be rediscovered by the Romantic historians of Catalonia's 19th-century Renaixença in their quest to reconstruct a heroic past, and so they were at last enshrined in, among other places, the street names of Barcelona's Eixample.

Then, at the end of the eighth century, the Franks began to drive southwards against the Muslims from across the mountains. In 801, Charlemagne's son, Louis the Pious, took Barcelona and made it a bastion of the Marca Hispanica (Spanish March), the southern buffer of his father's empire. This gave Catalonia a trans-Pyrenean origin entirely different from that of the other Christian states in Spain; equally, it is for this reason that the closest relative of the Catalan language is Provençal, rather than the expected Castilian.

When the Frankish princes returned to their main business further north, loyal counts were left behind to rule sections of the Catalan lands. Around 885, one of these, Count Guifré el Pilós (that's Wilfred 'the Hairy' to you and me), succeeded in gaining title to several of the Catalan territories, in a kind of a power play. Because of that, his successors were able to make Barcelona their capital, thereby setting the seal on the city's future.

A century after Wilfred, in 985, a Muslim army attacked and sacked Barcelona. The hairy count's great-grandson, Count Borrell II, requested aid from his theoretical feudal lord, the Frankish king. He received no reply, and so repudiated all Frankish sovereignty over Catalonia. From then on – although the name was not yet in use – Catalonia was effectively independent, and the counts of Barcelona were free to forge its destiny.

FROM COUNTS TO KINGS

In the first century of the new millennium, Catalonia was consolidated as a political entity. The Catalan counties retained from their Frankish origins a French system of aristocratic feudalism – another difference from the rest of Iberia – but also had a peasantry who were notably independent and resistant to noble demands. And it was in the 1060s that the country's distinctive legal code, known as the Usatges, was established.

At around this same time, the devout counts of Barcelona and many lesser nobles as well, also endowed monasteries and churches throughout the region. These provided the background to glorious Romanesque art, in the form of structures such as the Sant Pere de Rodes near Figueres, and the superb murals in the Museu Nacional on Montjuïc. There was also a flowering of scholarship at that time, reflecting Catalan contacts with Islamic cultures. In Barcelona, shipbuilding and commerce in grain and wine expanded, and a new trade developed in textiles. The city grew both inside its old Roman walls and outside them, where *vilanoves* (new towns) appeared at Sant Pere and La Ribera.

Catalonia – a name that gained currency in Latin in the 11th century – was also gaining more territory from the Muslims to the south, beyond the Penedès. For a long time, though, the realm of the Counts of Barcelona continued to look just as much to the north, across the Pyrenees. After 1035, during the reigns of the four Counts Ramon Berenguer, large areas of what is now southern France were acquired, either through marriage or with Arab booty. In 1112, the union of Ramon Berenguer III 'the Great' (1093-1131) with Princess Dolça of Provence extended his authority as far as the Rhône. A more significant marriage occurred in 1137, when Ramon Berenguer IV (1131-62) wed Petronella, heir to the throne of Aragon. This

Sleazy does it

Barcelona's legendary low-life district, the Barrio Chino (or Barri Xinès), was long one of its most celebrated features, especially for foreigners. Even quite recently, no British or French journalist could visit Barcelona without mentioning at least one encounter with an over-the-top, Dolly Parton-coiffed transsexual prostitute on the lower Rambla. It was an essential part of the Barcelona mix, an extra dose of sauce, but the schemes and alterations of the 1990s have transformed this area maybe more completely than any other part of town: they may not have made it much more salubrious, but the old-style, spectacular Chino sleaze has been swept into history, to an extent that would have been unimaginable just a few years ago.

The Chino never had precise boundaries, but its core was the lower Raval, between C/Sant Pau and the sea. There were already brothels clustered around the Drassanes, then a barracks for soldiers and sailors, in the 1740s, and by the late 19th century it had more or less officially decided to tolerate (and so confine) prostitution within the lower Raval. Around the brothels there grew up a ragged assortment of bars, cabarets and gambling houses. The Chino really took off, though, with Barcelona's great boom during the World War I. Formerly penny-pinching Catalan manufacturers found themselves with money to burn, and they were in a hurry to try out forbidden pleasures. This was the great era of the opulent cabarets and dance halls along C/Nou de la Rambla, with the tango as the music of choice. Grandest of all was the Eden Concert (where the Hotel Gaudí now stands), where millionaires hob-nobbed with gangsters.

Barcelona was the favourite refuge from the war for drifters and low-lifes from all over Europe. By the 1920s, the Chino enjoyed a status similar to that of Marseille in the 1970s as the hub of drug-trafficking and most other illegal dealings around the Mediterranean. Around its big cabarets were scores of other venues of every size and catering to every taste: brothels from the luxurious to the wretched offering every kind of sexual practice stood alongside strip clubs, gay bars, illegal casinos, drag shows, porn publishers and drug dens. By the 1930s the epicentre of the Chino was the C/del Cid, site of the era's most famously on-the-edge cabaret, La Criolla.

There was always a fantasy aspect to go with the lurid realities. The spiralling growth in this underworld after 1914 was watched with a mix of horror and fascination by respectable Barcelona, which imagined all kinds of horrors. In 1925 journalist Francesc Madrid wrote a series of exposés of 'vice' in the wonderfully titled tabloid magazine *El Escándalo* and, inspired by a film he'd seen featuring white slavery in the Chinatown of San Francisco, first referred to these streets as being like a 'Barrio Chino'. Catalans, of course, like to be cosmopolitan, so the name soon caught on, even though the area had nothing Chinese about it. It soon became a tourist attraction, and visitors – including Cocteau and Hemingway – came down to take a look. One penniless Frenchman, Jean Genet, became part of the Chino himself, as Barcelona's most famous rent boy, and in his *Thief's Journal* wrote one of the classics of Chino literature.

would, in the long term, bind Catalonia into Iberia. The uniting of the two dynasties created a powerful entity known as the Crown of Aragon, each element retaining its separate institutions, and ruled by monarchs known as the count-kings. Since Aragon was already a kingdom, it was given precedence and its name was often used to refer to the state, but the court language was Catalan and the centre of government remained in Barcelona. At the beginning of the following century, however, the dynasty lost virtually all its lands north of the Pyrenees to France, when Count-King Pere I 'the Catholic' was killed at the battle of Muret in 1213. This was a blessing in disguise. In future, the Catalan-Aragonese state would be oriented

decisively towards the Mediterranean and the south, and was able to embark on two centuries of imperialism equalled in vigour only by Barcelona's growing commercial enterprise.

ALL THE KINGS' MED

Pere I's successor was the most expansionist of the Count-Kings. Jaume I 'the Conqueror' (1213-76) abandoned any idea of further adventures in Provence and joined decisively in the campaign against the Muslims to the south, taking control of Mallorca in 1229, Ibiza in 1235 and then, at much greater cost, Valencia in 1238. He made it the third part of the Crown of Aragon. This made Barcelona the centre of an empire that spanned the Mediterranean.

The Civil War and Franco's victory brought the extravagant years of the Chino to an end, and in the first years of the new regime the district became just a place of poverty and squalor. Despite its usual puritanism, though, the Franco regime – perhaps with a military attitude to bodily needs – never really sought to close down the Chino entirely, and even oversaw a certain revival in the 1950s via its cooperation treaty with the USA, which led to regular visits by the US Sixth Fleet, creating a whole new market for prostitution that was reflected in the emergence of 'girly bars' with names like 'St Louis' and 'Kentucky'

on C/Sant Pau and across the Rambla on C/Escudellers. Then, amid the post-Franco freedoms of the late 1970s, the Chino experienced a last mini-boom, partly through the rediscovery of its kitsch appeal, with its wildly camp drag shows in among the sleazy old bars. The invasion of heroin in the '80s, though, brought a much heavier, more violent atmosphere, which could put off even the most determined slummer. The, in the pre-Olympic build-up the Socialist city council – for whom no challenge is too great – finally decided really to get to grips with the Chino and with the Raval as a whole.

Throughout the 1990s, brothels and squalid hotels have been closed down, and entire blocks of decrepit old flats swept away in giant renovation schemes like the Rambla del Raval. At the same time, the area's ethnic make-up was changing radically with the influx of migrants from North Africa, Pakistan and other parts of the world. Today, the district is scarcely more affluent then when the effort started. It remains a street crime hotspot, but the sex industry has largely moved on to the small newspaper ads and to squalid roadsides further out of town, so that, of the old decadence, only a few glimmering traces – like the shops still selling 'showgirl outfits' on Nou de la Rambla – remain.

The city grew tremendously under Jaume I, and in the mid 13th century he ordered that a new, second city wall be constructed, along the line of the Rambla, bringing La Ribera and the other *vilanoves* within the city. In 1274 he also gave Barcelona a form of representative self-government, the Consell de Cent, a council of 100 citizens that would exist for more than 400 years. In Catalonia, royal powers were limited by the Cort, a parliament with a permanent standing committee known as the Generalitat.

The count-kings commanded a powerful fleet and a mercenary army, centred on the Almogàvers, fast-moving bands of irregular warriors who had been hardened in the battles with the Muslims on the Catalan frontier. The stuff of another set of heroic legends – such as their pre-battle ritual of beating their swords against rocks to produce showers of sparks, with the battle-cry '*Desperta ferro!*' ('Awaken, iron!') – the Almogàvers made themselves feared equally by Christians and Muslims as they travelled the Mediterranean conquering, plundering and enslaving in the name of God and the Crown of Aragon.

In 1282, Pere II 'the Great' sent his armies into Sicily; Catalan domination over the island would last for nearly 150 years. The Catalan empire reached its greatest strength under Jaume II 'the Just' (1291-1327), as both Corsica (1323) and Sardinia (1324) were added to the Crown of Aragon, although the latter would never submit to Catalan rule and would be a constant focus of revolt.

GOLDEN TOWN
The Crown of Aragon was often at war with Arab rulers, but its capital flourished through commerce with every part of the Mediterranean, Christian and Muslim. Catalan ships also sailed into the Atlantic, to England and Flanders. Their ventures were actively supported by the count-kings and burghers of Barcelona, and regulated by the first-ever code of maritime law, the Llibre del Consolat de Mar (written 1258-72), an early example of the Catalans' tendency to legalism, the influence of which extended far beyond their own territories. By the late 13th century, nearly 130 consulates ringed the Mediterranean, engaged in a complex system of trade that involved spices, coral, grain, slaves, metals, wool and other textiles, olive oil, salt fish and leather goods.

Not surprisingly, this age of power and prestige was also the great era of building in medieval Barcelona. The Catalan Gothic style reached its peak between the reigns of Jaume 'the Just' and Pere III 'the Ceremonious' (1336-87). The count-kings' imperial conquests may have been ephemeral, but their talent for permanence in building can still be admired today. Between 1290 and 1340, the construction of most of Barcelona's major Gothic buildings was initiated. Religious edifices such as the cathedral, Santa Maria del Mar and Santa Maria del Pi were matched by civil buildings such as the Saló de Tinell and the Llotja, the old market and stock exchange. As a result, Barcelona today contains the most important nucleus of Gothic civil architecture anywhere in Europe.

The ships of the Catalan navy were built in the monumental Drassanes shipyards, begun by Pere II and completed under Pere III in 1378. In 1359 Pere III also built the third (and final) city wall, along the line of the modern Paral.lel, Ronda Sant Pau and Ronda Sant Antoni. This gave the 'old city' of Barcelona its definitive shape. La Ribera, 'the waterfront', was the centre of trade and industry in 14th-century Barcelona. Once unloaded at the beach, wares were taken to the Llotja. Just inland, the Carrer Montcada was the street par excellence where newly enriched merchants could display their wealth in opulent Gothic palaces. All around were the workers of the various craft guilds, grouped together in their own streets.

'At the very top of society some women became very powerful.'

Women's domains in this Barcelona were initially limited to home, market, convent or brothel, although in 1249 they won the right to inherit property, and women were at one time the main textile workers. At the very top of society some women became very powerful, as it was quite common – unusually for that era – for Catalan count-kings to delegate their authority to their queens when they went away on long campaigns.

The Catalan 'Golden Age' was also an era of cultural greatness. Catalonia was one of the first areas in Europe to use its vernacular language as well as Latin, in written form and as a language of culture. The oldest written texts in Catalan are the *Homílies d'Organyà*, translations from the Bible dating from the 12th century. Not just monks, but also the court and the aristocracy attained an unusual level of literacy, and Jaume I wrote his own autobiography, the *Llibre dels Feits* or 'Book of Deeds', which recounted in dramatic style his achievements and conquests.

Incipient Catalan literature was given a vital thrust by the unique figure of Ramon Llull (1235-1316). After a debauched youth, he experienced a series of religious visions and then turned to more serious pursuits. He was the first man in post-Roman Europe to write philosophy in a vernacular language. Steeped in Arabic and Hebrew writings, he brought together Christian, Islamic, Jewish and classical ideas, and also wrote a vast amount on other subjects – from theories of chivalry to poetry and visionary tales.

In doing so Llull effectively created Catalan as a literary language. Catalan translations from Greek and Latin were also undertaken at this time. In the very twilight of the Golden Age, in 1490, the Valencian Joanot Martorell published *Tirant Lo Blanc*, a bawdy tale that is believed to be the first European novel.

REVOLT AND COLLAPSE

Barcelona was not, however, a peaceful and harmonious place as the 14th century wore on. Social unrest and violence were common: grain riots, popular uprisings, attacks on Jews and gang warfare were rampant. An ongoing struggle took place between two political factions, the Biga (representing the most established merchants) and the Busca (largely composed of smaller tradesmen).

The extraordinary prosperity of the medieval period, though, was not to last. The count-kings had overextended Barcelona's resources, and overinvested in far-off ports. By 1400, the effort to maintain their conquests by force, especially in Sardinia, had exhausted the spirit and the coffers of the Catalan imperialist drive. The Black Death, which had arrived in the 1340s, had also had a devastating impact. This only intensified the bitterness of social conflicts between the aristocracy, merchants, peasants and the urban poor.

In 1410, Martí I 'the Humane' died without an heir, bringing to an end the line of counts of Barcelona unbroken since Guifré el Pilós. After much deliberation between Church and aristocracy the Crown of Aragon was passed to a member of a Castilian noble family, the Trastámaras: Fernando de Antequera (1410-16).

His son, Alfons V 'the Magnanimous' (1416-58), undertook one more conquest, of Naples, but the empire was under ever greater pressure, and Barcelona merchants were unable to compete with the Genoese and Venetians. At home, in the 1460s, the effects of war and catastrophic famine led to a collapse into civil war and peasant revolt. The population was depleted to such an extent that Barcelona would not regain the population level it had in 1400 (40,000) until the 18th century.

In 1469, an important union for Spain initiated another woeful period in Barcelona's history, dubbed by some Catalan historians the *decadència*, which would lead to the end of Catalonia as a separate entity. In that year,

Ferdinand of Aragon (reigned 1479-1516) married Isabella of Castile (1476-1506), and so united the different Spanish kingdoms, even though they would retain their separate institutions for another two centuries.

EAST OF EDEN

As Catalonia's fortunes had declined, those of Castile had risen. While Catalonia was impoverished and in chaos, Castile had become larger and richer, and was now on the crest of a wave of expansion. In 1492, Granada, the last Muslim foothold in Spain, was conquered, and as Isabella decreed the expulsion of all Jews from Castile and Aragon, Columbus discovered America.

It was Castile's seafaring orientation towards the Atlantic, rather than the Mediterranean, that confirmed Catalonia's decline. The discovery of the New World was a disaster for Catalan commerce: trade shifted decisively away from the Mediterranean, and Catalans were officially barred from participating in the exploitation of the new empire until the 1770s. The weight of Castile within the monarchy was increased, and it very soon became the seat of government.

In 1516, the Spanish crown passed to the House of Habsburg, via Ferdinand and Isabella's grandson, Emperor Charles V. His son, Philip II of Spain, established Madrid as the capital of all his dominions. Catalonia was managed by appointed viceroys, the power of its institutions restricted, with a down-at-heel aristocracy and a meagre cultural life.

GRIM REAPERS

While Castilian Spain went through its 'Golden Century', Catalonia was left more and more on the margins. Worse was to come, however, in the following century, with two national revolts – both heroic defeats – that have since acquired a central role in Catalan nationalist mythology.

The problem for the Spanish monarchy was that, whereas Castile was an absolute monarchy and so could be taxed at will, in the former Aragonese territories, and especially Catalonia, royal authority kept coming up against a mass of local rights and privileges. As the Habsburgs' empire became bogged down in endless wars and expenses that not even American gold could meet, the Count-Duke of Olivares, the formidable great minister of King Philip IV (1621-65), resolved to extract more money and troops from the non-Castilian dominions of the crown. The Catalans, however, felt they were taxed quite enough already.

In 1640, a mass of peasants, later dubbed *els Segadors* (the Reapers), gathered on the Rambla in Barcelona, outside the *porta ferrissa* (iron gate) in the second wall. They rioted against

Charles II.

royal authority, surged into the city and seized and murdered the viceroy, the Marqués de Santa Coloma. This began the general uprising known as the *Guerra dels Segadors*, the Reapers' War. The authorities of the Generalitat, led by its president, Pau Claris, feared the violent reaction of the poor and, lacking the confidence to declare Catalonia independent, appealed for protection from Louis XIII of France. But French armies were unable to defend Catalonia adequately, and in 1652 a destitute Barcelona capitulated to the equally exhausted army of Philip IV. In 1659, France and Spain made peace with a treaty that gave the Catalan territory of Roussillon, near Perpignan, to France. After the revolt, Philip IV and his ministers were surprisingly magnanimous, allowing the Catalans to retain what was left of their institutions despite their disloyalty. This war provided the Catalans with their national anthem, *Els Segadors*.

THE REIGN IN SPAIN

Fifty years later came the second of the great national rebellions, the War of the Spanish Succession, which would represent the last time Catalonia sought to regain its national freedom by force. In 1700, Charles II of Spain died without an heir. Castile accepted the grandson of Louis XIV of France, Philip of Anjou, as King Philip V of Spain (1700-46). The alternative candidate, Archduke Charles of Austria, vowed to restore the traditional rights of the former Aragonese territories, and so won their allegiance. He also had the support, in his fight against France, of Britain, Holland and Austria.

Once again, though, Catalonia had backed the wrong horse, and was let down in its choice of allies. In 1713, Britain and the Dutch made peace with France and withdrew their aid, leaving the Catalans stranded with no possibility of victory. After a 13-month siege in which every citizen was called to arms, Barcelona fell to the French and Spanish armies on 11 September 1714.

The most heroic defeat of all, this date marked the most decisive political reverse in Barcelona's history, and is now commemorated as Catalan National Day, the Diada. Some of Barcelona's resisters were buried next to the church of Santa Maria del Mar in the Born, in the Fossar de les Moreres.

In 1715, Philip V issued his decree of Nova Planta, abolishing all the remaining separate institutions of the Crown of Aragon and so, in effect, creating 'Spain' as a single, unitary state. Large-scale 'Castilianisation' of the country was initiated, and Castilian replaced the Catalan language in all official documents.

In Barcelona, extra measures were taken to keep the city under firm control. The crumbling medieval walls and the castle on Montjuïc were refurbished with new ramparts, and a massive new citadel was built on the eastern side of the old city, where the Parc de la Ciutadella is today. To make space for it, though, thousands of people had to be expelled from La Ribera and forcibly rehoused in the Barceloneta, Barcelona's first-ever planned housing scheme, with its barrack-like street plan that was unmistakably provided by French military engineers. This citadel soon became the most hated symbol of the city's subordination.

RETAIL THERAPY
Politically subjugated and without a significant native ruling class, following the departure of many of its remaining aristocrats to serve the monarchy in Madrid, Catalonia nevertheless revived in the 18th century. Catalans continued speaking their own language, and developed independent commercial initiatives. Ironically, the Bourbons, by abolishing legal differences between Catalonia and the rest of Spain, also removed the earlier restrictions on Catalan trade, especially with the colonies. The strength of Barcelona's guilds enabled it to maintain its artisan industries, and the city revived after the official authorisation to trade with the Americas by King Charles III in 1778.

Shipping picked up again, and in the last years of the 18th century Barcelona had a booming export trade to the New World in wines and spirits from Catalan vineyards, and textiles, wool and silk. In 1780, a merchant called Erasme de Gómina opened Barcelona's

first true factory, a hand-powered weaving mill in C/Riera Alta with 800 workers. In the next decade, Catalan trade with Spanish America quadrupled; Barcelona's population had grown from around 30,000 in 1720 to close to 100,000 by the end of the century.

This prosperity was reflected in a new wave of building in the city. Neo-classical mansions appeared, notably on C/Ample and the Rambla. The greatest transformation, though, was in the Rambla itself. Until the 1770s, it had been no more than a dusty, dry riverbed where country people came to sell their produce, lined on the Raval side mostly with giant religious houses and on the other with Jaume I's second wall. In 1775, the captain-general, the Marqués de la Mina, embarked on an ambitious scheme to demolish the wall and turn the Rambla into a smooth, paved promenade. Beyond the Rambla, the previously semi-rural Raval was becoming densely populated.

Barcelona's expansion was briefly interrupted by the French invasion of 1808. Napoleon sought to appeal to Catalans by offering them national recognition within his empire, but, curiously, met with very little response. After six years of turmoil, Barcelona's business class resumed its projects with the restoration of the Bourbon monarchy.

GETTING UP STEAM
On his restoration, Ferdinand VII (1808-33) attempted to reinstate the absolute monarchy of his youth and reimpose his authority over Spain's American colonies, but failed to do either. On his death he was succeeded by his three-year-old daughter Isabel II (1833-68), but the throne was also claimed by his brother Carlos, who was supported by the most reactionary sectors in the country.

To defend Isabel's rights, the Regent, Ferdinand's widow Queen María Cristina, was obliged to seek the support of liberals, and so granted a very limited form of constitution. Thus began Spain's Carlist Wars These would have a powerful impact in conservative rural

Philip V.

Catalonia, where Don Carlos's faction won a considerable following, in part because of its support for traditional local rights and customs.

While this see-saw struggle went on around the country, in Barcelona a liberal-minded local administration, freed from subordination to the military, was able to engage in some city planning, opening up the soon-to-be fashionable C/Ferran and Plaça Sant Jaume in the 1820s, and later adding the Plaça Reial. A fundamental change came in 1836, when the governmental leaders in Madrid decreed the *desamortización* (disentailment) of Spain's monasteries. In Barcelona, where convents and religious houses still took up great sections of the Raval and the Rambla, a huge area was freed for development.

The Rambla took on the appearance it roughly retains today, while the Raval, the main district for new industry in a Barcelona still contained within its walls, rapidly filled up with tenements and textile mills several storeys high. In 1832, the first steam-driven factory in Spain was built on C/Tallers, sparking resistance from hand-spinners and weavers.

Most of the city's factories were still relatively small, however, and Catalan manufacturers were very aware that they were at a disadvantage in competing with the industries of Britain and northern Europe. For decades, their political motto would be protectionism rather than any kind of Catalan nationalism, as they demanded of Madrid that the Spanish textile markets should be sealed against foreign competition.

'Barcelona's people were notably rebellious, and liberal, republican and utopian groups proliferated'

Also, they did not have the city to themselves. Not only did the anti-industrial Carlists threaten them from the countryside, but Barcelona soon became a centre of radical ideas. Its people were notably rebellious, and liberal, republican and utopian socialist groups proliferated between sporadic bursts of repression. In 1842, a liberal revolt, the *Jamancia*, took over Barcelona, and barricades went up around the city. This would be the last occasion Barcelona was bombarded from the castle on Montjuïc, as the army was left struggling to regain control.

The Catalan language, by this time, had been relegated to secondary status, spoken on every street but rarely written or used in cultured discourse. Then, in 1833, Bonaventura Carles Aribau published his *Oda a la Pàtria*, a romantic Catalan eulogy to the country, its language and its past. This poem had an extraordinary impact,

and is traditionally credited with initiating the *renaixença* (rebirth) of Catalan heritage and culture. The year 1848 was a high point for Barcelona, with the inauguration of the first railway in Spain, from Barcelona to Mataró, and the opening of the Liceu opera house.

SETTING AN EIXAMPLE
The optimism of Barcelona's new middle class was counterpointed by two persistent obstacles: the weakness of the Spanish economy as a whole, and the instability of their own society, reflected in atrocious labour relations. No consideration was given to the manpower behind the industrial surge: the underpaid, overworked men, women and children who lived in appalling conditions in high-rise slums within the cramped city. In 1855, the first general strike took place in Barcelona. The captain-general, Zapatero, inaugurating a long cycle of conflict, refused to permit any workers' organisations, and bloodily suppressed all resistance.

One response to the city's problems that had almost universal support in Barcelona was the demolition of the city walls, which had imposed a stifling restriction on its growth. For years, however, the Spanish state refused to relinquish this hold on the city. To find space, larger factories were established in villages around Barcelona, such as Sants and Poblenou. In 1854, permission finally came for the demolition of the citadel and the walls. The work began with enthusiastic popular participation, crowds of volunteers joining in at weekends. After this, Barcelona at last broke out of the space it had occupied since the 14th century and spread outward into its new *eixample* (extension), according to a plan by Ildefons Cerdà (*see p123* **The man with the plan**).

In 1868, Isabel II, once a symbol of liberalism, was overthrown by a progressive revolt. During the six years of upheaval that followed, power in Madrid would be held by a provisional government, a constitutional monarchy under an Italian prince and then later under a federal republic. Workers were free to organise, and in November 1868 Giuseppe Fanelli, an Italian emissary of Bakunin, brought the ideas of anarchism to Barcelona. Given the radical nature of the town, it is not surprising that he found ready support in Catalonia. In 1870, the first-ever Spanish workers' congress took place in Barcelona. The radical forces, though, found themselves divided between warring factions. The established classes of society were also feeling increasingly threatened, and called for the restoration of order. Thus, the Republic proclaimed in 1873 was unable to establish its authority, and ultimately succumbed to a coup.

Protest city

Preparing the barricades, 1909.

Barcelona is an inherently theatrical city, spread out like a great stage between Tibidabo, Montjüic and the sea. In its most vibrant and turbulent era from the 1880s to 1939, when it showed more hunger for new ideas than just about any other city in Europe, all the currents that turned up in town vied to show themselves on the streets as well as in print or talk. Crowds were something Barcelona was known for, and its many street gatherings ranged from mass celebrations to bitter confrontations, sometimes on the same day.

For the well-heeled classes of the 1900s, the Eixample was their showcase for their own taste, and thus, in their view, a display of modernity, status and sophistication; the Passeig de Gràcia was then virtually traffic-free and a real promenade, and everyone in 'society' took a turn there on Sundays to show off their finery. The ragged and revolutionary marked out their space too, and in radical outbursts such as the Setmana Tràgica of 1909 and general strike of 1917, the Raval was barricaded off into a no-go area for government and police. For most of better-off Barcelona, though, these were only passing episodes; until, that is, the CNT's first true general strike in February 1919. By then, living standards that had plummeted in the galloping inflation at the end of World War I were even worse, and workers flocked to join the union. Then, a strike over union recognition at the company which supplied most of the city's electricity spread to the whole city.

SERRANO SCAM

In 1874, the Bourbon dynasty yet again found its way back to power when Alfonso XII took the throne. Workers' organisations were again suppressed. The middle classes, however, felt their confidence renewed. The 1870s saw a frenzied boom in stock speculation – called the *febre d'or* (gold fever) – and the take-off of construction in the Eixample. From the 1880s, Modernisme became the preferred style of the new district, the perfect expression for the self-confidence, romanticism and strength of the industrial class.

Barcelona felt it needed to show the world all that it had achieved, and that it was more than just a 'second city'. So, in 1885, an exhibition promoter named Eugenio Serrano de Casanova proposed to the city council the holding of an international exhibition, like the ones that were doing so well in London, Paris and Vienna. Serrano, though, was not all he said he was, and

he ultimately made off with large amounts of public funds. But, by then, the city fathers had fully committed themselves to the project. The Universal Exhibition of 1888 was used as a pretext for the final conversion of the Ciutadella into a park; giant efforts had to be made to get everything ready in time, a feat that led the mayor, Francesc Rius i Taulet, to exclaim that 'the Catalan people are the yankees of Europe'. The first of Barcelona's three great efforts to demonstrate its status to the world, the 1888 Exhibition signified the consecration of the Modernista style, the demise of provincial, dowdy Barcelona and its rebirth as a modern city to be reckoned with.

THE CITY OF THE NEW CENTURY

As 1900 approached, there were few cities where the new century was regarded with greater anticipation than in Barcelona. The Catalan *renaixença* continued, and acquired

On the night of 21 February all power was cut – Barcelona came to a juddering halt – and the streets suddenly emptied as respectable citizens locked themselves indoors fearing a general throat-cutting. To restore confidence and reclaim the streets the government brought in the army and set up a local militia called the *somatén*. Its first patrols were led by some of Barcelona's most prominent businessmen – in their best clothes and with shotguns in hand. After two months, a huge, rowdy crowd of strikers met in the Arenes bullring in Plaça d'Espanya, where they were persuaded to accept a partial settlement. However, employers failed to honour it and the strike proved only the curtain-raiser to four years of bleak drama, as CNT activists and the employers' hired gunmen (the most notorious a gang run by a former German spy known as the 'Baron de Koening', and operating from a bar on Ronda Sant Antoni) sought to eliminate each other.

This back-street war was finally ended by Primo de Rivera's coup in 1923. But Barcelona regained its taste for demonstrations at the end of the '20s, when it was racked by mass protests from just about every sector of society – from students to sports fans – that gradually knocked away the teetering confidence in the regime. Through the 1930s demonstrations were something of a Barcelona fixture: one day Catalanists, the next fringe Marxists. It

was hard to get noticed in that kind of an atmosphere, but the CNT's activists sought to make the maximum impact in their many strikes; one favourite tactic was to seize a tram at the top of C/Muntaner, set fire to it, and then launch it unstoppably down the long slope to Plaça Universitat. Another memorable episode took place in 1934 when a general strike dragged on for months in Zaragoza, and the Barcelona CNT offered to look after the strikers' children. Thousands flocked to train stations in order to welcome the '*niños de Zaragoza*', amid emotional affirmations of solidarity.

The most dramatic street event of all, though, came in July 1936, in two days of bitter fighting followed by huge jubilation when it became clear that, in Barcelona at least, the uprising had been beaten. In the first year of the Civil War, in the city where, as Orwell famously recalled, the 'wealthy classes had practically ceased to exist', the many divisions in the republican camp – communists, anarchists, Catalanists – often seemed to devote as much of their energy to organising competing rallies around the Plaça Catalunya as they did to fighting the Francoists; something they later realised to their cost. As if to drive the point home, when Franco's army finally took Barcelona in January 1939, it marked its victory as emphatically as possible with a giant open-air mass right in the plaça.

a more political tone. In 1892, a draft plan for Catalan autonomy – called the *Bases de Manresa* – was drawn up. Middle-class opinion was becoming more sympathetic to political Catalanism. A decisive moment came in 1898, when the underlying weakness of the Spanish state was abruptly made plain, despite the superficial prosperity of the first years of the Bourbon restoration.

Spain was soon manoeuvred into a short war with the United States, in which it very quickly lost its remaining colonies in Cuba, the Philippines and Puerto Rico. Catalan industrialists, horrified at losing the lucrative Cuban market, feared the state might never reform itself. So, many decided to support a conservative nationalist movement called the Lliga Regionalista (Regionalist League). Led by Enric Prat de la Riba and the politician-financier Francesc Cambó, it promised national revival and a modern, efficient government.

Amidst this turmoil, the city continued to grow, and it had officially incorporated most of the surrounding smaller communities by 1897, reaching a population of over half a million.

Catalan letters were also thriving: the Institut d'Estudis Catalans (Institute of Catalan Studies) was founded in 1906, and Pompeu Fabra set out to create the first Catalan dictionary. Literature in the region had acquired a new maturity, and in 1905 Victor Català (a pseudonym used by a woman, Caterina Albert) shocked the country with the publication of *Solitud*, a darkly modern novel of a woman's sexual awakening. By then, Barcelona had a vibrant artistic community, from architects and painters such as Rusiñol and Casas to penniless bohemians who hung round them, including the young Picasso.

Barcelona's bohemians were also drawn to the increasingly wild nightlife of the Raval (*see p10* **Sleazy does it**). Around the cabarets, though, were also the poorest of the working class, for whom conditions had only continued to decline. Barcelona had some of the worst overcrowding and highest mortality rates of any city in Europe. These conditions led to growing anger, and in 1893 more than 20 people were killed in a series of anarchist bombings. The most notorious of these attacks came when a bomb was thrown into the stalls of the Liceu during a performance of *William Tell*. The perpetrators acted alone, but the authorities seized the opportunity to round up all the usual suspects – mostly anarchists and radicals – several of whom were tortured and executed in the castle above Barcelona. The city seethed, until 1906, when a Catalan anarchist tried to assassinate King Alfonso XIII on his wedding day. A few years later, in 1909, the city's rage culminated in the explosive outburst known as *Setmana Tràgica* (Tragic Week). It began as a protest against the conscription of troops for the colonial war in Morocco, but soon it had spiralled into a general riot, with the destruction of churches by excited mobs. A number of suspected culprits were summarily executed, including the anarchist Francesc Ferrer, accused of 'moral responsibility' even though he was not in Barcelona at the time.

> **'Barcelona also became the most amenable place of refuge for anyone who wished to avoid the war.'**

These events dented the optimism of the Catalanists of the Lliga, but in 1914 they secured from Madrid the administrative union, – known as the *mancomunitat* – of the four Catalan provinces, the first joint government of any kind in Catalonia in 200 years. Unfortunately, the Lliga's plans for a respectable Catalonia were to be obstructed by a further surge in social tensions.

TALKIN' ABOUT REVOLUTION

Spain's neutral status during World War I gave a huge boost to the Spanish – and especially the Catalan – economy. Exports soared as Catalonia's manufacturers made millions supplying uniforms to the French army. Barcelona's industry was at last able to diversify from textiles into engineering, chemicals and other more modern sectors.

Barcelona also became the most amenable place of refuge for anyone in Europe who wished to avoid the war. It acquired an international refugee community, which included avant-garde artists Sonia and Robert Delaunay, Francis Picabia, Marie Laurencin and Albert Gleizes, and was a bolt-hole for all kinds of low-life from

around Europe. The Raval area would shortly be dubbed the *Barrio Chino*, or 'Chinatown', identifying it as an area of sin and perdition.

The most regular patrons of the lavish new cabarets were industrialists, and many of the war profits were spent immediately in very conspicuous consumption. Along with creating millionaires, the skyrocketing inflation caused by the war drove thousands from rural Spain into the cities. Barcelona doubled in size in 20 years to become the largest city in Spain, and, finally, the fulcrum of Spanish politics.

Workers' wages, meanwhile, had lost half their real value. The chief channel of protest in Barcelona was the anarchist workers' union, the Confederación Nacional del Trabajo (CNT). The CNT and the socialist Union General de Trabajadores (UGT) launched a joint general strike in 1917, coordinated with a campaign by the Lliga and other liberal politicians for political reform. However, the politicians quickly withdrew at the prospect of serious social unrest. Inflation continued to intensify, and employers refused to recognise the CNT, so in 1919 Barcelona was paralysed for four months by a CNT general strike as the union demanded recognition (*see p18* **Protest city**). The strike quickly descended into violence as some employers hired gunmen to kill union leaders. Eventually union activists replied in kind, and a virtual guerrilla warfare developed between the CNT, the employers and the state. More than 800 people were killed on the city's streets in the space of five years.

In 1923, in response both to the chaos in Barcelona and a crisis in the war in Morocco, the captain-general of Barcelona, Miguel Primo de Rivera, staged a coup and established a military dictatorship under King Alfonso XIII. The CNT, exhausted from the struggle, was nearly completely suppressed. Conservative Catalanists, longing for an end to disorder and the revolutionary threat, initially supported the coup, but were rewarded by the abolition of the *mancomunitat* and a vindictive campaign by the Primo regime against the Catalan language and national symbols.

This, however, achieved the opposite of its desired effect, as it helped to radicalise and popularise Catalan nationalism. This was also, though, a highly politicised society, in which new magazines and forums for discussion – despite the restrictions of the dictatorship – found a ready audience.

After the terrible struggles of the previous years, the 1920s were, at last, a time of notable prosperity for many in Barcelona, as some of the wealth recently accumulated filtered through the economy. A prime motor of Barcelona's prosperity in the 1920s was the International

Exhibition of 1929, the second of the city's great showcase events. It had been proposed by Cambó and Catalan business groups, but Primo de Rivera saw that it could also serve as a propaganda event for his regime. A huge number of public projects were undertaken in association with the main event, including the post office in Via Laietana, the Estació de França and Barcelona's first Metro line, from Plaça Catalunya to Plaça d'Espanya. Thousands of migrant workers came from southern Spain to build them, many living in decrepit housing or shanty towns on the city fringes. By 1930, Barcelona was very different from the place it had been in 1910; it contained more than a million people, and its urban sprawl had crossed into neighbouring towns such as Hospitalet and Santa Coloma.

For the Exhibition itself, Montjuïc and Plaça d'Espanya were comprehensively redeveloped, with grand halls by Puig i Cadafalch and other local architects in the style of the Catalan neo-classical movement *Noucentisme*, a backward-looking reaction to the excesses of Modernisme. They contrasted strikingly, though, and the German pavilion by Mies van der Rohe (the Pavelló Barcelona), emphatically announced the international trend toward rationalism.

THE REPUBLIC SUPPRESSED

Despite the Exhibition's success, in January 1930 Primo de Rivera resigned. The king appointed another soldier, General Berenguer, as prime minister, with the mission of restoring stability. The dictatorship, though, had fatally discredited the old regime, and a protest movement spread across Catalonia against the monarchy. In early 1931, Berenguer called local elections as a first step towards a restoration of constitutional rule. The outcome was a complete surprise, for republicans were elected in all of Spain's cities. Ecstatic crowds poured into the streets, and Alfonso XIII abdicated. On 14 April 1931, the Second Spanish Republic was proclaimed.

The Republic came in amid mass euphoria. This was especially true in Catalonia, where it was associated with hopes for both social change and national reaffirmation. The clear winner of the elections in the country had been the Esquerra Republicana, a leftist Catalanist group led by Francesc Macià. A raffish, elderly figure, Macià was one of the first politicians in Spain to win genuine affection from ordinary people. He declared Catalonia independent, but he later agreed to accept autonomy within the Spanish Republic.

The Generalitat was re-established as a government that would, potentially, acquire wide powers. All aspects of Catalan culture were then in expansion, and a popular press

in Catalan gained wide readership. Barcelona, by then, had become a small but notable centre of the avant-garde.

In Madrid, the Republic's first government was a coalition of republicans and socialists led by Manuel Azaña. Its overriding goal was to modernise Spanish society through liberal-democratic reforms, but as social tensions intensified the coalition collapsed, and a right-wing republican party, with support from the traditional Spanish right, secured power after new elections in 1933. For Catalonia, the prospect of a return to right-wing rule prompted fears that it would abrogate the Generalitat's hard-won powers. On 6 October 1934, while a general strike was launched against the central government in Asturias and some other parts of Spain, Lluís Companys, who had been leader of the Generalitat since Macià's death the previous year, declared Catalonia independent. This 'uprising', however, turned out to be a bit of a farce, for the Generalitat had no means of resisting the army, and the 'Catalan Republic' was rapidly suppressed.

As feared, the Generalitat was suspended and its leaders imprisoned. Over the following year, fascism became a real threat, as political positions became polarised throughout Spain. Then, in February 1936, fresh elections were won by the Popular Front of the left. Soon, the Generalitat was reinstated, and in Catalonia the next few months were, surprisingly peaceful. Elsewhere in Spain, though, tensions reached the bursting point, and right-wing politicians, refusing to accept the loss of power, talked openly of the need for the military to intervene. In July, the stadium on Montjuïc was the site of the Popular Olympics, a leftist alternative to the main Olympics of that year in Nazi Germany. On 18 July, however, army generals launched a coup against the Republic and its left-wing governments, expecting no resistance.

UP IN ARMS

In Barcelona, militants from the unions and leftist parties, on alert for weeks, poured into the streets to oppose the troops in fierce fighting. Over the course of 19 July the military were gradually worn down, and finally surrendered in the Hotel Colón on Plaça Catalunya (by the corner with Passeig de Gràcia, the site of which is now occupied by the Radio Nacional de España building). Opinions have always differed as to who could claim most credit for this remarkable popular victory: militants claimed it was the 'people in arms' who defeated the army, while others stress the importance of the police remaining loyal to the Generalitat. The likely truth, though, is that they actually encouraged each other.

Tension released, the city was taken over by the revolution. People's militias of the revived CNT, different Marxist parties and other left-wing factions marched off to Aragon, led by streetfighters such as the anarchists Durruti and García Oliver, to continue the battle. But, while the army rising had failed in Spain's major cities, it had won footholds in Castile, Aragon and the south, although in the heady atmosphere of Barcelona in July 1936 it was often assumed that resistance could not last, and that the people's victory was inevitable.

Far from the front, Barcelona was the centre of the revolution in republican Spain, the only proletarian city. Its middle class avoided the streets, where, as Orwell recorded in his *Homage to Catalonia*, workers' clothing was all there was to be seen. Barcelona became a magnet for leftists from around the world, including writers such as André Malraux, Hemingway and Octavio Paz. Industries and public services were collectivised, including cinemas, phone system and food distribution. Ad hoc 'control patrols' of the revolutionary militias roamed the streets supposedly checking for suspected right-wing agents but sometimes carrying out summary executions, a practice that was condemned by many leftist leaders.

The alliance between the different left-wing groups was unstable and riddled with tensions. The communists, who had extra leverage because the Soviet Union was the only country prepared to give the Spanish Republic arms, demanded the integration of the loosely organised militias into a conventional army under a strong central authority. The following months saw continual political infighting between the discontented CNT, the radical-Marxist party Partit Obrer d'Unificació Marxista (POUM), and the communists. Co-operation broke down totally in May 1937, when republican and communist troops seized the telephone building in Plaça Catalunya (on the corner of Portal de l'Angel) from a CNT committee, sparking the confused war-within-the-civil-war witnessed by Orwell from the roof of the Teatre Poliorama. A temporary agreement was patched up, but a short while afterwards the POUM was banned, and the CNT excluded from power. A new republican central government was formed under Dr Juan Negrín, a socialist allied to the communists.

The war gradually became more of a conventional conflict. This did little to improve the Republic's position, for the nationalists, under General Francisco Franco, and their German and Italian allies had been gaining ground. Madrid was under siege, and the capital of the Republic was moved to Valencia, and then to Barcelona, in November 1937.

Refugees poured into Catalonia, leading to food shortages, while the lack of armaments ground down morale. The fighting was fierce; Barcelona was the first major city in Europe to be subjected to sustained intensive bombing, and the city was pummelled throughout 1938, most damagingly by Italian bombers based in Mallorca. The Basque Country and Asturias had quickly fell to Franco, and in March 1938 his troops reached the Mediterranean near Castellón, cutting the main republican zone in two. The republic had one last throw of the dice, in the Battle of the Ebro in summer 1938, when for months the Popular Army struggled unsuccesfully to retake control of the river. After that, it was all over. Barcelona fell to the Francoist army on 26 January 1939. Half a million refugees fled to France, to be interned in barbed-wire camps along the beaches.

THE FRANCO YEARS

In Catalonia the Franco regime was iron-fisted and especially vengeful. Thousands of Catlan republicans were executed, including the president of the Generalitat Lluís Companys. Exile and deportation became the fate of thousands more. Publishing, teaching and any other public cultural expression in Catalan, including even speaking it in the street, were prohibited, and every Catalanist monument in the city was dismantled. All independent political activity was suspended; censorship and the secret police were a constant presence, and the resulting atmosphere of fear and suspicion was to mark many who lived through it. The entire political and cultural development of the country during the previous century and a half was thus brought to an abrupt halt.

The epic of the Spanish Civil War is known worldwide; but more present in the collective memory of Barcelona, is the long *posguerra* or post-war period, which lasted nearly two long decades after 1939. The city itself was impoverished, and food and electricity were rationed; it would not regain the standard of living it had experienced in 1936 until the mid 1950s. And still migrants in flight from the brutal poverty of the south flowed into the hungry city, occupying precarious shanty towns around Montjuïc and other areas in the outskirts. Reconstruction of the nearly 2,000 buildings destroyed by bombing was slow, for the regime built little during its first few years in power other than monumental showpieces and the vulgar basilica on top of Tibidabo, which was intended to expiate Barcelona's 'sinful' role during the war.

Some underground political movements were able to operate. Anarchist urban guerrillas such as the Sabaté brothers attempted to carry on

The serenos

If you've ever been kept awake by a neighbour's roaring TV, then you'd have appreciated the services of the *vigilante*. Until the 1970s, there was a patrolling nightwatchman for every four streets, who would have gently rapped on the door with his *chuzo* (a metal-tipped stick) and called for silence. The Spanish Corps of Night Watchmen was officially created in 1844, although they've been traced back to as far as 1785 in Múrcia. They came to be known colloquially as *serenos* because one of their duties as they patrolled the streets was to shout out the time and weather conditions to those indoors – and this being Spain, the weather report was usually '*sereno*'. If it was raining heavily, the *sereno's* meteorological report meant those who worked in the open air could roll over and go back to sleep, or at least knew they would have to whip out the sou'wester and gumboots.

Unfortunately, the business of shouting out the time throughout the night was not exactly conducive to a good night's sleep for anybody, and with the advent of alarm clocks this duty was swiftly dropped, but it was the *serenos* who called the doctor for the sick, or who fetched medicine from the all-night pharmacy. Other duties included catching thieves, preventing burglaries and preventing 'scandals' – i.e. no drunken snogging on the way back from the cabaret – and, it is said, some had a rather more sinister duty during Franco's era, acting as moles to report on suspected dissidents.

As the *serenos* were armed only with a whistle and the *chuzo*, they had various code phrases for discreetly summoning their colleagues if they suspected danger. They also kept the keys for every house on their beat; they would lock the doors at ten and

open them at five or six in the morning. Anyone arriving or wanting to leave during those hours would simply clap or shout and the *sereno* would turn up with his keys and then light their way with his torch. Also within their remit was to try and prevent that most rampant of Spanish misdemeanours: pissing in the street. Many have tried to contain this tradition, though, and history does not record where the *vigilantes* themselves answered the call of nature.

---

armed resistance, and March 1951 saw the last gasp of the pre-war labour movement in a general tram strike, the only major strike during the harshest years of the regime. It was fiercely repressed, but also achieved some of its goals. Clandestine Catalanist groups undertook small acts of resistance and rebellion, including underground publications and secret theatre performances. Some Catalan high culture was tolerated: the poet Salvador Espriu promoted a certain resurgence of Catalan literature, and the young Antoni Tàpies held his first solo exhibition in 1949. For a great many people,

though, the only remaining public focus of national sentiment – of any collective excitement – was Barcelona football club, which took on an extraordinary importance at this time, above all in its biannual meetings with the 'team of the regime', Real Madrid.

As a fascist survivor, the Franco regime was subject to a UN embargo after World War II. Years of international isolation and attempted self-sufficiency came to an end in 1953, when the United States and the Vatican saw to it that this anti-communist state was at least partially re-admitted to the western fold. Even a limited

Franco is dead...

TIRED OF FRANQUISME

After the years of repression and the years of development, 1966 marked the beginning of what became known as *tardofranquisme* (late Francoism). Having made its opening to the outside world, the regime was losing its grip, and labour, youth and student movements began to emerge from beneath the shroud of repression. Nevertheless, the Franco regime never hesitated to show its strength. Strikes and demonstrations were dealt with savagely, and just months before the dictator's death a Catalan anarchist named Puig Antich became the last person to be executed in Spain by the traditional method of the garrotte.

In 1973, Franco's closest follower, Admiral Carrero Blanco, was assassinated by a bomb planted by the Basque terrorist group ETA, leaving no one to guard over the core values of the regime. Change was in the air.

GENERALISIMO TO GENERALITAT

When Franco died on 20 November 1975, the people of Barcelona took to the streets in celebration, and it is said that not a bottle of cava was left in the city by evening. However, no one knew quite what was about to happen. The Bourbon monarchy was restored, under King Juan Carlos, but his attitude and his intentions were not clear. In 1976, he made a little-known Francoist bureaucrat, Adolfo Suárez, prime minister, charged with leading the country to democracy.

Understandably, the first months and years of Spain's 'transition' were a difficult period. Demonstrations were repressed by the police with considerable brutality, and far-right groups threatened violence. However, political parties were legalised, and June 1977 saw the first democratic elections since 1936. They were won across Spain by Suárez's own new party, the Union de Centro Democratico (UCD), and in Catalonia by a mixture of socialists, communists and nationalist groups.

It was, again, not clear how Suárez expected to deal with the demands of Catalonia, but shortly after the elections he surprised everyone by going to visit the exiled president of the Generalitat, Josep Tarradellas. His office was the only institution of the old Republic to be so recognised, perhaps because Suárez astutely identified the old man (a veteran of the pre-civil war government) as a fellow conservative. Tarradellas was invited to return as provisional president of a restored Generalitat, and arrived amid huge crowds in October 1977.

The following year, the first free elections took place in Barcelona. They were won by the Socialist Party, with Narcis Serra elected as mayor. The party has retained control of the

opening to the outside world meant that foreign money began to enter the country, and the regime relaxed some control over its population. In 1959, the Plan de Estabilización (Stabilisation Plan), drawn up by Catholic technocrats of the Opus Dei, brought Spain definitively within the western economy, throwing its doors wide open to tourism and foreign investment.

Two years earlier, in 1957, José María de Porcioles was appointed Mayor of Barcelona, and he would hold that title for more than 15 years. Porcioles is now regarded as the very personification of the damage inflicted on the city by the Franco regime. During that time development ignored the city's natural beauty and historic character. It was buried in drab, utilitarian high-rises and threaded by roads that held no concern for the beauty destroyed in the process. Many valuable historic buildings – including the once grand cafés of the Plaça Catalunya – were torn down to make way for ugly modern business blocks.

Barcelona Ajuntament ever since. 1980 saw yet another set of elections, to the restored Generalitat, won by Jordi Pujol and his party Convergència i Unió. Pujol and his party have kept power throughout the 1980s and '90s. Imprisoned for Catalanist activities in 1960, Pujol represents a strain of conservative nationalism that goes back to Prat de la Riba. Facing each other across Plaça Sant Jaume, the Generalitat and Ajuntament are the two constants of modern Catalan politics.

CITY OF DESIGN

Inseparable from the restoration of democracy was a complete change in the city's atmosphere. In the 1970s, new freedoms – in culture, in sexuality, in work – were explored, and newly released energies expressed in a multitude of ways. Barcelona soon began to look different too, as the inherent dowdiness of the Franco years was swept away by a new Catalan style: postmodern, high-tech, punkish, comic strip, minimalist and tautly fashionable. In the 1980s, design mania struck the city, a product of the rebirth of Barcelona's artistic, artisan and architectural traditions.

This emphasis on slick, fresh style began on a street and underground level, but the special feature of Barcelona was the extent to which it was taken up by public authorities, and above all the Ajuntament, as a central part of their drive to reverse the policies of the previous regime. The highly educated technocrats who led the socialist city administration began to 'recover' the city from its neglected state, and in doing so enlisted the elite of the Catalan intellectual and artistic community to help. A rolling programme of urban renewal was initiated, beginning with the open spaces and public art programme and low-level initiatives, such as the campaign in which hundreds of historic façades were given an overdue facelift.

This ambitious, emphatically modern approach to urban problems acquired greater focus after Barcelona's bid to host the 1992 Olympic Games was accepted. Far more than just a sports event, the Games were to be Barcelona's third great effort to cast aside suggestions of second-city status and show the world what it could do. The exhibitions of 1888 and 1929 had seen developments in the Ciutadella and on and around Montjuïc; the Olympics provided an opening for work on a citywide scale. Taking advantage of the public and private investment, Barcelona planned an all-new orientation toward the sea, in a programme of urban renovation of a scope unseen in Europe since the post-World War II reconstruction.

Along with the creation of the new Barcelona in bricks and mortar came a city-sponsored promotion of Barcelona-as-concept, a seductive

...long live the king.

cocktail of architecture, imagination, tradition, style, nightlife and primary colours. This was perhaps the most spectacular – certainly the most deliberate – of Barcelona's many reinventions of itself; it also succeeded in good part because this image of creativity and vivacity fitted an idea many of Barcelona's citizens had always had of their town, as if the drab decades had been just a bad dream.

Inseparable from all this was Pasqual Maragall, mayor of Barcelona from 1982 to 1997, a tireless 'Mr Barcelona' who appeared in every possible forum to expound his vision of the role of cities, and who intervened personally to set the guidelines for projects or secure the participation of major international architects. In the process, Barcelona was transformed into an international reference point in urban affairs.

ENDGAMES

The Games were finally held in July-August 1992 and universally hailed a success. From then onwards, confidence picked up, the city's relentless self-promotion seemed actually to be attracting investment and Barcelona and Catalonia rode out Spain's post-1992 recession better than any other part of the country. The Ajuntament announced still more large-scale projects, such as the Old Port and the Raval. Maragall's personal popularity meant he was able to stand aside from the corruption scandals that dragged down his socialist allies in the central government of Felipe González after 14 years in office, and enabled the right-wing Partido Popular (PP) of José María Aznar to take power in Madrid after the elections of 1996.

From 1993 to 1999 the support of the Catalan nationalists in the Madrid parliament was essential to keep minority socialist and then PP central governments in power, a situation that enabled Jordi Pujol and his Convergència party to build up a pivotal role in Spanish affairs. In return for this cooperation Pujol sought more powers for the Generalitat, gaining a reputation as the most artful operator in Spanish politics. This image of canny agility went down well with his core following in Catalonia, but only added to his status as something of a hate-figure in many other parts of Spain.

In the last few years, the political panorama has been changeable. In Barcelona city politics, Pasqual Maragall stood down amid general surprise in 1997, after winning a fifth term. He was succeeded as mayor by his then little-known deputy, Joan Clos, who, however, held on to the Ajuntament with an increased majority in the next city elections in 1999. Maragall meanwhile declared his intention to challenge his old rival Jordi Pujol as socialist candidate for president of the Generalitat: in the October 1999 elections, the socialists won more votes than Convergència, but fewer seats in the Catalan parliament.

To stay in power, Pujol called on the local PP to return the favour he had done for the government in Madrid by supporting his minority administration. Then, in the Spanish general election in May 2000, Aznar and the PP gained an absolute majority. Freed from the much-resented need for horse-trading with the nationalists, the Aznar government has displayed a new and sometimes belligerent assertiveness, notably in calling for Spain to regain a sense of 'national unity' and reaffirming the powers of central government over the regions in the face of a decentralisation that, it feels, has gone too far. Pujol, his leverage gone, and dependent on the PP to retain power himself, was forced to retreat from his power-broker status, and placed in the uncomfortable position of having to simultaneously cooperate and argue with a central government that frequently challenges cherished Catalanist

Artur Mas (left) and **Jordi Pujol** shake on it.

ideals. Behind the policy details, old Catalan dilemmas of just how much separateness would be possible within Spain, and just what it is that Catalans want have not gone away. The tensions between nationalism and conservatism within Pujol's government are apparent, and his more nationalist supporters are disgruntled at Convergència's subservience to the PP.

In 2001 Jordi Pujol announced that, after 23 years in power, his current term would be his last. To the suprise of some, he named his current deputy, Artur Mas as his chosen successor for Generalitat president. Mas has already called for a new Autonomy Statute for Catalonia, to replace the current one, which was written in 1980. So far, though, there's been little sign that the Aznar government will react favourably to this demand. In the end, the most likely beneficiary of this ongoing argument in the next Catalan elections (which are scheduled to be held by October 2003) will be Pasqual Maragall, who will once again try to win the Generalitat for the socialists.

Key events

c15 BC Barcino founded by Roman soldiers.
cAD 350 Roman stone city walls built.
415 Barcelona briefly capital of Visigoths.
719 Muslims attack and seize Barcelona.
801 Barcelona taken by Franks.
985 Muslims sack Barcelona; Count Borrell II renounces Frankish sovereignty.
1035-76 Count Ramon Berenguer I of Barcelona extends his possessions into southern France.
1137 Count Ramon Berenguer IV marries Petronella of Aragon, uniting the two states in the Crown of Aragon.
c1160 *Homílies d'Organyà*, first Catalan texts, written.
1213 Pere I is killed and virtually all his lands north of the Pyrenees are seized by France.
1229 Jaume I conquers Mallorca, then Ibiza (1235) and Valencia (1238); second city wall built in Barcelona.
1274 Consell de Cent, municipal government of Barcelona, established.
1282 Pere II conquers Sicily.
1298 Gothic cathedral begun. Population of city c40,000.
1323-4 Conquest of Corsica and Sardinia.
1347-8 Black Death cuts population by half.
1462-72 Catalan civil war.
1479 Ferdinand II inherits Crown of Aragon, and with his wife Isabella unites the Spanish kingdoms.
1492 Final expulsion of Jews, and discovery of America.
1522 Catalans refused permission to trade in America.
1640 Catalan national revolt, the Guerra dels Segadors.
1652 Barcelona falls to Spanish army.
1702 War of Spanish Succession begins.
1714 Barcelona falls to Franco-Spanish army after siege.
1715 Nova Planta decree abolishes Catalan institutions; new ramparts and citadel built around Barcelona. Population c33,000.
1808-13 French occupation.
1814 Restoration of Ferdinand VII.
1833 Aribau publishes *Oda a la Pàtria*, beginning of Catalan cultural renaissance. Carlist wars begin.
1836-7 Dissolution of Barcelona monasteries.
1839 First workers' associations formed in Barcelona.
1842-4 Barcelona bombarded for the last time from Montjuïc, to quell Jamancia revolt.

1854 Demolition of Barcelona city walls.
1855 First general strike is violently suppressed.
1859 Cerdà plan for the Eixample approved.
1868 September: revolution overthrows Isabel II. November: first anarchist meetings held in Barcelona.
1873 First Spanish Republic.
1874 Bourbon monarchy restored under Alfonso XII.
1882 Work begins on the Sagrada Família.
1888 Barcelona Universal Exhibition.
1899 FC Barcelona founded; first electric trams.
1900 Population of Barcelona 537,354.
1909 Setmana Tràgica, anti-church and anti-army riots.
1910 CNT anarchist workers' union founded.
1921 First Barcelona Metro line opened.
1923 Primo de Rivera establishes dictatorship in Spain.
1929 Barcelona International Exhibition.
1930 Population 1,005,565. Fall of Primo de Rivera.
1931 14 April: Second Spanish Republic.
1934 October: Generalitat attempts revolt against new right-wing government in Madrid, and is then suspended.
1936 February: Popular Front wins Spanish elections; Catalan Generalitat restored. 19 July: military uprising against left-wing government is defeated in Barcelona.
1937 May: fighting within the republican camp in Barcelona.
1939 26 January: Barcelona taken by Franco's army.
1959 Stabilisation Plan opens up Spanish economy.
1975 20 November: Franco dies.
1977 First democratic general elections in Spain since 1936; provisional Catalan Generalitat re-established.
1978 First democratic local elections in Barcelona won by Socialists.
1980 Generalitat fully re-established under Jordi Pujol.
1982 Pasqual Maragall becomes mayor.
1992 Olympics Games held in Barcelona.
1996 Partido Popular wins Spanish elections.
1997 Joan Clos replaces Maragall as mayor.
1999 Jordi Pujol wins sixth term as president of the Generalitat.
2000 Partido Popular wins absolute majority in the Madrid parliament.

Barcelona Today

Never a city to rest upon its laurels.

Barcelona seems to have a knack for trophies. A decade after the Olympics and several years after receiving the Royal Institute of British Architects' gold medal (awarded for the first time ever to a city), came the 2002 Venice Biennial special prize for urban planning. The results of a 2002 BBC survey, meanwhile, included the city as one of the world's top 50 places to visit before one dies. The upcoming and much hyped events of 2004 promise to attract further applause, record numbers of visitors keep streaming in, business is booming on many fronts and relative social harmony reigns throughout the city.

POSITIVE ENERGIES

In short, most would agree that the city is doing well. So well, in fact, that sometimes one hears bizarre explanations for its success, such as the one given prior to the World Buddhist Conference, held here in the mid 1990s (only the third time the massive event had ever been staged outside of India or Tibet). The conference's selection committee apparently chose Barcelona because of the city's unique

and promising 'energy field'. More commonly given reasons for the city's rise include the social and cultural rebirth following years of dictatorship, and pure economics: Barcelona enjoys one of the most robust economies in Spain. When you get right down to it, however, the greatest measure of responsibility for Barcelona's good health clearly rests with the group of able socialists who have held the reins of city government for the last 25 years.

These left-leaning technocrats (or *'progres'* in local argot), many of them products of the 1960s, are currently led by a discreetly mannered, former anaesthetist, Mayor Joan Clos. Raised on a farm and educated in both Barcelona and Edinburgh, Clos got his start in Barcelona politics as director of public health before moving on to become Councillor of the Old City. Under his tutelage huge changes were carried out, most of them for the better. Among the best works were the 'ventilation' of the claustrophobic Raval by the Rambla del Raval; the addition of the MACBA to the same area, and the new housing projects that were constructed in Sant Pere.

What Fòrum?

FORUM 2004

As Mayor, Clos inherited momentum from his
very active predecessor, Pasqual Maragall.
The largest lump by far of this inheritance is
the Fòrum Universal de les Cultures 2004.
The Fòrum is an ambitious attempt to bring
together as many manifestations as possible
of the world's cultures, all under the benign
umbrella of peace, environmental sustainability
and social justice. The road to the Fòrum has
been less than smooth, unfortunately. There has
been considerable confusion over exactly what
it will be, as well as vehement criticism from
some groups that it is little more than a thinly
disguised property development scheme. Large
international developers certainly have their
fingers in the pie, and a small city of luxury
residential towers has risen around the Fòrum
zone at the sea end of the Avinguda Diagonal.
The area now has its own name, Diagonal-Mar,
and a brand new metro station. Indeed, millions
of euros have been pumped into this project.
More, according to some estimates, than Berlin
spent on urban development over several years.

With all the controversy, though, there's
no question that the work being carried out
in preparation for the event – the creation of
new parks, beaches and health facilities, the
construction of a high-speed train station
(connecting the city with Madrid and Paris) and
the cleaning up of the long-abused Besós River
– will vastly improve the quality of life locally.

DRIVING FORCES

All of this intense activity taking place in the
Fòrum area highlights a peculiar feature of the
city: Barcelona, unlike many of its European
and American counterparts, has long avoided
creating a concentrated business district. No
area fills up with stressed office workers during
the day only to become a ghost town at night.
Instead, there are what city planners like to
call 'zones of centrality', pockets of dense
office or commercial space that are knitted into
residential neighbourhoods. A recently created
example is the 22@ district in Poblenou, a zone
near the future Fòrum and one specifically
designed by the city council to attract high-tech
companies. The strategy behind this planning

is to combat the number one woe of all cities – mobility. Ideally, the thinking goes, one should be able to walk to work. Though the idea is sound, and may one day truly bear fruit, in practice Barcelona is still unfortunately plagued by the same abuse of private vehicles as most other cities, as anyone who has spent a day in the Eixample, for instance, will tell you.

EAST OF CENTRE
The fact that Barcelona has, for the most part, maintained or improved the quality of life for its residents, and the fact that its empowered neighbourhoods give the city something of the aspect of a federation of villages, neatly mirrors an emerging role the city is creating for itself on the international scene. Much in the model of a city-state, Barcelona has become the champion of a worldwide network of cities fighting to gain more economic and decision-making freedom from central governments. This organisation – known as United Cities and Local Governments – has recently chosen Barcelona to be its world headquarters. As vice-president of the UCLG, Mayor Clos has popped up at such events as the Johannesburg Earth Summit and United Nations assemblies, arguing, among other things, that city governments are the most appropriate bodies to deal with local environmental issues.

In many respects, it seems only fitting that Barcelona should take on such a fight. As the capital of a country-within-a-country (Catalonia within Spain), the city's relations with the Spanish central government have never been exactly easy. Relations have only worsened since the right-of-centre Spanish president, José María Aznar, and his Partido Popular (PP) have enjoyed an absolute majority in parliament, a state of affairs that limits Barcelona's ability

to influence important infrastructure decisions. The most notable example of this is the struggle to enlarge the city's airport to allow more intercontinental flights (in 2002, Barcelona's airport was second only to that of Beijing in terms of increase of visitors), and the linking of the high-speed train with the airport.

ALL CHANGE
Regional elections in the spring of 2003, meanwhile, will bring changes. If not to city politics (Clos has no significant rivals and the city's voters, at any rate, are firmly left of centre), then definitely to the leadership of the Catalan autonomous government, the Generalitat. Unlike the city council, which is very healthy in fiscal terms, the Generalitat – which has been led by the wily conservative Jordi Pujol for the last 20 years – is desperately in need of an honest auditor, and has been racked by a series of embarrassing financial scandals. Pujol himself will not seek re-election. His heir apparent, the stiff and uncharismatic Artur Mas, will in all likelihood lose to the more famous former city mayor, Pasqual Maragall. Should this come to pass, then the synergy between Maragall and his former protégé Clos might well augur an even brighter future for the city and for Catalonia.

The city, at any rate, has plenty of cards up its sleeve. Having hosted the very successful Year of Gaudi in 2002, which was presumably responsible for a more than 30 per cent increase in tourism, 2003 has been declared the Year of Sport. The city will yet again be the scene of important international sporting competitions, namely, the World Swimming Championships, the European Field Hockey Championships and the World Police and Fire Games. In other words, more trophies are assured.

Barcelona by numbers

1	ranking of Marc as name for newborn Catalans	41.7%	Catalans with Internet access at home
2	ranking of Maria as name for newborn Catalans	40%	Catalans who use home Internet access to look at porn
73%	Catalans 'proud to be Spanish'	60%	Catalans who would like to see bullfighting banned
82%	Catalans 'proud to be Catalan'		
232	calories in a *crema catalana*	217	inhabitants per doctor in Catalonia
260	skyscrapers in Barcelona	600+	inhabitants per doctor in UK
138	projected years needed, in total, to complete Sagrada Familia	34%	Catalans who own a musical instrument
30%	Catalans between 18 and 27 who admit to having tried marijuana at least once.	8.9%	Catalans who play a musical instrument
35%	roof terraces in Old City thought to have marijuana plants on them	15,000	total arrests clocked up by 500 bagsnatchers and pickpockets known to Barcelona police.

Talking a dying language

A couple of anecdotes should suffice to give an idea of the enormous linguistic change that Barcelona has undergone in the last hundred years or so. Towards the end of the 19th century, the Italian anarchist Giuseppe Fanelli came to Spain to help organise the burgeoning workers' movement of the time, but found it impossible to learn Spanish in Barcelona because so much Catalan was spoken here. Eventually, he had to move elsewhere in order to do so. In 1971, though, when the renowned Catalan writer Mercè Rodoreda returned to Barcelona after three decades of political exile, she immediately decided to move out to the country for because she said she no longer felt at home in the city. Her move was partly due to the fact that Barcelona had become 'bilingual', meaning that Spanish was now as widely spoken as Catalan.

In other words, between Fanelli's arrival and Rodoreda's return, there had been a massive increase in the use of Spanish in Barcelona, and the causes are not hard to find: first, the imposition of this language and the corresponding banning of Catalan in all public and private fields by a fascist dictatorship that lasted thirty-six years; second, the migration into the city of over half a million people from the poorest areas of Spain, who sought work and a new life in industrialised Catalonia.

With the full legalisation of Catalan after democracy, a host of political parties, unions and NGOs tried to redress the balance as regards its public use. It is thanks to their efforts that, as you travel around the city, you will find that most public transport information, for example, is written in Catalan (and usually in Spanish and English too). The station announcements on the metro are exclusively in Catalan, as are the indications in the municipal car parks as to whether or not they are full. Within Catalonia, some Spanish supermarket chains have labelled their brands exclusively in Catalan; most restaurants put their main menus in Catalan, and Catalan is the only language used for signs in most hospitals, in all city council buildings, and, by the by, on a whole bunch of toilet doors.

More importantly, according to the most recent survey available (1996), 73 per cent of Barcelona's citizens can now speak Catalan, and a mere 3 per cent don't understand it at all. Why, then, did one of the country's leading linguists, Joan Solà, recently declare publicly that the decline in daily use of Catalan in Barcelona heralded the language's extinction? The decline could be due to the tendency of *barcelonins* to switch to Spanish as soon as they suspect that they are not addressing a native Catalan speaker. Or to the increasing use of Spanish as a group language among young people, despite Catalan being the language of education at every level. Whatever, the fact is that Barcelona's delicate linguistic situation is by no means resolved, and that the words of the contemporary Catalan poet Màrius Sampere may well turn out to be more than just a bit of ironic bravado: 'How I adore writing in a dying language.'

Architecture

Buildings are Barcelona's art, and rooftops its museums.

A clear line of continuity can be traced between generations of Catalan architects. Even though ideas, attitudes and trends are taken in from abroad, they are almost always assimilated by the strong local culture. This is because, in Catalonia seemingly more than anywhere, national identity is expressed through architecture in the same way that in other countries it is expressed through art or music. Periods when architecture flourishes have generally reflected eras of increased Catalan freedoms and wealth. With those elements, it seems, inevitably comes a reinforcement of collective civic pride.

Catalan builders have always had a penchant for decorating surfaces, and a preoccupation with texture and the use of fine materials and finishes. This is combined with a simplicity of line and sense of sobriety often seen as distinguishing Catalan character from that of the rest of Spain. Other common elements are references to the traditional architecture of rural Catalonia – the large *masia* farmhouses, with chalet-type tile roofs, massive stone walls and round-arched

doorways, a style maintained by anonymous builders for centuries – and to the powerful constructions of Catalan Romanesque and Gothic. There has also long been a close relationship between architects and craftsmen in the production of buildings, especially in the working of metal and wood.

The revival of Catalan culture and the city of Barcelona since 1975 have been accompanied by dynamic expansion in architecture, as is well known world-wide. Modern Catalans want to contribute to their architectural heritage today, rather than merely to preserve it as a relic of the past. Contemporary buildings are daringly constructed alongside (even within) old ones, and this mix of old and new is a prime characteristic of many of the most successful projects in Barcelona in the past two decades.

The importance of architecture here is also reflected in public attitudes; Barcelona residents take a keen interest in their buildings. A range of architectural guides is available, some in English (*see p323*) and informative leaflets on building styles are also provided (in English) at tourist offices (*see pp318-9*).

ROMAN TO GOTHIC

The Roman citadel of Barcino was founded
on the hill of Mons Taber, just behind the
cathedral, which to this day remains the
religious and civic heart of the city. The
Roman settlement left an important legacy
in the fourth-century city wall, fragments of
which are visible around the Old City.

Barcelona's next occupiers, the Visigoths,
left little in the city, although a trio of fine
Visigothic churches survives nearby in
Terrassa. When the Catalan state began to
form under the Counts of Barcelona from the
ninth century, the dominant architecture of
this new community was massive, simple
Romanesque. In the Pyrenean valleys there
are hundreds of fine Romanesque buildings,
notably at **Sant Pere de Rodes**, **Ripoll**,
Sant Joan de les Abadesses and **Besalú**.
There are, however, relatively few in Barcelona.
On the right-hand side of the cathedral, looking
at the main façade, is the 13th-century chapel
of **Santa Llúcia**, incorporated into the later
structure, while tucked away near Plaça
Catalunya is the church of **Santa Anna** and
in La Ribera there is the tiny travellers' chapel,
the **Capella d'en Marcús**. The city's greatest
Romanesque monument is the beautifully plain
12th-century church and cloister of **Sant Pau
del Camp**, built as part of a larger monastery.

By the 13th century, Barcelona was the
capital of a trading empire, and growing
rapidly. The settlements called *ravals* or
vilanoves that had sprung up outside the
Roman walls were brought within the city by
the building of Jaume I's second set of walls,
which extended Barcelona west to the Rambla.

This commercial growth and political
eminence formed the background to the
great flowering of Catalan Gothic, with the
construction of many of Barcelona's most
important civic and religious buildings. The
cathedral was begun in 1298, in place of an
11th-century building. Work began on the
Ajuntament (Casa de la Ciutat) and **Palau
de la Generalitat** in 1372 and 1403
respectively. Major additions were made to the
Palau Reial of the Catalan-Aragonese kings,
especially the **Saló del Tinell** of 1359-62, and
the great hall of the **Llotja** or trading exchange
was finished in 1380-92. Many of Barcelona's
finest buildings were built or completed in these
years, in the midst of the crisis that followed
the turmoil of the Black Death.

Catalan Gothic has characteristics that
distinguish it from northern, classic Gothic. It
is simpler, and gives more prominence to solid,
plain walls between towers and columns, rather
than the empty spaces between intricate flying
buttresses that were the trademarks of the great

The majesty of **Santa Maria del Mar**.

French cathedrals. This means that the
Catalan buildings appear much more massive.
In façades, as much emphasis is given to
horizontals as to verticals; octagonal towers end
in cornices and flat roofs, not spires. Decorative
intricacies are mainly confined to windows,
portals, arches and gargoyles. Many churches
have no aisles but only a single nave, the classic
example of this design being the beautiful
Santa Maria del Pi in Plaça del Pi, built
between 1322 and 1453.

This style has ever since provided the
historic benchmark for Catalan architecture.
It is simple and robust, yet elegant and
practical. Innovative, sophisticated techniques
were developed: the use of transverse arches
supporting timber roofs allowed the spanning
of great halls uninterrupted by columns, a
system used in the Saló del Tinell. Designed
by Pere III's court architect Guillem Carbonell,
it has some of the largest pure masonry arches
in Europe, the elegance and sheer scale of which
give the space tremendous splendour. The
Drassanes, built from 1378 as the royal
shipyards (and now the **Museu Marítim**),
is really just a very beautiful shed, but its
enormous parallel aisles make this one of
the most imposing spaces in the city.

La Ribera, the Vilanova del Mar, was the
commercial centre of the city, and gained the
magnificent masterpiece of Catalan Gothic,
Santa Maria del Mar, built between 1329-
84. Its superb proportions are based on a
series of squares imposed on one another,

with three aisles of almost equal height. The interior is quite staggering in its austerity.

The domestic architecture of medieval Barcelona, at least that of its noble and merchant residences, can be seen at its best in the line of palaces along **Carrer Montcada**, next to Santa Maria. Built by the city's merchant elite at the height of their confidence and wealth, they conform to a very Mediterranean style of urban palace, making maximum use of space. In most of the buildings, a plain exterior is presented to the street with heavy doors opening into an imposing patio on one side of which a grand external staircase leads to the main rooms on the first floor (*planta noble*), which often have elegant open loggias. Many of these palaces now house some of Barcelona's most visited cultural institutions.

MARKING TIME
By the beginning of the 16th century, political and economic decline meant there were far fewer patrons for new construction in the city. While a good deal was built over the subsequent 300 years, there was little of distinctive Catalan style. Among those of some note, the **Palau del Lloctinent** was built for the royal viceroys on Plaça del Rei in the 1550s. The Italian Renaissance style main façade was added to the **Generalitat** in 1596. The Church built lavishly during this time, with baroque convents and churches along La Rambla (of which the **Betlem** (1680-1729), at the corner of C/Carme, is the most important survivor). Later baroque churches include **Sant Felip Neri** (1721-52) and **La Mercè** (1765-75).

Another addition, after the siege of Barcelona in 1714, was new military architecture, since the city was encased in ramparts and fortresses. Examples remain in the **Castell de Montjuïc**, the buildings in the **Ciutadella** – one now the Catalan parliament – and the **Barceloneta**.

A more positive 18th-century alteration was the conversion of the Rambla into a paved promenade, begun in 1775 with the demolition of Jaume I's second wall. Neo-classical palaces were built alongside: **La Virreina** and the **Palau Moja** (at the corner of C/Portaferrisa) both date from the 1770s. Also from that time but in a less classical style is the **Gremial dels Velers** (Candlemakers' Guild) at Via Laietana 50, with its two-toned stucco decoration.

It was not, however, until the closure of the monasteries in the 1820s and '30s that major rebuilding on the Rambla could begin. Most of the first structures that replaced them were still in international, neo-classical styles. The site that is now the **Mercat de la Boqueria** was first remodelled in 1836-40 as Plaça Sant Josep

to a design by Francesc Daniel Molina, based on the English Regency style of John Nash. It is now buried beneath the 1870s market building, but its Doric colonnade can still be detected. Molina also designed the **Plaça Reial**, begun in 1848. Other fine examples from the same era are the collonaded **Porxos d'en Xifré**, the 1836 blocks opposite the Llotja on Passeig Isabel II, by the Port Vell.

BIRTH OF THE MODERN CITY
In the 1850s, Barcelona was able to expand physically, with the demolition of the walls, and psychologically, with economic expansion and the cultural reawakening of the Catalan Renaixença. And from the first, one could see in operation one of the characteristics of modern Barcelona – audacious planning. The city would spread outwards and be connected up to Gràcia and other outlying towns through the great grid of the **Eixample**, designed by **Ildefons Cerdà** (1815-75). An engineer by trade, Cerdà was also a radical influenced by utopian socialist ideas, concerned with the cramped, unhealthy conditions of workers' housing in the old city.

His plan, begun in 1859, was closely related to visionary rationalist ideas of its time, with its love of straight lines and uniform grids. In keeping with this style, Cerdà placed two of its main avenues along a geographic parallel and added a meridian. Cerdà's central aim was to alleviate overpopulation while encouraging social equality by using quadrangular blocks of a standard size, with strict building controls to ensure that they were built up on only two sides, to a limited height, leaving a garden in between. Each district would be of 20 blocks, containing all community necessities.

In the event, though, this idealised use of urban space was scarcely ever achieved, for the private developers who actually built the Eixample regarded Cerdà's restrictions on their property as pointless interference. Buildings went up to much more than the planned heights, and in practice all the blocks from Plaça Catalunya to the Diagonal have been enclosed, with very few inner gardens withstanding the onslaught of construction.

However, the construction of the Eixample saw the refinement of a specific type of building: the apartment block, with giant flats on the *principal* floor (first above the ground), often with large glassed-in galleries for the drawing room, and small flats above. The area's growth also provided perfect conditions for the pre-eminence of the most famous of Catalan architectural styles, **Modernisme**, the very distinct local variant of art nouveau. (For more information on the movement and

All that glitters

Barcelona has always been associated with fine architecture. The 'new' Barcelona created since the late '70s – not from any one grand plan but through a constant, open-ended stream of partial schemes – enjoys great press internationally. Even locals, after years of feelgood propaganda designed to convince them that onwards and upwards is always the best path, are often loath to appear stick-in-the-muds and query the merits of the next big project. Over time, though, as grand project-ism has been enshrined as a self-justifying official obsession, it has become an ever more valid question to ask just what and for whom all Barcelona's urban regeneration is for, and to look more critically at its results. The much-applauded social objectives of the early projects – the 'recovery' of Barcelona for its citizens after the neglect of the Franco era, and the creation of open spaces – are now hard to make out amid the relentless, immensely successful promotional operation that is Barcelona Incorporated.

One of the most lauded aims of the main programme – to renovate the old city without displacing its living communities or disturbing its traditional fabric – has been only patchily achieved, and is much less visible in many areas than gentrification.

Fòrum 2004

In addition to its landmark new architecture Barcelona has unquestionably acquired a deal of architectural dross.

There is a great irony here, in that many of the features of Barcelona most appreciated by foreigners (and, in their more romantic moments, by locals not signed up with official bodies) are to do with the city's unique character. Its attraction is its individuality and unpredictability, its asymmetries and idiosyncrasies, and in architecture, the very distinctiveness of the Catalan tradition itself,

its proponents, the most famous of whom was Antoni Gaudí, *see chapter* **Modernisme**.) Most Modernista architects, in love with curves, had in fact initially decried Cerdà's project as a horror, but it was later to become the ultimate showcase for their imaginative feats. Equally, the interplay between the straight lines of the Eixample's roads and buildings and the disorderly tangle of the older city has become an essential part of Barcelona's identity.

As well as an openness to ambitious planning, another recurring feature of modern Barcelona is the limited political and financial resources available to put these big schemes into effect, due among other things to Barcelona's not being the capital of a state. The city's favoured means of breaking out of this anomalous, second-city status and giving a kick-start to development has been to organise a big international event to raise some cash. Each one of these massive fundraisers has left a distinctive stamp on Barcelona: the first, the **Universal Exhibition of 1888**, definitively established Modernisme as the

favourite architectural style of the city, above all in the buildings around the Ciutadella (most of which were designed by Domènech i Muntaner). The surviving example is the **Museu de Zoologia**, in a building that was constructed to hold the exhibition's restaurant.

THE 20TH CENTURY

By the 1910s, Modernisme had become too extreme for the Barcelona middle class, and the later buildings (including those by Gaudi) were often met with derision. The new 'proper' style for Catalan architecture was Noucentisme, which stressed the importance of classical proportions. However, it failed to produce anything of note: the primary surviving buildings in this style are those of the 1929 Exhibition, Barcelona's second 'big event', which was also the excuse for the bizarre, neo-baroque **Palau Nacional**.

The 1929 Exhibition also brought to Barcelona one of the most important buildings of the century: Mies van der Rohe's German Pavilion, the **Pavelló Barcelona**, rebuilt near its historic openness to decoration and to the playful, quirky or eccentric. Many of its renovation schemes, on the other hand, have often seemed directed, by accident or design, towards ironing out the edges of this urban mix, towards making this a more off-the-peg, standardised, neat-and-tidy, international city.

A certain ideal of urban uniformity was implicit in many of Barcelona's historic 'grand plans', and has continued to underlie many schemes since 1975. In extending Cerdà's grid down to the sea, for example, Oriol Bohigas' design for the Vila Olímpica did away with much of the raggedy old industrial barri of Poblenou. This same idea is now being extended in Diagonal-Mar. Each scheme, of course, has its spectacular, prize-winning headline building by a big-name architect to concentrate the attention, but in the background, here and in many other areas, new streets are filled with bland, production-line blocks, often built over what were once some of the more individual, characterful parts of the city. This has been the case in the last few years, as the planning obsession has been extended to districts previously left untouched. The sheer scale and pace of Barcelona's building schemes has meant that architectural finer points have often been dispensed with. Famous Modernista

buildings, of course, are preserved to be showcased, but elsewhere – the flanks of Montjüic, the Turó de la Rovira – atmospheric streets and squares and distinctive, small-scale older buildings are swept away to be replaced by drab, uniform beige blocks in a utilitarian, cost-cutting brutalist style that is no longer fashionable anywhere.

Barcelona's latest great event is the global Fòrum Universal de les Cultures in 2004. If this orgy of good intentions goes to plan, after every issue under the sun has been duly chewed over for five months, on the last day Dubya and Osama will fall into a hug in front of a tearful crowd in the vast new convention centre as the world looks forward to a new and peaceful future, all thanks to the foresight of the Ajuntament de Barcelona. Behind the noble sentiments, however, those who call the shots in Barcelona do not deny that, for them, the main attraction of the Fòrum is that it will help along the Diagonal-Mar project, the latest grand design in their rather unfraternal effort to maximize the city's competitiveness. One motif of the Fòrum, supposedly, is to celebrate cultural diversity. The pulse of the new Barcelona, though, as manifest in the dreary tower blocks of Diagonal-Mar, seems to be to override the dense, imaginative texture of the city itself.

its original location in 1986. Even today it looks modern in its challenge to conventional ideas of space, and its impact at the time was extraordinary. Mies had a strong influence on the hottest trend in Catalan architecture of the 1930s, which, reacting against Modernisme and nearly all earlier Catalan styles, was emphatically functionalist. Its leading figures were Josep Lluís Sert and the GATCPAC collective (Group of Catalan Architects and Technicians for the Progress of Contemporary Architecture), who struggled to introduce the ideas of their friend Le Corbusier and the International Style. Under the Republic, Sert built a sanatorium off C/Tallers, and the **Casa Bloc**, a workers' housing project at Passeig Torres i Bages 91-105 in Sant Andreu. In collaboration with Le Corbusier the GATCPAC also produced a plan for the radical redesign of the whole of Barcelona as a 'functional city', the Pla Macià of 1933. Surviving drawings for the scheme present this plan as an entirely new stark Barcelona that closely resembles a Soviet-era Siberian town, so few regret that it

never got off the drawing board. In 1937, Sert also built the Spanish Republic's pavilion for that year's Paris Exhibition, since rebuilt in Barcelona as the **Pavelló de la República** in Vall d'Hebron. His finest work, however, came much later, in the **Fundació Joan Miró**, built in the 1970s after he had spent years in exile in the United States.

BARCELONA'S THIRD STYLE

The Franco years had an enormous impact on the city: as the economy expanded at breakneck speed in the 1960s, Barcelona received a massive influx of migrants, in a context of unchecked property speculation and minimal planning controls. The city was ringed by a chaotic mass of high-rise suburbs. Another legacy of the era are some ostentatiously tall office blocks, especially on the Diagonal and around Plaça Francesc Macià.

Hence, when an all-new democratic city administration finally took over the reins of Barcelona at the end of the 1970s, there was a great deal for it to do. But, even though a generation of Catalan architects had been chafing at Francoist restrictions for years, the tone set early on by Barcelona's since-ubiquitous chief planner Oriol Bohigas was one of 'architectural realism', with a powerful combination of imagination and practicality. Budgets were limited, so it was decided that resources should not initially be concentrated on buildings, but on the gaps between them, by creating a string of fresh, contemporary parks and squares, augmented with original artwork. From that moment, Barcelona placed itself in the forefront of international urban design.

Barcelona's renewal programme took on a more ambitious shape in advance of the 1992 Olympics, helped by a booming late-1980s economy. The third and most spectacular of the city's great events, the Barcelona games were intended to be stylish and innovative, and to provide focus for a sweeping renovation of the city. The three main Olympic sites – **Vila Olímpica**, **Montjuïc** and **Vall d'Hebron** – are each quite individual. The Vila Olímpica had the most comprehensive masterplan, which sought to extend Cerdà's grid down to the seafront. The main project on Montjuïc was the transformation of the existing 1929 stadium, but alongside it there is also Arata Isozaki's **Palau Sant Jordi**, with its space-frame roof. Vall d'Hebron is the least successful of the three sites, but Esteve Bonell's **Velòdrom** is still one of the finest (not to mention the earliest) of the city's sports buildings. Perhaps an indication of the city's optimism, it was constructed even before the city made its Olympic bid in 1984.

Even after the Olympics, the city continued to expand through the '90s, as one major scheme followed another. Post-1992, the focus

shifted to the Raval and the Port Vell (old port), and then more recently to the Diagonal-Mar area in the north of the city. Many striking buildings are by local architects, such as Helio Piñón and Albert Viaplana, whose work combines fluid, elegant lines with a modern use of materials. This can be seen in the controversial 1983 **Plaça dels Països Catalans** and the daring transformations of historic buildings such as the old Casa de la Caritat (now the **Centre de Cultura Contemporània**) and in new projects like **Maremàgnum** in the port. Others are by international names: Richard Meier's bold white **MACBA**, or Norman Foster's **Torre de Collserola** on Tibidabo. Another major project, the giant, box-like **Auditori**, is by Madrid-based architect Rafael Moneo.

The latest architectural changes are associated with the polemical **Fòrum Universal de les Cultures** planned for 2004. The main activity is along the shoreline of Diagonal-Mar, with the construction of seaside high-rises and the development of the city's second-largest park, already under construction atop a huge landfill. Again, internationally famous architects have been invited to endow the city with new wonders: the main **Edifici Fòrum** convention centre – a flat, glittering triangle – is by Swiss architect Jacques Herzog. French architect Jean Nouvel has designed a blatantly phallic 142-metre (466-foot) skyscraper, the **Torre Agbar**, for the nearby Plaça de les Glòries. All this dynamic new architecture has come to represent a 'third style' incorporated into the city's identity. It sits comfortably alongside Gothic and Modernisme, but is far more diffuse and eclectic than either.

Pavelló de la República: a masterpiece of Rationalist architecture. *See p37.*

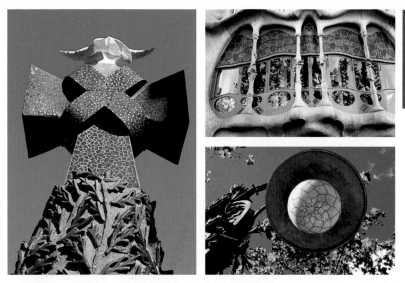

Modernisme

Art nouveau given an indefinable Catalan éclat.

For all Catalonia's long and varied traditions in architecture and the arts, no style is more identified with it than Modernisme. This is in part due to the enormous modern popularity of its most famous proponent, Gaudí – and with its mix of unrestrained decoration, eccentric unpredictability, dedicated craftsmanship and solid practicality, Modernisme can also be seen as matching certain archetypes of Catalan character. For some 25 years, during one of the most formative periods in Barcelona's history – from the mid 1880s to around 1908, Modernisme dominated every area of the arts and, above all, architecture, leaving an indelible stamp on the city.

To some extent Modernisme was the Catalan variant of art nouveau. The late 19th century was a time of uncertainty in the arts and architecture across Europe, as a range of new pressures – the huge expansion of cities, dramatic social upheavals, the rise of new nationalisms and political currents – all created special tensions, while the introduction of iron and steel and other new materials demanded a new architectural language. Art nouveau

emerged as the end of the century approached, encompassing some of these concerns and contradictions. Its influence spread quickly all over Europe and to the Americas; from around 1890 to 1914 it became the leading movement in the decorative and fine arts, integrating spectacularly in architecture. In Catalonia, its influence merged forcefully with the growth of the cultural and political movement of the Catalan Renaixença, to produce what became known as Modernisme (always confusing, since 'modernism' in English usually refers to 20th-century functional styles).

Influenced by a variety of mainly French and British currents – Ruskin, William Morris and the Arts and Crafts movement, Viollet-le-Duc and French symbolism – Modernisme was nevertheless a passionately nationalist and self-consciously indigenous expression that made

▶ Many of the buildings mentioned in this chapter are described in more detail in the **Sightseeing** chapters, particularly **The Eixample**, see p111.

On the tiles

Of the many architects who went to work for Antoni Gaudí, only one was able to find his way out from under the master's eccentric dominance to make a mark of his own. Josep Maria Jujol was born in 1879, the year Gaudí began to work as an assistant to the Sagrada Familia's first architect, Francisco de Paula del Villar. Like so many of Gaudí's close-knit circle, he was born in Tarragona, studied architecture in Barcelona, and was a pious Catholic, a fact that was not at all contradictory to a highly creative conception of building design.

By the time Jujol came to work for Gaudí, in 1904, many of the great monuments of the Modernista style had already been built. This did not impede Jujol from influencing his mentor in fundamental ways, something ignored by official history until only a few decades ago. Jujol is now celebrated for giving Gaudí's work a greater quality of surface design, thanks to his particular sensibility for sculpture and painting. At **La Pedrera** he is now given credit for the extraordinary wrought-iron balconies and the beautiful frescoes in the courtyards, recently restored, and, while Gaudí had used his trademark 'trencadís' broken tile technique before Jujol came along, the young assistant was to take it to new heights at **Park Güell**. It was Jujol who came up with the fascinating collages of glass and ceramics that adorn the ceiling of the covered area supported by thick columns. Around the open square above, on the famous undulating bench, he worked with a team of masons to cover the surface in whimsical fashion, picking out combinations of colours and shapes from piles of used ceramic, to create the culminating moment of the trencadís method.

As an independent architect, Jujol was unable to secure wealthy private patrons in Barcelona with the ease of his predecessors, and his most important work in Barcelona

was only begun in 1923. The **Casa Planells** at Avda Diagonal 332 has a heavy, rounded stone façade punctuated by brickwork, and an interesting system of grilles and shutters to filter light and air, although the upper two floors were completed by another architect.

Jujol's most challenging work, however, was done outside Barcelona, in Sant Joan Despí. The **Torre de la Creu** from 1913 is unmissable, hovering over the present-day train station. It was originally conceived as two mirror-image homes for his aunt, which were joined in a later renovation. This small suburb has many other Jujol buildings, including **Can Negre**, an old farmhouse that Jujol renovated for the owner, adding delicate details like a surrealistic staircase. Now a community centre, it can be visited alone or as part of a town-wide Jujol tour on the last Sunday of each month.

Jujol eventually found solace in small commissions in his home province of Tarragona. The **Teatre Metropol** on the Tarragona Rambla is nondescript on the outside, but within the small, elegantly renovated theatre there are beautiful Jujolian touches. Happy to find refuge in obscure rural projects, Jujol worked on a magnificent religious sanctuary in Montferri and came up with a church for the tiny village of Vistabella, near the home of his parents. Completed in 1923, it is a masterpiece, with soft textures complementing radical structural asymmetry. Both buildings are worth seeking out, although a car and a good map are essential. Jujol continued to work in humility until his death in 1949, plying his trade far from the cosmopolitan lights of Barcelona.

Centre Jujol–Can Negre

Plaça Catalunya s/n, Sant Joan Despí (93 373 73 63). RENFE from Plaça Catalunya. **Open** 9am-2pm, 4-8pm Tue-Fri; 5.30-8pm Sat; noon-2pm Sun.

use of, and in many cases revived, Catalan traditions of design and craftwork. Its artists strove to revalue the best of Catalan art, showing enormous interest in the Romanesque and Gothic of the Catalan Golden Age. Domènech i Muntaner, for example, took great pains to combine iron frame construction with the same distinctive Catalan styles of brick that had been employed in the Middle Ages, regarding them as an 'expression of the Catalan earth'. Like art nouveau artists elsewhere, Modernistas sought to integrate fine and decorative arts, and gave as much weight to furniture and glasswork as to painting, sculpture and architecture.

All art nouveau had a tendency to look backwards and forwards at the same time, combining a love of decoration and also of craftsmanship with new industrial techniques and materials, and so it was in Catalonia. Modernista architects, even as they constructed a nostalgic and legendary vision of the ideal Catalan motherland, and plunged into an experimentation with the new technologies of the age. Encouraged by their wealthy patrons, they began to design works of iron and glass, introduced electricity, water and gas piping to their building plans. They were the first to tile bathroom and kitchen walls, made a point of allowing natural light and fresh air into all rooms, and toyed with the most advanced, revolutionary expressionism.

Catalan Modernista creativity was at its peak from 1888 to 1908. The Eixample is the style's foremost display case, with the greatest concentration of art nouveau in Europe (the Ajuntament's *Quadrat d'Or* book is a good architectural guide, and you can find it in many local book stores), but Modernista buildings and details can be found in innumerable other locations around Barcelona and Catalonia: in streets behind the Paral.lel or villas on Tibidabo, in shop interiors or dark hallways and in the cava cellars of the Penedès.

International interest in Gaudí often eclipses the fact that there were many other remarkable architects and designers working at that time; it is still less appreciated that Modernisme was much more than an architectural style. The movement included painters such as **Ramón Casas**, **Santiago Rusiñol** and **Isidre Nonell**, sculptors such as **Josep Llimona**, **Miquel Blay** and **Eusebi Arnau**, and furniture makers like the superb Mallorcan, **Gaspar Homar**; and, much more than any other form of art nouveau, it extended into literature, thought and music, marking a whole generation of Catalan writers, poets, composers and philosophers. Although it was in architecture that it found its most splendid

and lasting expression, it is clear in retrospect that Modernisme was an artistic movement in the fullest sense of the word.

GAUDÍ
Seen as the genius of the Modernista movement, Antoni Gaudí i Cornet was really a one-off, an unclassifiable figure. His work was a product of the social and cultural context of the time, but also of his own unique perception of the world, together with a deep patriotic devotion to all things Catalan. Unlike Domènech i Montaner and Puig i Cadafalch, who were both public figures who took an active part in politics and other fields, Gaudí, after being fairly sociable as a youth, became increasingly eccentric, leading a semi-monastic existence lost in his own obsessions.

Born in Reus in 1852, he qualified as an architect in 1878. His first architectural work was as assistant to Josep Fontseré on the building of the **Parc de la Ciutadella** in the 1870s. The gates and fountain of the park are attributed to him, and around the same time he also designed the lamp-posts in the **Plaça Reial**. His first major commission was for the **Casa Vicens** in Gràcia, which he built from 1883 and 1888 for Manuel Vicens, a tile manufacturer. An orientalist fantasy, it is structurally fairly conventional, but Gaudí's control of the use of surface material already stands out in the building's exuberant neo-Moorish decoration and multicoloured tiling and in the superbly elaborate ironwork on the gates. The house, originally half its current size, was enlarged in the 1920s by another architect, who had the decency to respect the original Gaudí design. Gaudí's **Col.legi de les Teresianes** convent school (1888-9) is more restrained, but has great clarity and fluidity.

An event of crucial importance in Gaudí's life came in 1878, when he met Eusebi Güell, heir to one of the largest industrial fortunes in Catalonia. Güell had been impressed by some of Gaudí's early furniture, and the pair also discovered that they shared many ideas on religion, philanthropy and the socially redemptive role of architecture. Güell placed utter confidence in his architect, allowing him to work with complete liberty. Gaudí produced several buildings for Güell, the first being the **Palau Güell** (1886-8), a darkly impressive, historicist building that established his reputation, and the crypt at **Colònia Güell** outside Barcelona, one of his most structurally experimental and surprising buildings.

In 1883, Gaudí became involved in the design of the **Sagrada Família**, begun the previous year. He would eventually devote himself to it entirely. Gaudí was profoundly religious, and an extreme Catholic conservative; part of his

Modernisme

Hotel España
Domènech designed the bar, Eusebi Arnau the curvaceous fireplace and the main dining room is adorned with water nymph murals by Ramon Casas. *See p54.*

Palau Güell
Behind the striking features of the exterior is a wonderful Gaudí interior. *See p91.*

Palau de la Música Catalana
Domènech's extraordinary concert hall is the epitome of Modernisme; the explosion in tile, sculpture and glass makes any event here special. *See p96.*

Museu de Zoologia
Domènech's 'Castle of Three Dragons' sums up the fairy-tale side of Modernisme, but was also highly innovative in its use of iron, glass and brick. *See p96.*

Museu d'Art Modern
Painting by Rusiñol, Casas and Nonell, and decorative art including the spectacular inlaid wood furniture of Gaspar Homar. *See p95.*

Manzana de la Discordia
Gaudí's utterly original Casa Batlló, Puig i Cadafalch's cautious, medievalist Casa Ametller and the lush curves of Domènech i Montaner's Casa Lleó Morera. *See p117.*

La Pedrera
A fine contrast to the Sagrada Família: Gaudí's most successful combination of imagination and radical architectural innovation. *See p113.*

Fàbrica Casaramona
Puig's former textile mill is a prime example of Modernista industrial building. *See p102.*

La Sagrada Família
Modernisme's most eccentric, ambitious monument. *See p112.*

Hospital de Sant Pau
One of the most successful examples of the application of Modernista style and vivid decoration to a very practical purpose. *See p116.*

Park Güell
An incomplete, tantalising vision of Gaudí's ideal world. *See p121.*

obsession with the building was a belief that it would help redeem Barcelona from the sins of secularism and from the modern era (some conservative Catalan Catholics have long been campaigning for him to be made a saint). From 1908 until his death he worked on no other projects, often sleeping on-site, a shabby, white-haired hermit, producing visionary ideas that his assistants had to 'interpret' into drawings.

The Sagrada Família became the testing ground for Gaudí's ideas on structure and form. His boyhood interest in nature began to take form, and what had previously provided external decorative motifs became the inspiration for the structure of his buildings.

In his greatest years, Gaudí combined other commissions with his cathedral. **La Pedrera** (also known as **Casa Milà**), begun in 1905, was his most complete project. In a prime location on a corner of Passeig de Gràcia, it has an aquatic feel about it: the balconies resemble seaweed, and the undulating façade the sea. The roof resembles an imaginary landscape inhabited by mysterious figures. The **Casa Batlló**, on the other side of Passeig de Gràcia, was an existing building that Gaudí remodelled in 1905-7; the roof looks like a reptilian creature perched high above the street.

Gaudí's later work has a uniquely dreamlike quality. His fascination with natural forms found full expression in the **Park Güell** (1900-14), where he blurs the distinction between natural and artificial forms in a series of colonnades winding up the hill. These paths lead up to the large central terrace projecting over a hall. The terrace benches are covered in some of the finest examples of *trencadís* (broken mosaic work), mostly by Jujol (*see p40* **On the tiles**).

In June 1926, Antoni Gaudí was run over by a tram on the Gran Via. Nobody recognised the down-at-heel old man, and he was taken to a public ward in the old Hospital de Santa Creu in the Raval, where he died. When his identity was discovered, Barcelona gave its most famous architect an elaborate funeral.

DOMÈNECH I MONTANER
A vital, decisive, boost was given to Modernista architecture as the style of turn-of-the-century Barcelona by the **Universal Exhibition of 1888**. The most important buildings commissioned for the show were planned by **Lluís Domènech i Montaner** (1850-1923), then far more prominent than Gaudí as a propagandist for Modernisme in all its forms and much more of a classic Modernista architect. Most of the Exhibition buildings no longer exist, but one that remains is the **Castell dels Tres Dragons** in the Ciutadella park,

La Pedrera.
See p113.

Palau de la Música Catalana.

designed to be the exhibition restaurant and now the **Museu de Zoología**. It already demonstrated many key features of Modernista style: the use of structural ironwork allowed greater freedom in the creation of openings, arches and windows.

Domènech was one of the first Modernista architects to develop the idea of the 'total work', working closely with large teams of craftsmen and designers on every aspect of a building. His greatest creations are the **Hospital de Sant Pau**, built as small 'pavilions' within a garden to avoid the usual visual and emotional effect of a monolithic hospital, and the fabulous **Palau de la Música Catalana**, an extraordinary display of outrageous decoration.

Domènech also left behind several impressive constructions in Reus, near Tarragona, most notably the elaborate and ornate mansions known respectively as **Casa Navàs** and **Casa Rull**. Similarly grand are his spectacular

pavilions at the **Institut Pere Mata**, a pyschiatric hospital and the forerunner of the Hospital de Sant Pau.

PUIG I CADAFALCH

Third in the trio of leading Modernista architects was **Josep Puig i Cadafalch** (1867-1957), who showed a strong neo-Gothic influence in such buildings as the **Casa de les Punxes** ('House of Spikes', officially the **Casa Terrades**) in the Diagonal, combined with many traditional Catalan touches. Nearby on Passeig de Sant Joan, at No.108, is another of his masterpieces, the **Casa Macaya,** its inner courtyard inspired by the medieval palaces of C/Montcada. Puig was responsible for some of the best industrial architecture of the time, an area in which Modernisme excelled: the Fundació La Caixa's cultural centre recently moved from Casa Macaya to another of Puig i Cadafalch's striking creations, the **Fábrica Casaramona** at Montjuïc, built as a textile mill; and outside Barcelona he designed the extraordinary **Caves Codorniu** wine cellars. His best-known work, however, is the **Casa Amatller**, between Domènech's **Casa Lleó Morera** and Gaudí's **Casa Batlló** in the **Manzana de la Discòrdia**.

Puig was also a renowned art historian, archaeologist and an active politician. From 1917 to 1923 he served as the president of the Mancomunitat, the semi-autonomous government of Catalonia. Unlike Domènech or Gaudí, however, Puig never allowed ethics to interfere with success, as he unashamedly used his influence to extort contracts from the city.

These are the famous names of Modernista architecture, but there were many others, for the style caught on with extraordinary vigour throughout Catalonia. Some of the most engaging architects are the least known internationally, such as Gaudí's assistant **Josep Maria Jujol**. Enormously impressive apartment blocks and mansions were built in the Eixample by **Joan Rubió i Bellver** (Casa Golferichs, Gran Via 491), **Salvador Valeri** (Casa Comalat, Av. Diagonal 442) and **Josep Vilaseca**. North of Barcelona is La Garriga, Catalonia's Baden-Baden, where **MJ Raspall** built exuberant summer houses for the rich and fashionable families of the time, and there are dainty Modernista residences in many towns along the coast, such as Canet and Arenys de Mar. Some of the finest Modernista industrial architecture is in Terrassa, designed by the municipal architect **Lluís Moncunill** (1868-1931), while another very local architect, **Cèsar Martinell**, built co-operative cellars that are true 'wine cathedrals' in Falset, Gandesa and many other towns in southern Catalonia.

Accommodation

Accommodation   46

Features

The best Hotels   47
The magnificent seven   58

Accommodation

Take advantage of Barcelona's hotel fever and hit the sack in a family-run *pensión* or dream away in a Modernista masterpiece.

Barcelona is bursting with hotels for all types of travellers, from five-star connoisseurs wanting a mud wrap to weary backpackers simply looking for a pillow and a shower. Though the city already has over 200 hotels to choose from, more than 60 more – mostly luxury – will be built by 2005 in conjunction with the hyped Fòrum 2004 (*see p30*). Barcelona is, without doubt, an increasingly popular city to visit, but it remains to be seen if it can absorb a 50 per cent increase in the number of available beds. The weakened world economy and September 11 temporarily set back tourism here; hotel occupancy levels, especially at five-star establishments, dropped noticeably. But the city rebounded, and now the planes and trains headed to Barcelona are filling up again. The tourism pipeline is fed by a growing number of cheap flights to the city, and by the relentless promotion of its trade fairs.

The low season has all but dwindled down to the winter months of November, January and February, yet even these months can book up for trade fairs, sporting events and festivals. During busy times and at the height of the summer season, it can be tough to find a room. Booking in advance – by at least two weeks – is strongly advised, but if you do arrive in the city without a reservation, the **tourist offices** in Plaça Catalunya and Plaça Sant Jaume (*see p319*) can usually hunt down a room. There's no commission, but a deposit is required. Some private booking services are listed here and the tourist offices can provide a complete list of all accommodation in Barcelona.

Many of the cheaper hotels, particularly those in the Barri Gòtic, will not accept reservations, although this is beginning to change. However, even as the accommodation selection has increased, so have the prices. Once one of Europe's most reasonably priced destinations, Barcelona is getting more expensive. It still has an interesting selection of budget rooms, but most of its new hotels are expensive, and there's less available than ever before in the moderate price range.

THE PLACE TO BE

The highest concentration of hotels is located in the **Old City**, which comprises three areas: the **Barri Gòtic**, the **Raval**, and **Sant Pere** and the **Born**. While the narrow streets of these districts ooze Barcelona charm, watch your bag, as petty crime abounds. Hotels on or near **La Rambla** are especially convenient for the city's sights, but can be noisy and are subject to the greatest fluctuations in price.

For a more sedate hotel experience, select a place to stay in the **Eixample**. With its fair share of designer shops, restaurants and world-class architecture, the Eixample is home to some of the city's more pleasant *pensiones* and most luxurious hotels.

In recent years, hotels and *pensiones* have popped up in other Barcelona neighbourhoods, including villagey **Gràcia**, uptown **Zona Alta** and working-class **Sants**. Hotels in these areas offer a taste of authentic residential life and are never more than 20 minutes or so from the city centre, thanks to Barcelona's manageable size and efficient transportation system.

STAR STRUCK

Barcelona has a unique way of rating its accommodation, and deciphering the system can be confusing. The Generalitat, the regional government, has divided accommodation into two official categories: hotels (H) and *pensiones* (P). A hotel, star-rated one to five, must have en suite bathrooms in every room. Ratings are based on general quality and services rather than price. *Pensiones*, usually cheaper and, often family-run, are star-rated one or two. *Pensiones* are not required to have en suite bathrooms or restaurants, but many have been renovated in recent years to include bathrooms in at least some of the rooms.

One thing potentially baffling to tourists is that *pensiones* are also known as *hostales* or *residencias*. However, do not confuse *hostales* with youth hostels, which are known as *albergues* (*see p70*).

As previously mentioned, rooms don't come cheap. For a double room per night, expect to pay €30-€55 for a budget *pensión*, €50-€150 for a mid-range establishment and from €150 to more than €400 for a five-star, top-of-the-range hotel. This is a guideline only, since prices can vary considerably depending on the time of year, demand and special offers.

All hotel and *pensión* bills are subject to seven per cent IVA (value added tax) on top of the basic price; this is normally quoted

The best **Hotels**

Antique addicts

Check into the new wing of the family-run **Hostal Girona**, decorated with antiques, oriental rugs and original Modernista tile floors (*see p64*). The **Hotel Mesón Castilla** also has plenty of interesting pieces (*see p55*), though nothing to match the ancient art of the **Hotel Claris** (*see p60*).

Bar flies

Hotel Barcelona House, which has its own private entrance to a happening watering-hole (*see p50*), or for something a little classier, sip a Martini at the **Hotel Majestic** (*see p61*).

Stylish budgeteers

The **Hotel Confort** (*see p67*) in Gràcia shines more brightly than its two stars, and feng shui doesn't come any cheaper than at the **Banys Orientals** (*see p57*).

Animal lovers

The **Hostal Rey Don Jaime I** (*see p50*) and **Acropolis Guest House** (*see p67*) both welcome well-behaved pets, or if you don't have your own there's always Benji at the **Hostal Fontanella** (*see p64*).

Water babies

Take the plunge at **Hotel Claris** (*see p60*), **Hotel Arts** (*see p59*), **Barcelona Plaza** (*see p67*), or **Hotel Regente** (*see p61*).

separately on bills. The hotels and *pensiones* listed here are divided according to the basic high-season, weekday rate of a double room including tax. Breakfast is not included in the price unless otherwise stated.

BOOKING A ROOM

When booking a hotel, to be sure your room has natural light or a view, ask for an outside room (*habitación exterior*), which will usually face the street. Many of Barcelona's buildings are constructed around a central patio or air shaft, and the inside rooms (*habitación interior*) around them can be quite gloomy, albeit quieter. However, there are some cases where an inward-facing room is the best option because it will look on to large, open-air patios or gardens; we have tried to mention these hotels where possible.

For flat rental agencies, *see p69*; for student and youth accommodation services, *see p319*.

Barcelona On-Line

*Gran Via de les Corts Catalanes 662, Eixample (93 343 79 93/fax 93 317 11 55/www.barcelona -on-line.es). Metro Passeig de Gràcia. **Open** 9am-2pm, 4-7pm Mon-Fri; 9am-2pm Sat. **Map** p342 D5.*
This booking agency can reserve hotel rooms and private apartments in Barcelona and its surroundings online, over the phone or at their Eixample office. The service is free and the staff multilingual. Ask about special offers and last-minute deals.

Europerator

*Gran Via de les Corts Catalanes 561, Eixample (93 451 03 32/fax 93 451 14/www.europerator.org). Metro Urgell. **Open** 9.30am-2pm, 4-8pm Mon-Fri; 9.30am-2pm Sat. **Credit** AmEx, MC, V. **Map** p342 C5.*
A good resource when rooms are hard to come by, Europerator offers a room search service. It deals with one- to five-star hotels and *pensiones* and can also book apartments and aparthotels in downtown Barcelona, Sitges, Castelldefels, Gavá and the Costa Brava. The multilingual staff speak English, French, German, Italian, Spanish and Catalan and the company charges no booking fees or commission.

Hotel Connect

*28 St Albans Lane, London, NW11 7QE (00 44 (0)20 8731 7000/fax 00 44 (0)20 8731 7003/ www.hotelconnect.co.uk). **Open** 8am-8pm Mon-Fri. **Credit** MC, V.*
This London-based booking agency offers a selection of more than 50 Barcelona hotels, rated from two to five stars. Reservations can be made online or by phone and offers are posted on the website each month. No booking fees and no commission.

TUI Viajes

*Vestíbulo, Estació de Sants, Sants (93 491 44 63/ www.tuiviajes.com). Metro Sants Estació. **Open** 8am-10pm daily. **Credit** AmEx, DC, MC, V. **Map** p341 A4.*
Located in the central hall of Sants train station, this agency can book a room for you at most of Barcelona's hotels (from one to five stars) and at some of the city's *pensiones*. For a reservation, which includes a city map and directions to your accommodation, you will be charged a small fee of €3. **Branches** throughout the city.

Barri Gòtic & La Rambla

Expensive

Hotel Catalonia Albinoni

*Avda Portal de l'Àngel 17 (93 318 41 41/fax 93 301 26 31/www.hoteles-catalonia.es). Metro Catalunya. **Rates** single €126.20-€165.80; double €159.40- €178.70. **Credit** AmEx, DC, MC, V. **Map** p344 B2.*
This converted 19th-century neo-classical palace retains much of its original structure, including a grand marble staircase in an internal courtyard and a carriage entrance that has become the reception

and bar. However, after such an impressive display in the public spaces, many of the rooms are small and disappointing. The 18 rooms with private terraces over the back patio are slightly smaller than those facing the pedestrian street, Portal de l'Angel. Bustling with activity by day, you could hear a pin drop on this promenade most nights.

Hotel services *Air-conditioning. Bar. Disabled: adapted rooms (2). Garden. Laundry. Multilingual staff. Ticket agency.* **Room services** *Minibar. Room service (7pm-midnight). Safe. Telephone. TV: pay movies/satellite.*

Hotel Colón

Avda de la Catedral 7 (93 301 14 04/fax 93 317 29 15/www.hotelcolon.es). Metro Jaume I. **Rates** single €165.80; double €235.40; suite €374.50. **Credit** AmEx, DC, MC, V. **Map** p344 B2.

With touches of old-world luxury, this 147-room hotel has a superb location opposite the cathedral, with matchless views of the Sunday *sardana* dancing or Thursday's antique market. There's a good restaurant and relaxing piano bar, and staff are friendly and efficient. Guests at the not-as-luxurious sister hotel around the corner, the Regencia Colón (€139-€158.40 double), can use the Colón's facilities.

Hotel services *Air-conditioning. Babysitting. Bar. Laundry. Limousine service. Multilingual staff. Restaurant.* **Room services** *Dataport. Minibar. Room service (24hrs). Safe. Telephone. TV: pay movies/satellite.*

Branch: Hotel Regencia Colón C/Sacristans 13, Barri Gòtic (93 318 98 58).

Hotel Hesperia Metropol

C/Ample 31 (93 310 51 00/fax 93 319 12 76/ www.hoteles-hesperia.es). Metro Jaume I. **Rates** single €95.20-€133.75; double €107-€143.20. **Credit** AmEx, DC, MC, V. **Map** p345 B4.

Although renovated, this 19th-century hotel retains its old charm and also pays homage to some of the city's artistic alumni with replicas of some of Gaudí's furniture in the lobby, a Gaudí-inspired reception counter and Dalí prints scattered throughout. Half the 71 rooms look on to C/Ample and C/Gignàs, which are surprisingly quiet and tranquil for old-city streets near the port. Interior rooms can be gloomy unless they are on the top floor. There is a very good buffet breakfast.

Hotel services *Air-conditioning. Laundry. Multilingual staff.* **Room services** *Minibar. Room service (7.30-11pm). Safe. Telephone. TV: satellite.*

Hotel Laietana Palace

Via Laietana 17 (93 268 79 40/fax 93 319 02 45). Metro Jaume I. **Rates** single €166.90-€214; double €180-€245; suite €337. **Credit** AmEx, DC, MC, V. **Map** p344 B2.

A brand new hotel on one of the city's main thoroughfares, the Laietana Palace sits between Port Vell and the cathedral. Its 62 rooms are stylish and tasteful, with marble-tiled floors. The rooms at the back have unobstructed views of a large section of Roman wall, while the front rooms overlook busy

Via Laietana, but are equipped with soundproofed windows. The lobby has neo-classical features, including mosaic floors and busts.

Hotel services *Air-conditioning. Bar. Disabled: adapted rooms (1). Laundry. Multilingual staff. Restaurant.* **Room services** *Dataport. Minibar. Room service (24hrs). Safe. Telephone. TV: satellite.*

Hotel Le Meridien Barcelona

La Rambla 111 (93 318 62 00/fax 93 301 77 76/ www.lemeridien-barcelona.com). Metro Liceu. **Rates** single €344.40-€417.30; double €374.50-€449.40; suite €535-€1,926. **Credit** AmEx, DC, MC, V. **Map** p344 A2.

A central location on the Rambla (just off Plaça Catalunya) and luxurious decor have combined to make this 212-room hotel a first choice for celebs, including Pavarotti, Sting and Oasis. Given this fact, it's unsurprising that its prices have reached such high levels. Its fine restaurant, Le Patio, serves Mediterranean food and its intimate bar offers live jazz nightly. The suites have large terraces with views of the city. The interior design of the rooms (all of which have just been renovated) is warm and elegant. Guests get free use of a nearby gym.

Hotel services *Air-conditioning. Babysitting. Bar. Car park. Car rental. Disabled: adapted rooms (4). Laundry. Limousine service. Multilingual staff. Non-smoking rooms. Restaurant. Safe. Ticket agency.* **Room services** *Dataport. Minibar. Room service (24hrs). Telephone. TV: satellite/VCR.*

Hotel Oriente

La Rambla 45-7, Barri Gòtic (93 302 25 58/fax 93 412 38 19/www.husa.es). Metro Drassanes. **Rates** single €102.70; double €140.20; triple €174.40. **Credit** AmEx, DC, MC, V. **Map** p345 A3.

Inaugurated in 1842 as Barcelona's first ever 'grand hotel', the Oriente was built from an old Franciscan monastery; remnants of the old pillars are still visible in the ballroom. Brass door plaques indicate the rooms where notable guests – Toscanini, Maria Callas, General Grant, among others – once stayed. The old-world dining room (serving a good buffet breakfast) and elegant ballroom (now a lounge) are a reminder of this glorious past, but the hotel is now a far cry from the glamour of its heyday. Its 142 rooms are spacious, if rather spartan, although many are furnished with antiques.

Hotel services *Bar. Conference facilities. Fax. Laundry. Lifts. Multilingual staff.* **Room services** *Safe. Telephone. TV: satellite.*

Hotel Rivoli Ramblas

La Rambla 128 (93 302 66 43/reservations 93 412 09 88/fax 93 317 50 53/www.rivolihotels.com). Metro Catalunya or Liceu. **Rates** (incl breakfast) single €108.20-€298.30; double €120.20-€298.80; suite €316-€364. **Credit** AmEx, DC, MC, V. **Map** p344 A2.

The peaceful Rivoli is a world apart from the bustle on La Rambla. The rooms are comfortable and classy, with soundproofed windows blocking out most of the noise in the rooms facing the street. The

The eccentric charm of **Hostal Parisien**. *See p51.*

Blue Moon cocktail bar is a relaxing place to begin or end the evening. Residents can use the rooftop pool at nearby branch, Hotel Ambassador.
Hotel services *Air-conditioning. Babysitting. Bar. Car park. Fitness centre (gym/sauna/solarium). Laundry. Limousine service. Multilingual staff. Restaurant. Terrace. Ticket agency.* **Room services** *Minibar. Room service (7am-11pm). Safe. Telephone. TV: satellite.*
Branch: Hotel Ambassador C/Pintor Fortuny 13, Raval (93 412 05 30).

Mid-range

Hostal Jardí
Plaça Sant Josep Oriol 1 (93 301 59 00/fax 93 318 36 64). Metro Liceu. **Rates** single €60-€75; double €70-€75. **Credit** AmEx, DC, MC, V. **Map** p345 A3.
Though prices have risen recently, this is still one of the most popular mid-range options in Barcelona. Rooms vary in size; go for those with a view over the leafy *plaça*. All have bathrooms, with either a bath (big or small) or a shower. The decor is fresh and crisp, and there is a sunny breakfast room that looks over the square. Book well in advance.
Hotel services *Air-conditioning. Safe.* **Room services** *Telephone.*

Hostal Rey Don Jaime I
C/Jaume I 11 (tel/fax 93 310 62 08). Metro Jaume I. **Rates** single €42; double €61; triple €81. **Credit** AmEx, DC, MC, V. **Map** p345 B3.
Don Jaime sits on the main artery through the centre of the Old City. The hotel is more spacious than you might first imagine, with a few large rooms suitable for groups and families. Basic but clean, all 30 rooms have new bathrooms. Some of the inside rooms can be gloomy, so it's best to go for an outside one (though those on C/Jaume I can be noisy).
Hotel services *Lounge. Multilingual staff. Safe. TV.* **Room services** *Telephone.*

Hotel Barcelona House
C/Escudellers 19 (93 301 82 95/fax 93 412 41 29/ reservas@hotelbarcelonahouse.com). Metro Drassanes. **Rates** (incl breakfast) single €26.50-€32.30; double €51.80-€64.60; triple €74.50-€84.10. **Credit** AmEx, DC, MC, V. **Map** p345 A3-B3.
Bars along this notorious pedestrian thoroughfare run the gamut from very seedy to funky, so the rooms facing the street provide colourful views, and can also be noisy. Rooms vary in style, with chunky porcelain sinks and baths, 1950s-style furniture and antique beds. Most rooms have complete bathrooms. It is particularly popular with the Euro-rail, backpacking set. Guests can use the hotel's direct access to the popular bar-club Café Royale until around midnight, depending on when the bar's doorman decides to lock the door.
Hotel services *Bar. Laundry. Multilingual staff. Restaurant. Safe.* **Room services** *Telephone.*

Hotel Cortés
C/Santa Anna 25 (93 317 91 12/fax 93 412 66 08). Metro Catalunya. **Rates** (incl breakfast) single €58.70; double €97.80. **Credit** AmEx, MC, V. **Map** p344 B2.
With a useful location and friendly service, the small and comfortable Hotel Cortés (43 rooms in all) is a good choice. The back rooms face a peaceful, sunny courtyard that is closed at night; the rooms facing the street (which is also generally very quiet at night) have balconies. Cortés has a typical, Barcelona-style bar-restaurant right next door, where breakfast is served for the guests. If the Cortés is fully booked, its sister hotel, the Cataluña, is just across the street.
Hotel services *Air-conditioning. Bar. Laundry. Multilingual staff. Restaurant.* **Room services** *Safe. Telephone. TV.*
Branch: Hotel Cataluña C/Santa Ana 24, Barri Gòtic (93 301 91 20).

Hotel Ramblas

La Rambla 33 (93 301 57 00/fax 93 412 25 07/
www.ramblashoteles.com). Metro Liceu. **Rates** (incl
breakfast) single €112.50-€138.20; double €128.60-
€154.30; triple €167.20-€186.50. **Credit** AmEx, MC,
V. **Map** p345 A3-4.

The Ramblas occupies an attractive 18th-century
building with a tiled Modernista façade. Rooms are
spacious and comfortable; those on the eighth and
ninth floors have large terraces. The front rooms
have views of the Rambla and the port, while those
at the back look out towards Montjuïc and the roof
of Gaudí's Palau Güell.

Hotel services *Air-conditioning. Bar. Laundry.*
Room services *Minibar. Room service (breakfast*
only). Safe. Telephone. TV: satellite.

Hotel Suizo

Plaça de l'Àngel 12 (93 310 61 08/fax 93 315 04 61/
www.gargallo-hotels.com). Metro Jaume I. **Rates**
single €103.80; double €125.20; triple €164.80.
Credit AmEx, DC, MC, V. **Map** p345 B3.

Although freshly renovated, the Suizo's old-style
charm remains. There's a cosy little bar with lots of
wood and white lace curtains where continental
breakfast is served; or, until construction is finished
on a larger room upstairs, guests can enjoy a heartier buffet at the Hotel Gótico across the street. All
rooms enjoy plenty of natural light and good views,
although those above Plaça de l'Angel and C/Jaume
are noisier than those over C/Llibreteria.

Hotel services *Air-conditioning. Coffee bar.*
Disabled: adapted rooms (2). Laundry. Multilingual
staff. **Room services** *Minibar. Safe.*
Telephone. TV.

Husa Internacional

La Rambla 78-80 (93 302 25 66/fax 93 317 61 90/
www.husa.es). Metro Liceu. **Rates** (incl breakfast)
single €55.60-€56.70; double €100.60-€102.60;
triple €130.50-€133.75. **Credit** AmEx, DC, MC,
V. **Map** p345 A3.

Built in 1894, this La Rambla institution recently
went through a full refurbishment. A good buffet is
served in a bright and elegant breakfast room, and
there's additional seating on balconies overlooking
the busy promenade below. In spite of the noise,
rooms facing the street are tremendously popular.
Also available are rooms facing a sleepy back street;
the quietest (also the darkest) rooms are those facing interior light shafts.

Hotel services *Bar. Multilingual staff.* **Room**
services *Safe. Telephone. TV.*

Budget

Hostal Lausanne

Avda Portal de l'Àngel 24 (93 302 11 39). Metro
Catalunya. **Rates** single €25-€35; double €45-€55;
triple €60-€70. **No credit cards. Map** p344 B2.

This 17-room, family-run *pensión* is on the first
floor of a fine old building. It has high ceilings and
ample rooms, some of which have balconies

overlooking the wide, pedestrian Portal de l'Àngel.
It's clean, bright and basic, with a big sitting room.
The reception is open 24 hours.

Hotel services *Lounge. Multilingual staff. Safe.*
Telephone. Terrace. TV.

Hostal Maldà

C/del Pi 5, 1° 1ª (93 317 30 02). Metro Liceu. **Rates**
single €12; double €26; triple €36. **No credit cards.**
Map p344 B2.

This comfortable *pensión* in the heart of the Barri
Gòtic is a find in every sense: access is through one
of the entrances to a shopping arcade (a guard will
let you in at night), where you will likely be given a
beaming welcome. There are no en suite facilities,
but the four communal bathrooms are clean. The
atmosphere is friendly and homey and some of the
rooms conserve the old building's original mosaic
tiles. Rooms face either a pedestrian street of shops
or a very quiet, sun-filled patio.

Hotel services *Lounge. Refrigerator. Telephone.*
TV: satellite.

Hostal Noya

La Rambla 133, 1° (93 301 48 31). Metro
Catalunya. **Rates** single €20-22; double €30-€35.
No credit cards. Map p344 A2.

This modest *pensión* is good value for its choice location right on the Rambla, just off Plaça Catalunya.
It's basic and clean (although also a bit rundown);
half of the rooms face either the crowds (Rambla-
side) or a bright patio at the back, while the rest are
inward-facing and quite dark. Most worrying of all
is the fact that only one communal bathroom serves
all 15 rooms. But it's very cheap.

Hotel services *Telephone.*

Hostal Palermo

C/Boqueria 21 (tel/fax 93 302 40 02). Metro Liceu.
Rates single €42; double €57; triple €81. **Credit** DC,
MC, V. **Map** p345 A3.

Hostal Palermo is a cheerful place with 34 clean,
recently refurbished rooms, most of which have en
suite bathrooms. The interior rooms mostly overlook a bright patio that is very quiet at night
(although during the day it is used by a bar). But
whichever room you get is a bit of a game of roulette,
since there's one room that looks on to a dark air
shaft. To be sure of a good view, ask for one of the
rooms that enjoy glimpses of the 14th-century
Gothic church, Santa Maria del Pi.

Hotel services *Laundry.*

Hostal Parisien

La Rambla 114 (tel/fax 93 301 62 83). Metro Liceu.
Rates single €20-€30; double €38.50. **No credit**
cards. Map p344 A2.

An extroverted parrot called Fede greets guests in
the Hostal Parisien lobby, which is done up in an
odd jumble of eccentric knick-knacks: a Mardi Gras
mask, a fluffy heart mirror, a leopard skin bikini and
cowboy hat ensemble. The 13 rooms (facing La
Rambla or a narrow street at the back) are well maintained, and the eight bathrooms are clean and have

been recently refurbished. Service is friendly and the location is excellent, but the plethora of long-term guests means it's hard to get a single room. **Hotel services** *Lounge. Multilingual staff. Safe. Telephone. TV: satellite.*

Hostal Rembrandt

C/Portaferrissa 23, pral 1º (tel/fax 93 318 10 11). Metro Liceu. **Rates** single €25; double €45-€60; triple €65-€75. **No credit cards. Map** p344 B2.
Popular with backpackers, the cheerful Rembrandt has 29 spotlessly clean rooms. The foyer opens on to a communal patio. The amenable owners will allow up to five people in a room at reasonable prices. **Hotel services** *Multilingual staff. Refrigerator. Safe. Telephone. TV.*

Hotel Toledano

La Rambla 138, 4º (93 301 08 72/fax 93 412 31 42/ www.hoteltoledano.com). Metro Catalunya. **Rates** single €34.30; double €56.70; triple €71.70. **Credit** AmEx, DC, MC, V. **Map** p344 A2.
The light-filled rooms at this modest hotel are high up from the Rambla, which means the hotel is quiet and has good views. There's a somewhat chintzy lounge area with a sunny balcony, and the rooms are strictly functional, although some have air-con and all have private bathrooms. Rooms at the back provide glimpses of the cathedral, although, for this, the Hostal Residencia Capitol, upstairs in the same building and run by the same people, is better. The reception for both is on the fourth floor. **Hotel services** *Multilingual staff. Safe.* **Room services** *Telephone. TV: satellite.*

The well-located **Pensión Segre**.

Pensión-Hostal Mari-Luz

C/Palau 4 (phone/fax 93 317 34 63). Metro Liceu. **Rates** double €34-€40; 4-6-person rooms €13-€16 per person. **Credit** AmEx, DC, MC, V. **Map** p345 B3.
Mari-Luz and Simón take great care of their lodgers in this clean and friendly *pensión*. The 15 rooms – two of which have en suite showers – are plain but quiet, and some face a gorgeous and sunny courtyard. There's a comfortable little lounge area, which the owners have been known to quickly convert into a bedroom for desperate travellers in need of urgent accommodation. But be warned that the lounge is a few flights up and there's no lift. **Hotel services** *Lockers. Lounge. Safe.* **Room services** *Telephone.*
Branch: Pensión Fernando C/Ferran 31, Barri Gòtic (93 301 79 93).

Pensión Segre

C/Simó Oller 1 (93 315 07 09). Metro Drassanes. **Rates** single €20; double €35-€45. **No credit cards. Map** p345 B4.
All but four of the 24 functional rooms here have balconies overlooking a fairly quiet street. An added benefit is that Pensión Segre is three minutes' walk from the port and beach, and just around the corner from the Plaça del Duc de Medinaceli where Almodóvar shot scenes for *All About My Mother*. About half of the rooms have full bathrooms and a lounge is under construction (the owners hope to have it finished by summer 2003). There is a lift. **Hotel services** *Concierge. Telephone.*

Pensión Vitoria

C/Palla 8, pral (tel/fax 93 302 08 34). Metro Liceu. **Rates** single €10-€12; double €25-€35; triple €30-€40. **Credit** MC, V. **Map** p344 B2.
Close to the Plaça del Pi, the Vitoria has ten light and airy double rooms with balconies and two dark, inward-facing single rooms. Two of the doubles have en suite bathrooms with showers, while the rest of the rooms share one bathroom. The best room in the house is the corner double, which has three balconies and a bathroom. Despite the basic facilities, the *pensión* has a loyal bunch of repeat guests, so it's a good idea to book early. **Hotel services** *Multilingual staff. TV.*

Residencia Victòria

C/Comtal 9, 1º 1ª (93 318 07 60/93 317 45 97/ victoria@atriumhotels.com). Metro Catalunya or Urquinaona. **Rates** single €29; double €39-€42; triple €52. **No credit cards. Map** p344 B2.
This spacious and peaceful *pensión* offers communal cooking and washing facilities. Rare for budget accommodation, it also has a pleasant little outdoor terrace. Rooms are very basic, clean and light; all but two rooms have balconies, but none has an en suite bathroom. Personable service keeps the clientele coming back year after year, so make sure to book early to guarantee a room. **Hotel services** *Kitchen. Laundry. Lift. Lounge. Telephone. Terrace. TV.*

Mid-range

Hostal Gat Raval

*C/Joaquín Costa 44, 2ª (93 481 66 70/www.
gataccommodation.com). Metro Universitat.*
Rates single €31-€39.60; double €45-€71.70.
Credit AmEx, MC, V. **Map** p342 C5.

With its lime-green doors and woodwork, clean
white walls, and original lighting consisting of
blown-up photos of Barcelona street scenes, this is
a fun, friendly and bright place to stay. Most of the
rooms don't have bathrooms, but the communal
facilities are clean and new. While there's no air-con,
fans keep the rooms comfortable. Staff are friendly
and helpful and there is handy computer access for
hotel guests in the lobby.
Hotel services *Internet access. Safe. Telephone.*
Room services *TV.*

Hostal-Residencia Ramos

*C/Hospital 36 (93 302 07 23/fax 93 302 04 30).
Metro Liceu.* **Rates** single €38-€45; double
€58-€69; triple €78-€88. **Credit** AmEx, DC, MC, V.
Map p344-5 A2-3.

Another off-Rambla hotel, the Ramos occupies the
first and second floors of a charming old building
with a tiled entrance and elegant staircase. Renovated
in the past few years, this *pensión* is in excellent condition. All rooms are a good size and have bathrooms,
and slightly more expensive rooms at the front look
over the church and trees of Plaça Sant Agustí (two
outside corner rooms have two balconies). It's excellent value for money and, not surprisingly, attracts
a string of regular guests, although we have received
reports of occasionally unhelpful staff.
Hotel services *Air-conditioning. Multilingual staff.
Safe. Terrace.* **Room services** *Room service (10am-
6pm). Telephone. TV.*

Hotel Aneto

*C/Carme 38 (93 301 99 89/fax 93 301 98 62).
Metro Liceu.* **Rates** (incl breakfast) single €52.50;
double €80.20. **Credit** AmEx, MC, V. **Map** p344 A2.

With the MACBA, the Boqueria market and the
Rambla almost on its doorstep, this small hotel is
ideally located and has a friendly staff. Its 15 rooms
– all with bathrooms – are basic and comfortable.
The best rooms are the exterior ones at the front on
C/Carme, with their view of the Antic Hospital.
Hotel services *Air-conditioning.* **Room services**
Telephone. TV.

Hotel España

*C/Sant Pau 9-11 (93 318 17 58/fax 93 317 11
34/www.hotelespanya.com). Metro Liceu.* **Rates**
(incl breakfast) single €45; double €86. **Credit**
AmEx, DC, MC, V. **Map** p345 A3.

The España is a Modernista landmark, with lower
floors designed by Domènech i Montaner in 1902.
The main restaurant (good for lunch) is decorated
with floral tiling and elaborate woodwork, and the

Hotel España: a Modernista landmark.

larger dining room beyond it features extravagant
murals of river nymphs by Ramon Casas. The rooms
can come as a disappointment after all this; they
vary in size and some are poky and rather gloomy,
although several open on to a bright interior patio.
Hotel services *Air-conditioning. Multilingual staff.
Restaurant. Safe. TV room.* **Room services**
Telephone. TV.

Hotel Gaudí

*C/Nou de la Rambla 12 (93 317 90 32/fax 93 412
26 36/www.hotelgaudi.es). Metro Liceu.* **Rates** single
€96.30-€123; double €128.40-€160.50; triple €165.80-
€208.60; quadruple €197.20-€230.15. **Credit** AmEx,
DC, MC, V. **Map** p345 A3.

True to its name, this tastefully renovated hotel has
a Gaudí-inspired café-bar and a staircase encrusted
with *trencadís* (smashed tiles), with delicate iron
handrails in the lobby. Some of the 73 rooms look
directly on to Gaudí's Palau Güell on the other side
of the road. Rooms with large, sunny terraces are
also available. The rooms are clean, comfortable and
simply decorated and the staff are friendly. This is
a popular choice for British travellers.
Hotel services *Air-conditioning. Babysitting. Bar.
Car park. Disabled: adapted rooms (2). Fitness centre
(gym). Multilingual staff. Restaurant.* **Room
services** *Room service (noon-midnight). Telephone.
TV: satellite.*

Hotel Mesón Castilla

*C/Valldonzella 5 (93 318 21 82/fax 93 412 40 20/
www.mesoncastilla.com). Metro Universitat.* **Rates**
(incl breakfast) single €99.60; double €125.10; triple
€167; quadruple €200.10. **Credit** AmEx, DC, MC, V.
Map p344 A1.

This old-world-style hotel could pass as a museum
of artisan antiques with its murals and assorted furniture. It has 57 individually decorated rooms, some
of which are furnished with handpainted wardrobes,
beds and bedside tables. Some rear rooms have terraces, and the three large rooms, with up to four
beds, are great for families with children. Most
rooms have minibars. Breakfast is served in a bright
dining room or on the beautifully tiled patio, which
has a lovely view of the MACBA.
Hotel services *Air-conditioning. Car park.
Laundry. Multilingual staff. Safe. Terrace.*
Room services *Telephone. TV: satellite.*

Hotel Peninsular

*C/Sant Pau 34-36 (93 302 31 38/fax 93 412 36 99).
Metro Liceu.* **Rates** (incl breakfast) single €45;
double €65; triple €80; quadruple €105. **Credit** MC,
V. **Map** p344 A3.

Hotel Peninsular is a grand old hotel and part of a
former monastery. Although it has been modernised, a unique atmosphere remains: wicker furniture imparts a colonial feel while monastic
tranquillity surrounds the beautiful inner courtyard
that has plants hanging throughout. All of the
Peninsular's 85 rooms have en suite baths or showers and are accessed from the courtyard, although

those that also have windows facing the street can
be noisy at night. A continental breakfast is served
in a high-ceilinged, old-style hall with skylights.
Hotel services *Air-conditioning. Multilingual staff.
Safe. Terrace. TV room.* **Room services**
Telephone.

Hotel Principal

*C/Junta de Comerç 8 (93 318 89 74/fax 93 412 08
19/www.hotelprincipal.es). Metro Liceu.* **Rates** (incl
breakfast) single €71.60; double €91-€107.40; triple
€117.70; quadruple €131. **Credit** AmEx, DC, MC, V.
Map p345 A3.

The Principal distinguishes itself by the ornate furniture in its 120 completely renovated bedrooms, all
of which have modernised bathrooms. A continental breakfast is served in a comfortable, if dark,
breakfast room. The best rooms are those facing the
street (all of which have balconies); however, it bears
mentioning that the two popular bars on this otherwise peaceful street don't close until around 2am.
Hotel services *Air-conditioning. Bar. Disabled:
adapted rooms (3). Multilingual staff.* **Room
services** *Safe. Telephone. TV.*

Hotel Sant Agustí

*Plaça Sant Agustí 3 (93 318 16 58/fax 93 317 29
28/www.hotelsa.com). Metro Liceu.* **Rates** (incl
breakfast) single €96.80; double €128.40-€144.40;
triple €160.50. **Credit** AmEx, DC, MC, V.
Map p345 A3.

One of the oldest continuously functioning hotels in
Barcelona, the Sant Agustí has been owned and run
by the Tura-Monistrol family for well over 100

The monastic tranquillity of **Hotel Peninsular**.

years. It has had two major facelifts in the past decade but retains some old-world charm: top-floor rooms have oak-beamed ceilings and romantic views over the city's rooftops. Rooms are comfortable, three of which have two bathrooms each and sleep up to six. The interior rooms are surprisingly bright, thanks to a large central patio.

Hotel services *Air-conditioning. Babysitting. Bar. Dataport. Disabled: adapted rooms (2). Laundry. Multilingual staff. Restaurant (dinner only).* **Room services** *Room service (9.30-11am). Safe. Telephone. TV: satellite.*

Budget

Hostal La Terrassa

C/Junta de Comerç 11 (93 302 51 74/fax 93 301 21 88). Metro Liceu. **Rates** single €18; double €28-€34; triple €36-€45. **Credit** DC, MC, V. **Map** p345 A3.

La Terrassa is basic and clean; about half the rooms have en suite bathrooms, although, in some cases, they are only separated by a wall for privacy. There's a bright patio out back, but it's lower than the surrounding buildings, so you might be treated to views of laundry hung out to dry. While a few bars have just opened up along this street, it is still fairly quiet, making the street-side rooms with balconies the recommended choice.

Hotel services *Lounge. Multilingual staff. Safe. Telephone. Terrace. TV.*

Hostal Opera

C/Sant Pau 20 (93 318 82 01/ info@hostalopera. com). Metro Liceu. **Rates** single €31; double €50. **Credit** MC, V. **Map** p345 A3.

As the name indicates, this *pensión* is right beside the Liceu opera house, just off the Rambla. All rooms have been renovated recently and enjoy abundant natural light, private bathrooms, central heating and air conditioning; those at the back are the best and quietest. A lounge with satellite TV and internet access has just been added.

Hotel services *Air-conditioning. Disabled: adapted rooms (6). Lift. Lounge. Multilingual staff. Safe. Telephone. TV.*

Hosteria Grau

C/Ramelleres 27 (93 301 81 35/fax 93 317 68 25/ www.intercom.es/grau). Metro Catalunya. **Rates** single €29; double €46.50-€67.40; apartment €70.60-€133.70. **Credit** AmEx, DC, MC, V. **Map** p344 A1.

This pleasant *pensión* – with its tiled spiral staircase and rustic lounge/mezzanine with reading lamps and internet access – has an artisan charm about it, and provides a relaxing place to write a postcard home. Rooms are clean and quiet, but inside rooms are dark. It has direct access to a funky little café (Café-Bar Centric) next door. The Grau family also owns two apartments, each big enough for six people, situated in another building along the same quiet, conveniently located street.

Hotel services *Bar. Multilingual staff. Telephone. TV lounge.*

Sant Pere & the Born

Mid-range

Banys Orientals

C/Argenteria 37 (93 268 84 60/fax 93 268 84 61/ www.hotelbanysorientals.com) Metro Jaume 1. **Rates** single €87; double €91. **Credit** AmEx, DC, MC, V. **Map** p345 B3.

You know you're somewhere stylish when there are slide projections behind reception. This new and effortlessly cool hotel is a breath of fresh air to Barcelona's hotel scene, combining an oriental shades-of-grey minimalism with thoughtful touches, like bottles of complimentary mineral water on every landing. The only complaint might be that the dim lighting is so hip as to be impossible to read by; otherwise this place is perfect for price and location.

Hotel services *Air-conditioning. Disabled: adapted rooms (1).* **Room services** *Telephone. TV: satellite.*

Hostal Orleans

Avda Marquès de l'Argentera 13 (93 319 73 82/fax 93 319 22 19). Metro Barceloneta. **Rates** single €24-€39; double €45-€54; triple €55-68. **Credit** AmEx, DC, MC, V. **Map** p341 E6.

This family-run hostel near the Port and the Parc de la Ciutadella has 17 good-sized rooms with en suite facilities, including some with balconies (which can be noisy). All are clean, but the upper-floor rooms are more modern. There are special rates for triples or quadruples; weekly rates can also be negotiated. Not all rooms have telephones.

Hotel services *Laundry. Multilingual staff. Telephone.* **Room services** *TV.*

Hotel Catalonia Princesa

C/Rec Comtal 16-18 (93 268 8600/fax 93 268 8491/www.hoteles-catalonia.es). Metro Arc de Triomf. **Rates** single €95-€132; double €115-€145. **Credit** AmEx, DC, MC, V. **Map** p344 C2.

Everything but the building itself is new at this comfortable and tasteful hotel that opened in the summer of 2002. There are 89 double rooms and a suite,

Banys Orientals: minimalist chic.

all of which are impeccably clean, and have excellent natural light, facing either a sunny atrium or the quiet residential street out front. To add to this, the food – especially the buffet breakfast – in the restaurant downstairs is very good. Throughout the hotel, there are elegant details such as arched windows and a skylight above the restaurant.

Hotel services *Air conditioning. Bar. Internet Access. Laundry. Restaurant.* **Room services** *Dataport. Minibar. Room service (7-10.30am). Telephone. TV: (satellite).*

Hotel Triunfo

Passeig Picasso 22 (tel/fax 93 315 08 60). Metro Arc de Triomf. **Rates** single €39-€41; double €61-€65; triple €75-85. **Credit** MC, V. **Map** p343 E6.
Located on the fringe of the Born, this hotel has six rooms with balconies that have views of the Parc de la Ciutadella. The rest of the 15 rooms, all with bathrooms, are bright and airy and face quietly away from the street.

Hotel services *Air-conditioning. Safe.* **Room services** *Telephone. TV.*

The magnificent seven

There's a lot of pathos and more than a little eccentricity involved in any explanation of the unique Hispanos Siete Suiza. An elegant, 19-room aparthotel, the Hispanos opened in 2001 as the result of a bequest from a wealthy local physician. Dr Melchor Colet lost his wife to cancer in 1974, and devoted the rest of his days to the search for a cure. He started a foundation to raise money for the effort, and, upon his death, left his entire estate to that organisation. The Hispanos Siete Suiza is one of the foundation's money raising projects. All of the hotel's profits go towards medical grants, publications and cancer research.

The hotel's unusual name comes from one of the doctor's great loves – his collection of cars. Over his lifetime, he acquired seven magnificent, limited-edition cars built in the 1920s by the Spanish manufacturer, Hispanos Suiza.

The doctor's beloved cars are on display in the lovely, cream-coloured bar and lounge area. The hotel's trademark – a heron – is the Hispanos Suiza hood ornament. While the hotel has a medical aim, its ambience is far from sterile. The apartments are first-rate and well thought-out for longer stays in the city or for weekend visits with a family. Each apartment has a marble-lined, fully-equipped kitchen that overlooks a dining table and a sitting area with cream-coloured furnishings, parquet floors and a terrace. Each suite includes two bedrooms, one with a double bed and a private bath and the other with twin beds and a massage shower.

The fixtures in the hotel are Gaudí-inspired. Windows are designed to appear shattered and curvaceous, metal banisters and barstools are bone-like. The white-linen restaurant, La Cúpula, is located in a loft-like space above the domed lounge area. Behind the menu is renowned Barcelona culinary genius, Carles Gaig. Even if you never spend

a night at the Hispanos, a meal in the La Cúpula is bound to be good, and is less expensive than his well-known main restaurant, Gaig. On Thursday, Friday and Saturday nights, live music gives the hotel and its worthy cause a lovely sound.

Hispanos Siete Suiza

C/Sicilia 255, Eixample (93 208 20 51/ fax 93 208 20 52/www.hispanos7suiza.com). Metro Sagrada Familia. **Rates** *(incl breakfast)* apartments 1 person €144.50-€267.50; 2 people €160.50-€267.50; 3 people €177-€300; 4 people €191.20-€321; up to 6 people €385.20-€530. **Credit** AmEx, DC, MC, V. **Map** p339 E3.
Hotel services *Air-conditioning. Bar. Car park. Disabled: adapted rooms (1). Multilingual staff. Non-smoking floor. Restaurant.* **Room services** *Dataport. Minibar. Room service (24hrs). Safe. Telephone. TV: satellite/DVD hire.*

Hotel Urquinaona

Ronda de Sant Pere 24 (93 268 13 36/fax 93 295 41 37/www.barcelonahotel.com/urquinaona). Metro Urquinaona. **Rates** single €75.40; double €95.70; triple €123.10. **Credit** MC, V. **Map** p344 B1.

This spick-and-span, recently remodelled hotel offers the kind of comfort and facilities that usually cost considerably more, including cushy large beds. All 18 rooms are spacious and brightly decorated, with brand spanking new bathrooms.
Hotel services *Air-conditioning. Laundry. Multilingual staff.* **Room services** *Refrigerator. Room service (breakfast only). Safe. Telephone. TV: satellite.*

Pensió 2000

C/Sant Pere Més Alt 6, 1º (93 310 74 66/fax 93 319 42 52/www.pensio2000.com). Metro Urquinaona. **Rates** single €36.10-€47; double €45.20-€58.70; triple €63.20-€76.70; quadruple €78.20-€91.70. **Credit** MC, V. **Map** p344 B2.

This spacious *pensión* – run by the friendly Orlando and Manuela – is perfect for classical music lovers as it's located directly in front of the stunning Palau de la Mùsica and in the same building as a school full of music students, frequently to be heard practising. Three of the seven spacious, yellow-walled rooms have balconies looking on to the Palau, and these share a bathroom. Breakfast is served at tables in the rooms or on the outdoor patio.
Hotel services *Laundry. Lounge. Multilingual staff. TV.* **Room services** *Room service (8-10.30am).*

Budget

Pensión Francia

C/Rera Palau 4 (93 319 03 76). Metro Barceloneta. **Rates** single €26.70; double €40.60-€53.50; triple €53.50-€64.20. **Credit** AmEx, DC, MC, V. **Map** p345 C4.

Just off Plaça Ollés, in the Born, the Francia is a friendly, peaceful, 20-room *pensión*. Exceptionally clean and bright (even the woodwork is painted white), most of the rooms have beautifully tiled floors and there is a comfortable lounge in which to read one of the many books kept at reception. Rooms vary in size and most have showers or baths (communal facilities are spotlessly clean). It's generally quiet (especially the larger rooms looking over the tiny Passatge Palau), and, unusually for this price range, all rooms have TVs. Excellent value.
Hotel services *Telephone.* **Room services** *TV.*

Ports & shoreline

Expensive

Hotel Arts

C/Marina 19-21 (93 221 10 00/fax 93 221 10 70/ www.ritzcarlton.com). Metro Ciutadella-Vila Olímpica. **Rates** standard room €332-€428; club room €481; suite €444-€578; club suite €645; apartment €1,177-€2,222. **Credit** AmEx, DC, MC, V. **Map** p343 F7.

Plush robes and Bang & Olufsen CD players that open when you clap your hands are among the standard perks awaiting guests at the Hotel Arts. Owned by the Ritz-Carlton, the 44-storey glass-and-steel hotel is only 100 metres from the beach, affording the pastel, contemporary rooms striking views of either the city or the sea. Even seasoned world travellers are dazzled by the top-notch service, art-filled hallways and Barcelona's only beachfront pool, overlooking Frank Gehry´s bronze fish sculpture. At the top of the building is 'The Club' – a private area for those guests who want even more comfort and exceptional service – along with 27 luxury duplex apartments with round-the-clock butler service. The delicious Sunday brunch served at Café Veranda includes sushi.
Hotel services *Air-conditioning. Babysitting. Bar. Beauty salon. Car park. Disabled: adapted rooms (5). Fitness centre (gym/sauna/massage). Garden. Laundry. Limousine service. Multilingual staff. Non-smoking floor. Pool (outdoor). Restaurants. Ticket agency.* **Room services** *CD player. Minibar. Room service (24hrs). Safe. Telephone. TV: satellite.*

Grand Marina Hotel

Edificio World Trade Center, Moll de Barcelona (93 603 9030/fax 93 603 90 90/www.grandmarina hotel.com). Metro Drassanes. **Rates** single €187.25-€256.80; double €374.50-€508.25; suite €695.50-€1605. **Credit** AmEx, DC, MC, V. **Map** p342 C7.

For business travellers, this five-star hotel that forms one side of the World Trade Center (at the end of the pier in Port Vell), could not be more convenient; although tourists also enjoy its proximity to the Old City and the fact it has little noise from streets and crowds. All of the 235 rooms are spacious, each with warm lighting and decor. There is a rooftop gym and swimming pool, an elegant piano bar with live music nightly, a Japanese restaurant under an inspiring glass structure and a fine restaurant serving Mediterranean cuisine.
Hotel services *Air-conditioning. Bar. Beauty salon. Business centre. Car park. Disabled: adapted rooms (4). Fitness centre (gym). Laundry. Limousine service. Non-smoking floor. Restaurants. Safe. Pool (outdoor). Terrace.* **Room services** *Minibar. Room service (24hrs). Telephone. TV: satellite/pay movies.*

Poble Sec

Mid-range

Hotel Nuevo Triunfo

C/Cabanes 34 (93 442 59 33/fax 93 443 21 10). Metro Paral.lel. **Rates** single €53.50-€55.70; double €84.50-€102.80. **Credit** AmEx, MC, V. **Map** p342 C6.

Located off a quiet residential street at the base of Montjuïc, the Nuevo Triunfo, run by Ramón and Maria, is central, but away from the hustle and bustle. Its 40 rooms are all simply decorated, with good bathrooms; some have private terraces. A continental breakfast is available.

Hotel services *Air-conditioning. Disabled: adapted rooms (1). Multilingual staff. Safe.* **Room services** *Telephone. TV: satellite.*

Hotel Paral.lel
C/Poeta Cabanyes 5 (93 329 11 04/www.nnhotels.es). Metro Paral.lel. **Rates** single €64.90-€70.20; double €87.20-€106. **Credit** AmEx, DC, MC, V. **Map** p341 B6.
Although from the outside this hotel looks like an office building with its black and grey colour scheme, inside it's comfortable and bright and has friendly, multilingual staff. It's popular with business people and useful for tourists, too, being reasonably central, and there are a couple of family suites. The rooms facing Avda Paral.lel and C/Poeta Cabanyes have double-glazing to keep noise levels down, while the rooms at the back face a quiet patio. **Hotel services** *Air-conditioning. Disabled: adapted rooms (1). Laundry. Multilingual staff.* **Room services** *Safe. Telephone. TV: satellite.*

Eixample

Expensive

Hilton Barcelona
Avda Diagonal 589-91 (93 495 77 77/fax 93 495 77 00/www.hilton.com). Metro Maria Cristina. **Rates** single €256.80-€326.35; double €288.90-€331.70; suite €342.20-€433.35. **Credit** AmEx, DC, MC, V. **Map** p337 B2-3.
This modern white tower is a sound five-star choice for business travellers wanting to be close to the airport and to the financial and commercial district on Diagonal. Recently renovated rooms feature seductive lighting, creature comforts such as PlayStation and a cool decorative scheme of grey, white and steel with touches of strong colour. When guests are not meeting in one of the 18 new, state-of-the art conference rooms, they congregate in the Atrium Piano Bar for live music and chat.
Hotel services *Air-conditioning. Babysitting. Bar. Business centre. Car park. Disabled: adapted rooms (3). Fitness centre (gym). Laundry. Limousine service. Multilingual staff. Non-smoking floor. Restaurants. Safe. Terrace.* **Room services** *Minibar. Room service (24hrs). Telephone. TV: satellite/VCR/pay movies.*

Hotel Caledonian
Gran Via de les Corts Catalanes 574 (93 453 02 00/ fax 93 451 77 03/www.hotel-caledonian.com). Metro Universitat. **Rates** (incl breakfast) single €110.20-€224.70; double €150.90-€224.70; suite €165-€240. **Credit** AmEx, DC, MC, V. **Map** p314 C5.
Your basic three-star independent hotel, the Caledonian is favoured by business travellers for its location: ten minutes walking to Plaça Catalunya and 15 minutes in the other direction to Plaça Espanya and the trade fair grounds. Constructed during the 1992 Olympic madness, the Caledonian has friendly staff and 50 well-equipped rooms.

Hotel services *Air-conditioning. Babysitting. Bar. Disabled: adapted rooms (1). Laundry.* **Room services** *Minibar. Safe. Telephone. TV: cable.*

Hotel Claris
C/Pau Claris 150 (93 487 62 62/fax 93 215 79 70/ www.derbyhotels.es). Metro Passeig de Gràcia. **Rates** single €306-€341.30; double €341.30-€378.80; suite €447-€964. **Credit** AmEx, DC, MC, V. **Map** p338 D4.
Close, but not too close, to the bustle of Passeig de Gràcia, this elegant, 124-room hotel is ideal for lovers of comfort and art. Owner Jordi Clos, who runs the city´s Museu Egipci, displays over 300 pieces from his private art collection in the Claris's guestrooms, hallways and small museum. Housed in the 19th-century Vedruna Palace, the Claris successfully mixes contemporary design with antique furniture and pre-Columbian art. Original Andy Warhols liven up the East 47 bar-restaurant. Another fringe benefit is the glorious rooftop pool and solarium.
Hotel services *Air-conditioning. Babysitting. Bar. Business centre. Car park. Disabled: adapted rooms (15). Fitness centre (gym/sauna). Laundry. Limousine service. Multilingual staff. Non-smoking floor. Pool (outdoor). Restaurants. Ticket agency.* **Room services** *Minibar. Room service (24hrs). Safe. Telephone. TV: satellite.*

Hotel Condes de Barcelona
C/Passeig de Gràcia 73-75 (93 467 47 86/fax 93 467 47 85/www.condesdebarcelona.com). Metro Passeig de Gràcia. **Rates** single €174.40-€222; double €190.50-€276; suite €321-€539. **Credit** AmEx, DC, MC, V. **Map** p338 D4.
Made up of two buildings facing each other on C/Mallorca at the intersection of Passeig de Gràcia, the four-star, family-owned Condes has somewhat of a split personality. The building on the north side occupies a 19th-century palace and has a somewhat dated, old-world feel. A plush dipping pool sits on the roof. The newer building, called 'The Centre', was refurbished in a modern style shortly before the 1992 Olympics. Rooms on the seventh floor have terraces and a bird's eye view of La Pedrera. Hotel guests can use the facilities of both locations. The rooms themselves are all similar, with hardwood floors and marble bathrooms.
Hotel services *Air-conditioning. Bar. Disabled: adapted rooms (2). Laundry. Multilingual staff. Pool (outdoor) Restaurant. Solarium.* **Room services** *Minibar. Room service (6am-midnight). Safe. Telephone. TV: satellite.*

Hotel Inglaterra
C/Pelai 14 (93 505 11 00/fax 93 505 11 09/ www.hotel-inglaterra.com). Metro Universitat. **Rates** single €176.55; double €214; triple €252.50. **Credit** AmEx, DC, MC, V. **Map** p344 A1.
The three-star cousin of the Hotel Majestic (*see p61*), the Inglaterra is surrounded by fast food restaurants and groovy clothing shops just off the Plaça Catalunya. Yet, once inside the hotel's stylish lobby, peace reigns. The Inglaterra's 55 comfortable, creamy rooms have lovely bathrooms. Oriental

drawings are embedded in the headboards. On the sixth floor, next to the sundeck, is room 601, an especially large space with its own rooftop terrace.
Hotel services *Air-conditioning. Bar. Disabled: adapted rooms (1). Laundry. Multilingual staff. Safe. Ticket agency.* **Room services** *Minibar. Room service (7.30am-10.45pm). Telephone. TV: satellite.*

Hotel Majestic

Passeig de Gràcia 68 (93 488 17 17/fax 93 487 97 90/www.hotelmajestic.es). Metro Passeig de Gràcia. **Rates** single €171.20-€278.20; double €187.25-€342.40; triple €227-€390; suite €385.20-€572.45. **Credit** AmEx, DC, MC, V. **Map** p338 D4.

Always abustle with activity, the Majestic is straddled on Passeig de Gràcia by Chanel, Armani and Roberto Verino boutiques. An over-the-top fresh flower arrangement and huge, sparkling chandelier greet guests in the lobby, and the bar has a romantic feel. Though some rooms are small, they are well-appointed and soundproofed from the city traffic. The hot/cold breakfast buffet in the basement is excellent, and the coffee always hot. Drolma, the hotel's restaurant, is possibly the best in the city, and is also possibly the most expensive.
Hotel services *Air-conditioning. Babysitting. Bar. Business centre. Car park. Disabled: adapted rooms (4). Fitness centre (gym). Laundry. Limousine service. Non-smoking floors. Pool (outdoor). Restaurants.* **Room services** *Minibar. Room service (24hrs). Safe. Telephone. TV: satellite/pay movies.*

Hotel Podium

C/Bailèn 4 (93 265 02 02/reservations 902 11 51 16/fax 93 265 05 06/www.nh-hotels.com). Metro Arc de Triomf. **Rates** single €160.50; double €207.60-€249.30; suite €497.55. **Credit** AmEx, DC, MC, V. **Map** p315 E5.

A ten-minute walk from Plaça Catalunya, the quiet 145-room Podium is part of the reliable NH chain, which has 11 other hotels scattered around Barcelona. The stylish lobby with green marble floors, original artwork and contemporary furniture is stocked with international papers. This place tends to attract business clients and tourist groups. Housed in a 20th-century palace, the Podium has a rooftop pool, sauna and gym. Interior rooms face an old convent and cloister, with the spires of the Sagrada Familia off in the distance. The generous bathroom kit is well nickable.
Hotel services *Air-conditioning. Babysitting. Bar. Car park. Disabled: adapted rooms (6). Fitness centre (gym/sauna). Laundry. Limousine service. Multilingual staff. Non-smoking rooms. Pool (outdoor). Restaurant. Safe.* **Room services** *Minibar. Room service (24hrs). Telephone. TV: satellite/pay movies.*

Hotel Regente

Rambla Catalunya 76 (93 487 59 89/reservations 902 102 120/93 481 73 50/fax 93 487 32 27/www.hcchotels.com). Metro Passeig de Gràcia/FGC Provença. **Rates** single €112.35-€204.40; double €132.70-€248.20. **Credit** AmEx, DC, MC, V. **Map** p338 D4.

As if to encourage you to burn off the calories from those big Barcelona dinners, the Regente includes an exercise bike in every room. The 79-room, four-star hotel occupies a renovated 1913 Modernista mansion designed by Evarist Juncosa. Rooms on the sixth and seventh floors have terraces with great views and many of the lower rooms have grand wrought-iron balconies. Peer down at the Eixample from the rooftop pool. The Regente's sister hotel, the St Moritz, is also reliable and well located (93 412 15 00, C/Diputació 262).
Hotel services *Air-conditioning. Babysitting. Bar. Disabled: adapted rooms (2). Fitness centre (gym/ sauna/solarium). Laundry. Limousine service. Multilingual staff. Pool (outdoor). Ticket agency.* **Room services** *Minibar. Room service (11.30am-1.45pm & 7.15-10.45pm). Safe. Telephone. TV: satellite.*

Ritz Hotel

Gran Via de les Corts Catalanes 668 (93 318 52 00/ fax 93 317 36 40/www.ritzbcn.com). Metro Passeig de Gràcia. **Rates** single €358.45; double €406.60; triple €508.25; suite €535-€2,600. **Credit** AmEx, DC, MC, V. **Map** p342 D5.

Based on the philosophy of Swiss hotelier César Ritz, this classic landmark hotel pampers guests with five-star luxury. Inaugurated in 1919, the Ritz's old-world elegance has attracted such celebrity guests as Salvador Dalí, Frank Sinatra, Ava Gardner and Roger Moore. Even non-guests can stop in for proper afternoon tea in the lavish Bar Hall or to sip a cocktail at the Scotch Bar downstairs. Precocious Romain Fornell, the 26-year-old chef at the sumptuous restaurant Diana, is the youngest chef ever to be awarded a Michelin star.
Hotel services *Air-conditioning. Babysitting. Bar. Business centre. Garden. Fitness centre (gym/massage/sauna). Laundry. Limousine service. Multilingual staff. Non-smoking floor. Restaurant. Ticket agency.* **Room services** *Minibar. Room service (24hrs). Safe. Telephone. TV: satellite.*

Mid-range

Hotel Astoria

C/París 203 (93 209 83 11/fax 93 202 30 08/ www.derbyhotels.es). Metro Diagonal. **Rates** single €124.10-€168; double €134.80-€185.10. **Credit** AmEx, DC, MC, V. **Map** p345 B3.

Only a block away from bustling Diagonal, this three-star old timer offers guests a glimpse of the past. Originally built in 1952 and renovated in the 1990s by the Derby Hotel group (whose star is the Hotel Claris, *see p60*), the Astoria features a sprawling lobby decked out with marble floors, cosy leather armchairs and painted frescoes. Black and white chequered floors spice up the fairly basic rooms. In the morning, the hotel's wooden bar becomes a breakfast buffet that is well worth waking up for. Astoria's partner hotel, Hotel Balmes, has a lovely interior garden and duplex rooms (93 451 19 14, C/Mallorca 216).

Hotel services *Air-conditioning. Babysitting. Bar. Car park. Fitness centre (gym). Laundry. Limousine service. Non-smoking rooms. Restaurant.* **Room services** *Dataport. Minibar. Room service (7am-midnight). Telephone. TV: cable/satellite.*

Hostal Ciudad Condal

C/Mallorca 255, pral (93 215 10 40/fax 93 487 04 59). Metro Passeig de Gràcia/FGC Provença. **Rates** single €58.85-€80.25; double €91-€112.40; triple €107-€123. **Credit** AmEx, DC, MC, V. **Map** p339 F4.

The Ciudad Condal offers 15 clean but sparse rooms, all with high ceilings and private baths. Its best rooms – the four double rooms overlooking a lush interior garden – are the most expensive, but worth it if the view matters to you. The building's gorgeous façade forms part of the Modernista block designed by Josep Vilaseca i Casanovas (not to be confused with Gaudí's Casa Batlló). There is no lift.
Hotel services *Bar. Car park. Safe.* **Room services** *Telephone. TV.*

Hostal Plaza

C/Fontanella 18 (tel/fax 93 301 01 39/www.plaza hostel.com). Metro Urquinaona or Plaça Catalunya. **Rates** single €35-€65; double €58-€75; triple €68-€91. **Credit** AmEx, DC, MC, V. **Map** p344 B1.

Pricey for what it is, but centrally located, the Hostal Plaza is run by a family of Hispanic-Americans from Miami. Their Florida roots are visible in the reception and bar in the bright floral cushions, bamboo chairs, incense burners and La Habana posters. The 17 rooms are clean and 14 of them have private showers. Guests can use the computer, the kitchenette and the gold-painted communal fridge.
Hotel services *Internet access. Laundry. Microwave. Multilingual staff. Safe. TV room.*
Branch: Hotel Duques de Bergara C/Bergara 11, Eixample (93 301 51 51/fax 93 317 34 42).

Hotel Actual

C/Rosselló 238 (93 552 05 50/fax 93 552 05 55/ www.hotelactual.com). Metro Diagonal. **Rates** single €108-€171; double €119-€180. **Credit** AmEx, DC, MC, V. **Map** p337 B4.

A chic lobby in shades of white and chocolate brown sets the stage for this magazine-pretty newcomer, owned by the Gimeno sisters (of the design and household store, Gimeno, just around the corner on Passeig de Gràcia). The 29 rooms have a minimalist design, with black headboards, velvet curtains and grey slate bathrooms. Modest perks for business travellers include a shoe shining machine in the lobby, a reading room and internet access.
Hotel services *Air-conditioning. Bar. Disabled: adapted rooms (2). Laundry. Limousine service.*
Room services *Minibar. Room service (7am-3pm). Safe. Telephone. TV: satellite.*

Hotel Ginebra

Rambla Catalunya 1, 3° 1ª (93 317 10 63/fax 93 317 55 65/hotelginebra@telefonica.net). Metro Catalunya. **Rates** single €38.60; double €60.10. **Credit** DC, MC, V. **Map** p344 B1.

With a prime location on the third floor of a graceful building, this two-star family-run hotel has cool white walls, white tile floors and a decor featuring folk art, plastic flowers and a random bird feeder or two. The 12 rooms are clean, with functional, private bathrooms. Five of the rooms (numbers 402-406) have good views over Plaça Catalunya.
Hotel services *Air-conditioning. Safe. Snack bar.* **Room services** *Telephone. TV: satellite.*

Hotel Gran Via

Gran Via de les Corts Catalanes 642 (93 318 19 00/ fax 93 318 99 97/www.nnhotels.es). Metro Passeig de Gràcia. **Rates** single €70-€88; double €110; triple €145; quadruple €170. **Credit** AmEx, DC, MC, V. **Map** p342 D5.

The Gran Via has an excellent central location. Its 53 rooms occupy a bourgeois palace that was built in 1870 and converted into a hotel in 1936. Previously the headquarters of Barcelona's Círculo Artístico, the Gran Via showcases some of the original Spanish art and heavy, gilded antiques. An impressive main stairway leads up to a gallery of arches and a pleasant outdoor patio looking over a typical Eixample courtyard. The rooms themselves are on the spartan side. The hotel belongs to the same chain as the Hotel Paral.lel (*see p60*).
Hotel services *Air-conditioning.* **Room services** *Minibar. Safe. Telephone. TV: satellite.*

Hotel Pelayo

C/Pelai 9, 1° (93 302 37 27/fax 93 412 31 68/ www.hotelpelayo.com). Metro Universitat. **Rates** single €54; double €75; triple €90. **Credit** MC, V. **Map** p344 A1.

Reached via a long, somewhat mysterious vestibule and up an elevator to the first floor, the Pelayo feels more like a family-run *pensión* than a typical hotel. If you get lucky, you'll avoid one of the seven stuffy interior rooms (most of them singles) and will get a space with a window overlooking the interior courtyard or C/Pelai (although you'll need earplugs to drown out the traffic). All rooms are en suite.
Hotel services *Air-conditioning. Laundry. Multilingual staff.* **Room services** *Safe. Telephone. TV.*

Hotel Sant'Ángelo

C/Consell de Cent 74 (93 423 46 47/fax 93 423 88 40/www.nh-hoteles.es). Metro Rocafort or Tarragona. **Rates** single €102- €113; double €124-€150; triple €174-€210; junior suite €172-€208. **Credit** AmEx, DC, MC, V. **Map** p341 B5.

This intimate, 50-room business hotel is located just next to Joan Miró park, just a few metres from the trade fair. It has all the bells and whistles for a business client, including express check-out and direct modem connections. The rooms are done in calm pastels, with modern touches of grey, light blue and wood. The two junior suites include jacuzzis.
Hotel services *Air-conditioning. Bar. Car park. Disabled: adapted room. Laundry. Non-smoking rooms. Restaurant. Safe.* **Room services** *Minibar. Room service (8am-4pm). Telephone. TV: cable/pay movies.*

Hotel Splendid

C/Muntaner 2 (93 451 21 42/fax 93 323 16 84/
www.hotel-splendid.com). Metro Universitat. **Rates**
single €80-€150; double €130-€170. **Credit** AmEx,
DC, MC, V. **Map** p342 C5.
Decorated in cheerful blues and yellows, this Best
Western hotel has 43 rooms that vary in size, but all
have a minibar, TV and internet access. A hot buffet breakfast is available, and there is a little bar.
Hotel services *Air-conditioning. Bar. Car park.*
Disabled: adapted rooms (1). Laundry. Multilingual
staff. Non-smoking rooms. **Room services** *Minibar.*
Room service (10.30am-11pm). Safe. Telephone. TV:
satellite/pay movies.

Budget

Hostal Eden

C/Balmes 55, 1° (93 454 73 63/fax 93 452 66 21/
www.hostaleden.net). Metro Passeig de Gràcia.
Rates single €25-€41; double €33-€57; triple €39-
€77 ; quadruple €44-€87. **Credit** AmEx, MC, V.
Map p338 D4.
Though it's certainly no Eden, this 32-room *pensión*
does have some perks: free internet access, a commonroom with snacks on offer and a DVD player,
and big triangular-shaped bathtubs in some of the
double and triple rooms. Glass half empty: the paint

is chipping, interior rooms are dark and C/Balmes
is noisy. Glass half full: room numbers 114 and 115
face the patio, and beautiful morning light streams
in through their huge windows.
Hotel services *Air-conditioning. Internet access.*
Multilingual staff. Telephone. Ticket agency. **Room**
services *Safe. TV.*

Hostal Fontanella

Via Laietana 71, 2ª (tel/fax 93 317 59 43). Metro
Urquinaona. **Rates** single €29-€35; double €45-€58;
triple €70-€81; quadruple €78.75-€87.50. **Credit**
AmEx, DC, MC, V. **Map** p337 B1.
The owner's fluffy pet chow, Benji, stands guard at
the reception of this bustling *pensión* located on highly trafficked Via Laietana. The building's Modernista
lift is worth a visit all on its own. The *pensión*'s 11
clean rooms are decorated with pastel-coloured stucco walls and floral bedspreads and drapes. Only
three rooms lack a private bath or shower. Owner
Encarna gives the hostel her personal touch.
Hotel services *Laundry. Safe.* **Room services**
TV: satellite.

Hostal Girona

C/Girona 24, 1° 1ª (93 265 02 59/fax 93 265 85
32/hostalgirona.com). Metro Urquinaona. **Rates**
single €22-€35; double €46-€60. **Credit** MC, V.
Map p344 C1.

Hostal Girona.

Oozing Eixample charm, the Hostal Girona combines pretty painted rooms, antiques, Modernista tiled floors and oriental rugs. The family that owns the place all but doubled the number of rooms last year when they renovated the space across the hall. Ask for the new part, which has brand-new bathrooms and a cosy, red reception area. The original *pensión* is set to be spruced up in 2003. Not all rooms have a bathroom, so ask in advance. The building dates to the 19th century and has a spectacular double marble staircase.
Hotel services *Telephone.* **Room services** *TV: satellite.*

Hostal Goya

C/Pau Claris 74, 1° (93 302 25 65/fax 93 412 04 35/www.hostalgoya.com). Metro Urquinaona. **Rates** single €25-€30; double €42-€68.50; suite €82.50. **Credit** MC, V. **Map** p342 D5.
This *pensión* is like two in one. Upstairs, 12 rooms preserve the original floor tiles, but the roar of the traffic outside echoes through the halls. Downstairs, happily, recent renovations have created seven quiet, creamy-hued rooms with new bathrooms and bedspreads, air-conditioning and parquet floors. The modern living area includes comfy chenille armchairs and a library. Prices reflect the difference between what you get upstairs and down.
Hotel services *Safe. TV room.*

Hostal de Ribagorza

C/Trafalgar 39 (93 319 19 68/fax 93 319 19 68/ hostalribagorza@terra.es) Metro Urquinaona. **Rates** double €40-€55; triple €47.5-€65. **Credit** AmEx, MC, V. **Map** p344 C2.
Lace curtains and fresh flowers are some of the special touches found at this *pensión* run by Pedro Iglesias and family. Located near the Palau de la Música, the Ribagorza is entered through an impressive Modernista lobby with unique carved wooden doors. The 11 rooms have televisions and lofty ceilings. Room 106 has a very nice light-filled gallery.
Hotel services *Safe. Telephone.* **Room services** *TV.*

Hostal-Residencia Oliva

Passeig de Gràcia 32, 4° (93 488 01 62/fax 93 487 04 97). Metro Passeig de Gràcia. **Rates** single €26; double €48-€55; triple €78. **No credit cards. Map** p342 D5.
The adventure at this *pensión* begins in the lift; a Modernista masterpiece of carved wood with a comfortable bench. The hostel itself sits at the top of the building's luminous, oval-shaped interior patio. The 16 rooms are nicely decorated with a feminine touch and all have a television. Some rooms overlook the picturesque but noisy Passeig de Gràcia. Only the singles lack private baths. The Oliva is a sound choice for its reasonable price and good location just above Adolfo Dominguez.
Hotel services *Lounge. Telephone. TV.*

Hostal San Remo

C/Ausiàs Marc 19, 1° 2ª (93 302 19 89/fax 93 301 07 74). Metro Urquinaona. **Rates** single €27; double €51-€54; triple €54-€69. **Credit** MC, V. **Map** p344 C1.

Hostal-Residencia Oliva: uplifting.

Owner Roser keeps this modest, seven-room *pensión* sparkling. Located in the wholesale textile district, the San Remo is positioned at the corner of a stately Eixample building. Four of the rooms have exterior views and balconies, but all seven are large and serene, with televisions and simple en suite bathrooms. The only exception is the popular triple/quadruple room where the bathroom is separate, though it does have a seating area with a sofa and lots of sunlight.
Hotel services *Air-conditioning. Safe. Telephone. TV.* **Room services** *TV.*

Pensión Rondas

C/Girona 4, 3° 2ª (93 232 51 02/fax 93 232 12 25). Metro Urquinaona. **Rates** single €30; double €42. **No credit cards. Map** p344 C1.
Brother and sister team David and Sonia run this rather basic *pensión* on the top floor of a quiet Eixample building. Expect absolutely no frills, just clean, small rooms; some with bathrooms and some without. Of the 11 rooms, two doubles overlook an open-air patio.
Hotel services *Telephone.*

Gràcia

Expensive

Catalonia Córcega

C/Córcega 368 (93 208 19 19/fax 39 208 0857/
www.hoteles-catalonia.es). Metro Verdaguer. **Rates**
single €126-€166; double €160-€179. **Credit** AmEx,
MC, V.

On the border between Gràcia and the Eixample,
this four-star hotel is located in an old residential
building that was renovated in 2001. Though the
original antique doors were preserved, the new look
has a modern edge. Especially nice is the restaurant,
which is illuminated by a skylight. The 79 rooms
have parquet flooring and marble bathrooms, and
two suites have private terraces.

Hotel services *Air-conditioning. Babysitting. Bar.*
Disabled: adapted rooms (2). Laundry. Restaurant.
Safe. **Room services** *Minibar. Room service*
(10am-10pm). Telephone. TV: satellite/pay movies.

Mid-range

Hotel Confort

Travessera de Gràcia 72 (93 238 68 28/fax 93 238
73 29/www.mediumhoteles.com). Metro Diagonal or
Fontana. **Rates** single €96; double €108. **Credit**
AmEx, DC, MC, V.

A modern glass, steel and marble portico welcomes
guests to this pristine newcomer, inaugurated in
June 2001. Popular with business travellers, the 36-
room Confort is more stylish than its two stars
would seem to indicate. The peach-hued hallways
feature halogen lighting and contemporary artworks.

The rooms have light wood furnishings and marble
bathrooms. You can enjoy the cold breakfast buffet
in the creamy dining room or on the large terrace at
the back, surrounded by ficus trees.

Budget

Acropolis Guest House

C/Verdi 254 (93 284 8187/fax 93 284 8187/
acropolis@telefonica.net). Metro Lesseps. **Rates**
single €21-€36; double €36-€50; triple €54-€70.
No credit cards. Map p339 D3.

Just a stone's throw from Park Güell, in a quiet residential neighbourhood, this gorgeous old house has
ten sunny rooms; four with terraces and two with en
suite facilities. The decor is eclectic, with a hotchpotch of old furniture and crystal chandeliers that
provide a comfortable, laidback atmosphere. Guests
are welcome to use the fully-equipped kitchen and
can take their meals either out back in the plant-filled
garden, on the sunny front porch or in the newly renovated dining room. Vegetarian oriental dishes (prepared by the Japanese owner) are available on
request. Pets are welcome, for an additional fee.

Hotel services *Cooking facilities. Telephone.*

Sants

Expensive

Hotel Catalonia Barcelona Plaza

Plaça Espanya 6-8 (93 426 26 00/fax 93 426 04 00/
www.hoteles-catalonia.es). Metro Plaça Espanya.
Rates single €159-€218; double €199-€251; suite
€299-€390. **Credit** AmEx, DC, MC, V. **Map** p341 A5.

The shiny new **Hotel Confort**.

Alberg Mare de Déu de Montserrat: beautiful, sunny and peaceful. *See p70.*

Rising up beside Plaça Espanya and its magical fountain, this 347-room hotel couldn't be better situated for attending events at Barcelona's Fira trade fair. Standard rooms have a burgundy, cream and blue colour scheme, and some have amazing views of Montjuïc. Though the hotel has the feel of a convention hall, its breakfast buffet is exceptional and includes over 300 options, including freshly baked bread, freshly squeezed juice, a wide range of *embutidos* (cold cuts) and diet alternatives. There's also an in-house travel agency and a rooftop pool.
Hotel services *Air-conditioning. Babysitting. Bar. Business centre. Car park. Disabled: adapted rooms (4). Fitness centre (gym/massage/sauna). Laundry. Limousine service. Multilingual staff. Pool (outdoor). Restaurant. Terrace.* **Room services** *Minibar. Room service (24hrs). Safe. Telephone. TV: satellite/pay movies.*

Mid-range

Hotel Onix

C/Llançà 30 (93 426 00 87/fax 93 426 19 81). Metro Espanya. **Rates** *single €83-€125; double €94-€156.* **Credit** AmEx, DC, MC, V. **Map** p341 B5.
Just two blocks from the Fira de Barcelona trade fair, this 80-room hotel has business on its mind. Piped-in music livens the peaceful, fully-equipped rooms,

decorated with salmon-coloured accents. Some rooms overlook the soon to be renovated Arenas bullring while others face an interior patio. On the roof is a tiny pool and sundeck.
Hotel services *Air-conditioning. Bar. Car park. Disabled: adapted rooms (3). Laundry. Multilingual staff. Pool (outdoor). Ticket agency.* **Room services** *Minibar. Refrigerator. Room service (8am-11pm). Safe. Telephone. TV: satellite.*

Budget

Pensión Sants

C/Antoni de Capmany 82 (93 331 37 00/ fax 93 421 68 64). Metro Plaça de Sants. **Rates** single €23-€26; double €32-€39. **Credit** MC, V. **Map** p341 A4.
This large, recently renovated *pensión* occupies a seven-storey building just a stone's throw from Sants station. The 76 rooms are bright – including those at the rear – and impeccably clean, though completely lacking in decoration. Almost all have en suite baths and some have balconies. To avoid street noise and get a spectacular view, ask for a room on the upper floors (all singles are on the seventh floor), preferably with a balcony.
Hotel services *Safe. TV.* **Room services** *Telephone.*

Zona Alta

Expensive

Hotel Alimara

C/Berruguete 126 (tel/fax 93 427 00 00/fax 93 427 92 92/www.alimarahotel.com). Metro Montbau. **Rates** (incl breakfast) single €88-€153; double €113-€171; suite €171-€249. **Credit** AmEx, DC, V.
Convenient for those coming to Barcelona by car, the Alimara is located off the Ronda ring road and near the wonderful Parc del Laberint. Designed by Barcelona architect Oscar Tusquets in time for the '92 Olympics, the Alimara is well connected to the city centre, with a metro stop right out front. All 156 contemporary rooms have stunning views of the city, the Collserola forest or the hotel garden with its mimosa and acacia trees. Better still are the panoramic vistas from the glass lift. Reduced weekend rates. **Hotel services** *Air-conditioning. Bar. Car park. Disabled: adapted rooms (4). Garden. Laundry. Multilingual staff. Non-smoking rooms. Restaurant. Ticket agency.* **Room services** *Minibar. Room service (7am-1am). Safe. Telephone. TV: pay movies.*

Mid-range

Hotel Guillermo Tell

C/Guillem Tell 49 (93 415 40 00/fax 93 217 34 65/ www.hotelguillermohotel.com). Metro Fontana or Lesseps/FGC Plaça Molina. **Rates** single €79-€125; double €87-€139; suite €116-€185. **Credit** MC, V. **Map** p338 D2.
Situated just off Plaça Molina, this hotel offers a glimpse of residential life in Barcelona's uptown Sant Gervasi neighbourhood. Nevertheless, this 61-room, independent hotel is still just three metro stops away from Plaça Catalunya. The rooms are modern – with wood accents and French blue bedspreads and curtains – and those overlooking C/Guillem Tell are the largest. Colonial teak furniture decorates the lobby and breakfast area, filled mostly with business travellers during the week and tourists at weekends. **Hotel services** *Air-conditioning. Bar. Car park. Disabled: adapted rooms (2). Laundry. Restaurant. Safe.* **Room services** *Minibar. Telephone. TV.*

Hotel Via Augusta

Via Augusta 63 (93 217 92 50/fax 93 237 77 14/ reservas@hotelviaaugusta.com). Metro Fontana/FGC Gràcia. **Rates** single €50-€66; double €72-82; triple €103. **Credit** AmEx, DC, MC, V. **Map** p338 D3.
Sporting a freshly cleaned façade, the handsome Hotel Via Augusta straddles the neighbourhoods of Gràcia and Sant Gervasi. Good value for money, this friendly, popular hotel has 56 rooms with en suite bathrooms. Though the rooms are a bit dated, combining chequered tile floors with tired-looking bedspreads, renovations are planned for 2003. In the plus column are the professional staff, the outdoor terrace, the rooftop summer solarium and internet service. Rooms facing Via Augusta can be noisy.

Hotel services *Air-conditioning. Disabled: adapted rooms (1). Laundry. Multilingual staff. Ticket agency.* **Room services** *Safe. Telephone. TV: satellite.*

Apartment hotels

Apartment hotels are made up of self-contained small flats with kitchen facilities and maid service. They are useful for slightly longer stays, and usually offer reduced monthly or longer-term rates. *See also p58* **The magnificent seven.**

Aparthotel Bertran

C/Bertran 150, Zona Alta (93 212 75 50/fax 93 418 71 03/www.hotelbertran.com). Metro Vallcarca/FGC Tibidabo. **Rates** single €85-€95; double €105-€115. **Credit** AmEx, DC, MC, V.
Though the furnishings are a bit drab (brown bedcovers and curtains with white tiled floors), the spic-and-span Bertran has friendly staff, a small rooftop pool, decent kitchenettes and a sundeck. Located in the quiet residential area of Putxet, near Avenida Tibidabo and the Ronda ring roads, the Bertran has 30 spacious apartments, seven of which have ample terraces. Ask for the C/Bertran side.
Hotel services *Air-conditioning. Car park. Fitness centre (gym). Laundry. Multilingual staff. Pool (outdoor). Safe. Ticket agency.* **Room services** *Refrigerator. Telephone. TV: satellite.*

Atenea Aparthotel

C/Joan Güell 207-211, Zona Alta (93 490 66 40/fax 93 490 64 20/www.apartahotelatenea.com). Metro Les Corts. **Rates** single studio or apartment €20-€156; double studio or apartment €136-€180; third person supplement €24. **Credit** AmEx, DC, MC, V. **Map** p337 A3.
This large (105 apartments), 1990s aparthotel offers four-star facilities, with a bar, restaurant and conference rooms, in the heart of the business district. The flats are efficiently organised with first-rate technology, although they lack character. A food shopping service is available.
Hotel services *Air-conditioning. Bar. Car park. Disabled: adapted rooms (4). Multilingual staff. Restaurant.* **Room services** *Room service (7am-11pm). Safe. Telephone. TV: satellite.*

Apartment/room rentals

Barcelona Allotjament

C/Pelai 12, pral B, Eixample (tel/fax 93 268 43 57/ www.barcelona-allotjament.com). Metro Universitat or Catalunya. **Open** *Sept-July* 10am-2pm, 5-7pm Mon-Thur; 10am-2pm Fri. Closed afternoons July & all Aug. **No credit cards**. **Map** p344 A1.
Rooms with local families (B&B, half-board or full-board), in shared student flats, aparthotels, hotels or private apartments can be booked through Barcelona Allotjament. Short-term B&B rates start at €18 per day (for students); long-term (course-length) B&B stays cost €331 upwards per month, plus a €103 agency fee.

Habit Servei

C/Muntaner 200, 2° 3ª, Eixample (93 209 50 45/ fax 93 414 54 25/www.habitservei.com). FGC Provença/Metro Hospital Clínic. **Open** 10am-2pm, 3-7.30pm Mon-Fri. **Credit** DC, MC, V. **Map** p338 C3.

This agency can find rooms in flats for visitors staying at least two weeks. Rates range from €310 to €365 a month for a flatshare, and are around €300 for a room in a private house. Whole flats, with widely varying prices, are also available. The agency fee (€139 for a shared flat and €209 for an entire flat) is payable only when a suitable place is found, and a deposit is returned at the end of the stay. Popular with Erasmus students.

Youth hostels

Rates can vary by season. For student and youth services and websites that can take reservations for hostels, *see p317.*

Alberg Mare de Déu de Montserrat

Passeig de la Mare de Déu del Coll 41-51, Horta (93 210 51 51/fax 93 210 07 98/www.tujuca.com). Metro Vallcarca. **Open** *Hostel* 8am-midnight daily (ring for entry after hours). *Reception* 8am-3.30pm, 4.30-11pm daily. **Rates** (incl breakfast) €15 under-25s; €18 over-25s. **Credit** DC, MC,V.

This peaceful and sunny hostel, housed in a beautiful old building that has served alternately as private mansion, hospital and orphanage, is situated some way from the centre, but not far from Park Güell. Rooms (all well-kept and clean) sleep two to 12 people. Many of the rooms have pleasant views of the city and the hostel's gorgeous gardens. The spacious double-height lounge area has cherubs painted on the ceilings and stained glass framing the large windows. There is ample on-site parking space. IYHF cards are required.
Hotel services *Car park. Dining room. Disabled: adapted rooms (1). Games room. Internet access. Laundry. Multilingual staff. Safe. Telephone. TV/video room.*

Albergue Kabul

Plaça Reial 17, Barri Gòtic (93 318 51 90/fax 93 301 40 34/www.kabul-hostel.com). Metro Liceu. **Open** 24hrs daily. **Rates** €14-€21 per person. **No credit cards. Map** p345 A3.

This popular hostel couldn't be better positioned for backpackers looking to be in the middle of all the action. Albergue Kabul is just completing a two-year renovation to expand its communal areas and improve services, while also leaving the hostel's rustic look – wood tables, brick masonry – in place. Breakfast fare includes scrambled eggs with chorizo, as well as the standard continental menu. The communal washing facilities are particularly excellent. Reservations are not accepted.
Hotel services *Billiard table. Café-restaurant. Laundry. Lounge. Multilingual staff. Safe. Telephone.* **Room services** *Lockers.*

Hostal Hedy Holiday

C/Buenaventura Muñoz 4, Eixample (93 300 57 85/ fax 93 300 94 44/www.hedyhostal.com). Metro Arc de Triomf. **Rates** (incl breakfast) €16-€18 per person; double €20-€22. **Credit** AmEx, DC, MC, V. **Map** p343 E6.

Located beside the Parc de la Ciutadella, this hostel is spacious and has good facilities, including a bar-restaurant with internet-connected computers. All rooms have central heating, and large lockers. Rooms sleep two, six or ten. Staff are helpful and friendly.
Hotel services *Air-conditioning. Bar. Cafeteria. Internet access. Laundry. Lockers. Lounge. Multilingual staff. Telephone. TV.*

Itaca Alberg-Hostel

C/Ripoll 21, Barri Gòtic (93 301 97 51/www.itaca hostel.com). Metro Urquinaona. **Open** *Reception* 7am-4am daily. **Rates** dormitory €17; twin €40. **No credit cards. Map** p344 B2.

This funky, colourful hostel is located on a very quiet street a stone's throw from the cathedral. Murals, sofas, and a steady stream of music in the lobby make for a welcoming (if loud) atmosphere. There is a communal kitchen, a small breakfast room, help-yourself bookshelves, games and internet access. It has 33 beds in five airy dormitories, all with balconies, and one private room with twin beds and an equally private bathroom.
Hotel services *Air-conditioning. Internet access. Kitchen. Lockers. Café-lounge.*

Campsites

For more information on campsites not far from the city, get the *Catalunya Campings* brochure from the Palau Robert (*see p319*). As well as the rates listed below, there are extra charges for cars, motorbikes, caravans, tents and light.

Estrella de Mar

Autovia de Castelldefels km 16.7, Castelldefels (93 633 07 84/fax 93 633 03 70). **Open** *Reception* 9am-1.30pm, 3.30pm-midnight daily. *Campsite* 7.30am-midnight daily. **Rates** €4.50 per person; € 3.25 under-10s. *Tent/caravan/car* €4.50. **Credit** MC, V.

This campsite lies between Barcelona and Sitges, within five minutes' walking distance from the beach. Basic service includes a bar, restaurant and supermarket, which are only open from Friday to Sunday. There is a swimming pool and the 95 bus heading into Barcelona stops just out front.

Masnou

Carretera N2, km 633, El Masnou, Outer Limits (tel/fax 93 555 15 03). **Open** *Reception* Winter 9am-1pm, 3-7pm daily. Summer 8am-10pm daily. *Campsite* 7am-11.30pm daily. **Rates** €4.80 *per person/tent/car;* €3.80 under-10s. **No credit cards.**

Near the coast north of Barcelona, this small campsite has a bar, restaurant and supermarket (open June to September), kids' playground and pools. There's a sandy beach nearby, as well as diving and sailing. Double rooms (€30) can also be rented.

Sightseeing

Introduction	72
Barri Gòtic	75
Raval	86
Sant Pere & the Born	92
Barceloneta & the Ports	99
Montjuïc	104
The Eixample	111
Gràcia & Other Districts	119

Features

Don't miss The city's greatest sights	74
Walk this way Roman Barcelona	80
How to dance the *sardana*	83
How to hold on to your wallet	89
Walk this way medieval trading	92
1714 and all that	98
A place in the sun	100
Colonic denigration	102
Death on the mountain	109
The last great temple	112
Walk this way Modernisme	116
The man with the plan	123
A walk in the woods	126
Top ten Works of street art	128

Introduction

A long weekend will never seem shorter.

It's almost impossible to exaggerate Barcelona's charms, and ever since its makeover for the 1992 Olympics when the city emerged blinking into the limelight, it has been one of the world's most celebrated cities. Along with a grand mix of tradition, modernity, style, unique architecture and vivid streetlife, Barcelona has a compactness that makes it easy to explore, with many sights within enjoyable walking distance of each other. Even the key sights that are not close to the centre – the **Park Güell**, for example, or the monastery at **Pedralbes** – are served by easy-to-use, cheap and frequent buses and the metro.

The Olympics were not the first catalyst for change: since the 1970s the city has undergone an unprecedented physical transformation, in a burst of urban renovation unequalled in Europe. Areas such as **Montjuïc**, the **Port Olímpic** and the **beach** were rebuilt or created from next to nothing, and since then the pace has not let up. The spectacular old harbour, **Port Vell** was reinvented, and dramatic urban surgery performed in the Raval. Attention now has turned to the Diagonal-Mar project, in the

north. In the process, though, the identities of individual *barris* have been pushed and pulled, and sometimes changed beyond recognition.

The **Old City**, described here in chapters Barri Gòtic, Raval and Sant Pere & the Born, is a labyrinthine mass of narrow streets bordered by Avda Paral.lel, the **Parc de la Ciutadella**, Plaça Catalunya and the sea. This is the area that once fell within the medieval walls and, until 150 years ago, made up the entire city. At its heart is the **Barri Gòtic** (Gothic Quarter), a body of interconnecting streets and buildings from Barcelona's Golden Age. Its twisting maze of streets first were held inside the original Roman walls; then, as the city's own wealth increased in the Middle Ages, new communities developed outside the old Roman perimeter. These areas, **La Mercè**, **Sant Pere** and **La Ribera**, were brought within the city with the building of a second wall in the 13th century. The area south of this wall, on the other side of the riverbed later to become the Rambla, was the **Raval**, enclosed within a third city wall built in the 14th century.

Touch down and hit the ground running.

Barcelona's city walls stayed up far longer than most, and consequently the city grew little between 1450 and 1800. The first modern industries developed inside the walls, but factories also appeared in small towns on the surrounding plain, such as **Gràcia**, **Sants**, **Sant Martí** and **Sant Andreu**. The walls finally came down in the 1860s, and Barcelona extended across the plain following Ildefons Cerdà's plan for the **Eixample** (see p111). With its long, straight streets, this became the city's second great characteristic district, and a showcase for the location of the greatest works of Modernisme – although there are others to be found in many parts of the city. Beyond the Eixample lie the green mountains of **Montjuïc** and, at the centre of the great ridge of the Serra de Collserola, **Tibidabo**, both towering above Barcelona and providing wonderful views.

Barcelona has entered squarely into the post-industrial age, as a city with big ambitions. Most of its factories are now tucked away in the **Zona Franca**, the industrial zone between Montjuïc and the airport. Within the city, and especially in the **Poblenou** area, old factories that had not moved out have been encouraged to do so, while the shells of those that did leave have become art spaces, sports centres, studios, clubs, bars or restaurants.

Discount schemes

A variety of discount schemes offer reduced admission to many attractions. Where these discounts apply, it is indicated in the listings below and throughout the guide with the abbreviations **BC** (Barcelona Card), **BT** (Bus Turístic), **RM** (Ruta del Modernisme) and **Articket**. For tourist offices, see p319, and for regular city transport, see p302.

Articket

Rates €15.
The Articket gives a discount of around 50% to the following major museums and art galleries: **MNAC** (see p108), which includes the **Museu d'Art Modern** (see p95), **MACBA** (see p91), the **Fundació Miró** (see p106), **Espai Gaudí-La Pedrera** (see p113), the **Fundació Tàpies** (see p115) and the **CCCB** (see p90). The ticket is valid for three months from the date of purchase, and available from participating venues, tourist offices (see p319). and via Tel-entrada (see p208).

Barcelona Card

Rates 1 day €16.25; €13.20 concessions. Two days €19.25; €16.25 concessions. 3 days €22.25; €19.25 concessions. 4 days €24; €21 concessions. 5 days €26; €23 concessions.
For the time stipulated, the Barcelona Card gives you unlimited transport on the metro and city buses, and

discounts on the airport bus and cable cars, as well as discounted entry to a wide variety of museums, theatres and clubs. There are discounted prices at several shops and restaurants (a great comes with the card). It is sold in the airport, at tourist offices (see p319) and at branches of El Corte Inglés (see p182).

Ruta del Modernisme

Centre del Modernisme, Casa Amatller, Passeig de Gràcia 41, Eixample (93 488 01 39/www.bcn.es). Metro Passeig de Gràcia. **Open** 10am-7pm Mon-Sat; 10am-2pm Sun. **Rates** €7.50; €4 concessions. **No credit cards. Map** p340 D5.
Multi-access ticket giving 50% discount on entry to many Modernista buildings (and at some restaurants); a guidebook is available, and guided tours are often included. Ticket is valid for 30 days.

Tours

See also **www.saboroso.com** for a half-day, English-speaking food tour of the city.

Barcelona by Bicycle

Un Cotxe Menys, C/Esparteria 3, La Ribera (93 268 21 05). Metro Barceloneta. **Tours** 10am Sat, Sun. **Rates** €20. **No credit cards. Map** p345 C3-4.
This bicycle shop offers tours of the city, bike hire included, lasting 2½hrs. Booking essential.

Barcelona Tours

93 317 64 54. **Tours** May-Sept 9am-9pm daily. Oct-Apr 9am-8pm daily. Approx every 15-20mins. **Tickets** 1 day €16; €10 4-14s. 2 days €20; €13 4-14s. Free under-4s. Available on board bus. **No credit cards.**
Open-topped tourist buses with stops around the city and an informed recorded commentary via headphones. The entire route (without stopping) takes three hours, and is one-way. Not as frequent as the Bus Turístic (see below), but far less crowded and covering most of the same sights.

Bus Turístic

Tours Apr-Oct 9am-9pm daily. Nov-Mar 9am-7pm daily. Approx every 10mins. **Tickets** 1 day €15; €9 4-12s. 2 days €29; €12 4-12s. Free under-4s. Available from tourist offices or on board bus. **No credit cards.**
The rival open-topped tourist buses, with two circular routes, both running through Plaça Catalunya: the northern (red) route passes La Pedrera, Sagrada Família, Park Güell, Tibidabo and Pedralbes; the southern (blue) route takes in Montjuïc, Port Vell, Vila Olímpica and the Barri Gòtic. Both routes are one-way. Ticket holders get discount vouchers for a large range of attractions.

Mike's Bike Tours

C/Escudellers 48 (93 301 36 12/www.mikes biketours.com). Metro Drassanes. **Tours** Mar-mid Apr 12.30pm daily. Mid Apr-July 11.30am & 4.30pm. Aug 4pm. Sept-mid Dec 12.30pm. **Rates** €24; €22 concessions. **No credit cards. Map** p345 A3.

The city's greatest sights

Cathedral
Part Disney, part Hammer House, wholly impressive (*see p79*).

Fundació Joan Miró
Bold and colourful paintings in an unbeatable location (*see p106*).

Hospital Sant Pau
Possibly Modernisme's greatest civic work (*see p116*).

MACBA
Catalonia's most important modern art collection (*see p91*).

La Manzana de la Discordia
Buildings by three of the city's greatest architects in discordant harmony (*see p117*).

Museu Picasso
A revealing overview of the artist's formative years (*see p95*).

Nou Camp football stadium
Scene of many a bloody battle with the *merengues* from Madrid (*see p122*).

Palau de la Música
The frothiest of all the Modernista buildings, and utterly unmissable (*see p96*).

La Pedrera
An aquatic apartment block with top class exhibition space (*see p113*).

Park Güell
Fantastical buildings, sweeping views and everybody's favourite dragon (*see p121*).

Sagrada Família
Gaudí's unfinished masterpiece (*see p112-3*).

Santa Maria del Mar
The people's cathedral (*see p98*).

Park Güell's dragon.

This friendly company offers half-day bike tours of the Old City, Sagrada Família and Ciutadella park, with a pitstop at the beach. Rad.

My Favourite Things
93 329 53 51/637 26 54 05/www.myft.net.
Walking tours of the city (€25-€30), with routes based on food, design and architecture. Phone or check out the funky website for details.

Museu d'Història tours
Museu d'Història de la Ciutat, C/Veguer 2, Barri Gòtic (93 315 11 11). Metro Jaume I. **Tours** *Nit al Museu* (June-Sept) 9pm Tue, Wed. **Tickets** €6. **Advance tickets** Servi-Caixa. **No credit cards.** **Map** p345 B3.
On occasional Saturdays throughout the year, the Museu d'Historia runs walking tours on various

themes, including Roman, literary and industrial Barcelona. In summer, the Nit al Museu, is a particularly good night tour around the buildings of Plaça del Rei. The night tours have the added attraction of spectacular mood, as the city is especially beautiful after dark. Always check timings.

Walking tours
906 301 282/93 319 02 22. **Tours** 10am (English), noon (Catalan/Spanish) Sat, Sun. **Tickets** €7.50; €3 4-12s. **Discounts** BC, BT. **No credit cards. Map** p344 B1.
This company for those who like thinking on their feet offers pleasant, informative tours of about 1½ hours around the Barri Gòtic. Numbers are limited, and the tours are popular, so book ahead via the tourist offices. The meeting point is the tourist office in Plaça Catalunya (*see p319*).

Barri Gòtic

Shadowy medieval alleys, grand churches and ancient ruins abound in the political and religious heart of the Old City.

Maps p344-p345

When Barcelona began to flourish under the Catalan Counts, its social and political core continued to be here, on the site of the Roman settlement Barcino, in the same place where it was under the Romans (*see p80* **Walk this way: Roman Barcelona**). This neighbourhood represents one of the most complete surviving ensembles of medieval buildings – from churches to private residences – in Europe, although the idea of it as a 'Gothic Quarter' is a fairly recent invention, having come about in the 1920s. To help the image stick, a few touches were made then to enhance the area's 'Gothicness'. One of the most photographed features of the Barri Gòtic, the **Bridge of Sighs** across C/Bisbe from the Generalitat, is actually a 20th-century addition, built to look old in 1928.

The main square of the Old City is the Plaça Sant Jaume, which contains both the city hall (**Ajuntament**, *see p79*) and the seat of the Catalan regional government (**Palau de la Generalitat**, *see p81*), standing opposite each other in occasional rivalry. They have not always done so: the square was only opened up in 1823, after which the present neo-classical

façade was added to the Ajuntament. That of the Generalitat is older, from 1598 to 1602. The greater part of both buildings, however, was built in the early 15th century, and both of their original main entrances open on to the street now called Bisbe Irurita on one side of the *plaça*, and Ciutat on the other.

The roads running into the square, particularly **C/Ferran**, are useful navigation points for getting around the confusing twists and turns of the medieval alleys hereabouts. Above C/Ferran is the **C/Call**, which, together with its continuation **C/Llibreteria**, used to be the Cardus Maximus, the main thoroughfare for the Roman town. This road leads down to the **Plaça de l'Àngel**, so named for an angel said to have descended in 879 on the procession taking Santa Eulàlia's remains to the cathedral as it ground to a halt. The angel pointed at one of the bishops present until he returned something he had stolen from the coffin and the cortège was able to move again. A statue of the angel sits above the disused bank in the square.

The Gothic **cathedral** is the third cathedral to be built on the site; the first was built in the sixth century. Many buildings around here represent history written in stone. In C/Santa

Waiting for the bars to open in **Plaça Reial**. *See p76.*

Llúcia, just in front of the cathedral, is **Casa de l'Ardiaca**, originally a 15th-century residence, it has a superb tiled patio. Today it houses the city archives. It was renovated recently, but in a previous renovation in the 1870s, it acquired its curious letterbox by Domènech i Montaner showing swallows and a tortoise, believed by some to symbolise the contrast between the 'swiftness of truth and the law's delay', or by others, more prosaically, to be a reflection on the postal service.

On the other side of Plaça Nova from the Casa de l'Ardiaca is the **Col.legi d'Arquitectes**, with architectural exhibitions and a sandblasted mural designed by Picasso (*see p79*). In front of the cathedral, on the right as you come out, is the **Museu Diocesà**, housing religious art (*see p79*), and continuing around the side of the cathedral brings you to the little-visited but fascinating **Museu Frederic Marès** (*see p81*).

A little further along is the 16th-century **Arxiu de la Corona d'Arago** building, also known as the **Palau del Lloctinent**, with a lovely Renaissance patio seen at its best during **L'Ou Com Balla** at Corpus Christi (*see p213*). This has another exit to the superbly preserved medieval square, the **Plaça del Rei**. Around the square are some of Barcelona's most historically important buildings – the **chapel of Santa Àgata**, the 16th-century watchtower of King Martí (**Mirador del Rei Martí**) and the former royal palace (**Palau Reial**). Some parts of the palace are said to date back to the tenth century, and there have been many remarkable additions to it since, notably the 14th-century Saló del Tinell, a medieval banqueting hall that is a definitive work of Catalan Gothic. It is here that Ferdinand and Isabella are said to have received Columbus on his first return from America. Most of the sections of the Palau Reial now form part of the **Museu d'Història de la Ciutat** (*see p79*).

The narrow streets bounded by Carrers Banys Nous, Call and Bisbe once housed a rich Jewish ghetto, or *call*. At the corner of C/Sant Domènec del Call and C/Marlet is the medieval **synagogue**, recently restored and now open to the public (*see p83*). At C/Marlet 1 is a 12th-century inscription from a long-demolished house. Hebrew inscriptions can also be seen on stones set into the eastern wall of the **Plaça Sant Iu**, across from the cathedral, and at ankle level in the south-west corner of the Plaça del Rei.

To walk around this area is to delight in what is perhaps the most satisfying and peaceful part of the Barri Gòtic. Near the centre of the Call is the beautiful little **Plaça Sant Felip Neri**, with a fine baroque church and a

soothing fountain. Close by are the leafily attractive **Plaça del Pi** and **Plaça Sant Josep Oriol**, where there are some great pavement bars, and where painters exhibit their work at weekends. The squares are separated by **Santa Maria del Pi**, one of Barcelona's most distinguished – but least visited – Gothic churches, with a magnificent rose window.

Despite the expansion of Barcelona into the Eixample, the old centre has remained a hub of cultural, social and political life. In C/Montsió, a narrow street off Portal de l'Àngel, is the **Els Quatre Gats** café (*see p169*), legendary haunt of Picasso and other artists and bohemians. Between C/Portaferrissa and Plaça del Pi lies **C/Petritxol**, one of the most charming streets of the Barri Gòtic, known for its traditional *granges* offering coffee and cakes, but which also houses the **Sala Parés** (*see p228*), the city's oldest art gallery, where Rusiñol, Casas and the young Picasso all exhibited. On the other side of C/Portaferrissa, heading up C/Bot, you come to the sorely mistreated **Plaça Vila de Madrid**, where there are the excavated remains of a Roman necropolis. Between here and the Plaça Catalunya is the marvellous little Romanesque church of **Santa Anna**, begun in 1141 as part of a monastery then outside the walls, and with an exquisite 14th-century cloister.

Back on the seaward side of the Barri Gòtic, if you walk from Plaça Sant Jaume up C/Ciutat, to the left of the Ajuntament, and turn down the narrow alley of C/Hércules, you will come to **Plaça Sant Just**, a fascinating old square with a Gothic water fountain from 1367 and the grand church of **Sants Just i Pastor**, built in the 14th century on the site of a chapel founded by Charlemagne's son Louis the Pious.

The area between here and the port is called **La Mercè**, and has a different atmosphere from the Barri Gòtic proper – shabbier and with less prosperous shops. Its heart is the **Plaça Reial**, known for its bars and cheap hotels, and a favourite spot for a drink or an outdoor meal – provided you don't mind the odd drunk and are prepared to keep an eye on your bags. An addition from the 1840s, the *plaça* has the **Tres Gràcies** fountain in the centre and **lamp-posts** designed by the young Gaudí. On Sunday mornings a coin and stamp market is held here. Plaça Reial has had a dangerous reputation in the past, but has been made safer by heavy policing, and the opening of new restaurants and clubs.

This once prosperous area became steadily more run-down throughout the 20th century. The city authorities made huge efforts to change this, particularly in the 1990s, when new squares were opened up: **Plaça George**

Ajuntament de Barcelona.
See p79.

A point of interest

Walking down La Rambla, on the right, quite near the Columbus monument, lies the Cultural Information Point of the Autonomous Government of Catalonia.

There you will find addresses, data and information on cultural activities, literary awards, art prizes, museums, the Filmotheque, theatre, exhibitions...

Rambla de Santa Mònica, 7
08002 Barcelona
publinfo@correu.gencat.net
http://cultura.gencat.net
Fax: 93 316 28 11

012 atenció ciutadana

Generalitat de Catalunya
Departament de Cultura

Orwell on C/Escudellers, known as the 'Plaça del Trippy' by the youthful crowd that hangs out there and the subject of much heated debate when CCTV was recently introduced (the irony of which was lost on no one), and **Plaça Joaquim Xirau**, off the Rambla. Another tactic was the siting of parts of the Universitat Pompeu Fabra on the lower Rambla.

The grand porticoes of some of the buildings around the church of **La Mercè**, once the merchants' mansions, are testimony to the former wealth of the area before the building of the Eixample. There are also a dwindling number of lively *tascas* (small traditional tapas bars) on C/Mercè. Beyond C/Ample and the Mercè you emerge from narrow alleys on to the **Passeig de Colom**, where a few shipping offices and ships' chandlers still recall the dockside atmosphere of former decades. The pretty **Plaça Duc de Medinaceli**, off to one side, was the setting for some of the scenes in Almodóvar's *All About My Mother*. Monolithic on Passeig de Colom is the army headquarters, the **Capitanía General**, with a façade that has the dubious distinction of being the one construction in Barcelona directly attributable to the dictatorship of Primo de Rivera.

Ajuntament de Barcelona

Plaça Sant Jaume (93 402 70 00/special visits 93 402 73 64/www.bcn.es). Metro Liceu or Jaume I. **Open** 8.30am-2.30pm Mon-Fri. *Visits* 10am-1.30pm Sun. **Admission** free. **Map** p345 B3.
Few bother to visit the Casa de la Ciutat, or City Hall, but its rooms contain some wonderful sculpture and remarkable decoration. The centrepiece of the Ajuntament is the stately 15th-century Saló de Cent, flanked by the semicircular Saló de la Reina Regent, where council meetings are still held, and the Saló de Cròniques, spectacularly painted with murals by Josep Maria Sert. The old entrance on C/Ciutat is a work of Catalan Gothic contrasting completely with the main entrance in the rather dull neo-classical façade. On Sundays there are guided tours (in different languages) every 20 minutes, or visitors can go it alone.

Catedral de Barcelona

Pla de la Seu (93 315 15 54). Metro Jaume I. **Open** *Cathedral* 8am-1.30pm, 5-7.30pm Mon-Fri; 8am-1.30pm, 5-7.30pm Sat. *Cloister* 9am-1.15pm, 4-7pm daily. *Museum* 10am-1pm daily. **Admission** *Cathedral & cloister* free. *Museum* €1. *Lift to roof* €1.05. *Choir* 90¢. **No credit cards. Map** p345 B3.
The cathedral dates from between 1298 and 1430, except for a neo-Gothic façade added in 1913 during the 'rediscovery' of medieval Barcelona. Not all is Gothic: in the far right corner of the cathedral, looking at the façade, is the older and simpler Romanesque chapel of Santa Llúcia. The most striking aspect of the cathedral is its volume: it has three naves of near-equal width. It contains many images, paintings and sculptures, and an intricately carved choir built in the 1390s. The cathedral museum, in the 17th-century chapter house, has paintings and sculptures, including works by the Gothic masters Jaume Huguet, Bernat Martorell and Bartolomé Bermejo. In the crypt is the alabaster tomb of Santa Eulàlia, local Christian martyr and first patron saint of Barcelona. The cloister, bathed in light filtered through arches, palms and fountains, is the most attractive section of the cathedral, and an atmospheric retreat from the city. It contains some white geese, which are said to represent the purity of Santa Eulàlia. Inside the cathedral, there is also a lift to the roof, for a magnificent view of the Old City. Visitors are asked not to enter on Saturday and Sunday afternoons, when there is mass.

Col.legi d'Arquitectes

Plaça Nova 5 (93 301 50 00/www.coac.net). *Metro Jaume I.* **Open** 10am-9pm Mon-Fri; 10am-2pm Sat. **Admission** free. **Map** p344 B2.
The College of Architects, opposite the cathedral, hosts interesting exhibitions on 20th-century architecture. The sandblasted stick-figure mural on the façade was designed by Picasso in the 1950s, but executed by other artists.

Museu del Calçat

Plaça Sant Felip Neri 5 (93 301 45 33). Metro Jaume I. **Open** 11am-2pm Tue-Sun. **Admission** €2; €1.50 concessions; free under-7s. **No credit cards. Map** p345 B3.
One of only three in the world, this footwear museum displays the cobbler's craft through originals and reproductions from Roman times to the present day. Highlights include embroidered satin dress shoes from the 19th century, and the enormous shoe made from the mould for the Columbus statue at the foot of the Ramblas. Shoes worn by the famous include pairs donated by the first Catalan to climb Everest, whose boots took local shoemaking to new heights.

Museu Diocesà

Avda de la Catedral 4 (93 315 22 13). Metro Jaume I. **Open** 10am-2pm, 5-8pm Tue-Sat; 11am-2pm Sun. **Admission** €1.90. **Credit** (shop only) V. **Map** p344 B2.
A rather disorganised collection of religious art, including a group of sculpted virgins on the top floor, altarpieces by Bernat Martorell and murals from Polinyà. The building itself is interesting, and includes the Pia Almoina, a former almshouse, stuck on to a Renaissance canon's residence, which in turn was built inside a Roman tower.

Museu d'Història de la Ciutat

Plaça del Rei 1 (93 315 11 11). Metro Jaume I. **Open** *June-Sept* 10am-8pm Tue-Sat; 10am-2pm Sun. *Oct-May* 10am-2pm, 4-8pm Tue-Sat; 10am-2pm Sun. **Guided tours** by appointment. **Admission** €3.50; €2 concessions; free under-15s. Free 4-8pm 1st Sat of the mth. **Discounts** BC. **No credit cards. Map** p345 B3.

Extensive remains of the Roman city of Barcino form a giant labyrinthine cellar beneath the museum, with the streets and villa layouts still visible. A visit to the remains takes you right underneath the Plaça del Rei and winds as far as the cathedral itself, beneath which there is a fourth-century baptistery. Busts, monuments and other sculptures found in the excavations are also on display. The admission fee also gives you access to the Santa Àgata chapel, with its 15th-century altarpiece by Jaume Huguet, one of the greatest Catalan painters in medieval times.

The museum runs an impressive virtual reality presentation, *Barcelona: Una Història Virtual*, on the city's history, with English commentary (shows last approx 30mins). There's also a well-stocked

Walk this way Roman Barcelona

Duration: 45 minutes.

In 15 BC Roman soldiers established a colony on a small hill called the **Mons Taber**, later to become the settlement of **Barcino**. Medieval Barcelona and all subsequent buildings in the Barri Gòtic were constructed on top of that, and many a local resident has set out to make over a bathroom and turned up a bit of ancient masonry. Barcino has had an unappreciated impact on every subsequent era: many of Barcelona's most familiar streets – C/Hospital, even Passeig de Gràcia – follow the line of Roman roads. The best way to get an idea of the Roman town is to walk the line of its walls. Along the route all kinds of Roman remains can be found, poking out from where they were re-used or built over by medieval and later builders.

A logical place to start a walk is at **C/Paradís**, between the cathedral and Plaça Sant Jaume, where a round millstone is set into the paving to mark what was believed to be the precise centre of the Mons Taber. It is here that you'll find the remains of the **Temple Romà d'Augusti** (*see p83*). Where C/Paradís meets the Plaça Sant Jaume was where Barcino's two main thoroughfares used to meet, and the road left, **C/Llibreteria**, began life as the **Cardus Maximus**, the main road to Rome. Just off this road is the Plaça del Rei and the extraordinary **Museu d'Història de la Ciutat**, below which you can visit the largest underground excavation of a Roman site in Europe.

Rejoining C/Llibreteria, turn left at **C/Tapineria** to reach **Plaça Ramon Berenguer el Gran** and the largest surviving stretch of ancient wall, incorporated into the medieval Palau Reial. Continue on along Tapineria, where there are many sections of Roman building, to **Avda Catedral**. The massive twin-drum gate on C/Bisbe, while often retouched, has not changed in its basic shape since it was the main gate of the Roman town. To its left you can see fragments of an aqueduct, and at its front

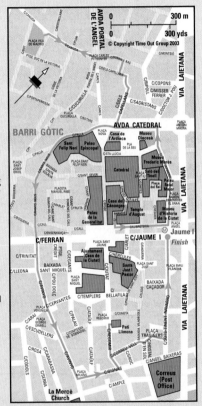

Joan Brossa's bronze letters, spelling out 'Barcino'. If you take a detour up C/Capellans to **C/Duran i Bas**, you can see another four arches of an aqueduct; heading left and straight over the Avda Portal de l'Àngel is the Roman necropolis in **Plaça Vila de Madrid**, with the tombs clearly visible. In accordance with Roman custom these had to be outside the city walls.

bookshop and information centre with leaflets in English. The museum runs the Monestir de Pedralbes (see p125) and the Museu Verdaguer (see p126) and tickets are valid for all three. From October to December 2003 'Hispania from the Via Augusta' will exhibit pieces charting the road from Rome. See p74 for the museum's walking tours of Gothic and Roman Barcelona.

Returning to the cathedral, turn right into **C/Palla**. A little way along, a large chunk of wall is visible, only discovered when a building was demolished in the 1980s. Palla runs into **C/Banys Nous**, where at No.16 there is a centre for disabled children, which inside contains a piece of wall with a relief of legs and feet (try to phone ahead, 93 318 14 81, for a viewing time). At No.4 is **La Granja** (see p169), a lovely old café with yet another stretch of Roman wall at the back. Beyond there is the junction with **C/Call**, the other end of the Cardus, and so the opposite side of the Roman town from Llibreteria-Tapineria. The staff of the clothes wholesalers at C/Call 1 are also used to people wandering in to examine their piece of Roman tower.

Carry on across C/Ferran and down **C/Avinyó**, the next continuation of the perimeter. At the back of **El Gallo Kiriko**, the Pakistani restaurant at No.19, there is a cosy cave-like dining room at the back, two sides of which are formed by portions of the Roman wall.

From **C/Milans**, turn left on to **C/Gignás** – near the junction with **C/Regomir** there are remains of the fourth sea gate of the town, which would have faced the beach, and the Roman shipyard. Take a detour up C/Regomir to visit one of the most important relics of Barcino, the **Pati Llimona** (see p81), then continue walking up **C/Correu Vell**, where there are more fragments of wall, to reach one of the most impressive relics of Roman Barcelona in the small, shady **Plaça Traginers**: a Roman tower, one corner of the ancient wall, in a remarkable state of preservation, despite having had a medieval house built on top of it. Turn up **C/Sots-Tinent Navarro** – with a massive stretch of Roman rampart – to end the walk at Plaça de l'Àngel.

Museu Frederic Marès

Plaça Sant Iu 5-6 (93 310 58 00). Metro Jaume I. **Open** 10am-7pm Tue-Sat; 10am-3pm Sun. **Admission** €3; €1.50 concessions; free under-16s. Free 3-7pm Wed, 1st Sun of the mth. **Guided tours** noon Sun. **Discounts** BC, BT. **Credit** (shop only) AmEx, MC, V. **Map** p345 B3.

Trained as a sculptor (his figurative bronzes and marbles are found all over Barcelona), Frederic Marès dedicated his 97 years to gathering every imaginable type of object, now displayed in one of the most engaging museums of the city. Created for Marès by the city in the 1940s, the museum contains his personal collection of religious sculpture, with legions of sculpted virgins, crucifixions and saints on the lower floors. Marès even collected clothing for saints. The Museu Sentimental on the top floor contains his more extraordinary collections: everything from iron keys, ceramics and tobacco pipes to pocket watches, early daguerreotypes and Torah pointers. Especially beautiful is the Sala Femenina, in a room once belonging to the medieval royal palace: fans, sewing scissors, nutcrackers and perfume flasks give a charming image of 19th-century bourgeois taste.

The museum has completed the first part of a judicious renovation programme, bringing some coherence to Marès' collecting and making it possible to appreciate the real quality of the pieces. When the basement is completed, religious sculpture from different periods will be more clearly organised. The renovation has also opened Marès' own study and library upstairs. The museum hosts interesting and unusual temporary shows, which from April 2003 to February 2004 will include an exhibition of the museum's 19th-century photography.

Palau de la Generalitat

Plaça Sant Jaume (93 402 46 17/www.gencat.es). Metro Liceu or Jaume I. **Guided tours** 10.30am-1.30pm 2nd & 4th Sun of the mth; also 8am-3pm Mon-Fri by appointment. **Admission** free. **Map** p345 B3.

Inside, the finest features are the Pati de Tarongers ('Orange Tree Patio'), and the magnificent chapel of Sant Jordi of 1432-4, the masterpiece of Catalan architect Marc Safont. Like the Ajuntament, the Generalitat has a Gothic side entrance, with a beautiful relief of Sant Jordi, patron saint of Catalonia, made by Pere Johan in 1418. The Generalitat is traditionally open to the public on Sant Jordi (23 April), when its patios are spectacularly decorated with red roses, and queues are huge; it normally also opens on 11 September (Catalan National Day) and 24 September (La Mercè).

Pati Llimona

C/Regomir 3 (93 268 47 00). Metro Jaume I. **Open** 9am-2pm, 4.30-8.30pm Mon-Fri; 10am-2pm Sat, Sun. **Exhibitions** 10am-2pm, 4-8pm Mon-Fri; 10am-2pm, 5-9pm Sat. Closed Aug. **Admission** free. **Map** p342 D5.

One of the oldest continuously occupied sites in Barcelona, incorporating part of a round tower that dates from the first Roman settlement, and later

Sightseeing

Ar**t**ICKET BCN

Visit **6** art centres in Barcelona for **15 €**

Museu d'Art Contemporani de Barcelona

Fundació Joan Miró

FUNDACIÓ ANTONI TÀPIES
BARCELONA

Centre de Cultura Contemporània de Barcelona

FUNDACIÓ CAIXA CATALUNYA

Ticket valid for three months
www.telentrada.com
From abroad (+34) 93 326 29 48
Ticket offices at the art centers.

902 10 12 12 **TEL**·ENTRADA
CAIXA CATALUNYA

Roman baths and then a 15th-century residence. The excavated foundations are visible from the street under glass. It is now used as a civic centre.

Sinagoga Shlomo Ben Adret

C/Marlet 5 (93 317 07 90/www.calldebarcelona.org). Metro Jaume I. **Open** 11am-2pm, 4-7pm Tue-Sat; 11am-2pm Sun. **Admission** free. **Map** p345 B3.
The remains of what was Barcelona's main synagogue until 1391 are now open to the public. Admission is free but a €2 donation is encouraged.

Temple Romà d'Augusti

C/Paradis 10 (information Museu d'Història de la Ciutat 93 315 11 11). Metro Jaume I. **Open** 10am-2pm, 4-8pm Tue-Sat; 10am-3pm Sun. **Admission** free. **Map** p342 D5.

The Centre Excursionista de Catalunya (a hiking club) contains four fluted Corinthian columns that formed the rear corner of the Temple of Augustus, built in the first century BC as the hub of the town's Forum. Opening hours can vary.

La Rambla

The mile-long boulevard that cuts a swathe through the Old City and leads down to the port can be at best delightful (buzzing with life and colour), and at worst wretched (a charmless thoroughfare crammed with tourists in search of some rumoured essence). The truth is that La Rambla has as many guises as the human statues that line its path. It changes by the

Sightseeing

How to dance the *sardana*

After the transporting passion and sweat of flamenco, or the athletic leaps of the Aragonese *jota*, Catalonia's emblematic folk dance, the *sardana*, can look a bit wimpy. The gentle, bobbing steps get a lot of stick from other regions of Spain, where the mere mention of *sardana* can result in hoots of derision, swiftly followed by an impression of a shuffling geriatric groping for the zimmer frame. But, as any aficionado will tell you, the joy of *sardana* is in taking part, rather than watching; it is a dance of co-existence and solidarity, not spectacle.

In theory, anyone must be allowed to join in. In practice, it is not a good idea to barge in on a circle beyond your level, so choose carefully, and make sure you break into the left of a man so as not to commit the gaffe of breaking up a couple. Dancers don the traditional *tabarner* espadrille with ribbons, and join hands in a circle to begin the series of tiny, intricate steps forward and back, crossing to the left and right. Except for formal occasions, all their street shoes and belongings are piled up in the middle, so that

they are, in best disco tradition, dancing around their handbags.

Sardanes can be quite lengthy and consist of interchanging sequences of eight *curts* (short sets) when dancers hold their arms low, and 16 *llargs* (long sets) when arms are held aloft. One person in the ring takes charge of counting out the sets but the dance is also musically accompanied by a traditional band known as a *cobla*. This consists of 11 musicians playing 12 instruments – the drummer also plays the recorder – including double bass, trumpets and trombones, alongside reed instruments known as the *tible* and *tenora*. To follow the structure of the *sardana*, listen out for the *flabiol* (recorder) flourishes, which mark the counterpoints for the dancers.

Sardanes are a stock feature of all traditional festivals and take place every weekend in front of the cathedral (6.30-8.30pm Sat, noon-2pm Sun) and in Plaça Sant Jaume (6pm-8pm Sun). For more information and details of classes, contact the Federació Sardanista (93 319 76 37).

hour, the day, the season. Les Rambles (technically plural, composed of one Rambla after another, end to end) is best experienced by day, when everything is in full, vibrant flow. It used to be said that it was an obligation for every true Barcelona citizen to walk down the Rambla at least once a day. Nowadays, many locals are blasé about the place, but the avenue remains one of Barcelona's essential attractions. There are many ways of *ramblejant* – a specific verb for going along the Rambla – from a saunter to a purposeful stride, but the best way to get a feel for the place is to take a seat at one of the pavement cafés and simply watch.

A *rambla* is an urban feature virtually unique to Catalonia, and there is one in most towns in this area of Spain. Originally, the Rambla of Barcelona, like most of its smaller equivalents, was a seasonal riverbed, running along the western edge of the 13th-century city, the name deriving from *ramla*, an Arabic word for sand. From the Middle Ages to the baroque era a great many churches and convents were built along this riverbed, some of which have given their names to sections of it: as one descends from Plaça Catalunya, it is successively called **Rambla de Canaletes**, **Rambla dels Estudis** (or **dels Ocells**), **Rambla de Sant Josep** (or **de les Flors**), **Rambla dels Caputxins** and **Rambla de Santa Mònica**.

The Rambla also served as the meeting ground for city and country dwellers, for on the far side of these church buildings lay the still scarcely built-up Raval, 'the city outside the walls', and rural Catalonia. At the fountain on the corner with C/Portaferrissa, once a city gateway, there is an artist's impression in tiles of this space beside the wall, which became a natural marketplace. From these beginnings sprang La Boqueria, Spain's largest market, and still on the Rambla today.

The Rambla took on its recognisable present form between approximately 1770 and 1860. The second city wall came down in 1775, and the Rambla was gradually paved and turned into a boulevard. Seats were available to strollers for rent in the late 18th century. The avenue acquired its definitive shape after the closure of the monasteries in the 1830s, which made swathes of land available for new building. No longer on the city's edge, the Rambla became a wide path through its heart.

As well as having five names, the Rambla is divided into territories. The first part – at the top, by Plaça Catalunya – has belonged by unwritten agreement to groups of men perpetually engaged in a *tertulia*, a classic Iberian half-conversation, half-argument about anything from politics to football. The **Font de Canaletes** drinking fountain is beside them; if

La Rambla…

you drink from it, the legend goes, you'll return to Barcelona. Here, too, is where Barça fans converge to celebrate their triumphs.

Next comes perhaps the best-loved section of the boulevard, known as Rambla de les Flors for its line of magnificent flower stalls, open into the night. To the right is the **Palau de la Virreina** exhibition and cultural information centre, and the superb **Boqueria** market; don't linger near the entrance, however – the food here is expensive and non-Catalans are liable to be ripped off with rotten fruit and rottener prices. There's more fun to be had inside, where the sheep's heads leer and the crayfish make futile bids for freedom. A little further is the **Pla de l'Os** (or **Pla de la Boqueria**), centrepoint of the Rambla, with a pavement mosaic created in 1976 by Joan Miró. On the left, where more streets run off into the Barri Gòtic, is the extraordinary **Bruno Quadros** building (1883), with umbrellas on the wall and a Chinese dragon protruding over the street.

...home of the brave.

and, at weekends, stalls selling bric-a-brac and craftwork, alongside fortune tellers and tarot readers catering to an incorrigible local interest in all things astrological. As well as the human statues there are buskers, clowns, puppeteers, dancers and musicians. There's street theatre of another kind in the shape of the three-card sharpers or hustlers with three walnut shells and a pea under one of them, challenging you to a bet. Then finally it's a short skip to the port, and the **Monument a Colom** (*see p101*).

Centre d'Art Santa Mònica

La Rambla 7 (93 316 28 10/www.cultura.gencat.es/ casm/index.htm). Metro Drassanes. **Open** 11am-2pm, 5-8pm Mon-Sat; 11am-3pm Sun. **Admission** usually free. **Map** p345 A4.

Since this 17th-century monastery was renovated as a centre for contemporary art in the 1980s it has had its ups and downs, ceding much of its importance to the MACBA in recent years. The redesign, by architects Piñón and Viaplana, is difficult enough for installation artists, and is near impossible when it comes to showing painting. From March to May 2003 there will be an exhibition of Ron Arad's industrial design, to coincide with Barcelona's Year of Design.

Museu de l'Eròtica

La Rambla 96 bis (93 318 98 65/www.erotica- museum.com). Metro Liceu. **Open** *June-Sept* 10am-midnight daily. *Oct-May* 11am-9pm daily. **Admission** €7.50; €6.50 concessions. **Discounts** BT. **Credit** AmEx, MC, V. **Map** p345 A3.

This private museum's shabby display diminishes some genuine rarities of erotica, including Japanese drawings, 19th-century engravings by German Peter Fendi and compelling photos of brothels in Barcelona's Barrio Chino in the decadent 1930s. Other curiosities include S&M apparatus and simulated erotic telephone lines, but until things are sharpened up, the Eròtica is something of an embarrassment in a city with true connoisseurship for the bawdy.

Palau de la Virreina

La Rambla 99 (93 301 77 75/www.bcn.es/icub). Metro Liceu. **Open** 11am-8.30pm Mon-Sat; 11am-3pm Sun. **Admission** €3; €1.50 concessions, Wed; free under-16s. **No credit cards**. **Map** p344 A2.

This neo-classical palace takes its name from the wife of a viceroy of Peru, who lived in it after its completion in the 1770s. Once the city council's main exhibition space, the Virreina handed over all significant programming to the MACBA in the late 1990s. Now, under the direction of Cuban critic Iván de la Nuez, it has made a strong comeback, with the upstairs dedicated to one-off exhibitions and the smaller downstairs gallery focused on historical and contemporary photography. La Virreina also has information on cultural events in Barcelona. Temporary exhibitions in 2003 are largely designed to coincide thematically with Barcelona's Year of Design, but there will also be a display of Latin American photography from June to September.

The lower half of the Ramblas is far more restrained, flowing between the sober façade of the **Liceu** opera house and the rather more *fin-de-siècle* (architecturally and atmospherically) **Cafè de l'Opera** (*see p167*), Barcelona's second most famous café after the Zurich. On the right is C/Nou de la Rambla (where you'll find Gaudí's **Palau Güell** (*see p91*), and then the promenade widens into the Rambla de Santa Mònica. Here you hit the stretch that for years was a thriving prostitution belt. You will still see a few lycra-and-furred transvestites, but official clean-up efforts have greatly reduced the visibility (if not the existence) of street soliciting. Renovations, including a 1980s arts centre, the **Centre d'Art Santa Mònica** (*see p85*), have diluted the sleaziness of this part of the Rambla – although this is still one of the areas where you need to be most wary of pickpockets and bag-snatchers.

Further towards the port and the Colom column are the **Museu de Cera** (*see p222*)

Raval

For years it lay in Barcelona's gutter, but always looking at the stars.

Raval is the original medieval name for the area now sandwiched between Avda Paral.lel and La Rambla, adapted from an Arabic word meaning somewhere 'outside the walls'. When a wall was built down the north side of La Rambla in the 13th century the area was still a largely unpopulated expanse of farmland with just the odd farmhouse. Only around the monastery of Sant Pau del Camp had a small medieval village sprung up. Over the centuries it came to be used for functional spillover from the city. It centred around the Barri Gòtic, hosting monasteries, religious hospitals and activities considered too dangerous or noxious to be allowed inside the city, such as brickmaking or slaughtering. This continued to be the case even after a further defensive wall was built in the 14th century; though only a small part of the wall still exists, that early fortification defines the Raval's current limits. With early industrialisation it became Barcelona's working-class district, reaching an estimated density of over 100,000 people per square kilometre in the 1930s. In short order, it earned a reputation for seedy lowlife and became Barcelona's haven for urban decadence, wild nightlife and prostitution. The nickname '**Barrio Chino**' (*Barri Xino*

in Catalan) was coined in the 1920s by a journalist comparing it to San Francisco's Chinatown, referring to its underworld feel rather than any Chinese population. In recent years, though, urban reform has altered the neighbourhood's grimy face, but it has not entirely lost its rough character. It still has a hard edge, and it's advisable to be wary of pickpockets and purse snatchers, especially along C/Sant Pau. Street prostitution is still common on C/Sant Rafael.

The Raval can be divided into three sections. The first part to take on an urban character was the middle swath – a long triangle defined by C/Hospital below and C/Carme above. The streets meet at the Plaça Pedró, where the tiny Romanesque chapel of **Sant Llàtzer** sits. From La Rambla, this area is accessed along either street or through the **Boqueria** market, itself the site of the Sant Josep monastery until the sale of church lands in the 1830s led to its destruction. Behind the market is the huge **Antic Hospital de la Santa Creu**, which served the needs of the city from the 15th century until it finally closed in 1926. Since then it has been converted to host various important governmental institutions and offices including Catalonia's

Palau Güell. *See p91.*

main library, the headquarters of the Catalan studies institute and **La Capella**, an attractive exhibition space (*see p90*).

The upper Raval, from C/Carme towards Plaça Catalunya, has been massively impacted by the large-scale official projects designed for the rejuvenation of the area. Most notable is the cultural complex that includes the **MACBA** (Museu d'Art Contemporani de Barcelona) and the **CCCB** (Centre de Cultura Contemporània de Barcelona), built in what was once the almshouse, the **Casa de la Caritat** (*see p90*). Across the street, the new Faculty of History and Geography building for the University of Barcelona is under construction. Opposite the MACBA is the 16th-century **Convent dels Àngels**, now headquarters of the FAD design institute. The area never had the same lowlife reputation as the lower Raval, in spite of lingering street prostitution along C/Joaquín Costa. In recent years the upper Raval has become one of Barcelona's hippest places to be, with a plethora of late-night bars and laid-back restaurants.

Below C/Hospital the Raval is a confusion of identities, as stately heritage buildings, the darker side of the Chino, new waves of immigration and partially completed urban reform projects clash. The main thoroughfare of the lower Raval, C/Nou de la Rambla, is home to a peculiar addition from the 1880s, the **Palau Güell**, built by Gaudí for Eusebi Güell. It was a very eccentric decision of Güell's to have his new residence located in what was then an unfashionable area, and he often had trouble persuading dinner guests to take up his invitations. Nearby, in C/Sant Pau, is another Modernista landmark, the **Hotel España** (*see p54*), designed by Domènech i Montaner. In the lower corner were the ***drassanes*** (shipyards) now home to the **Museu Marítim** (*see p101*). Along the Paral.lel side of this impressive Gothic edifice remains the only large section of Barcelona's third city wall, built by Pere IV the Ceremonious in the 14th century. The area nearby took centuries to build up, and as late as 1800 much of it still consisted of small gardens. A trace of this earlier Raval is suggested by the name of one of the most beautiful pockets of peace in the district, the tenth-century Romanesque church of **Sant Pau del Camp** (*see p91*). Iberian remains dating to 200 BC have been found next to it, making it one of the oldest known parts of Barcelona.

When industry first began in the late 18th century, this was the area where most land was available. Even more land came into use when liberal governments dissolved the monasteries in 1836. Early industry, mainly textile mills, thus had to grow within the cramped confines

Antic Hospital. *See p90.*

of the still-walled Raval. Some of the strange, barrack-like buildings known as *cases-fàbriques* (residential factories) from that time can still be seen in streets such as C/Riereta, despite recent demolitions. Workers lived alongside them, often in appalling conditions. Then known to most people as the *Quinto* or Fifth District, this was the area where the underclasses took refuge, and it became the centre of revolutionary Barcelona, a perennial breeding ground for anarchists and other radicals. Numerous conspiracies were hatched here, riots and revolts began here, and whole streets became no-go areas for the police after dark.

The other notorious aspect of the lower Raval was the emergence of low-life, drug trafficking and the sex industry, with high-class brothels for the rich and cheap dives for the poor. The Chino's heyday was in the 1920s and '30s, but it managed to survive in muted form during the Franco years. Hundreds of bars, low-rent eateries and cheap *hostals* lined streets such as Nou de la Rambla, catering to a transient population of grifters. Jean Genet's flea-infested account of the flea-infested late '20s in *Thief's Journal* (1949) and others like André Pieyre de Mandiargues' *The Margin* (1967) perpetuated this reputation, as have the Carvalho detective books by Raval-born writer Manuel Vázquez Montalbán, published since the 1970s.

In recent years, the Raval has changed enormously, perhaps more than anywhere else in Barcelona. Industry has been largely pushed out. The former hotbed of radical politics is but

How to hold on to your wallet

Barcelona has a shocking and perhaps deserved reputation for petty crime, but (and this is a big 'but') take a look at some of the tourists in the queue outside the Museu Picasso, and you realise just how easy life is for those who've decided to make a living from relieving people of their handbags.

Barcelona is not a violent city; actual physical assaults are rare, and the vast majority of thefts could be avoided with a little common sense. Don't carry anything valuable, don't wear your bag on your back or your camera slung over a shoulder, and beware of anyone jostling you or trying to distract you. Be aware, too, of the following well-worn repertoire of favourite tricks:

Losing possession

'Hey! You English? You know David Beckham?' Followed by chummy mock football tackle, leaving you one wallet lighter.

Cut the mustard

'What's that on your shoulder? Can I help you wipe it off while my friend picks your pocket?'

Unlucky heather

Beware she of the headscarf and many skirts. Particularly adept at helping you find the change for your smart new nosegay.

Victim support

You will meet many victims of crime; they're the ones waving a photocopied 'police report' and asking you to lend them some cash to help them get home. Don't.

The metro escalator shuffle

The person in front of you bends to tie his shoelace, and in the ensuing mock domino effect his friend behind you steadies himself by thrusting one hand into your pocket.

Hunt the lady

Guessing which cup the pea's under may look easy, and my, aren't people winning a lot? But they're all in it together, see.

Snogging

It may be that you are so sexually attractive that strangers in clubs can't resist a quick tongue sarnie, or it may be that they're interested in what else is in your trousers.

Grab it and run

Your basic bag snatch. That's why God gave us pockets.

Passport control

'Can I see your passport, sir?' 'Can I see your ID, officer?'

Sightseeing

---

a shadow of its pre-Franco self. The biggest change of all has been in the Chino, a prime target of the Ajuntament's urban renewal schemes. In the late 1970s serious problems were caused by the arrival of heroin. The old, semi-tolerated petty criminality became more threatening, affecting the morale of Barcelona residents and the success of the tourist trade. Spurred on by the approaching Olympics, the authorities set about the problem with their customary clean-sweep approach. Before 1992 the cheapest *hostals* were closed, and whole blocks associated with drug dealers or prostitution were demolished. The people displaced were often transferred to newer flats on the outskirts of town, out of sight and out of mind. Student residences, a sports centre and office blocks were constructed, and a new police station was built.

Most dramatic of all was the plan to create a '*Raval obert al cel*' – 'a Raval open to the sky'. The most tangible result so far is the **Rambla del Raval**, completed in 2000 as a sweeping, palm-lined boulevard. Just below the new *rambla*, Avda Drassanes, near the **Monument**

a Colom, was actually created in an earlier attempt to 'open up' the Raval, under Franco's mayor Porcioles in the 1960s (one thing that Franco's administrators and modern planners could agree on was that the Chino must go), but only got as far as C/Nou de la Rambla. The new *rambla* extends the effort, bulldozing all before it up to C/Hospital. Entire streets have vanished in its wake. The current grand project, situated halfway along it, is the '*Illa de la Rambla del Raval*' – a block is slowly being demolished to make way for a complex containing shops, offices and a luxury 11-storey hotel.

Some of these changes have undeniably been for the best, but their cumulative effect has been to leave one of the most singular parts of the city looking strangely empty. Another, equally unpredicted change in the area has been the appearance of a sizeable Muslim community, mostly from Pakistan and North Africa. This is now one of the city's most multicultural areas, where halal butcher shops catering to expat North Africans sit alongside Pakistani groceries, Indonesian barbers and *carnisseries* selling pig parts to Catalans.

If it's cultural, and it's contemporary, it's at the **CCCB**.

Antic Hospital de la Santa Creu & La Capella

C/Carme 47-C/Hospital 56 (no phone). Metro Liceu. **Open** 9am-8pm Mon-Fri; 9am-2pm Sat. *La Capella (93 442 71 71)* noon-2pm, 4-8pm Tue-Sat; 11am-2pm Sun. **Admission** free. **Map** p344 A2.

The buildings of this former hospital, with entrances on both C/Carme and C/Hospital, combine a 15th-century Gothic core – including a beautifully shady colonnaded courtyard – with baroque and classical additions. The original hospital was founded on this site in 1024 and remained the city's main hospital until its medical facilities moved to the Hospital Sant Pau near the Sagrada Família in the 1930s. Gaudí died here in 1926.

Around the courtyard is the Escola Massana (an arts and crafts school) and the Biblioteca de Catalunya, with impressive arched Gothic ceilings (it cannot be properly visited without a library card). Towards C/Carme, the Institut d'Estudis Catalans occupies a baroque building from the late 17th century, the Casa de Convalescència, with fascinating ceramic murals in the entrance hall. In an impressive Gothic building that used to be the hospital's church is La Capella, now used to display exhibits of contemporary art; the choir balcony and side chapels are still visible. In spring 2003 an exhibition of art magazines will be followed by a show of recent photography from Latin America. Late autumn 2003 will see a show of young artists from Iceland; part of an exchange with Catalonia.

CCCB (Centre de Cultura Contemporània de Barcelona)

C/Montalegre 5 (93 306 41 00/www.cccb.org). Metro Catalunya. **Open** *Mid June-mid Sept* 11am-8pm Tue-Sat; 11am-3pm Sun. *Mid Sept-mid June* 11am-2pm, 4-8pm Tue, Thur, Fri; 11am-8pm Wed, Sat; 11am-7pm Sun. **Admission** *1 exhibition* €4; €3 concessions. *2 exhibitions* €5.50; €4 concessions. *Wed* €2.50. Free under-16s. **Discounts** Articket, BC, BT. **Credit** MC, V. **Map** p344 A1.

The CCCB occupies part of the Casa de la Caritat, built in 1802 on the site of a medieval monastery to serve as the city's main workhouse. The massive façade and part of the courtyard remain from the old building, while the rest was rebuilt in 1994 by architects Piñón and Viaplana, resulting in a dramatic combination of original elements with the imposing curtain wall in the cloister. As a contemporary culture centre it picks up on whatever falls through the cracks elsewhere in Barcelona, including urban culture, early 20th-century art and thematic shows on TV or cinema. The series *Fars* (Lighthouses) links famous 20th-century writers and cultural personalities with their cities and contexts.

Until May 2003 Fantasies of the Harem examines western myth and iconography of the harem. From May to August the exhibition 'Junk Culture' will be on display here. Other scheduled activities include a festival of video art, an alternative cinema festival, the extremely popular Sónar music festival (*see p213*) and other spin-off music events (including a contemporary music series that runs through November), along with dance events. There is also a good bookshop with urban-related topics.

MACBA (Museu d'Art Contemporani de Barcelona)

Plaça dels Àngels 1 (93 412 08 10/www.macba.es). *Metro Catalunya.* **Open** *June-Sept* 11am-8pm Mon, Wed-Fri; 10am-8pm Sat; 10am-3pm Sun. *Oct-May* 11am-7.30pm Mon, Wed-Fri; 10am-8pm Sat; 10am-3pm Sun. **Guided tours** *Oct-May only* 6pm Wed, Sat; noon Sun. **Admission** *Museum* €5.50; €4 concessions. *Temporary exhibitions* €4; €3 concessions. *Combined ticket* €7; €5.50 concessions. **Discounts** Articket, BC, BT. **Credit** (shop only) MC, V. **Map** p344 A1.

For some years the MACBA's main draw was, for many, Richard Meier's building itself, with its crisp geometry and spanking white façade, its airy transitional spaces and never-ending ramps between floors. MACBA's content now holds its own on the international stage, though, largely thanks to director Manuel Borja-Villel, who has enabled MACBA to do what no Barcelona museum has ever done: show contemporary art and collect it with certain criteria. Borja is allied to the current reinterpretation of socio-political art of the 1960s and '70s, giving it a decidedly southern European flavour.

The collection begins with pieces from the 1940s, although earlier works by Paul Klee, Alexander Calder and Catalan sculptor Leandre Cristòfol are also on display. The work from the 1940s to the '60s is mostly painting, with Spanish expressionists such as Saura and Tàpies alongside Dubuffet. Basque sculptors Jorge Oteiza and Eduardo Chillida are fully represented. Collections from the past 40 years are more international, with work by Joseph Beuys, Robert Rauschenberg, Piero Manzoni and Christian Boltanski, along with recent acquisitions of Tony Oursler, South African William Kentridge, and Gerhard Richter's monumental *48 Portraits*. The contemporary Spanish collection includes a review of Catalan painting (Ferran Garcia Sevilla, Miquel Barceló) and sculpture (Sergi Aguilar, Susana Solano), plus conceptual artists Muntadas, Francesc Torres, as well as Eulàlia Valldosera, one of Spain's sharpest emerging creators. For temporary shows in 2003, Spanish content includes a web-based project by Dora Garcia in the spring. There are also large retrospective exhibitions by Richard Hamilton (March-June) and Fluxus guru Robert Filliou (April-June), while the video and performance-based work of American Adrian Piper will be shown in the autumn. Late in the year and into 2004 the show *Disagreements* will take a look at Spanish art with political intentions.

Palau Güell

C/Nou de la Rambla 3-5 (93 317 39 74). Metro Liceu. **Guided tours** (subject to change) *Mar-Oct* 10am-6.15pm Mon-Sat. *Nov-Feb* 10am-4.30pm Mon-Sat. **Admission** €3; €1.50 concessions; free under-6s. **Discount** RM. **No credit cards. Map** p345 A3.

Go all modern at **MACBA**.

This vaguely medievalist palace was built in 1886-8 as a residence for Gaudí's patron Eusebi Güell. It was Gaudí's first major commission for Güell, and one of the first buildings in which he revealed the originality of his ideas. Once past the fortress-like façade and dark entrance halls, one finds an interior in impeccable condition, with lavish wooden ceilings, dozens of snake-eye stone pillars and original furniture. The roof terrace is a garden of decorated chimneys, each one different from the other. Visits are by guided tour only, and tickets for afternoon visits must be bought in the morning.

Sant Pau del Camp

C/Sant Pau 101 (93 441 00 01). Metro Paral.lel. **Open** 5-8pm Mon, Wed, Thur; 10am-1pm Sat. **Admission** free. **Map** p342 C6.

This site has been used for holy purposes for at least 1,000 years. Archaeologists have determined that a monastery stood here before 912 AD. As one of Barcelona's oldest surviving churches (in English its name means St Paul's in the Field) it is a fine example of the Catalan Romanesque style. It lacks the towering grandeur of later churches like the cathedral or Santa Maria del Mar; it is rounded in on itself, giving a sense of intimacy and protection to worshippers. The church is typified by three aisles and a triple apse, particularly beautiful from without. The small cloister features extraordinary Visigoth capitals and triple-lobed arches, unique among similar monasteries in the style.

Sant Pere & the Born

Barcelona's most happening neighbourhood is also its prettiest.

Maps p344-p345

The neighbourhoods of Sant Pere and the Born fit loosely within the district known as La Ribera, although this name is used less frequently nowadays. *Ribera* means waterfront, and recalls the time before permanent quays were built, when the shoreline reached much further inland. Originally contained, like the Barri Gòtic, within the second, 13th-century, city wall, this is one of the most engaging districts of the Old City. It has, though, fallen victim to two historic acts of urban vandalism. The first took place after the 1714 siege, when the victors razed one whole corner of the Ribera in order to construct the fortress of the Ciutadella, now the **Parc de la Ciutadella** (*see p97*). The second occurred when the Via

Laietana was struck through the *barri* in 1907, in line with the contemporary theory of 'ventilating' insanitary city districts by driving wide avenues through them.

In Barcelona's Golden Age, from the 12th century onwards, La Ribera was both the favourite residential area of the city's merchant elite and the principal centre of commerce and trade. The **Plaça de l'Àngel**, now a rather nondescript space on Via Laietana near the Jaume I metro station, is all that remains of the Plaça del Blat, the 'wheat square' where all grain brought into the city was traded. This was its commercial and popular heart, where virtually everybody came at least once a day.

Below the Ronda Sant Pere lies the district of Sant Pere, originally centred around the

---

Walk this way medieval trading

Duration: 45 minutes

From **Plaça de l'Àngel**, site of the Plaça del Blat, the grain market, cross Via Laietana to **C/Bòria**, a name that probably means 'outskirts' or 'suburbs', since it was outside the original city. C/Bòria continues into the evocative little **Plaça de la Llana**, old centre of wool (*llana*) trading in the city, now an animated meeting place for the Dominican community. Alleys to the left were associated with food trades: **C/Mercaders** ('traders', probably in grain), **C/Oli** ('olive oil') just off it, and **C/Semoleres**, where semolina was made. To the right on Bòria is **C/Pou de la Cadena** ('well with a chain'), a reminder that water was essential for textile working.

After Plaça de la Llana the Roman road's name becomes **C/Corders** ('ropemakers'), and then **C/Carders** ('carders', or combers of wool). Where the name changes there is a tiny square, Placeta Marcús, with a smaller Romanesque chapel, the **Capella d'en Marcús**, built in the early 12th century to give shelter to travellers who arrived after the city gates had closed for the night. Bernat Marcús, who paid for it, is also said to have organised the first postal service in Europe, and it was from here that his riders set off north. The chapel is rarely open.

Carry on a little way along C/Carders to **Plaça Sant Agustí Vell**, different parts of which date from many periods, from the Middle Ages to the 19th century: just off it, on **C/Basses de Sant Pere** as it leads away to the left, there is an intact 14th-century house. Retrace your steps down C/Carders, to turn left into **C/Blanqueria** ('bleaching'). Here wool was washed before being spun. At **C/Assaonadors** ('tanners'), turn right. At the end of this street, behind the Marcús chapel, is a statue of John the Baptist, patron saint of the tanners' guild.

Now you are at the top of **C/Montcada**, one of Barcelona's great museum centres and a beautiful street in itself. The first of the line of medieval merchants' palaces you reach after crossing C/Princesa is the **Palau Berenguer d'Aguilar**, home of the **Museu Picasso**, which has also taken over four more palaces. Opposite is one of the finest and largest palaces, the **Palau dels Marquesos de Lió**, now the **Museu Tèxtil**, with a fine café. To the right is the milliners' street **C/Sombrerers**; opposite it is Barcelona's narrowest street, **C/Mosques** ('flies'), not even wide enough for an adult to lie across, and now closed off with an iron gate because too many people were pissing in it at night.

monastery of **Sant Pere de les Puelles**, which still stands, if greatly altered, in Plaça de Sant Pere. This was Barcelona's main centre of textile production for centuries, and to this day streets like Sant Pere Més Baix and Sant Pere Més Alt contain many textile wholesalers and retailers. The area may be medieval in origin, but its finest monument is one of the most extraordinary works of Modernisme, the **Palau de la Música Catalana**, facing C/Sant Pere Més Alt (*see p96*). Less noticed on the same street is a curious feature, the **Passatge de les Manufactures**, a narrow 19th-century arcade between C/Sant Pere Més Alt and C/Ortigosa.

Like other parts of the Old City, Sant Pere looks very run-down in places, but, as elsewhere, it too is undergoing dramatic renovation, with the gradual opening up of a continuation of the Avda Francesc Cambó, which will eventually swing around to meet up with C/Allada Vermell, a wide street formed when a block was demolished in 1994. The district's market, **Mercat de Santa Caterina** – one of Barcelona's oldest – is being completely rebuilt, and remains of the medieval

Santa Caterina convent will be shown behind glass at one end. In the meantime its stallholders have been relocated along Passeig Lluís Companys, by the park. Another convent nearby is the **Convent de Sant Agustí**, now a civic centre, on C/Comerç. The entrance contains a magical 'light sculpture' by James Turrell, commissioned by the Ajuntament in the 1980s and best seen after dark.

At the bottom of Sant Pere, where C/Carders meets C/Montcada, is the Placeta d'en Marcús, with a small chapel, the 12th-century **Capella d'en Marcús**, built as part of an inn for travellers. From this tiny square C/Montcada, one of the unmissable streets of old Barcelona, leads into the Born. It is lined with a succession of medieval palaces, the greatest of which house a variety of museums, including the **Museu Tèxtil** (*see p96*), the **Museu Barbier-Mueller** of pre-Columbian art and, above all, the **Museu Picasso** (for both, *see p95*).

'Born' originally meant 'joust' or 'list', and in the Middle Ages and for many centuries thereafter the neighbourhood's main artery, the **Passeig del Born**, was the centre for the

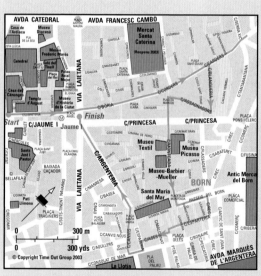

found, and **C/Formatgeria**, where one would have gone for cheese. After that is **C/Vidrieria**, where glass was stored and sold. Esparteria runs into C/Ases, which crosses **C/Malcuinat** ('badly cooked'). Turn left into **C/Espaseria** ('sword-making') to emerge out of ancient alleys on to the open space of Pla del Palau. Turn right, and then right again into **C/Canvis Vells** ('old exchange'). A tiny street to the left, **C/Panses**, has an archway above it, with a stone sculpture of a face over the second floor. This face, called a *carabassa*, indicated the existence of a legalised brothel.

C/Montcada ends at **Passeig del Born**, a hub of the city's trading for 400 years.

Turn left, and on the left is **C/Flassaders** ('blanket makers'), and to the right **C/Rec**, the old irrigation canal. Go down Rec to turn right into **C/Esparteria**, where *espart* (hemp) was woven. Turnings off it include **C/Calders**, where smelting furnaces would have been

At the end of Canvis Vells you come to **Plaça Santa Maria** and La Ribera's superb parish church, **Santa Maria del Mar**: on the left-hand side is **C/Abaixadors** ('unloaders'), where porters would unload goods, and from the square **C/Argenteria** ('silverware') leads back to the Plaça de l'Àngel.

city's festivals, processions, tournaments, carnivals and the burning of heretics by the Inquisition. At one end of the square is the old **Born market**, a magnificent 1870s wrought-iron structure that used to be Barcelona's main wholesale food market. It closed in the '70s, and the market was transferred elsewhere. Plans to turn it into a library have been thwarted with the discovery of medieval remains (*see p98* **1714 and all that**).

At the other end of the Passeig from the market stands the greatest of all Catalan Gothic buildings, the magnificent church of **Santa Maria del Mar** (*see p98*). On one side of it, a square was opened in 1989 on the site where it is believed the last defenders of the city were executed after the fall of Barcelona to the Spanish army in 1714. Called the **Fossar de les Moreres** (the 'Mulberry Graveyard'), the square is inscribed with emphatic patriotic poetry, and nationalist demonstrations converge here every year on Catalan National Day, 11 September. The square is seen as a monument itself, so the recent addition of a tall structure curving over the C/Santa Maria and holding an 'eternal flame' to commemorate the victims has been badly received, not least by the original architect of the square, Carme Fiol.

From the Born and Santa Maria, tiny streets lead through centuries-old arches and the little **Plaça de les Olles** to the harbourside avenue and another symbol of La Ribera, the **Llotja** (Exchange). Its outer shell is neo-classical, added in the 18th century, but its core is a superb 1380s Gothic hall, sadly closed to the public, save for occasional functions organised through the Chamber of Commerce. Until the exchange moved to the Passeig de Gràcia in 1994, this was the oldest continuously functioning stock exchange in Europe.

Museu d'Art Modern

Edifici del Parlament, Parc de la Ciutadella (93 319 57 28/www.mnac.es). Metro Ciutadella. **Open** 10am-7pm Tue-Sat; 10am-2.30pm Sun. **Guided tours** noon Sat, Sun. **Admission** €3; €1.50 concessions; free under-7s. **Discounts** Articket, BC. **Credit** (shop only) V. **Map** p343 E6.

Slowly being squeezed out as the Catalan parliament (with which it shares a building) expands, the Modern Art Museum is eventually due to move hook, line and sinker to the upper floors of the MNAC building in Montjuïc (*see p108*). This was slated for completion in 2003, but seems unlikely to happen until 2004. The theme of the collection is not 20th-century art, but Catalan art and design from the mid 19th century to the 1930s. It is, therefore, the main showcase for the burst of Modernista creativity.

The galleries begin with the Romantic painter Marià Fortuny, whose liking for oriental exoticism and ostentatious detail led to his *Odalisque* (1861).

After the realism of the Olot school, there is some impressionist-influenced work by Ramon Casas and Santiago Rusiñol, the main Modernista painters. Casas' famous image painted for the Els Quatre Gats café, of himself and the café's owner Pere Romeu riding a tandem, gives a vivid sense of the vibrant spirit of the close of the 19th century. Modernisme refused to discriminate between fine and decorative arts, and a major attraction is the superb selection of furniture and decorative objects by the likes of Gaudí, Puig i Cadafalch and talented furniture maker Gaspar Homar. Josep Llimona and the neo-classicist Josep Clarà represent figurative sculpture, although at the time of writing much of Clarà's work had been moved into storage in readiness for the eventual move. Painters include Isidre Nonell (who influenced Picasso's Blue Period), Joaquim Mir and Josep de Togores.

Museu Barbier-Mueller d'Art Precolombí

C/Montcada 14 (93 319 76 03). Metro Jaume I. **Open** 10am-6pm Tue-Sat; 10am-3pm Sun. **Admission** €3; €1.50 concessions. *Combined admission with Museu Tèxtil* €3.50; €2 concessions. Free under-16s. Free 1st Sun of the mth. **Discounts** BC. **Credit** (shop only) AmEx, MC, V. **Map** p345 C3.

A regularly changing selection of pieces from the superb collection of pre-Columbian art in the Barbier-Mueller museum in Geneva. Though Columbus's famed voyage took place in 1492, this museum demonstrates how much of what is described as 'pre-Columbian' comes from well beyond that date, as the subjugation of indigenous cultures by the *conquistadores* lasted for decades. The rooms are uncomfortably dark with exhibits spotlit in a cliché of tribal art presentation, but the collection is impressive, highlighted by extraordinary pieces from Central America, the Andes and the lower Amazon.

Museu de Geologia

Passeig Picasso, Parc de la Ciutadella (93 319 68 95). Metro Arc de Triomf. **Open** 10am-2pm Tue, Wed, Fri-Sun; 10am-6.30pm Thur. **Guided tours** by appointment (93 319 69 12). **Admission** *Combined ticket with Museu de Zoologia* €3.50; €1.50 concessions; free under-16s. Free 1st Sun of the mth. **Discounts** BC. **No credit cards. Map** p343 E6.

A rather dry display of minerals, painstakingly classified alongside explanations of geological phenomena found in Catalonia, with a rather more interesting selection from the museum's collection of 300,000 fossils, including fossilised bones, many found locally. In 2003 the geology museum will have its 125th anniversary. Along with the zoology museum (*see p96*) it is now known collectively as the Museu de Ciències Naturals de la Ciutadella and admission covers both.

Museu Picasso

C/Montcada 15-23 (93 319 63 10/www.museu picasso.bcn.es). Metro Jaume I. **Open** 10am-7.45pm Tue-Sat; 10am-2.45pm Sun. **Admission** *Permanent collection only* €4.80; €2.40 concessions. *With*

temporary exhibition €7.80; €4.50 concessions.
Free under-12s; free (museum only) 1st Sun of the
mth. **Discounts** BC. **Credit** (shop only) AmEx,
MC, V. **Map** p345 C3.

The permanent collection at the Picasso will be
closed from February to mid April 2003, while the
final phase of the museum's expansion is under way.
The plan is to show as much as possible of the more
than 3,000 paintings, drawings and other work, as
well as temporary shows, which in 2003 will include
a display of over 400 pictures showing the role of
caricature in Picasso's work.

The permanent collection is testimony to the vital
formative years that the teenage Picasso spent at
Barcelona's art school (where his father taught),
and where he began to hang out with Catalonia's
fin-de-siècle avant-garde. The museum arose out of
a donation to the city by Picasso's secretary and life-
long friend Jaume Sabartès (seen in a Blue Period
painting from 1901). It graces a tight row of
medieval courtyard-palaces, appropriately just five
minutes away from the old art school building, La
Llotja. The main entrance is at the elegant Palau
Berenguer d'Aguilar, though you can also get tickets a few metres down the street if the queue gets
too long. Since opening in 1963, it has expanded to
incorporate adjacent mansions: the later but also
impressive Palaus Meca and Castellet, the baroque
Casa Mauri and the early Gothic Casa Finestres.

The seamless presentation of Picasso's development from 1890 to 1904, from deft pre-adolescent
portraits to sketchy landscapes to intense innova-
tions in blue, is unbeatable. Then it leaps to a gallery
of mature cubist paintings from 1917, and completes
with a jump to oils from the late 1950s, including the
complete series of studies based on Velázquez'
famous *Las Meninas*. The culmination of Picasso's
early genius in *Les Demoiselles d'Avignon* (1907) and
the first cubist paintings from the time (many of
them done in Catalonia), as well as his collage and
sculpture, are completely absent, although the imminent expansion could change all that.

Museu Tèxtil i d'Indumentària

C/Montcada 12 (93 319 76 03/93 310 45 16/
www.museutextil.bcn.es). Metro Jaume I. **Open**
10am-6pm Tue-Sat; 10am-3pm Sun. **Guided tours**
by appointment (93 280 50 20). **Admission** €3.50;
€1.50 concessions. *Combined admission with Museu*
Barbier-Mueller €3.50; €2 concessions. Free under-
16s; free 1st Sun of the mth. **Discounts** BC.
Credit (shop only) AmEx, MC, V. **Map** p345 C3.

Through the handsome medieval courtyard of this
C/Montcada palace, right across from the Picasso
Museum, visitors come to the elegant displays of
the Textile and Clothing museum. The collection
occupies two adjacent buildings, the Palau Nadal
and Palau dels Marquesos de Lliò; the latter retains
some of its 13th-century wooden ceilings. Items
include medieval Hispano-Arab textiles, liturgical
vestments and the city's lace and embroidery collection. The real highlight are the historic fashions
– from baroque to 20th-century – that collector

Manuel Rocamora donated in the 1960s, one of the
finest collections of their type anywhere. Recent
important donations include one from Spanish
designer Cristóbal Balenciaga, famous for the 1958
baby doll dress and pill box hat, and from February
to May 2003 there will be a exhibition of Belgian
fashion. The museum shop is a great place to pick
up presents, and there's a wonderful outdoor café.

Museu de la Xocolata

Antic Convent de Sant Agustí, Plaça Pons i Clerch
(93 268 78 78/www.museudelaxocolata.com). Metro
Jaume I. **Open** 10am-7pm Mon, Wed-Sat; 10am-3pm
Sun. **Admission** €3.60; €3.10 concessions; free
under-7s. **No credit cards. Map** p345 C3.

An irresistible overview of one of man's greatest
weaknesses. Alongside some rather dry explanations of chocolate's New World origins, its use in
medicine and as an aphrodisiac, and its arrival in
Europe, there are some extraordinary *monas* (huge,
elaborate chocolate sculptures made for Easter), here
in giant form; a life-size chocolate Tintin and Snowy;
a smaller scale Sagrada Família; a virgin and child
and Columbus's ship.

Museu de Zoologia

Passeig Picasso, Parc de la Ciutadella (93 319 69
12/ www.museuzoologia.bcn.es). Metro Arc de
Triomf. **Open** 10am-2pm Tue, Wed, Fri-Sun; 10am-
6pm Thur. **Admission** C*ombined admission with*
Museu de Geologia €3.50; €1.50 concessions; free
under-16s; free 1st Sun of the mth. **Discounts**
BC. **No credit cards. Map** p343 E6.

Another of the city's older museums, the Zoology
Museum occupies the much-loved 'Castell dels Tres
Dragons', built by Domènech i Montaner as the café-
restaurant for the 1888 Exhibition. The separation
between structure and glass façade predates the
curtain walls of the modern movement. Downstairs
is the Whale Room (with a whale skeleton), which
is also where temporary shows are organised; from
May 2003 a year-long show called 'The Other
Architects' looks at the relation between the construction of homes in the animal and bird kingdoms,
and the architecture of man. The upper floor has a
collection of dissected and preserved animals displayed according to group and species.

Palau de la Mùsica Catalana

C/Sant Francesc de Paula 2 (93 295 72 00/
www.palaumusica.org). Metro Urquinaona.
Open Box office 10am-9pm Mon-Sat. **Guided tours**
10am-3.30pm daily. **Admission** €7; €6 concessions.
Credit (minimum €20) MC, V. **Map** p344 B-C2.

Domènech i Montaner's Palace of Catalan Music was
built in 1905-8, and is without a doubt the most fantastical Modernista creation in the city. The façade,
with its bare brick, busts and mosaic friezes representing Catalan musical traditions and composers,
is impressive enough, but it is surpassed by the
building's staggering interior. Decoration erupts
everywhere: the ceiling centrepiece is of multicoloured stained glass; 18 half-mosaic, half-relief
figures representing the musical muses appear out

Verdant delights aplenty in the **Parc de la Ciutadella**.

of the back of the stage; and on one side, massive Wagnerian carved horses ride out to accompany a bust of Beethoven. The old Palau has been bursting under the pressure of the musical activity going on inside it, and an extension and renovation project by Oscar Tusquets in the 1980s is being followed by yet more alterations by the same architect.

The best way to see the Palau is to go to a concert (*see p96*), but guided tours are available in English, Catalan or Spanish every 30 minutes or so. They begin with a rather tedious video, which can make the remaining tour a bit rushed, and parts of the building (such as the exterior decoration) are not touched upon. Be sure to ask plenty of questions; guides are very knowledgeable, but need to be drawn out of their pat routine.

Parc de la Ciutadella

Passeig Picasso (no phone). Metro Arc de Triomf or Barceloneta. **Open** *Apr-Sept* 8am-10pm daily. *Oct-Mar* 8am-8pm daily. **Map** p343 E6.
Barcelona's most historic park, the Ciutadella, occupies the site of the loathed 18th-century citadel. It was created for the 1888 Exhibition and just outside it is the Arc de Triomf, which formed the main entrance to the Exhibition. Although formally laid out, the park is large enough to provide a verdant oasis within the confines of busy thoroughfares such as Passeig Picasso and Passeig Pujades.

Surprisingly extensive, the park also contains a host of attractions: the Museu d'Art Modern, the Museu de Geologia and Museu de Zoologia. In the middle of the park there is a lake with boats for hire (€2 per person, per half hour). Beside the lake is the Cascade, an ornamental fountain on which the young Gaudí worked as assistant to Josep Fontseré, the architect of the park. The Zoo (*see p219*), at least part of which is due to move to the Diagonal-Mar area by 2004, currently takes up over half the park's space. Not to be missed are Fontseré's Umbracle (literally, 'shade house'), built in the 1880s with a cast-iron structure reminiscent of his Mercat del Born on C/Comerç and restored to provide a pocket of tropical forest in the city, and the elegant Hivernacle (winter garden), with a fine café (*see p175*).

Sala Montcada

C/Montcada 14 (93 310 06 99). Metro Jaume I. **Open** 11am-8pm Tue-Sat. **Admission** free. **Map** p345 C3.
Another groundbreaking exhibition space for contemporary art from the Fundació la Caixa. Each year a different curator develops a mixed programme of Spanish and international artists; until July 2003 Cicle Ficcions brings to the fore work by Quebecois Luc Courchesne, Cuban Carlos Garaioca and the Muscovite AES Group.

Santa Maria del Mar

Plaça de Santa Maria (93 310 23 90). Metro Jaume I. **Open** 9am-1.30pm, 4.30-8pm Mon-Sat; 10am-1.30pm, 4.30-8pm Sun. **Admission** free. **Map** p345 C3.

It's perhaps thanks to the group of anti-clerical anarchists who set this magnificent basilica ablaze in 1936 that its superb features can be appreciated – without the wooden baroque images that clutter so many Spanish churches, the simplicity of its lines can emerge. Built remarkably quickly for a medieval building, between 1329 and 1384, it has an unusual unity of style. Inside, two rows of slim, perfectly proportioned columns soar up to fan vaults, creating a wonderful atmosphere of space and peace. There's also some superb stained glass, particularly the great 15th-century rose window above the main door. The incongruous modern window at the other end was a 1997 addition, belatedly celebrating the Olympics.

1714 and all that

The iron structure of the Antic Mercat del Born at the end of the Passeig del Born has stood empty and more or less abandoned since the '70s, when the market closed down and the neighbourhood settled into a decade or two of gentle decline, little suspecting the rude awakening coming at the end of the '90s, and giving no hint of the polemical riches that lay beneath its surface, until 1998, when Mayor Joan Clos announced plans to build a provincial library on the site, respecting the original structure, and bringing an estimated 10,000 visitors to the area each day. Local shopkeepers were delighted.

There was a catch, however. It was common knowledge that below the surface of the empty market lay archaeological remains dating from the destruction of the Ribera neighbourhood between 1714 and 1716 to make way for the repressive Ciutadella fortress. As recently as 1991, during construction of a subterranean car park in front of the market, similar remains had been found, excavated then ripped out without a second thought. Before work could begin, the archaeologists were summoned.

It turned out that the ruins were in excellent condition; they were, after all, only 200 years old and had been covered up for most of that time. Street plans, houses, shops, 'palaces' (a rather grandiose term for the elegant mansions of the type that house the Picasso and Textile museums in nearby C/Montcada). Moreover, contemporary tax records made it possible to identify all of it. Here was an area the size of a football pitch that could be excavated in its entirety. This was prime

medieval real estate, suddenly looming from the dust like the lost city of Atlantis.

And there the problems began. After all, 1714 is etched on the collective Catalan conscious in the same way as 1066 in England or 1789 in France. Ironically, the day Felipe V's troops marched into Barcelona was 11 September, a day of barbarity and bloodshed that is also commemorated as Catalonia's national day, and a proud moment in the small nation's fortunes (despite the fact that it was a crushing defeat for the home side at the hands of the Castilian invaders).

To rip up the ruins would be to desecrate the memory of those brave martyrs, argued some. What better memorial than a library to celebrate Catalan identity and spirit, argued others. It was billed as a struggle between archaeologists and architects, although of course it was really a political issue, as is anything related to Catalan national identity. For their part, the archaeologists weren't too bothered. 'We don't need it,' announced the director of the Catalan Archaeology Society. 'We've studied it, we've photographed, we've catalogued it. Now we can cover it up again.'

For a while there was even the possibility of sharing the glory, with a compromise library-cum-monument incorporating the ruins below a glass floor. Finally this too was discounted, and space for the library has at last been found behind the Estació de França. The project is expected to be completed around 2007. In the meantime, the fate of the ruins is uncertain and the empty market looms over deserted medieval streets, leaking water into 21st-century puddles.

Barceloneta & the Ports

Caught between the city and the deep blue sea.

Port Vell

It's easy to forget that Barcelona is built around a port, and even more so that it is by the sea. Unlike the great harbour cities – San Francisco, Hong Kong, Sydney – the sea seems to have been added on as sort of an urban afterthought. Perhaps this is because you rarely glimpse it from the city centre; even from the harbour front the Mediterranean is little more than a rumour, whispering between the masts of yachts moored in the marina and in the mournful horn of the passenger ferries. It wasn't always thus, for in the days when the sea lapped around the foot of the Ramblas, the shipyards, or *drassanes*, were fully operative and the port and city were one. Back then they were linked by the Barrio Chino's exotic maze of warehouses, factories and seafaring foreigners. Even as recently as 1980 the industrial port occupied what is now the leisure marina. Now the 14th-century *drassanes* have become the **Museu Marítim** (*see p101*) and the nearest waves are half a mile away as the gull flies. Even so the city's identity is still closely tied to the sea that has brought it so much prosperity, though nowadays it's more as an aquatic leisure centre than anything else. It's there mostly for the visiting hordes pouring out of the monolithic cruise ships that stop briefly in Barcelona for lightning tourist strikes.

Locals joke that for years people have puzzled over the orientation of the Christopher Columbus statue (known simply as **Colom**) at the foot of the Ramblas, which sternly points east, rather than west. Perhaps he's just telling all those cruise ships to get out of his port (*see p102* **Colonic denigration**). Or perhaps, having done so much for world trade himself, he's pointing to the **World Trade Center**, a charmless architectural allusion to a ship at the end of Moll de Barcelona housing offices, a conference centre and five-star hotel, and that juts out into the port with all the warmth and appeal of a conger eel. This is where the passenger ferries depart, and unless you're going to the Balearics there's little reason to head this way, except to gasp at the huge drawbridge, the largest of its type in the world (beating Rotterdam by about a metre) that is humbly named the **Porta d'Europa**. The bridge is part of the ongoing expansion of the industrial port. Another development is the new

harbour mouth, due to be finished in early 2003, which will create a more direct link between the sea and the leisure marina, separating the ships from the boats, as it were. It will also be used for the 2003 World Swimming Championships.

From Colom, cross **Moll de la Fusta** (literally, 'wood wharf'), and head right to cross the harbour on the **Golondrinas** boat trips (*see p100*) or veer left to the 1918, three-masted schooner *Santa Eulàlia*. Entrance is free if you've kept your ticket for the maritime museum. Look out for the shoals of shark-like dog fish that cruise the waters, waiting for the occasional breadcrumb or the offbalance tourist. Ahead stands the **Maremàgnum** shopping and entertainment centre, joined to the bottom of the Ramblas by an undulating wooden footbridge called the **Rambla del Mar**, which swivels aside to let yachts in and out. Maremàgnum's gaping mouth is topped by a series of curving mirrored panels that give great reflective photos over the quay to the port beyond. Beyond the mouth you're swallowed up into the whale-like insides, pulsating with chain boutiques and fast food emporia, while on the roof is an open-air mini-golf course, surrounded by infamous music bars usually heaving with adolescent exchange students and perplexed Northern European businessmen. Further along

Heading across the **Rambla del Mar**.

A place in the sun

If you want to hit the beach while you are in Barcelona, you are faced with three choices: slightly grubby **Barceloneta** beach; marginally less so **Nova Icària**, **Mar Bella** and **Bogatell**, or heading out of town – either north, where **Montgat**, **Premià**, **Mataró** and **Arenys** all have nicer, cleaner beaches; or south, to the wide expanses of **Castelldefels** and the queer and quaint seaside resort of **Sitges** (*see p277*).

Barceloneta is charming off season, when the water doesn't glisten with suntan oil and there is less detritus floating in it. In high season the beach is overcrowded, dusty, litter-strewn and post-apocalyptic, particularly round the beach shacks (*chiringuitos*) that play garage, house and salsa and serve

drinks and food to crowds of wide-eyed travellers trying to relive Goa. Water quality varies from crystal clear to hazy, depending on wind, tide and recent rain, although in general the water is usually clean enough for swimming. Towards the southern end of the beach is an unofficial nudist area. An official nudist area can be found on the southern half of **Nova Mar Bella** beach, beyond the sailing club and screened off by a reed-covered dune – though this doesn't deter the handful of nature lovers who can usually be found carefully studying the local fauna with more than the usual amount of interest. The beach restaurants here are rather better than those on Barceloneta beach, though in general, like everywhere else, they founder in the difficult relationship between a good meal, a good deal and a good view.

Whichever city beach you go to, watch out for thieves, who act with impunity in broad daylight on even the most crowded beaches. If you leave anything unattended, or even out of your field of vision while you sleep, snog or sunbathe, don't be surprised to find it gone. During the summer, a police caravan is usually stationed conveniently by **Nova Icària** beach to deal with the huge numbers of reported thefts.

is the fantastic **Aquàrium** (*see p219*) and the less fantastic **IMAX** cinema, while on the road that leads back to dry land (and to Roy Lichtenstein's towering pop-art *Barcelona Head*), stands a modern replica of Narcis Monturiol's *Ictíneo*, one of the first successful submarines, which was made of wood and had its maiden voyage around the port in 1860.

Beyond this is the marina – with some very luxurious yachts – and a line of waterside restaurants. The *tinglados*, the huge dock storage sheds that once dominated **Passeig Joan de Borbó**, have nearly all been pulled down to open up an entirely new, positively gracious harbourside promenade on this side of Barceloneta. One exception is the **Palau de Mar**, a converted warehouse that now hosts a clutch of restaurants and the **Museu d'Història de Catalunya**. Set down into the pavement around here, you will see the names of all the winds of the Catalan coast, carved by sculptor Lothar Baumgarten. If you continue beyond here, you can go through Barceloneta to Port Olímpic and the city's beaches.

Catamaran Orsom

Moll de Espanya, Maremàgnum (93 225 82 60/ www.barcelona-orsom.com). Metro Drassanes or Barceloneta. **Maremàgnum to Port Olímpic** (approx 1hr 30mins) *June-Sept* 3 daily. *Oct-May* 2 daily. All sailings subject to weather conditions. **Tickets** €5-€12; free under-4s. **Credit** MC, V. **Map** p342 D7.

The catamaran takes you past the breakwater, at which point the engine is turned off and the sail hoisted for a peaceful float along the coast to Port Olímpic and back. Occasionally, there are live jazz evenings, where the boat simply drifts around Port Vell accompanied by gentle bossanova; phone ahead to check. The catamaran can also be chartered for private groups of up to 100 people for full- or half-day sailings to Sitges.

Las Golondrinas

Moll de Drassanes (93 442 31 06/www.las golondrinas.com). Metro Drassanes. **Drassanes to breakwater & return** (35mins) *July-late Sept* every 35-45mins 11am-8pm daily. *Late Sept-June* (no stop at the breakwater) hourly 11.45am-5pm Mon-Fri; every 35min (phone to check times) Sat, Sun. **Tickets** €3.50, €1.75 concessions; free under-4s.

Drassanes to Port Olímpic & return (1hr 30mins) *July-Sept* 11.30pm, 1.30pm, 4.30pm, 6.30pm, 8.30pm daily. *Apr-June* 11.30pm, 1.30pm, 4.30pm Mon-Fri; 11.30pm, 1.30pm, 4.30pm, 6.30pm Sat, Sun. *Oct-Mar* 11.30am, 1.30pm Mon-Fri; 11.30am, 1.30pm, 4.30pm Sat, Sun. **Tickets** €8.10; €3.70-€6.10 concessions; free under-4s. *Both* **Discounts** BC, BT. **Credit** MC, V. **Map** p342 C7.

The double-decker 'Swallow Boats' run short trips around the harbour from the jetty in front of the Columbus monument. A modern, motor-catamaran with a glass bottom makes a longer trip to the Port Olímpic and back. There are cheaper operators further along, opposite Maremàgnum, but proceed with caution (unless you are a strong swimmer).

Monument a Colom

Plaça Portal de la Pau (93 302 52 24). Metro Drassanes. **Open** *June-late Sept* 9am-8.30pm daily. *Late Sept-Mar* 10am-1.30pm, 3.30-6.30pm Mon-Fri; 10am-6.30pm Sat, Sun. *Apr, May* 10am-1.30pm, 3.30-7.30pm Mon-Fri; 10am-7.30pm Sat, Sun. **Admission** €1.80; €1.20 concessions; free under-4s. **Discounts** BC, BT. **No credit cards. Map** p345 A4.

The tardis-like 60m (197ft) Columbus column, built for the 1888 exhibition, contains a lift up to the viewing platform at the explorer's feet, for a unique view of the port and La Rambla. It is not for the claustrophobic, and holds only four at a time.

Museu Marítim

Avda de les Drassanes (93 342 99 29/www.diba.es/mmaritim). Metro Drassanes. **Open** 10am-7pm daily. **Admission** €5.50; €2.70 concessions; free under-7s. **Discounts** BC, BT. **Credit** MC, V. **Map** p345 A4.

The impressive Gothic arches of the giant *drassanes*, the medieval shipyards that house the Maritime Museum, are worth seeing in themselves, and the collection inside is one of the city's most attractive. The highlight is the full-scale reproduction of the *Royal Galley*, the flagship of Don Juan de Austria at the Battle of Lepanto against the Turks in 1571. This battle and the subsequent history of Barcelona's port are presented in a series of unashamedly audience-pleasing historical simulations, with headphone commentary (also in English). Visitors are caught in a storm on a 19th-century ship, take a steamer to Buenos Aires and go underwater in the *Ictineo*, the prototype submarine of Catalan inventor Narcís Monturiol. The museum has pleasure boats, fishing craft, figureheads, explanations of boat-building techniques and a section on map-making and navigation. Admission also gets you on board the historical *Santa Eulàlia* sailing ship docked nearby at the Moll de la Fusta. The first phase of a long-term restoration project is reaching completion, increasing the space available for temporary exhibitions, as well as adding glass walls to open up several of the spaces, including the workshops where the museum's ships and boats are restored. Temporary exhibitions for 2003 include one on lighthouses.

Transbordador Aeri

Miramar, Parc de Montjuïc to Torre de Jaume I, Port Vell to Torre de Sant Sebastià, Barceloneta (93 441 48 20). World Trade Center: Metro Drassanes. **Open** *Mid June-mid Sept* 11am-8pm daily. *Mid Sept-mid Oct, Mar-mid June* 10.45am-7pm daily. *Mid Oct-Feb* 10.30am-5.45pm daily. **Tickets** €7.50 single; €9 return; free under-3s. **No credit cards.** **Map** p342 C-D7.

The rickety, swaying cablecar that goes from Barceloneta beach to Montjuïc, stopping halfway at the World Trade Center, gives fantastic, bird's-eye views of the port. Keep your eyes on the view, not on the 1929 Eiffel-like girders, however.

Horn's *Wounded Star. See p103.*

Barceloneta

In the 19th century Barceloneta (or 'little Barcelona') became a dockers' and fishermen's district, and even today it has a very distinct character to the rest of the city. Originally just a spit of sand jutting out into the sea, ending in a small, rocky island, it was turned into a virtual shanty town by the inhabitants of La Ribera, who were evicted without compensation to make way for the new citadel in 1714, and were forced to live in makeshift shelters on the beach. Only in the 1750s did the authorities finally decide to rehouse them, when Flemish army engineer Prosper Verboom drew up the groundplan of regimented blocks that still exists today – though the original intention was to build two-storey buildings – the four-storey blocks make the area claustrophobic. Cut off from the rest of the city by road and railway lines, Barceloneta has retained a distinctive, working-class identity, complete with its exuberant local celebrations, including the

Sightseeing

local *festa major* (*see p216*) and its Carnival, with weeping widows and sardine-burying. The promenade to the beach between the marina and Barceloneta is an esplanade lined with palm trees. At the top is the municipal **Sant Sebastià swimming pool**, hugely popular with locals, not least because you can see the sea as you swim. A new outdoor pool is due to open in time for the 2003 World Swimming Championships. Next door, the **Club Natació de Barcelona** (*see p268*) is a private swimming, sailing and sports centre, where the favoured form of transport is the *patí*. Sharing the same name as a rollerskate, this is a small, one-person catamaran that, uniquely, doesn't have a rudder. Further along, the new entrance to the marina is currently under redevelopment as a leisure area, to be crowned

Colonic denigration

From heroic explorer to slave-owning proto-colonialist in the space of a few decades; no, history has not been kind to Christopher Columbus. Barcelona is one of the few places in the world that still heaps glory on the man, and in fact for many years Catalans propagated the theory that Columbus was not actually Genoese but Catalan.

The **Monument a Colom** (*see p101*) is the most obvious and eye-catching tribute to Columbus. Positioned at the bottom of La Rambla, the statue, perched atop a 60-metre (197-foot) column, points dramatically towards the sea as if to say, 'Look, that's where I got screwed'. Those who are paying attention may note that Columbus is facing in the wrong direction – towards Mallorca, actually – and historians will respond that this was a deliberate statement by the people of Barcelona on their denial of a piece of the American pie as punishment for their unwillingness to accept the hegemony of the Catholic kings.

Commissioned for the 1888 exhibition at the peak of the Catalan *Renaixença*, and built using bronze from melted-down cannons from the Castell de Montjuïc, the monument's base is adorned with non-politically correct bas-reliefs of mainly Catalan missionaries 'converting' the natives to Christianity. In a wonderfully typical piece of Catalan theatre of the absurd, the statue of Columbus was ceremonially married to the Statue of Liberty on St Valentine's Day in 1992. A replica of his flagship, the *Nao de Santa María*, sat in Barcelona's port for many years. Its presence wasn't particularly welcome to local anarchists, who set fire to it twice in the late '80s as a symbolic protest against Spain's joining of Nato. Faced with a potentially life-threatening tourist trap, the port authorities opted to take a radical approach: they towed it out to sea and scuttled it.

If you make your way to the Saló del Tinell, a splendid, cavernous hall built in 1362 spanned by 15-metre (49-foot) arches, and now part of the **Museu d'Historia de la Ciutat** (*see p79*), you can see the place where Columbus allegedly met Ferdinand and Isabel on his triumphant return from the New World. Legend has it that in the square outside, Columbus introduced the six natives whome he had brought back as proof of his discovery. The baptismal font used to christen them is in the Cathedral. It was, until recently, still the favoured place to christen the offspring of the Catalan middle classes. A plaque next to the font celebrates the baptism of 'the first Christians of the New World'; the tale of what happened to them later is one of history's great tragedies. Columbus' subsequent fall from grace and the atrocious behaviour of the European *conquistadores* over the next few centuries add a tragic coda to the story of Barcelona's most famous adopted son.

The **Museu d'Història de Catalunya**.

by a new hotel in the shape of a sail, designed by the ever-controversial Catalan architect Ricard Bofill. After public outcry he was obliged to reduce the original 150 metres (490 feet) to a marginally less priapic 88 metres (290 feet), though delays mean that building is unlikely to start before 2004.

In the opposite direction, heading towards the Port Olímpic, the promenade along the beach is popular with joggers and Rollerbladers. The stack of rusting metal cubes towering above the palm trees is Rebecca Horn's sculpture *Wounded Star,* a memento of the beach shacks (*chiringuitos*) that used to serve great seafood here before being swept away by Olympic regeneration. A handful have gingerly reappeared.

For Barceloneta, the massive reworking of the old port – and the transformation of Passeig Joan de Borbó from dockyard service road to waterside promenade – has in effect meant a complete reorientation from looking out to sea to overlooking the port. Some former *chiringuito* owners have been encouraged to reopen, albeit alongside smart all-new restaurants on the new harbourside *passeig* and in the **Palau de Mar**, while other dock buildings have been torn down to open up a view of the harbour and Montjuïc.

Museu d'Història de Catalunya

Plaça Pau Vila 3 (93 225 47 00/www.cultura.gencat. es/museus/mhc). Metro Barceloneta. **Open** 10am-7pm Tue, Thur-Sat; 10am-8pm Wed; 10am-2.30pm Sun. **Admission** €3; €2.10 concessions; free under-7s. **Guided tours** noon Sun. **Discounts** BC, BT. **Credit** (shop only) MC, V. **Map** p345 C4.

Not a museum in the sense of a large collection of treasured objects, but rather an overview from prehistory to the present, with dynamic displays. A multitude of materials is used to keep you entertained – texts, photographs, real objects, reproductions, videos and animated models. There are also hands-on exhibits, a waterwheel and armour. Large temporary exhibitions deal with Catalonia's past and present, but are often of specialised interest. In 2003 they include a centenary exhibition on the poet Carles Fages de Climent (1902-68); the last of a series of exhibitions devoted to Catalan political parties, and an exploration of the links between Catalonia and Occitania in the time of the Cathars.

Following criticism of certain key omissions in the museum's narrative, such as the extensive impact of immigration from the rest of Spain since the 1930s, director Jaume Sobrequés, a socialist historian, has promised to modernise the entire museum. No firm date has been fixed, though work is due to start sometime in 2003, which will lead to some parts of the museum being temporarily inaccessible. The library upstairs has English material, and English tours are available for groups. The top-floor café has an unbeatable view and a reasonable *menú del día*. There is also an imaginative gift shop.

Vila Olímpica

Among the many legacies of the Olympic Games, the Vila Olímpica was one of the most ambitious, creating a new, residential *barrio* from scratch on reclaimed industrial land. Not since Cerdà or Gaudí has anyone had such an impact on the face of Barcelona as Oriol Bohigas, Josep Martorell, Albert Puigdomènech and long-time English resident David Mackay. These architects were entrusted with the overall design of the all-new district, to be built on reclaimed industrial land. Constructed in just two years, it was initially named Nova Icària to recall the utopian socialist community that briefly existed in the area in the last century, but the name didn't stick. They built some 2,000 apartments, which it was hoped would provide low-cost housing after the athletes had gone, although economic realities have dictated otherwise.

Ildefons Cerdà's original concept for the Eixample was taken as an inspiration, with semi-open blocks built around gardens. The final effect is of a rather cold suburb, although the waterway parallel to C/Moscou and the red brick of **Plaça Tirant lo Blanc** soften the harshness. There are few corner shops or cafés, and the spiky metal pergolas on Avda Icària look like a grim parody of trees. However, a touch of humour can be found in the same park, in the enormous six-metre (20-foot) sculpture of the lower half of a human body. Created by Basque artist Eduardo Úrculo, it has inevitably become known as *el culo de Úrculo* (Úrculo's arse). The Vila's open spaces are colonised by cyclists and Rollerbladers at weekends. The most successful part of the Vila is the **Port Olímpic**, the leisure marina (with 743 mooring spaces) that grew up from nothing over the last two decades. It's now heaving with bars and restaurants. On the far side are the Olympic beaches, which will eventually link up with the new Diagonal-Mar district to the north.

Montjuïc

The hill is alive with music, sport, art and architecture.

Montjuïc is Barcelona's most distinguishing geographical feature, casting its shadow over the entire port area. The hill offers numerous options for colourful strolls through its sprawl of thematic parks, and around its museums, sporting facilities and oddities like the massive cemetery to the south. The area's name is probably a result of its use by medieval Jews as a burial site, (*juïc* being a variation on the Catalan *jueu*) and many of those old tombstones are now in the **Museu Militar** (*see p108*). Its history goes even further back, however. According to legend, Barcelona was founded by Hercules and populated by the crew of the ninth ship (*barca nona*) that went with him on his travels, after which Hercules sat on Montjuïc to admire his creation. In terms of less mythical history, archaeologists have found a prehistoric Iberian storage site on its flank, and the Romans built the first port for the colony of Barcino near the cemetery entrance.

Montjuïc has not always had pleasant associations. The fortress capping it, built in the 17th century, soon became a symbol of the suppression of Catalan liberties. As a prison and torture centre for rebels and radicals, it inspired fear and loathing for two centuries. Here many republicans were executed after the Civil War, including Generalitat President Lluís Companys (who now has a monument in the cemetery). Only at the end of the 19th century did the military finally cede its jealous control over the land, allowing for the construction of housing on its lower slopes.

The definitive step to turn the mountain into a leisure zone came with the 1929 Expo. The long axis drawn up from **Plaça Espanya** is still the most popular access to the park, with the climb now eased by a sequence of open-air escalators. Plaça Espanya itself is ennobled by the disused **Las Arenas** bullring with its Moorish arches, now scheduled to be remade into a shopping and leisure centre designed by architect Richard Rogers. On the other side of the square, two Venetian-style towers announce the beginning of the **Fira**, the trade show area, with numerous pavilions from 1929 and newer ones used for conventions and congresses. Further up, the rebuilt Mies van der Rohe **Pavelló Barcelona** (*see p108*), a modernist classic, contrasts sharply with the many neo-classical structures in the area. Behind it is the

Poble Espanyol (*see p110*), a throwback from 1929 dedicated to Spanish crafts and architecture, while across the street Puig i Cadafalch's Modernista factory has been converted into a new home for the Fundació La Caixa cultural centre, called **CaixaForum** (*see p105*).

Presiding over it all is the bombastic **Palau Nacional**, where the **Museu Nacional d'Art de Catalunya** (*see p108*) art museum is now located. At nightfall the entire setting is illuminated by Carles Buïgas' water-and-light spectacular, the **Font Màgica** (*see p106*), still operating with its complex original mechanisms. Other buildings erected for the 1929 World's Fair have been converted into the **Museu d'Arqueologie** and the **Ciutat del Teatre** complex, to the left of the Palau Nacional going up. From the same period are the nearby **Teatre Grec**, used for summer concerts during the Grec festival, and the beautifully restored **Jardins de Laribal**, designed by French landscape architect JCN Forestier; the **Museu Etnològic**, a typical 1970s construction, sits just above (*see p107*).

In spite of the glowing effects of 1929, by the 1940s Montjuïc was inhabited by thousands of immigrant workers from the rest of Spain. Some squatted in precarious shacks, while others rented brick and plaster sheds laid out along improvised streets. These *barraques* thrived until the last few stragglers moved out in the '70s. Energetic visitors eager to walk up the hill can follow the same steep routes these residents once took home, whether off Avda Paral.lel up C/Nou de la Rambla, or straight up C/Margarit in Poble Sec, the most direct route: the stairway at the top leaves you just a short distance from the **Fundació Miró** and the Olympic Stadium area. An easier way up to the same point is the **funicular** (*see p106*), leaving from the Paral.lel metro station and linking up with the **Telefèric cable car** to the Castell. A more circuitous and dizzying way up the hill for those with no fear of heights is to take the **Transbordador Aeri cablecar** across the harbour to the corner of the mountain called **Miramar**. Here, work on a five-star hotel has begun; incredibly, the current road will disappear and a tunnel will run beneath the hotel gardens, making for a bit of construction chaos in the area throughout 2003.

The astonishing, swirling **Calatrava** communications tower.

Montjuïc's **Anella Olímpica** (Olympic Ring), is a compact hub of buildings in contrasting styles that was the heart of the 1992 Olympic Games. The **Estadi Olímpic** – home to the city's 'second' football team, Espanyol – although entirely new, was built within the façade of a 1929 stadium by a design team led by Federico Correa and Alfonso Milà. Next to it is the most original and attractive of the Olympic facilities, Arata Isozaki's **Palau Sant Jordi** indoor arena, with its undulating façade evoking Gaudí and a high-tech interior featuring a transparent roof. It now regularly serves as a venue for concerts and other events; a swimming pool will be set inside it for the FINA World Swimming Championships in July 2003. In the *plaça* in front locals gather on Sundays for family walks and picnics, next to Santiago Calatrava's remarkable, Brancusi-inspired communications tower. Across the square is Barcelona's best swimming pool, the **Piscina Bernat Picornell** (*see p268*), while further down is the INEFC physical education institute, featuring architect Ricardo Bofill's trademark Doric columns.

Despite all the activity on the mountain and its proximity to the city centre, it's surprisingly easy to find peaceful, shaded places among the many green areas. Below Miramar, on the steep flank nearest the port, are the **Jardíns Mossèn Costa i Llobera** (*see p107*), which abound in tropical plants, but particularly cacti. Not far above it all are the **Jardíns del Mirador**, from where there is a spectacular view out over the harbour. The old amusement park across the street is being converted into another botanically thematic garden. Walk down towards the funicular station and you will reach the **Jardins Cinto Verdaguer**, with a beautiful pond, flowers and more views. The creative biospheres of the **Jardí Botànic** (*see p107*) just above the Olympic Stadium, are still too young to fully enjoy.

CaixaForum

Casaramona, Avda Marquès de Comillas 6-8 (93 476 86 00/www.fundacio.lacaixa.es). Metro Plaça Espanya. **Open** 10am-8pm Tue-Sat; 11am-3pm Sun. Closed Aug. **Admission** free. **Credit** (shop) AmEx, DC, MC, V. **Map** p341 A5.

Catalonia's largest savings bank, La Caixa, has a high-profile cultural foundation with an excellent collection of international contemporary art and a Spain-wide exhibitions programme that also touches on ethnology and archaeology. The main cultural centre in Barcelona moved to this, the renovated Casaramona textile mill, in 2001, while the former centre at the Casa Macaya in the Eixample is now temporary home to the foundation's large science museum. The much larger Casaramona is now called CaixaForum: its exterior is distinguished by creative brickwork, with an entrance plaza designed by Arata Isozaki. The massive interior floor space allows for key pieces of the permanent collection, such as installations by Joseph Beuys and Jannis Kounellis, to be viewed at all times.

Temporary shows in 2003 include an April to August exhibition on ancient Nubians, coinciding with another on 19th-century Spanish photography.

The CaixaForum also houses Barcelona's best documentary centre for video and media art, and runs an excellent programme of music (early music in the spring, non-commercial world music in the autumn).

Font Màgica de Montjuïc
Plaça d'Espanya (93 291 40 42/www.bcn.es/fonts). *Metro Espanya.* **Fountain** *May-Sept* 8pm-midnight Thur-Sun; music every 30mins 9.30pm-midnight. *Mar, Apr, Oct-early Jan* 7-9pm Fri, Sat; music every 30mins 7-9pm. **Map** p341 A5.

Still using its original art deco waterworks, the 'magic fountain' works its wonders with 3,600 pieces of tubing and over 4,500 light bulbs. Summer evenings after nightfall, the multiple founts swell and dance to various hits ranging from Whitney Houston to the '1812 Overture', showing off its kaleidoscope of pastel colours while searchlights play in a giant fan pattern over the palace dome.

Fundació Joan Miró
Parc de Montjuïc (93 329 19 08/www.bcn.fjmiro.es). *Metro Paral.lel, then Funicular de Montjuïc/61 bus.* **Open** *July-Sept* 10am-8pm Tue, Wed, Fri, Sat; 10am-9.30pm Thur; 10am-2.30pm Sun. *Oct-June* 10am-7pm Tue, Wed, Fri, Sat; 10am-9.30pm Thur; 10am-2.30pm Sun. **Guided tours** 12.30pm Sat, Sun. **Admission** *All exhibitions* €7.20; €3.90 concessions. *Permanent exhibitions* €3.60; €1.80 concessions. Free under-14s. **Discounts** Articket, BC, BT. **Credit** AmEx, DC, MC, V. **Map** p341 B6.

White walls, rustic tile floors and an elegant system of roof arches make this one of the world's great museum buildings. The foundation houses a collection of more than 225 paintings, 150 sculptures and all Miró's graphic work, plus some 5,000 drawings. The permanent collection, highlighting Miró's trademark use of primary colours and simplified organic forms symbolising stars, the moon, birds and women, occupies the second half of the exhibition space. It begins with a large tapestry created with Josep Royo, then, on the way to the sculpture gallery, is Alexander Calder's reconstructed *Mercury Fountain*, originally seen at the Spanish Republic's Pavilion at the 1937 Paris Fair. In other works, Miró is shown as a cubist (*Street in Pedralbes*, 1917), naïve (*Portrait of a Young Girl*, 1919) or surrealist (*Man and Woman in Front of a Pile of Excrement*, 1935), while the Sala Pilar Juncosa features early depictions of Mont-roig, where Miró summered; an early surrealist work (*The Lion*, 1925) has recently been loaned by a private collector. Large, simpler, black-outlined paintings are from the final period, while more sculpture is found on the roof terrace.

In 2003 there will be fewer temporary shows as the exhibition space undergoes renovations until late spring. Afterwards there will be an exhibition of the Languedoc-Roussillon FRAC collection, from just across the border. The Espai 13 in the basement features young contemporary artists in a unique cycle entitled Psychodrome. The adjacent outdoor sculpture garden has fine work by Catalan artists such as Jaume Plensa, Pep Duran and Perejaume. The Foundation hosts other activities, especially contemporary music and children's theatre, and has a good café (which doesn't require a museum ticket).

Funicular de Montjuïc
Metro Paral.lel to Avda Miramar (93 443 08 59). *Metro Paral.lel.* **Open** 8am-8pm Mon-Fri; 9am-8pm Sat, Sun. **Tickets** as metro. **Map** p341 B/C6.

The funicular is now integrated into the general city transport system, meaning from the Paral.lel metro station you can transfer directly on to this cogwheeled train. It is mostly underground, but brings you out well placed for the Fundació Joan Miró and connects with the Telefèric (cable car) to the top.

Galeria Olímpica
Estadi Olímpic, Parc de Montjuïc (93 426 06 60/ *www.fundaciobarcelonaolimpica.es). Metro Espanya/* *bus all routes to Plaça d'Espanya.* **Open** *Apr-Sept* 10am-2pm, 4-7pm Mon-Fri. *Oct-Mar* (by appt) 10am-1pm, 4-6pm Mon-Fri. **Admission** €2.40. **Discounts** BC, BT. **Credit** AmEx, MC, V. **Map** p341 A6.

A hotchpotch of imagery and paraphernalia commemorating the 1992 Olympics, including the costumes from the opening ceremony and the full array of marketing items featuring the ubiquitous mascot Cobi. It offers little for true sports fans, however.

Jardí Botànic
Doctor Font i Quer (93 426 49 35). Metro Espanya. **Open** *Apr-June, Sept, Oct* 10am-5pm daily. *Nov-Mar, July, Aug* 10am-3pm daily. **Admission** €3; €1.50 concessions; free under-16s. Free last Sat of mth. **No credit cards. Map** p341 A6-7.

CaixaForum. *See p105.*

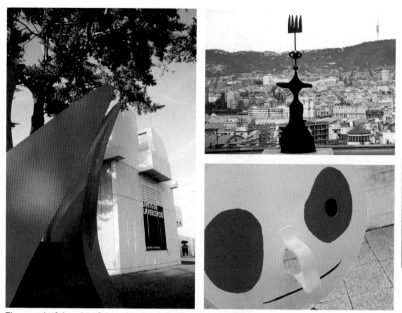

The wonderful, colourful world of the **Fundació Joan Miró**. See p106.

The Jardí Botànic was opened in 1999, and still needs a few years for its long, meticulously tailored slope of plantings to mature. A visit is still worthwhile, however, if only to take in the typical species from the Mediterranean area and the Canary Islands, and from parts of the world compatible with the Barcelona climate (Chile, California, Australia and South Africa). Many shrubs and flowers complement the truly beautiful tree varieties.

Jardíns Mossèn Costa i Llobera

Ctra de Miramar 1 (93 413 44 80). Metro Paral.lel or Drassanes. **Open** 10am-sunset daily. **Admission** free. **Map** p341 B7.

One of the lovelier gardens on Montjuïc, this one is dedicated to cacti and other exotic species. The microclimate on the port side of Montjuïc sustains more than 800 species, including a 200-year-old Backeberg cactus native to the high Andes, its long white hairs punctuated by orange spines.

Museu d'Arqueologia de Catalunya

Passeig de Santa Madrona 39-41(93 423 21 49/56 01/www.mac.es). Metro Poble Sec/55 bus. **Open** 9.30am-7pm Tue-Sat; 10am-2.30pm Sun. **Admission** €2.40; €1.80 concessions; free under-16s. **Discounts** BC. **Credit** (shop only) MC, V. **Map** p341 B6.

The Palace of Decorative Arts holds one of the city's finest scientific museums, filled with artefacts from digs all over Mediterranean Spain, starting with the Palaeolithic period and moving on through subse-

quent eras, with relics of Greek, Punic, Roman and Visigoth colonisers, up to the early Middle Ages. Roman work includes original floor mosaics, and a reconstructed Pompeian palace room. There are also monumental Greek and Roman pieces, including a sarcophagus showing the rape of Persephone and Roman funerary *stelae*. Upstairs small temporary exhibitions are displayed, along with a huge statue of a sexually charged Priapus. A few galleries are dedicated to the Majorcan Talaiotic cave culture, and there is a very good display on the Iberians, the pre-Hellenic, pre-Roman inhabitants of south-eastern Spain, whose level of decorative sophistication has been re-evaluated in recent years. Lovely terracotta goddesses and some beautiful jewellery taken from a dig on Ibiza recall the Carthaginian presence in the Balearics, and a large gallery is dedicated to interesting Greek remains found at Empúries.

Museu Etnològic

Passeig de Santa Madrona 16-22 (93 424 68 07/ www.museuetnologic.bcn.es). Metro Poble Sec/55 bus. **Open** 10am-7pm Tue, Thur; 10am-2pm Wed, Fri-Sun. **Admission** €3; €1.50 concessions; free under-12s. **Discounts** BC. **No credit cards. Map** p341 A6.

This museum holds massive collections from non-European cultures, totalling more than 30,000 pieces altogether. This is all shown on a rotating basis, with special emphasis increasingly given to contemporary cultures. Early 2003 will feature a look at the gypsies of Poland, while from April onward there will be an ethnographic interpretation of Catalan daily life in the 1940s.

Museu Militar

Castell de Montjuïc, Parc de Montjuïc (93 329 86 13). Metro Paral.lel, then Funicular & Telefèric de Montjuïc. **Open** *mid Mar-mid Nov* 9.30am-8pm Tue-Sun. *Mid Nov-mid Mar* 9.30am-5pm Tue-Sun; 9.30am-8pm Sat, Sun. **Admission** €2.50; free under-15s. **Discounts** BC. **No credit cards.** **Map** p341 B7.

Under fire since 2001 when the gift shop was found to be selling objects with Franco-era and Nazi symbolism; the Military Museum was already controversial for the portrait gallery of repressive generals and Franco's equestrian statue, which now have been stored away. The city is pushing hard to reconvert it into a less-glorifying, more critical place for the understanding of human conflict. The museum occupies the 17th-century fortress overlooking the city on the top of Montjuïc, which was used to bombard rather than protect Barcelona in past conflicts, and as a prison and place of execution, the castle has strong repressive associations. However, its selection of historic weapons is quite impressive: armour, swords and lances; muskets (beautiful Moroccan *moukhala*), rifles and pistols; and menacing crossbows. Other highlights include 23,000 lead soldiers representing a Spanish division of the 1920s. Oddly, a display of Jewish tombstones from the mountain's desecrated medieval cemetery is the only direct reminder of death within its thick walls.

MNAC (Museu Nacional d'Art de Catalunya)

Palau Nacional, Parc de Montjuïc (93 622 03 60/ www.mnac.es). Metro Espanya/bus all routes to Plaça d'Espanya, then escalator. **Open** 10am-7pm Tue-Sat; 10am-2.30pm Sun. **Admission** *All exhibitions* €6; €4.20 concs; free under-7s. *Permanent exhibitions* €4.80; €3.36 concessions. *Temporary exhibitions* €4.20; €2.10-€3.80 concessions. **Discounts** Articket, BC, BT. **Credit** (shop only) V. **Map** p341 A6.

Built as a 'temporary pavilion' for the 1929 Exhibition, the Palau Nacional nevertheless looks like the baroque palace of some absolute monarch. Its long process of refurbishing has been directed by Italian architect Gae Aulenti, of Musée d'Orsay fame. Here the undisputed star is the Romanesque. In the first decades of the 20th century, some art historians realised that scores of solitary tenth-century churches in the Pyrenees were falling into ruin, and with them the extraordinary Romanesque mural paintings of the Pantocrator (Christ in Majesty, the Virgin and biblical stories), which had served to instruct doubting villagers in the basics of the faith). Entire chunks of buildings were 'saved' by private collectors to be set up elsewhere, but in Catalonia the laborious task was begun of removing murals intact from church apses. The result is a series of images of timeless power. The display comprises 21 sections in loose chronological order, with the murals set into

freestanding wood supports or reconstructed church interiors. One highlight is the tremendous Crist de Taüll, from the 12th-century church of Sant Climent de Taüll.

Another treasure, from the church of Santa Maria de Taüll (in the same village), has an apse of the Epiphany and Three Kings and a wall of the Last Judgement, packed with images of purgatory. Original 'graffiti' scratchings – probably by monks – of animals, crosses and labyrinths have been preserved on some columns, and there are also some carvings and sculptures.

The Gothic collection here is excellent. You can follow the evolution of Catalan Gothic painting, including altarpieces on wood panels and alabaster sculptures pulled from parish churches in Barcelona. Highlights are the works of the Catalan masters of the Golden Age: Bernat Martorell and Jaume Huguet. Works in the Renaissance and baroque collections include a few non-Spanish masters (Tintoretto, Rubens, De la Tour) mixed in with national figures such as Zurbarán and Goya.

High-quality temporary shows are presented in the basement: in 2003 these include a show from January to May of Hispano-Flemish painting, followed by a major review of Catalan Romantic painter Marià Fortuny, opening in October. Restoration continues on the upper floors, where the excellent photography holdings and the collections of the Museu d'Art Modern, currently in the Ciutadella, will finally be installed in late 2004. The museum has good English labelling and a helpful English language guidebook.

Pavelló Barcelona (Pavelló Mies van der Rohe)

Avda Marqués de Comillas (93 423 40 16/ www.miesbcn.com). Metro Espanya. **Open** 10am-8pm daily. **Admission** €3; €1.50 concs; free under-18s. **Credit** (shop only) MC, V. **Map** p341 A5.

Mies van der Rohe built the German Pavilion for the 1929 Exhibition not as an exhibit but as a simple reception space, set off by his trademark 'Barcelona Chair'. The pavilion was a founding monument of modern rationalist architecture, with its flowing floor plan and a revolutionary use of materials: pure sculpted space. Though demolished after the Exhibition, a fine replica was built on the same site in 1986. Purists may think of it as a pastiche of the original, but the simplicity of the design combined with the warm tones of the marble and expressive Georg Kolbe sculpture in the pond remain a striking demonstration of what rationalist architecture could do before it was reduced to production-line clichés.

Poble Espanyol

Avda Marqués de Comillas (93 325 78 66/ www.poble-espanyol.com). Metro Espanya/bus all routes to Plaça d'Espanya. **Open** 9am-8pm Mon; 9am-2am Tue-Thur; 9am-4am Fri, Sat; 9am-midnight Sun. **Admission** €7; €4.40 concessions; €3.70 7-12s; €14 family ticket; free under-7s. **Discount** BC, BT. **Credit** AmEx, MC, V. **Map** p341 A5.

Death on the mountain

Montjuïc is Barcelona's most lively public park, blending gardens with museums and sporting facilities. Yet for centuries, before the city began to conceive of the mountain as a premium leisure zone, Montjuïc had more sombre connotations; if someone merely mentioned the name, *barcelonins* thought of death, frequently of a violent nature.

The name *juïc* itself comes from a medieval Catalan word referring to things Jewish. Until the devastating pogroms of 1391 the thriving local Jewish population used the mountain as a burial site – which according to religious precepts had to be set apart from populated areas. The original tombs were near the summit, and the dead were given simple headstones with Hebrew inscriptions. After the definitive expulsion of the Jews in 1492 many of these stones were grabbed for use in 'new' construction (as seen in the walls of the former Archive of the Crown of Aragon building just to the east of the cathedral, built using the headstones in the 16th century). An entire room has been set aside for a number of these tombstones in the **Museu Militar** (*see p108*), with good translations. In addition, a new project to spiff up the top of the mountain will restore part of the cemetery alongside walking areas and old quarries.

The entire south-west corner of Montjuïc is occupied by the stepped terraces of the present-day cemetery. When it first opened in 1883 it was a quiet, out-of-the-way spot looking out over unused beaches; nowadays the bustling container port in the Zona Franca and the noisy ring road make it a far from hospitable site for other-worldly slumber. Its saving graces are the numerous pantheons featuring fine neo-Gothic architecture and Modernista sculptures (a favourite theme

is the disconsolate angel slumped over the tomb). A newer and more pleasant part of the cemetery is set into the **Fossar de la Pedrera**, an atmospheric memorial park in a former quarry. On the far end of the grassy meadow, the dead of the International Brigades from the Civil War are remembered, while another corner has a Holocaust and concentration camp memorial.

This is also where the Catalan 'martyrs' of the Civil War are honoured, featuring a 1980s monument to Lluís Companys, the Catalan president executed by Franco's military tribunals on 15 October 1940. Arrested by the Gestapo in France after the Civil War, he was extradited, summarily tried, and sent to death by firing squad at Montjuïc's castle (his final words are said to have been '*Visca Catalunya!*' – 'Long live Catalonia'). His ignominious end only reinforced the castle's negative symbolism for most Catalans, not least because it had been used for so long as more of a repressive outpost against the locals than as a defensive fortress against any outside invasion.

Another Catalan to be executed on Montjuïc was the famed educational reformer Francesc Ferrer i Guardia, founder of Barcelona's 'Modern School' in 1902. Unjustly accused of having instigated violent protests against the war in Morocco, in 1909 he was arrested and given a farcical trial and condemned to death. Known as the 'Spanish Dreyfus' for the widespread protests his case inspired across Europe, he faced the firing squad in the castle moats on 13 October of that year. The sculpture of Ferrer i Guardia just above the **Palau Nacional**, at the top of the escalators, is a replica of the monument erected in his honour by the City of Brussels in 1911.

As part of the preparations for the 1929 Exhibition, someone had the bright idea of building, in one enclosed area, examples of traditional architecture from every region in Spain. The result was the Poble Espanyol, or 'Spanish village'. Inside it, a Castilian square leads to an Andalucian church, then to village houses from Aragon, and so on. There are numerous bars and restaurants (including vegetarian), and 60-plus shops. Many are workshops in which craftspeople make and sell Spanish folk artefacts, such as ceramics, embroidery, fans, metalwork and candles. Some of the work is quite attractive, some tacky, and prices are generally high. Outside, street performers recreate bits of Catalan and Spanish folklore; there are children's shows, and the 'Barcelona Experience', an audio-visual history presentation (available in English).

The Poble has an unmistakeable tourist-trap air, but it has been working hard to raise its cultural level, as with the inclusion of the Fran Daurel collection of contemporary art; a quality museum of Iberian arts and crafts will finally be opened in spring 2003. It also tries hard to promote itself as a nightspot, with bars, restaurants, clubs and a flamenco show, and dance bands and music groups perform regularly in the main square. The grand entrance houses the bar that was once the pinnacle of Barcelona design-bardom, Torres de Avila, while one of the city's most popular clubs, La Terrrazza (or Discothèque, in its winter incarnation), is located at the back (see p257 for both).

Telefèric de Montjuïc

Estació Funicular, Avda Miramar (93 443 08 59/ www.tmd.net). Metro Paral.lel, then Funicular de Montjuïc/20, 36, 57, 64 bus. **Open** *June-mid Sept* 11.15am-9pm daily. *Mid Sept-Oct, Apr, May* 11am-7.15pm daily. *Nov-Mar* 11am-7.15pm Sat, Sun. **Tickets** €3.20 single; €4.50 return; €3.50 child return. **Discounts** BT. **No credit cards. Map** p341 B6.
This cable car line runs between the funicular station and the castle at the top. Each car holds four people, and offers superb if vertiginous views.

Tren Montjüic

Plaça d'Espanya (information Transporte Ciutat Comtal 93 415 60 20). Metro Espanya/bus all routes to Plaça d'Espanya. **Open** *Mid Apr-mid Sept* 10am-9pm daily. Closed mid Sept-mid Apr. **Frequency** hourly Mon-Fri; every 30mins Sat, Sun. **Tickets** *All-day* €3; €2.40 concessions. **Discounts** BT. **No credit cards. Map** p341 A/B5.
It's not a train but is in an open trolley pulled by a truck, which goes up Montjüic to Miramar, passing all the hilltop sights along the way.

Poble Sec & Paral.lel

The *barri* lining the side of the hill and ending at **Avda Paral.lel** is called **Poble Sec**. The name means 'dry village', which is explained by the fact that it was 1894 before the poor local workers saw the installation of the area's first water fountain (still standing in C/Margarit). They celebrated by dancing in the streets. By 1914 some 5,000 people lived in shanty towns up where the district meets Montjüic. The name Avda Paral.lel derives from the fact that it coincides exactly with 41° 44' latitude north, one of Ildefons Cerdà's more eccentric conceits. The avenue was the prime centre of Barcelona nightlife – often called the city's 'Montmartre' – in the first half of the 20th century, and was full of theatres, nightclubs and music halls. A statue on the corner with C/Nou de la Rambla commemorates Raquel Meller, a legendary star of the street who went on to equal celebrity around the world. She stands outside Barcelona's notorious modern live-porn venue, the Bagdad. Apart from this, most of its cabarets have disappeared, although there are still theatres and cinemas along the Paral.lel. A real end of an era came in 1997 when El Molino, the most celebrated of the avenue's traditional, vulgar old music halls, suddenly shut up shop. It seemed to symbolise the change in the neighbourhood.

On the stretch of the Paral.lel opposite the city walls three tall chimneys stand amid modern office blocks. They are all that remain of the Anglo-Canadian-owned power station that is known locally as *La Canadença* ('The Canadian'). This was the centre of the city's largest general strike, in 1919. Beside the chimneys an open space has been created and dubbed the **Parc de les Tres Xemeneies**. It is now particularly popular with skateboarders and Pakistani ex-pat cricketers.

Today, Poble Sec is a friendly, working-class area of quiet, relaxed streets and leafy squares. Towards the Paral.lel are some distinguished Modernista buildings, which local legend has maintained were built for *artistas* from the nude cabarets by their rich sugar daddies. At C/Tapioles 12 is a beautiful, narrow wooden Modernista door with typically writhing ironwork, while at C/Elkano 4 is **La Casa de les Rajoles**, with a peculiar mosaic façade.

Refugi Antiaeri del Poble Sec

C/Nou de la Rambla 175 (93 319 02 22). Metro Paral.lel. **Open** (guided tour & by appt only) 11am-12.30pm Sat. **Admission** €3.30; free under-7s. **Meeting place** Biblioteca Francesc Boix, C/Blai. **Map** p341 B6.
Barcelona was viciously air bombed during the Civil War, a fact that has long been suppressed. As Poble Sec was particularly targeted, a large air-raid shelter was built into the mountain at the top of Nou de la Rambla; at the time of its construction it was one of about 1,200 such shelters in the city. Recently rediscovered, it is worth a visit as an emblem of its time. Groups are taken through every Saturday, but advance reservation must be made by phone.

The Eixample

Where Gaudí meets Gucci.

The Eixample ('extension') is the spiritual heart of Barcelona, a grand expression of the city's enduring love of the artistic gesture and urban planning. The area and its rich concentration of sights has been recognised by UNESCO, although traffic, as always, is a problem as streets that were designed for the stately passing of a horse-drawn carriage find themselves subjected to the rigours of the frenetic traffic overload typical of most Mediterranean cities. The gateway to the Eixample is the **Plaça Catalunya**, Barcelona's focal point, once ringed by old cafes, but now dominated by the monolithic façade of **El Corte Inglés** (*see p182*). Here, you can find the underground city **tourist office**, and catch the open-topped **tourist bus** at the beginning of its journey. Leading up from the plaça is the **Passeig de Gràcia**, a smart shopping boulevard, which is known for its magnificent wrought-iron lamp-posts designed by Gaudí, and by the ceramic mosaic benches that grace the length of what is undoubtedly one of the most beautiful streets in the world.

The history of the Eixample begins with the razing of the restrictive medieval walls of the Old City in the middle of the 19th century, a symbolic as well as physical opening up of the town, which gave the bourgeoisie, enriched by rapid industrialisation, the chance to engage in a sustained game of one-upmanship to see who could commission the most spectacular buildings to express their growing confidence. Alongside the emergence of an extraordinary generation of artists, the result was the birth of Modernisme, Catalonia's answer to art nouveau. Modernisme was an artistic movement that elevated expressive individualism to new heights, where organic, flowing shapes happily co-existed with wedding-cake, neo-Gothic castle turrets and Moorish minarets. The importance that the Modernistas gave to decorative and fine arts is reflected in countless shopfronts, hallways and panelling or stained glass.

After considerable controversy, including interventions by the central government in Madrid (*see* **The man with a plan,** *p123*), the city authorities opted to build the Eixample as an enormous grid based on a design by

Ildefons Cerdà. Using straight lines, parallels, diagonals and meridians, Cerdà's design is a perfect example of 19th-century rationalism. His system gives the area a monumental, urban feel reminiscent of downtown Manhattan, yet maintains a human scale that makes it almost impossible for walkers to get lost as long as they stick to the oft-used reference points of *mar* (sea) or *muntanya* (mountain). The more utopian features of the plan, however – building on only two sides of each block, height limits of just two or three storeys, and gardens in the middle of the blocks – were quickly superseded by the realities of property speculation. Most of the bucolic interior courtyards were converted into car parks, workshops or shopping centres. In 1985 a plan to reclaim these courtyards was set into motion, and now over a third of them have reverted to their original status as interior gardens, giving residents a respite from the busy traffic outside their front doors. The garden around the **Torre de les Aigües** water tower at C/Llúria 56 and the patio at **Passatge Permanyer** at C/Pau Claris 120 give you a glimpse of just how attractive the architect's plan could have been. At the same time, much effort has been made over recent years to restore the Eixample's buildings – some of which are crumbling dangerously away – to their former glory.

Thanks to the railway that used to run down the street that is now C/Balmes, the Eixample has traditionally been divided into two halves, the more fashionable **Dreta** (right), which contains the most distinguished Modernista architecture, the main museums and shopping avenues, and the **Esquerra** (left), which was built slightly later, and contains some great markets and a few less well-known Modernista sights. Together they all form the essence of Barcelona life: busy and beautiful; eccentric but, at the same time, logical.

The Dreta

The great avenue of the **Passeig de Gràcia** is the centre of the district. It is famous for its architectural masterpieces, built as elegant residences with buildings by Gaudí, Puig i Cadafalch and Domènech i Montaner. Two of the most beautiful of these are Gaudí's **La Pedrera** (*see p113*) and the **Manzana de la**

▶ *See also chapter* **Modernisme,** *p39.*

Sightseeing

The last great temple

Barcelona's most emblematic symbol and Gaudí's best-known work was neither begun nor finished by the great man. In the 1860s a private religious society came up with the idea of a church whose very funding would be an act of piety, calling it an 'expiatory temple'. The first stones were laid under the direction of Francisco de Paula del Villar in 1882, and Gaudí took over a year later. The young architect never was to do a full set of technical drawings, concentrating instead on its conceptual meanings for more than 40 years until his death. Only the neo-Gothic crypt (where Gaudí is buried), the apse and the four towers of the Nativity façade along C/Marina were completed in his lifetime, and its continuation is a source of constant polemic. Many find the contemporary construction coldly clinical in comparison to the early work, while others condemn the sculptures on the Josep Maria Subirachs Passion façade (on C/Sardenya) as out of step with Gaudí's spirit. Gaudí, however, saw the church as a collective effort, and refused, throughout his life, to treat the endeavour as an individual project.

Laid out like the great Gothic cathedrals with a multi-aisled central nave and a transept defining a cross, the church is charged with symbolism. The trademark sets of four towers are dedicated to the apostles; four more will one day be raised across the main Glory façade facing C/Mallorca. The most thrilling part of any visit (for those with no fear of heights) involves climbing their tight spiral staircases and enjoying the vertiginous views from the top; a lift can also be taken. Eventually, a large central spire dedicated to Christ will be built to a monumental height of 170 metres (550 feet). Four more domes for each evangelist will flank it, along with another in honour of the Virgin Mary. Plans are that one day the blocks of flats facing the church on C/Mallorca will be demolished to make way for an entrance esplanade, with traffic sent through a tunnel.

Over the years, work on the temple has often been stalled, but it has accelerated since the 1980s, thanks to money from tourists. Currently, the exteriors are being completed, featuring figures by Japanese sculptor Etsuro Sotoo. The interior is now a forest of columns, each made with stone from a different quarry. These hold up the vaults of the main nave, for the first time giving the Sagrada Família a substantial roof; the idea

Discordia (*see p117*). The Passeig de Gràcia and the parallel **Rambla Catalunya** are both fashionable shopping streets, while shopping for art has traditionally been concentrated close by in C/Consell de Cent between Balmes and Rambla Catalunya. Nearby is one of the most impressive of the city's art spaces, the **Fundació Antoni Tàpies** (*see p115*).

As well as the most renowned Modernista buildings, the streets around Passeig de Gràcia are full of other extraordinary examples of architecture from that period. The section of the Eixample between C/Muntaner and C/Roger de Flor has been labelled the **Quadrat d'Or** or 'Golden Square' of Modernisme, and plaques have been placed on 150 protected buildings. Particularly of note are the hallway and exuberant decoration of **Casa Comalat**, designed by Salvador Valeri in 1906 (Avda Diagonal 442-C/Còrsega 316). Also on Avda Diagonal are three characteristic buildings by Puig i Cadafalch: the **Palau Baró de Quadras** (No.373); the **Casa Terrades** (Nos.416-20) – an extraordinary neo-Gothic fantasy with pointed towers that gained it the alternative name of **Casa de les Punxes** ('House of Spikes') – and the playful **Can Serra** (on the corner with Rambla Catalunya), where a fairytale façade wraps around a smooth, black glossy structure. The **Casa Casas** at Passeig

is to celebrate the first mass inside on St Joseph's day (19 March) in 2007 – which would represent the 125th anniversary of the beginning of construction. Officials from the church's foundation now venture that it all could be completed by 2015.

The museum in the basement contains models and a history of the project, as well as a selection of early drawings and photographs. Original casts for the sculptural work, along with alabaster and stone bits pulled off the building for reasons of erosion or damage, fill display cases like dinosaur fossils in a palaeontology exhibition. Another curious piece is the catenary model for the Colònia Güell, an imaginative way of calculating effective

arches. Other temporary exhibits are usually set up in the temple's transitional spaces above. Gaudí himself is buried beneath the nave of the basilica, and steps towards his canonisation have been taken by Catalan bishops, an idea the humble architect would surely have abhorred.

Temple Expiatori de la Sagrada Família

C/Mallorca 401 (93 207 30 31/www.sagrada familia.org). Metro Sagrada Família. **Open** *May-Sept* 9am-8pm daily. *Oct-Apr* 9am-6pm daily. **Admission** €8; €5 concessions; free under-10s. *Lift to spires* €1.50. **Discounts** BC, BT, RM. **Credit** (shop only) MC, V. **Map** p339 F4.

de Gràcia 96 was home to one of Barcelona's greatest painters, Ramon Casas, and is now home to a design shop, **Vinçon**, which boasts an original, imposing carved fireplace and a patio at the back that gives you an interesting perspective of **La Pedrera** next door. Not far away – in the block on the corner of C/València and C/Bruc – is a market by Rovira i Trias, the **Mercat de la Concepció**, which has lovely tilework on its roof. Here it is possible to buy flowers 24 hours a day.

The streets above the Diagonal are mainly residential, and for the most part were built after 1910, but with some striking Modernista buildings such as Puig i Cadafalch's 1901

Palau Macaya, now a cultural centre of the **Fundació la Caixa** (Passeig de Sant Joan 108, 93 476 86 00) and the temporary home of parts of the Science Museum until 2004. The area is dominated, though, by the towering mass of the **Sagrada Família**. Not far away is another great Modernista project, Domènech i Montaner's **Hospital de Sant Pau** (*see p116*).

Espai Gaudí – La Pedrera

Passeig de Gràcia 92-C/Provença 261-5 (93 484 59 95/www.caixacat.es/fundcat.html). Metro Diagonal. **Open** 10am-8pm daily. **Admission** €6; €3 concessions. **Guided tours** (English) 5.30pm Mon-Fri. **Discounts** Articket, BC, BT, RM. **Credit** MC, V. **Map** p338 D4.

Built entirely with columns and parabolic arches, with no supporting walls, and supposedly without a single straight line or right-angled corner, this curving, globular apartment block contrasts strikingly with the angularity of much of the Eixample. Its revolutionary features were not appreciated by the Milà family – who paid for it – nor by contemporary opinion, which christened it La Pedrera ('the Stone Quarry'). These days it's run by Fundació Caixa de Catalunya as a cultural centre and the building features three complementary exhibition spaces. Access to the free art gallery is via the spectacular main entrance and staircase. The space itself is an excellent example of a Gaudí interior: fabulous plaster ceiling reliefs recall the building's marine-life themes, while heavy stone columns punctuate the open spaces. Temporary shows in the gallery frequently include some of the most important names in the history of art. Highlights in 2003 include a major retrospective of the work of Kandinsky and a rare collection of Renaissance drawings from the Bibliothèque Nationale in Paris.

The Pis de la Pedrera ('Pedrera flat') on the fourth floor is a finely tuned reconstruction of a Modernista flat interior (with only the floorplan by Gaudí) from the first decades of the 20th century. Notable is the bedroom suite by famed furniture designer Gaspar Homar, and the detailed re-creation of the kitchen and other service areas. An adjacent space focuses on everyday life in Barcelona during the same period. The Espai Gaudí on the top floor occupies a space once partially open to dry residents' washing, beneath Gaudí's inspiring sequence of flat brick, Gothic-style arches. The Espai offers Barcelona's best systematic overview of the architect's œuvre; drawings, photos, models and audio-visual displays give a brief yet clear idea of each of the master's important buildings, with special emphasis on La Pedrera itself. Above is the building's unmissable roof terrace with its extraordinary warrior-like figures (actually ventilation shafts and chimneys).

Fundació Antoni Tàpies

C/Aragó 255 (93 487 03 15/museu@ftapies.com). Metro Passeig de Gràcia. **Open** 10am-8pm Tue-Sun. **Admission** €4.20; €2.10 concessions; free under-16s. **Discounts** Articket, BC, RM. **Credit** MC, V. **Map** p338 D4.

Rather than create a shrine to himself, Antoni Tàpies had the sense to approve a line of programming not overtly related to his style. Thus, the idiosyncratic three-floor gallery takes up a renovated early Modernista industrial building from the 1880s by Domènech i Montaner. A selection of Tàpies' own work is often shown on the upper floor, and sometimes throughout the entire space. The winding tube sculpture on the roof, visible from the street, is entitled *Núvol i Cadira* ('Cloud and Chair') and reflects Tàpies' long fascination with eastern mysticism; the library contains a fine collection of material on oriental art. Exhibitions in 2003 include one dedicated to Turner Prize-winning British artist

Casa de les Punxes. *See p112.*

Steve McQueen and pieces by eight artists from different countries concerned with the relationship between technology and public and private spaces under the title *Indivisuales*.

Fundació Francisco Godia

C/Valencia 284 pral (93 272 31 80/www.fundacion fgodia.org). Metro Passeig de Gràcia. **Open** 10am-8pm Mon, Wed-Sun. **Admission** €4.50; €2.10 concessions; free under-5s. *Combined ticket with Museu Egipci* €8.50; €6.50 concessions. **Discounts** BC. **Credit** (shop only) MC, V. **Map** p338 D4.

Francisco Godia united two apparently incongruous passions: he was a Formula 1 racing car driver (for Maserati) and an avid art collector. This cosy private museum indicates his principal art interests:

Walk this way Modernisme

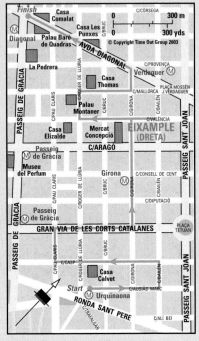

Duration: 1 hour 30 minutes

The grander (or more outrageous) Modernista buildings are easy to find, but one of the most striking things about the style is the way it appears at so many points in the city's fabric, often in unexpected places. This route covers a selection of lesser-known Modernista creations. The buildings are nearly all private but it's often possible to look in the entrances; most also require repair work, however, so there's always a risk they may be under scaffolding.

The walk begins at Plaça Urquinaona. From there, go along C/Ausiàs Marc. At No.20 is **Casa Manuel Felip**, designed in 1901 by the little-known architect, Telmo Fernández, with tall graceful galleries to the left and right connecting the first and second floors. At No.31 is the **Farmàcia Nordbeck** (1905), with its rich dark wood exterior. Modernisme and pharmacies were peculiarly closely associated in the Eixample.

At the next corner, with C/Girona, is **Casa Antoni Roger** (1890), at Nos.33-5, by one of the more prominent (and bombastic) Modernista architects, Enric Sagnier. On the next block, at Nos.42-6, is **Casa Antonia Burés** (1906), a truly extraordinary building by another forgotten architect, Juli Batllevell. Two magnificent stone columns in the shape of trees seem to be holding up the building, anticipating the same motif in the Parc Güell.

Turn left at C/Bailen, then left again into C/Casp, and walk back two and a half blocks. At No.48 is Gaudí's **Casa Calvet** (1900), which now contains an excellent restaurant of the same name (*see p151*). The symmetrical

façade seems very un-Gaudí-like, but the interlacing wrought-iron strips around the gallery – with mushroom motifs – and immense iron doorknockers betray the master's touch. Just after the next block,

medieval religious art, historic Spanish ceramics and modern painting. Medieval standouts include Alejo de Vahía's *Pietà* sculptural group. The modern collection has works by Joan Miró, Julio González and sculptor Manolo Hugué, to whom a temporary show will be dedicated in late 2003. Other shows in 2003 include a major exhibition of traditional African art from private collections around Barcelona. The collection continues to expand through purchases, many of them the works of contemporary artists.

Hospital de la Santa Creu i Sant Pau

C/Sant Antoni Maria Claret 167 (93 291 90 00). Metro Hospital de Sant Pau. **Map** p339 F4.

Domènech i Montaner's wonderful hospital up near the Sagrada Família is a match for its better-known religious neighbour for anyone interested in architecture. Begun in 1901 as a long-overdue replacement for the old hospital in the Raval, it was not finished until 1930, by the architect's son. Modernisme's greatest civic work, the 'garden city' comprises 17 pavilions, each with its own exuberant collection of sculpture, murals and mosaics and all connected by subterranean tunnels.

To create an atmosphere yet more distinct from the streets around the hospital, Domènech set the building at 45° from the rest of Cerdà's grid (of which he was emphatically not a fan). As a place to nurse the sick, it really is wonderful – a combination of the utilitarian and the beautiful. Alas, though, it will not be for much longer: Domènech's design is considered unsuitable for modern medicine, and work has begun on an ugly set of buildings at the furthest end of the grounds from the current entrance. The old pavilions will be used for research,

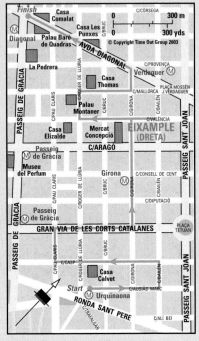

Sightseeing

at C/Casp 22, is **Casa Llorenç Camprubí** (1901). The long, narrow windows in the first-floor gallery and neo-Gothic windows give a superb impression of verticality.

Turn back and left up C/Pau Claris. On the corner with Gran Via, is another extravagant Modernista pharmacy, **Farmàcia Vilardell** (1914). From there, walk along Gran Via three blocks, cross over and turn left into C/Girona. **Casa Jacinta Ruiz**, designed by Ramon Viñolas in 1909, is at No.54. Glassed-in *galeries* characterise most Modernista houses, but here the spectacular four-storey gallery takes up the entire façade, and, with its clean lines, is almost modern rather than Modernista. The delicate wrought-iron balconies are gorgeous.

Another block up, at C/Girona 73, on the corner of C/Consell de Cent, is **Forn Serrat**, also known as **Forn Vidal**. This bakery looks a little run-down; outside, though, it has curving woodwork framing a picture of a girl holding bales of wheat and ears of corn – a classic example of the Modernista tendency to round off work with a grand flourish.

At C/Girona 86, in the next block, is **Casa Isabel Pomar** (1906), an almost bizarrely narrow building by Joan Rubió i Bellver. Its neo-Gothic roof and pinnacle, like a church in the sky, may have been an architect's joke. Cross C/Aragó, and continue to C/València. Turn right to the next corner (C/Bailen) and the marvellous **Casa Manuel Llopis** (1902), No.339, by Antoni Gallissà and Gaudí's collaborator Josep Maria Jujol. It has angular galleries running almost the whole height of the building, with elaborate thin brickwork.

If you retrace your steps along C/València and then continue for another two blocks, at the corner with C/Roger de Llúria you will come upon a veritable explosion of Modernista architecture. At No.312 is **Casa Villanueva** (1909), with thin graceful columns, elaborate glass galleries and a needle-topped tower. Opposite, at No.285, **Casa Jaume Forn** (1909) has beautiful stained glass and a magnificent carved door. Also on this crossing is the **Queviures Murrià** grocery (*see p200*), with its tiled advertising posters (created from designs by Ramon Casas) still in place. Down the street at C/Roger de Llúria 74 is one more pharmacy, **Farmàcia Argelaguet** (1904), which has fine stained glass and floral decoration on the walls.

At the next junction uphill, C/Roger de Llúria-C/Mallorca, are two major buildings by Domènech i Montaner. To the left, at C/Mallorca 278, is the **Palau Montaner** (1893), built for his own family and now used as government offices. At No.291 is **Casa Thomas** (1905), now, fittingly, home to the **BD** design company and shop (*see p189*). Much less known is the elegant **Casa Dolors Xiró** (1913), at C/Mallorca 302, by Josep Barenys. Turn left on Girona and left again on to Avda Diagonal. After a block you will come to Puig i Cadafalch's neo-Gothic fantasy house, the **Casa Terrades** (also called Casa de les Punxes), on your right, and his **Palau Baró de Quadras** on your left. A couple of blocks beyond that is the splendid **Casa Comalat** by Salvador Valeri (1911), now home to nightclub **Distrito Diagonal**.

but it is hoped that the public will still be free to wander through the courtyards and gardens and guided tours will be available through advance booking (93 488 20 78).

La Manzana de la Discordia

Passeig de Gràcia 35-45 (93 488 01 39). Metro Passeig de Gràcia. **Map** p338 D4.
The name is a pun; in Spanish '*manzana*' means 'apple' as well as 'block' and here refers both to the Apple of Discord that Paris gave to Aphrodite, and also to the wildly clashing styles of this showcase of Modernista architecture. At No.35, on the corner of C/Consell de Cent, is Domènech's Casa Lleó Morera, a classic Modernista building of exuberantly convoluted, decorative forms. Three doors up, at No.41, is Puig's Gothic-influenced Casa Amatller, and next to that Gaudí's Casa Batlló, rising like a

giant fish out of the pavement. Most Modernista masterpieces are privately owned and therefore have restricted access, but the Centre del Modernisme (located in the wonderful surroundings of the lobby of the Casa Amatller) organises a Ruta del Modernisme tour, which allows access to certain monuments with a multi-ticket. Following the huge success of the International Year of Gaudi in 2002, the Casa Batlló will remain open another year. After paying the €10 entrance fee, the public will get a chance to wander through the extraordinary interiors and see how some lived in *fin-de-siècle* Barcelona.

Museu de Carrosses Fúnebres

C/Sancho de Avila 2 (93 484 17 20). Metro Marina. **Open** 10am-1pm, 4-6pm Mon-Fri; 10am-1pm Sat, Sun (weekends call to confirm). **Admission** free. **Map** p343 F5.

Adjacent to the municipal Sancho de Avila funerary services, a dull basement holds this unusual and handsome (if grim and dark) collection of historic funeral carriages. Ask at the desk and someone will take you down to view some 20 horse-drawn carriages and a few motorised vehicles, which were used in Barcelona from the 18th century up to the 1970s. Carriages vary from ornate white hearses for children and 'single people' (presumably virgins) to a windowless black-velour mourning carriage that carried the unfortunate 'second wife' (mistress). It's one of the most unusual museums in the city.

Museu del Perfum

Passeig de Gràcia 39, Eixample (93 215 72 38/www.perfum-museum.com). Metro Passeig de Gràcia. **Open** 10.30am-1.30pm, 4.30-8pm Mon-Fri; 11am-1.30pm Sat. **Admission** free. **Map** p338 D4.
In a back room of the Regia perfumery (*see p203*) are hundreds of scent bottles, dating from pre-dynastic Egypt to the present. When owner Ramon Planas moved his shop here in 1960, he began gathering what is now viewed as one of the world's finest collections. Many flasks trace the period before perfumes were labelled, including Egyptian, Greek and Roman vials, flasks and bottles. The rest are shown by brands (Guerlain, Dior, 4711), as well as limited-edition bottles, such as a Dalí creation for Schiaparelli, and a prized art nouveau flask by René Lalique for the Coty Cyclamen brand. Yes, it seems that this one is for the ladies.

Museu Egipci de Barcelona

C/Valencia 284 (93 488 01 88/www.fundclos.com). Metro Passeig de Gràcia. **Open** 10am-8pm Mon-Sat; 10am-2pm Sun. **Admission** *Museum* €5.50; €4.50 concessions; free under-5s. *Guided tours* €11.50; €10 concessions. *Combined ticket with Fundació Godia* €8.50; €6.50 concessions. **Discounts** BC. **Credit** MC, V. **Map** p338 D4.
Jordi Clos was still a teenager when his fascination for Ancient Egypt was first sparked. Now that he's a successful hotelier, Clos pours his passion and free time into Barcelona's Egyptian Museum. Run by Clos's prestigious archaeological foundation, which is reputable enough to be allowed to conduct official digs in Egypt and run university programmes, the museum is the ideal showcase for a well-chosen collection that includes religious statuary, mummies, jewellery and elements from everyday life spanning over 3,000 years of Nile-drenched culture. The oldest objects include pre-dynastic ceramics (3,500 BC), while some of the outstanding pieces are the friezes from the Tomb of Iny (Fifth or Sixth Dynasty), a stele representing Cleopatra VII, and the little mummy of the Girl of Kemet, from the Ptolemaic period. Dramatic re-creations of burial settings and X-rays of mummified animals enhance the display. In 2003 an exhibition will focus on the lives of two of history's most famous star-crossed lovers: Nefertiti and Akhenaton. The gift shop is a gold mine of related books, games and trinkets.

Parc de l'Estació del Nord

C/Nàpols (no phone). Metro Arc de Triomf. **Open** 10am-sunset daily. **Map** p343 E/F5/6.
A striking park behind the bus station; an open, grassy crescent with very few trees or benches, just flat ceramic forms in turquoise and cobalt, swooping and curving through the park – a landscape sculpture by Beverly Pepper.

The Esquerra

This side of the Eixample quickly became the new area for some activities of the city that the middle classes did not want to see on their doorsteps. A huge slaughterhouse was built in the extreme left of the area, knocked down and replaced by the **Parc Joan Miró** in 1979 (*see below*). The functional **Hospital Clínic** was sited on two blocks between C/Còrsega and C/Provença, and further out still on C/Entença is the city's 1905 **Modelo** prison, the relocation of which outside the city is currently under way. There are two good markets, the **Ninot**, by the hospital, and the **Mercat de Sant Antoni**, on the edge of the Raval, which is taken over by an excellent second-hand book market every Sunday morning. This is also an area for academic institutions, from the vast **Escola Industrial** on C/Comte d'Urgell to the original **Universitat** central building on Plaça Universitat, constructed in 1842.
Modernista architecture does extend over into the Esquerra (as the Quadrat d'Or concept recognises), with such superb examples as the **Casa Societat Torres Germans** (C/Paris 180-2) from 1905, and the Moorish influenced **Casa Golferichs** (Gran Vía 491) built by Joan Rubió, one of Gaudí's chief collaborators in 1901. The district also contains the city's main concentration of gay nightlife around the crossing of C/Consell de Cent and C/Muntaner – the area known as the 'Gaixample'. Beyond the hospital the outer Eixample has no great sights, but leads up to Plaça Francesc Macià, developed since the 1960s as the centre of a new business district, and the main crossroads of affluent Barcelona. Beyond the office blocks of the *plaça* lie the fashionable business, shopping and residential areas of the Zona Alta.

Parc Joan Miró (Parc de l'Escorxador)

C/Tarragona (no phone). Metro Tarragona or Espanya. **Open** 10am-sunset daily. **Map** p341 B4/5.
The Miró park, built on the site of a huge slaughterhouse (*escorxador*), mainly comprises stubby palmera trees, around half of which have been uprooted as work continues on an underground reservoir. It is still worth a visit, however, for Miró's huge phallic sculpture *Dona i Ocell* ('Woman and Bird') rising out of a shallow pool.

Gràcia & Other Districts

From the red flags of Gràcia to the blue chips of Diagonal-Mar.

Emerging from the Eixample into Gràcia, the change in atmosphere is striking. The neighbourhood is overwhelmingly low-rise and dotted with squares on a welcome human scale. Until the late 19th century Gràcia was not much more than a village, and distinct from Barcelona not only in its geography. It was known as a radical centre of anarchism and revolution, with place names such as Mercat de la Llibertat, Plaça de la Revolució and C/Fraternitat. Political activism is still strong within the *barri*, and dozens of properties have been taken over by the Okupas – a squatters' movement with an arsenal of axes to grind from anti-globalisation to the tyranny of television.

Gràcia's independent attitude is also reflected in its strong attachment to traditions such as its *festa major*, the biggest in Barcelona, which for a few days in August makes the *barri* a centre for the whole city (*see p214*). The district contains many small factories and workshops, and has a sizeable gypsy community. It's home to students and a substantial creative colony of artists, actors, musicians, photographers and designers, who seem to spend their all of their days hanging out in its café terraces.

Perhaps unsurprisingly, given its artsy quotient, there are many cultural venues around, including the **Centre Artesà Tradicionarius** for folk music and dance, as well as theatres such as the innovative **Sala Beckett** and two of the most enterprising cinemas in Barcelona, the **Verdi** and **Verdi Park**. The district is also home to the **Gràcia Territori Sonor** experimental music collective, which performs at Sónar and other festivals.

Among the most lively of Gràcia's many squares are **Plaça Rius i Taulet**, site of the pre-1897 town hall and dominated by a lofty clock tower designed by Rovira i Trias; **Plaça de la Virreina**, with its village-like church; **Plaça del Sol**; and the peaceful **Plaça Rovira i Trias**, with an appealing bronze statue of this underrated architect himself (*see p123* **The man with the plan**).

Plaça del Diamant has a rather ugly sculpture to commemorate *The Time of the Doves*, the celebrated novel written by Mercè Rodoreda and named (in Catalan) after the square, as well as a Civil War air-raid shelter, recently discovered, which is scheduled to become a peace museum. A more recent square

A mosaic of influences at **Casa Vicens**.

called, true to the tenor of Gràcia's hippy subculture and nomenclature, **Plaça John Lennon**, is designed for kids.

The reason most visitors come to Gràcia, though, is to see Gaudí's astonishing **Park Güell** (*see p121*). Its colourful sculptures spread across the Tibidabo side above Plaça Lesseps, and across the busy Travessera de Dalt. But the district contains other Modernista gems, including one of Gaudí's earliest and most fascinating works, the **Casa Vicens** of 1883-8, hidden away in C/Carolines. As a private residence it is not open to visitors, but the castellated red brickwork and colourful tiled exterior with Indian and Mudéjar influences should not be missed; see, too, the spiky wrought-iron leaves on the gates. A slightly less exotic form of Modernisme is represented by Domènech's **Casa Fuster** (1908-11) at C/Gran de Gràcia 2-4, and by the work of Francesc Berenguer, one of Gaudí's assistants, who designed the Mercat de la Llibertat and the old town hall in Plaça Rius i Taulet.

The fantastical world of **Park Güell**.

Park Güell

C/Olot (Casa-Museu Gaudí 93 219 38 11). Metro Lesseps/24, 25, bus. **Open** *Park* 10am-sunset daily. *Museum* Apr-Sept 10am-7.45pm daily. Oct-Mar 10am-5.45pm daily. **Admission** *Museum* €4. **Discounts** RM. **Credit** (shop only) MC, V. **Map** p339 E2.

Based on the design of garden cities in England (hence the spelling of 'park'), with which Gaudí's patron Eusebi Güell was fascinated, the Park Güell was intended to be an upmarket residential area overlooking the city. Gaudí was to design the basic structure and main public areas; the houses were to be designed by other architects. It was early days for Gaudí, however, and his ideas were still considered too radical for much of the city's bourgeoisie, few plots were sold, and the development was never finished. The most complete part is the entrance to what is now a city-owned park, with its gingerbread houses flanking the gate and the mosaic dragon fountain; one of the city's most enduring symbols. The park is utterly magical, with twisted pathways and avenues of columns intertwined with the natural structure of the hillside. At the centre is the great esplanade, with an undulating bench covered in *trencadís* (mosaic formed with broken tiles) – much of it not the work of Gaudí but of his overshadowed but talented assistant Josep Maria Jujol (*see chapter* **Modernisme**). Gaudí lived for several years in one of the two houses built on the site (not designed by himself); it is now the Casa-Museu Gaudí. The park stretches well beyond the area designed by Gaudí, into the wooded hillside. Guided tours are available, sometimes in English. The best way to get to the park is on bus 24; if you go via Lesseps metro, be prepared for a steep uphill walk.

Sants

In the days when Barcelona's gates shut at 9pm every night, hostels, inns and smithies grew up around the city to cater for latecomers. During the 19th century it became a major industrial centre, the site for giant textile factories such as Joan Güell's **Vapor Vell** (now a library), the Muntades brothers' **L'Espanya Industrial** – which, thanks largely to the strength of a local neighbourhood campaign, became a futuristic park in 1985 (*see below*) – and **Can Batlló**. Few of the people who admire Gaudí's work in the Casa Batlló, the Palau Güell or the Park Güell give much attention to the fact that it was these factories and the workers in them that produced the wealth necessary to support such projects. Sants was also a centre of labour militancy, and in 1855 the first general strike in Catalonia broke out there. Practically all Sants' industrial centres have since disappeared.

The first port of call for most passing through the area is the **Estació de Sants**. In front of it is the ferociously modern **Plaça**

dels **Països Catalans**, created by Helio Piñón and Albert Viaplana in 1983 on a site where, they claimed, nothing could be planted because of the amount of industrial waste in the soil. An open, concreted space, with shelter provided not by trees but steel ramps and canopies, it is loved by skateboarders and those interested in urban design, but reckons on few other admirers. On the other side of the station are the more appealing squares of **Sants** and **Peiró**. The first Catalan film, *Baralla en un café* ('brawl in a café') was shot in the latter, in 1898. Near the Plaça de Sants is a complex called **Les Cotxeres**, an old tram depot now converted into a multifunctional community and arts centre. From there, C/Creu Coberta, an old Roman road once known as the Camí d'Espanya, 'the road to Spain', runs to Plaça d'Espanya, where C/Tarragona, to the left, sharply marks the end of Sants and the beginning of the Eixample. This street has been changed totally by pre- and post-Olympic projects, and now has rows of high-rise office towers, but is still dominated by the **Parc Joan Miró** and Miró's wonderful, towering sculpture *Dona i Ocell*.

Parc de l'Espanya Industrial

Passeig de Antoni (no phone). Metro Sants-Estació. **Open** 10am-sunset daily. **Map** p341 A4.

The most postmodern of Barcelona's new parks, with ten watchtowers looking out over a boating lake; at night, lit up, it gives the impression that some strange warship has managed to dock by Sants train station. Despite its periodic falls into disrepair – when the lake dries up to a muddy puddle and the place needs a good rake – this is one of the 1980s parks most liked by the public. Boats can be hired (during the months where there *is* a lake), and kids play on Andrés Nagel's *Gran Drac de Sant Jordi* dragon sculpture.

Les Corts

Without a love of the beautiful game, it takes some perseverance to find much charm in Les Corts. It's even harder to discern the origins of its name, 'the farmsheds', amid the row upon row of functional apartment blocks, unless you want to make some allegorical comparison to utilitarian buildings. However, **Plaça del Carme** and **Plaça de la Concòrdia** – remnants of the old village of Les Corts which was annexed to Barcelona in 1867 – still evoke the atmosphere of another era. Still, for most Barcelona residents, Les Corts is synonymous with **Fútbol Club Barcelona**, whose massive sports complex takes up a great deal of the district's space (*see also p265*). Curiously, at night the area becomes the haunt of prostitutes, transvestites and their customers.

Sightseeing

The view from **Tibidabo**.

Norman Foster's **Torre de Collserola**.

Nou Camp – FC Barcelona

Nou Camp, Avda Arístides Maillol, access 9,
Les Corts (93 496 36 00/36 08). Metro Maria
Cristina or Collblanc. **Open** 10am-6.30pm
Mon-Sat; 10am-2pm Sun. **Admission** €4.80.
Guided tour €8.90. **Discounts** BC, BT.
No credit cards. Map p337 A3.

Nou Camp is the largest football stadium in Europe,
and a shrine to Barcelona FC. There's a club museum, and visitors can take a guided tour around the
stadium locker rooms, out through the tunnels and
on to the pitch, where they can sit on the players'
benches. The museum contains a vast collection of
paraphernalia that has accumulated since Swiss
immigrant Johan Gamper founded Barça in 1899.
The shiniest silver in the trophy case belongs to the
European Cup trophies from 1979, 1982, 1989 and
1997, and the club's greatest treasure, the 1992
European Cup won at Wembley. Appropriately
enough, the museum bought Wembley memorabilia at auction – goalposts, the royal box, historic
lighting fixtures – for a future re-creation of the
glorious moment. The extensive display has been
magnificently enhanced by Pablo Ornaque's first-
class collection of world soccer souvenirs, including sculptures, posters, magazines, uniforms, boots
and balls, often shown in historical re-creations.
Even if you don't take a tour, you can still step out
into the stands for a peaceful view of the cavernous,
empty stadium (its capacity is 115,000).

Tibidabo

Tibidabo is just one peak of the huge Collserola
mountain range that dominates the landward
side of the city. During his temptation of Christ,
the Devil took him to a high mountain, with
all the world below, and offered to give him
everything in return for a little divine adoration.
To name the peak towering over Barcelona after
the words spoken (*tibi dabo* is Latin for 'To thee
I will give') may seem an example of typical
Catalan boastfulness, but the view from the top
on a clear day is truly magnificent. The city is
laid out as though in miniature, with familiar
towers and roads easily discernible, all framed
by Montjuïc and a vibrant blue sea. On those
days when the traffic smog blots out the details,
it's not quite as good, but at least the air is fresh.

Getting up there, by the clanking old
Tramvia Blau (Blue Tram) and then the
Funicular de Tibidabo, is part of the fun
(*see p124*). The square between the tram and
the Funicular is one of the best places in town
for an al fresco drink or meal, and at the very
top of the Funicular is a great **funfair** (*see
p124*). For a limitless view, ascend the giant
needle of Norman Foster's communications
tower, the **Torre de Collserola** (*see p124*).

The man with the plan

There's a well-dressed man who sits day after day on a bench in the Plaça Rovira i Trias at the far edge of Gràcia. You can find him in the same spot he has inhabited for the last 13 years, with impeccable posture, a three-piece suit, a newspaper tucked in his left pocket and a dreamer's look. His friends range from an alcoholic confidant who sits beside him and whispers secrets in his ear, to young children who climb on his strong shoulders, rub the fine-trimmed goatee and dress him in funny hats. On the ground in front of this life-size bronze statue of Antoni Rovira i Trias is a plaque with a cryptic, unfamiliar Barcelona map and a quote in French that translates to 'the design of a city is the work of time more than any architect'. His prediction was only to be partly right.

Like two belligerent siblings, Barcelona and Madrid have found always reasons to be at each other's throats, Barna playing the role of the mischievous, yet overpowered younger brother. After a long siege, King Felipe V sacked Barcelona in 1714 because it had supported a British-Austrian contender for the Spanish throne. Barcelona was then confined within her city walls by the fortresses of Montjuïc and Ciutadella. When Madrid finally allowed the walls to be torn down in 1854 Barcelona resembled a cartoon character – blowing steam, swelling dangerously and about to burst. Residents tore down the stones with a passion, leaving very little of the old walls standing. Haphazard expansion efforts started immediately, despite the fact that it was clear that an organised plan was needed for the expansion ('*eixample*' is the Catalan word for expansion).

In 1859 the Ajuntament convoked the most illustrious architects of the day with a competition for a city plan. Antoni Rovira i Trias emerged as the victor, with a project whereby the city would radiate from Plaça Catalunya, with main thoroughfares shooting out every 20 degrees or so. It was a popular conception of urban planning that created suburban areas for the rich, and the design received widespread support from Barcelona's citizens and the architectural guild.

Work was about to begin when Madrid informed the Ajuntament that the project would, instead, proceed based on plans by *its* preferred candidate: a truck engineer named Idelfons Cerdà. He proposed to fill the space with an enormous grid of blocks with bevelled corners, crossed by three major thoroughfares forming an X with a line down the middle. The decision was highly unpopular and resulted in widespread protests, all of which fell on deaf ears. The rest, as they say, is history.

Retrospectively, Cerdà's visionary, utopian design gave Barcelona a more even urban fabric with markets, schools and hospitals as focal points. But there still remains a glimmer of resentment about Madrid's imposed decision, and that glimmer took form in 1990 when the Ajuntament commissioned Catalan artist Joaquim Camps to construct a sculpture in tribute to the defeated plan. Rovira i Trias himself died in 1889 at the age of 73, leaving behind a variety of distinguished architecture, from the Geology Museum in Parc de la Ciutadella to the Sant Antoni market. The latter is the only market in Barcelona that follows Cerdà's original ideas, so it would seem that Rovira i Trias didn't hold a grudge. Cerdà, on the other hand, died embittered and destitute, due to Madrid's failure to pay his fees and the continual perversion of his plans for commercial speculation, most lamentably with the abolishment of several proposed parks and public spaces. Rovira i Trias will never achieve Cerdà's posthumous fame, but if his statue's air of tranquillity is anything to go by, perhaps it was better that destiny touched another man and left this plan on a humble plaque in a secluded corner of Gràcia.

Sightseeing

Next to the funfair is a church, built in an extravagantly bombastic style and completed under Franco's orders in 1940 to atone for Barcelona's 'sins' during the Spanish Civil War. It is not well loved by locals.

Funicular de Tibidabo

Plaça Doctor Andreu to Plaça Tibidabo (93 211 79 42). FGC Avda Tibidabo, then Tramvia Blau. **Open** *End Mar-May* 10.45am-7.15pm Sat, Sun. *Begin June* 10.45am-5.15pm Thur, Fri; 10.45am-8.15pm Sat, Sun. *End June* 10.45am-6.15pm Thur, Fri; 10.45am-8.15pm Sat, Sun. *July* 10.45am-8.15pm Mon-Thur; 10.45am-9.15pm Fri; 10.45am-10.15pm Sat, Sun. *Aug* 10.45am-10.15pm Mon-Thur; 10.45am-11.15pm Sat, Sun. *Begin Sept* 10.45am-8.15pm Mon-Fri; 10.45am-9.15pm Sat, Sun. *End Sept* 10.45am-9.15pm Sat, Sun. *Oct* 10.45am-7.15pm Sat, Sun. *Nov-begin Mar* 10.45am-6.15pm Sat, Sun. **Tickets** single €2; return €3. **No credit cards**.

The Funicular that takes you from the end of the tramline to the very top of the mountain is art deco-esque, like much of the funfair. Each train has two halves, one pointing down and one up, and from the 'down' end you get a panoramic view of the city.

Museu d'Autòmates del Tibidabo

Parc d'Atraccions del Tibidabo (93 211 79 42). FGC Avda Tibidabo, then Tramvia Blau & Funicular de Tibidabo. **Open** Same as Funicular above. **Admission** €10 (incl 6 funfair rides). **Credit** MC, V.

This collection of fairground coin-operated machines from the early 20th century inside the Tibidabo funfair contains some of the finest examples of automata in the world. Entertaining scenarios include machines that have fantastical depictions of hell; to the sound of roaring flames repentant maidens slide slowly into the pit, prodded by naked devils, and the saucy *La Monyos,* named after a famed eccentric who cruised the Rambla nearly a century ago: she claps her hands, shakes her shoulders and winks, pigtails flying. Unfortunately, you have to buy a ticket for the funfair to enter, and it doesn't come cheap.

Torre de Collserola

Ctra de Vallvidrera al Tibidabo (93 406 93 54/ www.torredecollserola.es). FCG Peu Funicular, then Funicular. **Open** *July-Sept* 11am-2.30pm, 3.30-8pm Wed-Fri; 11am-8pm Sat, Sun. *May, June, Oct* 11am-2.30pm, 3.30-7pm Wed-Fri; 11am-7pm Sat, Sun. *Nov-Apr* 11am-2.30pm, 3.30-6pm Wed-Fri; 11am-6pm Sat, Sun. **Admission** €4.40; €3.70 concessions; free under-7s. **Credit** V.

If you have no fear of heights, you can join the crowds queuing to take the lift up to the observation deck of Norman Foster's 288m (945ft) high communications tower for a fabulous panoramic view. Built in 1992 to take TV signals to the world, the tower itself arouses very different feelings among visitors and locals (and it's visible from pretty much everywhere in the city), but there's no disputing the breathtaking views from the top.

Zona Alta

Zona Alta (literally, 'upper zone', or simply 'uptown') is the name given collectively to a series of smart neighbourhoods, including **Sant Gervasi**, **Sarrià**, **Pedralbes** and **Putxet**, that fan out across the area above the Diagonal and to the left of Gràcia on the map. There are few major sights around here other than the **Palau Reial** and its museums and the remarkable **Pedralbes Monastery** (*see p125*), with its religious paintings and lovely architecture. The centre of Sarrià and the streets of old Pedralbes around the monastery still retain an appreciable flavour of what were quite sleepy country towns until well into the 20th century.

The Zona Alta holds several interesting works by Gaudí. From wealthy Pedralbes, a walk down Avda de Pedralbes leads to his wonderful gatehouse and gates, the **Pavellons de la Finca Güell** at No.15, with a fierce-looking wrought-iron dragon. In the garden of the **Palau Reial de Pedralbes** on Avda Diagonal, a former Güell residence, there is a delightful Gaudí fountain, and back on the other side of the Zona Alta off the Plaça Bonanova, near Tibidabo FGC station, is the remarkable Gothic **Torre Bellesguard**, or **Figueres**. Further into town near Putxet is Gaudí's larger, more sober design, the **Col.legi de les Teresianes** (C/Ganduxer 85-105).

The Palau de Pedralbes (or **Palau Reial**) also contains two interesting museums, the **Museu de Ceràmica** and **Museu de les Arts Decoratives** (*see p125*). Around it, stretching out on either side of the Diagonal, is the bleakly functional **Zona Universitària**, chosen as the area for the expansion of Barcelona's main university in the 1950s. On the fringes of the city, at the very end of the Diagonal, is the pretty **Parc de Cervantes** with a magnificent rose garden and a striking Andreu Alfaro sculpture, *Dos Rombs* ('Two Rhomboids'). From the park, a turn back along the Diagonal toward Plaça Maria Cristina and Plaça Francesc Macià will take you to an area that is Barcelona's main business section and, increasingly, its shopping district.

Close to Plaça Francesc Macià is the small, popular **Turó Parc**, laid out in a semi-formal style, with plaques of poetry set among the bronze statuary to inspire contemplation. To the right of it on the map is Sant Gervasi, an area that had its moment of glory as the most fashionable night-time meeting point in early 1990s Barcelona. The **Jardins de la Tamarita**, at the foot of Avda Tibidabo, is a tranquil and verdant dog-free oasis with a pleasant children's playground, and nearby is where the **Tramvia Blau** (*see p127*) starts its clanking journey up the hill, past the **Museu**

de la Ciència (which will be closed throughout 2003, *see p127*), to the **Funicular de Tibidabo**. Further north, above the Parc Güell, is the extraordinary **Parc de la Creueta del Coll**, an old quarry that has been turned into a swimming pool (*see p126*).

Monestir de Pedralbes Col.lecció Thyssen-Bornemisza

Baixada del Monestir 9 (93 280 14 34/www.museo thyssen.org). FGC Reina Elisenda. **Open** 10am-2pm Tue-Sun. **Admission** *Monastery* €4; €2.50 concessions. *Col.lecció Thyssen* €3.50; €2.30 concessions. *Combined ticket* €5.50; €3.50 concessions; free under-12s. **Discounts** BC, BT. **Credit** (shop only) AmEx, DC, MC, V. **Map** p337 A1. The days of this harmonious setting for these 90 or so religious paintings from the remarkable Thyssen art collection are sadly numbered; the late Baron Thyssen's wife declared in early 2003 that the public visiting hours for the convent were too limited and that the collection is to move in 2004 to the MNAC on Montjuïc (*see p108*). Currently occupying a former dormitory on one side of the 14th-century cloister, the collection has Italian paintings from the 13th to the 17th centuries – an important influence in Catalonia – and European baroque works. There is one true masterpiece: Fra Angelico's *Madonna of Humility* (c1430s). Notable paintings include a small *Nativity* (c1325) by Taddeo Gaddi, a subtle *Madonna and Child* (1545) by Titian, and a

Torre Bellesguard.

A walk in the woods

Since the city's sudden haste to rotate and turn its gaze upon the Mediterranean in time for the Olympics, the vast **Parc de Collserola**, to its landward side, has been all but forgotten. More of a series of forested hills than a park, its shady paths through holm oaks and pines open out to spectacular views and teem with birds and wildlife. It is most easily reached by FGC train on the Terrassa-Sabadell line from Plaça Catalunya or Passeig de Gràcia, getting off at **Baixador de Vallvidrera** station. A ten-minute walk from the station up into the woods (there is an information board just outside the station) will take you to the **Vil.la Joana** (*pictured*), an old *masia* covered in bougainvillea and containing the **Museu Verdaguer** (93 204 78

05/93 319 02 22; open by appointment Tue-Fri; 10am-2pm Sat, Sun; admission free) dedicated to 19th-century Catalan poet Jacint Verdaguer, who used this as his summer home. Just beyond the Vil.la Joana is the park's **information centre** (93 280 35 52, open 9.30am-3pm daily) with basic free maps of the area, or more detailed maps for sale. Almost all the information is in Catalan but staff are very helpful. There is also a snack bar and an exhibition area.

Should the centre be closed when you arrive, six itineraries are clearly marked and colour coded. None involves difficult walking and at a very gentle pace green will take around 15 minutes, yellow 20, orange 45, blue 45, red 1 hour 15 minutes and purple 2 hours 15 minutes. Just under halfway round the purple route there are two excellent lunch options in traditional Catalan country restaurants: Can Cortes (93 674 04 35), which also has a pool, and Can Casas (93 589 18 68) further down the hill. At both it is possible just to have a drink.

Zurbaran crucifixion. Other highlights are portraits of saints by Lucas Cranach the Elder and Tiepolo's *Way to Golgotha* (c1728). Velázquez's *Queen Maria Anna of Austria* (1655-7) is magnificent.

The wonderfully preserved convent is more than worth a visit in itself. Founded in 1326, it is still home to the 'Poor Clares', whose nuns mould their contemplation to the schedules of visitors. A tour of the building provides a fascinating glimpse of life in a medieval convent: the pharmacy, the kitchens and the huge refectory with its vaulted ceiling have all been preserved. The main attraction is the magnificent, entirely intact, three-storey Gothic cloister. To one side is the tiny chapel of Sant Miquel, with striking murals from 1343 by Ferrer Bassa, a Catalan painter who was a student of Giotto.

Museu de Ceràmica & Museu de les Arts Decoratives

Palau Reial de Pedralbes, Avda Diagonal 686 (Ceràmica 93 280 16 21/Arts Decoratives 93 280 50 24). Metro Palau Reial. **Open** 10am-6pm Tue-Sat; 10am-3pm Sun. **Guided tours** by appointment. **Admission** *Both museums* €3.50; €2 concessions. *Temporary exhibition* €3; €1.50 concessions. *Combined ticket* €4.80; €2.40 concessions; free under-16s. **Discounts** BC, BT. **No credit cards.** **Map** p337 A2.

The Palau Reial on the Diagonal was originally built as a residence for the family of Gaudi's patron Eusebi Güell, and in one corner of the gardens is a famous iron gate designed by Gaudi. It became a royal palace and was greatly expanded in the 1920s, when it was given to King Alfonso XIII. It now houses two separate museums, both accessible on the same ticket; although there is a project under way to create an applied arts museum near Plaça de les Glòries for 2004, which will in theory include both collections. The Ceramics Museum has an exceptionally fine Spanish ceramics collection stretching back several centuries, expertly organised by sharply varying regional and historical styles. Especially beautiful are the medieval dishes, mostly for everyday use, such as those from Manises near Valencia. Catalan holdings feature two popular tile murals from the 18th century: *La Xocolatada* depicts chocolate-drinking at a garden party, while the other presents a chaotic baroque bullfight. Upstairs, highlights of the selection of 20th-century Spanish work are the refined simplicity of Catalan master Josep Llorens Artigas and pieces by Picasso and Miró. Excellent temporary exhibitions of contemporary ceramics are also mounted.

The other wing of the building is occupied by the museum of decorative arts. The palace's original painted walls provide a warm setting for furniture and decorative objects from the Middle Ages on, with styles from Gothic to romanticism, Catalan Modernisme, art deco and the present. Quality is high, although only a small portion of the first-class collections of decorative clocks, Catalan glasswork (comparable to the Venetian style) and other artefacts is shown at any one time. Visitors can also look down into the palace's sumptuously decorated oval throne room. Until July 2003 a temporary exhibition in the museum contemplates the idea of 'Design and Architecture for Flexible Living'.

Museu de la Ciència

C/Teodor Roviralta 55 (93 212 60 50/ www.fundacio.lacaixa.es). FGC Avda Tibidabo, then Tramvia Blau.
The Science Museum will remain closed until early 2004 while it undergoes what promises to be a remarkable expansion, making it the largest science museum in Europe. Meanwhile, some of its exhibits and activities are housed in the Fundació la Caixa's cultural centre in the Palau Macaya (*see p105*).

Parc de la Creueta del Coll

C/Mare de Déu del Coll (no phone). Metro Penitents. **Open** *May-Aug* 10am-9pm daily. *Apr, Sept* 10am-8pm daily. *Mar, Oct* 10am-7pm daily. *Nov-Feb* 10am-6pm daily. **Admission** free.
An impressive park created from an old quarry by Josep Martorell and David Mackay in 1987. It has a large lake with an artificial beach and modern sculpture: an Ellsworth Kelly and a monumental piece by Eduardo Chillida, *In Praise of Water*, hanging from cables. Occasionally, the lake is drained for cleaning, leaving the whole park looking a bit dejected.

Tramvia Blau

Avda Tibidabo to Plaça Doctor Andreu (93 318 70 74). FGC Avda Tibidabo. **Open** *July-mid Sept* 10am-8pm daily. *June, last 2wks Sept* 10am-8pm Sat, Sun. *Oct-May* 10am-6pm Sat, Sun. *Easter week* 10am-6pm daily. **Frequency** 30mins Mon-Fri; 15mins Sat, Sun. **Tickets** single €2; return €2.90; 20 trips €20. **No credit cards**.
The lovely old 'blue trams' have been creakily climbing up Avda Tibidabo between the FGC station and Plaça Doctor Andreu since 1902. At the top you can

Who goes there? **Pavellons de la Finca Güell**. *See p124.*

Sightseeing

Works of street art

Barcelona began a lively programme of public sculpture in the 1980s, and has continued since then to include public art in all urban projects. Some of the best of it follows:

Roy Lichtenstein
Barcelona Head, 1992
Lichtenstein's tall sculpture features his trademark use of the Benday-dot technique, only here as ceramic plates in homage to Gaudí's *trencadís* technique, though the face is classic cubist, neatly throwing Picasso into the mix. On Passeig Colom at the foot of Via Laietana, opposite the post office. (*Pictured centre.*)

James Turrell
Light sculpture, 1992
Turrell has turned the entrance of the Convent de Sant Agustí civic centre into a handsome piece where the architecture supports volumes of coloured light. Effectively invisible by day and cleverly seductive after dark. Look through the slats in the door at C/Comerç 36.

Rebecca Horn
Wounded Star, 1992
This stack of rusty container-like cubes on Barceloneta beach is Horn's homage to the beach restaurants that were demolished on this very site during the pre-Olympic wrecking ball frenzy. The piece once had sparks of light inside serving as a kind of crippled lighthouse, but those haven't worked for years.

Antoni Llena
David-Goliath, Goliath-David, 1993
This white face in an enormous kite is one of the better pieces in the Vila Olímpica, in the Parc de Carles I. Llena is a Catalan artist who often works with torn paper. (*Pictured left.*)

Richard Serra
The Wall, 1984
Serra's *Tilted Arc* in New York, from the same year, was forced down by the mob, mostly because it cut a square in half. This one features two curved, white concrete walls and you can walk through them. On the Plaça de la Palmera, in the Verneda neighbourhood.

Claes Oldenburg and Coosje van Bruggen
Matches, 1992
Truly one of the most successful public sculptures in the city. A huge steel matchbook in colours recalling Miró on one corner of the intersection, with used matches twisted out of shape on the others. On Avda Cardenal Vidal i Barraquer in Vall d'Hebron. (*Pictured right.*)

Joan Brossa
Visual Poem, 1984
Brossa was one of the most vital Catalan poets of the 20th century, producing 'poem objects' as early as the '50s. In this case a large letter 'A' disintegrates in stages down a grassy slope dotted with concrete punctuation marks. Beside the Velòdrom d'Horta.

take in the view, have a meal or a drink, or catch the Funicular to the funfair (*see p124*). In months when the tram only operates at weekends, a bus service runs instead during the week.

Poblenou & beyond

Poblenou and the surrounding area used to be a farming and fishing community, and later a centre for heavy industry. This brought the usual problems – child labour, disease, overcrowding, noise, smells, smoke – and the usual responses: co-operatives, unions, strikes and other conflicts. In the 1960s the neighbourhood began to change character as factories folded, moved to the Zona Franca in the south or got out of the city altogether. Today Poblenou has become a laboratory for post-industrial experiments. Old factories are now schools, civic centres, workshops and open spaces. Recently, there has been a tremendous push by the artistic community, particularly, to make this *the* area in which to live and work, and as a result a handful of achingly trendy clubs and bars have opened up.

Heading seawards from the centre of Poblenou there are still unchanged parts: the lovely **Rambla del Poblenou** compares favourably with the more famous one in the city centre, and the area around **Plaça Prim** has kept its village atmosphere, although even this is undergoing some ominous construction work. In the midst of it is the city's oldest and most atmospheric cemetery, the **Cementiri de l'Est**, with the extraordinary sculpture *El bes de la mort* ('Kiss of Death') as its highlight. Nearby is **Plaça de les Glòries**, which, according to designer Ildefons Cerdà's dream

Eduardo Chillida
Elegy to Water, 1987
Hanging from large cables near a public pool that has been carved into a former quarry. The heavy hook-like forms are in the typical style of Chillida, the great Basque master who died in 2002. There's also a piece by Ellsworth Kelly in the same Parc la Creueta del Coll.

Piñón and Viaplana
Plaça dels Països Catalans, 1987
Not a public art piece but a sort of sculpted public square in front of the Sants train station. The designed elements and finishing materials are a classic example of the Barcelona hard square, with nary a blade of grass in sight. Critics called it chicken coop design, though there is no doubt that the architects' radical approach is definitely compelling.

Perejaume
Roof, 1990
This is perhaps the oddest work in the sculpture garden beside the Joan Miró Foundation. Catalan artist Perejaume took the typical roof tiles of a country house and arranged them at ground level, suggesting that the residence was somewhere below, beneath the earth.

for the Eixample, should have been the centre of the city, with his rigid blocks continuing north along the coast almost as far as the Besòs river. What with one thing and another (unrest, civil war, dictatorship), these plans never came to pass, and now the *plaça* is just a suffocating traffic hub, and the area north of it stands as a monument to the stagnation of the Franco years. One breath of fresh air in the area is the **Parc del Clot**, and, just beyond it, the **Plaça de Valentí Almirall**, with the old town hall of Sant Marti and a 17th-century building that used to be the Hospital de Sant Joan de Malta, somewhat at odds with the modern buildings that have mushroomed around them.

Further north, up C/Sagrera, the entrance to a former giant truck factory now leads to the charming **Parc de la Pegaso**. The area also has a fine piece of recent architecture, the supremely elegant **Pont de Calatrava** bridge – designed by Santiago Calatrava – which links to Poblenou via C/Bac de Roda.

Diagonal-Mar

As 2004 approaches, the massively promoted Fòrum Universal de Cultures promises to change the area out of all recognition. The most radical changes are gathering momentum in the area on the north side of Poblenou along the coast towards the Besòs river. This is what is now known as Diagonal-Mar, the latest focus of attention of the city planners. The name is emblazoned everywhere, on buses, hoardings and in magazines, in an attempt to thrust it into the city's consciousness and ensure its successful completion. The starting point of the scheme has been the extension all the way to the sea of **Avda Diagonal**, which – contrary to the Cerdà plan – used to fizzle out just east of Glòries. Construction work is well under way for skyscraping hotels, a new marina, where certain sections of the city zoo are to be housed, a new business district, snappily called '22@', and new beaches and parks.

Beyond this, due north of the city and spanning both banks of the Besòs river, **Sant Adrià del Besòs** is famous for two things. The first is the district of **La Mina**, notorious as a hotbed of crime and poverty (although it is hoped it will benefit from the Fòrum 2004). The second is the **Feria de Abril** (*see p212*), which is now held in the Diagonal-Mar development zone (and will be for the next few years). North of Sant Adrià, **Badalona** is famous for its basketball team, **Joventut Badalona**, which has won the European Basketball Cup, something its rival FC Barcelona has never managed. It also has its own traditions, with a great *festa major* in May, climaxing with the *cremada del dimoni*, when a huge devil is burned on the beach.

Horta & around

Incorporated into Barcelona in 1904, the aptly named **Horta** (market garden) has retained many rural features, including some very well-preserved traditional farmhouses known as '*masies*'. The medieval **Can Cortada**, in C/Campoamor, shows at a glance that these houses also served as fortresses; **Can Mariner**, in C/d'Horta, is said to date back to 1050. Horta's abundant water supply once made it the laundry room of respectable Barcelona, with a whole community of *bugaderes* or washerwomen – as the open-air stone tanks along the lovely C/Aiguafreda attest.

South of here and joined to Gràcia by the long Avda Mare de Déu de Montserrat, the neighbourhood of **Guinardó** largely consists of just two big parks. One, the **Parc de les Aigües**, contains an entertaining sculpture of a buried submarine by Josep Maria Riera, and Barcelona's most eccentrically beautiful municipal district headquarters, the **Casa de les Altures**, a neo-Arabic fantasy from 1890. The other, **Parc del Guinardó**, is one of the city's oldest parks, opened in 1920. Escalators have been installed in some of the district's steeper streets to save residents' legs.

The **Vall d'Hebron**, just above Horta along the Ronda de Dalt ring road on the flanks of Collserola, was one of the city's four main venues for Olympic events, and so it has inherited centres for tennis, archery and cycling, at the **Velòdrom**. Around the sports venues are some very striking examples of

For the kids: **Turó Parc**. *See p125*.

street sculpture, such as Claes Oldenburg's spectacular *Matches*, near the tennis centre, and Joan Brossa's *Visual Poem*, by the Velòdrom. There is also a reconstruction of the **Pavelló de la República** from 1937 (*see p131*). One of the area's most distinctive assets is much older: the delightful, semi-concealed **Parc del Laberint** from 1791 – testimony to this hillside's much earlier role as a site for aristocratic country residences (*see below*). For most locals, though, the Vall d'Hebron means above all the **Ciutat Sanitària**, the largest hospital in the city and the place where many first saw the light of day.

Parc del Laberint

C/Germans Desvalls, Passeig Vall d'Hebron (no phone). Metro Montbau. **Open** 10am-sunset daily. **Admission** €1.75; €1.05 concessions Mon, Tue, Thur-Sat; free under-6s, over-65s. Free Wed, Sun. Originally the grounds of a large, sprawling mansion (which has long since been demolished), this atmospheric park is densely wooded with pines. It features hidden charms including, tucked away at the centre, an 18th-century formal garden with a deliberately picturesque fantasy element, including a romantic stream and waterfall. There's much to

Sightseeing

explore, but, be careful – the maze that gives the park its name has often proved a match for cynics who thought it was only a game for children.

Pavelló de la República

Avda Cardenal Vidal y Barraquer (93 428 54 57). *Metro Montbau.* **Open** 9am-8pm Mon-Fri. **Admission** free.

This is actually a copy of the Spanish pavilion for the Paris Exhibition of 1937. The original building was an emblematic work of rationalist architecture designed by Josep Lluís Sert, and once held Picasso's *Guernica* and Alexander Calder's *Mercury Fountain* (which is now, in reconstructed form, at the Fundació Miró, *see p106*). Austerely functionalist, the pavilion forms a curious pair with Oldenburg's *Matches* across the street. It houses a private research library, but most of the building is open.

The outer limits

Beyond the district of Sants and completely integrated into Barcelona's transport network, **L'Hospitalet de Llobregat** nevertheless asserts its identity with 'L'H' stickers on cars, and by having street signs pointing to 'Barcelona' even though the invisible boundary is only a few blocks away. With its a large Andalucian-born population (most street signs are in Spanish rather than Catalan), it is Catalonia's main centre for flamenco; among the many *peñas* (clubs) are **Tertulia Flamenca** (C/Calderon de la Barca 12, 93 437 20 44), which also runs guitar classes. Equally, L'Hospitalet has plenty of bars and restaurants with good Andalucian specialities, and a thriving cultural life, with good productions at the **Teatre Joventut** (C/Joventut 10, 93 448 12 10) and, occasionally, some excellent exhibitions at the **Tecla Sala** gallery.

Heading eastwards out of Barcelona along the Meridiana, which, like the Paral.lel, derives its name from solar co-ordinates, **Sant Andreu** is to the right, and **Nou Barris** to the left. Sant

Andreu was another of the industrial and working-class hubs of the city. Much altered in the 1960s, it has seen some recent renovations: on Passeig Torres i Bages, at Nos.91-105, Josep Lluís Sert's **Casa Bloc**, a rationalist block of flats that was one of the main contributions to Barcelona of the brief republican era, has been restored, and, just off the Meridiana, a lovely wine press has been installed in Plaça d'en Xandri. Two recent shopping areas are **La Maquinista** (*see p183*), built on the grounds of a long-defunct train station, and Heron City, which also has a multi-screen cinema.

Nou Barris (nine neighbourhoods) has a different make-up. In the 1950s, when the flow of migration into the city was at its height, a number of ramshackle settlements were built here, followed by tower blocks. The price is now being paid, as flats that are scarcely 40 years old have already fallen into ruins and are being demolished. Services of all kinds are deficient and although the city has provided parks, sculptures and services – the **Can Dragó** sports complex has the biggest public swimming pool in Barcelona, and a **Parc Central** was completed in 1999 – overall these areas represent what is very much the 'other side' of the new Barcelona. Crowded and unattractive, this is the part of the city that most tourists do not encounter.

Tecla Sala Centre Cultural

Avda Josep Tarradellas 44, Hospitalet de Llobregat (93 338 57 71). *Metro La Torrassa.* **Open** 11am-2pm, 5-8pm Tue-Sat; 11am-2pm Sun. **Admission** free.

Tecla Sala is an attractive converted factory with exhibitions of international contemporary art. In 2003 these will include Modernista Anglada Camarasa and photographer Fernando Scianna. Barcelona's magnetism tends to condemn all sub-urban museums to anonymity, even when shows are top-notch, but those who make the journey out here are generally rewarded.

Think scientific at the **Museu de la Ciència**. *See p127.*

salsitas

Creative Cuisine.
Top dj's, Visuals, Drinks...

Restaurant until 01.00h - Drinks until 3.00h
Nou de la Rambla 22
t. 93 318 08 40.

danzatoria

Chic crowd & Drinks in four different rooms,
and terraces in the downhill Garden
in a centenary style house. Decorated with
the latest fashionable design...

Av. Tibidabo 61 t. 93 211 62 61 Wed to Sun from 23.00h to 03.00h

club danzatoria

Design dance club.
Beside the sea. Two dance floors with
the latest sexiest house music...

Ramón trias Fargas 2-4 (beside Hotel Arts).
t. 93 224 04 80

s:pic

Exogen - Exozen.
Restaurant, Asiatic Lounge Club, Cocktail Bar,
Young designers showroom...

c. Ribera 10 - Born.
t. 93 310 15 95 . From Thursday to Friday

Eat, Drink, Shop

Restaurants	**134**
Cafés & Bars	**165**
Shops & Services	**181**

Features

The best Restaurants	137
Treading a fine wine	138
Eating by design	153
Menu glossary	154
A bread winner	157
Catalan cuisine	160
The best Cocktails	165
Dens of yore	166
How to drink absinthe	173
Some like it hot	177
Some like it cold	180
I should cocoa	182
Street of dreams	192
The best Objects of desire	196
The herbalisers	202
Market analysis	204
The best Shops	206

Restaurants

Barcelona's chefs take over the world, or at least its recipes.

Barcelona's preoccupation with being at the cutting edge of design and cool has a way of seeping into every area of life here; including those it does nothing to enhance. In recent years, the city's restaurant scene has been the latest in a long list of fashion victims, and many of the newer places will spend longer deciding the shape of that season's dinner plates than the elements of that week's menu.

Of course there are plenty of restaurants 'de tota la vida' – restaurants that have been around forever, have a crowd of loyal regulars and a reputation that has run through generations, such as **Can Culleretes** (*see p135*), **La Parra** (*see p163*), **Gaig** (*see p163*) or **Can Solé** (*see p161*) – but there is little rising up to meet them. New restaurants open with concepts rather than cuisines, with DJs where once there were pianos and with kangaroo where there was once milk-fed lamb; which is all well and good until they dash your hopes of getting a 21st-century salad or professional service. Those who get the balance right waste no time in opening new branches, and much as it goes against the grain to recommend chains, anything belonging to the **Tragaluz** group, for example (*see p153*, **Agua** *p159* and **Bestial** *p161*), is likely to uphold excellent culinary standards.

Authentic international cuisine is gaining ground only very slowly; unaccustomed local palates and the difficulty of sourcing key ingredients mean that it can be difficult to find really good Indian, say, or Italian, food. Middle Eastern and Japanese restaurants have been rather more successful, along with a growing number of Latin American places. What is really taking hold, however, is the idea of the fusion restaurant. Here it pays to think long and hard before eating in smaller, cheaper restaurants, where cooks are unlikely to have the experience or training to turn out dishes from Thailand, Japan, Mexico and Italy with equal panache.

Apart from the Pakistani restaurants, that abound in the Raval, most of the ethnic variety is to be found in Gràcia. Japanese restaurants, being relatively expensive, are mainly found in the Eixample or Zona Alta, where most of the top-end restaurants are clustered, while seafood restaurants, for the most part, are in and around Barceloneta and the ports (with some notable exceptions). Catalan restaurants are evenly spread throughout the city, as is an impressive variety of vegetarian restaurants.

HOW

When dining out in Barcelona, you may occasionally feel hurried – often the pudding menu appears on the table before the main course has been cleared – but this is actually a reflection of the local tendency to rattle through the food; any lingering is done afterwards, with coffee and brandy. In cheaper restaurants, it's also not unusual for waiters to bring out dishes as they are ready, so you may get your main course while someone else at your table is still on their starter, or you might find two courses put in front of you at once.

WHEN

Lunch starts around 2pm and goes on until about 3.30 or 4pm, and dinner is served from 9pm until about 11.30pm or midnight. Some open earlier in the evening, but arriving before

Café de l'Acadèmia.
See p135.

9.30 or 10pm generally means you will be dining alone or in the company of foreign tourists. Reserving a table is generally a good idea not only on Friday and Saturday nights, but also on Sunday evenings and Monday lunchtimes when few restaurants are open. Many also close for lengthy holidays, including about a week over Easter, two or three weeks in August or early September, and often the first week in January. We have listed closures of more than a week where possible, but restaurants are fickle, particularly on the issue of summer holidays, so call to check.

PRICES AND PAYMENT

The price guidelines used here are indications of the cost of an average starter, main course and dessert – not including wine, service or cover charge. € is used for anything under €20; €€ for €20-€30; €€€ for €30-€45, and €€€€ means the average meal will set you back over €45. Eating out in Barcelona is not as cheap as it used to be, but low mark-up on wines keeps the cost relatively low for Northern Europeans and Americans. All but the upmarket restaurants are required by law to serve an economical fixed-price *menú del día* (*menú* is not to be confused with the menu, which is *la carta*) at lunchtime – usually consisting of a starter, main course, dessert, bread and something to drink. The idea is to provide cheaper meals for the workers, and while it can be a real bargain, it is not by any means a taster menu or a showcase for the chef's greatest hits. It's generally worth shelling out an extra couple of euros here; a €9 *menú* is often exponentially better than a €7 *menú*.

Laws governing the issue of prices are routinely flouted, but legally, menus must declare if the seven per cent IVA (VAT) is included in prices or not (it rarely is), and also if there is a cover charge (which is generally expressed as a charge for bread). Waiters in Spain earn a respectable salary, so tipping tends to be a matter of a couple of euros, rather than the ten per cent expected elsewhere.

For more detailed information on the city's eating and drinking scene, see Time Out's *Barcelona Eating & Drinking Guide*.

Along with reviews of 300 bars, cafés and restaurants, the guide has location maps and details of opening times, prices and transport.

Ample 24

C/Ample 24 (93 319 19 27). Metro Barceloneta or Drassanes. **Open** 1-4.30pm, 7pm-midnight Mon-Fri; 7pm-midnight Sat, Sun. **Average** €. **Credit** AmEx, DC, MC, V. **Map** p345 B4.

Starters include a Spanish take on scrambled egg on toast; bursting with chunks of *botifarra*, asparagus, shrimps and garlic. Mains are simpler, including grilled salmon marinated in orange, honey and soy sauce or a rich rabbit stew. Desserts are not quite as creative, nor are they really needed after such huge portions. This is an elegant little spot for a quiet lunch; note that there is no à la carte during the day, just a set menu for €9.

Ateneu Gastronomic

Plaça de Sant Miquel 2 bis (93 302 11 98). Metro Liceu or Jaume I. **Open** 1-4pm, 8.30-11.30pm Mon-Fri; 8pm-midnight Sat. Closed 3wks Aug. **Average** €€. **Credit** AmEx, DC, MC, V. **Map** p345 B3.

A 'gastronomic club', with a colonial look – lots of columns, palms and wicker lampshades – where old standards are given funky twists; steamed asparagus is served with a bittersweet passion fruit reduction and a sorbet is infused with a cigar for those who can't wait. The wine list is staggeringly long and there is a superb value lunch *menú* for €7.80 on weekdays you can tuck into French onion soup, roast beef and fig ice-cream.

Café de l'Acadèmia

C/Lledó 1 (93 319 82 53/93 315 00 26). Metro Jaume I. **Open** 9am-noon, 1.30-4pm, 8.45-11.30pm Mon-Fri. Closed 2wks Aug. **Average** €€. **Credit** AmEx, MC, V. **Map** p345 B3.

One of the most reliable restaurants in the city, with a menu that reads like a primer of modern Catalan food; *lassanya freda* is layers of *escalivada* with marinated anchovies, or there is risotto with foie gras, roast guinea fowl, tender pink duck breast and more, all at eminently reasonable prices. Candlelit tables on one of the prettiest squares of the Old City are worth booking ahead for.

Can Culleretes

C/Quintana 5 (93 317 30 22). Metro Liceu. **Open** 1.30-4pm, 9-11pm Tue-Sat; 1.30-4pm Sun; closed Mon. Closed 3wks July. **Average** €€. **Credit** MC, V. **Map** p345 A3.

Barri Gòtic

Agut

C/Gignàs 16 (93 315 17 09). Metro Jaume I. **Open** 1.30-4pm, 9pm-midnight Tue-Sat; 1.30-4pm Sun. Closed Aug. **Average** €€. **Credit** MC, V. **Map** p345 B4.

Agut has the air of a restaurant that's seen it all, and the combination of its location on a slightly insalubrious street and its well-heeled clientele means that it probably has. Fresh pasta, meat and fish dishes are consistently excellent, and puddings are light and creative. The many oil paintings hung around the walls serve as reminders of Agut's time as a meeting place for artists and writers.

Eat, Drink, Shop

taxidermista...cafè restaurant
Plaça Reial 8   08002 Barcelona   tel. 93 412 45 36

The second oldest restaurant in Spain has been going since 1786 and still sees few unfilled tables in its rambling series of dining rooms (six at last count). Traditional dishes like roast *lechón* (suckling pig), *cuixa d'oca amb pomes* (goose leg with apples) and a three-course menu of daisy-fresh seafood are served up with friendly efficiency. Prices are unbeatable, particularly for wine; unfortunately all Barcelona is aware of this, so it pays to reserve.

El Gran Café

C/Avinyó 9 (93 318 79 86). Metro Liceu. **Open** 1-4pm, 8pm-midnight Mon-Sat. **Average** €€. **Credit** AmEx, DC, MC, V. **Map** p345 B3.
Old-fashioned service and a menu that won't frighten the horses conspire to make this comfortable brasserie the sort of place your mother would love. Unusually for these parts, butter comes with bread and vegetables come with everything (even, endearingly, salad). Reliably competent standards include steak tartare, roast beef, duck magret and osso buco.

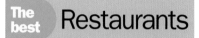

The best Restaurants

For dining al fresco
Agua (see p159); **La Balsa** (see p163); **Bestial** (see p161); **Café de l'Acàdemia** (see p135); **La Venta** (see p164) and **La Verònica** (see p141).

For breaking the bank
Abac (see p145); **El Bulli** (see p164); **Ca l'Isidre** (see p142); **Comerç 24** (see p147); **Gaig** (see p163) and **Ot** (see p158).

For bankrupts
Bar Salvador (see p146); **Can Culleretes** (see p135); **Casa Delfin** (see p146); **Envalira** (see p157); **Mesón David** (see p143) and **Pla dels Àngels** (see p143).

For seafood
Botafumeiro (see p157); **Cal Pep** (see p146); **Can Maño** (see p161); **Can Solé** (see p161); **Casa Leopoldo** (see p142) and **Passadis del Pep** (see p147).

For a *menú del dia*
Ateneu Gastronomic (see p135); **La Casa de la Rioja** (see p142); **La Cova d'en Vidalet** (see p157); **Pou Dols** (see p137); **Sagarra** (see p145); **Silenus** (see p145) and **Sukur** (see p141).

For scrumptious elegance
Bestial (see p161); **Casa Calvet** (see p151); **Laurak** (see p158); **Els Pescadors** (see p163); **Tragaluz** (see p153) and **Windsor** (see p153).

Mastroqué
C/Codols 29 (93 301 79 42). Metro Drassanes or Jaume I. **Open** 1.30-3.30pm, 9-11.30pm Mon-Fri; 9-11.30pm Sat. Closed 3wks Aug. **Average** €€. **Credit** MC, V. **Map** p345 B4.
Tucked away down a dark, narrow street and through a small entrance lies this deceptively spacious restaurant, with ochre walls, wooden beams and a quietly cool crowd of regulars. A small but interesting selection of Provençal and Catalan *platillos* includes *trinxat* (see p160), black pudding with onion marmalade and duck in more guises than you might consider feasible.

Mercè Vins
C/Amargós 1 (93 302 60 56). Metro Urquinaona. **Open** 8am-5pm Mon-Thur; 8am-5pm, 9pm-midnight Fri. **Average** €. **Credit** V. **Map** p344 B2.
A cosy lunch restaurant with yellow walls, fresh flowers and fabulously friendly staff. Outside breakfast hours there is a set menu only (€7.40). This features interesting Catalan dishes such as *trinxat de la Cerdanya* (think bubble and squeak with bacon) to start, followed by *gall dindi* (turkey) with roquefort sauce or *llom* (pork) with almonds and prunes. On Friday nights, *pa amb tomàquet* (see p160) is served with hams and cheeses.

Mesón Jesús
C/Cecs de la Boqueria 4 (93 317 46 98). Metro Liceu. **Open** 1-4pm, 8-11pm Mon-Fri. Closed Aug-early Sept. **Average** €. **Credit** MC, V. **Map** p345 A3.
The menu is limited and never changes, but dishes are reliably good and inexpensive to boot – try the sautéed green beans with ham to start, then superb grilled prawns or a tasty *zarzuela* (fish stew). The feel is authentic Castilian, with gingham tablecloths, oak barrels and farming implements hung around the walls, while the waitresses are incessantly cheerful and especially obliging when it comes to children. There are no reservations so it's wise to arrive early.

Pla
C/Bellafila 5 (93 412 65 52). Metro Jaume I. **Open** 9pm-midnight Mon-Thur, Sun; 9pm-1am Fri, Sat. **Average** €€. **Credit** MC, V. **Map** p345 B3.
Pla fills a baffling vacuum in the city's dining scene, in that it manages to strike a perfect balance between a consummately cool ambience and excellent food. The menu is a modish mix of Mediterranean and oriental dishes: curries, sushi and crêpes all figure, accompanied by fabulous salads and rich, creative sauces. Not a place for stuffy diners; music is at a level which very nearly inhibits conversation and waiters are of the school which pulls up a chair.

Pou Dols
C/Baixada de Sant Miquel 6 (93 412 05 79). Metro Liceu or Jaume I. **Open** 1-4pm, 9-11.30pm Tue-Sat. Closed 3wks Aug. **Average** €€€. **Credit** AmEx, DC, MC, V. **Map** p345 B3.
A smart, brilliant-white interior and cuisine so nouvelle it's passé don't usually add up to good value,

Treading a fine wine

Catalan wine has come on in leaps and bounds over the past decade or so, which is just as well, really, for there are few wine lists in Barcelona restaurants to offer a great deal beyond the produce of the region, let alone the country. It's worth arming yourself with a little knowledge before you set out.

Most of the new wave Catalan chardonnays and merlots are exported, but even if you do have the knowledge to untangle your macabeos from your tempranillos you'll still be faced with the problem of finding a wine to go with the ambient temperature and food. The style of wines coming out of the region gives no hint at its climate and gastronomy, and full-bodied heavily oaked reds still far outnumber crisp fragrant whites.

That's the bad news. The good news is that quality is generally pretty good; Catalonia is one of the most exciting and progressive wine regions in Spain and prices are comparatively low. To start a meal, the most obvious aperitif will be a glass of cava, the local sparkler, produced by a method similar to champagne. Given the widespread improvement in quality in recent years, picking the producer – Codorníu and Freixenet

being the biggest and most ubiquitous labels – is probably less important than sorting out the confusing array of styles. *Extra brut* is the driest, followed in ascending order of sugar levels by *brut*, *extra seco* (often off-dry), *seco* (may in fact be medium sweet), *semi seco* (sweet), and *dulce* (very sweet).

Catalan whites (*blanco* in Spanish, *blanc* in Catalan) can be uninspiring and if there is something from Galicia on the list (Rias Baixas is the main region to look for), grab it. The extra cost will be worth it. Going local, however, your best bet is the Penedès region and the white wines of Miguel Torres are always top quality. A glass of Torres' fragrant Vina Esmeralda is an unbeatable antidote to heat stress. Another Penedès producer making excellent whites and rosés is Joan Raventos Rosell. Look out too for the Heretat Vall-Ventos name.

Good quality reds (*tinto/negre*) are a lot easier to find and can easily be split up according to how much oak flavour you like. *Vino joven* generally has no oak in it and Albet I Noya's *tempranillo joven* is a great example of this young fruit-only style of wine. Then going up the wood (and expense) scale there are *crianzas*, *reservas*, and *gran reservas*.

If the list is divided by region, here is a rough guide to what you can expect. Priorat is home to full-bodied (and fully priced) reds – one of the most critically acclaimed is Clos L'Obac, the flagship wine from Costers del Siurana. The same producer also makes an impressive sweet lightly fortified red called Dolc de l'Obac. Penedès is cava territory but also makes increasingly impressive reds and fresh citrusy whites. Ex-restaurateur Jean Leon's red *reserva* is considered to be one of the best cabernet-based wines in Spain. Costers del Segre, meanwhile, is veering towards New World fruity style reds, and if you like plenty of toasty wood Clamor is a delicious single vineyard California-style red from Raimat. The same *bodega* makes a very good merlot rosé (*rosado/rosat*). If you prefer to head to relatively undiscovered territory, Tarragona and Terra Alta are the two regions to watch for.

Finally, if you have room and your hotel is within staggering distance, you could try a sweet moscatel with your *crema catalana* or a glass of Tarragona Clásico (once known as 'poor man's port' in Britain) with cheese.

but Pou Dols' set lunch, at €9.90, has to be one of the best deals around. Going à la carte, crab and asparagus cannelloni drizzled with mango sauce are delicate parcels of delight, or try the seared sea bream with tiny squid and baby broad beans. Desserts are sublime: light fruit soups and peppery aubergine purée served with lime sorbet are as delicious as they are unusual.

Les Quinze Nits
Plaça Reial 6 (93 317 30 75). Metro Liceu.
Open 1-3.45pm, 8.30-11.30pm daily. **Average** €. **Credit** MC, V. **Map** p345 A3.
A ferociously popular chain of restaurants, whose bargain basement prices are utterly incongruous in such sleek settings. Starters are a sophisticated lot including superb salads, but things tend to slide from there – meat and fish mains can be overcooked and dishes such as paella taste as if they were produced in large quantities. The lengthy queues to get in, however, are testimony to the fact that sometimes you do get more than you pay for.
Branches: La Dolça Herminia, C/Magdalenes 27 (93 317 06 76); La Fonda, C/Escudellers 10 (93 301 75 15) and throughout the city.

El Salón
C/Hostal d'en Sol 6-8 (93 315 21 59). Metro Jaume I. **Open** 2-4pm, 9pm-midnight Mon-Sat. Closed 2wks Aug. **Average** €€. **Credit** AmEx, MC, V. **Map** p345 B4.
A quirky, baroque dining room with a bar at one end and a bohemian feel, although the acoustics can be a bit trying at busy times. The menu defies all attempts at labelling, but look forward to venison with parsnips and redcurrant sauce; a goulash made with clams, or satay lamb and chicken with coconut rice. Blackcurrant and almond crumble with cream provides a final flourish.

Taxidermista
Plaça Reial 8 (93 412 45 36). Metro Liceu.
Open noon-2am Tue-Sun. *Meals served* 1.30-4pm, 8.30-12.30pm. Closed 2wks Jan. **Average** €€. **Credit** DC, MC, V. **Map** p345 A3.
Taxidermista's immense popularity with tourists doesn't do it any favours, which is a pity, for it has good food and an interesting history. It was once a taxidermist's, counting Dalí among its regular customers, and before that a natural history museum. The Franco-Catalan menu does not change often and generally features *rèmol* (turbot) with cider sauce and apple purée, or poularde stuffed with *espinacas a la catalana* and served with leek crisps.

International

La Locanda
C/Doctor Joaquim Pou 4 (93 317 46 09). Metro Jaume I or Urquinaona. **Open** 1.15-4.30pm, 8.15-midnight Tue-Sun. **Average** €€. **Credit** MC, V. **Map** p344 B2.
One of precious few decent Italian restaurants in town, La Locanda is pricier than most, but seems to take more care sourcing authentic, fresh and top-quality ingredients. Pasta, gnocchi and focaccia are made in house; carpaccios and pizzas are also good. An all-Italian wine list is slightly overpriced, but respite is to be found in a reasonable house red.

Eat, Drink, Shop

Pou Dols. *See p137.*

LOMBARDO
Restaurants

< LOMBARDO

Five minutes from Plaza Catalunya on Barcelona's top shopping boulevard. Relaxed atmosphere and delicious modern Catalan cuisine.
Summer terrace.

Rambla Catalunya, 49-51
Tel. 93 487 48 42

TALLER DE TAPAS >

Just off the Ramblas by the Plaça del Pi. Lively tapas restaurant with open kitchen and exceptional seafood. Outside terrace.

Pl. Sant Josep Oriol, 9 (Pl. del Pi)
Tel. 93 302 62 43

< LOMBARDO

Next to Barcelona football stadium. Beautiful restaurant with groundbreaking design. Eclectic Mediterranean cuisine and a relaxing garden.

Travessera de les Corts, 64-68
Tel. 93 448 35 52

El Paraguayo

C/Parc 1 (93 302 14 41). Metro Drassanes.
Open 1-4pm, 8pm-midnight Tue-Sun. **Average**
€€€. **Credit** AmEx, DC, MC, V. **Map** p345 A4.
Carnivore heaven – chunks of beef, blackened on the
outside and oozing red at the centre, are served on
wooden boards, with only a bowl of garlicky
chimichurri as a token nod to plant life. Well, side
dishes do include a selection of salads, corn on the
cob and yucca chips. The warm, pine interior is covered in South American art, and there is friendly,
informal service. Did we mention the meat?

Peimong

*C/Templers 6-10 (93 318 28 73). Metro Jaume
I.* **Open** 1-4.30pm, 8-11.30pm Tue-Sun. **Average**
€. **Credit** MC, V. **Map** p345 B3.
Not, perhaps, the fanciest-looking restaurant around
(think Peruvian gimcracks and strip lighting) or
indeed the fanciest-looking food, but it sure tastes
like the real thing. Try the *ceviche* for an explosion
of lime and coriander or the spicy corn tamales.
Service is particularly friendly, there are two types
of Peruvian beer and even – for the very nostalgic
or the hypoglycaemic – Inca Kola.

Polenta

C/Ample 51 (93 268 14 29). Metro Jaume I.
Open 7pm-midnight Mon-Thur, Sun; 7pm-1am
Fri, Sat; 1.30pm-midnight Sun. **Average** €.
Credit AmEx, MC, V. **Map** p345 B4.
The menu globetrots from Argentine beef with
chimichurri and chicken with mole sauce through
polenta and osso buco and on down to tempura and
teriyaki. The restaurant, where deep and funky
colours prevail and contrast with the exposed
stonework, is small and relaxed with an eclectic
music selection and magazines to read.

Shunka

*C/Sagristans 5 (93 412 49 91). Metro Jaume
I.* **Open** 1.30-3.30pm, 8.30-11.30pm Tue-Fri;
2-4pm, 8.30-11.30pm Sat, Sun. **Average** €€.
Credit AmEx, DC, MC, V. **Map** p344 B2.
One of the best Japanese restaurants in the city.
Sushi, sashimi, tempuras, udon noodles with prawns
and vegetables or a sublime nigiri zushi are all pro-
fessionally prepared (right in front of you, should
you get one of the coveted seats at the bar overlooking the kitchen). Desserts include creamy green
tea ice-cream and sake truffles. Prices have risen
recently, but the set lunch is still a bargain at €12.70.

Sukur

C/Avinyó 42 (93 301 01 02). Metro Jaume I.
Open 1.30-4pm, 9-12.30am Mon-Sat. **Average**
€€. **Map** p345 B4.
A colourful hotchpotch of ethnic influences with low
Moroccan tables at the back, terracotta walls, olive
green paintwork and shifting diaphanous curtains
between tables. Tajines, couscous, stuffed vine
leaves and Greek salad are mainstays of a frequently
changing menu, as is the *brie*: not what it seems but
a fritter of tuna, egg, aubergine and olives.

La Verònica

C/Avinyó 25 (93 412 11 22). Metro Liceu.
Open 7.30pm-12.30am Tue-Fri; 1pm-1am Sat,
Sun. Closed 2wks Feb, 2wks Aug. **Average**
€. **Credit** MC, V. **Map** p345 B3.
A colourful, elegantly constructed space with food
to match: thin, crispy pizzas and designer salads.
During the summer, tourists fill the outside tables
on Plaça George Orwell, but late nights and winter
months draw a fashionably clad, mainly gay, local
crowd, to munch on such delights as carrot and
parsnip shavings doused in ginger vinaigrette.

Vegetarian

Govinda

*Plaça Vila de Madrid 4-5 (93 318 77 29). Metro
Liceu.* **Open** 1-4pm Mon; 1-4pm, 8-11pm Tue-Thur; 1-
4pm, 8-11.45pm Fri, Sat; 1-4pm Sun. Closed 2wks Aug.
Average €. **Credit** AmEx, DC, MC, V. **Map** p344 A2.
Going à la carte in this Hindu restaurant is surprisingly expensive, although the thalis are a good way
to sample a wide range of Indian titbits. The weekday set lunch (€8.40) is the more popular option, and
includes a basic salad buffet, spicy soups, and mains
such as pumpkin patties with walnuts and tomato
jam, finishing off with coconut pudding or rose petal
ice-cream. Note that no alcohol is served.

Juicy Jones

*C/Cardenal Casañas 7 (mobile 606 204 906).
Metro Liceu.* **Open** noon-midnight daily.
Average €. **No credit cards**. **Map** p345 A3.
The psychedelic graffiti and relaxed studenty vibe
here are a far cry from the dry, worthy feel that most
of the city's vegetarian restaurants enjoy. There are
substantial salads, *bocadillos* (try roast vegetables
with balsamic dressing) and gooey chocolate cake. As
the name suggests, the speciality is freshly squeezed
juices, fruity shakes and yoghurt smoothies.

Raval

Biblioteca

C/Junta de Comerç 28 (93 412 62 21). Metro Liceu.
Open 1-4pm, 9pm-midnight Tue-Sat. **Average** €€.
Credit AmEx, DC, MC, V. **Map** p345 A3.
Brought into being by a Spanish-Irish couple frus-
tated by the difficulty of finding decent cookery
books. The gang's all here from Escoffier to Oliver,
and the menu isn't a bad read either, combining Irish
and British heavyweights – roast beef and Yorkshire
pudding, oysters with Guinness, lamb with colcan-
non, venison pie – with light Mediterranean fish
dishes. The set lunch offers more basic fare of pasta
dishes and creative salads, but is good for €9.

El Cafetí

*C/Hospital 99 (end of passage) (93 329 24
19/www.elcafeti.com). Metro Liceu.* **Open** 1.30-
3.30pm, 9-11.30pm Tue-Sat; 1.30-3.30pm Sun.
Closed 2wks Aug. **Average** €€. **Credit** AmEx,
DC, MC, V. **Map** p342 C6.

Eat, Drink, Shop

Entering this romantic hideaway at the end of the Passatge Bernadí Martorell feels, in the nicest possible way, like straying into someone's sitting room. An extensive menu changes with the seasons, but might include duck with wild mushrooms, rabbit with mustard sauce, various paellas and myriad other seafood dishes. A framed article by Ken Livingstone describes it as a mayoral favourite.

Ca l'Estevet

C/Valldonzella 46 (93 302 41 86). Metro Universitat. **Open** *1.30-4pm, 8.30-11pm Mon-Sat. Closed 2wks Aug.* **Average** €€. **Credit** AmEx, DC, MC, V. **Map** p344 A1.
The signed photos and artistic doodlings around the walls are vestiges of a time when Estevet was the place for writers, artists and politicians to meet; and it seems that little has changed since. The menu features the same *filet de Café Paris* (served in a buttery, herby sauce with wild mushrooms) and succulent kid that it always did. The food at times is secondary to the atmosphere; starters can be spartan and desserts tend towards the pre-packaged, but it's an unbeatable place to hang out with friends.

Ca l'Isidre

C/Flors 12 (93 441 11 39/93 442 57 20). Metro Paral.lel. **Open** *1.30-4pm, 8.30-11pm Mon-Sat. Closed 2wks Aug.* **Average** €€€€. **Credit** AmEx, DC, MC, V. **Map** p342 C6.
A top-flight, family-run restaurant, whose secret has been to draw the maximum potential out of high-quality market-bought ingredients, served in disarmingly straightforward dishes. Catalan, Spanish and European classics, featuring magnificent local lamb, or fine foie gras and masterfully prepared seafood from Atlantic *angulas* (eels) to a tuna fillet. Only puddings break with the tendency towards understatement, with daughter and master pastry chef Núria elaborating some of the most deliciously creative desserts imaginable.

La Casa de la Rioja

C/Peu de la Creu 8-10 (93 443 33 63). Metro Catalunya. **Open** *1-4pm, 9-11pm Mon-Sat.* **Average** €. **Credit** AmEx, MC, V. **Map** p342 C5.
Showcasing the cuisine of the La Rioja region, this colourful, sharp-edged restaurant is not quite the jaw-dropping bargain it was when it opened a couple of years ago, but still provides some of the best-value food around, particularly in its €8.15 lunch *menú*. There are great salads (try crab and salmon), *cazuelitos* (little terracotta dishes of stews) and other hearty fare, all eclipsed by ambrosial desserts such as home-made chocolate and pistachio ice-cream, or an inspired Roquefort cheesecake.

Casa Leopoldo

C/Sant Rafael 24 (93 441 69 42). Metro Liceu or Paral.lel. **Open** *1.30-4pm, 8.30-11pm Tue-Sat; 1.30-4pm Sun. Closed Aug.* **Average** €€€. **Credit** AmEx, DC, MC, V. **Map** p342 C6.
Bullfighting paraphernalia, wooden fittings, tiles and red gingham give this Barcelona classic plenty

Casa Leopoldo: traditional food...

of old-style charm, and traditional food is still the order of the day with generous and excellent fish, shellfish, steaks and homey stews. For some of the seafood, and particularly the fish of the day, you might want to put your bank manager on speed dial, however; the shabbiness of the surrounding area does little to affect the prices.

Elisabets

C/Elisabets 2-4 (93 317 58 26). Metro Catalunya. **Open** *7.30am-10pm Mon-Thur, Sat; 7.30am-2am Fri. Closed 3wks Aug.* **Average** €. **No credit cards**. **Map** p344 A2.
Traditional and supercheap Catalan dishes are the order of the day; as well as a long list of generous *bocadillos*, there are rabbit stews, chicken cooked in beer, *botifarra* sausage with eye-watering *all i oli*, and so on. An unpretentious but friendly place to have lunch among the denizens of the Raval and those on their way back from the MACBA.

La Fragua

Rambla del Raval 15 (93 442 80 97). Metro Liceu or Sant Antoni. **Open** *Mar-Oct 1-4pm, 8pm-1am Tue-Sun. Nov-Feb 8pm-1am Tue-Sun.* **Average** €. **Credit** AmEx, DC, MC, V. **Map** p342 C6.
Rural simplicity incarnate, serving food to match. Salads, stews, steaks and sausages, with a brief vegetarian section consisting of various omelettes and

...and thoroughly modern prices.

delicious spinach rolls with pinenuts and raisins. It's cheap and basic, making it a good budget option, especially in summer, when there are tables out on the lively Rambla del Raval. The set menu is normally worth a try at €8.50 (without wine), and it's available in the evenings.

La Gardunya

C/Jerusalem 18 (93 302 43 23). Metro Liceu. **Open** 1-4pm, 8pm-1am Mon-Sat. **Average** €. **Credit** AmEx, DC, MC, V. **Map** p344 A2.
A tall, thin, glass and steel building, funkily decorated, with a mosaic of stone and sand set into the floor and a colourful spiral staircase leading up to a mezzanine. Grab a table up there to get a view into La Boqueria market, and watch your *sardinas* or *manitas de cabrito* (kid's trotters) being haggled over. Livelier at lunchtime (with both market workers and customers) than at night, despite the pull of a good €11.50 set dinner.

Hotel España

C/Sant Pau 9 (93 318 17 58). Metro Liceu. **Open** 1-4pm, 8.30pm-midnight daily. **Average** €€. **Credit** AmEx, DC, MC, V. **Map** p342 C6.
A magnificent Modernista interior with floral tiled mosaics, original lamps and an impressive ceiling, conceived by architect Domènech i Montaner in 1902, and Ramon Casas underwater murals in the

back dining room, are all let down by the mediocre food. However, there is an €8 menu, which is a low-risk way to bask in the splendid decor.

Lupino

C/Carme 33 (93 412 36 97). Metro Liceu. **Open** 1-4pm, 9pm-midnight Mon-Thur, Sun; 1-4pm, 9pm-1am Fri-Sat. **Average** €€. **Credit** AmEx, MC, V. **Map** p344 A2.
Sky-high production values meant that this restaurant-cocktail bar was all the rage when it opened back in 2002, although its retro-futuristic airport lounge look with waiters dressed like mortuary attendants had already fallen out of favour a year later, such are the vagaries of fashion. The food is still good, however: lamb with couscous or chicken with ginger and sesame, with the odd nod to trad Spanish – stir-fried vegetables with strips of *membrillo* (quince jelly) – are surprisingly cheap, and surprisingly tasty.

Mama Café

C/Doctor Dou 10 (93 301 29 40). Metro Catalunya or Liceu. **Open** 1pm-1am Mon-Sat. **Average** €. **Credit** DC, MC, V. **Map** p344 A2.
Very much of its *barri*, with Rajasthani wallhangings, slide projections and trip hop, the Mama Café provides healthy, Mediterranean dishes to a wildly diverse crowd. Dreadlocks settle in next to blue rinses to chow down on succulent chicken and wild mushroom brochettes, salmon cooked in zingy lemon rosemary oil or maybe a warm goat's cheese salad with pear and orange vinaigrette. The staff are charming and the seats comfy, but the semi-transparent walls of the lavatory demand a certain amount of courage.

Mesón David

C/Carretas 63 (93 441 59 34). Metro Paral.lel. **Open** 1-4pm, 8pm-midnight Mon, Tue, Thur-Sun. Closed Aug. **Average** €. **Credit** AmEx, MC, V. **Map** p342 C6.
Ordering here can be a bit of a lottery, but favourites such as *pulpo gallego* (octopus Galician-style), *trucha navarra* (a whole trout stuffed with *jamón serrano* and cheese, lightly breaded and fried) or *lechazo* (a sticky, tender-roasted pork knuckle) are safe bets, as are lamb dishes – and at these absurdly low prices, you can't go too far wrong. Tips are tossed into a large metal pot behind the counter and a bell is rung, at which point everyone in the restaurant stops eating and cheers.

Pla dels Àngels

C/Ferlandina 23 (93 329 40 47). Metro Universitat. **Open** 1.30-4pm, 9-11pm Mon-Thur, Sun; 1.30-4pm, 9pm-midnight Fri, Sat. **Average** €. **Credit** DC, MC, V. **Map** p342 C5.
In keeping with its position smack in front of the MACBA, Pla dels Àngels is artistically and colourfully decorated, and buzzes with animated conversation. A short menu comprises imaginative salads, great spaghetti and gnocchi dishes, carpaccios of duck, salmon or octopus and a few meat

Eat, Drink, Shop

dishes – chicken with tiger nut sauce, or stout little hamburgers. Prices are admirably reasonable for what is often excellent cooking.

Sagarra

C/Xuclà 9 (93 301 06 04). Metro Liceu. **Open** 1-4pm Mon; 1-4pm, 8-11pm Tue-Sat. **Average** €. **Credit** AmEx, DC, MC, V. **Map** p344 A2.
An excellent-value lunch *menú* gets you Greek salad to start or maybe asparagus with romesco sauce, followed by chicken parcels or pork with *sobrassada* (spicy Mallorcan sausage) and a pudding, all for €7.75. A la carte options include eminently reasonable *a la brasa* rabbit, quail and kid, or duck served with a bittersweet tomato confit. The main dining room is large and airy with windows overlooking C/Pintor Fortuny, while a smaller bar area looks over C/Xuclà and is a sunny spot for tapas or breakfast.

Silenus

C/Àngels 8 (93 302 26 80). Metro Liceu. **Open** 1.30-4pm, 8.30-11.45pm Mon-Sat. **Average** €€. **Credit** AmEx, DC, MC, V. **Map** p344 A2.
The ghost of a clock is projected on a far wall; the faded leaves of a book float up high; the ceiling twinkles with little lights, and wisps of wild flowers sit in glass jars. Not the lair of the Faerie Queen, but a thoroughly modern restaurant, where the aesthetic reigns supreme. A lunchtime *degustación* (€14.80) affords tiny portions of every delight on the menu; expect doll's house paella, tuna with couscous and pink peppercorns and paper-thin slices of pork cheeks with apple and a chocolatey port gravy.

International

Fil Manila

C/Ramelleres 3 (93 318 64 87). Metro Catalunya. **Open** 11.30am-4.30pm, 8-11.30pm Mon, Wed-Sun. **Average** €. **No credit cards. Map** p344 A2.
A neat and tidy little Filipino restaurant with an almighty tome of a menu, simplified only slightly by being divided into sections: grilled, barbecue, sizzling, rice and noodle dishes, and so on. Start with *tinola* (chicken and ginger soup) or *lumpiang Shanghai* (tiny crispy pork rolls), then maybe the spicy strips of beef served spitting on a hotplate with vegetables and a mountain of egg-fried rice. Ask for dishes 'Filipino style' to have the heat left in.

Punjab Restaurante

C/Joaquín Costa 1B (93 443 35 72). Metro Liceu. **Open** 11am-midnight daily. **Average** €. **No credit cards. Map** p342 C5.
Absurdly cheap and gloriously, unintentionally kitsch (those tablecloths are the real thing), the Punjab offers a salad, curry with rice, naan and a pudding for an unbeatable €3.50. Anyone prepared to go the extra euro is rewarded with a wider choice involving tandooris, birianis and couscous dishes. A recent Latin liaison in the kitchen has brought about an incongruous list of South American dishes.

Umita

C/Pintor Fortuny 15 (93 301 23 22). Metro Liceu. **Open** 1-4pm, 9pm-12.30am Mon-Sat. **Average** €€. **Credit** AmEx, MC, V. **Map** p344 A2.
Nikkei is the name given to the food that results when Japanese immigration impacts on local cuisine; normally Latin American, and here Peruvian. The most celebrated coupling of the two cultures comes in the form of *ceviche*, here tangy and fresh. At lunchtime there are two *menús*: one (€9) involving main courses such as pork with figs and puréed *boniato*, and another (€12) made up of sushi, sashimi and *gyoza* dumplings.

Vegetarian

L'Hortet

C/Pintor Fortuny 32 (93 317 61 89). Metro Liceu. **Open** 1.15-4pm, 8.30-11pm daily. **Average** €. **Credit** MC, V. **Map** p344 A2.
In time-honoured rustic style – beams, rusty horseshoes and healthy investment in the terracotta and gingham industries – L'Hortet manages to be one of the cosiest vegetarian places around. The set lunch is not cheap, but does offer four courses; generally soup or salad, then maybe artichokes with *romesco*, a pasta dish and baked cheesecake or apple compôte to finish.

Sésamo

C/Sant Antoni Abat 52 (93 441 64 11). Metro Sant Antoni. **Open** 1.30-4.30pm Mon; 1.30-4pm, 9-11.30pm Wed-Sun. Closed Aug. **Average** €. **Credit** MC, V. **Map** p342 C5.
The two course €8 lunch menu consists of excellent soups, salads, lasagnes, quiches and rice dishes. At night a healthy range of dishes à la carte includes crêpes stuffed with sautéed vegetables or gnocchetti with tomato, onion and ricotta. The wine list is not extensive but it's still decent. Mornings, there's muesli, fresh juices and home-made cakes. Music tends toward trendy, mellow electronica, and the decor is marked by an orderly grove of tall, bamboo-like lamps which lean over diners in the main room.

Sant Pere & the Born

Abac

C/Rec 79-89 (93 319 66 00). Metro Barceloneta. **Open** 8.30-10.30pm Mon; 1.30-3.30pm, 8.30-10.30pm Tue-Sat. Closed 2wks Aug. **Average** €€€€. **Credit** AmEx, DC, MC, V. **Map** p345 C4.
Blond wood, bare walls and unfussy furniture provide the perfect backdrop to elaborate dishes and impeccable service. The *menú degustación* is an absurdly indulgent series of dishes such as tuna with broccoli cream and caviar; langoustines on a bed of couscous with artichoke crisps, or scallops with braised endive and wild mushroom sauce. Puddings hit the only duff note: a rather bland selection of milk-based desserts not greatly suited

Eat, Drink, Shop

Espai Sucre. See p147.

to rounding off a heavy meal. Better to sample some of the superb cheeses and hold out for the fantastic petits fours.

Bar Salvador

C/Canvis Nous 8 (93 310 10 41). Metro Jaume I or Barceloneta. **Open** 9am-5pm Mon-Fri. **Average** €. **Credit** MC, V. **Map** p345 B4.
An old-school *bodega* dishing out good, cheap, uncomplicated Catalan food to the working masses; battered *calamars* to start, or raviolis al Roquefort, then perhaps knuckle of veal, *botifarra* with haricot beans or cod with *samfaina*. Another winner is roast pork with rosemary and onions and fat, fluffy potato wedges. The drinking options are a fiery house wine from the barrel or beer; here both tend to be drunk from glass *porrones* held aloft – a skill best practised at home.

Brasserie Flo

C/Jonqueres 10 (93 319 31 02). Metro Urquinaona. **Open** 1.30-4pm daily; 8.30pm-12.30am Mon-Thur, Sun; 8pm-1am Fri, Sat. **Average** €€. **Credit** AmEx, DC, MC, V. **Map** p344 B2.
Parlour palms and '20s posters; waiters with cloths draped over their arms and trays wielded at shoulder height; you get the picture. The house specialty is a huge platter of seafood, but a Catholic range of dishes runs from carpaccio to ostrich. Gallic treats for pudding include *îles flotantes* and profiteroles. The set dinner menu at €22.70 is good value and includes wine.

Cal Pep

Plaça de les Olles 8 (93 310 79 61). Metro Barceloneta. **Open** 8-11.45pm Mon; 1.30-4pm, 8-11.45pm Tue-Sat. Closed Aug. **Average** €€. **Credit** AmEx, DC, MC, V. **Map** p344 C4.
Get here early for the coveted seats at the front, where the bar bends round; otherwise you can expect to have waiting customers breathing down your neck, such is the reputation of Cal Pep. The seafood *raciones* can be exceptional – don't miss the creamy, garlicky squid or the expensive but fabulous prawns. Book well ahead for a table in the brick-lined room at the back.

Casa Delfín

Passeig del Born 36 (93 319 50 88). Metro Barceloneta. **Open** 7am-5pm Mon-Sat. Closed 3wks Aug. **Average** €. **Credit** MC, V. **Map** p345 C3.
While the beautiful people sun themselves at the tables outside, inside is still a jovial workmen's canteen, serving simple but tasty meat and fish at lunchtimes only. The extensive *menú del día* is still good value, with great sardines, fresh tuna and, during the season, roast artichokes. Stews and soups are not quite as good, however, and some of the salad options tend to be overdressed.

Comerç 24

C/Comerç 24 (93 319 21 02). Metro Arc de Triomf. **Open** 1.30-3.30pm, 8.30pm-12.30am Tue-Fri. Closed 3wks Aug. **Average** €€€. **Credit** MC, V. **Map** p345 C3.

Chef Carles Abellan has created his own version of Ferran Adrià's famous tasting menu (*see p164*), playing with flavours and deconstructing traditional favourites (DIY tortilla: just dip the ingredients into a warm egg-yolk spume). A selection of tiny dishes roams the globe: tuna sashimi and seaweed on a wafer-thin pizza crust; Puy lentils with bacon and foie gras; or squid stuffed with *botifarra* and anise. Steel girders and jailhouse-grey paint punctuated with bursts of yellow and red provide some industrial chic.

Coses de Menjar

Pla de Palau 7 (93 310 60 01). Metro Jaume I or Barceloneta. **Open** 1.30-4pm, 9-11.30pm Mon-Thur, Sun; 1.30-4pm, 9pm-midnight Fri, Sat. **Average** €€. **Credit** MC, V. **Map** p345 C4.
As with sister restaurants Pla dels Àngels and Semproniana (*see p143 and p153*), the formula here is quirky, charming decor with food coming a reasonable second. Chandeliers are made from wine glasses, menus are glued to wine bottles and bent forks become napkin rings. The regular menu can be a tad overpriced, but from the reduced lunch menu starters such as courgettes stuffed with wild mushrooms are less than €3 and mains such as tender calves' liver with onion and walnut are only €4.25.

L'Econòmic

Plaça Sant Agustí Vell 13 (93 319 64 94). Metro Arc de Triomf. **Open** 12.30-4.30pm Mon-Fri. Closed Aug. **Average** €. **No credit cards**. **Map** p344 C2.

As you'd expect, old favourites such as *escudella* (stew), *galtes de ternera* (calves' cheek) and roast rabbit are nothing if not cheap, and there's an unusually good range of puddings, including a dreamy lemon mousse. It's a deep, narrow restaurant lined with Andalucian tiles and the owner's oil paintings; always packed, but there are chairs on the pretty *plaça* outside for anyone waiting for a table.

Espai Sucre

C/Princesa 53 (93 268 16 30). Metro Jaume I. **Open** 9-11.30pm Tue-Sat. Closed Aug. **Average** €€€. **Credit** MC, V. **Map** p345 C3.
Prepare the palate with a small savoury dish – couscous with fried skate, perhaps, or a lentil broth with grilled foie gras – in preparation for a series of light and artfully constructed desserts, in possibly the only pudding restaurant in the world. The sheer number of flavours in one dish – a soup of shredded lychee holds a lozenge of ice-cream, infused with apple, celery and eucalyptus and sprinkled with ground cloves and more – can sometimes be dizzying; the key is not to analyse the parts, but enjoy the sum.

Mundial Bar

Plaça Sant Agustí Vell 1 (93 319 90 56). Metro Arc de Triomf or Jaume I. **Open** 10am-11.30pm Tue-Sat; 11am-4pm Sun. Closed 2wks Aug. **Average** €. **Credit** MC, V. **Map** p344 C2.
A welcome antidote to many of the fussy, touristy, seafood restaurants hereabouts, Mundial is a no-nonsense bar-restaurant run by three generations of an extremely welcoming family. Be warned that some of the fare on offer does not seem to be freshly prepared, but the *parrillada* (€24 for two), a towering heap of langoustines, prawns, clams, razor clams, octopus and more, is a fantastic bargain.

Passadís del Pep

Pla del Palau 2 (93 310 10 21). Metro Barceloneta. **Open** 1.30-3.30pm, 9-11.30pm Mon-Sat. Closed 3wks Aug. **Average** €€€€. **Credit** AmEx, DC, MC, V. **Map** p345 C4.
Hidden down a long corridor and invisible from the street, once inside this upmarket seafood restaurant is a blast of colour and activity. There's no written menu, but charming waiters will bring a selection of excellent seafood dishes, including some outstanding paellas or a lobster *fideuà*. Wine (generally cava) is included in the price, which hovers around €75 per head, but is dependent on the market.

El Pebre Blau

C/Banys Vells 21 (93 319 13 08). Metro Jaume I. **Open** 8.30pm-midnight daily. **Average** €€. **Credit** MC, V. **Map** p345 C3.
Soft lighting and a cascade of colourful light-shades work their magic against the Gothic arches of this former stable. A French-Moroccan menu includes plenty of tajines, curries and an emphasis on duck. Try the goat's cheese in a tuile basket with ginger marmalade for dessert. Service is, seemingly without exception, young, attentive and charming, and Edith Piaf provides the final touch.

Eat, Drink, Shop

Pucca.

Branch: L'Ou Com Balla, C/Banys Vells 20, Born (93 310 53 78).

Pla de la Garsa

C/Assaonadors 13 (93 315 24 13). Metro Jaume I. **Open** 8pm-1am daily. **Average** €€. **Credit** AmEx, MC, V. **Map** p345 C3.

High-quality cheeses from around Spain, pâtés and cold meats are all to be found in this elegant 16th-century dairy, as well as local specialities such as *greixera menorquina* (Menorcan leek tart). For a selection, along with samplers of dishes based on traditional recipes, some dating back to medieval times, there is a taster menu at €13 per person (minimum two people). Desserts are similarly based on local traditions and vary according to the religious calendar.

Pucca

Passeig Picasso 32 (93 268 72 36). Metro Arc de Triomf. **Open** 1.30-4.30pm, 9pm-midnight. Tue-Sat; 1.30-4.30pm Sun. **Average** €€. **Credit** MC, V. **Map** p343 E6.

If it weren't for the overwhelming percentage of punters sporting Freitag bags and Beckham fins, you could be forgiven for mistaking Pucca's minimalism for 'sixties railway station' (with acoustics to match). The globe-trotting food, however, is superb, with influences and flown-in ingredients from Thailand, Indonesia, Mexico and elsewhere. Try the *tom ka gai* chicken soup or *gule kambing*,

an aromatic lamb stew, and perhaps a hollowed-out baby pineapple filled with ice-cream for dessert.

La Reina

C/Sant Antoni dels Sombrerers 3 (93 319 53 71). Metro Jaume I or Barceloneta. **Open** 8.30pm-midnight Mon-Thur, Sun; 8.30pm-1am Fri, Sat. **Average** €€. **Credit** MC, V. **Map** p345 C3.

It would seem red-and-black is the new black. La Reina's peculiar Dracula-chic sweeps on to the dark, narrow street by way of a crimson carpet and flickering candles, spooking passers-by. Toothsome pleasures inside include a tender duck magret with caramelised apples and a generous tuna steak with aubergine and black olives (both served rare, naturally). Desserts are similarly good – try the chocolate tart topped with a sublime passion fruit cream.

Santa Maria

C/Comerç 17 (93 315 12 27). Metro Arc de Triomf. **Open** 1.30-3.30pm, 8.30pm-midnight Tue-Sat. Closed 3wks Aug. **Average** €€. **Credit** V. **Map** p345 C3.

At the vanguard of the new wave of designer tapas restaurants, Santa Maria offers saucers of tuna *mojama* (thinly sliced and cured), or tiny bowls of perfectly al dente fried rice with chicken and vegetables, as well as minuscule versions of perfectly prepared international standards such as sushi and falafel, but the desserts are where things get really interesting. Expect the unexpected.

Senyor Parellada

C/Argenteria 37 (93 310 50 94). Metro Jaume I.
Open 1-3.45pm, 8.30-11.45pm Mon-Sat. **Average**
€. **Credit** AmEx, DC, MC, V. **Map** p345 B3.
Senyor Parellada has been around forever, but after
a makeover a couple of years back it now serves
smaller dishes at lower prices, with only a slight dip
in quality. Tasty Catalan favourites include plenty
of seafood, or the ferociously good *xai a les dotze
cabeces d'all* (lamb with 12 heads of garlic). Paellas
and *fideuàs* are where the changes become more
obvious, though, as those are not dishes that benefit from mass production.

International

Bunga Raya

*C/Assaonadors 7 (93 319 31 69). Metro Jaume
I.* **Open** 8pm-midnight Tue-Sun. **Average** €.
No credit cards. **Map** p345 C3.
The great-value set dinner involves beef rendang,
chicken curry, lamb satay, squid and various pickles, sambal and coconut, as well as a beer and a
dessert, all for less than €12. A narrow downstairs
dining room has Malaysian tourist posters on the
bamboo-lined walls, and often a Malaysian video
providing the soundtrack, while the upstairs room
is airy and peaceful. A friendly British-owned
place, where service treads the critical line between
relaxed and slow.

El Celler de Macondo

C/Consellers 4 (93 319 43 72). Metro Jaume I.
Open *Apr-Oct* 1pm-1am daily. *Nov-Mar* 6pm-1am
Mon, Tue, Thur-Sun. **Average** €. **Credit** AmEx,
DC, MC, V. **Map** p345 B4.
Macondo was the name of the imaginary village in
One Hundred Years of Solitude, fans of which will
recognise myriad other references from the butter-
flies on the menus to the names of the dishes. A spe-
ciality is 'arepizzas' – made with an *arepa* (a Latin
American corn cake) base and a variety of toppings.
There's also a good wine list, with plenty of Chilean
and Argentinian offerings.

Habana Vieja

*C/Banys Vells 2 (93 268 25 04). Metro Jaume
I.* **Open** 10am-4pm, 8.30pm-midnight Mon-Thur;
8pm-1am Fri, Sat; 1pm-1am Sun. **Average** €€.
Credit AmEx, DC, MC, V. Map p345 C3.
Like it says, this is a taste of old Havana; *ropa vieja*
(tender shredded beef, cooked with mild chillies) and
arroz congrí (rice with black beans) are comple-
mented with authentic trimmings – *machuquillos de
Elleguá* (fried balls of minced pork and plantain) are
much better than they sound. For some really indulgent comfort food, finish with the *torrejas Habana
Vieja*: slices of bread dipped in egg and fried with
cinnamon, and accompany it all with a Mojito.

Little Italy

*C/Rec 30 (93 319 79 73). Metro Barceloneta or
Jaume I.* **Open** 1-4pm, 9pm-midnight Mon-Sat.

Closed 2wks Aug. **Average** €€. **Credit** AmEx,
DC, MC, V. **Map** p345 C3.
Apart from a short list of pasta and risotto *primi*,
this is not so much Little Italy as Little
Mediterranean, with an emphasis on good, fresh
market produce. This is also one of few places in
town to make a decent salad and serve your main
course with, heaven forfend, vegetables. Its split-
level, candlelit dining room and, above all, its jazz –
live on Wednesday and Thursday; recorded Ella,
Louis and friends the rest of the week – attract a
slightly older, diverse crowd.

Al Passatore

Pla del Palau 8 (93 319 78 51). Metro Barceloneta.
Open 1pm-12.30am Mon-Wed; 1pm-1am Thur-Sun.
Average €. **Credit** MC, V. **Map** p345 C4.
The pizzas, which were always good, have grown
exponentially of late and are now officially unfin-
ishable. The rest – the pasta, the risottos, the cheap
set lunch – were never really up to par and have
remained on the back seat. The restaurant's enormous popularity means that there is usually a queue,
although this has diminished since the licence for
their pavement tables was revoked after neighbours
complained of noise. It's hoped it will be regained in
time for summer 2003.
Branches: Al Passatore, Moll de Gregal 25, Vila
Olímpica (93 225 00 47); Plaça Antonio López 6 (93 310
67 17); Montello, Via Laietana 42 (93 310 35 26).

Teranga

C/Nau 9 (93 310 33 65). Metro Jaume I.
Open 1-5pm, 9pm-1am Mon, Wed-Sun.
Average €. **No credit cards**. **Map** p345 B3.
The simple Senegalese food here is somewhat variable; spicy spinach on a bed of sweet potato is delicious, as is the ginger and pineapple juice, but
dumplings are bland and the lamb stew is occasionally uninspired. Still, it's difficult to cavil in the
face of such low prices. It's also a funky place just
for a beer, and in summer, there are tables outside
on a quiet square, away from the main Born rat run.

Vegetarian

Comme Bio

*Via Laietana 28 (93 319 89 68/www.commebio.es).
Metro Jaume I.* **Open** 1-3.45pm, 8.30-11pm daily.
Average €. **Credit** AmEx, DC, MC, V. **Map** p345 B3.
Corporate vegetarianism is an unusual hybrid, but
the Comme Bio chain is living proof that such a
concept exists. The €8.90 set lunch is not exactly
a bargain, and nor is it prepared with too much
love, but it's nice to get stuck into a salad buffet
with no fear of coming across a bit of tuna or ham.
Having said that, the slightly more complex à la
carte dishes, such as wild mushroom ragout or
spinach and ricotta pancakes, do include a couple
made with organic meat.
Branches: Gran Via de les Corts Catalanes 603,
08007, Eixample (93 301 03 76); Biocenter, C/Pintor
Fortuny 25, Raval (93 301 45 83).

Tragaluz: the original and best of Barcelona's design restaurants. *See p153.*

Eixample

Alboroque

C/Mallorca 304, (93 458 08 55). Metro Verdaguer.
Open 1-4pm Mon-Wed; 1-4pm, 8-11.30pm Thur-Sat.
Closed 2wks Aug. **Average** €. **Credit** MC, V.
Map p339 E4.
Classical music, tasteful decor and immaculate service from an all-girl team accompany some of the best food you'll find in this price range. The cooking is light and fresh, with starters such as camembert croquettes, or a spinach and mushroom salad; main courses include combinations such as sea bass with beetroot, or rabbit in red wine.

Alkimia

C/Indústria 70 (93 207 61 15). Metro Sagrada Família. **Open** 1.30-3.30pm, 9-11pm Mon-Fri;
9-11pm Sat. Closed 2wks Aug. **Average** €€€.
Credit AmEx, DC, MC, V. **Map** p339 E3.
An excellent wine cellar and richly diverse menu comprising creative collages of taste and colour spun off from Catalan and Provençal standards make this a restaurant on the rise. Start with a salad of luxury lettuces, beetroot purée and warm sliced squid, and then expect main courses involving game, wild rice or baked fish in unexpected combinations. A great way to explore is the gourmet menu, with four savoury courses and a couple of desserts.

El Asador de Burgos

C/Bruc 118 (93 207 31 60). Metro Verdaguer. **Open**
1-4pm, 8.30-11pm Mon-Sat. Closed Aug. **Average**
€€€. **Credit** AmEx, DC, MC, V. **Map** p339 D4.

A Romeo y Julieta Corona hangs heavy in the foyer, where bejewelled and besuited *barcelonins*, some with their moss green raglans hanging cape-like from their shoulders, wait patiently with talk of skiing, schools and high finance. This bastion of traditional Castilian cooking is all about meat; tender racks of honey-sweet lamb and suckling piggies hot from the huge wood-fired oven. On the wine list, hefty *gran reservas* rule the roost, but the good house red is more sensibly priced.

Casa Calvet

C/Casp 48 (93 412 40 12). Metro Urquinaona.
Open 1-3.30pm, 8.30-11pm Mon-Sat. Closed
Aug. **Average** €€€. **Credit** AmEx, DC,
MC, V. **Map** p344 C1.
This elegant restaurant sits inside Gaudí's Casa Calvet, one of his more understated projects, with an interior full of glorious detail in the carpentry, stained glass and tiles. The food is also a delight; modern Catalan dishes include pea soup with little chunks of squid; smoked foie gras with mango sauce; succulent pigeon with Szechuan pepper and roast fennel, and tasty lamb meatballs with creamy risotto. Puddings are supremely good – try the pine nut tart with foamed crema catalana – and the wine list is encyclopaedic.

Cata 1.81

C/Valencia 181 (93 323 68 18). Metro Passeig de Gràcia or Hospital Clínic. **Open** 6pm-midnight Mon-Thur; 6pm-1am Fri, Sat. Closed last 3wks Aug. **Average** €. **Credit** AmEx, DC, MC, V.
Map p338 C4.

Eating by design

Biscuits with bite-mark instructions on the surface, a nutritional snack with seeds inside allowing you to reforest by defecation – these are some of the odd-ball inventions by Barcelona designer Martí Guixé, who uses food as a vehicle for his sharply ironic commentary on contemporary life.

True to his Catalan roots, and combining a love of design, eccentricity and a nose for business, Guixé combines commercial projects for multinationals like the Camper footwear company with unusual prototypes working more as conceptual exercises than practical solutions to real problems. His unsettled life – he lives between Berlin and Barcelona and exhibits throughout the world – has brought him to reflect upon such themes as culinary multiculturalism, new forms of convenience food, or the importance of eating and drinking in nocturnal socialising. The tapa, that very Spanish collage of ingredients, tastes and ideas, is his paradigm of our time, so much so that he calls himself a 'tapaist', combining existing realities into new ones.

He is no pretentious culinary connoisseur, however; see, for example, his ongoing 'Spamt' project. Taking on that universally maligned lunchmeat, Guixé has converted Catalonia's emblematic *pa amb tomàquet* into Spamt (éS Pa AMb Tomàquet). His many variations include a travelling bread with tomato kit, a pre-made mix in a roll-on tube, not to mention an elaborate performance piece where visitors at gallery openings are converted into improvisational cooks. Another popular performance is the SSK-Snack Bar Wall, where edible panels are stuck to a gallery wall with Nutella, with eating instructions printed on the food itself with squid ink.

Guixé does occasionally come up with commercially viable products, such as a series of elegant canvas aprons with an elaborate geometric folding system. His art gallery in Barcelona, Galeria H$_2$O (*see p230*), has produced a number of his ideas for sale, including a Spamt kit and a creative colouring recipe book, both for children. His onslaught of design ideas can also be seen on www.guixe.com or in a new glossy book, *1:1*.

'Cata' means tasting, and is the raison d'être of this brightly lit and slightly austere-looking little place. Oenophiles flock to try 25cl decanters of whatever takes their fancy from the impressive wine list, saucer-sized portions of food: dinky little hamburgers with tiny cones of chips, salted foie with strawberry sauce, and miniature parcels of cheese and tomato; treacly pigs' trotters with figs, walnuts and honey ice-cream. Hugely popular among Catalan gastronomic luminaries, who, sadly, get the best of the service.

Semproniana

C/Rosselló 148 (93 453 18 20). *Metro Hospital Clínic.* **Open** 1.30-4pm, 9-11.30pm Mon-Thur; 1.30-4pm, 9pm-midnight Fri, Sat. **Average** €€. **Credit** MC, V. **Map** p338 C4.
A colourful wonderland of floaty gauze drapes, twigs glittering with glass pendants, dusty ancient books, with coat hooks and napkin rings made from contorted cutlery glinting in the candlelight. The capricious wording of the menu makes roast pigeon 'the bird which flies on the ground', and a dense chocolate mousse 'delirium tremens'. The food, which might also include a creamy courgette soup or a hunk of cod with *calçots*, is not at all bad, but rarely a match for the atmosphere.

Tragaluz

Passatge de la Concepció 5 (93 487 01 96). Metro Diagonal. **Open** 1.30-4pm, 8.30pm-midnight Mon-Wed, Sun; 1.30-4pm, 8.30pm-1am Thur-Sat. **Average** €€€. **Credit** AmEx, DC, MC, V. **Map** p338 D4.
Faultless in its design, presentation and culinary execution, Tragaluz sets the standards for mid-range modern Mediterranean cuisine. Try a warm duck salad to start, or a creamy cauliflower soup with lychee granita and *jamón ibérico*, followed by tender, flaky sea bass with an onion millefeuille and tomato marmalade. Puddings are spectacularly good; try apricot and strawberry soup with iced yoghurt and Szechuan pepper. Downstairs, lighter meals are served all day, and the group also runs a Japanese restaurant across the street.
Branches: throughout the city.

Windsor

C/Còrsega 286 (93 415 84 83). *Metro Diagonal.* **Open** 1.15-4pm, 8.30-11pm Mon-Fri; 8.30-11pm Sat. Closed Aug. **Average** €€€. **Credit** AmEx, DC, MC, V. **Map** p338 D4.
The dishes on offer here are unreconstructed Catalan, consummately executed and wholly dependent on what's in season, from artichoke soup with cod mousse to venison cannelloni with black truffle sauce or pigeon risotto. The list of puddings, each accompanied by different suggestions for dessert wines, is a real highlight. La Selva Negra is a triumphant paean to current vogues – Black Forest gâteau presented as stacked slabs of chocolate cake next to swirls of cherry sorbet and vanilla cream foam. Very postmodern. Very good.

Eat, Drink, Shop

Menu glossary

Essential terminology

Catalan	Spanish	
una cullera	*una cuchara*	a spoon
una forquilla	*un tenedor*	a fork
un ganivet	*un cuchillo*	a knife
una ampolla de	*una botella de*	a bottle of
una altra	*otra*	another (one)
més	*más*	more
pa	*pan*	bread
oli d'oliva	*aceite de oliva*	olive oil
sal i pebre	*sal y pimienta*	salt and pepper
amanida	*ensalada*	salad
truita	*tortilla*	omelette

(note: **truita** can also mean trout)

la nota	*la cuenta*	the bill
un cendrer	*un cenicero*	an ashtray
vi negre/	*vino tinto/*	red/rosé/
rosat/blanc	*rosado/blanco*	white wine
bon profit	*aproveche*	Enjoy your meal
sóc	*soy*	I'm a
vegetarià/ana	*vegetariano/a*	vegetarian
diabètic/a	*diabético/a*	diabetic

Cooking terms

a la brasa	*a la brasa*	chargrilled
a la graella/	*a la plancha*	grilled on a hot
planxa		metal plate
a la romana	*a la romana*	fried in batter
al forn	*al horno*	baked
al vapor	*al vapor*	steamed
fregit	*frito*	fried
rostit	*asado*	roast
ben fet	*bien hecho*	well done
a punt	*medio hecho*	medium
poc fet	*poco hecho*	rare

Carn i aviram/Carne y aves/ Meat & poultry

ànec	*pato*	duck
bou	*buey*	beef
cabrit	*cabrito*	kid
conill	*conejo*	rabbit
embotits	*embotidos*	cold cuts
fetge	*higado*	liver
gall dindi	*pavo*	turkey
garrí	*cochinillo*	suckling pig
guatlla	*codorniz*	quail
llebre	*liebre*	hare
llengua	*lengua*	tongue
llom	*lomo*	loin (usu. pork)
oca	*oca*	goose
ous	*huevos*	eggs
perdiu	*perdiz*	partridge
pernil (serrà)	*jamón serrano*	dry-cured ham
pernil dolç	*jamón york*	cooked ham
peus de porc	*manos de cerdo*	pigs' trotters
pichón	*colomí*	pigeon
pintada	*gallina de Guinea*	Guinea fowl
pollastre	*pollo*	chicken
porc	*cerdo*	pork
porc senglar	*jabalí*	wild boar
vedella	*ternera*	veal
xai/be	*cordero*	lamb

Peix i marisc/Pescado y mariscos/Fish & seafood

anxoves	*anchoas*	anchovies
bacallà	*bacalao*	salt cod
besuc	*besugo*	sea bream
caballa	*verat*	mackerel
calamarsos	*calamares*	squid

International

Al Diwan

C/Valencia 218 (93 454 07 12). Metro Passeig de Gràcia. **Open** 1-4pm, 8.30pm-midnight Mon-Fri; 8.30pm-midnight Sat. Closed Aug. **Average** €€. **Credit** AmEx, DC, MC, V. **Map** p338 C4.
Unadulterated *Carry On Up The Lebanon* with a billowing tented ceiling, bright wool rugs on the walls, photos of bejewelled belly dancers, goatskins on the floor and seductive lighting. The all-day special menu is fantastic value at just under €15, as is the excellent mezze selection. For €7 the lunch menu brings forth yet more wonders of the Orient; tabbouleh or *warak arich* (stuffed vine leaves) to start,

then perhaps the *sabanegh* (beef with spinach, rice and pine nuts) or spiced chicken wings.

El Rodizio

C/Consell de Cent 403 (93 265 51 12). Metro Girona. **Open** 1-4pm, 8.30pm-midnight Mon-Thur; 1-4pm, 8.30pm-1am Fri, Sat; 1-4pm Sun. **Average** €. **Credit** MC, V. **Map** p339 E5.
Loosely based on a Brazilian *rodizio* (where huge skewers of meat are carved at your table until you beg them to stop), the only difference here is that you help yourself. Every sort of meat turns slowly under a grill; just point at what you want, then help yourself to the fantastic range of salads and vegetables, and even a huge pan of paella. Prices rose a fair bit in 2002, but remain low.

cloïsses	almejas	clams
cranc	cangrejo	crab
escamarlans	cigalas	crayfish
escopinyes	berberechos	cockles
espardenyes	espardeñas	sea cucumbers
gambes	gambas	prawns
llagosta	langosta	spiny lobster
llagostins	langostinos	langoustines
llamàntol	bogavante	lobster
llenguado	lenguado	sole
llobarro	lubina	sea bass
lluç	merluza	hake
moll	salmonete	red mullet
musclos	mejillones	mussels
navalles	navajas	razor clams
percebes	percebes	barnacles
pop	pulpo	octopus
rap	rape	monkfish
rèmol	rodaballo	turbot
salmó	salmón	salmon
sardines	sardinas	sardines
sípia	sepia	squid
tallarines	tallarinas	wedge clams
tonyina	atún	tuna
truita	trucha	trout

(note: **truita** can also mean an omelette)

Verdures/Legumbres/Vegetables

albergínia	berenjena	aubergine
all	ajo	garlic
alvocat	aguacate	avocado
bolets	setas	wild mushrooms
carbassós	calabacines	courgette
carxofes	alcahofas	artichokes
ceba	cebolla	onion
cigrons	garbanzos	chick peas
col	col	cabbage
enciam	lechuga	lettuce
endivies	endivias	chicory
espinacs	espinacas	spinach
mongetes blanques	judías blancas	haricot beans
mongetes verdes	judías verdes	French beans
pastanagues	zanahorias	carrot
patates	patatas	potatoes
pebrots	pimientos	peppers
pèsols	guisantes	peas
porros	puerros	leek
tomàquets	tomates	tomatoes
xampinyons	champiñones	mushrooms

Postres/Postres/Desserts

flam	flan	crème caramel
formatge	queso	cheese
gelat	helado	ice-cream
música	música	dried fruit and nuts, served with moscatell
pastís	pastel	cake
tarta	tarta	tart

Fruïta/Fruta/Fruit

figues	higos	figs
gerds	frambuesas	raspberries
maduixes	fresas	strawberries
pera	pera	pear
pinya	piña	pineapple
plàtan	plátano	banana
poma	manzana	apple
préssec	melocotón	peach
prunes	ciruelas	plums
raïm	uvas	grapes
taronja	naranja	orange

Eat, Drink, Shop

Thai Gardens

C/Diputació 273 (93 487 98 98). Metro Passeig de Gràcia. **Open** 1-4pm, 8pm-midnight daily. **Average** €€. **Credit** AmEx, DC, MC, V. **Map** p342 D5.

Trickling fountains, palms, lilies, triangular floor cushions and waitresses in national dress have all been successfully imported, but certain key ingredients have proved harder to track down; missing flavours are lemon-grass and galangal, and there are some incongruous substitutions (celery features highly). The food is otherwise pretty good, however, although local tastes are reflected in the mildness of most curries. For something a bit spicier, avoid the *degustación*, and pick the dishes with the heat warning signs from the à la carte.

Vegetarian

L'Atzavara

C/Muntaner 109 (93 454 59 25). Metro Diagonal or Hospital Clínic. **Open** 1-4pm Mon-Sat. Closed 3wks Aug. **Average** €. **Credit** AmEx, MC, V. **Map** p338 D4.

L'Atzavara can get absolutely jammed at lunchtime when a daily-changing three course menu (€7.80) offers staples (veggie burgers and mushroom stroganoff) as well as more interesting dishes like *estofado* (stew) *de seitan*. The place itself is pretty characterless, as though so much care has gone into the food that there's just no imagination left for the decoration. It's bright and barn-like and

A bread winner

International reporters looked on baffled at a recent anti-globalisation demonstration in Valencia, as protesters handed out slices of bread rubbed with ripe tomato and drizzled with olive oil. What coded call to arms was this? The Catalan red and gold flag, Quatre Barres, made vegetal? Or some kind of international soup kitchen, braced, like the Red Cross, to provide succour and sustenance to those fighting the good fight? No, this was *pa amb tomàquet*, bread with tomato, Catalonia's simplest and most emblematic of dishes, used as a reminder that local produce is the best produce, and that even the mighty emperors of fast-food stand no chance in a cultural battle.

In a recent book, Mallorcan resident Tomàs Graves, son of the poet Robert, tries to claw back some of the cultural identity of his island from the sunburned hordes of Northern Europeans with an entire tome on the subject. The title, *Volem pa amb oli*, means 'We want bread and oil' and refers to the cry that went up in their banned language from the hunger-striking Mallorcans imprisoned under Franco. This is not the only book on the topic; in 1984 Leopoldo Pomès published a (not entirely serious) work, entitled *The Theory and Practice of Bread With Tomato*.

The key, apparently, lies in the tomato. It has to be good, and it has to be ripe. Very ripe. Bread, too, can benefit from just the right amount of ageing – a day is about spot on. *Pa amb tomàquet* is good with anything, but especially ham, cheese or anchovies, and washed down with copious quantities of hearty red wine. A *llesqueria* is a place that specialises in such delights; *llesca* means 'slice', and if the bread is toasted, it becomes a '*torrada*'. Good *llesqueries* include **La Vinateria del Call** (*see p170*) and **Mercè Vins** (*see p137*) in the Barri Gòtic or **La Tinaja** (*see p176*) or **Pla de la Garsa** (*see p149*) in the Born. Restaurants that serve excellent *llesques* along with heartier *a la brasa* fare include **La Bodegueta** (C/Blai 47, 93 442 08 46) and **La Tomaquera** (*see p163*) in Poble Sec or **La Parra** (*see p163*) in Sants.

cheered only slightly by the chicken-wire decorations, blazing a lonely trail in lowly rustic chic.

Gràcia

Botafumeiro

C/Gran de Gràcia 81 (93 218 42 30/ www.botafumeiro.es). Metro Fontana. **Open** 1pm-1am daily. Closed 3wks Aug. **Average** €€€€. **Credit** AmEx, DC, MC, V. **Map** p338 D3.
Reports both ecstatic and negative fly in on this legendary seafood restaurant, but we found the service excellent and the shellfish divine. The efficiency of the operation is staggering, but is also Botafumeiro's least likeable aspect. Squadrons of waiters wear white jackets with gold nautical trim to match the gilt-edged decor, and every last metre of space put to good use adds to the impersonal experience. However, the juicy lobster and shellfish salad is superbly fresh, as are fish dishes such as baked sea bass smothered in onions, mushrooms, garlic and flat-leaf parsley, or sole in a delicious buttery cava sauce with langoustines.

La Cova d'en Vidalet

C/Torrent d'en Vidalet 22 (93 213 55 30). Metro Fontana or Joanic. **Open** 1.30-3.30pm Mon; 1.30-3.30pm, 9-11pm Tue-Thur; 9pm-midnight Fri, Sat. Closed 3wks Aug. **Average** €€. **Credit** MC, V. **Map** p339 E3.
A quiet, understated little place with lace curtains, pale yellow walls and a French air to its decor, its wonderful service and its rich food. Duck breast, foie gras and entrecôte loom large on the menu, alongside monkfish ragoût, hake en papillote, partridge and gourmet burgers with Roquefort sauce. The lunch menu is exceptionally good value at €6.60.

Envalira

Plaça del Sol 13 (93 218 58 13). Metro Fontana. **Open** 1.30-4pm, 9pm-midnight Tue-Sat; 1.30-5pm Sun. Closed Aug. **Average** €€. **Credit** AmEx, MC, V. **Map** p338 D3.
Envalira is no looker, with its Artex-coated walls, stone cladding painted brown, energy-saving lightbulbs, but there is a decent selection of Catalan, Basque and Galician favourites with fish cooked

Ot.

every which way, thick, tender steaks, game dishes and pile-'em-high salads. This is a good place, too, to try out traditional desserts – *crema catalana, tarta de Santiago, flan,* and so on – which, like everything else here, are own-made, delicious and keenly priced.

Jean Luc Figueras

C/Santa Teresa 10 (93 415 28 77). Metro Diagonal. **Open** 1.30-3.30pm, 8.30-11.30pm Mon-Fri; 8.30-11.30pm Sat. Closed 2wks Aug. **Average** €€€€. **Credit** AmEx, DC, MC, V. **Map** p338 D4.
Jean Luc Figueras' perfectly executed classics are rendered unforgettable through wonderful sauces and innovative combinations, such as roast guinea fowl with cardamom. The long *menú de degustación* is perfectly balanced, with highlights including a salad of partridge, black truffle and foie with Armagnac prunes, Laguiole fondue with bonito brochettes, or red mullet *escabeche* marinated with orange. Desserts, such as the parfait of peanuts and caramelised banana with milk chocolate sorbet, are sumptuous combinations of temperature and texture.

Laurak

C/Granada del Penedès 14-16 (93 218 71 65). FCG Gràcia. **Open** 1-4pm, 9-11.30pm Mon-Sat. **Average** €€€. **Credit** AmEx, DC, MC, V. **Map** p338 D3.
A sleek, ocean-liner-style cocktail bar opens out to a spacious and quiet dining room where Basque specialities such as black pudding from Besain, Idiazábal cheese, and imaginatively crafted combinations of duck foie gras with toffee-glazed banana, or red mullet with a sesame crust and black olive vinaigrette are gracefully served. The puddings are supremely luxurious, especially the pistachio biscuit with praline mousse and chocolate *crocante*.

Octubre

C/Julián Romea 18 (93 218 25 18). FCG Gràcia. **Open** 1.30-3.30pm, 9-11pm Mon-Fri; 9-11pm Sat. Closed Aug. **Average** €. **Credit** MC, V. **Map** p338 D3.
A tiny restaurant run by one man with devotion and resolve to offer seasonally changing Catalan dishes at very low prices. Thus sizzling *patates Eivissenques* (Ibizan potatoes) accompanied by clams, green peppers and *sobrassada* (Mallorcan spicy sausage), to start, or *amanida Carnestoltes* (Carnival salad), to follow with *frisée, botifarra, romesco* sauce and tortilla with haricot beans. To follow, you might get duck stew with red wine, cabbage and a tasty mushroom sauce, or tender sea bass on a bed of young garlic and onions.

Ot

C/Torres 25 (93 284 77 52). Metro Diagonal or Verdaguer. **Open** 2-4pm, 9-11pm Mon-Fri; 9-11pm Sat. Closed 3wks Aug. **Average** €€€€. **Credit** MC, V. **Map** p339 E3.
It's difficult to find food this good in such a fresh, relaxed atmosphere. There is no menu; waiters will recommend wine and bring a selection of dishes which might include prawn tempura with curry foam; tuna tataki wrapped in a gossamer-thin sheet of pineapple, or ravioli of smoked aubergine served with pancetta in a *turrón* 'soup'. Spectacular puddings sometimes include an improbably delicious thyme ice-cream with a balsamic vinegar reduction.

Roig Robí

C/Sèneca 20 (93 218 92 22). Metro Diagonal. **Open** 1.30-4pm, 9-11.30pm Mon-Fri; 9-11.30pm Sat. Closed 2wks Aug. **Average** €€€€. **Credit** AmEx, DC, MC, V. **Map** p338 D3.

Lots of seagrass matting and a little garden terrace are all very zen, except on quiet nights when patrolling waiters, constantly tweaking and watching, can be rather unsettling – like dining out under police escort. A short menu is wide in scope, with fish, meat, game and rice options. The speciality is the succulent prawns with crispy shredded leek, but duck breast with pistachio sauce is also excellent. Leave room for desserts: yoghurt with apple ice-cream and Calvados jelly is not to be missed.

International

Cantina Machito

C/Torrijos 47 (93 217 34 14). Metro Fontana or Joanic. **Open** 1-4pm, 7pm-1.30am daily. **Average** €. **Credit** MC, V. **Map** p339 E3.
With fabulous Margaritas and some of the most authentic Mexican food around, the colourful, family-run Cantina Machito serves great classics (*quesadillas, burritos* and so on), as well as *mole poblano* (shredded turkey breast smothered in a chilli mole sauce) and tender lamb *al pastor*, all accompanied by beans, salsas and salads. For dessert, the lime and tequila mousse is to die for.

Figaro

C/Ros de Olano 4 bis (93 237 43 53). Metro Fontana. **Open** 1.30-4pm, 8.30pm-1am Mon, Wed-Fri; 1.30-4pm Tue; 8.30pm-1am Sat, Sun. **Average** €. **Credit** MC, V. **Map** p338 D3.
This popular 'spaghetteria' serves simple, elegant Italian meals in an intimate setting. The lunchtime *menú del dia* (€8.50) offers authentic pastas, salads and carpaccios. At night the menu opens with salads combining such delicious ingredients as rocket and provolone, or pear and parmesan. Popular spaghetti sauces include puttanesca or just plain old ragu, while the carpaccios, either veal or salmon, are favourites with the steady stream of groovy locals. Panna cotta or superb platters of Italian cheeses provide the perfect finale.

La Gavina

C/Ros de Olano 17 (93 415 74 50). Metro Fontana. **Open** 1pm-2am Tue-Sun. **Average** €. **No credit cards. Map** p338 D3.
The perfect place for a speedy, substantial pizza fix at any time of day. A very popular local joint with tiny, tightly packed tables, and angels on the ceilings and walls, along with an unusual mix of matadors' outfits, guns and a truly enormous nut. Served on wooden platters, the crispy pizzas range from a plainish tomato and mozzarella, through to *pulpo* (octopus) or the Hawaiian, with ham, pineapple, prawns and caviar.

Lahore

C/Torrent de l'Olla 159 (93 218 95 11). Metro Fontana. **Open** 8pm-midnight Mon; noon-4pm, 8pm-midnight Tue-Sun. **Average** €. **Credit** MC, V. **Map** p338 D3.

No red flock wallpaper, no tapestries of maharajahs in compromising positions with doe-eyed lovelies, no sitar soundtrack; instead, grey tiling and formica, and a fabulously obliging Pakistani family who will rustle up anything you fancy whether it's on the menu or not. The offer is made redundant by the range of dansak, bhuna, mughlai, korma, biriani and tandoori dishes, alongside a few lesser-known treats.

SoNaMu

Passatge Josep Llovera 11 (93 209 65 83). FCG Muntaner. **Open** 1.30-3.30pm, 8.30-11.30pm Mon-Fri; 8.30-11.30pm Sat. Closed 1wk Aug. **Average** €. **Credit** DC, MC, V. **Map** p338 C3.
SoNaMu offers Korean and Japanese specialities of consistently good quality. The *dolsot* is a searingly hot stone bowl filled with rice, meat and vegetables; there are also different kinds of sushi and a selection of Korean-style barbecued meat. If you want a quick, healthy lunch, try one of the bento boxes: each contains four or five treats, such as steamed *gyoza* dumplings, a stack of vegetable and prawn tempura, sushi, sashimi, wasabi, and seaweed and noodle salad.

Vegetarian

L'Illa de Gràcia

C/Sant Domènec 19 (93 238 02 29). Metro Diagonal. **Open** 1-4pm, 9pm-midnight Tue-Fri; 2-4pm, 9pm-midnight Sat, Sun. Closed 2wks Aug. **Average** €. **Credit** DC, MC, V. **Map** p338 D3.
The minimalist decor, dark wooden slab tables and exposed brick walls make L'Illa de Gràcia one of the few vegetarian restaurants in Barcelona to make any concession to style or ambience. The extensive menu features no fewer than 14 different salads as well as dishes such as pan-fried tofu with alfalfa and wild rice, plus several filled crêpes and home-made cakes.

Barceloneta & the Ports

Agua

Passeig Marítim 30 (93 225 12 72). Metro Barceloneta. **Open** 1.30-4pm, 8.30pm-midnight Mon-Thur; 1.30-4pm, 8.30pm-1am Fri; 1.30-5pm, 8.30pm-1am Sat; 1.30-5pm, 8.30pm-midnight Sun. **Average** €€. **Credit** AmEx, MC, V. **Map** p343 F7.
The relaxed and sunny interior, good food reasonably priced, and large terrace on the beach, all mean one thing: book ahead. There are colourful prints on the walls, squidgy sofas and newspapers to amuse you while you wait amid a young and informal crowd. The menu rarely changes (if it ain't broke…); specialities include grilled turbot with noodles cut from squid, a thick steak with red wine gravy, salmon tartare with leeks, and scrummy puddings like marron glacé mousse and apricot crumble.

Can Majó

C/Almirall Aixada 23 (93 221 54 55/93 221 58 18). Metro Barceloneta. **Open** 1-4pm, 8-11.30pm Tue-Sat; 1-4pm Sun. **Average** €€. **Credit** AmEx, DC, MC, V. **Map** p342 D7.

Eat, Drink, Shop

Catalan cuisine

Many dishes apparently from other cuisines – risotto, *canelons*, *raviolis* – are as entrenched in the Catalan culinary tradition as their own. Two names borrowed from the French, which frequently appear on Catalan menus, are *foie* (as opposed to *fetge/higado* or foie gras), which has come to mean hare, duck or goose liver prepared with liqueur, salt and sugar.

a la llauna literally, 'in the tin' – baked on a metal tray with garlic, tomato, paprika and wine

all i oli garlic crushed with olive oil to form a mayonnaise-like texture, similar to aïoli

amanida catalana/*ensalada catalana* mixed salad with a selection of cold meats

arròs negre/*arroz negro* 'black rice', seafood rice cooked in squid ink

botifarra/*butifarra* Catalan sausage: variants include *botifarra negre* (blood sausage) and *blanca* (mixed with egg)

botifarra amb mongetes/*butifarra con judías* sausage with haricot beans

calçots a variety of large spring onion, available only from December to spring, and eaten char-grilled, with *romesco* sauce

carn d'olla traditional Christmas dish of various meats stewed with *escudella*

conill amb cargols/*conejo con caracoles* rabbit with snails

crema catalana custard dessert with burnt sugar topping, similar to crème brûlée

escalivada/*escalibada* grilled and peeled peppers, onions and aubergine

escudella winter stew of meat and vegetables

espinacs a la catalana/*espinacas a la catalana* spinach fried in olive oil with garlic, raisins and pine nuts

esqueixada summer salad of marinated salt cod with onions, olives and tomato

fideuà/*fideuá* paella made with vermicelli instead of rice

mar i muntanya a combination of meat and seafood in the same dish

mel i mató curd cheese with honey

pa amb tomàquet/*pan con tomate* bread prepared with tomato, oil and salt

picada a mix of nuts, garlic, parsley, bread, chicken liver and little chilli peppers, which is often used to enrich and thicken dishes

romesco a spicy sauce from the coast south of Barcelona, made with crushed almonds and hazelnuts, tomatoes, oil and a special type of red pepper (*nyora*)

samfaina a mix of onion, garlic, aubergine and red and green peppers (similar to ratatouille), often accompanies grilled meat and fish.

sarsuela/*zarzuela* fish and seafood stew

sípia amb mandonguilles/*sepia con albóndigas* cuttlefish with meatballs

suquet de peix/*suquet de pescado* fish and potato soup

torrades/*tostadas* toasted *pa amb tomàquet*

xató salad containing tuna, anchovies and cod, with a romesco-type sauce

Eat, Drink, Shop

Can Majó avoids the nautical trappings so beloved of seafood places the world 'round, with a smart, clean feel and cream and green walls. Start by sharing a 'pica-pica' plate of shellfish, then move on to one of the excellent paellas or *fideuàs*. Fish is also expertly prepared; cod comes with clams and *salsa verde* (made with garlic and parsley) and the *suquet* is a triumph; a sizzling panful of monkfish, hake, mussels, clams, prawns and potatoes. The service, at worst, is endearingly forgetful.

Can Maño

C/Baluard 12 (93 319 30 82). Metro Barceloneta.
Open 8am-11am, noon-4pm, 8pm-midnight Mon-Fri; 8am-4pm Sat. **Average** €. **No credit cards.**
Map p343 E7.
Strip lighting, tiny formica tables, uncomfortable chairs and yet still there's a queue. The seafood is what draws them in: superbly fresh and at knock-down prices. The friendly waiters reel off the daily specials at lightning speed, but you can't go wrong with the fat, succulent prawns cooked in garlic, or the soft, creamy squid with parsley. In the mornings you can also get mammoth truckers' breakfasts.

Can Solé

C/Sant Carles 4 (93 221 50 12). Metro Barceloneta.
Open 1.30-4pm, 8-11pm Tue-Sat; 1.30-4pm Sun.
Closed 2wks Aug. **Average** €€€. **Credit** AmEx, DC, MC, V. **Map** p343 E7.
Paellas and *fideuàs* are the main event in this elegant century-old seafood restaurant, but are joined by a host of other delights such as monkfish soup, lobster stew, tiny wild octopuses, Palamòs prawns, the freshest fish, and every crustacean served to the peak of perfection. The sea-blue walls heave with awards, photos and mementos of regular customers (including Joan Miró and Santiago Rusiñol) while the bustle of the open kitchen adds to Can Solé's friendly atmosphere.

Ruccula

World Trade Center, Moll de Barcelona (93 508 82 68). Metro Drassanes. **Open** 1.30-4pm, 8.30pm-midnight Mon-Sat; 1-4pm Sun. **Average** €€.
Credit AmEx, DC, MC, V. **Map** p342 C7.
Ruccula's situation in the WTC affords it great views over the port, but its stark brown and grey decor and largely business clientele make for rather staid surroundings and give no hint at the delights about to emerge from the kitchen – a huge, creamy portion of *besugo* (sea bream) with wedge clams and peppercorns and a rich, flavoursome monkfish and potato *suquet* to name but two. Rice dishes, too, are excellent – try partridge and artichoke risotto, but leave room for the elaborate desserts.

Set Portes

Passeig d'Isabel II 14 (93 319 30 33/93 319 29 50/www.7puertas.com). Metro Barceloneta.
Open 1pm-1am daily. **Average** €€.
Credit AmEx, DC, MC, V. **Map** p345 C4.
Without doubt, this is the city's most famous temple to the paella, and there is always a queue of

hungry pilgrims outside. Despite its popularity, Set Portes has managed to maintain the quality of its seafood and rice dishes, although the vastness of the place can be offputting – as can the house pianist playing *Three Times a Lady* on the baby grand.

Suquet de l'Almirall

Passeig Joan de Borbó 65 (93 221 62 33). Metro Barceloneta. **Open** 1-4pm, 9-11pm Tue-Sat; 1-4pm Sun. **Average** €€. **Credit** MC, V. **Map** p342 D7.
There is a pretty terrace but it's almost a shame to miss the cosy ochre interior decorated with aquarelles of wonderfully po-faced fish. The best way to eat here is to try one of the set menus, which include a seven-course sampler, the 'blind menu' of seven tapas and a rice dish, or the light *pica-pica* with tomato *coca* bread, red pepper *escalivada* with anchovies, battered cod croquettes, fried fish, a huge bowl of steamed shellfish, rock-salted king prawns, and a knockout *fideuà* with lobster.

Torre de Altamar

Passeig Joan de Borbó 88 (93 221 0007). Metro Barceloneta. **Open** 8.30-11.30pm Mon; 1-3.30pm, 8.30-11.30pm Tue-Sat. **Average** €€€€. **Credit** AmEx, MC, V. **Map** p342 D7.
Spiked on the top of the cablecar tower, at the top of a dizzying 75-metre lift ride, this wildly fashionable restaurant has spectacular views and assimilates all that is currently hip (Shanghai Lil and Twiggy do *Blade Runner*) but the steeply priced food – a fairly limited selection of fish and seafood – is less impressive. The average customer, a mobile-wielding uptowner, notices neither that the food could be better nor that the view could not.

Xiringuitó Escribà

Litoral Mar 42, Platja Bogatell, (93 221 07 29). Metro Ciutadella-Vila Olímpica. **Open** *June-Sept* 1-4.30pm, 9-11pm daily; *Oct-Mar* 1-4.30pm Tue-Sun. **Average** €€€. **Credit** MC, V.
Smack on the beach and with excellent food, this would be heaven but for the unpredictable service. The specialities are rice dishes and *fideuà*, with wonderful starters: a warm salad with tender partridge *escabeche*, for example, or young artichokes with scallops and baby broad beans. The desserts are spectacular if you have the patience of Job.

International

Bestial

C/Ramón Trias Fargas 2-4 (93 224 04 07). Metro Barceloneta. **Open** 1.30-4pm Mon; 1.30-4pm, 8.30-midnight Tue-Thur; 1.30-5pm, 8.30pm-1am Fri, Sat. **Average** €€. **Credit** AmEx, MC, V. **Map** p343 F7.
A sleek new addition from the Tragaluz people (*see p153*), sitting under Frank Gehry's glittering giant fish. The architecture is something to behold; the planes of its low, stark structure extend seamlessly to a tiered wooden terrace on the beach, like a Le Corbusier holiday home. The food is top-of-the-range Italian: tuna with black olive risotto; rocket

Eat, Drink, Shop

Gaig. *See p163*.

salad with Parma ham and a poached egg, and fabulous fresh pasta dishes. Leave room for own-made tiramisu or *sorbete de limoncello*.

dZI

Passeig de Joan de Borbó 76 (93 221 21 82).
Metro Barceloneta. **Open** 1-4pm, 8pm-midnight
daily. **Average** €€. **Credit** AmEx, DC, MC,
V. **Map** p345 C4.

A refreshing change from all the seafood restaurants hereabouts, dZI has food from all over Asia, with Mongolian and Tibetan dishes as well as the usual Chinese and Japanese, all rendered rather prosaically in English on the menu. Try the chicken with black mushrooms, water chestnuts and rice baked in a banana leaf, the green curry soup or the spicy tiger prawns. Waiters are unerringly polite, and the shady terrace has a great view of the port.

Poble Sec & Sants

Elche

C/Vilà i Vilà 71 (93 441 30 89). Metro Paral.lel.
Open 1-4.30pm, 8pm-midnight Mon-Thur;
1-4.30pm, 8pm-12.30am Fri; 1pm-12.30am Sat;
1pm-midnight Sun. **Average** €€. **Credit** AmEx,
MC, V. **Map** p342 C6.

A family-run paella restaurant where wonderfully friendly management contrasts with a baffling ineptitude on the part of the waiting staff. A pity, really, for the starters (which can be had in half-portions) are delectable. The paellas, *fideuàs* and rice broths are among the best in the city. The split-level restaurant is slightly lacking in character, and the piped-in music doesn't really help.
Branch: L'Elche al Moll, Maremàgnum, Moll d'Espanya, Port Vell (93 225 81 17).

La Parra

C/Joanot Martorell 3 (93 332 51 34). Metro
Hostafrancs. **Open** 8.30pm-midnight Tue-Fri;
2-4.30pm, 8.30pm-midnight Sat; 2-4.30pm Sun.
Closed Aug. **Average** €€. **Credit** MC, V.
Map p341 A4.

This 19th-century coaching inn now houses one of the city's best restaurants for Catalan *a la brasa* cooking. Boulders of meat, still spitting from the fierce wood-fired grill, are served on slabs of wood and accompanied by ferociously strong *all i oli*. Lamb (actually mutton, and none the worse for it) is served alongside goat, horse, beef and rabbit, but the tastiest dish might just be the succulent *galtes* (pig's cheeks). The cosy and traditionally decorated interior is the perfect place to be on a cold winter's night, while in summer the eponymous vine provides cool shade on the peaceful terrace.

La Tomaquera

C/Margarit 58 (no phone). Metro Poble Sec.
Open 1.30-3.45pm, 8.30-10.45pm Tue-Sat. Closed
Aug. **Average** €. **No credit cards. Map** 341 E6.

A world of red gingham and bright lighting, where staff will bark instructions at you, many of which are reproduced on the walls. There is no booking

and no telephone, there is only house wine, there is only *a la brasa* meat – and if you don't like it, you can go elsewhere. *Barcelonins* obviously do like it, for they come in droves to tuck into huge portions of perfectly cooked meat served with weapons-grade *all i oli*.

International

Il Golfo di Napoli

C/Lleida 38 (93 423 53 83). Metro Plaça Espanya
or Poble Sec. **Open** 1-4pm, 8pm-midnight Mon-Sat.
Credit AmEx, DC, MC, V. **Map** p341 B5.

Once you're past the mournful lobster peering through brackish water in the window and your eyes have adapted to the bright lighting things start to improve dramatically. Run by a family of Neapolitans, Il Golfo di Napoli offers some of the most authentic Italian food around, with fabulous own-made pasta, great crispy pizzas and a range of antipasti which would make meals in themselves.

Horta & Poblenou

Gaig

Passeig Maragall 402 (93 429 10 17). Metro
Horta. **Open** 1.30-4pm, 9-11pm Tue-Sat; 1.30-
4pm Sun. Closed 3wks Aug. **Average** €€€€.
Credit AmEx, DC, MC, V.

Carles Gaig, to whose family this restaurant has belonged for 130 years, believes that more than three elements on a plate is too much. But, oh, what elements! From the crayfish tempura *amuse-gueule*, served with a dip of creamed leek salted with a piece of pancetta, through to a shotglass holding layers of tangy lemon syrup, crema catalana mousse, caramel ice-cream and topped with burnt sugar (to be eaten by plunging the spoon all the way down), every dish is as surprising and perfectly composed as the last.

Els Pescadors

Plaça Prim 1 (93 225 20 18). Metro Poblenou.
Open 1-3.45pm, 8pm-midnight daily. **Average**
€€€. **Credit** AmEx, DC, MC, V.

Els Pescadors encapsulates the best of modern and traditional Barcelona; one dining room is beautifully old-fashioned, with marble-topped tables, wooden chairs and dressers decked with spirits; the other is sharp-edged, red and steely grey. The dichotomy is reflected in the food, where the emphasis is on superbly fresh, locally caught fish, prepared using age-old methods, and given the occasional twist.

Zona Alta

La Balsa

C/Infanta Isabel 4 (93 211 50 48). FCG Av Tibidabo.
Open 9-11.30pm Mon; 2-3.30pm, 9-11.30pm Tue-Sat.
Average €€€. **Credit** AmEx, MC, V.

The location among the mansions of high society; the sniffy parking attendant, the award-winning

Eat, Drink, Shop

building amid lush gardens ablaze with geraniums: all of this might lead you to expect fancy forkfuls of minimal food. Not so. The menu, like the restaurant, has a country feel to it, and is more likely to feature enormous portions of Catalan classics than itsy-bitsy polenta bites. On cold winter nights, a log fire crackles, while in summer nowhere is as pretty as the verdant, jasmine-scented terrace.

Neichel

C/Beltrán i Rózpide 1-5 bis (93 203 84 08). Metro Maria Cristina. **Open** 1-3.30pm, 8.30-11.30pm Tue-Sat. Closed Aug. **Average** €€€€. **Credit** AmEx, DC, MC, V.
A superb restaurant very slightly let down by slow service and an overformal air. An extensive menu features velvety, divine prawns with wild mushrooms; delicious spoonfuls of lobster and prawn tartar in a blaze of marine and vegetable life, including baby eels and asparagus, and venison with rhubarb and fruits of the forest. Servings are generous, so take care if you want to make the most of the fantastic cheese and dessert trolleys.

La Venta

Plaça Doctor Andreu 1 (93 212 64 55). FCG Avda Tibidabo, then Tramvia Blau. **Open** 1.30-3.15pm, 9-11.15pm Mon-Sat. **Average** €€€. **Credit** AmEx, DC, MC, V.
The rambling building, set high above the city in the square below the Tibidabo cable car, has out-door terraces and a glassed-in conservatory that create an airy, out-of-the-city feel. Starters include delicacies such as *erizos de mar gratinados* (sea urchins au gratin) or baby broad bean and fresh mozzarella salad. Steaks and rack of lamb are specialities, or there is delicate monkfish wrapped in filo pastry with pesto and tomato coulis.

Vivanda

C/Major de Sarrià 134 (93 205 47 17). Metro FCG Reina Elisenda. **Open** 9-11.30pm Mon; 1-3.30pm, 9-11.30pm Tue-Sat. **Average** €€. **Credit** DC, MC, V. **Map** 337 B1.
Starters include fish soup, shellfish salads and seasonal vegetables, while the main courses featured are grilled monkfish, hake or tuna with light, creative sauces, and a couple of foie options. The reliable approach is followed through in Catalan standards like *botifarra*, veal and duck, as well as the seasonal game. There is also an excellent value set lunch at €11.25.

International

Ken

C/Benet i Mateu 53 (93 203 20 44). FGC Les Tres Torres. **Open** 1.30-4pm, 8.30pm-midnight Tue-Sun. Closed Aug. **Average** €€. **Credit** MC, V. **Map** 337 B2.
Book a seat at the counter for a show of culinary theatre in this Japanese restaurant specialising in *a la plancha*. The *planchas* in question are two wide griddles which become the stage for a performance of frying, tossing, chopping, teasing and effortless artistry. Aside from the usual Japanese dishes, the speciality is seafood; clams, scallops, langoustines and squid. For the undecided, there are three set menus comprising fish, meat and noodle dishes.

Out of town

El Bulli

Cala Montjoi (972 15 04 57/www.elbulli.com). By car A7 or N11 north (7km/4.5 miles from Roses)/by train RENFE from Sants or Passeig de Gràcia to Figueres, then bus to Roses, then taxi. **Open** Apr-June 8-10pm Wed-Sun. June-Sept 8-10pm daily. Closed Oct-Mar. **Average** €€€. **Credit** AmEx, DC, MC, V.
A couple of hours' drive north of Barcelona, but nevertheless worth a mention as one of the most talked-about restaurants in the world. Head chef and *patron*, Ferran Adrià, has created a legendary tasting menu, with up to 35 dishes; each a wispy mouthful of exquisite delight. He is never one to sit still, but among those miniature treats that have hovered around the menu for a couple of seasons is Kellogg's Paella; where toasted grains of impossibly light rice are served with a tiny jug of liquid to be poured over them for an extraordinary transformation of taste (and, it goes without saying, a snap, crackle and pop). Expect to pay around €125 a head without wine, but prepare to be blown away.

La Balsa. *See p163.*

Cafés & Bars

From taking tea to dancing with the green fairy.

Though not yet scientifically proven, there is a substantial body of evidence to suggest that the narrower the street, the more interesting the bar. With one or two notable exceptions, such as **Schilling** (*see p169*) or **Cafè de l'Opera** (*see p167*), most bars and cafés along well-trodden tourist thoroughfares will belong to the corporate monsters with decor and prices set by a head office in Zurich. A little exploring off the beaten track brings untold rewards in the shape of ancient taverns, sharp-edged designer bars and an awful lot of quirky, recycled chic.

Many visitors to the city are disappointed by the lack of tapas bars. Catalonia doesn't really do tapas in the way that other regions of Spain do, although there are are lot of Basque bars bedecked with platters of *pintxos*; small pieces of bread topped with some ingenious culinary combination. The trays are generally brought out at particular times, often around 1pm and again at 8pm. *Pintxos* come impaled with toothpicks – keep these on your plate, so that the barman knows how many you had.

What tapas bars there are can be quite intimidating unless you know exactly what you want. Don't be afraid to seek guidance, but some of the more standard offerings will include *tortilla* (potato omelette), *patatas bravas* (fried potatoes in a spicy red sauce and garlic mayonnaise), *ensaladilla* (Russian salad), small pork skewers (*pinchos morunos*), prawns and garlic (*gambas al ajillo*), mussels in a tomato and onion sauce (*mejillones a la marinera*), squid fried in batter (*chocos*), steamed clams with garlic and parsley (*almejas al vapor*), octopus (*pulpo*) and little green peppers (*pimientos del padrón*), which are good to share with friends since they constitute a kind of culinary Russian roulette – not all are hot, but one or two have a vicious bite.

RULES OF THE GAME

Except in very busy bars, or when sitting outside, you won't usually be required to pay until you leave. If you have trouble attracting a waiter's attention, a loud but polite '*oiga*' or, in Catalan, '*escolti*', is perfectly acceptable. Tipping is not obligatory, but it's customary to leave a few coins if you've been served at a table. On the vexed question of throwing detritus on the floor (cigarette ends, paper napkins, olive pits and so on), it's safest to keep an eye on what the locals are doing.

Barri Gòtic

Arc Café

C/Carabassa 19 (93 302 52 04). Metro Jaume I.
Open 9am-1am Mon-Thur; 9am-3am Fri; 11am-3am Sat; 11am-1am Sun. **Credit** MC, V. **Map** p345 B4
With plenty of newspapers to flick through and floor-to-ceiling windows, this is a great place for breakfast (options run from muesli to fry-ups). From 1pm onwards, these are supplanted by a reasonable selection of Mediterranean dishes and the odd special; a Thai curry or lamb with couscous. The café has also become a nerve centre for the locals' campaign to save its historic street from the evil developers.

L'Ascensor

C/Bellafila 3 (93 318 53 47). Metro Jaume I. **Open** 6.30pm-2.30am Mon-Thur, Sun; 6.30pm-3am Fri, Sat. **No credit cards**. **Map** p345 B3.
Enter through the eponymous mahogany lift with its original sliding doors and bevelled glass, into this low-ceilinged den. The gently quaint decor (gilt lamps, marble tables with wicker chairs and lots of dark wood) is redolent of *fin-de-siècle* Paris, but the funky sounds and fortifying Mojitos and Caipirinhas drag it, rather confused, into the 21st century.

The best Cocktails

Barcelona Rouge
Absinthe goes into the mix for a night you won't forget (*see p255*).

Boadas
The original and best (*see p171*).

Dry Martini
Watch what these boys can do with a twist of lemon (*see p179*).

Flash Flash
Cocktails don't come any more retro (*see p179*).

Ginger
Stylish, relaxed and unfailingly friendly (*see p169*).

Stinger
Your mother would like it and, weirdly, so would your teenage brother (*see p179*).

The Bagel Shop

C/Canuda 25 (93 302 41 61). Metro Catalunya.
Open 9.30am-9.30pm Mon-Sat; 11am-4pm Sun.
No credit cards. Map p344 B2.
A cramped but jolly little joint, with a useful spread of bagels, cakes and more to eat in or take away. The Sunday brunch menu is hugely popular with the local expat community: eggs and bagels; bacon and bagels; pancakes and maple syrup and bagels… you get the picture.

Bar Celta

C/Mercè 16 (93 315 00 06). Metro Drassanes.
Open noon-midnight Mon-Sat. **Credit** MC, V.
Map p345 B4.
No messing but plenty of mess (a mixture of screwed-up napkins, toothpicks and olive stones) make for a surprisingly enjoyable tapas bar. Huge platters laden with good – and inexpensive – seafood glow under fluorescent lighting along the counter, where fishermen rub shoulders with the more intrepid tourists.

Bar del Pi

Plaça Sant Josep Oriol 1 (93 302 21 23). Metro Liceu. **Open** 9am-11pm Mon, Wed-Sat; 10am-10pm Sun. **Credit** MC, V. **Map** p344 A2.
These must be the most coveted terrace tables in Barcelona, in a picturesque square in the heart of the Barri Gòtic labyrinth. Inside, space is cramped, but there is still room for the old piano at the back to help foster the friendly atmosphere. Tapas are basic but good, and there are decent own-made cakes.

Bar Pinotxo

La Boqueria 66-67, La Rambla 91 (93 317 17 31).
Metro Liceu. **Open** 6am-4pm Mon-Sat. **No credit cards. Map** 344 A2.
Using the freshest of market produce (seriously – you want it, they go buy it), Pinotxo produces deceptively classy dishes from a spit 'n' sawdust market bar. Hover for a seat, then put your lunch in their hands; there's no menu but the day's dishes are invariably excellent, and might include duck magret with figs or a sumptuous tuna stew.

Dens of yore

Barcelona's tradition of political resistance runs deep. From the peasant uprisings in 1640 to the modern anti-globalisation movements, *barcelonins* have always had a zeal for plotting and denouncing their oppressors, and, as anyone who has attended so much as a union meeting knows, it can be thirsty work. Barcelona retains a fair few taverns that gave liquid courage and nourishment to various revolutionaries over the last century. They tend to be the oldest and most atmospheric bars in town, meaning a visit is not only for the political of heart.

On the bottom floor of Puig i Cadafalch's stunning neo-Gothic Casa Martí, **Els Quatre Gats** (*pictured, and see p169*) was the cradle of early 1900s artistic powerhouses like Pablo Picasso, Ramon Casas and Santiago Rusiñol. Picasso was only a teenager when he frequented the bar, but would later become the most revolutionary figure in modern art and a political radical with his anti-fascist masterpiece, *Guernica*. At around the same time, the famous Modernista haunt **London**

Bar (*see p252*) started as a hangout for cabaret singers and lion-tamers from the circus, but changed dramatically in the late 1960s and '70s, when its back room filled with bohemians and radical student thinkers of the Catalan independence gatherings typical during the wane of Franco's dictatorship.

Nearby is the legendary **Marsella** (*see p252*), which opened its doors in 1820 and has long been serving absinthe to factory workers, prostitutes and literati alike. When anarchism achieved its most widespread support in the 1930s, the Raval was its seat, and the Marsella was a favourite destination after nearby meetings at the largest anarchist club in town, the **Agrupación Faros** at Avda Mistral 17. Meanwhile, the favoured Barri Gòtic haunt was the bar **El Túnel** (C/Ample 33, 93 315 2759), an old tavern that was home to many an anti-Franco conspirator during the last century. When the bar was raided, as it frequently was, the customers would escape through the celebrated passageway to C/Gignàs.

Bilbao-Berria

Plaça Nova 3 (93 317 0124). Metro Jaume I.
Open 9am-midnight daily. **Credit** AmEx, MC,
V. **Map** p344 B2.
With tables outside overlooking the cathedral
square, this is a useful meeting point. Choose from
the dozens of fresh and colourful *pintxos* lining the
counter, or order a *cazuelito* – a small earthenware
dish – of one of the delicacies (usually seafood) on
display at the end of the bar. The excellent restaurant downstairs specialises in Basque favourites.

Bliss

Plaça Sant Just 4 (93 268 10 22). Metro Jaume I.
Open 11am-midnight Mon-Fri; 2pm-midnight Sat;
5-10pm Sun. *June-Aug* 11am-midnight Mon-Fri;
2pm-midnight Sat. **Credit** MC, V. **Map** p345 B3.
Bliss has three spaces: one for lunch; another for
lounging on animal-print sofas leafing through the
selection of magazines and finally tables outside on
the tiny Plaça Sant Just. There's a reasonable *menú
del día* at lunchtime, while filled baguettes, 'pizze-
tas', cakes and brownies are available all day.

El Bosc de les Fades

*Passatge de la Banca (93 317 26 49). Metro
Drassanes.* **Open** 10.30am-1.30am Mon-Thur,
Sun; 10.30am-2.30am Fri, Sat. **No credit cards.**
Map p345 A4.
The 'fairies' forest' requires a very particular mood.
As you grope in the semi-darkness you might
chance upon a pointy-eared elf (an escapee from the
nearby wax museum) kneeling in silent prayer at a
waterfall. Or perhaps you'd care to sup in the castle
kitchen, complete with inglenook and hanging caul-
dron. A very surreal drinking experience.

Café La Cereria

*Baixada de Sant Miquel 3-5 (93 301 85 10).
Metro Liceu.* **Open** 9.30am-11.30pm Mon-Sat.
No credit cards. **Map** p345 B3.
Expect creative, healthy sandwiches, milkshakes,
fresh juices, a long list of herbal teas and *mate* in
this friendly and buzzing café. It's run as a co-operative and many of the waiters are co-owners. There
are tables outside in the covered Passatge Crèdit.

Cafè d'Estiu

*Museu Frederic Marès, Plaça Sant Iu 5 (93 310 30
14). Metro Jaume I.* **Open** *Apr-Sept* 10am-10pm Tue-
Sun. Closed Oct-Mar. **Credit** MC, V. **Map** p345 B3.
The tables of the Museu Marès' café sit outdoors in
a quiet Gothic courtyard next to a fishpond and in
the shadows of ancient orange trees. On offer is a
selection of drinks and light snacks, but only in summer – as its name, 'summer café', indicates.

Café de l'Opera

*La Rambla 74 (93 317 75 85/93 302 41 80). Metro
Liceu.* **Open** 8am-2.15am Mon-Thur, Sun; 8am-
2.45am Fri, Sat. **No credit cards.** **Map** p345 B3.
A Rambla institution, where *fin-de-siècle* opera goers
from the Liceu over the road used to head to discuss
the show. With two salons upstairs and many of its

Ginger. *See p169.*

original fittings, it's still an elegant place for breakfast or an early evening drink, with a short list of
tapas and a long list of beers.

Café Zurich

Plaça Catalunya 1 (93 317 91 53). Metro Catalunya.
Open *May-Oct* 8am-1am Mon-Fri; 10am-1am Sat,
Sun. *Nov-Apr* 8am-11pm Mon-Fri; 8am-midnight Sat,
Sun. **No credit cards.** **Map** p344 B1.
The original and much-loved Zurich was torn down
to make way for the El Triangle shopping centre.
This, its modern-day incarnation, is decorated with
generic, old-style fittings. Unsurprisingly, it misses
the mark somewhat, but still enjoys a sunny, sprawl-
ing terrace on which to while away an afternoon.

Casa de Molinero

C/Mercè 13 (93 310 33 83). Metro Drassanes. **Open**
6pm-2am daily. **No credit cards.** **Map** p345 B4.
Worlds apart from the slickly designed bars that pepper the city, this old-style tapas bar is brightly lit, with
whitewashed walls and rustic decor. Along with the
others on this street, it presents an unreconstructed
and very Spanish face. Enjoy chorizo *al diablo* (set
alight in alcohol) and the opaque alcoholic concoction
known as *leche de pantera* ('panther's milk').

Círculo Maldá

C/Pi 5 (93 412 43 86). Metro Liceu. **Open** 7pm-1am
Tue-Thur; 7pm-2am Fri, Sat; 6pm-midnight Sun.
No credit cards. **Map** p344 B2.
Hidden upstairs next to the cinema in the 17th-cen-
tury Maldá palace is this elegant bar, where the tall
ceilings, baroque furniture and chequered floor tiles
of the former drawing room whisk you to another
era. One of the current Maldás, a musician, now runs
the bar and occasionally performs with musical
friends. On other nights the playlist includes Tom
Waits, Van Morrison and other mellow favourites.

Ginger

C/Palma de Sant Just 1 (93 310 53 09). Metro Jaume I. **Open** 7pm-3am Tue-Sat. Closed 2wks Aug. **Credit** AmEx, V. **Map** p345 B3

A new and happy amalgam of cocktail and tapas bar, where you can sink into lemon-coloured leather sofas to chat in quiet corners, or perch daintily at one of the art deco bars. Within weeks of opening, Ginger had a loyal following for its sophisticated selection of wines and food (try the wild mushroom filo or the apple tartlet with foie gras) and its unstuffy vibe.

Glaciar

Plaça Reial 3 (93 302 11 63). Metro Liceu. **Open** 4pm-2.15am Mon-Sat; 9am-2.15am Sun. **No credit cards. Map** p345 A3.

Inside, the high ceilings and old dark wood provide the sort of ambience that resists the vagaries of fashion, but Glaciar's real selling point (and it sure ain't the loos) is its terrace on the Plaça Reial. Locals and resident foreigners still congregate here in time-honoured fashion, to people-watch and meet friends.

La Granja

C/Banys Nous 4 (93 302 69 75). Metro Liceu. **Open** 9.30am-2pm, 5-9.30pm Mon-Sat; 5-10pm Sun. Closed 3wks Aug/Sept. **No credit cards. Map** p345 B3.

An old-fashioned café filled with yellowing photos and antiques and with its very own section of Roman wall. The tarry-thick hot chocolate and especially the *suís*, topped with whipped cream, will be too much for unaccustomed palates; but the *xocolata amb café*, a mocha espresso, or the *xocolata picant*, with chilli, pack a mid-afternoon energy punch.

Leticia

C/Còdols 21 (93 302 00 74). Metro Drassanes. **Open** 7pm-2.30am Mon, Wed, Thur, Sun; 7pm-3am Fri, Sat. **Credit** MC, V. **Map** p345 A4.

One of the friendliest, most relaxed bars in the city, with miniature art exhibitions, a sofa and cosy banquettes at the back on which to chat, play chess and chill out to gentle trip hop, lounge and jazz. There's a good range of simple dishes and own-made cakes, plenty of teas and reasonably priced cocktails.

La Palma

C/Palma de Sant Just 7 (93 315 06 56). Metro Jaume I. **Open** 8am-3.30pm, 7-10pm Mon-Thur; 8am-3.30pm, 7-11pm Fri; 7-11pm Sat. **No credit cards. Map** p345 B3.

A quiet, unchanged *bodega* with a local feel; this is not a place to be brandishing a camera and making impossible demands in a foreign tongue. The paintings on the walls are by the Internos, a group of artists who used to meet up here in the 1950s.

Pilé 43

C/Aglà 4 (93 317 39 02). Metro Liceu. **Open** 8.30pm-2am Mon-Thur, Sun; 8.30pm-3am Fri, Sat. **No credit cards. Map** p345 A3.

From the '70s vinyl chairs and smoked glass coffee tables to the lava lamps and the pendant light fittings, almost everything in this bar is for sale. All

well and good when there are plenty of people in to give it some life, but at other times there's no escaping the feeling that you're just drinking in a shop.

El Portalón

C/Banys Nous 20 (93 302 11 87). Metro Liceu. **Open** 9am-midnight Mon-Sat. Closed Aug. **No credit cards. Map** p345 B3.

An unreconstructed *bodega* with a faded, run-down feel as well as a still discernible rustic charm. This place was created in the 1860s from the stables of a medieval palace. Ever since, it's been offering traditional tapas and wine to a group of regulars, who sit chatting under massive clusters of garlic.

Els Quatre Gats

C/Montsió 3 bis (93 302 41 40). Metro Catalunya. **Open** 9am-2am daily. **Credit** AmEx, DC, MC, V. **Map** p344 B2.

This is a Modernista masterpiece and former haunt of artistic Barcelona. Santiago Rusiñol and Ramon Casas painted pictures for it, and the menu cover was Picasso's first paid commission. It closed in 1903, and was used as a textile warehouse until it was restored and reopened in the 1980s, with reproductions by contemporary artists of the original paintings. It's now more smart than bohemian, but it's still an unmissable stop on the city tour.

Rabipelao

C/Mercè 26 (93 319 92 31). Metro Drassanes. **Open** 9pm-2am Mon-Thur, Sun; 8pm-3am Fri, Sat. **No credit cards. Map** p345 B4.

This is a tiny, friendly joint, with Andalucian tiling and an assortment of junk hanging from the walls: a bicycle wheel, the guts of a forgotten typewriter, rolls of film and dog-eared books. Intermittent projections slice through the blood-red shadows deep at the back, while staff dole out cocktails and *bocadillos* to a mish-mash of urban irregulars.

Schilling

C/Ferran 23 (93 317 67 87). Metro Liceu. **Open** 10am-2.15am Mon-Sat; noon-2.15am Sun. **Credit** V. **Map** p345 A3.

Vying for recognition with the grand cafés of European society, Schilling is in fact an upstart from the '90s. Spacious and utterly elegant, with a particularly large gay clientele, it is no longer as fashionable as it was, although the snobby waiters appear not to have realised. Nonetheless, it is an unbeatable spot for watching the world go by, with windows overlooking the thoroughfare of C/Ferran.

Shanghai

C/Aglà 9 (no phone). Metro Liceu. **Open** 7pm-2.30am Mon-Thur, Sun; 7pm-3am Fri, Sat. **No credit cards. Map** p345 A3.

A saucy little mock-oriental drinking hole off C/Escudellers, Shanghai mixes down-at-heel glamour with laid-back eccentricity. From the tasselled light fittings to the shattered corner of the huge mirror, it's scruffily beguiling, although the cocktails can take forever to appear.

Venus Delicatessen

C/Avinyó 25 (93 301 15 85). Metro Liceu.
Open noon-midnight Mon-Sat. Closed 2wks Nov.
No credit cards. Map p345 B3.
Naïve art sits prettily with marble tables and che-quered floors, and there are plenty of newspapers and magazines to flick through. Nonchalant staff can be a bit trying, but they will at least serve you light meals at any point throughout the day, which makes Venus a useful place to know about.

La Vinateria del Call

C/Sant Domènec del Call 9 (93 302 60 92). Metro Jaume I or Liceu. **Open** 6pm-1am Mon-Sat. Closed 1wk Aug. **Credit** AmEx, DC, MC, V. **Map** p345 B3.
The narrow entrance to this deep restaurant-bar, fur-nished with dark wood and dusty bottles, has some-thing of the Dickensian tavern about it, but once inside there's an eclectic music selection – from sevil-lanas to raï – and lively multilingual staff. The wine list and range of hams and cheeses are outstanding; try the *cecina de ciervo* – thin slices of cured venison.

Vinissim

C/Sant Domènec del Call 12 (93 301 45 75). Metro Jaume I. **Open** 8.30am-11pm Tue-Fri; noon-midnight Sat; noon-5pm Sun. **Credit** MC,V. **Map** p345 B3.
Owned by the same people as La Vinateria (*see above*) and run with the same degree of knowledge-able enthusiasm for wine and good food, Vinissim is the daytime option. Painted in warm funky colours and bathed in sunlight, it also has tables out-side on the bright Placeta Manuel Ribé.

Xaloc

C/Palla 13 (93 301 19 90). Metro Liceu or Urquinaona. **Open** 9am-midnight Mon-Thur, Sun; 9am-1am Fri, Sat. **Credit** AmEx, DC, MC, V. **Map** p344 B2
Part café, part deli with a top-notch range of wine, ham, charcuterie and cheese for sale. The tapas are also good, and come in generous portions; try the *morcilla* (black pudding) with caramelised onions or a hearty cabbage tortilla.

Xocoa

C/Petritxol 11 (93 301 11 97). Metro Liceu. **Open** 9am-9pm Mon-Sat. **Credit** MC, V. **Map** p344 A2.
As well as cocoa (*xocoa*) led delights (including a 'chocolate survival kit' with everything the addict needs for a month) there are sublime fruit tarts, cheesecake, tarte tatin and all manner of breakfasty pastries; croissants, magdalenas, brioche and huge Mallorcan *ensaimadas*. Chocolate is the thing, how-ever, here and in the shop next door, or the fabulous Wonkaesque branch nearby at C/Bot 4.

Raval

Bar Bodega Fortuny

C/Pintor Fortuny 31 (93 317 98 92). Metro Catalunya. **Open** 9am-1am Tue-Sun. Closed 1wk Aug, 1wk Dec. **No credit cards. Map** p344 A2.

The old barrels of this former *bodega* sit alongside playful pop art designs and a collection of toy robots. With a largish gay clientele, and a lot of regulars who all appear to know one another, this is a relaxed place, especially good for lunch. Food is global fusion, with an emphasis on Greek.

Bar Kasparo

Plaça Vicenç Martorell 4 (93 302 20 72/ www.kasparo.com). Metro Catalunya. **Open** *May-Aug* 9am-midnight daily. *Sept-Mar* 9am-11pm daily. Closed 2wks Dec/Jan. **No credit cards. Map** p344 A2.
This friendly café is run by two Australian sisters, with almost all its seating outside under an arcade. The square itself is sunny and traffic-free with a playground for kids. Their parents can kick back with the papers and a long but healthy lunch.

Bar Mendizábal

C/Junta de Comerç 2 (no phone). Metro Liceu. **Open** 8am-1am daily. **No credit cards. Map** p345 A3.
Little more than a colourful pavement stall, Mendizábal has been around for decades. More than two leaning on the bar is a crowd, so best to take a seat in the tiny square to enjoy fabulous juice combinations, milkshakes and ever so slightly overpriced soup, tortilla and *bocadillos*.

Bar Muy Buenas

C/Carme 63 (93 442 50 53). Metro Liceu. **Open** 7.30am-2.30am Mon-Sat; 6pm-2.30am Sun. **Credit** AmEx, MC, V. **Map** p344 A2.

Vinissim.

Swooping Modernista woodwork, a marble bar (originally a trough for salting cod) and the original beer taps – one side for the barman to pull pints, one for the customers to help themselves to water – have remained in this welcoming little split-level bar. Friendly staff serve falafel, hummus, lentil soup and home-made cakes in the evenings, and there are poetry readings on Wednesdays.

Bar Pastis

C/Santa Mònica 4 (93 318 79 80). Metro Drassanes.
Open 7.30pm-2.30am Mon-Thur, Sun; 7.30pm-3.30am Fri, Sat. **Credit** AmEx, MC, V. **Map** p345 A4.
This tiny, smoky classic from the '40s has a louche Marseilles feel, floor-to-ceiling indecipherable oil paintings (painted by the original owner when drunk), Edith Piaf monopolising the stereo and free-flowing Pastis and absinthe. Don't miss the fabulous French *chanteuse* on Sunday nights.

Bar Ra

Plaça de la Gardunya 3 (93 301 41 63). Metro Liceu.
Open 1.30-4pm, 9pm-midnight Mon-Sat; 10.30am-6pm. **Credit** AmEx, V. **Map** p344 A2.
Bar Ra has recently branched out into the Sunday brunch market, and foreigners craving something more than the standard croissant will be delighted by the bacon, eggs, toast, juice, muesli, yoghurt and oatmeal on offer. Lunch and dinner range from Mexican to Thai to West Indian fare, served on a buzzing terrace at the back of the Boqueria. Reservations are only taken for dinner: at lunchtime take your place in the queue that sits along the wall.

Bar 68

C/Sant Pau 68 (93 441 31 15). Metro Paral.lel.
Open *Bar* 8pm-2am Tue-Thur; 8pm-3am Fri, Sat. *Restaurant* 9-11.30pm Tue-Sat. **No credit cards**. **Map** p342 C6.
A sparely decorated high-ceilinged room, where recycled lamps hanging above the bar cast a dim orange glow. Mediterranean food is served downstairs or up on the tiny mezzanine, but this is predominantly just an easygoing place to meet up with friends. A DJ plays rare groove, mellow funk and jazz in all its forms.

Boadas

C/Tallers 1 (93 318 95 92). Metro Catalunya.
Open noon-2am Mon-Thur; noon-3am Fri, Sat.
No credit cards. **Map** p342 C/D5
This tiny cocktail bar is difficult to spot, but it needs no neon sign – locals know where it is. While the crowds rage just outside on La Rambla, inside, this 1930s institution is cool and relaxing with black-jacketed and professional barmen. The daytime clientele are usually well dressed and elderly, while the night-time patrons are a more varied bunch, creating a livelier atmosphere.

Buenas Migas

Plaça Bonsuccés 6 (93 319 13 80). Metro Liceu.
Open 9am-9pm daily. **Credit** AmEx, MC, V.
Map p344 A2.
'Good crumbs' (from a phrase meaning 'to get along well') has a wholesome look, with lots of pine, gingham and Kilner jars. The speciality is focaccia with

Bar Muy Buenas. *See p170.*

Eat, Drink, Shop

a variety of toppings, although the apple crumble, brownies and carrot cake are also delicious. Tables outside sprawl across the square.
Branch: Baixada de Santa Clara 2, off Plaça del Rei, Barri Gòtic (93 319 13 80).

El Café Que Pone Muebles Navarro
C/Riera Alta 4-6 (no phone). Metro Sant Antoni.
Open 6pm-1am Tue-Thur, Sun; 6pm-3am Fri, Sat.
No credit cards. **Map** p342 C5.
Muebles Navarro was the name of the furniture shop that stood here for many years, hence the peculiar name of the café – not unlike a quirky furniture shop itself, with long white spaces and mismatched sofas and tables everywhere. A cool place to sip on a cocktail, with generous *bocadillos* and cheesecake.

Casa Almirall
C/Joaquín Costa 33 (no phone). Metro Universitat.
Open 7pm-2.30am Mon-Thur, Sun; 7pm-3am Fri, Sat. **No credit cards**. **Map** p342 C5.
Opened in 1860, the Almirall is the second oldest bar in the city after Marsella. The bar for all seasons, its Modernista woodwork, soft lighting and deep sofas give it a cosy feel in winter, while its glass front opens up for the summer months.

La Confitería
C/Sant Pau 128 (93 443 04 58). Metro Paral.lel. **Open** 6pm-3am Mon-Sat; 6pm-2am Sun. **No credit cards**. **Map** p342 C6.
An ageing but highly polished bar, bursting with character and charmingly done up with old chan-deliers, Modernista wood panelling and murals of rural scenes dating from its days as a sweetshop (*confitería*). A second, more modern, space at the back attracts a younger crowd.

Escribà
La Rambla 83 (93 301 60 27). Metro Liceu.
Open 8.30am-9pm daily. **Credit** (over €9) MC, V. **Map** p345 A3.
If you think this lovely Modernista façade with its colourful mosaic tiles is a treat in itself, just wait until you sample some of the home-made chocolates and pastries waiting inside. It also sells local *moscatell* in cute, decorative bottles and has a handful of tables outside in the shade of a narrow street.

Granja M Viader
C/Xuclà 4-6 (93 318 34 86). Metro Liceu or Catalunya. **Open** 5-8.45pm Mon; 9am-1.45pm, 5-8.45pm Tue-Sat. Closed 1wk Aug. **Credit** AmEx, MC, V. **Map** p344 A2.
The oldest of the city's *granjes* (literally, farms): cafés that specialise in dairy products and sweet delights such as thick hot chocolate topped with whipped cream. An evocative place with century-old fittings and enamel adverts, where marble-topped tables scrape across richly decorated tiles. A huge hit with the old ladies of the neighbourhood.

Horiginal
C/Ferlandina 29 (93 443 39 98). Metro Sant Antoni. **Open** 8.30pm-1am Mon-Thur; 8.30pm-2am Fri, Sat; 6pm-2am Sun. **Credit** MC, V. **Map** p342 C5.

Euskal Extea. *See p175.*

How to drink absinthe

On any given night, Marsella – Barcelona's temple to absinthe since the heady days of Jean Genet and his thieving, whoring cohorts – will be peopled on one side by sallow foreigners sliding slowly under the table, their eyes rolling back; and on the other side by Jean-Paul Belmondo lookalikes discussing the nature of Catalan identity. Therein lies the secret to drinking absinthe. Poise.

The 'green fairy' was popular with writers and artists such as Baudelaire, Toulouse-Lautrec, Oscar Wilde, Gauguin and Van Gogh and, taken in excess, is said to affect the vision in a way that may have inspired the latter's paintings. It is similar to Pastis or Pernod and contains many of the same essential oils – of star anise, juniper and nutmeg, among others – but with one vital and allegedly pyschoactive ingredient: wormwood. Wormwood was originally used to get rid of worms in humans, and was also said to have antimalarial properties. Some of its less desirable effects are thought to include delirium and hallucinations, and are the reason for absinthe's illegal status in most countries. Admittedly, the levels of this herb have been much reduced nowadays, and absinthe's high alcohol content means that alcohol poisoning is likely to hit long before any other ingredient can reach levels of toxicity, but its effect is still unique and not to be taken lightly.

The preferred way to serve it is to balance a sugar lump on a specially designed flat, slotted spoon that rests on the top of the glass. Cold water is then trickled over the sugar, turning the absinthe opaque and offsetting the bitterness. A flashier method involves soaking the sugar in the alcohol and setting fire to it so that it drips into the glass, although the cognoscenti will point out that the sugar cannot then dissolve. It can be ordered in many bars – including **Leticia** (*see p169*) and **Bar Pastis** (*see p171*) – but the *ne plus ultra* of *absenta* bars, with its own brand and secret formula, is **Marsella** (*see p252*).

A relaxed and colourful café, with shelves of poetry (all for sale), monthly art exhibitions, an excellent mix of music (jazz, flamenco and more) and clients ranging from laid-back locals to book-reading travellers. The tables outside look over the MACBA and the square, and the Mexican chef serves up Oaxaca-style cuisine.

Iposa
C/Floristes de la Rambla 14 (93 318 60 86). Metro Liceu. **Open** 1pm-2.30am Mon-Thur; 8.30pm-2am Fri, Sat; 6pm-2am Sun. **Credit** MC, V. **Map** p344 A2.
A welcoming open-fronted bar with a scattering of tables outside on a leafy square. An eclectic music policy picks up the prevailing mood, which is almost invariably relaxed. The fantastic 'Formula' menu gets you an imaginative main course, a drink and a coffee for a paltry €5.

La Ruta dels Elefants
C/Hospital 48 (no phone). Metro Liceu. **Open** 5pm-2am Mon-Thur, Sun; 5pm-3am Fri, Sat. **Admission** free. **No credit cards**. **Map** p344 A2.
Forcibly quelled by various fines and a ban on the chaotic concerts that used to pack out its innermost depths, La Ruta is no longer the anything-goes traveller/street performer bar it once was. None the less

the alternative crowd still gives it an offbeat atmosphere unusual so close to La Rambla. Opening hours occasionally vary by an hour or two according to the owner's whim.

Els Tres Tombs
Ronda Sant Antoni 2 (93 443 41 11). Metro Sant Antoni. **Open** 6am-2am daily. **No credit cards**. **Map** p342 C5.
Not a graveyard in sight; the name refers to 'the three circuits' of the area performed by a procession of men on horseback during the Festa dels Tres Tombs in January. This lively bar-restaurant with great tapas and a sunny outside terrace is always busy, but especially during the Sunday book market at the nearby Mercat Sant Antoni.

Born & Sant Pere

The Clansman
C/Vigatans 13 (93 319 71 69). Metro Jaume I. **Open** (can vary for sporting events) 6pm-3am Mon-Thur, Sun; 6pm-4am Fri, Sat. **Credit** MC, V. **Map** p345 C3.
Hankering after a packet of prawn cocktail Golden Wonder and a pint of Newkie Brown? Missing the

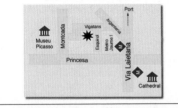

Va de Vi. See p176.

footy and the smell of B&H? Well, there are worse places to fill a pint-sized hole, and apart from the tartan barstools it's all quite tasteful, with a low-ceilinged, cosy feel.

Espai Barroc
C/Montcada 20 (93 310 06 73). Metro Jaume I. **Open** 8pm-2am Tue-Sat; 6-10pm Sun. **Credit** MC, V. **Map** p345 C3.
A spectacular bar housed deep within the 17th-century Palau Dalmases (step through the heavy wooden doors to the back of the courtyard). Baroque furniture and paintings and displays of flowers, fruit and aromatic herbs give it the look of an Italian still life. Classical music enhances the experience.

La Estrella de Plata
Pla del Palau 9 (93 319 60 07). Metro Barceloneta. **Open** 8.30pm-midnight Mon; 1.30-4pm, 8.30pm-midnight Tue-Sat. **Credit** MC, V. **Map** p345 C4.
Time was the reputation for world-class tapas here would draw in aficionados from far and wide, a following now limited to wealthy uptowners (witness the serried ranks of Audis) and a babel of Eurotrash. While the tapas (bar the odd exception such as artichoke hearts stuffed with quails' eggs) have lost their edge, the prices have made healthy progress.

Euskal Extea
Placeta Montcada 1-3 (93 310 21 85). Metro Jaume I. **Open** *Bar* 9am-11.30pm Tue-Sat; 12.45-3.30pm Sun. *Restaurant* 1-3.30pm, 9-11.30pm Tue-Sat. Closed Aug. **Credit** MC, V. **Map** p345 C3.
Platters laden with dainty Basque morsels – from a sublime hake mousse to *botifarra* with Cabrales cheese – appear on the bar at about midday and 7pm, while the restaurant at the back is a superb place to sample more substantial Basque fare, and does a great lunch menu for €9. Our only complaint is that wine is served in thimbles.

L'Hivernacle
Parc de la Ciutadella (93 295 40 17). Metro Arc de Triomf. **Open** 10am-midnight daily. **Credit** AmEx, DC, MC, V. **Map** p343 E6.

An utterly unique place for a drink, in the elegant late 19th-century iron and glass palmhouse at the entrance to the Parc de la Ciutadella. With three parts (one shaded room, one unshaded and a terrace), the Hivernacle hosts exhibitions and occasional jazz and classical concerts. A good place to let kids run around, with a rare children's menu.

La Idea
Plaça Comercial 2 (93 268 87 87/www.idea born.com). Metro Jaume I. **Open** 9am-11am Mon-Thur; 9am-3am Fri; 10am-3am Sat; 10am-10pm Sun. **No credit cards. Map** p345 C3.
Predating the trend for cocooning, La Idea has a sitting-room feel, with a selection of books for sale on global themes, newspapers and a chilled-out area downstairs with floor cushions. It's also a relaxed place to surf the net, with plenty of computers (€3 per hr). Upstairs a floor-to-ceiling canvas bears the UN Universal Declaration of Human Rights.

Miramelindo
Passeig del Born 15 (93 310 37 27). Metro Jaume I. **Open** 8pm-2.30am Mon-Thur; 8pm-3am Fri, Sat; 7.30pm-2.30am Sun. **No credit cards. Map** p345 C3.
It's ironic that Miramelindo is considered such a Barcelona classic, and yet if you added a swirly carpet you'd have a London pub; mirrors, lots of wood, a fireplace of sorts, tables jostling for space and people three-deep at the bar. A short cocktail list and aproned waiters give it a little Mediterranean pzazz.

La Morera
Plaça Fossar de les Moreres 5 (mobile 617 810 312). Metro Jaume I. **Open** 5pm-12.30am Tue, Wed, Sun; 5pm-3am Thur-Sat. **Credit** AmEx, MC, V. **No credit cards. Map** p345 C4.
A more popular recent addition than the 'Eternal Flame' (to remember the martyrs of 1714) that lights the other side of the square, these young *llesqueria* has a vaguely Moroccan feel, with deep pink walls, candles and low tables and stools. The choice of wines is impressive and panes of glass set into the floor provide a window into a larger room below.

Mudanzas

C/Vidriería 15 (93 319 11 37). Metro Jaume I.
Open 10am-2.30am Mon-Thur, Sun; 10am-3am
Fri, Sat. **Credit** MC, V. **Map** p345 C3.
Few of the many cafés and bars surrounding the
increasingly trendy Born area manage to capture
the relaxed ambience of this bar, with its chequered
tiled floor and marble-topped tables. There's a rack
of newspapers and magazines, many in English,
and some tables outside.

El Nus

C/Mirallers 5 (93 319 53 55). Metro Jaume I.
Open 7.30pm-2.30am Mon, Tue, Thur; 7.30pm-3am
Fri, Sat. **No credit cards. Map** p345 C4.
White lace curtains, stone walls, dusty chandeliers,
wood and the liberal use of red paint make this a
charming place to enjoy a quiet drink, while low-key
jazz plays in the background. The sage-looking gent
pondering the crowd from a large black and white
photo fixed to the ceiling is the bar's original owner.

Orígens 99,9%

C/Vidriería 6-8 (93 310 75 31). Metro Jaume I.
Open 1.30pm-1.30am daily. **Credit** AmEx, MC,
V. **Map** p345 C3.
The last of the glassmakers that used to line this
street finally closed in 2002 and Orígens took its
place, retaining much of the original glass in display
cases. Half shop/half café, the name refers to the
provenance of its stock, which is almost completely
Catalan. The menu comes with entertaining explanations of the diminutive sampler dishes, their history, connected proverbs and relevant folklore.

Ribborn

*C/Antic de Sant Joan 3 (93 310 71 48). Metro Jaume
I.* **Open** 10pm-2.30am Tue-Thur, Sun; 10pm-3am Fri,
Sat. **Credit** MC, V. **Map** p345 C3/4.
The perfect palliative for the Born's airs, Ribborn is
noisy, lively and unpretentious. Relaxed locals,
bathed in a dim red glow, shout above old funk like
James Brown, or chill to great live sounds. The staff
mix a fine cocktail and there is Guinness on tap.

Suau

*Passeig del Born 30 (93 310 63 54). Metro Jaume I
or Barceloneta.* **Open** 3pm-1.30am Mon-Thur; 3pm-
3am Fri; 7pm-3am Sat; 4.30pm-2am Sun. **No credit
cards. Map** p345 C3.
The locals' powerful lobby for undisturbed sleep
means that Suau's outside terrace (along with all the
others hereabouts) has to be cleared as the witching
hour approaches. If the downstairs space – with gar-
ish Tutankhamen mural – becomes too cramped,
there's another, usually empty, room upstairs. Tarot
reading and imported beers (among them Leffe and
Chimay) are available.

Tèxtil Cafè

*C/Montcada 12-14 (93 268 25 98). Metro Jaume
I.* **Open** *Apr-Oct* 10am-midnight Tue-Sun. *Nov-Mar*
10am-9pm Tue-Thur; 10am-midnight Fri-Sun.
Credit MC, V. **Map** p345 C3.

In the courtyard of a graceful 14th-century palace
(which now houses the Textile and Barbier-Mueller
museums) is this peaceful oasis; an elegant place for
a coffee in the shade , or under gas heaters in winter, with decent breakfast and lunch menus. The
array of newspapers improves the patience of those
waiting to be served, which can take forever.

La Tinaja

C/Espartería 9 (93 310 22 50). Metro Jaume I.
Open 2pm-2am Tue-Sat. **Credit** AmEx, DC, MC,
V. **Map** p345 C4.
The old crocks hanging like swallows' nests from
the beams, the collection of wrought-iron implements and the lofty stone arches create an appealing *rus in urbe* atmosphere – a near perfect spot to
sample the standard *llesquería* menu, washed down
with a good value bottle of wine. Finish off with the
fine *tarta de Santiago*: almond cake on to which you
pour the accompanying glass of *moscatell*.

Txirimiri

C/Princesa 11 (93 310 18 05). Metro Jaume I.
Open 11.30am-midnight Tue-Sun. Closed 2wks
Sept, 2wks Jan. **Credit** MC, V. **Map** p345 C3.
Pintxo heaven would be a big airy place, where the
excellent Basque tapas would be free, you'd always
get a seat and the relaxed staff would welcome you
with radiant smiles. Perhaps there would also be
occasional visits from a Zeppo-like jester to twist
balloons and perform magic tricks. Alas, they still
make you pay at Txirimiri.

Va de Vi

C/Banys Vells 16 (93 319 29 00). Metro Jaume I.
Open 6pm-1am Mon-Wed, Sun; 6pm-2am Thur;
6pm-3am Fri, Sat. **Credit** MC, V. **Map** p345 C3.
Run by an artist who has a taste for wine and
an eye for Gothic extravagance, Va de Vi, with its
16th-century arches, candles and heavy drapery,
mixes atmospheric sophistication with relaxed
informality. The wine list includes numerous
unusual bottles, many of which are available in a
small tasting measure (*cata*), and the *llesquería*
fare maintains the high standard.

La Vinya del Senyor

*Plaça Santa Maria 5 (93 310 33 79). Metro
Barceloneta or Jaume I.* **Open** noon-1am Tue-Thur;
noon-1.30am Fri, Sat; noon-midnight Sun. **Credit**
AmEx, MC, V. **Map** p345 C4.
This elegant little wine-taster's bar has tables outdoors from which to contemplate the majestic coun-
terposition of verticals and plain space in the
façade of Santa Maria del Mar. With a superb list
of more than 300 wines and selected cavas, sher-
ries and *moscatells*, changed every 15 days, the
Iberian ham and French cheese come in very handy
for their qualities of absorption.

El Xampanyet

C/Montcada 22 (93 319 70 03). Metro Jaume I.
Open noon-4pm, 6.30-11.30pm Tue-Sat; noon-4pm
Sun. Closed Aug. **Credit** MC, V. **Map** p345 C3.

Run by the same family since the 1930s, this little 'champagne bar' is one of the eternal attractions on this ancient street. It's lined with coloured tiles, barrels and antique curios, and there are a few marble tables; nearly always full. El Xampanyet has three specialities: anchovies, fresh cider and 'champagne' (a pretty plain cava, if truth be told, but very refreshing all the same).

Barceloneta & the ports

Port Olímpic has a strip of cheesy, overpriced, neon-lit bars with little to choose between them. Useful for stag nights but not a great deal else.

Can Ganassa
Plaça de la Barceloneta 4-6 (93 225 19 97). Metro Barceloneta. **Open** *June-Sept* 9am-1.30am Mon, Tue, Thur-Sun. *Oct-May* 9am-11pm Mon, Tue, Thur-Sun. **No credit cards. Map** p343 D/E7.
It's smoky, it's noisy, it's full of gruff old men competing to be heard above the fruit machines – we love it. And besides, there are tables outside. Good tapas are nearly all on display, so you don't need to worry about flexing your Catalan, just point. Try the 'bomba Ganassa'; a huge potato and bacon croquette served with *all i oli* and a fiery chilli sauce.

Can Paixano
C/Reina Cristina 7 (93 310 08 39). Metro Barceloneta. **Open** 9am-10.30pm Mon-Sat. **No credit cards. Map** p345 C4.
There's no sign outside, and besides, this narrow, smoky buzzing bar hidden among the electronic shops is known universally as the 'champagne bar'. Bargain-basement cava flows at all hours but to order a bottle you must now accompany it with at least two of the similarly cheap *bocadillos*.

Jai-ca
C/Ginebra 13 (93 319 50 02). Metro Barceloneta. **Open** 9am-midnight Tue-Thur, Sun; 9am-1am Fri, Sat. **Credit** MC, V. **Map** p343 E7.
The jumble of tables in the tight space inside this no-nonsense tapas bar spills out on to a pleasant, shaded terrace. Its location on the corner of two quiet streets, the fresh breeze wafting through, the informality and the permanently stopped clock all conspire to make for a laze-inducing atmosphere – a perfect pre- or post-beach stop-off.

Luz de Gas – Port Vell
Opposite the Palau de Mar (93 209 77 11/ www.luzdegas.com). Metro Barceloneta or Jaume I. **Open** *Mar-Oct* noon-3am Mon-Sat; 11am-3am Sun. Closed Nov-Feb. **Credit** AmEx, MC, V. **Map** p342 D7.
This floating bar is docked in the Port Vell alongside a promenade buzzing with strollers, cyclers and Rollerbladers. Catch some sun over a cold drink on the upper deck, or rest in the shade on the lower. With nightfall, candles are brought out, wine is uncorked and the scene develops an air of romance, marred only by the cheesy music selection.

Some like it hot

Spanish coffee is very strong and generally excellent. The three basic types are *café solo* (*cafè sol* in Catalan, and also known simply as '*café*'), a small strong black coffee; *cortado/tallat*, the same but with a little milk; and *café con leche/cafè amb llet*, a white coffee, but with more milk and less water than in northern Europe or America. Cappuccinos have yet to really catch on, and whipped cream as a substitute for foam is not unheard of. Then there's *café americano* (a tall black coffee diluted with more water), and spiked coffee: a *carajillo*, which is a short, black coffee with a liberal dash of brandy. If you want another type of liqueur, you have to specify, such as *carajillo de ron* (rum) or *carajillo de whisky*. A *trifásico* is a *carajillo* with a bit of milk. Decaffeinated coffee (*descafeinado*) is widely available, but ask for it *de máquina* (from the machine) if you don't want a sachet of Nescafé with hot milk. To stand out as a true *guiri* (faintly disdainful term for Northern Europeans and Americans), ask for *café con leche* any time after mid-morning.

Tea, on the whole, is abysmal; weak, tasteless and given that special railway buffet flavour with the UHT milk used routinely in Spain. If you cannot live without it, make sure you ask for cold milk on the side (*leche fría aparte*) or run the risk of getting a glass of hot milk and a teabag. Herbal teas, such as chamomile (*manzanilla*), lime flower tea (*tila*) and mint (*menta*), are generally easier to find.

La Miranda del Museu
Museu d'Història de Catalunya, Plaça Pau Vila 3 (93 225 50 07). Metro Barceloneta. **Open** 10am-7pm Tue-Sat; 10am-12.30am Sun. **Credit** MC, V. **Map** p345 C4.
In a city well known for its wonderful views, this top-floor café has one of the best, especially as the sun sinks down behind Montjuïc, bathing the city in a lustrous orange glow. The enormous terrace is perfect for young children to let off steam, and there is also a great value set lunch. You don't need a museum ticket; just take the lift to the top floor.

El Vaso de Oro
C/Balboa 6 (93 319 30 98). Metro Barceloneta. **Open** 9am-midnight daily. Closed Sept. **No credit cards. Map** p343 E7.
Its charm lies in the decor – like a bar on some down at heel 1950s cruise ship, with liveried staff,

Dry Martini. See p179.

cramped layout and dark wooden fittings. It's always noisy and bustling and has some of the best tapas in town, especially the *patatas bravas*. Get there early for a seat in the wings, otherwise it's standing room only.

Poble Sec

Bar Primavera
C/Nou de la Rambla 192 (93 329 30 62). Metro Paral.lel. **Open** *Apr-Oct* 8am-10pm Tue-Sun. *Nov-Mar* 8am-7pm Tue-Sun. **No credit cards**. **Map** p341 B6.
At the very end of C/Nou de la Rambla, where it hits the slope of Montjuïc, is this peaceful leafy terrace looking down on the city below. There is no indoor seating but shade is provided by the vines creeping overhead. With a small bar serving rudimentary *bocadillos* and snacks, this is the perfect place for a pit stop on the climb up the hill.

Fundació Joan Miró
Parc de Montjuïc (93 329 07 68). Metro Paral.lel, then Funicular de Montjuïc. **Open** 10am-7pm Mon-Sat; 10am-2.30pm Sun. **Credit** MC, V. **Map** p341 B6.
One of very few decent places to have lunch or a coffee on Montjuïc lies inside the Miró museum (you don't need to pay the entrance fee). In summer, sit in the grassy courtyard in the company of the artist's goblin ceramics and a bronze female statue, with a good choice of inventive sandwiches (like smoked salmon and avocado with radish sauce) or more substantial dishes at lunchtime.

Quimet i Quimet
C/Poeta Cabanyes 25 (93 442 31 42). Metro Paral.lel. **Open** noon-4pm, 7-10.30pm Tue-Sat; noon-4pm Sun. **Credit** MC,V. **Map** p341 B6.
The most is made of very limited space in lovely old *bodega*: shelves reaching the ceiling are stocked with dusty bottles of wine, beer, liqueurs and cava,

ranging from bargain-basement to the stuff of a connoisseur's dreams. There are only three tables and nowhere to sit, however, and it can get overwhelmingly crowded.

Eixample

La Barcelonina de Vins i Esperits
C/Valencia 304 (93 215 70 83). Metro Passeig de Gràcia. **Open** 6pm-2am Mon-Fri; 7.30pm-2am Fri, Sat. **Credit** V. **Map** p339 E4.
A wine bar with a difference; it's utterly unpretentious. The TV is on, the clientele as scruffy as the Eixample allows and you're not expected to know the first thing about wine. There is also a selection of assorted meats and cheeses.

La Bodegueta
Rambla de Catalunya 100 (93 215 48 94). Metro Diagonal/FGC Provença. **Open** 8am-2am Mon-Sat; 6.30pm-1am Sun. Closed 2wks Aug. **No credit cards**. **Map** p338 D4.
Dwarfed by the swanky designer palaces around it, this downstairs bar is a much-loved classic of the *barrio*, with old rose petal tiles and stacks of old-time charm. It's especially crowded around lunch, with, inevitably, more suits than overalls these days.

Café Torino
Passeig de Gràcia 59 (93 487 75 71). Metro Passeig de Gràcia. **Open** 8am-11pm Mon-Thur, Sun; 9am-1.30am Fri, Sat. **No credit cards**. **Map** p344 B1.
The original Café Torino, a wonderful Modernista flight of fancy, only exists in the fading photographs on the walls; whether they are there to boast of its glorious past or as a sackcloth for mindless '60s destruction is unclear. The place is a useful refuelling stop on the way to more fortunate architectural gems, with decent coffee and good *bocadillos*.

Casa Alfonso
C/Roger de Llúria 6 (93 301 97 83). Metro Urquinaona. **Open** 9am-midnight Mon-Thur; 9am-1am Fri; noon-1am Sat. Closed 2wks Aug. **Credit** AmEx, DC, MC, V. **Map** p344 C1.
In the same family since it opened back in 1935, Casa Alfonso has a refined, old-fashioned air; monochrome murals of early 20th-century Barcelona decorate the walls, *jamones* hang from the high ceiling, and glass-fronted cupboards display bottles of oil and wine. Locals pop in for fine tapas and the selection of *embotits* and other charcuterie. There are more tables in the room at the back amid the exhibition of slightly questionable art.

Cervecería Catalana
C/Mallorca 236 (93 216 0368). Metro Passeig de Gràcia. **Open** 7.30-1.30am Mon-Fri; 9-1.30am Sat, Sun. **Credit** AmEx, DC, MC, V. **Map** p338 D4.
One of the best of the enormous tapas barns found all over the Eixample: perfect for those looking for the tapas experience but who aren't sure they're ready for sawdust on the floor. There's not a lot of character, but there is a fantastic selection of tapas.

Dry Martini

C/Aribau 162-6 (93 217 50 72). FCG Provença.
Open 1pm-2.30am Mon-Thur, 6pm-2.30am Sun;
1pm-3am Fri, Sat. **Credit** AmEx, DC, MC, V.
Map p342 C5.
All the trappings of a trad cocktail bar – professional bow-tied staff, leather banquettes, the odd drinking antique and wooden cabinets displaying a century's worth of bottles – but none of the stuffiness; the music owes more to trip hop than middle-aged crowd pleasers, and the barmen welcome all comers. There are plans to start serving Mediterranean and Japanese food at lunchtime.

Laie Libreria Cafè

C/Pau Claris 85 (93 302 73 10). Metro Urquinaona.
Open *Café* 9am-1am Mon-Fri; 10am-1am Sat.
Bookshop 10.30am-9pm Mon-Sat. **Credit** AmEx,
DC, MC, V. **Map** p344 B1.
The layout at the front is a bit cramped, but the covered patio at the back is perfect; airy, spacious and decorated with photographs of last century's literary giants. There is a buffet breakfast of pastries, eggs, fruit and *bocadillos*, a light lunch menu and more substantial restaurant fare at night. If nothing strikes your fancy in the bookshop downstairs, there's a selection of magazines and papers to read.

Stinger

C/Còrsega 338 (93 217 71 87). Metro Diagonal.
Open 6.30pm-3am Mon-Fri; 7.30pm-3.30am Sat.
Credit MC, V. **Map** p338 D4.
For a place so firmly entrenched in the Barcelona scene, Stinger doesn't take itself too seriously. Sure, the glossy black bar, velvet seating and moody yellow lighting are cocktail-bar cliché, but the unwritten rule that only Brazilian bossa should be played is flouted routinely and not always fortuitously. Prepare to rock.

Valor Chocolatería

*Rambla Catalunya 46 (93 487 62 46). Metro Passeig
de Gràcia.* **Open** 8.30am-1pm, 3.30-10pm Mon-Thur;
9am-1pm, 3.30pm-2am Fri, Sat; 9am-1pm, 3.30-11pm
Sun. **No credit cards. Map** p345 D3.
From chocolate fondues with a plate of fruit for dunking to the standard steaming mugful, chocolate in all its guises is taken very seriously here. Cabinets chock full of home-made sweets tempt in passers-by, or at least the respectable elderly Catalan ladies among them.

Gràcia

La Baignoire

C/Verdi 4-6 (mobile 615 45 80 22). Metro Fontana.
Open 7pm-3am Mon, Wed-Sat; 6pm-2.30am Sun.
No credit cards. Map p338 D3.
As white as a bathtub and not much bigger, La Baignoire still manages to be comfortable, with slide projections and lounge music complementing the mellow vibe. Simple tapas and smiles from the staff are always available.

Bodega Manolo

*C/Torrent de les Flors 101 (93 284 43 77). Metro
Joanic.* **Open** 9.30am-7.30pm Tue, Wed; 9.30am-
11pm Thur, Fri; 12.30-4.30pm, 8pm-12.30am Sat;
10.30am-3pm Sun. Closed Aug. **No credit cards.**
Map p339 E3.
Another old family *bodega* with a faded, peeling charm, barrels on the wall and rows and rows of dusty bottles. Do not be fooled, however. Manolo specialises not only in wine, but in classy food; try the foie gras with pear and apple. At the other end of the scale, and also with its place, comes the 'Destroyer' hangover buster: eggs, bacon, sausage and chips.

Café del Sol

Plaça del Sol 16 (93 415 56 63). Metro Fontana.
Open 1pm-2.30am Mon-Thur, Sun; 1pm-3am Fri,
Sat. **No credit cards. Map** p338 D3.
Nursing a long drink on the terrace as the cadent sun casts summer shadows across Gràcia's liveliest square is heavenly. Being stuffed inside on a damp winter's night is more of an acquired taste, however; noisy, boisterous, three deep at the bar, but still kind of fun.

Casa Quimet

Rambla de Prat 9 (93 217 53 27). Metro Fontana.
Open 6.30pm-2am Tue-Sun. Closed Feb, Aug.
No credit cards. Map p338 D3.
Crumbling portraits and jazz posters cover every inch of wall, dozens of ancient guitars hang from the ceiling and ticking clocks compete to be heard over Billie Holliday. The other-worldly 'guitar bar' occasionally springs to life with an impromptu jam session, but at other times is a perfect study in melancholy.

Flash Flash

*C/Granada del Penedès 25 (93 237 09 90). FGC
Gràcia.* **Open** 1pm-1.30am daily. **Credit** AmEx,
DC, MC, V. **Map** p338 D3.
Opened in 1970, this bar was a design sensation in its day, with its white leatherette banquettes and walls imprinted with silhouettes of a life-size frolicking, Twiggyesque model. They call it a *tortilleria*, with more than 50 variations on the theme, including a handful of dessert tortillas.

La Fronda

*C/Verdi 15 (93 415 30 57). Metro Fontana or
Joanic.* **Open** 8pm-12.30am Mon, Wed, Thur,
Sun; 8pm-2.30am Fri, Sat. Closed Aug.
Credit V. **Map** p338 D3.
The wicker furniture, the leafy plants, the travel magazines fanned out along one side; there is something very colonial about La Fronda. The wine list is very reasonably priced, and there's a small selection of tapas, as well as excellent sandwiches, home-made cakes and ice-cream.

Mos

Via Augusta 112 (93 237 13 13). FGC Plaça Molina.
Open 7am-10pm Mon-Sat; 7.30am-10pm Sun.
Credit MC, V. **Map** p338 D3.

Eat, Drink, Shop

Tempting trays of hot and cold dishes that owe nothing to canteen cuisine, delectable desserts and even handmade chocolates; just point at what you want. It's weighed, marked on a ticket, you help yourself to drinks, then later tell the staff what you've had.

Salambó

C/Torrijos 51 (93 218 69 66). Metro Joanic.
Open noon-2.30am daily. **Credit** V. **Map** p339 E3.
By day, a large sophisticated split-level café serving coffee, teas and filled ciabatta to the *barri*'s more conservative element. By night, it's not exactly revolutionary, but the music goes up, and crowds from the Verdi cinema next door give it some life.

Sol Soler

Plaça del Sol 21 (93 217 44 40). Metro Fontana.
Open 1pm-2am daily. **No credit cards.**
Map p338 D3.
Its nod towards stylish design – plenty of mirrors, wood-lined walls, bistro lighting – contrasts with the student caff feel given to it by having too many tables and all the noisy *graciencs* sitting at them on a Saturday night. They come to taste the inventive salads (like tropical or Korean) and the roquefort quiche.

Sureny

Plaça Revolució 17 (93 213 75 56). Metro Joanic.
Open 8.30pm-midnight Tue-Thur; 8.30pm-1am Fri; 1-3.30pm, 8.30pm-1am Sat; 1-3.30pm, 8.30pm-midnight Sun. **Credit** V. **Map** p338 D3.
What Sureny lacks in the character of its brightly lit and bland decor, it more than makes up for in the quality of its gourmet tapas. As well as the run of the mill varieties, expect venison stew, foie with mango and wine, or partridge magret with chestnut purée, followed by, say, toffee pudding.

Other areas

Bar Tomás

C/Major de Sarrià 49, Zona Alta (93 203 10 77).
FGC Sarrià. **Open** 7.45am-10pm Mon, Tue, Thur-Sun. **No credit cards. Map** p337 B1.
Every now and then a foodstuff will assume iconic status; as *pa amb tomàquet* becomes a symbol for Catalonia, Bar Tomás' *patatas bravas* have become the emblematic tapa for Barcelona. Whether they actually merit the schlep across town or the queues on Sunday is irrelevant; until you've tried them, your Barcelona experience is incomplete.

La Esquinica

Passeig Fabra i Puig 296, Horta (93 358 25 19).
Metro Virrei Amat. **Open** 8am-midnight Tue-Fri; 8am-4pm, 6pm-midnight Sat; 8am-4pm Sun. Closed 2wks Aug. **No credit cards.**
Think of it not as a trek, but as a quest; queues outside are testament to the excellence of the tapas. Waiters will advise first-timers to start with *chocos* (creamy squid rings), *patatas bravas* with *all i oli*, *llonganissa* sausage and *tigres* (stuffed mussels). After which the world is your oyster, cockle or clam.

Some like it cold

Damm beer is ubiquitous in Catalonia, with **Estrella**, a strong lager, the most popular variety. Damm also produces an even stronger lager (**Voll Damm**) and a dark one (**Bock Damm**). For draught beer, ask for it *de barril/a pressió*. A *caña* is around half a (UK) pint, a *quinto* smaller still. Occasionally, you will find *jarras*, which are more like a pint. Shandy (*clara*), here made with bitter lemon, is refreshing and popular, and remains untouched by the stigma it has back home.

Among the wines, **Rioja** is well known, but in the north of Spain there are many excellent wines from other regions, such as the **Penedès** in Catalonia, Navarra or El Duero. Most of the wine is red (*tinto/negre*), but Galicia produces a good, slightly sparkling white wine (*vino turbio*). The Basques have a similar, clearer wine called **Txakolí** and, of course, Catalonia has its many **cavas**, of which *brut nature* is top of the range.

Of Spanish liquors and spirits, the most famous are the full-bodied, dark brandies, such as **Torres 5** or **10**, with names that reflect the number of years they've been aged. **Mascaró**, **Magno** and **Carlos III** are also good. Note that measures are enormous. **Anís** is popular, as is a range of very strong firewaters, including *orujo* and **absinthe** (*absenta*). Galician *orujo* is a digestif akin to French *eau de vie* or Italian *grappa*. It is distilled from what is left after wine grapes have been pressed.

Many bars offer freshly squeezed orange juice (though, peculiarly, it's more generally seen as something to drink after dinner by way of dessert), while *horchata* (tiger nut milk) makes a unique and refreshing drink in summer. Still water is *agua sin gas* and sparkling is *agua con gas*, not to be confused with *gaseosa*, which is a kind of lemonade.

Merbeyé

Plaça Doctor Andreu, Tibidabo (93 417 92 79).
FGC Av Tibidabo, then Tramvia Blau/60 bus.
Open noon-2.30am Mon-Thur; noon-3.30am Fri, Sat; noon-2am Sun. **Credit** MC, V.
If Humphrey Bogart had a cocktail bar, it would be something like this: bedecked in red velvet with monochrome prints of jazz luminaries on the walls, low lighting and a peaceful terrace. Later on the crowd crosses to the late-night disco in Mirablau.

Shops & Services

If you live to shop, welcome to paradise.

Given that La Rambla is the most famous street in the city, it offers a surprisingly limited range of potential purchases, unless you happen to be a collector of Mexican sombreros, rude postcards or plastic paella fridge magnets. If these aren't your bag, you'll do better almost anywhere else in the centre. Shops are concentrated in the Eixample and the Old City, and while Barcelona is no match for London or New York, there are several shopping areas that have their own distinct character.

Smarter, more expensive outlets are in the **Eixample**, along **Rambla de Catalunya**, **Passeig de Gràcia** and the central part of **Diagonal**. This is where to go if you want big-name glitz from names like Chanel, Antonio Miró or Adolfo Domínguez. The next stop on the way downtown – but light years away, aesthetically speaking – is the **Raval**. Home to commercial underdogs like second-hand shops and retro music stores, this area is gradually gaining momentum and showing the city that giant commercial centres aren't the only way to rejuvenate a neighbourhood.

The somewhat over-hyped **Born** district is the darling of recently graduated design students and although its shops can be pretentious (in terms of both content and price tags) the best of the bunch have a young, creative vibe and cutting-edge products. For one-of-a-kind purchases, however, no destination beats the **Barri Gòtic**, whose narrow streets hold delightfully quirky antique shops, unusual boutiques, and artisan workshops; those shops that are over 60 years old and that preserve their architectural heritage are awarded special brass pavement plaques from the Ajuntament.

Note that if you're paying by credit card, you usually have to show photographic ID, such as a passport or driving licence.

OPENING HOURS

The siesta tends to throw many visitors to the city, who gear up for an afternoon's shopping only to find that nobody's home. Most smaller shops close for lunch between about 2pm and 4.30pm on weekdays and – in a move that seems like financial suicide – quite a few still close on Saturday afternoons.

The regulation of Sunday and holiday opening hours is fiendishly complicated but generally speaking, small shops, restaurants, bakeries, flower stalls, convenience stores and

any shops in a tourist zone (like La Rambla or Maremàgnum) may open throughout the day, seven days a week. Shops are also permitted to open for at least 11 Sundays a year, including all four preceding Christmas.

SALES, TAX AND REFUNDS

Sales usually run from the second week in January to the end of February, and during July and August. The rate of sales tax (IVA) depends on the type of product: it's currently seven per cent on food, 16 per cent on most other items. In shops that display a 'Tax-Free Shopping' sticker on their door, non-EU residents can request a Tax-Free Cheque on purchases of over €150, which can then be reclaimed either as cash, a certified cheque or charge card credit at the airport in Terminal A (a handling fee will be deducted).

Returning goods, even when they are faulty, can be difficult in all but the largest stores. But all shops are required to provide a complaints book (ask for an *hoja de reclamación*). The mere act of asking for it sometimes does the trick, but, if not, take your copy of the completed form to the local consumer information office, OMIC (Ronda Sant Pau 43-45 (93 402 78 41/omic@mail.bcn.es), which may be able to help.

GETTING AROUND

A special shopping bus called **TombBús** (93 415 60 20) – 'tomb' means a round-trip, not necessarily around cemeteries – runs between Plaça de Catalunya (in front of Banc d'Espanya or El Corte Inglés) and Plaça Pius XII on Diagonal. The blue buses, complete with magazines and piped music, make 28 stops along the way; a single ticket costs €1.25, or a one-day travelcard is €5. Buses leave every seven minutes from 7.30am to 9.30pm on weekdays, and every 15 minutes from 9.30am to 9.30pm on Saturdays. Tickets are available on the bus or from tourist offices.

One-stop shopping

Barcelona Glòries

Avda Diagonal 208, Eixample (93 486 04 04).
Metro Glòries. **Open** *Shops* 10am-10pm Mon-Sat.
Map p337 A2.
When this giant commercial centre opened in 1995 it did much to revitalise a rather barren part of town. As well as offices, it houses 230 well-known shops,

3,500 parking spaces, a multiplex cinema (films are mostly dubbed into Spanish), bars and restaurants. It's also great for kids: there are pathways decorated with laser-triggered jets of coloured water that stop temporarily for passers by, there's plenty of park space, play areas and entertainment such as bouncy castles and trampolines.

Bulevard Rosa

Passeig de Gràcia 55, Eixample (93 378 91 91/ www.bulevardrosa.com). Metro Passeig de Gràcia. **Open** 10.30am-8.30pm Mon-Sat. **Credit** AmEx, DC, MC, V. **Map** p338 D4.

Bulevard Rosa is populated almost exclusively by ladies who carry their dogs in their handbags. This chi-chi uptown arcade opened in the 1980s amid the galeria boom and is still an efficient way to sample the wares of some 100 shops (mostly clothes boutiques and some larger chains) without having to subject your hairdo to the elements.

El Corte Inglés

Plaça Catalunya 14, Eixample (93 306 38 00/ www.elcorteingles.es). Metro Plaça Catalunya. **Open** 10am-10pm Mon-Sat. **Credit** AmEx, DC, MC, V. **Map** p344 B1.

Since its birth in 1940, this retail giant has methodically bludgeoned all the competition to become the only real department store in the whole country. Its services cover everything you might expect, from watch-mending to beauty treatments and cashing travellers' cheques. The titanic Plaça Catalunya branch has nine floors of fashion and home decor, plus a good supermarket in the basement and a seventh-floor café with fabulous views, while the branch on Portal de L'Àngel has six floors of music, electronics, mobile phone services, books, and sporting goods. If that's still not enough, try one of the out-of-town Hipercor hypermarkets.

Branches: El Corte Inglés Avda Diagonal 471-3, Eixample (93 419 20 20); Avda Diagonal 617-9, Eixample (93 366 71 00); Portal de l'Àngel 19, Barri Gòtic (93 306 38 00); **Hipercor** Avda Meridiana 350-356, Sant Andreu (93 346 38 11); C/Salvador Dalí 15-19, Cornella de Llobregat, Outer Limits (93 475 90 00).

L'Illa

Avda Diagonal 545-557, Eixample (93 444 00 00/ www.lilla.com). Metro Maria Cristina. **Open** 10am-9.30pm Mon-Sat. *Supermarkets* 9.30am-9.30pm Mon-Sat. **Map** p345 B3.

This gleaming white *supermanzana* (superblock) houses, among other things, over 100 big-name shops including FNAC and Decathlon, a food market on the ground floor, restaurants, a Caprabo hypermarket, and 6,000 sq m of green park – a space that is dwarfed 13 times over by L'Illa's car park.

I should cocoa

Chocolate is God's work. And man has never doubted it, from the Mayan priests who drank it as part of solemn rituals, to the 18th-century European nobles who paid princely sums for the imported delicacy. The price of chocolate was high well into the 19th century and the shops that made and distributed it were accordingly elegant affairs that prized quality and elaborate presentation. Barcelona at the time was a major port for South American trade, and Europe's first chocolate factory opened its doors here in 1780.

Founded in 1885, **Pastisseria Mauri** (Rambla Catalunya 102, 93 215 10 20) flaunts numerous treats in a classy Modernista store, with an elegantly painted ceiling. Highly recommendable is the 'choco-croc' – honey-glazed hazelnuts covered with dark chocolate, while not quite as classic but every bit as delicious are the wonders produced by the 'Mozart of chocolate' **Antoni Escribà**. He is famous for winning local Easter cake competitions that take on Cold War proportions as stores try to outdo each other with successively more fantastic creations. Although his Rambla shop (*see p199*) is

housed in a stylish Modernista building, the products are best sampled at the main Escribà store on the Gran Via, where one can catch a view of the bustling kitchen and sample the chocolate (try the *sacher* – a rich tart with apricot jam), as it is brought out by one of Escribà's three sons.

Bombones Blasi (C/Alfons XII, 26, 93 415 52 79) is a serendipitous discovery dating back to 1821. Tucked away on a sidestreet in Sant Gervasi, this proud family-run store may not be flashy, but the chocolate sure has soul. With a catalogue of over 500 varieties, there is never a dull moment for the palate, although allegiance often begins with a simple bite into the classic 70 per cent cocoa bar. Equally historic is **Fargas** (C/Pi 16, 93 302 03 42) in the Barri Gòtic, which opened its doors in 1823 and has been selling chocolate ever since from small, but charming wooden displays. The main counter houses a terrific variety of covered nuts and coffee beans, along with other vibrantly coloured dainties, but the real connoisseur should partake of the heavenly, dark truffles displayed in the window. Also dating back more than a century,

Eat, Drink, Shop

La Maquinista

Passeig de Potosí 2, Sant Andreu (902 24 88 42).
Metro Sant Andreu or Torras i Bages. **Open** 10am-
10pm Mon-Sat.
Built to breathe life into the Sant Andreu district, La
Maquinista is Catalonia's largest and newest mall.
The three levels of this open-air complex house 225
shops, ranging from top-rung designers (Adolfo
Domínguez, Purificación García) to ready-to-wear
fashions (Benetton, H&M). There's also a cinema, a
bowling alley and a Carrefour hypermarket.

Maremàgnum

Moll d'Espanya, Port Vell (93 225 81 00/
www.maremagnum.es). Metro Drassanes.
Open 11am-11pm daily. **Map** p342 D7.
Keep going after La Rambla, cross over the undulating wooden bridge, and you'll eventually end up
in this floating full stop. In 1995, the Maremàgnum
complex was a novelty, and its shops, discos, bars,
restaurants and rooftop mini golf course were *the*
places to hang out. As is the way of things, people
moved on, and now it can be eerily empty except
when ice-cream-munching families come on
Sundays to visit the cinemas or the aquarium. The
tilting, open spaces designed by Viaplana and Piñón
are an architectural wonder but their ingenious mirrors only reflect rows of tourist-orientated shops and
restaurants dreaming of past glory.

Antiques

The streets that surround C/Palla, in the Barri
Gòtic, are crowded with antique shops. A range
of more upmarket antiques are also found
around C/Consell de Cent in the Eixample, and
there are some less expensive shops around
C/Dos de Maig near **Els Encants** flea market
(*see p206*). Every Thursday, an **antiques**
market is held in front of the cathedral (*see*
p205) and dealers set up stands at the **Port**
Vell (*see p206*) at weekends.

Angel Batlle

C/Palla 23, Barri Gòtic (93 301 58 84). Metro Liceu.
Open 9am-1.30pm, 4-7.30pm Mon-Fri. **No credit**
cards. Map p344 B2.
Take a trip back in time at Angel Batlle, a movie-set
perfect shop for books and magazines from the 17th
to the 20th centuries, mainly on art, history and literature (in Spanish and Catalan). The shop's central
tables are piled high with wonderful 19th-century
prints, beautiful fashion plates, engravings, postcards, religious texts and maps.

L'Arca de l'Àvia

C/Banys Nous 20, Barri Gòtic (93 302 15 98). Metro
Liceu. **Open** 10am-2pm, 5-8pm Mon-Fri; 11am-2pm
Sat. **Credit** MC, V. **Map** p345 B3.

the venerable **Montserrat del Roc**
(C/Torrent de l'Olla, 81, 93 218 47 43)
in Gràcia has an agreeable feel of aged
authenticity. The Dorremadà family bought
the shop a century ago, and still uses the
original techniques, recipes and packaging.

For professionalism bordering on clinical
obsession, the serious chocolate
enthusiast should visit **Petit Plaisir**
(C/Rosselló 237, 93 217 45 18) in the
Eixample. A *maître chocolatier* prepares
the 68 varieties according to strict Belgian
traditions, and the resulting pleasures
are anything but *petit*.

The most outlandishly stocked store
in town, however, is **Cacao Sampaka**
(*see p199*), which has more varieties of
chocolate than anyone should be forced to
count. The *bonbons*, truffles, fruit/chocolate
combinations, dessert sauces, fondues,
drinkable chocolate and 18 varieties of
cocoa-based ice-cream are simply
astonishing, as are some of the fillings:
anchovy, cheese or curry among them. In
the back there is a tranquil café that serves
coffee, food and, yes, chocolate.

This gorgeous antique clothes shop is regularly plundered by magazine stylists for its beaded flapper dresses, boned corsets, silk shawls, puff sleeves and pin-tucked shirt fronts. Popular with brides looking for something special.

Bulevard dels Antiquaris

Passeig de Gràcia 55, Eixample (93 215 44 99).
Metro Passeig de Gràcia. **Open** *Sept-June* 9.30am-
1.30pm, 4.30-8.30pm Mon-Sat. *July, Aug* 10am-
1.30pm, 4.30-8.30pm Mon-Fri. **Credit** AmEx, MC,
V. **Map** p338 D4.

Up a stairway next to the Bulevard Rosa (*see p182*), this vast arcade houses 73 shops selling antiques, from fine art to alabaster Virgin Marys and art deco furniture. In Turn of the Century, you'll find miniature musical instruments from the 1930s and doll's furniture; Trik-Trak specialises in old tin toys.

Gothsland Galeria d'Art

C/Consell de Cent 331, Eixample (93 488 19 22).
Metro Passeig de Gràcia. **Open** 10am-1.30pm,
4.30-8.30pm Mon-Sat. **Credit** AmEx, DC, MC,
V. **Map** p342 D4-5.

Gothsland Galeria d'Art is a near-unique specialist in original Catalan Modernista art, furniture and decoration. A visit here might introduce you to a spectacular selection of fine furniture (including pieces by Gaspar Homar), polychrome terracotta sculptures by Casanovas, Pau Gargallo and Lambert Escaler, alabaster by Cipriani, Modernista vases and mirrors and 19th-century paintings.

Bookshops

As well as glossy coffee table jewellery, more in-depth books in English about Barcelona are on sale at the **Palau de la Virreina** on the Rambla, as well as the main **tourist office** on Plaça Catalunya and the Generalitat's **Palau Robert** on Passeig de Gràcia (for all, *see p319*). The **MACBA** bookshop (*see p91*) has a good collection of books and magazines (many in English) on architecture, art and culture, while **Laie Libreria Café** (*see p179*) has a more random, leftfield selection.

Casa del Llibre

C/Passeig de Gràcia 62, Eixample (93 272 34 80/
www.casadellibro.com). Metro Passeig de Gràcia.
Open 9.30am-9.30pm Mon-Sat. **Credit** AmEx, DC,
MC, V. **Map** p338 D4.

The 'House of the Book' belongs to a Spanish chain whose website lists more than 500,000 titles. The Barcelona shop has an extensive collection of books that cover a wide variety of subjects, as well as a tiny café where you can rest your feet. Section C is devoted to English-language bestsellers and literature.

FNAC

El Triangle, Plaça Catalunya 4, Eixample (93 344
18 00/www.fnac.es). Metro Plaça Catalunya. **Open**
10am-10pm Mon-Sat. **Credit** AmEx, MC, V. **Map**
p344 A1.

Not only does the buying power of this French-owned megastore ensure some of the lowest prices but also the biggest stocks, including a very decent range of titles in English (and French). The legions of helpful, multilingual staff – cruelly uniformed in green and mustard jerkins – are happy to order any books not in stock, or to point you to the galaxy of CDs, videos, cameras, computer games and other software on sale. Downstairs are concert ticket and film developing desks, a concert auditorium, and a great international newsstand where nobody ever stops you from browsing.
Branch: L'Illa, Avda Diagonal 549, Eixample
(93 444 59 00).

Specialist

Altaïr

Gran Via de les Corts Catalanes 616, Eixample
(93 342 71 71/www.altair.es). Metro Universitat.
Open 10am-2pm, 4.30-8.30pm Mon-Sat. **Credit**
AmEx, MC, V. **Map** p341 B5.

Al-taïr is Arabic for 'that which flies', and this specialist travel bookshop certainly lives up to its name. With more than 50,000 titles and an eponymous

Elephant. *See p186.*

monthly travel magazine, Altaïr has guidebooks and maps of Catalonia, Spain and the rest of the world, as well as anthropology and photography books and CDs. Many titles are in English.

BCN Books

C/Roger de Llúria 118, Eixample (93 476 33 43). Metro Passeig de Gràcia. **Open** 9am-2pm, 4-8pm Mon-Fri; 10am-2pm Sat. **Credit** MC, V. **Map** p342 D4.
An English-language bookshop, stocking predominantly teaching materials and travel guides, but also a reasonable selection of novels, computer manuals and so on. There is also a large selection of dictionaries and reference books.

Elephant

C/Creu dels Molers 12, Poble Sec (93 443 05 94). Metro Poble Sec. **Open** 10am-8pm daily. **No credit cards. Map** p341 B6.
This English bookshop offers overstock, second-hand and remainder books at good prices, including everything from baby books with tapes to who dunnits on CD, with a whole lot of cookbooks, dictionaries and classics in between. Friendly owners Frank and Jackie provide sofas for comfy browsing, and there's also a small café at the back.

Happy Books

Passeig de Gràcia 77, Eixample (93 487 00 31). Metro Passeig de Gràcia. **Open** 9.30am-9pm Mon-Sat. **Credit** AmEx, MC, V. **Map** p338 D4.
Fabulously cheap and with a cheerfully random selection, Happy Books is especially good for dictionaries and imported photographic books on art history, cookery and culture. Depending on the owners' mood, you may or may not find English language books in Zone E. The shop also stocks a wide range of calendars, diaries and address books, and have huge discounts during the sales.
Branch: C/ Pelai 20, Eixample (93 317 07 68).

Llibreria Quera

C/Petritxol 2, Barri Gòtic (93 318 07 43/ www.llibreriaquera.com). Metro Liceu. **Open** *Sept-July* 9.30am-1.30pm, 4.30-8pm Mon-Fri; 10am-1.30pm, 5-8pm Sat. *Aug* 10am-1.30pm, 4.30-8pm Mon-Fri. **Credit** MC, V. **Map** p344 A2.
If you're planning trips to the Catalan countryside and the Pyrenees, this is the ideal place to find good walking maps for every part of the country. Staff also have information on mountaineering and all kinds of outward-bound adventures.

Norma Comics

Passeig de Sant Joan 9, Eixample (93 244 8420/ www. normacomics.com). Metro Arc de Triomf. **Open** 10.30am-2pm, 5-8.30pm Mon-Sat. **Credit** AmEx, MC, V. **Map** p343 E5.
The largest comics shop in Barcelona: one floor is dedicated to European and US comics, another to Japanese manga, and there are special sections for Star Wars, model kits and the like, plus everything imaginable linked to *Lord of the Rings*.

El Ingenio. See p187.

Children

Clothes

For affordable everyday kids' wear try downstairs in **Zara** (*see p193*). **Galeries Maldà** (no phone, C/Portaferrissa 22), in the centre of the Barri Gòtic, is a small shopping centre with plenty of kids' stuff.

Du Pareil au Même

Rambla Catalunya 95, Eixample (93 487 14 49/ www.dpam.com). Metro Passeig de Gràcia. **Open** *Jan-July, Sept-Dec* 10.30am-8.30pm Mon-Sat. *Aug* 10.30am-2.30pm, 5-8.30pm Mon-Sat. **Credit** AmEx, MC, V. **Map** p338 D4.
New outfits arrive twice a week at this colourful shop. Du Pareil au Même is great for cheap and cheerful basics for youngsters aged zero to 14. The garments are surprisingly durable, but be aware that sizes tend to run small.

Menuts

C/Santa Anna 37, Barri Gòtic (93 301 90 83). Metro Catalunya. **Open** 5-8pm Mon; 10.30am-1.30pm, 5-8pm Tue-Fri; 10.30am-8pm Sat. **Credit** MC, V. **Map** p344 B2.
Munchkin-sized Menuts ('little ones' in Catalan) is stuffed with wonderful handmade baby and toddler clothes in traditional styles: smocked tops, crocheted hats and jackets, and dangerously cute knitted bootees. The very tiniest clothes, on display in the window, are for dolls.

Mullor Infants

Rambla Catalunya 102, Eixample (93 215 12 02).
Metro Diagonal. **Open** 10am-2pm, 4.15-8.15pm Mon-
Sat. **Credit** AmEx, MC, V. **Map** p338 D4.
All the essentials for the newborn are made by hand
in the adjacent workshop, including smocked dress-
es and over-the-top christening gowns.

Prénatal

Gran Via de les Corts Catalanes 611, Eixample
(93 302 05 25/www.prenatal.es). **Metro** Passeig de
Gràcia. **Open** 10am-8.30pm Mon-Sat. **Credit** AmEx,
DC, MC, V. **Map** p342 D5.
This French-owned chain has everything: good
quality pushchairs, cots, feeding bottles, toys, plus
clothes for the pregnant mum and for kids aged up
to eight. Branches include a large, central one in
Galeries Maldà on C/Portaferrissa in the Barri Gòtic.

Toys

Drap

C/Pi 14, Barri Gòtic (93 318 14 87). Metro Liceu.
Open 9.30am-1.30pm, 4.30-8.30pm Mon-Fri; 10am-
1.30pm, 5-8.30pm Sat. **Credit** AmEx, DC, MC, V.
Map p344 B2.
The name means rag (as in dolls), and Drap sells
everything related to dolls' houses, much of it handmade. You can buy a basic chair for €12, while the
custom-made houses can cost up to €900.

El Ingenio

C/Rauric 6, Barri Gòtic (93 317 71 38). Metro Liceu.
Open 10am-1.30pm, 4.15-8pm Mon-Fri; 10am-2pm,
5-8.30pm Sat. **Credit** AmEx MC, V. **Map** p345 A3.
A fabulous treasure-trove of ingenious magic tricks,
puppets, party decorations, juggling batons, and all
kinds of fripperous nonsense, from hobby horses to
squirt guns. The speciality is carnival outfits and
masks, whether of papier-mâché or leather, which
range from simple fake noses to the freakish, pump-
kin-like *capgrosses* (big heads) used at carnival time.

Joguines Foyé

C/Banys Nous 13, Barri Gòtic (93 302 03 89). Metro
Liceu. **Open** 10am-2pm, 4.30-8pm Mon-Fri; 10am-
2pm, 5-8.30pm Sat. Closed 2wks Aug. **Credit** AmEx,
MC, V. **Map** p345 B3.
This place runs the gamut from monochrome
Mickey Mouse dolls, tin cars and toy soldiers, to
elaborate china dolls, tricycles, tomato-shaped play
houses, hula hoops, walkie-talkies and a whole wall
of Playmobil toys for toddlers.

Joguines Monforte

Plaça Sant Josep Oriol 3, Barri Gòtic (93 318 22 85).
Metro Liceu. **Open** 9.30am-1.30pm, 4-8pm Mon-Sat.
Credit AmEx, MC, V. **Map** p345 A3.
Get thee behind me Playstation. This venerable old
toy shop concentrates on the quieter pursuits, stocking chess boards, jigsaw puzzles, wooden solitaire
and croquet sets, kites, and pile upon pile of board
games. It also stocks hand puppets and you can pick
up rare Smurfs (*barrufets*) for just €2.55.

Sardina Submarina

C/Cardenal Casañas 7, Barri Gòtic (93 317 11 79).
Metro Liceu. **Open** 10.30am-2pm, 4.30-8.30pm Mon-
Sat. **Credit** AmEx, MC, V. **Map** p345 A3.
Beautiful toys for babies to six-year-olds, mostly
made of soft fabric and wood rather than plastic.
The range includes play mats, baby gyms, con-
struction sets, nursery accessories and all manner
of charming, original board games.

Cleaning & repair

El Corte Inglés department store (*see p182*)
also has shoe repair and key-cutting.

Orange Lavanderie Self-Service

Plaça del Sol 11-12, Gràcia (mobile 639 140 229).
Metro Fontana. **Open** 7am-11pm daily. **No credit**
cards. Map p338 D3.
This busy Italian launderette franchise has state-of-
the-art change machines, as well as drinks, music
and TV. A small load will cost you €3.50 and the
dryers are €3.50 for 20 minutes.

Laundry

C/Escudellers 44, Barri Gòtic (no phone/www.watch
socksdry.com). Metro Drassanes or Jaume I. **Open**
9am-10pm Mon-Sat; 11am-8pm Sun. **No credit**
cards. Map p345 B3.
A self-service wash here costs €3 (plus 60¢ for soap)
and €1 for 12 minutes on the dryer; drop-off service
is €8 for six kilos of laundry. While it tumbles you
can play on the internet for 50¢ for 15 minutes.

Lavomatic

Plaça Joaquim Xirau 1, Barri Gòtic (93 342 51
19). Metro Drassanes. **Open** 9am-9pm Mon-Sat.
No credit cards. Map p344 A4.
This is a funky self-service launderette just off the
Rambla, where a seven-kilo load costs €3.75 and five
minutes on the dryer costs 75¢. Dry-cleaning and
home delivery also offered.
Branch: C/Consolat del Mar 43-45, Born
(93 268 47 68).

Tintorería Ferran

C/Ferran 11, Barri Gòtic (93 301 87 30). Metro
Liceu. **Open** 9am-2pm, 4.30-8pm Mon-Fri. **Credit**
V. **Map** p345 A3.
The claim here that it's 'cheaper than washing at
home' is dubious: six kilos washed, dried and folded will set you back a hefty €14.40. However, the
dry-cleaning service is very efficient and costs €6.75
for a jacket or €2.90 for a shirt, and there is also an
ironing and home delivery service.

Crafts & gifts

The most fertile ground for gift shops is,
naturally, around the big tourist sites such as
C/Montcada, next to the Picasso museum.
Some of the museum gift shops themselves are
especially worthy of mention: the **Espai Gaudí**

ENJOY THE BEST
BRANDS IN FASHION
AT REDUCED PRICES

COME AND ENJOY OUTLET SHOPPING IN THE COOL, SHADED STYLE OF A 19TH CENTURY CATALAN TOWN, EAT AT THE TERRACED RESTAURANTS OR SIMPLY SIT AT A CAFÉ AND COUNT YOUR SAVINGS.

AT LA ROCA VILLAGE YOU WILL DISCOVER OVER 50 STORES OF YOUR FAVOURITE SPANISH AND INTERNATIONAL DESIGNER NAMES IN FASHION, ACCESSORIES, BED AND BATH, SPORTSWEAR AND HOMEWARE OFFERING END OF SEASON COLLECTIONS. PRICES REDUCED BY UP TO 60% ALL YEAR ROUND. TERRACED RESTAURANTS AND CAFÉS. SUPERVISED CRÈCHE. FREE PARKING.

Exit 12 (Cardedeu)   A-7
Barcelona   Girona

For more information and opening hours please call:
(+34) 93 842 39 39 / www.larocavillage.com

LA ROCA VILLAGE

OUTLET SHOPPING

in La Pedrera (*see p113*) has all kinds of quality Gaudiana, from mouse pads to posters, glassware and reproduction pavement slabs from Passeig de Gràcia. The **Fundació Joan Miró** (*see p106*) stocks games and calendars in Miró's trademark primary colours, plus a good range of books, as does the **MACBA** (*see p91*), while the **Museu Tèxtil** (*see p96*) is great for quirky jewellery and scarves.

Art Escudellers

C/Escudellers 23-25, Barri Gòtic (93 412 68 01/ www.escudellers-art.com). Metro Drassanes. **Open** 11am-11pm daily. **Credit** AmEx, DC, MC, V. **Map** p345 A/B3.

You could do all your gift shopping in one blow at this enormous shop, then, to make things easier, make use of the worldwide shipping service. Artisan Spanish products (mainly ceramics) are grouped by region, from the latticed brown plates of Jaén to the splashy blue and green tiles of Granada. Everyday ware – such as smashable clay *huchas* (piggy banks) – can be found upstairs, while downstairs there are more exclusive pieces and hundreds of Spanish wines, which can be sampled at the bar.

Baraka

C/Canvis Vells 2, Born (93 268 42 20). Metro Jaume I. **Open** 10am-2pm, 5-8.30pm Mon-Fri; 11am-2pm, 5-8.30pm Sat. **Credit** AmEx, DC, MC, V. **Map** p345 C4.

'The only thing here that isn't from Morocco is me,' says co-owner Dani. Visitors will see that he is right, surrounded by leather babucha slippers, lamps, tagines, and rugs. Dani also stocks many CDs of Arabic music, books on Moroccan culture, kohl powder, henna, hookah pipe tobacco, and incense.

Caixa de Fang

C/Freneria 1, Barri Gòtic (93 315 1704). Metro Jaume I. **Open** 10am-8pm Mon-Sat. **Credit** AmEx, DC, MC, V. **Map** p345 B3.

A small ceramics shop – the *fang* refers to clay, not teeth – shining with glassware, glazed *azulejos* (tiles), cup-and-saucer sets inspired by Joan Miró, and all kinds of kitchenware. You can pick up a *crema catalana* ramekin for just 60¢.

Design & household

BD Ediciones de Diseño

Casa Thomas, C/Mallorca 291, Eixample (93 458 69 09/www.bdbarcelona.com). Metro Passeig de Gràcia. **Open** 10am-2pm, 4-8pm Mon-Fri; 10am-2pm, 4.30-8pm Sat. Closed 3wks Aug. **Credit** AmEx, DC, MC, V. **Map** p338 D4.

Located in a magnificent Modernista house built by Domènech i Muntaner in 1895, BD is an institution of the Barcelona design world. The shop is best known for its reproductions of classic designs by design deities like Gaudí, Dalí and Charles Mackintosh. This is the place to buy Gaudí's curving Calvet armchair or his Batlló bench. The stun-

ning art nouveau space also showcases works by contemporary big boys, such as Toni Miró, Javier Mariscal and the shop's co-founder, Oscar Tusquets.

Dom

Passeig de Gràcia 76, Eixample, (93 487 11 81/ www.id-dom.com). Metro Passeig de Gràcia. **Open** 10.30am-8.30pm Mon-Fri; 10.30am-9pm Sat. **Credit** DC, MC, V. **Map** p338 D4.

How many disco balls died to make this shop? Newly expanded, Dom is all about the most gigantic lava lamps you'll ever see, mirrorballs, pricey chrome gadgets and PVC furniture, comprising an approach to home decor that can only be described as corporate *Barbarella*.

Branch: C/Avinyó 7, Barri Gòtic (93 342 55 91).

Gemma Povo

C/Banys Nous 5-7, Barri Gòtic (93 301 34 76/www. gemmapova.com). Metro Liceu. **Open** 10am-1.30pm, 4.30-8pm Mon-Fri; 10am-1.30pm, 5-8.30pm Sat. Closed 2wks Aug. **Credit** AmEx, DC, MC, V. **Map** p345 B3.

A family-run, artisan shop specialising in wrought-iron lamps, wine racks, tables and bedsteads, all designed by the owner, who gives a slick twist to traditional rustic favourites. She also sells beautiful glassware and country house style furniture.

Gotham

C/Cervantes 7, Barri Gòtic (93 412 46 47/ www.gotham-bcn.com). Metro Jaume I. **Open** 10.30am-2pm, 5-8.30pm Mon-Sat. **Credit** DC, MC, V. **Map** p345 B3.

If Pedro Almodóvar were to open a furniture shop, this is what it would look like. Off-the-wall, retro furniture from the 1930s and '40s, in warm, almost cartoonish, colours, and great lamps, vases, glassware and other accessories from the '50s and '60s.

Ici et Là

Plaça Santa Maria del Mar 2, La Ribera (93 268 11 67/www.icietla.com). Metro Jaume I. **Open** 4.30-8.30pm Mon; 10.30am-8.30pm Tue-Sat. **Credit** AmEx, MC, V. **Map** p345 C3/4.

Whimsical butterfly lamps, padded velvet thrones, stone coffee tables or quartz crystal doorknobs: these pieces, sourced by a French and Spanish female collective, are about as affordable as new original design can be. Check out the horned and curlicued metal furniture by French artist, Pagart.

Pilma

Avda Diagonal 403, Eixample, (93 416 13 99/ www.pilma.com). Metro Diagonal. **Open** 10am-2pm, 4.30-8.30pm Mon-Sat. Closed 2wks Aug. **Credit** AmEx, DC, MC, V. **Map** p338 D4.

What started as a small cabinetmaker's workshop in the 1930s has transformed into a pillar of BCN design. Ramps connect the store's four levels, with sections devoted to furniture, lighting, gifts and kitchen/bathroom products. Even if you're not in the market for furnishings, this is a great place to keep up with cutting-edge design.

Eat, Drink, Shop

Maremàgnum. *See p183.*

Vinçon

Passeig de Gràcia 96, Eixample (93 215 60 50/ www.vincon.com). Metro Diagonal. **Open** 10am-8.30pm Mon-Sat. **Credit** AmEx, MC, V. **Map** p338 D4.

This revered temple to home design is all about names – and drops them regularly. Each major piece or collection is accompanied by a crib sheet on its creator, from big boys such as Mariscal to lesser known artists such as Skully, whose lamps shaded with foetal ultrasound scans are the very latest in cool. While most of the products in the lighting, kitchen, bathroom and kids' departments are affordable(ish), the large furnishings on the gorgeous Modernista upper floor can be prohibitively expensive. But if you're in town in December, watch out for Hipermercart, an art 'supermarket' that's hosted by Vinçon every year. Here, astute buyers can pick up originals by young artists for as little as €60. As part of its corporate expansion, Vinçon has opened a shop around the corner called TincÇon, Catalan for 'I'm sleepy' which is dedicated to the bedroom.
Branch: TincÇon Rosselló 246, Eixample (93 215 60 51)

Zeta

C/Avinyó 22, Barri Gòtic (93 412 51 86). Metro Jaume I or Liceu. **Open** 10.30am-2pm, 4.30-8.30pm Mon-Sat. **Credit** AmEx, DC, MC, V. **Map** p345 B3.

If you like your potato peeler and loo brush holder to have attitude, then Zeta is the shop for you. As well as accessories, it stocks large items such as furniture by Barcelona-based British designer Sig, and cheeky paintings by local satirist, Catman.

Fashion

Current holder of most fashionable street in town is **C/Avinyó**, with an impressive concentration of work by young local designers. Most high-street fashion chains are around **C/Portaferrissa** and **Portal de l'Àngel** in the Barri Gòtic; and **Passeig de Gràcia** and **Avda Diagonal** further uptown. The prices rise with the altitude.

4 Elements

C/Duc de la Victòria 5, Barri Gòtic (93 412 61 66). Metro Liceu. **Open** 10.30am-8.30pm Mon-Sat. **Credit** AmEx, MC, V. **Map** p344 B2.

4 Elements stocks great clubwear from the likes of Block 60, Seal Kay, Fake London and Josep Abril, and jewellery by Locking Shocking.

Inside

C/Llibreteria 19, Barri Gòtic (93 310 31 87). Metro Jaume I or Liceu. **Open** 10.30am-2pm, 4-8.30pm Mon-Sat. **Credit** MC, V. **Map** p345 B3.

The sizes are only for those who think lettuce is the only food group at this rapidly expanding chain with national and international labels such as Miró Jeans, Diesel, Fornarina and an unusual range of footwear by D&G, Adidas and Onitsuka Tiger.
Branch: C/Boters 11, Barri Gòtic (93 301 54 41); C/Tallers 21-23, Raval (93 301 53 03).

Jean-Pierre Bua

Avda Diagonal 469, Eixample (93 439 71 00/ www.jeanpierrebua.com). **Open** 10am-2pm, 4.30-8.30pm Mon-Sat. **Credit** AmEx, DC, MC, V. **Map** p338 C3.

The first, and for many years, the only Barcelona shop to sell avant-garde international designer fashion. Enjoy exclusive selections from Dries van Noten, Sybilla and Jean-Paul Gaultier.

Kwatra

C/Antic de Sant Joan 1, Born (93 268 08 04/ www.kwatra.com). Metro Barceloneta or Jaume I. **Open** 11am-2pm, 4-9pm Mon-Fri; 11am-9pm Sat. **Credit** DC, MC, V. **Map** p345 C3.

This is a bright, airy space in orange and white, and it's all about Nike. Former Nike employee, Robbie Pabla, uses his connections to nab limited series gear and trainers that can't be found elsewhere in the city, including lines like Speedsweep, Superfly and Rifts.

Loft Avignon

C/Avinyó 22, Barri Gòtic (93 301 24 20). Metro Jaume I or Liceu. **Open** 10.30am-2.30pm, 4.30-8.30pm Mon-Sat. **Credit** MC, V. **Map** p345 B3.

Clothes for men and women in mercilessly fashionable surroundings. Expect the likes of Vivienne Westwood, Byblos and Gaultier and shoes by Bikkembergs, Hudson and A Guardiani.
Branch: C/Boters 15, Barri Gòtic (93 412 59 10).

Mango

Passeig de Gràcia 65, Eixample (93 215 75 30/ www.mango.es/www.mangoshop.com). Metro Passeig de Gràcia. **Open** 10.15am-9pm Mon-Sat. **Credit** AmEx, DC, MC, V. **Map** p338 D4.

If your average Catalan girl isn't wearing something by Zara, then she's almost certainly wearing something by Mango. This unstoppable Spanish chain received its best press in England after Posh Spice shimmied about in a spray-on turquoise number. Many unsold items end up in the discount store, Mango 2 (C/Girona 37, 93 412 2935).
Branches: throughout the city.

El Mercadillo

C/Portaferrissa 17, Barri Gòtic (93 301 89 13). Metro Liceu. **Open** 11am-9pm Mon-Sat. **Credit** AmEx, DC, MC, V. **Map** p344 B2.

Pounding music, a life-size fibreglass camel and crowds of pierced teenagers mean it's hard to miss the entrance to El Mercadillo, Barcelona's grunge fashion arcade. If you have the patience to trawl through the tightly-packed rails, you could well find psycho-slut disco outfits, second-hand leather and suede jackets, denim and cheap urbanwear. The patio bar at the back looks cool but the service and coffee are both equally poor.

Noténom

C/Pau Claris 159, Eixample (93 487 60 84). Metro Passeig de Gràcia. **Open** 4.30-8.30pm Mon; 10.30am-8.30pm Tue-Fri; 11am-3pm, 4.30-8.30pm Sat. **Credit** AmEx, DC, MC, V. **Map** p338 D4.

Eat, Drink, Shop

Street of dreams

Poodle? Check. Pearls? Check. Platinum credit card and hair to match? Check and check.

Passeig de Gràcia is where shoppers go for glamour, and the last word in refinement; even the paving slabs and lampposts were designed by Gaudí. Starting at the top (on the left as you look down to the sea), there's **Gratacós** (No.108, 93 238 7353), a luxury draper's with famous window displays of mannequins wearing 'dresses' made from pinned and swathed materials. Opposite is the **Palau Robert** tourist office (*see p319*) with a useful book shop, and the **Gimeno** (*see p208*) smoking emporium, leading down to globalisation corner on C/Rosselló with a new Starbucks next to a Halifax bank.

Pause to take in the view of Gaudí's La Pedrera on the left, but don't waste too much valuable shopping time, as next door at No.96 the vast expanses of **Vinçon** (*see p191*) are waiting to be explored. Inside, the household designer goodies are Conran to the power of ten, and just for extra points, the building used to belong to the painter Ramon Casas.

Down past C/Provença on the right, is the incongruously dingy-looking **New Deal Factory Store** (*see p195*), selling – oh, the horror – discount designer seconds. On the same block, you can buy diaries for your lunch appointments at **Happy Books** (*see p186*), and admire the antique jewellery at the tiny **Novecento** (*see p197*). The block after C/Mallorca is an ivory satin train of bridal shops selling confetti-strewn fantasies, right next to a wedding list-friendly **Dom** (*see p189*).

Continuing down past C/València are the grand shopping arcades of **Bulevard dels Antiquaris** (*see 185*) and **Bulevard Rosa** (*see p182*). If there's still life left in the old credit card, you might pick up some designer threads at **Armand Basi** (*see p193*) or cross over the road to **Replay** (No.60, 93 467 72 24). Even if you're not interested in the clothes, it's worth a peep for the whacked-out jungle chic, with lily ponds, flying human-sized insects, and transformer pod changing rooms. **Burberry** (93 215 81 04) occupies the retail cemetery next door at No.56, where giants like Virgin Megastore and the Fashion Café have folded, evoking universal schadenfreude.

Over on the Manzana de la Discordia, **Bagués** jewellers (*see p195*) occupies Puig i Cadafalch's Casa Amatller, while **Loewe**'s (*see p196*) rinky-dink leather bags live at Domènech i Montaner's Casa Morera, to the disgust of many architectural purists, still up in arms about the destruction of the original windows to make way for Loewe's glitzy display cases.

From here it's all about fashion, and the flagship stores of high street giants such as **Adolfo Domínguez** (*see p193*), **Diesel** (No.19, 93 445 83 60), **Mango** (*see p191*) and **Zara** (*see p193*) are cheek by jowl with designer boutiques, the likes of Chanel or Hermès.

Just to finish with a bang, the end of the boulevard of broken bank accounts is marked by the queen bee of Spanish retail, **El Corte Inglés** (*see p182*), where you'll find everything and more, all under one roof.

Noténom (meaning 'nameless') is a collection of labels such as Exté, Comme des Garçons, Maurizio Pecoraso and D2. The two-level shop sells clothes and accessories for both sexes, and men in particular can get their hands on daring pieces that are difficult to locate anywhere else in town.

On Land

C/Princesa 25, Born (93 310 02 11/www.on-land.com). Metro Jaume I. **Open** 5-8.30pm Mon; 11am-2pm, 5-8.30pm Tue-Sat. Closed 1wk Aug. **Credit** AmEx, MC, V. **Map** p345 C3.

Selected items for men and women by On Land's own label plus Giménez and Zuazos' BoBa line of knitwear, bright cords from Josep Font II (his more affordable line) and sharp combos from Josep Abril. Also stocked are spray-on Petit Bateau T-shirts, and tops by popular local label Divinas Palabras, with cheeky slogans like 'Shopping makes me feel dirty'. Expect no mercy, however, if returning faulty goods.
Branch: C/Valencia 273, Eixample (93 215 56 25).

Overales & Bluyines

C/Rec 65, Born (93 319 29 76). Metro Barceloneta. **Open** 10.30am-8.30pm Mon-Sat. **Credit** AmEx, DC, MC, V. **Map** p345 C3.

A spacious shop with a post-industrial flavour, stocking vintage denim, Levi's Red Tab, Diesel and Paul Smith, as well as own label T-shirts and flatteringly cut jeans, which go for about €100 a pop. Also stocked are the coveted Freitag bags made out of recycled truck seatbelts and tarpaulin.

Tactic

C/Enric Granados 11, Eixample (93 451 03 87). Metro Plaça Universitat. **Open** 10.45am-2.30pm, 5-8.15pm Tue-Sat. **Credit** AmEx, MC, V. **Map** p338 C4.

Fashion for surfers and skaters, from the likes of Quiksilver, Ripcurl, Volcom and many others. It also specialises in snowboarding, windsurfing and kitesurfing: clothes and accessories for dudes.

Tribu

C/Avinyó 12, Barri Gòtic (93 318 65 10/ www.dresslab.com). Metro Jaume I. **Open** 11am-2.30pm, 4.30-8.30pm Mon-Sat. **Credit** AmEx, MC, V. **Map** p345 B3.

Tribu has a warren of showrooms that are filled with alternative clothes, shoes and accessories by internationally recognised names like Homeless, E-Play, Buffalo and Space Club, as well as local designers such as Spastor, the duo who became infamous for their dress made out of real chicken skin.

Trip Shop

C/Duc de la Victoria 13, Barri Gòtic (93 412 67 11). Metro Catalunya. **Open** 11am-2pm, 5-8.30pm Mon-Sat. **Credit** AmEx, DC, MC, V. **Map** p344 B2.

As much a hang-out as a shop, the name tells you all you need to know about the unbending clothes and music policy. If you can peel the staff's eyelids back for long enough, they'll guide you around great hip hop gear by Sir Benni Miles, South-Pole, Clench, Fubu and Phat Farm. Groovy.

Zara

C/Pelai 58, Eixample (93 301 09 78). Metro Catalunya. **Open** 10am-9pm Mon-Sat. **Credit** AmEx, DC, MC, V. **Map** p344 A1.

Now with some 500 shops in 30 countries, Zara's popular appeal lies in a constant influx of new designs and very affordable prices, which belie the relatively sophisticated look of many of the clothes. The secret lies in convincing copies of current catwalk designs, covering the gamut from sporty casuals to suits and slinky evening wear.
Branches: throughout the city.

[z]ink

C/Avinyo 14, Barri Gòtic (93 342 6288). Metro Jaume I or Liceu. **Open** 4.30-8.30pm Mon; 10.30am-2.30pm, 4.30-9pm Tue-Sat. **Credit** AmEx, DC, MC, V. **Map** p345 B3.

[z]ink is a deeply cool shop that receives regular makeovers from local artists. Stock includes Levi Red, Adidas classics, Junya Watanabe, Retrofame, and David Delfin, who controversially hit the headlines in 2002 by accessorizing with hangmen's nooses and head sacks.

Designer

Adolfo Domínguez

Passeig de Gràcia 32, Eixample (93 487 41 70/ www.adolfodominguez.es). Metro Passeig de Gràcia. **Open** 10am-8.30pm Mon-Sat. **Credit** AmEx, DC, MC, V. **Map** p342 D5.

Snapping at Zara's corporate heels comes another Galician retail giant, Adolfo Domínguez. Classic men's and women's designs are aimed squarely at the serious and stylish thirty- and fortysomethings. There is also the Linea U label, which includes fresher, more streetwise designs for younger people, most of which come in denim or linen.
Branches: Avda Diagonal 490, Gràcia (93 416 17 16); La Maquinista, C/Ciutat d'Asunción, Sant Andreu (93 360 8753); Passeig de Gràcia 89, Eixample (93 215 13 39).

Antonio Miró

C/Consell de Cent 349, Eixample (93 487 06 70/ www.antoniomiro.es). Metro Passeig de Gràcia. **Open** *Jan, Mar-July, Sept-Dec* 10am-8.30pm Mon-Sat. *Feb, Aug* 11am-2pm, 5-8pm Tue-Sat. **Credit** AmEx, DC, MC, V. **Map** p342 D5.

Probably the biggest name in Catalan fashion, Toni Miró makes slickly tailored urban clothing in between prestige projects such as designing the ceremonial outfits for the 1992 Olympics, or a backdrop for the Teatre Liceu. He tends to favour sober hues, although he now has a funkier label aimed at young people, called Miró Jeans (93 342 58 75, C/Provença 249 or C/Pi 11).

Armand Basi

Passeig de Gràcia 49, Eixample (93 215 14 21/ www.armandbasi.com). Metro Passeig de Gràcia. **Open** 10am-8.30pm Mon-Sat. **Credit** AmEx, DC, MC, V. **Map** p338 D4.

This Spanish designer's spring and summer 2003 collection, 'Spanglish', is a colourful, graffiti-influenced study of the Latinisation of the United States. Typically this both complements and contrasts with his previous season, which was a floatier affair inspired by Latin American magic realism. His flagship store also stocks his more traditional men's and women's classic collections.

Custo Barcelona

Plaça de les Olles 7, Born (93 268 78 93/www.custo-barcelona.com). Metro Jaume I. **Open** 10am-10pm Mon-Sat; 1-8pm Sun. **Credit** AmEx, DC, MC, V. **Map** p345 C4.

Although Catalan designer Custodio Dalmau designs general couture, it's his instantly recognisable, stretchy cotton tops that everyone wants. Bearing strident designs and glamorous faces, they have become so popular that you can expect to pay anything from €58 for a tank top to €270 for a more ambitious creation, that might contain up to eight different materials. The shop has recently expanded to include a denim section.

Giménez y Zuazo

C/Elisabets 20, Raval (93 412 33 81). Metro Catalunya. **Open** 10.30am-2.30pm, 5-8.30pm Mon-Fri; 10.30am-2pm Sat. **Credit** AmEx, MC, V. **Map** p344 A2.

The idea that really brought success to this award-winning duo was their second line of subtly quirky clothing called BoBa – a composite of *bonito* and *barato* (good and cheap) – consisting of T-shirts (about €40 each) and fashion in unusual fabrics. The joke is that *boba* also means silly or foolish, although in this case it proved to be anything but.
Branch: C/Rec 42, Born (93 310 67 43).

Josep Font

C/Provença 304, Eixample (93 487 21 10/ www.josepfont.com). Metro Diagonal. **Open** *Sept-July* 10am-8.30pm Mon-Sat. *Aug* 10am-2pm, 4.30-8.30pm Mon-Sat. **Credit** AmEx, MC, V. **Map** p338 D4.

Now well-established, this star of a crop of promising young designers produces hand-sewn garments, which often feature strong silhouettes and classic Spanish embroidery, and border on haute couture.

Designer bargains

New Deal Factory Store

Passeig de Gràcia 81, Eixample (93 215 03 80). Metro Passeig de Gràcia/22, 24, 28 bus. **Open** 10.30am-8.30pm Mon-Sat. **Credit** MC, V. **Map** p338 D4.

If you're not put off by the blaring radio, heaving rails and beige plasterboard, you could get up to 70 per cent off names like Moschino, Guess, Dolce & Gabbana, Versace or Ozbek.

Stockland

C/Comtal 22, Barri Gòtic (93 318 03 31). Metro Urquinaona. **Open** 10am-8.30pm Mon-Sat. **Credit** AmEx, DC, MC, V. **Map** p344 B2.

Originally known as Preu Bo ('good price'), this discount outlet is still living up to its former name, with nicely preserved end-of-lines by various designers, mostly Spanish, including Jordi Cuesta, Purificación Garcia and Jocomomola (Sybilla's younger range).
Branches: C/Balmes 308, Zona Alta (93 414 44 57); C/Craywinckel 5, Zona Alta (93 418 81 74).

Fashion accessories

Jewellery

Alea

C/Argentería 66, Born (93 310 13 73). Metro Jaume I. **Open** 10.30am-2.30pm, 5-8.30pm Tue-Sat. Closed 2 wks Aug. **Credit** AmEx, MC, V. **Map** p345 C3.

This tiny new showroom carries funky modern pieces in gold and silver as well as more unusual materials like enamel, methacrylate and glass. Check out the nuts, bolts and curled spring pieces by Miró Jeans, silver drop jewellery by Karen Hallam, and pendants like broken eggshells.

Bagués

Passeig de Gràcia 41, Eixample (93 216 01 73). Metro Passeig de Gràcia. **Open** 10am-8.30pm Mon-Fri; 10am-1.30pm, 5-8pm Sat. **Credit** AmEx, DC, MC, V. **Map** p338 D4.

This high-end jeweller's and watchmaker's, founded in 1839, sits in Puig i Cadafalch's Casa Amatller. Bagués is especially known for Modernista-inspired jewellery, and in 2002 it featured a homage to Gaudí with pieces by Lluís Masriera. Watch out for the high security double entrance – you must close one door and wait a little before the other will open.
Branch: C/Rambla de les Flors 105, Barri Gòtic (93 481 70 50).

Forvm Ferlandina

C/Ferlandina 31, Raval (93 441 80 18). Metro Universitat/24, 41, 55, 64, 91, 141 bus. **Open** 10.30am-2pm, 5-8.30pm Tue-Fri; 11am-2pm Sat. **Credit** AmEx, MC, V. **Map** p342 C5.

Near the MACBA, this work space and showroom features appropriately contemporary jewellery from leading designers. Some pieces are decidedly challenging while others are more practical and easier to wear. But is it jewellery or is it art?

Platamundi

C/Montcada 11, Born (93 268 10 94). Metro Jaume I. **Open** 10am-8pm Mon-Sat; 10am-3pm Sun. **Credit** AmEx, DC, MC, V. **Map** p345 C3.

Neat, affordable pieces in silver and other materials by local designers such as Ricard Domingo. The most popular lines combine silver with blue-hued enamels, notably the Gaudí-inspired rings, which will likely last a lot longer than a tourist T-shirt in your sartorial affections.
Branches: C/Hospital 37, Raval (93 317 13 89); Plaça Santa Maria 7, Born (93 310 10 87); C/Portaferrissa 22, Barri Gòtic (93 317 42 99).

Eat, Drink, Shop

Leather & luggage

Calpa
C/Ferran 53, Barri Gòtic (93 318 40 30). Metro Liceu.
Open 9.30am-2pm, 4.30-8pm Mon-Fri; 10am-2pm, 5-
8.30pm Sat. **Credit** AmEx, DC, MC, V. **Map** p345 B3.
This shop has bags of bags: from old-fashioned
leather suitcases to snap-shut doctors' valises and
affordable Kipling rucksacks and handbags.
Branch: Galeries Maldà, C/Pi 5, Barri Gòtic (93 412
58 22).

Casa Antich SCP
C/Consolat del Mar 27-31, La Ribera (93 310 43
91/ www.casaantich.com). Metro Jaume I. **Open**
9am-8pm Mon-Fri; 9.30am-8.30pm Sat. **Credit** DC,
MC, V. **Map** p345 B4.
Teetering stacks of hold-alls, briefcases, suitcases
and metal steamer trunks big enough to sleep in are
wall-to-wall here. Designs are mostly big names
such as Samsonite or Rimowa, but staff will also
make bags to your personal specifications.

Loewe
Passeig de Gràcia 35, Eixample (93 216 04 00/
www.loewe.com). Metro Passeig de Gràcia. **Open**
10am-8.30pm Mon-Sat. **Credit** AmEx, DC, MC, V.
Map p342 D5.
This top-of-the-range leather company has its main
Barcelona shop in Domènech i Montaner's Casa
Morera. Inside the shop there are two floors of high-
priced clothes and wonderfully supple leather and
sheepskin items, including bags, suitcases, scarves
and other accessories of superb quality. It can be
dangerously tempting to spend as much as €450 on
one of their power handbags.
Branches: Avda Diagonal 570, Eixample (93
200 09 20); Avda Diagonal 606, Eixample (93 240
51 04).

Lingerie & underwear

Look out for affordable swimwear and
underwear, sold as mix-and-match separates,
in high-street chains such as **Women's Secret**
(C/Portaferrissa 7-9, 93 318 92 42) or the
excellent **Oyshu** (Rambla de Catalunya 77, 93
488 36 01), which comes from the same stable
as the ever popular Zara.

Ciutad
Avda Portal de l'Àngel 14, Barri Gòtic (93 317
04 33). Metro Catalunya. **Open** 10am-8.30pm
Mon-Fri; 10.30am-9pm Sat. **Credit** AmEx, MC, V.
Map p344 B2.
A collection of combs and toilet articles are displayed over wooden dressing tables in this charming shop that has sold underwear and real bristle
brushes since 1892. The pretty bras and knickers,
along with swimwear and men's underpants, are
stashed behind the counter, so you'll have to ask for
what you want before trying it on.

The best Objects of desire

A Barça scarf
OK, so they never win anymore…
La Botiga del Barça (see p207).

A *botifarra*
The Catalan sausage *par excellence* and
everybody's favourite rude gesture (a vigorous
two-armed version of the finger). **La
Botifarrería de Santa María** (see p200).

A bottle of cava
Whatever you do, don't call it cheap
champagne. **La Catedral dels Vins i
Caves** (see p202).

Gaudí pavement slabs
Reproductions of the hexagonal swirling
fossils and plants that cover the Passeig de
Gràcia. **Espai Gaudí – La Pedrera** (see p187).

A shitting log
A smiling log (*caga tió*) dumps Christmas
presents on command. But will it catch on
back home? **Fira de Santa Llúcia** (see p218).

Camper shoes
Bendy soles and butter-soft leather.
Everyone's wearing them. **Camper** (see p197).

Capgrosses
Cheeky papier-mâché 'fatheads' for moments
of anonymous carnival madness. **El Ingenio**
(see p187).

Saffron
Get those paellas looking suitably yellow. It's
cheaper here, too. **Herboristeria del Rei** (see
p202, **The Herbalisers**).

Any over-designed household item
A set of fiendishly uncomfortable bicycle saddle
dinner chairs should do it. **Vinçon** (see p191).

Chupa Chups lollipop
Salvador Dalí designed the yellow daisy logo,
and these Catalan-invented 'sucky sucks' are
an essential accessory for clubbers and school
kids alike. Buy them at kiosks everywhere.

Janina

Rambla Catalunya 94, Eixample (93 215 04 84).
Metro Diagonal/FGC Provença. **Open** *Sept-July*
10am-8.30pm Mon-Sat. *Aug* 10am-2pm, 5-8.30pm
Mon-Sat. **Credit** AmEx, DC, MC, V. **Map** p338 D4.
A well-established shop that sells its own exclusive
silk and satin underwear, nightwear and robes, as
well as stockings by Risk and La Perla. A large selection of swimsuits and bikinis is also available.

Scarves & textiles

Although there are textile shops and workshops
all over the Old City, the largest concentration
is in the Born. Contact the tourist offices for
information about browsing the workshops or
taking a tour of the official 'Textile Itinerary'.

Atalanta Manufactura

Passeig de Born 10, Born (93 268 37 02). Metro
Jaume I. **Open** 5-8.30pm Mon; 10.30am-3pm,
5-8.30pm Tue-Fri; 11am-3pm, 5-8.30pm Sat.
Credit AmEx, DC, MC, V. **Map** p345 C3.
Judit Gallimo and Claudio Méndez produce luxurious hand-painted silk scarves, fans, shawls and ties
from their work shop at the back of this little corner
store. Their own designs are subtle and impres-
sionistic but they'll also print anything to order.

Rafael Teja

C/Santa Maria 18, Born (93 310 27 85). Metro
Jaume I. **Open** 10am-3pm, 5-9pm Tue-Sat; 11am-
3pm Sun. **Credit** AmEx, MC, V. **Map** p345 C3.
An unimaginable number of colourful scarves,
wraps, foulards and pashminas vie for attention in
this tiny two-floored shop. Materials include everything from heavily embroidered wool to luxurious
fringed silks but you can also pick up a simple winter scarf for about €15.
Branch: Conde de Salvatierra 10, Eixample
(93 237 70 59).

Second-hand

In the past couple of years, **C/Riera Baixa** in
the Raval has become a centre for second-hand
shops and innovative boutiques. The biggest is
Lailo at No.20 (93 441 37 49), which stocks
opera costumes, military jackets, '80s cocktail
dresses and endless racks of vintage leather
jackets and so on, while more specifically
fashion-oriented is **Recicla Recicla** at
No.13 (mobile 606 110 118), with vintage
Nike tracksuit tops and hip street gear. An
alternative second-hand clothes market is
held on the street every Saturday from May
to September and in December, and on the
first Saturday of every other month.

Novecento

Passeig de Gràcia 75, Eixample (93 215 11 83).
Metro Passeig de Gràcia. **Open** 10am-2pm, 4.30-8pm
Mon-Sat. **Credit** AmEx, DC, MC, V. **Map** p338 D4.

This small second-hand jewellery shop is an anom-
aly among all the smart chain stores. Its windows
are dripping with *bijouterie* from all eras including
Victorian art deco, retro '40s and belle époque, plus
more modern seconds and a few glass ornaments.

Smart & Clean

C/Xuclà 6, Raval (93 412 60 22/www.smartand
clean.com). Metro Catalunya. **Open** 10.30am-
1.30pm, 5-8.30pm Mon-Sat. **Credit** MC, V.
Map p344 A2.
Mods rule in this shrine to '60s and '70s UK fashion
and memorabilia, although the rockers do get a look
in as well. Next to ska, punk and northern soul on
vinyl, there are Fred Perry shirts, satchels, duffels,
Sta Press hipster slacks, drape jackets, penny loafers
and Doc Martens – perfect for wearing to the Vespa
runs and gigs advertised on the lovingly maintained
Smart & Clean website. Check it out.
Branch: C/Riera Baixa 7, Raval (no phone).

Shoes

If you're looking for shoe heaven you'll surely
find it on **Portal de L'Àngel** or **C/Pelai**,
where there's a great selection of shoe shops;
look out for chains such as **Casas**, **Scarpa**,
Mar Bessas or **Querol**, which have huge
stocks, although the models are often displayed
only in the window, so you'll have to drag the
assistants over to point at what you want to
try on. For traditional Catalan footwear, try
espardenyes (also called *alpargatas*), a type
of espadrille with ribbons attached.

Camper

El Triangle, C/Pelai 13-37, Eixample (93 302 41 24/
www.camper.com). Metro Plaça Catalunya. **Open**
10am-10pm Mon-Sat. **Credit** AmEx, DC, MC, V.
Map p344 A1.
The happy Camper phenomenon started in Mallorca,
where the Fluxá family produced shoes made of recycled tyres and canvas for field workers (*campers* in
Catalan.) The most popular lines in recent years have
maintained the basic philosophy of comfort and practicality and include the Pelota bowling shoes and the
mismatched Twin range. Look out for quirky messages such as 'Hispanic causing panic' on their soles.

Czar

Passeig del Born 20, Born (93 310 7222). Metro
Jaume I. **Open** 4-9pm Mon; 11.15am-2.30pm, 4-9pm
Tue-Sat. **Credit** DC, MC, V. **Map** p345 C3.
This ferociously hip little store specialises in design-
er trainers by Puma, Diesel and Adidas but also hard-
er-to-find labels such as Rizzo, Merrell, and Le Coq
Sportif. The first stop for trainers.

La Manual Alpargatera

C/Avinyó 7, Barri Gòtic (93 301 01 72). Metro Liceu.
Open *Jan-Sept, Dec* 9.30am-1.30pm, 4.30-8pm Mon-
Sat. *Oct, Nov* 9.30am-1.30pm, 4.30-8pm Mon-Fri; 10am-
1.30pm Sat. **Credit** AmEx, MC, V. **Map** p345 B3.

Eat, Drink, Shop

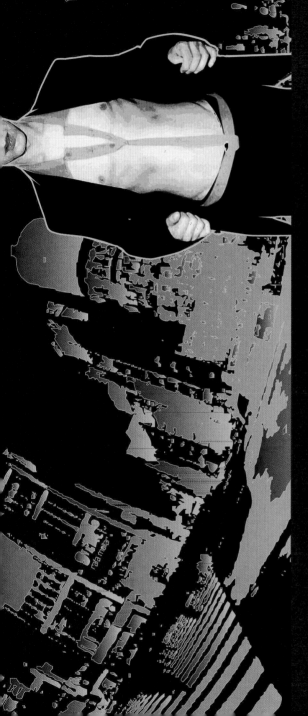

NOTÉNOM

PAU CLARIS 159 08037 BARCELONA T. 934 876 084

HOMBRE helmut lang d-squared levi's red p.a.r.o.s.h. kenzo new york industrie duffer of st. george byblos **MUJER** helmut lang comme des garçons comme des garçons holly p.a.r.o.s.h. maurizo pecoraro lebor gabala miriam ocariz lluís generó cacharel david delfín sonia rykiel **COMPLEMENTOS** helmut lang juan antonio lopez comme des garçons pirelli shoes **PERFUMES** the different company comme des garçons

This shop has famously shod the pope and Jack Nicholson, but prices are still rock bottom for these comfy traditional peasant espadrille shoes of canvas with coiled rope soles. The impressive stacks from floor-to-ceiling include the ribboned Tabarner model that Catalans wear to dance the *sardana*, but you can also have whatever you want made to order.

Muxart

C/Rosselló 230, Eixample (93 488 10 64/ www.muxart.com). Metro Diagonal. **Open** 10am-2pm, 4.30-8.30pm Mon-Fri; 10am-2pm, 5-8.30pm Sat. **Credit** AmEx, MC, V. **Map** p338 D4.

Get ready to drool. Barcelona's supreme shoe deity, Hermenegildo Muxart, whips up sharp, irresistible, sexy designs: from spike-heeled goatskin knee boots to attention-grabbing bags and accessories.
Branch: Rambla Catalunya 47, Eixample (93 467 74 23).

Royalty

Portal de l'Àngel 36, Barri Gòtic (93 317 16 32). Metro Catalunya. **Open** 10am-8.30pm Mon-Fri; 10am-9pm Sat. **Credit** AmEx, DC, MC, V. **Map** p344 B2.

This high street gallery has a pretty representative selection of major Spanish brands such as Ras, Camper, Pedro Garcia and Superga, plus international names such as Clarks and Timberland.
Branch: C/Calvet 23, Zona Alta (93 209 51 32).

Two Much Strong Ma Non Troppo Per Te

C/Avinyó 20, Barri Gòtic (93 412 52 14). Metro Jaume I. **Open** 11am-8.30pm Mon-Sat. **Credit** MC, V. **Map** p345 B3.

The messy tangle of Eurobabble that constitutes the shop's name is strangely at odds with the minimalist design of the shoes. Italian-made leather slip-ons, boots and smart trainers come mainly in a subdued palette of black, chocolate and beige, and shouldn't be Two Much Strong for anybody.

Vialis

C/Vidrieria 15, Born (93 319 94 91). Metro Barceloneta. **Open** 11am-9pm Mon-Sat. **Credit** AmEx, DC, MC, V. **Map** p345 C4.

Vialis uses buttery soft leather on supple soles that are bliss to walk on, whether in strappy sandals or chunky winter boots. This shop also stocks unusual trainers such as restyled versions of the famous '70s 'Munich' sneaker.

Flowers

The famous flower stalls along the Rambla de les Flors originated in the wonderful 19th-century custom of Boqueria market traders giving a free flower to their customers. There are also stands at the **Mercat de la Concepció**, on the corner of C/València and C/Bruc (map p339 E4), which are open all night, and many florists offer the Interflora delivery service.

Flors Navarro

C/Valencia 320, Eixample (93 457 40 99). Metro Verdaguer. **Open** 24hrs daily. **Credit** AmEx, MC, V. **Map** p338 D4.

Fresh-cut blooms, dried flower arrangements, bouquets, plants, and seedlings available 24 hours a day, plus a round-the-clock delivery service.

Food & drink

Pâtisseries and chocolate

For fabulous chocolates see also **Xocoa**. *See p170.*

Cacao Sampaka

C/Consell de Cent 292, Eixample (93 272 08 33/ www.cacaosampaka.com). Metro Passeig de Gràcia. **Open** 9am-9pm Mon-Sat; 5-9pm Sun. **Credit** AmEx, MC, V. **Map** p342 D5.

Ever tried curry chocolate? Mature Cabrales cheese bonbons? Chocolate and tomato jam? The taster café at the back offers 18 varieties of chocolate ice-cream, along with advice on chocolate fondue sets and which cava or wine to drink with your goodies. Call for information about their special gourmet dinners.

Caelum

C/Palla 8, Barri Gòtic (93 302 69 93). Metro Liceu. **Open** 5-8.30pm Mon; 10am-8.30pm Tue-Sat. *Café* 1-8.30pm Tue-Sat. **Credit** MC, V. **Map** p344 B2.

Monasteries and nunneries in Spain are famous for producing high-quality cakes, *yemas* (candied egg yolks) liqueurs or marzipan. Caelum stocks the best of these delicacies from around the country (which you can also sample in the downstairs café) on the site of some 15th-century Jewish baths.

Escribà

Gran Via de les Corts Catalanes 546, Eixample (93 454 75 35). Metro Urgell. **Open** 8am-9pm daily. **Credit** MC, V. **Map** p342 C5.

In the hands of Antoni Escribà, a cake can be anything from Mick Jagger's lips to an edible photograph of the lucky recipient or a mechanised sculpture. As the celebrity-spangled walls of his shops attest, this local Willy Wonka has made cakes for everyone from Dalí to Bruce Springsteen, and his prize-winning chocolate *monas* are displayed in the shop windows at Easter time.
Branch: La Rambla 83, Barri Gòtic (93 301 60 27).

Forn Boix

C/Xuclà 23, Raval (93 302 27 82). Metro Catalunya. **Open** 7am-9pm Mon-Sat. **No credit cards**. **Map** p344 A2.

Since 1920, this friendly bakery has specialised in wholewheat breads. As well as all the standard favourites, the range has grown to include Finnish 14-cereal bread and loaves with lemon, chocolate and walnut, apple, vegetables, onion and meaty *sobrassada*. For sweeter teeth, there's traditional *coques, polverons* and cream cakes.

General food stores

Colmado Afro-Latino

Via Laietana 15, Born (93 268 27 43). Metro Jaume I. **Open** 9am-9pm Mon-Sat; 10am-9pm Sun. **Credit** V. **Map** p345 B3.

Reasonably priced imported foods from Latin America, Africa and further afield are the attraction at this shop. Popular items include guava jam, *mate* from Argentina, *cachaça* from Brazil, Cameroonian palm wine, Peruvian beer, and open sacks of scoopable split peas, lentils, and popcorn.

Colmado Quilez

Rambla Catalunya 63, Eixample (93 215 23 56/ www.lafuente.es). Metro Passeig de Gràcia. **Open** *Jan-Sept* 9am-2pm Mon-Sat. *Oct-Dec* 9am-2pm, 4.30-8.30pm Mon-Sat. **Credit** MC, V. **Map** p338 D4.

Nearly 100 years old, this wonderful corner store is one of the monuments of the Eixample. The mirrored windows and walls are stacked rafter-high with a dazzling variety of olive oils, sweets, preserves, cheeses and Jabugo hams, plus every type of alcohol from saké to whiskies, cava and beers. These range from Trappist monk Chimay to Marston's Oyster stout. It also stocks its own gourmet label, Quilez, which includes Iranian Beluga caviar, cava, Kenyan coffee, *turrón*, saffon and anchovies.

Queviures Murrià

C/Roger de Llúria 85, Eixample (93 215 57 89). Metro Passeig de Gràcia. **Open** *Oct-June* 10am-2pm, 5-9pm Mon-Sat. *July-Sept* 10am-2pm Mon-Sat. Closed 2wks Aug. **Credit** MC, V. **Map** p338 D4.

This magnificent Modernista shop, photographed time and again for its original 1900s tiled decoration by Ramon Casas, and still run by the Murrià family, is not only an architectural attraction. Its wonderful food includes a superb range of individually sourced farmhouse cheeses, and more than 300 wines, including its own-label Cava Murrià.

Food specialities

La Botifarrería de Santa María

C/Santa María 4, Born (93 319 91 23). Metro Jaume I. **Open** 8.30am-2.30pm, 5.30-8.30pm Mon-Fri; 8.30am-3pm Sat. **Credit** AmEx, MC, V. **Map** p345 C3.

The beautifully arranged windows and counters of this porcine shrine glisten pinkly with artisan patés, herb-coated country salami, tender chorizo, top quality *pata negra* hams from Jabugo and, of course, the *botifarra* sausage, which Antoni Travé has raised to an art form. Apart from classics such as egg *botifarras* for Mardi Gras, the '*boti*' has been stuffed with everything from wild mushrooms or Roquefort to squid or coffee. There's even a sweet lemon and cinnamon *botifarra*, and it's no surprise to learn that some of the city's top restaurants buy here.

Casa del Bacalao

C/Comtal 8, Barri Gòtic (93 301 65 39). Metro Urquinaona. **Open** 9am-2.30pm, 4.30-8.30pm Mon-Sat. **Credit** AmEx, MC, V. **Map** p344 B2.

The 'house of cod' sells nothing else – salted and dried, with no chemical additives. Salt cod features in many Catalan and Spanish dishes, which require different parts of the fish: the cheek (*mejilla*) for Galician cod with 'green sauce' and broken-up pieces for Catalan *esqueixada*. The soft throat membrane (*kokotxas*) is a Basque delicacy. Staff can vacuum-pack your fish to take home, but to transform it from a skateboard into something cookable you'll need to soak it overnight (at least).

Casa Gispert

C/Sombrerers 23, Born (93 319 75 35/www. casagispert.com). Metro Jaume I. **Open** *Oct-Dec* 9.30am-2pm, 4-7.30pm Mon-Fri; 10am-2pm, 5-8pm Sat. *Jan-Sept* 9.30am-2pm, 4-7.30pm Mon-Thur; 10am-2pm, 5-8pm Sat. **Credit** DC, MC, V. **Map** p345 C3.

Founded in the 1850s, Casa Gispert is a wholesale outlet famous for top-quality nuts, dried fruit and coffee. All are roasted on site in the magnificent original wood-burning stove; you can delve into enormous baskets of almonds and hazelnuts, still warm from the oven. There are special packs for certain recipes, such as *romesco* sauce, or seasonal goodies, such as *coca de Sant Joan* in June or *panellets* at Hallowe'en. The packaging is also wonderful, and this is a great place to buy presents.

Formatgeria La Seu

C/Dagueria 16, Barri Gòtic (93 412 65 48). Metro Jaume I. **Open** 10pm-2pm, 5-8pm Tue-Fri; 10am-3pm, 5-8pm Sat. Closed 3wks Aug. **No credit cards.** **Map** p345 B3.

Scottish-born Katherine McLaughlin sells a tiny but carefully selected range of oils and cheese from small Spanish producers in this small shop, appropriately located in Barcelona's first buttermaking factory. Katherine also runs monthly cheese courses (taught in Spanish), and you can sample three cheeses with a small glass of wine for €2.

La Pineda

C/Pi 16, Barri Gòtic (93 302 43 93). Metro Liceu. **Open** 9am-3pm, 5-10pm Mon-Sat; 11am-3pm, 7-10pm Sun. **Credit** AmEx, DC, MC, V. **Map** p344 B2.

La Pineda has specialised in *jamón serrano* since 1930, together with other fine cold meats and a wide range of cheeses and wines. The shop – a charming Barri Gòtic survivor – also functions as a local *bodega*, with a few humble tables and stools where you can snack on these delicacies, washed down with a good Rioja.

Tot Formatge 2

Passeig del Born 13, Born (93 319 53 75). Metro Jaume I. **Open** *Sept-May* 8.30am-1.15pm, 4.30-7.30pm Mon-Fri; 9am-1.15pm Sat. *June-Aug* 8.30am-1.15pm, 4.30-7.30pm Mon-Fri. **No credit cards.** **Map** p345 C3.

Colmado Quilez.

Tot Formatge 2 is probably the most comprehensive cheese specialist in Barcelona, with cheeses from Catalonia and Spain, France, Italy and many other parts of Europe. Try *garrotxa*, a local cheese made from goat's milk, or the mild Catalan *mató* (curd cheese), which is made with honey.

Supermarkets

If you don't mind paying a little more, **El Corte Inglés** has a large basement supermarket and a 'gourmet' food section featuring such epicurean delights as Heinz tomato soup (*see p182*).

Champion

Rambla dels Estudis 113, La Rambla (93 302 48 24) Metro Catalunya. **Open** 9.15am-10pm Mon-Sat. **Credit** MC, V. **Map** p344 A2.
Apart from its unbeatable location at the top end of La Rambla, Champion really takes the super out of supermarket. Sluggish check-out lines and haphazard layout make for a frustrating experience. But on it's cheap, open late and has reasonable variety.

Superserveis

C/Avinyó 11-13, Barri Gòtic (93 317 53 91). Metro Jaume I. **Open** 8.45am-2pm, 5-8.30pm Mon-Sat. **Credit** MC, V. **Map** p345 B3.
Just about adequate for general supplies, the strength of this crowded shop is the range of hard-to-find imported food such as curry spices, poppadoms, burrito skins, Marmite, soy sauce and the like.

Wine

Craft shop **Art Escudellers** (*see p189*) has a good selection of wines in its cellar.

La Catedral dels Vins i Caves

Plaça Ramon Berenguer El Gran 1, Barri Gòtic (93 319 07 27). Metro Jaume I. **Open** 4.30-9pm Mon; 10am-2.30pm, 4.30-9pm Tue-Sat. **Credit** AmEx, DC, MC, V. **Map** p345 B3.
Since 1985, Senyor Joan has gathered more than 1,400 wines, cavas and spirits for sale in this charming and well-organised corner shop. Look out for the five varieties of absinthe.

The herbalisers

It's a quiet, slow-moving world of old fashioned weighing scales, racks of labelled glass jars holding mysterious secrets, rustling paper bags and shiny scoops, rather like an adult version of the corner sweet shop. And then there are the smells: the nose-tingling tang of rosemary; the mellow fragrance of camomile, or the sweet smell of star anis that floods the shop when the jar is opened.

Barcelona has around 140 or so of these *herbolaris* – a cross between a chemist's, a health shop, and your great-grandma's kitchen. They have enjoyed a renaissance since Barcelona's alternative health scene boomed about ten years ago, although evergreen festivals such as Sant Ponç (*see p212*) show that the tremendous variety of plant life in Catalonia has always inspired a strong herbal tradition. Famous local herbalists have included the Salvador dynasty and Pius Font i Quer, whose books are still used as botanical reference works today. The traditional colour for an *herbolari* is minty green, suggestive of the hundreds of dried herbs that form the backbone of the stock, although there are also myriad prepared lotions and potions, along with organic health and food products, and even make-up.

The recently restored **Herboristeria del Rei** was Barcelona's first *herbolari*, founded in 1818 by Josep Vilà as La Lineana, after the great Swedish botanist, Linné. Theatre designer Francesc Soler i Rovirosa designed the ornate balcony that winds around the shop at second-floor level, and lined the walls below with hundreds of tiny specimen drawers

Lavinia

Avda Diagonal 605, Eixample (93 363 44 45/
www.lavinia.es). Metro Maria Cristina. **Open**
10am-9pm Mon-Sat. **Credit** AmEx, DC, MC,
V. **Map** p337 A2.
This strikingly modern and massive space houses
thousands of wines, both local and international,
each and every one of them displayed horizontally.
A very efficient online operation is also offered (see
the website). There's also a club, a magazine and regular tasting events for wine enthusiasts.

Vila Viniteca

C/Agullers 7-9, Born (93 310 19 56/www.vila
viniteca.es). Metro Jaume 1. **Open** *Sept-July*
8.30am-2.30pm, 4.30-8.30pm Mon-Sat. *Aug* 8.30am-
2.30pm Mon-Sat. **Credit** AmEx, DC, MC, V.
Map p345 B4.
Since 1932, this friendly family business has built
up a stock of 3,500 wines, mostly from Spain but also
taking in favourites from Italy, South Africa and
California. Pick up one of the wonderful catalogues,
or ask about the wine-tasting courses.

all individually worked in marquetry or
decorated with miniature watercolours. In
1858, the shop became official herbalist
to Queen Isabel II, and changed its name
to Herboristeria del Rei; it stocks over
220 different herbs.

While there is a definite air of the
witches' coven about some *herbolaris*,
others try to suggest medical efficiency
with white coats and bright lights. In these
uncommunicative times, there is a growing
trend for shops like **Herbolari Farran**,
which have cut out the traditional over-the-
counter chit-chat by laying out most of
their products in mini-supermarket style.
Herbolari Farran has been serving a faithful
public since the 1940s. Its large basement
area also comprises a teashop, bookshop
and exhibition area, providing an all-round
health store service.

Herbolari Farran

Plaça Reial 18, Barri Gòtic (93 304 20
05). Metro Liceu. **Open** 9.30am-2pm,
4.30-8pm Mon-Sat. **Credit** MC, V.
Map p345 A3.

Herboristeria del Rei

C/Vidre 1, Barri Gòtic (93 318 05 12).
Metro Liceu. **Open** 5-8pm Mon; 10am-
2pm, 5-8pm Tue-Sat. **Credit** MC, V.
Map p345 A3.

Sephora. See p204.

Hair & beauty

Beauty treatments

Instituto Francis

Ronda de Sant Pere 18, Eixample (93 317 78 08).
Metro Catalunya. **Open** 9.30am-8pm Mon-Fri; 9am-
4pm Sat. **Credit** DC, MC, V. **Map** p344 B1.
Whether you want a wax or non-surgical body
reshaping, you can have it done on one of these eight
floors dedicated to pampering. But it ain't cheap.

Masajes a 1000

C/Mallorca 233, Eixample (93 215 85 85). Metro
Diagonal/FGC Provença. **Open** 7am-1am daily.
Credit AmEx, V. **Map** p338 D4.
Defiantly holding on to its *peseta*-era name, this efficient and economic beauty centre charges by a ticket system. One ticket (€3.60) gets you a half-hour
massage and siesta in an ergonomic chair, while 30
tickets buy a luxurious 90-minute 'four-hand' massage. It offers pedicures, manicures, hair and skin
care, as well as tanning, with no need to book ahead.

Cosmetics & perfumes

Regia

Passeig de Gràcia 39, Eixample (93 216 01 21/
www.regia.es/museo. Metro Passeig de Gràcia. **Open**
10am-8.30pm Mon-Fri; 10.30am-2pm, 5-8.30pm Sat.
Credit AmEx, DC, MC, V. **Map** p338 D4.
There's not just a good selection of perfumes and
cosmetics, but an outstanding perfume museum
that's hidden right at the back, past the offices.

Ranging from eighth-century BC Corinthian perfume pots to vintage Guerlain scent flasks, the history of perfume has never smelled sweeter.

Sephora

El Triangle, C/Pelai 13-39, Eixample (93 306 39 00). Metro Catalunya. **Open** 10am-10pm Mon-Sat. **Credit** AmEx, DC, MC, V. **Map** p344 A1.
The goodies in this French perfume and cosmetics hypermarket are all hidden downstairs, in a striking hall of black and white *Beetlejuice* stripes and red carpets. If you make it past the gloved ladies squirting promotional scents in your face, a vast landscape of perfumes, make-up, accessories and hair and skin products spreads out before you. Prices are excellent, especially for Sephora's own-brand products.
Branch: La Maquinista, C/Ciutat d'Asunción, Sant Andreu (93 360 87 21).

Hairdressers

Anthony Llobet

C/Sant Joaquim 28, Gràcia (93 415 42 10/mobile 639 931 555). Metro Fontana. **Open** 10.30am-3pm, 4-8pm Mon-Fri. Closed 2wks Aug. **Credit** MC, V. **Map** p338 D3.

Anthony and his staff speak English so there's no fear of getting a Ronaldo when you wanted a Beckham. A cut and blow dry costs upwards of €12 (for women) or €10.50 (for men) and there are face and body massages, nail art and extensions.

La Pelu

C/Argenteria 70-72, Born (93 310 48 07/ www.lapelu.com). Metro Jaume I. **Open** 11am-8pm Mon-Wed; 11am-9pm Thur, Fri; 11am-8pm Sat. **Credit** V. **Map** p345 C3.
Massively successful local chain of hairdressers started up by Llum Ventura. Apart from its trademark mullet à la mode, it is also famous for its monthly Full Moon sessions when the branch in C/Argenteria is open from 11pm to 2am, offering special theme nights (tarot readings, live music and comedy, among other things), reduced prices and drinks. Booking essential.
Branches: C/Tallers 35, Raval (93 301 48 07); C/Consell de Cent 259, Eixample (93 454 45 37).

Salva G

C/Avinyó 12, Barri Gòtic (93 302 69 86/www.salva-g.com). Metro Jaume I or Liceu. **Open** 9.30am-8.30pm Mon-Sat. **Credit** AmEx, MC, V. **Map** 343 B3.

Market analysis

It's often said that '*el mercat es el barrí*' (the market is the neighbourhood), and the recent demise of some of Barcelona's 40 local markets has deservedly given rise to much concern about the disintegration of community identity and colour.

Among Barcelona's better markets is **Mercat Sant Antoni**, near the Avda Paral.lel, housed in an ornate cross-shaped iron building with a clothes and Sunday book market around the outside. **Mercat de la Llibertat** in Gràcia has burst its confines and spread on to the streets, with many trestle tables heaving under garlic bulbs or nothing but melons, while **Mercat de la Concepció** on the corner of C/València and C/Bruc, is famous for flowers.

Markets open early (8am or before) and most close by about 2pm or 3pm, with afternoon opening only on Fridays. Monday is not a good day to go, as stocks are low and there is no fresh fish.

The largest and most famous market in Barcelona, though, is unquestionably **La Boqueria**. Pass through the 1914 cast iron and stained-glass portal – rather unromantically heralded by a Dunkin' Donuts – and you enter one of the greatest food markets in the world. Shuffling through the

crowds, the first stall you'll come to on the left is a kaleidoscopic display of neatly stacked fruits and vegetables, and although it's more expensive than the stalls further in, it does stock some hard-to-find fresh herbs such as coriander, tarragon and mint, along with star fruit, papaya and ginger, all garlanded with dark ropes of dried *nyora* peppers.

The stall on the right is a mecca for the hypoglycaemic, with treats such as candied fruits, jelly sweets, *higos chumbos* (Indian figs) or *caña dulce* (sugar cane sticks). Deeper into the labyrinth, it becomes clear that there is order in the madness: fruit and vegetables around the edge, olives and pickles next, moving to separate meat and chicken stalls, then bakeries and eggs, with fish and seafood in the centre. Just to add to the chaos, they are all periodically rearranged to accommodate repair work, although the roof is now finished.

If you can take the noise, some of the cheapest and most authentic bars in the city are under this roof and the tapas is, naturally, as fresh as they come. The cheapest fruit and vegetable stalls are those on the fringes of the market proper, in Plaça Sant Galdric.

Beyond the elaborate window displays at Salva G are über-stylish haircuts with a slightly punky edge, which cost from €16 for men and €27 for women. Makeovers are also offered, in the same vein.
Branch: Plaça de les Olles 4, Born (93 268 17 91).

Markets

There's a market for every mania. For details, call 010 for the council information lines. For details of Barcelona's **food markets**, see p204 **Market analysis**. On the first and third weekend of every month, merchants set up a food fair in the **Plaça del Pi** to sell their artisan food products, including honey and cheese. Also worth a glance is the stamp and coin market in the **Plaça Reial** on Sunday mornings.

Antiques Market

Plaça Nova, Barri Gòtic (93 302 70 45). Metro Jaume I. **Open** *Jan-July, Sept-Dec* 10am-9pm Thur. Closed Aug. **No credit cards. Map** p344 B2.
This Thursday antique market is located in front of the cathedral and dates from the Middle Ages. Vendors display pocket watches, antique lace, cam-

eras and a random assortment of jewellery among the bric-a-brac. Prices are tourist-oriented, so come prepared to bargain. Before Christmas the market transfers to the Portal de l'Àngel.

Art Market

Plaça Sant Josep Oriol, Barri Gòtic (no phone). Metro Liceu. **Open** 11am-10pm Sat; 11am-2pm Sun. **No credit cards. Map** p345 A3.
Every weekend since 1977, some 50 stalls have hawked art of variable quality here, ranging from tourist-friendly renderings of La Rambla to nudes, still-lifes and even abstract art.

Book & Coin Market

Mercat de Sant Antoni, C/Comte d'Urgell 1, Eixample (93 423 42 87). Metro Sant Antoni. **Open** 9am-2pm (approx) Sun. **No credit cards. Map** p342 C5.
This second-hand book and coin market is something of an institution in Barcelona. It takes place in Mercat de Sant Antoni, a wonderful iron building dating from 1876. At around 9am on Sunday mornings, jostling crowds gather to rummage through boxes of dusty tomes, old magazines and video games, as well as whole collections of old coins.

Back inside, the meat and fish stalls are kept firmly in order by cleaver-wielding ladies – most of whom still have a full complement of fingers – and there's many a grisly pile of tongues, tripe, sheeps' heads and skinned rabbits to behold. One step removed from the gore are the stalls for cheeses, *embutidos* (dried meats and sausages) and *jamones*, and the grocery stalls at the far end of the market are packed with prime *jamón de Jabugo*, which will set you back up to €90 a kilo. Just ask, and they'll let you try a slice of whatever you like.

Also at the back is Llorenç Petras' ever-popular woodland stall with wet sacks of snails, dried herbs and baskets overflowing with wild mushrooms (*bolets* in Catalan, *setas* in Spanish). Mushroom hunting is big business in Catalonia, and if you don't fancy a dawn trip to the hills yourself, then this is the place to buy orange-gilled *rovellons*, daffodil-like *llenegues*, delicate *gírgoles* or dried tree barks.

La Boqueria (Mercat de Sant Josep)

La Rambla 91, Barri Gòtic (93 318 25 84). Metro Liceu. **Open** 8am-8.30pm Mon-Sat. **Map** p344 A2.

The best Shops

For high-design homeware
Zeta (see p191); Ici et Là (see p189); Vinçon (see p191).

For drool-worthy jewellery
Platamundi (see p195); Alea (see p195); Forvm Ferlandina (see p195).

For tit-tight tart tops
Custo Barcelona (see p195); Giménez y Zuazo (see p195).

For second-hand helpings
Lailo (see p197); Novecento (see p197); Smart & Clean (see p197).

For the best intentions
Herboristeria del Rei (see p202); Herborlari Farran (see p202).

For the best chocolate
Cacao Sampaka (see p199); Pastisseria Mauri (see p182); Escribà (see p199).

For shoestring savvy
Mango 2 (see p191); Stockland (see p195); New Deal Factory Store (see p195).

For going up in smoke
Gimeno (see p208); L'Estanc de Laietana (see p208).

For smelling of roses
Sephora (see p204); Regia (see p203).

For smelling roses
Flors Navarro (see p199).

For firecracker flamenco
Etnomusic (see p206); FNAC (see p185).

Brocanters del Port Vell
Moll de les Drassanes, Port Vell (no phone). Metro Drassanes. **Open** 10am-9pm Sat, Sun. **No credit cards**. **Map** p345 A4.

Brocanters del Port Vell is a seafront bric-a-brac and antique market, held below the Columbus monument, that's great for shopping or just a wander and a look at the stalls. Popular with locals who are on the lookout for china, coins, collectors' records, costume jewellery, lace mantillas, pocket watches and even military gear. Many complain that the growing number of stalls selling video games and modern clothes have spoilt its character, but it's still a great place for bargains if you show up early.

Els Encants
C/Dos de Maig 186, Plaça de la Glòries, Eixample (93 246 30 30). Metro Glòries. **Open** 8.30am-6pm (auctions 7-9am) Mon, Wed, Fri, Sat. **No credit cards**. **Map** p343 F5.

The future of Els Encants (aka Mercat de Bellcaire) is uncertain in the face of council plans to resculpt and commercialise the entire area. It will eventually be moved and no doubt prettified, so enjoy the city's only authentic flea market while you can. It's a noisy affair place, especially when the morning auctions are under way. Past the fringes, lined by people hawking junk on cloths spread on the ground, you'll find real (and fake) antique furniture, second-hand clothes, tools, old British phone boxes, mountain bikes and heaps of fascinating junk. Try and avoid Saturdays, when it's very crowded, and be on your guard for pickpockets. The antique auctions are best either at 7am (when the commercial dealers buy) or at midday, when unsold goods drop dramatically in price. Although the market is officially open in the afternoons, many stalls pack up at midday; for the best stuff, get there early. And don't be shy to bargain.

Music

Large mainstream music shops can also be found in the huge Portal de l'Angel branch of **El Corte Inglés** (see p182) and the **FNAC** (see p185). C/Tallers, C/Bonsuccés and C/Riera Baixa in the Raval are dotted with speciality shops catering to all tastes and formats; some stock plenty of instruments and sheet music.

Discos Castelló
C/Tallers 3, 7, 9 & 79, Raval (93 318 20 41/ www.discos castello.es). Metro Catalunya. **Open** 10am-2pm, 4.30-8.30pm Mon-Sat. **Credit** AmEx, DC, MC, V. **Map** p344 A2.

This is actually a chain of small shops, each with a different emphasis. No.3 specialises in classical, while No.7 does rock, pop, heavy metal and jazz with a sprinkling of flamenco. The branch in Nou de la Rambla is good for ethnic music.
Branches: C/Nou de la Rambla 15, Raval (93 302 42 36); La Maquinista, C/Ciutat d'Asunción, Sant Andreu (93 360 80 78).

Edison's
C/Riera Baixa 9-10, Raval (93 441 96 74/ www.discos-edisons.com). Metro Liceu. **Open** 10.30am-2pm, 4.30-8.30pm Mon-Sat. **Credit** DC, MC, V. **Map** p342 C6.

Spread over two shops on opposite sides of the street, Edison's buys and sells vinyl LPs, singles and CDs, from the 1950s to the '90s, of all persuasions, from Kool and the Gang to Catalan new age.

Etnomusic
C/Bonsuccés 6, Raval (93 301 18 84/www.etno music.com). Metro Catalunya. **Open** 5-8pm Mon; 11am-2pm, 5-8pm Tue-Sat. **Credit** MC, V. **Map** p344 A2.

Eat, Drink, Shop

This ethnic music shop in the Raval has music from all over the planet, although most foreign visitors seem to be hunting for rare flamenco. Staff know their business and are extremely helpful.

New Phono
C/Ample 37, Barri Gòtic (93 315 13 61/ www.newphono.es). Metro Jaume I. **Open** 9.30am-2pm, 4.30-8pm Mon-Fri; 9.30am-2pm Sat. **Credit** AmEx, DC, MC, V. **Map** p345 B4.
Founded in 1834, this is one of the oldest shops in Spain, and specialises in the manufacture, sale and repair of musical instruments. The wide selection of guitars includes some fine ones by Ramirez, but prices can be high.

Opticians

Arense
Ronda Sant Pere 16, Eixample (93 301 82 90). Metro Catalunya. **Open** 10am-9pm Mon-Sat. **Credit** AmEx, DC, MC, V. **Map** p344 B1.
This full-service optician occupies a gorgeous Modernista space, built in 1874 as the art supply store Casa Teixidor. It sells big-name brands at reasonable prices and an optometrist works in the back behind a stained glass window. The downstairs lab turns specs around within two days.

Grand Optical
El Triangle, Plaça Catalunya 4, Eixample (93 304 16 40). Metro Catalunya. **Open** 10am-10pm Mon-Sat. **Credit** AmEx, MC, V. **Map** p344 B1.
Grand Optical has English-speaking staff who offer eye-tests, and can provide new glasses within two hours (or one hour if you have your prescription). Choose from two floors of designer frames – including big names like Police, Fred and Calvin Klein – and staff will refund the difference if you can find glasses at a cheaper price.

Photography

Arpi Foto Video
La Rambla 38-40 (93 301 74 04). Metro Drassanes or Liceu. **Open** 9am-2pm, 4-8pm Mon-Sat. **Credit** AmEx, DC, MC, V. **Map** p345 A3.
This specialist store caters for both the happy snapper tourist and the true camera buff. It sells disposable cameras and develops 24 colour prints in 24 hours for €6, but also stocks everything from projectors, to underwater Handycams, Polaroids and studio Hasselblads. It has a basic repair centre but queues can be long and slow.

Fotoprix
C/Pelai 6, Raval (93 318 20 36). Metro Universitat. **Open** 9.30am-8.30pm Mon-Fri; 10.30am-8.30pm Sat. **Credit** MC, V. **Map** p344 A1.
Fotoprix has more than 100 branches in the city, offering one-hour film developing, frames, albums and basic selections of film and cameras. To develop 24 colour prints in 24 hours costs €9.

Speciality shops

Alonso
C/Santa Anna 27, Barri Gòtic (93 317 60 85). Metro Catalunya. **Open** 10am-8pm Mon-Sat. **Credit** DC, MC, V. **Map** 342 B2.
This family-run glove shop preserves its ornate Modernista façade and has everything from driving gloves to delicate ivory silks for brides. It also stocks fringed silk shawls, lace mantillas and fans, which, according to Victoria Alonso, speak their own language: fanning quickly means 'I'm engaged'; fanning slowly – 'I'm married'; handle to the lips – 'kiss me'.

Cereria Subirà
Baixada de Llibreteria 7, Barri Gòtic (93 315 26 06). Metro Jaume I. **Open** 9am-1.30pm, 4-7.30pm Mon-Fri; 9am-1.30pm Sat. **Credit** AmEx, MC, V. **Map** p345 B3.
This charming candle store opened in 1761 and preserves much of its original decor, with steps swirling down from the mint green balustraded gallery, heralded by two torch-bearing black maidens.

Flora Albaicín
C/Canuda 3, Barri Gòtic (93 302 10 35). Metro Catalunya. **Open** 10.30am-1pm, 5-8pm Mon-Sat. **Credit** AmEx, MC, V. **Map** p344 A-B2.
Flamenco skirts, *sevillana* dresses, shoes, combs, shawls and men's riding boots jostle for space in this tiny shop. Outfits are also made to measure.

El Rei de la Magia
C/Princesa 11, La Ribera (93 319 39 20/ www.elreidelamagia.com). Metro Liceu. **Open** 10am-2pm, 5-8pm Mon-Fri; 11am-2pm Sat. **Credit** AmEx, MC, V. **Map** p345 B3.
As well as the obligatory rubber chickens and fake turds, this wonderful old joke and magic shop – founded in 1881 – specialises in illusion for practitioners of all levels, and tricks are also made on site. The basic drawer box costs about €19.50 and co-owner Jack, a performing magician from New York, will help you learn how to use it in the curtained-off back space. While you're there, ask Jack about the nearby magic workshop, or the new magic museum that is opening on C/Oli.

Sport

La Botiga del Barça
Maremàgnum, Moll d'Espanya, Port Vell (93 225 80 45). Metro Drassanes. **Open** 11am-11pm daily. **Credit** AmEx, DC, MC, V. **Map** p342 D7.
If your lust for FC Barcelona gear remains unsatisfied by the offerings on the Rambla, try their official outlet. Recently taken over by Nike, La Botiga has every permutation of Barça merchandise imaginable, from standard scarves, lighters and hats, to strips printed with your name while-u-wait and a range of classy items for your lovely home including claret-and-blue clocks and champagne flutes bearing the Barça shield.

Eat, Drink, Shop

El Rei de la Magia. *See p207.*

CASA FUNDADA EN 1881

Branches: Gran Via de les Corts Catalanes 418, Eixample (93 423 59 41); Museu del FC Barcelona, Nou Camp (93 490 68 43).

Decathlon
*C/Canuda 20, Barri Gòtic (93 342 61 61/
www.decathlon.es). Metro Catalunya.* **Open** 10am-9pm Mon-Fri; 10am-9.30pm Sat. **Credit** DC, MC, V. **Map** p344 B2.
Three floors of attire and equipment for every sport, from scuba diving to cycling. It is especially strong on hiking gear and has a trustworthy repair department for bicycles in the basement.
Branch: L'Illa, Avda Diagonal 549, Eixample (93 444 01 54).

Ticket agents

The best places to get advance tickets are often the venues themselves. Concert tickets for smaller venues may be sold in record shops; look out for details on posters. **FNAC** (*see p185*) has an efficient ticket desk for advance rock/pop concert tickets.

Servi-Caixa – La Caixa
902 33 22 11/www.servicaixa.com. **Credit** AmEx, DC, MC, V.
Next to the cash machines in branches of the biggest savings bank of all, the Caixa de Pensions (better known just as La Caixa), you'll find a machine called a Servi-Caixa. With a debit or credit card, you can use this to get T10 and T-50/30 travel cards (*see p305*), local information and tickets to a great many attractions and events, including Universal Studios Port Aventura, Barça football games, the Teatre Nacional and the Liceu, 24 hours a day. You can also order tickets by phone (many of the staff speak some English) or through the website.

Tel-entrada – Caixa Catalunya
902 10 12 12/www.telentrada.com. **Credit** MC, V.
Tel-entrada sells tickets for many theatres around Barcelona. You can buy them over the counter at all its branches. You can also book tickets by phone with a credit card (many of the staff speak reasonable English), but you must collect the tickets at the venue itself. You can also phone from outside Spain (on 34 93 479 99 20), or buy tickets on the internet.

Tobacco & cigars

L'Estanc de Laietana
Via Laietana 4, Born (93 310 10 34). Metro Jaume I. **Open** 9am-2pm, 4-8pm Mon-Fri; 10am-2pm Sat. **Credit** (gifts, not cigarettes) AmEx, MC, V. **Map** p345 B4.
This famous tobacconist stocks more than 100 brands of cigarettes and 100 types of rolling tobacco; the exceptional range of fine cigars is stored in an underground humidor at sea level.

Gimeno
La Rambla 100, Barri Gòtic (93 302 09 83). Metro Liceu. **Open** 9.30am-2pm, 4-8pm Mon-Fri; 10am-8.30pm Sat. **Credit** (gifts, not cigarettes) AmEx, DC, MC, V. **Map** p345 A3.
The puff daddy of them all, Gimeno has been a shrine to the weed since it opened 82 years ago. The shop specialises in Cuban cigars, along with pipes, smoking accessories, international cigarettes, cigars and tobacco products.

Travel services

Halcón Viajes
C/Aribau 34, Eixample (93 454 59 95/902 30 06 00/www.halcon-viajes.es). Metro Universitat. **Open** 9.30am-1.30pm, 4.30-8pm Mon-Fri; 10am-1pm Sat. **Credit** AmEx, DC, MC, V. **Map** p342 C5.
This company often has exclusive bargain deals on Air Europa's Spanish domestic and European flights. It also has a hotel booking service, and good deals on car rental.

Viajes Zeppelin
C/Villarroel 49 Bajos, Eixample (93 412 00 13/93 412 127 359/www.viajeszeppelin.com). Metro Urgell. **Open** *Sept-Apr* 9am-8pm Mon-Fri. *May-Aug* 9am-8pm Mon-Fri; 10am-1pm Sat. **Credit** AmEx, DC, MC, V. **Map** p342 C5.
A reliable agency with cheap schedule, and charter flights, excellent offers and an easy-to-use website.

Arts & Entertainment

Festivals & Events	**210**
Children	**219**
Film	**223**
Galleries	**227**
Gay & Lesbian	**231**
Music	**238**
Nightlife	**247**
Sport & Fitness	**263**
Theatre & Dance	**269**

Features

Getting high	211
The firestarters	215
There might be giants	216
Scream if you wanna go faster	220
It's the reel thing	225
Stiletto life	233
How to play your funky music	245
The best Festivals	246
Don't miss Nights out	247
Say cheese	249
Latin primers	258
How to be a Barça fan	264
Els Joglars	273

Festivals & Events

Barcelona gets a rise out of every occasion.

One of Barcelona's most lovable qualities is its enthusiasm for a get-together, and it hosts a near continuous cavalcade of festivals, fairs, games, parades and concerts. Anyone in town for big events like **Carnival** (*see p218*) or **Sant Joan** (*see p213*) may well wonder about the sober and reserved reputation of Catalans: the sight of them capering about as pyromaniac devils or formation dancing in drag will immediately dispel any such notions. Of course, some festivals are profoundly infused with a sense of nostalgia, such as the dying **Festa dels Tres Tombs** (*see p218*), kept on life support only through the loving efforts of various neighbourhood associations. Newer initiatives are generally focused on the performing arts, and festivals like **Sónar** (*see p213*), the **Grec** (*see p214*) and the **Marató de l'Espectacle** (*see p213*) are going from strength to strength. For a crash-course in Catalan traditions, you can't beat the neighbourhood celebrations (*festes majores*). The main one in Barcelona is the **Mercè** in September (*see p216*), though there are smaller, popular versions in Gràcia, Sants, Barceloneta and most local districts, involving an individual blend of concerts, street parties, human castles, parades of giants and fatheads, and the pandemonium of the *correfoc* (fire run). The main events are listed below.

INFORMATION

The best places for finding out what's going on are the tourist offices or the city's cultural information office in the Palau de la Virreina (*see p319*). Other good sources are the city's information phone line on 010, as well as its website at www.bcn.es – go to the cultural agenda section (available in English), and www.festes.org (Catalan only). Unless we've listed a separate information source, try these, and bear in mind that organisers are prone to change dates nearer the time. The daily papers also carry details, especially in their Friday or Saturday supplements. Events listed below that include public holidays (when many shops will be closed for the day) are marked *.

Spring

Festes de Sant Medir de Gràcia

Information: *www.santmedir.org. Gràcia to Sant Cugat and back, usually via Plaça Lesseps, Avda*

República Argentina & Carretera de l'Arrabassada. Starting point: Metro Fontana. **Date** 3 Mar. **Map** p338 D2/3.

A devout baker, Josep Vidal i Granés, started this charming tradition back in 1830. Decorated horses and carts gather around the Plaça Rius i Taulet in the early morning to ride up the winding Arrabassada road into the Collserola hills above Barcelona, ending at the Sant Medir Hermitage. (Alternatively, it's about an hour's pleasant walk through the woods from Sant Cugat – about 25 minutes from Plaça Catalunya by FGC train.) Here mass is celebrated, *sardanas* danced and barbecued *botifarras* are eaten with beans. Throughout the day, about 30 *colles* (neighbourhood groups) drive small processions of horse-drawn carts around Gràcia and other areas, notably Sarrià and Sants, throwing 100 tons of boiled sweets to the cheering crowds, who come armed with carrier bags to collect the goodies.

Setmana Santa* (Holy Week)

Date 13-20 Apr 2003.

In comparison to the overwhelmingly religious processions in Andalucia, Holy Week in Barcelona is a somewhat muted affair. The main event is the blessing of the palms on Palm Sunday, when the crowds around the Gothic cathedral are nearly impassable. The week beforehand, locals flock to the stalls along Rambla de Catalunya and outside all churches to buy natural palm fronds, some up to 2m (6ft) long, which are bleached and woven into intricate designs, along with traditional laurel, sugar rosaries and coloured ribbons. On Good Friday, a series of small processions and blessings takes place in front of the cathedral, starting with the Via Crucis in the morning, the blessing of the Christ of Lepanto in the afternoon, and a procession that sets out from the church of Sant Agusti in C/Hospital at around 5pm and arrives at the cathedral a couple of hours later. The big attraction for the kids is the elaborate chocolate *monas*: the local equivalent of the Easter egg, in the shape of animals, cartoon characters or houses.

Sant Jordi

La Rambla, & all over Barcelona. **Date** 23 Apr.

Sant Jordi (St George) was first the patron of the Catalan Cavalry, and the day was originally celebrated with jousting tournaments in the Born. He was later adopted as the patron saint of Catalonia, and the city abounds with statues and paintings of him in all his dragon-slaying glory (although it must be said that the dragon often looks suspiciously like a baby crocodile). It is said that as the drops of the dragon's blood fell, they turned into poppies, thus the popular custom of giving a red rose (they last

Getting high

At ground level, a *castell* (human castle) is a slightly more genteel version of a rugby scrum. First-time spectators naturally tend to focus on the more visible *tronc* (trunk) of wobbling bodies, but the real secret is in the base. '*Més pit!*' ('More chest!') bellows the man with the clipboard, demanding that the 100 or more people forming the core of the *pinya* (pine cone-shaped base) press in even more tightly towards the centre. Damp with sweat, and hidden in the middle of this straining, suffocating mass of bodies, are the stout *baixos* (bases) who'll be supporting up to nine levels of progressively lighter men, women and children. Bodies are squeezed and poked as climbers seek a good foothold in the *faixa* (the long sash wound tightly around the waist for back support), heads are clamped between the bony ankles of the next layer up, and to add to the indignity, some are buttressed from below by the helping hands wedged under their buttocks.

Given all of that – who'd be a *casteller*? Well, lots of people. *Castells* are enjoying a massive renaissance as a stock feature of the *festa major* of most areas, and especially during the Mercè: the floor plaques by the Ajuntament in the Plaça Sant Jaume commemorate recent past glories. Contests are held on Sundays between March and October, and the most charged atmosphere is easily at the bi-annual competitions in Tarragona, the traditional heartland of the *castellers*. Significantly, the town bullring (arch-symbol of 'Spanishness') is reappropriated for the event and, last year, was decorated in banners reading (in English) 'Catalonia is not Spain'. A more potent symbol of Catalan solidarity than the *castells* would be hard to find.

The history of this charming tradition is hazy. Some claim it evolved from the *moixiganga*, the religious dance that portrayed scenes from the Passion and ended with Christ rising up to heaven. Others say it was a medieval game of prowess or had a military origin as a technique for scaling high-walled castles. Either way, it has existed in Catalonia for more than 200 years.

Competitions usually feature several different *colles* who take turns to build up to five different towers. The formations are described in people per level so a *tres de nou* (a three by nine) has nine levels with three people per level, except for the penultimate level, which has one or two kids forming a base for the tiniest sprog of all, the *anxaneta*, who must raise his or her hand to show the tower is complete. The completion of each layer is marked by a flourish from the *gralles* (traditional reed pipes), but the maximum quota of points is not awarded unless the castle is correctly dismantled. Unsurprisingly, collapses are frequent, and the Red Cross paramedics are never far away with supplies of neck braces and stretchers.

Most difficult are the *castells* with only two people per level (known as *torres*) or with one per level (a *pillar*), but it goes the other way too, and a chunky *cinc de nou* (five by nine) is where it's at. Most prestigious of all, though, is the ten-level *castell*, which has only been achieved a handful of times, including October 2002, when it clinched first place at Tarragona for the Castellers de Vilafranca team.

longer than poppies) to your beloved on his feast day has been observed for at least five centuries. On this Catalan version of St Valentine's Day, men traditionally gave women a rose, and women reciprocated with a book. As it is now widely accepted that women can read, and that men might like flowers, many people give both. The tradition of the book only dates back to the last century when it was announced Day of the Book due to the curious factoid that both Cervantes and Shakespeare died on 23 April. This day accounts for 10% of Catalonia's total annual book sales, so wherever book stands are set up (mainly along Passeig de Gràcia, the Rambla and Rambla de Catalunya) throngs gather from midmorning on. This is also the day when the public traditionally troop down to the Palau de la Generalitat for the palace's own dazzling display of red roses.

Feria de Abril

Nova Mar Bella beach. Metro Besòs-Mar, then special buses. **Information** Federación de Entidades Culturales Andaluces en Cataluña (93 488 02 95/ www.fecac.com). **Date** 25 Apr-4 May 2003.
If you can't make it to Seville for the original of the ten-day Andalucian fiesta, this satellite version is a good substitute, as Barcelona's Andalucian population shows the locals how to party. Decorated *casetas* (marquees) offer food, drink and music, and there is plenty of opportunity to practise your *sevillanas* and flamenco, or just watch the experts. The traditional way to arrive is by horse and carriage, elaborately decorated with flowers, and there are riding exhibitions during the day. Alternatively, a special bus service runs to the venue, which is by the beach, a few kilometres from the Port Olimpic.

Festival de Música Antiga

CaixaForum, Avda Marquès de Comillas 6-8, Montjuïc (902 22 30 40/www.fundacio.lacaixa.es). Metro Plaça de Espanya. **Date** 26 & 27 Apr 2003. **Map** p341 A5.
This early music festival is the highpoint in Fundació la Caixa's admirable series of cultural events. Performers come from all over Europe and have included Thomas Zehetmair, Christophe Coin, Rinaldo Alessandrini, Andreas Staier and Musica Antiqua Köln. The accompanying fringe festival offers young performers the chance to practise and perform alongside more established musicians. You can get tickets in advance from Servi-Caixa.

Dia del Treball* (May Day)

Date 1 May.
On May Day committed unionists join marches organised by the main trade unions, along Passeig de Gràcia down to Plaça Sant Jaume – although in these apolitical times, for most workers it's just a day off to enjoy the arrival of spring.

Sant Ponç

C/Hospital, Raval. Metro Liceu. **Date** 11 May. **Map** p344-5 A2-3.
About 200 stalls of aromatic and medicinal herbs, candied fruits, syrups and artesan honey are set up along C/Hospital for this charming fair that has been traditional here since 1871. The original site was in front of Sant Miquel church which is thought to be built over an ancient temple to Flora, Roman goddess of nature and plants. Sant Ponç himself is a Christianised pagan god, and this patron saint of herbalists and beekeepers was worshipped in the nearby church of the Hospital de la Santa Creu. Since all things eco-friendly have become fashionable, Sant Ponç features an increasing number of stalls selling healthy and organic produce.

Festa de la Diversitat

Montjuïc. Metro Espanya. **Information** SOS Racisme (93 301 05 97/www.sosracisme.org). **Date** mid May 2003. **Map** p345 A-B4.
A laid-back celebration of the city's cultural and ethnic diversity at the foot of the Palau Nacional, attracting more than 50,000 visitors to its three days of concerts, conferences, music workshops, theatre and kids' activities. Local immigrant organisations set up stalls with food, clothes, jewellery and information, and there are daily workshops on capoeira, samba, henna and eastern gypsy music, and occasional big names such as Duquende or Cheb Balowski. Profits help sustain SOS Racisme in its fight against racism in Spain.

Barcelona Poesia

All over Barcelona. **Information** Institut de Cultura (93 301 77 75/www.bcn.es/icub). **Date** 8-14 May 2003.
The Jocs Florals (Floral Games) are named after the prizes for this annual poetry contest, started by King Joan I in 1393: a silver violet as third prize; a golden rose as second prize and, naturally, a real flower for the winner. Having died out by the mid 15th century, the games were resuscitated in 1859 as a vehicle for the promotion of the Catalan language, and prizes went to the most suitably florid paeans to the motherland. The Jocs are now combined with the annual International Poetry Festival and have expanded to a week of poetry, with thematic readings as well as a poetic walk through Barcelona. While most of the poems are still in Catalan, Spanish is also permitted and several foreign languages feature in the International Festival, held on the final day. Schools also hold their own mini-versions of the Jocs.

Festival de Flamenco de Ciutat Vella

Information: www.tallerdemusics.com. **Date** 19-24 May 2003.
If you've been left cold (not to mention many euros poorer) by cheesy tourist flamenco, then check out the dazzling virtuoso performers in the old city flamenco festival. Last year was centred around a homage to great contemporary performers including dancers 'El Güito' and Manolete, and famous local singer Duquende. The timing is designed to complement the Nou Barris Flamenco Festival (C/Doctor Pi i Molist 133) held a few days earlier.

Summer

Sónar

Information *93 442 29 72/www.sonar.es.*
Date 12-14 June 2003.

Sónar is a victim of its own success, and the blowout tenth anniversary celebrations of 2003 are unlikely to ease the overcrowding and transport issues that have hounded this delirious three-day International Festival of Advanced Music and Multimedia Art. It is a game of two halves: SónarDay and SónarNight. SónarDay runs from about midday to late evening and focuses on the trainspotting side of electronica: record fairs, conferences, exhibitions, soundlabs, interactive audio-visual installations and DJs playing hip hop, chillout and indietronics for light relief. The Raval is the main hub of activity, with the larger events in the CCCB and the new 1,500-person capacity SónarDome in Plaça dels Àngels, where the exhausted can flop down on the specially imported grass (take that as you will). SónarNight means a scramble for a shuttle ride (from the bottom of the La Rambla, included in the price of the ticket) out to the vast Polígon Pedrosa in Hospital de Llobregat. Recent performers include heavyweights like Carl Cox and Jeff Mills alongside the Pet Shop Boys. The full three-day pass costs around €92.

Marató de l'Espectacle

Mercat de les Flors, C/Lleida 59, Poble Sec. Metro Poble Sec or Espanya. **Information** Associació Marató de l'Espectacle (93 268 18 68/www.marato.com). **Date** 6-7 June 2003. **Map** p341 B6.

Celebrating its 20th anniversary in 2003, this unmissable performance marathon has lost none of its anarchic appeal. It's an action-packed explosion of theatre, dance, performance and circus skills, which takes place late into the night over two consecutive evenings. With more than 80 acts, mostly based in Spain, there's certainly no time to get bored, as the maximum time allotted to each act is ten minutes. While there are inevitable fluctuations in quality, the marathon is an interesting mosaic of talent. The audience mingles with the performers, drifting from fire-eater to drag queen to Shakepearean duo, stopping off for a break by the bar or to admire the avant-garde art installations in the foyer.

L'Ou Com Balla

Ateneu Barcelonès, C/Canuda 6; Casa de l'Ardiaca, C/Santa Llúcia 1; Cathedral cloisters; Museu Frederic Marès; all in Barri Gòtic. Metro Jaume I or Liceu/17, 19, 40, 45 bus. **Information** Institut de Cultura (93 301 77 75/www.bcn.es/icub). **Date** mid June 2003. **Map** p345 B3.

Before the 19th century, Corpus Christi was one of the most important celebrations in the year; since then it has lost a lot of its significance. The tradition of L'Ou Com Balla ('the egg that dances') continues: a hollowed-out egg is placed on the spout of a small fountain, where it spins and bobs, supported by the jet of water. Fountains are garlanded with spectac-ular flower displays, and a funnel-like structure guides the egg back on to the water spout whenever it falls off. L'Ou Com Balla can also be seen in the cathedral during Easter week.

Festa de la Música

All over Barcelona. **Information** Institut de Cultura (93 301 77 75/www.bcn.es/icub). **Date** 21 June 2003.

With so much music in Barcelona all year round, International Music Day may seem almost superfluous, especially since official support for it is minimal. Although hundreds of musicians take to the streets, it sometimes seems as if quality is playing second fiddle to quantity. Nevertheless, with every square, park, museum and cultural centre in the city involved, and all genres of music on show, it makes for a pleasant enough day.

Sant Joan*

All over Barcelona. **Date** night of 23 June.

Nominally Christian but with its roots in summer solstice celebrations, the eve of Sant Joan (St John the Baptist) is unmissable. Bonfires are built all over the city (*see p215* **The firestarters**), and for a week beforehand the June air is ripped apart by explosions, as every schoolkid in town spends their pocket money on terrifying bangers. Come the night itself, the city is a sonic boom of impromptu firework displays exploding from balconies and squares. There are big displays on Tibidabo, Montjuïc and down by the beach. Bands perform on the beach, and there are smaller events in squares across the city.

Nowadays, the huge bonfires that locals spontaneously built at road junctions in the city have been

L'Ou Com Balla.

banned after a few too many accidents, but fires still fill the *ramblas* of towns up and down the coast, and even in the city there are still one or two 'private initiatives'. It's obligatory to consume cava and *coca de Sant Joan*, a shallow, bread-like cake decorated with very sweet candied fruit. Specially laid on metro and FCG trains run continuously through the night.

Classics als Parcs
Information Parcs i Jardins (93 413 24 00/ www.bcn.es/parcsijardins). **Date** June-July.
On balmy evenings in early summer, what could be more pleasant than listening to classical music in some of the city's most attractive parks? There is a wide-ranging programme for small ensembles and soloists, and usually two or three concerts to choose from each week, in venues including Gaudí's Parc Güell, and the Ciutadella and Laberint parks.

Festival del Grec
Information Institut de Cultura (93 301 77 75/ www.bcn.es/grec). **Date** late June-July 2003.
The Grec, now in its 27th year, is Barcelona's main performing arts festival. Although performances are staged at venues all over the city, the festival takes its name from the mock-Greek, open-air theatre on Montjuïc, which hosts many of the main shows against the natural backdrop of an old quarry, complete with hanging greenery and stone seats.

In response to lacklustre attendance at the less mainstream performances, the decision to slim down the festival has paid off commercially but has severely restricted the content. Most of the theatre is in Catalan or Spanish. Dance is mostly contemporary and is similarly weighted to home-grown talent, although Mikhail Baryshnikov made a rare appearance last year. Music is usually strong on world, flamenco and jazz but last year included some unexpected choices such as De La Soul and Lou Reed. Tickets cost €15-€30 and can be bought from the special booth in Plaça Catalunya, from the Palau de la Virreina (*see p319*) or from Tel-entrada and branches of Caixa Catalunya.

Dies de Dansa
Information Associació Marató de l'Espectacle (93 268 18 68/www.marato.com). **Date** mid July 2003.
Three days of dance performances in various venues, day and night, featuring local and international dance companies. Some shows are free, particularly those held outdoors, and most generally last about 25 minutes. The most spectacular of the venues are Park Güell and the terrace of the Miró Foundation, but there also dynamic performances in and around the MACBA, the CaixaForum and the CCCB, where there are also choreography workshops and improvisational performances.

Festa Major de Gràcia
All over Gràcia. Metro Fontana. **Information** Festa Major de Gràcia (93 459 30 80/www.festa majordegracia.org). **Date** mid-late Aug 2003. **Map** p338 D-E2-3.

With little else going on in August, the Festa de Gràcia receives everybody's undivided party energy. This makes for some of the most exuberant and friendly local celebrations you'll see in Barcelona but it can get uncomfortably crowded on Friday and Saturday night. Around 25 Gràcia streets take part in the best-dressed street competition, when residents put in hundreds of hours turning balconies and pavements into lavishly decorated underwater kingdoms, spaceships or casinos. Despite their efforts, the upper section of C/Verdi is a consistent champion. Each street also lays on an open-air meal for all the neighbours, and a dance. Bigger concerts and events are centred on Plaça Rius i Taulet, Plaça de la Revolució, Plaça del Sol and Plaça de la Virreina. The festival opens with *gegants* and *castells* in Plaça Rius i Taulet, and climaxes on the last night with a *correfoc* and a *castell de focs* (castle of fireworks) in the same square.

Festa Major de Sants
All over Sants. Metro Plaça de Sants or Sants Estació. **Information** Federació Festa Major de Sants (93 490 62 14). **Date** 24-30 Aug 2003. **Map** p341 A4.
No sooner has Gràcia taken down its decorations than it is the turn of the district of Sants, though its *festa major* is less well known and more traditional. Major events, such as the *correfoc*, are held in the Parc de l'Espanya Industrial; others are centred on Plaça del Centre, C/Sant Antoni, Plaça de la Farga and Plaça Joan Peiro, behind Sants station.

Autumn

Diada National de Catalunya*
All over Barcelona. **Date** 11 Sept.
Rather than celebrating a victory, Catalan National Day commemorates Barcelona's disastrous fall to the Castilian/French army in the 1714 War of the Spanish Succession. This defeat led to the vicious repression of all Catalan institutions for the next 200 years, and in 1977, the first year the day could be celebrated openly after the dictatorship, over a million people took to the streets. It's now lost some of its vigour, but is still a day for national reaffirmation, with the Catalan flag displayed on buses and balconies. Catalan separatist groups hold a march, which usually attracts the attention of Spanish nationalists (including skinheads and neo-Nazis) and the riot police, and can sometimes degenerate into street skirmishing between the three groups.

B-Parade
From Montjuïc down to Avda Reina Maria Cristina & Plaça Espanya. **Information** 93 412 00 32/ www.b-parade.com. **Date** Sept 2003.
A direct descendant of the Berlin Love Parade, the rapidly growing B-Parade celebrates its third anniversary in 2003. The ambitious slogan is 'Music for a Better World', with the purported aim of promoting love, peace and harmony. Best of all: it's completely free. The result is huge crowds of people

The firestarters

Barcelona's traditions are thick with references to its pagan past, and even something as apparently respectable as the *sardana* (*see p83*) is suspected by some folklore historians to have started out as a witches' dance. Without exception, all of the earliest references to the *sardana* concern its complete prohibition, specifically within the vicinity of churches and religious buildings. The festival of Sant Joan in June (*see p213*), however, marking the summer solstice, is the ultimate expression of those atavistic urges. All pyromaniac tendencies come to the fore on *la nit del foc*, the 'night of fire', with huge bonfires lit on the beach and in the streets, fireworks exploding in all directions and drinking, music and dancing in an incredible outburst of unbridled pagan revelry.

From the time of the paleo-Catalan tribal sun cults, bonfires were associated with purification, and were originally built outside each dwelling to chase away evil spirits. In the Raval there was a custom of throwing live kittens to the flames, kitties being one of the favourite incarnations of the devil, along with snakes and goats. Some villages used to burn small witch figures or old boots in the hope that the terrible smell of burning leather would keep the witches at bay. As well as purification, the summer solstice fires were associated with regeneration, and couples who jumped over the flames of seven bonfires would marry before the end of the year and have a happy and fruitful union. Mothers who passed their babies over the flames made sure that their offspring would grow up strong and free of disease.

The tradition of the *correfoc* ('fire run') is linked to the pagan bestiary of Catalonia with *dracs* (dragons) and other fantastic creatures on the prowl. The largest *correfoc* in Barcelona is held for the Mercè (*see p216*) but is part of any major village festivities. To a pulsing drumbeat, a parade of infernal dragons studded with spitting fireworks comes belching flames – filling the streets with coloured smoke and the stink of sulphur. Whipping the crowd into a deliciously terrifying frenzy are their attendant *colla* (group) of *diables* (demons) who have come up from Hell to chase the screaming onlookers with blinding showers of sparks spinning from the top of their tridents. Anyone sufficiently protected in old cotton clothes, hats and bandanas can push through the crowds to dance in the devils' sparks or even kneel in the dragon's path to bellow, '*No passareu!*' ('You're not coming through!') After the flame-licked battle between good and evil is over, the revelry goes on long into the night.

Arts & Entertainment

There might be giants

It's a classic partnership. Call it ying and yang, call it good cop, bad cop, but one of the most popular elements of any Barcelona neighbourhood celebration is the parade of elaborate papier-mâché or fibreglass characters: the towering, sedate *gegants* (giants) accompanied by their little sidekicks, the squat, mischievous *nans* ('little ones' or dwarves) who are colloquially known as *capgrossos* or 'fatheads'.

Gegants rest on four wooden legs, rather like an enormous barstool, and are moved slowly forward by a person peeping out through a mesh in the skirts, which is why you sometimes see a medieval princess in a gleaming pair of Nikes. In contrast, the grinning *capgrossos* are free to scuttle about impishly, dance and interact with the crowd. These grotesque little Rumpelstiltskins are especially popular with children, who treat them rather like Mickey Mouse at Disneyland, mobbing them for hugs, photos and the sweets hidden in their pockets.

Catalan folklore expert Joan Amades wrote that: 'The *nans* are born out of a sense of opposition to the *gegants*, and only have reason to exist by their side.' *Gegants* are 'the majestic symbol of the force of *seny*,' *seny* being the much-vaunted Catalan characteristic of common sense. Its opposite quality, *rauxa* (raucousness), finds expression in the fatheads.

The *gegants* represent historic characters and the tradition dates from the 13th century, when the Church ordered their use in the Corpus Christi festival; the illiterate peasantry was proving slow to forget its pagan ways and the idea was to incorporate familiar pre-Christian figures into the enactment of scenes from the Bible.

The city's official giants, who represent King Jaume I and his queen, Violant of Hungary, are kept on display in the Palau de la Virreina alongside the city's apple-cheeked patron saint, Santa Eulàlia. In addition, each neighbourhood has its own set of emblematic

following sumptuously decorated floats blaring dance and electronica, culminating in the huge Urban Rave at the bottom of the hill. The 20 or so floats are laden with go-go dancers, transvestites and DJs. The parade starts at about 5pm by the Olympic Stadium and trails down past the Poble Espanyol to the fountains by Plaça Espanya. By nightfall there are around 100,000 people frugging to big-name DJs in the Firestiu space (9pm-5am).

Festa Major de la Barceloneta

All over Barceloneta. Metro Barceloneta.
Information Associació Veïns de la Barceloneta (93 221 72 44). **Date** late Sept 2003. **Map** p345 C4.
The proximity of the port and the beach make these local celebrations even more picturesque than most. All the usual ingredients are packed into Barceloneta's tight grid of narrow streets, including *castells*, *gegants* and a *correfoc*. Celebrations are led by the piratical, cannon-firing caricature of a French general, General Bum Bum (Boom Boom, possibly named after Prosper Verboom, the French army engineer who designed the *barri*), in a tradition said to date from 1881.

Festes de la Mercè*

All over Barcelona. Information tourist offices or www.bcn.es. **Date** around 24 Sept.
The biggest city in Catalonia has to stage the biggest *festa major*, and it is a matter of civic pride that Barcelona doesn't disappoint. It is called the Mercè after Our Lady of Mercy, who became one of the

patron saints of the city after seeing off a plague of locusts in 1637. The week-long celebrations have been dedicated to her name since 1871, and comprise a heady cocktail of everyone's favourite ingredients, the most traditional being medieval customs such as the human *castells* (castles), *gegants* (giants), *capgrosses* (bigheads) and the diabolic *correfoc* (fire run). The other ingredient is music, encompassing everything from traditional *sardanes* and *cobla* bands, to electronica, pop and crowd-pleasers like Manu Chao. An alternative music festival, Barcelona Acció Musical (known as the BAM), runs alongside with four nights of concerts. Last year's hits included Terry Callier, the Herbaliser and the Propellerheads, with shows in front of the cathedral, Plaça del Rei and the Rambla del Raval. Entrance is free except for performances in the echoing gulley of Estació de França train station (about €10). The Mercè features free admission to certain museums, public buildings, a firework competition on the beach and an air show.

Mostra de Vins i Caves de Catalunya

Maremàgnum, Moll d'Espanya, Port Vell. Metro Drassanes. **Information** INCAVI (93 487 67 38). **Date** as Mercè (*see above*). **Map** p342 D7.
The Penedès region, Catalonia's most important wine- and cava-producing area and home to cava labels such as Freixenet and Codorníu, is less than an hour from Barcelona. Coinciding with the Mercè, there are four days of tastings – for a small fee – of

characters such as the fisherman and his wife of Barceloneta, or the compère and topless chorus girl from the old El Molino music hall of Poble Sec. It's not all anthropomorphic though, and the outsized bestiary of Catalonia is a veritable zoo of mules, eagles, lions and dragons. Paganism lingers under the surface, and some outrageous displays are to be seen at the wild **La Patum** festival in the town of Berga (*see p299*).

Historically, *capgrossos* are much more recent than the *gegants*. *Capgrossos* made their first appearance in Valencia in 1589 as three couples – European, gypsy and African – allegedly representing the old tribes of Shem, Ham and Japhet. However, it was not until nearly three centuries later that *capgrossos* appeared in parades in Barcelona. Many popular personalities have cropped up such as *El Calvo* (Baldy), *El Artista* (the artist) and kiddies' favourite *El Patufet*, taken from an old comic book character. *Capgrossos* are no longer tied to any symbolism and can be anything from a washerwoman to a celebrity or political figure; there are over 70 off-the-peg models in stock at the specialist shop, El Ingenio (*see p187*), where an average fathead costs about 225.

wines and cavas from around 50 local producers, along with other Catalan specialities, including cheese, *embotits* (charcuterie) and anchovies.

Festival International de Jazz de Barcelona

Information The Project (93 481 70 40/www.the-project.net). **Date** mid Oct-mid Dec 2003.
Along with representing jazz in every form, the festival is gradually growing in scope to include some gospel, Dixieland, marching bands and 'Jazz in the Park' at Parc Diagonal-Mar. Big names in 2002 included Norah Jones, the Dave Holland Big Band and Gilberto Gil, along with about 15 other concerts at the Palau de la Música, Luz de Gas, Razzmatazz and L'Auditori. Get advance tickets from Tel-entrada (*see p208*) from €9-€36. The event overlaps with the more low-key Festival de Jazz de Ciutat Vella (Zingaria Produccions, 93 310 07 55), which puts on many free jazz concerts in bars and other small venues throughout the old city.

Festival de Músiques del Món

CaixaForum, Avda Marquès de Comillas 6-8, Montjuïc (902 22 30 40/www.fundacio.lacaixa.es). Metro Plaça de Espanya. **Date** Oct. **Map** p341 A5.
This 8th World Music Festival is organised by La Caixa's cultural foundation, and the CaixaForum hosts about 20 authentic indigenous concerts, workshops and conferences. Asian music of various latitudes features highly, but there are also major contributions from eastern Europe and north and sub-Saharan Africa alongside appearances from local folk outfits like Els Joglars (*see p273*). There's also 'Brunch with Jazz' in the cafeteria and family concerts (tickets about €2) are held at 12.30pm.

Tots Sants* (All Saints' Day)

All over Barcelona. **Date** 1 Nov.
On All Saints' Day many families make pilgrimages to the graves of their departed relatives. For those accustomed to church graveyards, the five-storey walls of numbered marble headstones can seem rather cramped and impersonal, and curiously reminiscent of municipal housing blocks. While for many the day means a businesslike spring clean with fresh flowers and kitchen cloths, for some – notably the gypsy community – the visit is an emotional affair with long vigils and lavish floral tributes. The day is known as the Castanyada, and it is customary to eat *castanyas* (roast chestnuts), *moniatos* (sweet potatoes) and *panellets*, small sweet cakes made from almonds and pine nuts. Always open to an excuse for another party, the Harry Potter generation of Catalans has embraced the custom of Hallowe'en on 31 October. Carved pumpkins are increasingly popular, and many a gory ghoul will be whooping it at the witching hour. Thanksgiving, surely, is just around the corner…

Winter

Fira de Santa Llúcia

Pla de la Seu & Avda de la Catedral. Metro Jaume I. **Dates** end Nov-23 Dec. **Map** p338 B2-3.

This Christmas fair dates from 1786, and if you can manage to squeeze through the crowds, you'll find around 400 stalls crammed with all manner of Christmas decorations and presents. The *pessebre* (nativity scene) is big in Catalonia and some 150 of the stalls are devoted to the necessary figurines, but among the donkeys and swaddling-wrapped babes is everybody's favourite: the *caganer*, or 'shitter'. This is a small figure crouching down, trousers around his ankles, with a lovingly sculpted turd steaming below. As a piece of caricature, the *caganer* is completely egalitarian, and everyone from nuns to Barça players has been caught with their pants down. To catch a live *caganer* in action, check out a *pastoret*, colourful theatre pieces that are a cross between pantomime, religious celebration and medieval mystery play. There's also a nativity scene contest, musical parades and exhibitions, including the popular life-size nativity scene in Plaça Sant Jaume – without a *caganer*, unfortunately.

Nadal* & Sant Esteve* (Christmas Day & Boxing Day)

All over Barcelona. **Dates** 25 & 26 Dec.
For further evidence of Catalonia's coprology, witness the Christmas Eve custom of the *caga tió* or shitting log. A log with smiling face and little red Santa hat is filled with sweets and presents and covered with a blanket; children then quite literally beat the crap out of it while singing, '*Caga tió, ametlles i torró, si no cagues bó, et donaré un cop de bastó.*' Which translates as, 'Shit log, almonds and nougat, if you don't shit well, I'll beat you with a stick.' Violence gets results, and the blanket is lifted to reveal a slew of little presents, and the proceedings are drawn to to a close by the appearance of a piece of toilet paper. These small presents have to see the kids through until the real goodies arrive with the Three Kings on 6th January. The Catalan equivalent of the Christmas midnight mass is the *missa del gall* (cockerel's mass) held at dawn when the cock crows. Later, the whole family enjoys a traditional Christmas feast of *escudella i carn d'olla* (a meaty stew with large pasta shells), seafood and truffled turkey, finishing with piles of nougat.

Cap d'Any (New Year's Eve)

Date 31 Dec & 1 Jan*.
As discos and bars charge outrageous admission for New Year parties, the mass public celebrations around the city are a better choice. Plaça Catalunya attracts the lion's share of the crowds, while for something less hectic the beaches are a safe bet, and wherever you are at midnight – well announced on TV and radio – you'll be expected to stop swilling cava and start stuffing 12 grapes into your mouth, one for every chime of the bell. Keep going until the New Year has been fully rung in, or it's bad luck. Don't forget to wear your lucky red underwear.

Cavalcada dels Reis

Route *Kings usually arrive at Moll de la Fusta, then parade up Via Laietana to Plaça Catalunya & continue to Passeig de Gràcia; the detailed route changes each year.* **Information** Centre d'Informació de la Virreina & 010. **Date** 5 Jan. **Map** p344-5 A-B1-4.
Scatology isn't confined to Christmas, and on Kings' Day, many bakeries sell traditional *tifas*: glistening turds made of cake, complete with sugar-spun flies on top. It's either that or a lump of edible coal. After that it's time to go down to the harbour to watch the Three Kings arrive by boat. The kings are then driven around town in an open carriage, throwing sweets. (Don't tell the kids, but there are usually three teams of kings working different beats; it's a big city for three travel-weary kings.) Routes are published in the newspapers.

Festa dels Tres Tombs

Sant Antoni. Metro Sant Antoni. **Date** 17 Jan.
Map p341-2 B-C5.
The iconography of Sant Antoni Abat shows him as victor over a pig (the medieval symbol of luxury), but through the Chinese whispers of history, he eventually came to be dubbed patron saint and holy protector of all domestic animals, especially horses, and muleteers. Although sadly waning in popularity, on his feast day it is still the custom to bring animals to the church of St Anthony to be blessed. Afterwards, horsemen in top hats and tails commemorate the occasion by riding three times (*tres tombs*, three turns) in a formal procession from Ronda Sant Antoni, through Plaça Catalunya, down La Rambla and along C/Nou de la Rambla.

Carnestoltes (Carnival)

All over Barcelona. **Date** 27 Feb-5 Mar.
Though you have to go to Sitges for a really outrageous carnival, there are still plenty of celebrations in Barcelona. The origins of carnival have been traced back to the 14th century, as an orgiastic outburst of overeating, overdrinking and underdressing prior to the privations of Lent. The opening of the ten-day event is presided over by Don Carnal and Rei Carnestoltes – the masked personifications of the carnival spirit. A few days later comes the *rua*, a traditional parade of floats through the city carrying figures in stunning outfits, amid a confusion of confetti, blunderbuss salvos and fireworks. There's dancing in Plaça Catalunya, concerts and a *Gran Botifarrada Popular* on the Rambla, when sausage is handed out. There are also children's fancy dress carnivals, and carnival is a big celebration in the city's markets, where the traders don costumes. The end of carnival on Ash Wednesday is marked by the burning of the effigy of Rei Carnestoltes and, more bizarrely, by the *Enterrament de la Sardina* (the Burial of the Sardine), which is most picturesquely celebrated in Barceloneta. Meanwhile the children carry sardines on little fishing rods to be buried on the beach. Nobody is quite sure why, but according to some the *sardina* is thought to be a phallic symbol, indicating the imminent abstinence of Lent, while others say it evolved from the original custom of burying a *cerdina* or small pig.

Children

Travel without tears.

With its magic fountains, fanciful dragon houses, chocolate museum and beaches, Barcelona is such a natural wonderland that it almost doesn't need any extras to win over its younger visitors. On top of that, Catalans are extremely indulgent with the little ones, so it comes as some surprise that the birth rate in Catalonia is one of the lowest in the world. One child per family is the norm. Perhaps because of this, without any unruly broods to control, parents simply whisk little Jordi or Montse along with the rest of the friends and family, whatever the occasion.

There is a distinct dearth of child-specific concessions and facilities: public transport is free only for children under four, and few metro stations are easily negotiable for those with pushchairs. There are also few babychanging facilities. Although restaurants rarely offer children's menus, many will provide small portions on request; but there's little need when tapas and kids were so clearly made for each other. Adapting to the local timetable might be more of a problem: most restaurants don't serve lunch before 2pm or dinner before 8pm.

Local beaches are reasonably clean and have plenty of lifeguards, showers, play areas and ice-cream kiosks, but beaches further out of town, in **Casteldefells** or **Sitges** (see p277), have shallower waters. Unfortunately, none has many public toilets.

Attractions

Streets don't get more exciting than **La Rambla**, and children love the bright flowers, caricature artists, human statues and street entertainers, while halfway down, nothing beats the **Boqueria** market for sheer gross-out value, with its skinned rabbits and eyeballs for sale. Over the wooden bridge, the **Maremàgnum** shopping centre is a magnet for families at the weekend with sea views, ice-cream and amusement arcades (see p183).

Sunday mornings are good for a visit to the **cathedral** when the square is packed with sardana dancers, and the bad-tempered geese who live inside the cloisters are unmissable. Older kids enjoy the challenge of navigating the labyrinthine streets of the Barri Gòtic and the Born, while the closed environment of **Poble Espanyol** (see p110), although slightly

naff, allows young kids off the reins to run about, and the glass blowers or shops frothing with flamenco dresses can be quite fun.

Other surefire hits are the **cable car** to Montjuïc, the **tram** to Tibidabo, the **open-topped buses**, the **swallow boats** (golondrinas) and the **catamaran** (for all, see section **Sightseeing**).

L'Aquàrium de Barcelona

Moll d'Espanya, Port Vell (93 221 74 74/ www.aquariumbcn.com). Metro Barceloneta. **Open** *July, Aug 9.30am-11pm daily. Sept-June 9.30am-9pm Mon-Fri; 9.30am-9.30pm Sat, Sun.* **Admission** €11.50; €7.70 concessions; free under-4s. **Advance tickets** Tel-entrada & Caixa de Catalunya. **Discounts** BC, BT. **Credit** MC, V. **Map** p342 D7.
The showpiece of the world's largest Mediterranean aquarium is the Oceanari, an 80m (260ft) underwater glass tunnel that allows you to walk through eerie shark-infested waters. Other large tanks are mainly based on local ecosytems such as the Costa Brava or underwater caves of the Medes islands. There are 50 interactive activities for young children, such as petting starfish or feeding a ray.

Parc d'Atraccions del Tibidabo

Plaça del Tibidabo, Tibidabo (93 211 79 42). FGC Av Tibidabo. **Open** *Last 2wks June 10am-5pm Thur, Fri; noon-8pm Sat, Sun. July noon-8pm Mon-Thur; noon-9pm Fri; noon-10pm Sat, Sun. Aug noon-10pm Mon-Thur; noon-11pm Fri-Sun. Sept noon-9pm Sat, Sun. Oct noon-7pm Sat, Sun; Nov-mid Mar noon-6pm Sat, Sun. Mid Mar-mid June noon-7pm Sat, Sun.* **Admission** *Six rides* €10. *Unlimited rides* €20; €4 children under 1m10cm tall. **Discounts** BC, BT. **Credit** MC, V.
Some of the rides date back to 1901 at this pine-scented, mountian-top fairground. Disneyland it is not, but all the old favourites (bumper cars, big wheel, ghost train) are here, and it's worth trying Aero Magic; a short, breathtaking ride on a train that skirts the mountain suspended beneath a rail. There's a wonderful collection of old fairground machines, and puppet shows on the hour.

Zoo de Barcelona

Parc de la Ciutadella, Born (93 225 67 80/ www.zoobarcelona.com). Metro Barceloneta or Ciutadella-Vila Olímpica. **Open** *(daily) Mar 10am-6pm. Apr 10am-7pm. May-Aug 9.30am-7.30pm. Sept 10am-7pm. Oct 10am-6pm. Nov-Feb 10am-5pm.* **Admission** €11.50; €5-€7 concessions. **Discounts** BC, BT. **Credit** MC, V. **Map** p343 E6.
This large but slightly shabby zoo is home to the most famous face of Barcelona: the scowling pink

chops of Snowflake (*Copito de Nieve*), the only albino gorilla in captivity and possibly in the world. Living in his shadow are chimps, penguins and elephants, along with giant anteaters and Chinese water dragons. There are pony rides (€2.50) and regular shows at the Dolphinarium. On Sundays there are special family mornings for children between four and 11.

Babysitting & childcare

These agencies employ qualified childminders, and can supply an English-speaker if necessary. Supervised daycare centres offer parents the chance of a few child-free hours.

Baby-Home

Diputació 188 (93 453 85 29). Metro Universitat or Urgell. **Open** 9am-1pm; 4-7.30pm Mon-Fri. **No credit cards. Map** p342 C5.
For babies under 12 months the basic hourly rate is €6.10, which drops to €5.60 for children over a year old. For night shifts, clients must pay for a taxi home.

Cinc Serveis

C/Pelai 50, 3° 1ª, Eixample (93 412 56 76/ 24hr mobile 639 36 11 11). Metro Catalunya. **Open** 9.30am-1.30pm, 4.30-8.30pm Mon-Fri. **No credit cards. Map** p344 A1.
For a child-free evening, the basic babysitting rate after 9pm is €9 per hour and the cost of the sitter's taxi home. Day and longer-term rates are cheaper.

Scream if you wanna go faster

Port Aventura is the home of all that is biggest, brightest and best. It claims that its Stampida is the fastest wooden track roller-coaster in the world; that its Sea Odyssey is the most technologically advanced underwater simulator in the world; that the Templo del Fuego uses more fire and water effects than any other attraction in the... well, you get the picture.

In 2002 Universal Studios acquired Port Aventura theme park as a component of the mighty beachside complex known as Universal Mediterrània: no longer a mere day trip but a fully fledged resort, with two themed hotels – the El Paso and the Port Aventura – and the newly opened Costa Caribe water park. This tropically landscaped indoor play area is designed to simulate a year-round Caribbean summer where visitors can lounge in turquoise lagoons and try out nine water rides. It can be entered separately or in conjunction with Port Aventura, although you'd need more than one day to do them both justice.

Port Aventura is still the main attraction, with 90 rides spread over five internationally themed areas: Mexico, the Far West, China, Polynesia and the Mediterranean. Roaming this time-space continuum to hug your kids are Universal Studios characters including the likes of Popeye, the Pink Panther and Inspector Gadget. The truly stomach-curdling Dragon Khan rollercoaster is one of the highlights with eight loops and G-forces that should only be attempted before lunch.

For the little ones there are the usual slew of carousels and spinning tea cups.

There are also 100 daily live shows and a spectacular lakeside 'Fiesta Aventura' with lights, music, fireworks and special effects.

Universal Studios – Port Aventura

977 77 90 90/www.portaventura.es. By car A2, then A7 to exit 35, or N340 (108km/67 miles)/by train RENFE from Sants or Passeig de Gràcia to Port Aventura (1hr 15mins). **Open** *Late Mar-mid June, mid Sept-Oct* 10am-7pm daily. *Mid June-mid Sept* 10am-midnight daily. *Nov-Dec* 10am-6pm Fri; 10am-7pm Sat, Sun. **Admission** *1 day* €32; €27 concessions. *2 consecutive days* €49; €39 concessions. *3 consecutive or alternate days* €60; €45 concessions. Free under-5s. *Night ticket* (mid June-mid Sept 7pm-midnight) €22.50; €18.50 concessions. **Credit** AmEx, DC, MC, V.

Happy Parc

*C/Comtes de Bell.lloc 74-8, Sants (93 490 08 35/
www.happyparc.com). Metro Sants Estació/bus all
routes to Estació de Sants.* **Open** 5-9pm Mon-Fri;
11am-9pm Sat, Sun. **Rates** €3.70 per hr daily; €1 each
subsequent 15mins. **No credit cards. Map** p345 A3.
Ball pools, twister slides and more at this giant
indoor fun park and drop-in daycare centre for kids
aged two to 12. (Maximum height: 1m45cm or
4ft7in.) It does private birthday party sessions for
groups of ten kids or more.
Branch: C/Pau Claris 97, Eixample (93 317 86 60).

Entertainment

It's hard to choose a best time to come to
Barcelona, but a festival as exciting as the
Mercè (*see p216*) or indeed any of the smaller
district *festes*, takes all the work out of child
entertainment. The fancy dress parades of
Carnival (*see p218*) in February are fun for
smaller kids while teenagers will enjoy the
fireworks and late-night beach parties of
Sant Joan (*see p213*) in June.

L'Auditori (*see p238*) has a cycle of
Concerts en Família from December to June,
where the kids can meet the musicians and
play with the instruments before and after
the performance. Every three months, the
Ajuntament presents a programme of special
entertainment for children aged three and
up, called **Espectacles Infantils + a prop**
(roughly, 'Children's performances closer to
you'). Events include concerts and marionette
and magic shows in neighbourhood civic
centres. Check with the venues about a
performance's suitability for non-Catalan-
or Spanish-speakers.

The **Verdi** cinema occasionally includes
undubbed English-language films in its
children's sessions on Saturday and Sunday
mornings, and the **Filmoteca** shows original-
language children's films on Sundays at 5pm.
On a rainy day, a good but pricey standby can
be the **IMAX** 3-D cinema, although films are
only shown in Spanish and Catalan, and tend
to be rather dreary. For all, *see chapter* **Film**.

Museums

The children's exhibitions at the **Museu de
Zoología** (*see p96*) in the Parc de la Ciutadella
will delight young zoologists, while budding
Ronaldos will head straight for the Barça
football museum in Les Corts, **Museu del
FC Barcelona** (*see p122*). Meanwhile, the
Museu Marítim (*see p101*) has life-size
models of boats and cabins, an audio-visual
Sea Adventure exhibition that simulates life
as a galley slave on the *Don Juan de Austria*
and a submarine jouney to the bottom of the

Zoo de Barcelona. *See p219.*

ocean. The **Museu de la Xocolata** (*see p96*)
has a delicious collection of giant chocolate
sculptures including cartoon figures, celebrities
and a giant steam train. There's also a colourful
workshop where children can play and make
their own chocolate figures.

While Barcelona builds one of the most
advanced science parks in Europe (to open in
2004), the **Museu de la Ciència** is closed. It
is maintaining a small temporary exhibition at
the **Palau Macaya** (*see p113*) but its excellent
interactive children's workshops, Clik dels Nens
and Toca Toca, have been cut due to lack of
space. The planetarium sessions currently
run in Catalan and Spanish only.

Many museums have workshops or events
for children throughout the year, and many
also take part in the **Estiu als Museus**
('Summer in the Museums') programme
from June to September, providing fun kids'
activities. Those for younger children tend
to be more accessible to non-Catalan-speakers.

Museu de Cera

Passatge de la Banca 7, Barri Gòtic (93 317 26 49/ www.museoceranbcn.com). Metro Drassanes. **Open** *July-Sept* 10am-10pm daily. *Oct-May* 10am-1.30pm, 4-7.30pm Mon-Fri; 11am-2pm, 4.30-8.30pm Sat, Sun. **Admission** €6.65; €3.75 children; free under-5s. **No credit cards. Map** p345 A4.

The Wax Museum belongs to the so-bad-it's-good category of entertainment. Just off La Rambla, it's worth a quick side-step to see some of the inhabitants, who do not appear to have been updated in a while: Jacko's skin tone is somewhat 1985, an alarmingly wizened Luke Skywalker looks older than Yoda; Henry VIII has been to Weightwatchers, and Cleopatra has been transformed into a Page Three lovely. Finish off with a final tribute to kitsch – a drink at the OTT museum café next door, El Bosc de les Fades (*see p167*).

(*see p167*)

Parks & playgrounds

Don't be fooled; green areas on Barcelona maps frequently turn out to be nothing more than turfed traffic islands, while kids' playgrounds are all too often handkerchief-sized fenced-in squares with a postmodern climbing frame and a horse on springs. Still, there are good places to go for playtime. The best are the lovely, hidden **Jardins de la Tamarita** next to the stop for the Tramvia Blau, the giant dragon slides of the **Espanya Industrial** park by Sants station (*see p121*), and the **Plaça Vicenç Martorell** in the Raval (map p344 A1-2).

For anything of real size, though, it has to be the wonderful **Parc de la Ciutadella** (*see p97*), where the rowing boats, shady gardens and zoo make for a fun and relaxed day out. One Saturday every May it also hosts the **Tamborinada** fair with puppet shows, magicians and circus acts. Gaudí's **Park Güell** (*see p119*) is short on grass but the bright gingerbread houses, winding coloured benches and stalactite caves are a surefire hit with kids, while further away, the delightfully quirky **Parc del Laberint** (*see p130*) has picnic areas and a deceptively simple maze.

Parc del Castell de l'Oreneta

Camí de Can Caralleu & Passatge Blada, Zona Alta (93 413 24 80/www.bcn.es/parcsijardins). By car Ronda de Dalt exit 9/by bus 30, 60, 66, 94. **Open** (daily) *May-Aug* 10am-9pm. *Apr, Sept* 10am-8pm. *Mar, Oct* 10am-7pm. *Nov-Feb* 10am-6pm.

On ten acres of old farmland in the foothills of the Collserola range, this verdant park has flowery fields and deliciously bosky glades. There are two signposted walks with wonderful views, plus picnic areas, pony rides for three- to 12-year-olds on Saturday and Sunday mornings (10am-2pm, €5), ping-pong tables and various playgrounds. On Sundays, you can hop aboard the miniature steam train (11am-2pm, €1.20).

Out of town

The **Teatre-Museu Dalí** in Figueres (*see p293*) is one of the few museums where the kids will want to spend more time than you do. They can put a coin in the slot to water the snails, experiment with the perspective cubes, climb the camel to look at Mae West and engage in all manner of surrealist activities. As well as the two water-parks mentioned below, Catalonia has four others: **Aqua Brava** (in Roses), **Aquadiver** (Platja d'Aro) and **Water World** (Lloret de Mar) along the Costa Brava and **Marineland** in Palafolls. *See also p220* **Scream if you wanna go faster.**

Catalunya en Miniatura

Can Balasch de Baix, Torrelles de Llobregat, Outer Limits (93 689 09 60/www.catalunyaen miniatura. com). By car N11 south to Sant Vicens dels Horts, then left to Torrelles de Llobregat (10km/6 miles)/by bus Oliveras from Plaça Espanya. **Open** *Apr-June, Sept* 10am-7pm daily. *July, Aug* 10am-8pm daily. *Oct, Mar* 10am-6pm daily. *Nov-Feb* 10am-6pm Tue-Sun. **Admission** €8.50; €5.40-€6 concessions. **Credit** MC, V.

An appropriately munchkin-sized train does a circuit of a meticulously recreated hit parade of scaled-down Catalan towns and monuments, from Montserrat to the Gaudí masterpiece of your choice – an unparalleled opportunity for cheesy photos. On Wednesdays at 1pm during the school term, clowns put on a show in the amphitheatre.

Isla de Fantasia

Finca Mas Brassó, Vilassar de Dalt, Outer Limits (93 751 45 53/www.illafantasia.com). By car N11 north to Premià de Mar, then left (24km/15 miles). **Open** *June-mid Sept* 10am-7pm Mon-Fri, Sun; 10am-7pm Sat. Closed mid Sept-May. **Admission** €12; €7 2-10s; free under-2s. **Credit** MC, V.

Port Aventura on a budget, this water park has dozens of excellent foam slides, kamikaze rides and rubber dinghy chutes, along with various pools, play parks and mini-golf. The atmosphere is very Spanish rather than touristy, and you are allowed to bring in your own food (picnic and barbecue areas provided) rather than being forced to eat in extortionate theme restaurants.

El Parc de les Aus

Carretera de Cabrils, Vilassar de Mar, Outer Limits (93 750 17 65/www.elparcdelesaus.com). By car N11 north to Vilassar de Mar, then left to park (24km/15 miles)/by train RENFE from Sants or Plaça Catalunya to Vilassar de Mar, then back. **Open** 10am-sunset daily. **Admission** €9.50; €6.50 3-12s; free under-3s. **Credit** AmEx, DC, MC, V.

Over 300 species of exotic birds live in this colourful botanical park, including cockatoos, geriatric parrots (some of them over 90 years old), flamingos and vultures. For younger children, there are also mini-train rides and a petting zoo.

Film

All films bright and beautiful, all features great and small.

What is it about Barcelona that makes foreign film-makers lose their powers of judgement? The Spanish and the Catalans seem to be able to use the city as a backdrop for everything from comedy to gore to TV detective series without any difficulty at all, to say nothing of interminable car ads. It has an urban backdrop for all occasions, from well-heeled to well dodgy, and some of the more picturesque parts of the Barri Gòtic are in an almost perpetual state of cinematic siege from itinerant film crews. Barcelona has even doubled for places as unlikely as Lisbon and Algiers. But bring in an English-speaking director, and whether it's the wackiness of Gaudí, the quaintness of the Old City or an excess of absinthe, they go into a spin. Whit Stillman's *Barcelona* (1994) was a love song to the city, but an inexplicable blip on his record between *Metropolitan* and *The Last Days of Disco*, while 2002 finally saw the release in Spain of *Gaudí Afternoon*, by *Desperately Seeking Susan* director Susan Seidelman, which, when it wasn't slouching awkwardly in and around many of Gaudí's key buildings, was skulking around the sleazy streets of the Barri Gòtic, presumably in search of a lost plot. The result had the audiences roaring with laughter, but for all the wrong

reasons. In contrast, when Pedro Almodóvar used Barcelona as the setting for *Todo Sobre Mi Madre* (*All About My Mother*) in 1999, he topped the Spanish film charts for months and won the Oscar for best foreign picture.

Already nationally revered, the Oscar boosted Almodóvar's bid for canonisation – and helped overcome something of a soggy period in his career. He has become a national treasure who could film ham curing and still pull in the punters. Behind him, though, come a whole new generation of major Spanish film-makers, who between them manage to chalk up around 100 feature films a year, and 150 co-productions, figures that would bring tears to the green-tinged eyes of many British producers.

Of the new wave of directors, though, only a handful will be familiar to subtitularly reluctant British audiences. Bigas Luna, perhaps, whose Spanish trilogy *Jamón Jamón, Huevos de Oro* (*Golden Balls*) and *La teta y la luna* (*The Tit and the Moon*) was a sensual and symbol-laden attempt to untangle the Spanish psyche; Julio Medem, whose outlook is more poetic and ethereal, although what started out as a fresh vision in his first film *Vacas*, has started to look a little formulaic in its insistent reliance on magical realism and whimsical charm with

Candles and *cañas* at **Cine Ambigú**. *See p226.*

the recent *Lucia y el Sexo*; and Álex de la Iglesia, who has avoided falling into a similar trap by leaping from genre to genre with the gleeful abandon of a psychotropic frog: so far he's covered sci-fi (*Accion Mutante*), horror (*El Día de la Bestia*), melodrama (*La Comunidad*) and now the western (*800 balas*), and he's showing no signs of flagging or a failing imagination. Look out, too, for Fernando León de Aranoa , who won a Goya (a Spanish Oscar) for his first film, *Barrio*, a hardhitting but often hilarious look at life in a marginalised suburb of Madrid, and whose second film, *Los Lunes al Sol*, about unemployment, promises to transform him into something of a Spanish Ken Loach. And of course Alejandro Amenábar, whose third film *The Others*, made in English and starring Nicole Kidman, transformed him overnight from geekish wunderkind to international cinema sophisticate.

In fact making films in English is slowly catching on, particularly in Catalonia, if not in the rest of Spain: Barcelona-based production company Filmax recently set up a subsidiary to make English-language horror films, though they have yet to reap much critical applause for their efforts. Catalan filmmakers Maria Ripoll and Ventura Pons have both made films in English recently, as has Isabel Coixet, whose *My Life Without Me* is her second in English, following the well-received Seattle slacker flick *Things I Never Told You* – though she reverted to Spanish for the best-forgotten 18th-century romance *A Los Que Aman* in between.

With so much national product, not to mention the enormous number of films coming from Latin America at the moment, particularly from Argentina and Mexico, Spanish cinema is in robust shape. There is still huge demand for American blockbusters, which account for all but a couple of the 25 top-grossing films each year, but alongside the mainstream, there is also a relatively large audience for slightly more alternative, independent work from all corners of the globe.

SEEING FILMS

There are dozens of cinemas in Barcelona, from flea-pit to space-cruiser, though the relentless invasion by popcorn-and-pap multi-screens is taking its toll on the smaller, more charming venues, one of which slips under every few years. The good news for non-Spanish speakers is that one or two prints of first-run films are usually shown in their original language with Spanish subtitles at the cinemas below.

Newspapers carry full details of screenings, as does the weekly *Guia del Ocio*. Subtitled films are marked VO for *versió original* or, in some cases, VOSE (*versió original subtitulado*

en espanyol). Some of the larger cinemas open at 11am, though most open at around 4pm. Early-evening screenings start between 7.30pm and 8.30pm, and later screenings between 10.15pm and 10.45pm. Weekend evenings can be very crowded, especially for recent releases, so turn up early. On Fridays and Saturdays, many cinemas also have a late-night session starting around 1am. All cinemas have a cheap night (*dia del espectador*), which is usually Monday, though sometimes Wednesday. You can also buy some tickets from the Internet through the service www.vealcine.com, and over the phone via Servi-Caixa (*see p208*).

Original-language cinemas

Icària Yelmo Cineplex

C/Salvador Espriu 61, Vila Olímpica (93 221 75 85/www.yelmocineplex.es). Metro Ciutadella-Vila Olímpica. **Tickets** €4 Mon, before 2pm Tue-Sun; €5.50 after 2.30pm Tue-Sun, late shows. **No credit cards. Map** 343 F7.
American-style cinema 15-screen multiplex in an American-style shopping mall beside the Port Olimpic showing mostly mainstream movies.

Maldà

C/Pi 5, Barri Gòtic (93 317 85 29). Metro Liceu. **Tickets** €4.50 Mon; €5.50 Tue-Fri; €5.75 Sat, Sun. **No credit cards. Map** 344 B2.
The slightly seedy-looking Maldà provides an excellent public service by showing double bills of fairly recent films, often thematically linked, at a little cheaper than the going rate. Great for when you've missed the first run, or want a second go at deciphering *Mulholland Drive*. Housed upstairs from the Galeries Maldà in an 18th-century palace, evident only in the elegant panelling bar.

Méliès Cinemes

C/Villaroel 102, Eixample (93 451 00 51). Metro Urgell. **Tickets** €3 Mon; €4.20 Tue-Sun. **No credit cards. Map** 342 C5.
The closest Barcelona has to an arthouse cinema, and also the cheapest in town, showing a constantly changing repertoire of watchable classics, ancient and reasonably modern. Up to eight films per week, changing regularly, with thematic cycles in summer.

Renoir-Floridablanca

C/Floridablanca 135, Eixample (93 228 93 93/www.cinesrenoir.es). Metro Sant Antoni. **Tickets** €4 Mon; €5.50, €4 concessions Tue-Sun; €4 late show Fri, Sat. **Credit** AmEx, MC, V. **Map** 342 C5.
A newly opened four-screen branch of the Renoir chain, showing reasonably interesting, off-beat Spanish and European films in their original language, with subtitles. Much more convenient than its six-screen sister cinema, which is lost in the wilds of Les Corts.
Branch: Renoir-Les Corts C/Eugeni d'Ors 12 , Les Corts (93 490 55 10).

It's the reel thing

It is a testament to Catalan industry, endeavour and imagination that Spain's first fiction film, *Riña en un café*, (*Brawl in a café*), was made in Catalonia by Fructuos Gelabert in 1897. Thereafter, a spirited evolution from travelogues to filmed theatre and historical biographies made Barcelona the centre of the Spanish film industry by 1936, when it boasted 114 cinemas equipped for sound, numerous production companies and the first female Spanish film-maker, Rosario Pi. The fascist victory in the Civil War saw many film-makers leave Barcelona and the Catalan language to suffer the centralising policies of Franco, but slowly the film industry was rebuilt, thanks largely to the wealthy and indulgent middle class that presided over the economic expansion and tourist boom of the '60s. Around that time a group of self-financing film-makers, led by Vicente Aranda – director of *Change of Sex* (1976), *Lovers* (1991) and *Juana La Loca* (2001) – formed the Barcelona School, and made films with a frank approach to sexual, some say sordid, themes as a riposte to the government-backed autocracy and censure of the Madrid Film School.

Following the reinstatement of the Generalitat in 1977, Catalan cinemas and production companies pandered to exploitation genres, but there was also a cathartic reinscription of Catalan history in expensive, historical epics such as Antoni Ribas' *La ciutat cremada* (*The burnt city*) in 1976, and the broaching of previously forbidden themes in films from new auteurs, such as Bigas Luna's *Bilbao* (1976), Francesc Bellmunt's *L'orgia* (*The orgy*) (1978), and Ventura Pons' *Ocaña, retrat intermitent*, (*Ocaña, intermittent portrait*), 1978, about a transvestite painter.

The declaration of autonomy in 1980 brought a stability that was later bolstered by the staging of the Olympic Games in 1992. It's worth mentioning, though, that cinema-going in Barcelona has declined dramatically in recent years, however, due to industry reticence about the commercial prospects of films made in Catalan and, conversely, the proliferation of Catalan language television channels. Recent collaborations between film and television companies such as TV3 and Canal 33 have intensified the battle against Madrid for control over funding and arrested this decline to the extent that Catalan cinema

has regained a reputation for quality literary adaptations, satirical social comedies and experimental documentaries.

Of the Catalan auteurs, Bellmunt and Bigas Luna may have faltered but Marc Recha's Rohmeresque *Pau i el seu germà*, (*Pau and his brother*), 2001, offered evidence of a major new talent, and Julio Wallovits and Roger Gual's Mametesque *Smoking Room* (2002) was an intelligent sleeper hit. Ventura Pons, who enjoyed a deserved breakout hit in all of Spain with his sarcastic but tender *El porqué de las cosas* (1994), continued to delight with *Anita no perd el tren* (*Anita takes a chance*), 2001, a bittersweet comedy about a cinema that's torn down to make way for a multiplex, while the best recent Spanish film was José Luis Guerín's *En Construcción* (*Work in Progress*) in 2001, a documentary about the revamping of Barcelona's red light district, the Barrio Chino. An impressionist contemplation of Catalan identity, ageing and rebirth, this exquisite film also functions as a forceful example of an enduring, evolving and uniquely Catalan sense of cinema.

Rex

*Gran Via de les Corts Catalanes 463, Eixample (93
423 10 60/www.grupbalana.com). Metro Rocafort.*
Tickets €5.30 Mon, Tue, Thur; €4.20 Wed; €5.60
Fri-Sun. **No credit cards. Map** 341 B5.

The nicest cinema is Barcelona only shows occasional films in English these days, unfortunately.
With its warm, red interior and '70s decor, this is a
reminder of what cinemas used to be like before the
multiplexes loomed over the scene.

Verdi

*C/Verdi 32, Gràcia (93 238 79 90/93 238 78
00/www.cinemes-verdi.com). Metro Fontana.*
Tickets €4 Mon; €5.50 Tue-Sun. **No credit
cards. Map** p338 D3.

The five-screen Verdi, and its four-screen annexe
Verdi Park on the next street over, are champions of
interesting but accessible cinema, with a lively, varied programme of films from around the world, particularly Asia and Europe. At peak times chaos
reigns, so arrive early and make sure you don't mis-
take the queue to go in for the ticket queue. The
neighbouring streets are full of pizza and falafel bars
for a cheap and cheerful post-film bite to eat.
Branch: Verdi Park C/Torrijos 49, Gràcia
(93 238 79 90).

Specialist cinemas

Cine Ambigú

*Sala Apolo, C/Nou de la Rambla 113, Paral.lel
(93 441 40 01/www.retinas.org). Metro Paral.lel.*
Shows 8.30pm, 10.30pm Tue. **Tickets** €4 or €6
(incl 1 drink). **No credit cards. Map** 342 C6.

European and Asian experimental cinema never
likely to get a wider distribution features in this old-
time music hall (and new-time techno club) every
Tuesday night, unless there's a concert, in which
case they switch to Wednesday. It's more like a
cabaret than a cinema, with small tables, candles
and a bar – although not overly comfortable. Two
screenings, at 8.30pm and 10.45pm.

Filmoteca de la Generalitat
de Catalunya

*Cinema Aquitania, Avda Sarrià 31-3,
Eixample (93 410 75 90/http://cultura.gencat.
net/filmo). Metro Hospital Clínic. Closed Aug.*
Tickets €2.70; €2 concessions; €33 block ticket
for 20 films. **Credit** (block tickets only) MC, V.
Map p338 C3.

This is film-buff nirvana, and a good place for filling gaps in your cinematic knowledge, though at
times the programme can be a little esoteric for
many tastes. Funded by the Catalan government,
the Filmoteca shows overlapping cycles of films
grouped by theme, country, style or director, from
all periods of cinematic history, as well as all nomi-
nations for Goyas (Spanish Oscars). There are three
screenings daily, usually at 5pm, 7.30pm and 10pm,
and latecomers are strictly not admitted. A fort-
nightly information sheet contains full programme

details and other notes, and kids' films are shown
on Sundays at 5pm. The Filmoteca also runs a
decent library of film-related books, videos and magazines, round the corner from the Centre d'Art Santa
Monica, at the bottom of the Ramblas.

IMAX Port Vell

*Moll d'Espanya, Port Vell (93 225 11 11/
www.imaxintengral.com). Metro Barceloneta
or Drassanes.* **Tickets** €6.60-€9.60 (also available
from Tel-entrada & Servi-Caixa). **Discount** BT.
Credit MC, V. **Map** 342 D7.

A white monolith squatting at one end of the port's
Maremagnum complex, and offering a choice of
mega-formats, including 3-D and towering OMNI-
MAX. The problem is that there are few decent films
made for these screens, so programmes rarely stray
from a repetitive round of nature films and uninspiring documentaries.

VOID/Sala Zelig

*C/Ferlandina 51, Raval (93 443 42 03/www.void-
bcn.com). Metro Sant Antoni or Universitat.*
Shows 9pm Wed-Sun. **Tickets** (incl 1 drink) €3.
No credit cards. Map 342 C5.

As well as renting out arthouse films on video
and DVD, the Raval branch of VOID has a small video
projection room and holds nightly screenings at 9pm
from Tuesday to Sunday. On Sundays the audience
turn up and choose what they want to see. The rest
of the week consists of vaguely avant-garde classics
from the catalogue. See the website for full details
of programmes and rental catalogue.

Festivals

There are an increasing number of film festivals
in Barcelona. Though none is as big or brash as
Sitges (*see below*), they all show interesting work
unlikely to be screened elsewhere. Most festivals
are held at cinemas around town and locations
like the **CCCB** (*see p87*). Every year new events
pop up, but the regulars include: **Asian** (April/
May), **Jewish** (May), **Women's** (June), **Gay
and Lesbian** (July and October), **Open Air
Shorts** (September), **Documentaries**
(October), **African** (November), **Alternative
Film** (November).

Festival Internacional de Cinema
de Catalunya, Sitges

*93 419 36 35/93 419 06 61/fax 93 439 73 80/
www.sitges.com/cinema.* **Advance tickets** from
Tel-entrada. **Date** 1st half of Oct.

The ten-day Sitges Film Festival offers the unique
and slightly disturbing combination of a quaint seaside town and gore, horror and sci-fi. This festival
is certainly not for the squeamish, as it offers a crazy
mix of geek-street retrospectives, Asian cyber-
scream arthouse and Hollywood blood-lust blockbusters. To give you an idea: in 2002, the best film
award went to *Dracula: Pages from a Virgin's Diary*,
and best director to David Cronenberg for *Spider*.

Galleries

Even Picasso went to Paris to get famous.

It's all contemporary at **Antonio de Barnola**. *See p228.*

Barcelona is a fine place for artists – and all creators – to live, but not necessarily the place to find artistic success. The weak local art market combined with poor public funding mean that artists are typically forced to seek sales in other places – Berlin and New York are the current faves – where their creative anxieties and career ambitions might come to some fruition. Those who are successful internationally – including the granddaddy Antoni Tàpies, the senior generation of Antoni Muntadas, Francesc Torres and Susana Solano, the mid-career crop led by Eulàlia Valldosera, Antoni Abad and Montserrat Soto, and younger lights like Carles Congost and Tere Recarens – tend to make it on their own, with little help from local dealers.

The Barcelona art scene is more an amalgam of isolated energies than a coherent, tangible whole. Artists are generally loath to engage each other intellectually or even to gather socially, as witnessed by the dearth of authentic art bars (the only thing close is **Kentucky**, *see p252*, the longtime late-night favourite). Artists tend to labour in solitude until an opening night (preferably their own) lures them from the cave.

Barcelona was a minor hotspot of the early 20th-century avant-garde, with Picasso, Miró and Dali as its guiding lights. The creative spirit that fostered them was all but paralysed after the Civil War and the advent of the dictatorship, but eventually the art world scraped back: the 1950s saw the emergence of *art informel* abstract painting, while conceptualism boomed in the '70s. Following the city's famously triumphant reawakening in the 1980s and '90s, the Barcelona art world has gone the way of extravagant self-promotion, which means, mainly, throwing money into museum construction and into ill-defined megashows like the **Triennial** (next scheduled for 2004).

A new generation of artists has come to share the benefits of globalised culture, participating in biennials and museum shows worldwide, though often at the expense of any recognisable artistic identity. The verve of Barcelona art-making has had little effect on local art finances. Amid the city's overall economic buoyancy, a flat art market has cut in on dealers' room to manoeuvre; even the most prestigious of local private galleries have lost their reputation as trendsetters, often descending into gimmickry and conservatism. Dealers are prone to jealous bickering. The lack of a half-decent local art fair only reinforces Madrid's ARCO as the premium Spanish gallery fair.

Public institutions and private foundations have picked up some of the slack, and together they make up a formidable phalanx on the contemporary art front. Innovative enough to usurp the role normally reserved for alternative spaces (the MACBA has been particularly committed to art with a socio-political bent), they have nevertheless given the city's art scene a rather top-heavy slant, cutting in on the artists' initiative.

There is no definitive guide to galleries and artistic activities. Listings appear in the weekly *Guía de Ocio* and in some newspapers, but are rarely comprehensive. The guides of the various rival gallery associations are only partial. The simplest plan is to go to a gallery district and do the rounds. All private galleries are closed on Sundays and Mondays. A few are now beginning to open in August, although most are closed. Exhibition openings typically take place around 8pm midweek.

Commercial galleries

The Barri Gòtic and the area centred on the Eixample's C/Consell de Cent are Barcelona's longest established gallery districts, but in recent years new clusters of contemporary spaces have developed in the Born and around the **MACBA** in the Raval.

Barri Gòtic

In addition to those listed below, the **Galeria Segovia Isaacs** (C/Palla 8, 93 302 29 80) is also of interest.

Antonio de Barnola

C/Palau 4 (93 412 22 14). Metro Liceu or Jaume I. **Open** 5-9pm Tue-Fri; noon-2pm, 5-9pm Sat. Closed Aug. **No credit cards. Map** p345 B3.
This handsome space presents impeccable shows of Spanish contemporary artists. Regulars include respected photographer Humberto Rivas, Catalan Mireya Masó and Madrid painter José Manuel Ballester, who applies his disturbing realism to modern architecture. American photographer Bill Beckley shows in spring 2003.

Artur Ramon

C/Palla 10, 23 & 25 (93 302 59 70). Metro Liceu. **Open** Oct-June 10am-1.30pm, 5-8pm Tue-Sat. July, Sept 10am-1.30pm, 5-8pm Tue-Fri. Closed Aug. **Credit** MC, V. **Map** p344/5 B2/3.
The best of the local dynasties dealing in historic art and objects, the Artur Ramon family has several spaces (on the same street). The finest shows are the exhibitions of historical Spanish and European arts and crafts, along with thematic shows culled from private collections – snuff bottles, Renaissance prints, Spanish masters – well presented at No.23.

Sala Parés

C/Petritxol 5 (93 318 70 08/www.salapares.com). Metro Liceu. **Open** Oct-May 10.30am-2pm, 4.30-8.30pm Mon-Sat; 11.30am-2pm Sun. June-Sept 10.30am-2pm, 4.30-8.30pm Mon-Sat. Closed 3wks Aug. **Credit** AmEx, MC, V. **Map** p344 A2.
The Sala Parés opened in 1840 and has long been a symbol for the Catalan bourgeoisie, who still make up the majority of its rather staid clientele. A hundred years ago it promoted the Catalan avant-garde, and it was here that Picasso had his first one-man show. Now the spacious renovated gallery specialises in figurative and historical painting. Nearby, at No.8, Galeria Trama offers contemporary work. **Branches**: Galeria Trama, C/Petritxol 8, Barri Gòtic (93 317 48 77); Galeria 18, C/Jacinto Benavente 18, Barri Gòtic (93 241 14 95); Edicions Margall, Rambla Catalunya 116, Eixample (93 415 96 92).

Raval

Other galleries showing paintings are **Galeria Ferran Cano** (Plaça dels Àngels 4, 93 310 15 48), and the **Cotthem Gallery** (C/Doctor Dou 15, 93 270 16 69), while the **Espai Vidre** (C/Àngels 8, 93 318 98 33) specialises in quality glasswork. The **FAD** design centre also does regular shows (Convent dels Àngels, Plaça dels Àngels 5-6, 93 443 75 20/www.fadweb.com).

Galeria dels Àngels

C/Àngels 16 (93 412 54 54/www.galeriadels angels.com). Metro Catalunya. **Open** noon-2pm, 5-8.30pm Tue-Sat. Closed Aug. **No credit cards. Map** p344 A2.
This narrow space is used by collector Emilio Álvarez, who shows his preferred artists, including abstract painters Miquel Mont and Santi Moix, and the photography-based work of Juan Urrios and Canadian Lynn Cohen. A nearby space (open only by appointment) is used for installations.

Ras Gallery

C/Doctor Dou 10 (93 412 71 99/www.actar.es). Metro Catalunya. **Open** 1-9pm Tue-Sat. **Credit** AmEx, MC, V. **Map** p344 A2.
Run by the Actar publishing house, Ras has a small architecture and design bookstore fronting a gallery with fine shows often related to new publications. Its exhibitions of original architectural drawings, photos and maquettes by contemporary masters are especially interesting.

Born

As well as the places listed here, you can also try **Centro Cultural Círculo de Arte** (C/Princesa 52, 93 268 88 20/21).

Galeria H₂0. *See p230.*

Galeria Maeght

C/Montcada 25 (93 310 42 45/www.maeght.com).
Metro Jaume I. **Open** 10am-2pm, 4-8pm Tue-Sat.
Credit AmEx, DC, MC, V. **Map** p345 C3.
The Paris-based Maeght gallery opened this handsome space in the 1970s. Occupying a Renaissance
palace near the Picasso museum, with a lovely courtyard and staircase, it shows high-powered Spanish
(Tàpies, Arroyo, Palazuelo) and European painters
and sculptors. Despite its prestigious name and digs,
though, the Maeght struggles for relevance on the
crowded Barcelona scene.

Metrònom

C/Fusina 9 (93 268 42 98). Metro Arc de Triomf
or Jaume I. **Open** 10am-2pm, 4.30-8.30pm Tue-Sat.
Closed Aug. **Map** p338 C3.
Run by collector Rafael Tous, this was Barcelona's
most lively art space back in the 1980s. After a brief
hiatus, it has recently won back some of its original
impetus, particularly through exhibitions that focus
on photography and multimedia installations. In
spring 2003 there will be a selection from Tous' conceptual art collection, followed by a show of sound
artists and 'The Deficit Show' into July; curated by
artist Gustavo Marrone, it will feature Barcelona-
based artists Javier Peñafiel, Joana Cera and Carles
Congost. It also has video and dance programmes
and organises a festival of contemporary music in
January beneath its gorgeous *belle époque* glass
ceiling. Work is not for sale. *See also p241.*

Eixample

Other worthwhile galleries in the area include
Galeria Metropolitana Barcelona (Rambla
Catalunya 50, pral 1ª, 93 487 40 42) and
Galeria Ignacio de Lassaleta (Rambla
Catalunya 47, 93 488 02 21), with its handsome
Modernista interior. The **Sala Vinçon** (Passeig
de Gràcia 96, 93 215 60 50/www.vincon.com) in
the Vinçon design store shows contemporary
art and design.

Galeria Carles Taché

C/Consell de Cent 290 (93 487 88 36/www.carles
tache.com). Metro Passeig de Gràcia. **Open** *Sept-*
June 10am-2pm, 4-8.30pm Tue-Sat. *July* 10am-2pm,
4-8.30pm Tue-Fri. Closed Aug. **No credit cards.**
Map p342 D5.
Carles Taché represents some of the most established senior Spanish painters, such as Arroyo,
Broto and Campano. Blue-chip internationals such
as Sean Scully and Tony Cragg can also be seen,
along with Catalan sculptor Jordi Colomer and the
clever pop of Carlos Pazos.

Galeria Estrany-de la Mota

Passatge Mercader 18 (93 215 70 51/www.estrany
delamota.com). FGC Provença. **Open** *Sept-June*
10.30am-1.30pm, 4.30-8.30pm Tue-Sat. *July* 10.30am-
1.30pm, 4.30-8.30pm Mon-Fri. Closed Aug.
No credit cards. Map p338 D4.
This iron-columned basement gallery works well for
Antoni Estrany's selection of neo-conceptualists,
including the intelligent photo-montages of
Montserrat Soto and the virtual sculpture and net.art
of Antoni Abad. International artists represented
include Thomas Ruff, Jean-Marc Bustamante and
Thomas Locher.

Galeria Joan Prats

Rambla Catalunya 54 (93 216 02 84/www.galeria
joanprats.com). Metro Passeig de Gràcia. **Open**
Sept-June 10.30am-1.30pm, 5-8.30pm Tue-Sat. *July*
10.30am-1.30pm, 5-8.30pm Tue-Fri. Closed Aug.
Credit AmEx, V. **Map** p342 D4.
This gallery was born out of the 1920s friendship
between Joan Prats, son of a fashionable hatmaker,
and the artist Joan Miró. Nowadays, the only rem-
nant of the original business is the name and the
headgear motifs on the shopfront; and the Prats'
Miró collection is now in the Fundació Miró. These
days, along with a crop of well-known painters, 'La
Prats' represents artists like the high-profile Eulàlia
Valldosera, and the quirky Catalan Perejaume, as
well as international artists like the British photographer Hannah Collins. The nearby branch on
C/Balmes has limited-edition prints.
Branch: Joan Prats-Artgràfic, C/Balmes 54 (93
488 13 98).

Kowasa Gallery

C/Mallorca 235 (93 487 35 88/www.kowasa.com).
FGC Provença. **Open** 11am-2pm, 5-8.30pm Tue-Sat.
Closed Aug. **Credit** AmEx, MC, V. **Map** p338 D4.

Arts & Entertainment

This photography gallery is located above the excellent bookshop of the same name. Its two spaces are used for Spanish and international artists like Martí Llorens, Ramon David and the famed Civil War chronicler Agustí Centelles. The gallery has works by hundreds of photographers, among them Nadar, Cartier-Bresson and John Coplans.

Galeria Toni Tàpies

C/Consell de Cent 282 (93 487 64 02/
www.tonitapies.com). Metro Passeig de Gràcia.
Open 10am-2pm, 4-8pm Mon-Fri; 11am-2pm, 5-8.30pm Sat. **Credit** MC, V. **Map** p339 F4.
Run by the son of the prestigious Catalan painter, this gallery shows young Catalan artists Tere Recarens and Martí Anson, along with established creators Jaume Plensa and daddy Tàpies himself (showing in early 2003); there are shows by foreign artists as well, including Canadian Jana Sterbak. The gallery also produces limited-edition prints.

Gràcia & Zona Alta

Fundació Foto Colectània

C/Julián Romea 6 (93 217 16 26/www.colectania.es).
FGC Gràcia. **Open** 5-8.30pm Mon; 11am-2pm, 5-8.30pm Tue-Sat. **No credit cards**. **Map** p338 D3.
This private photography foundation is dedicated to the promotion of photography collecting. Shows in the large, handsome space emphasise collections of other important galleries and museums, including major Spanish and Portuguese photographers since the 1950s. Work from the fabulous collection of Spaniard Enrique Ordóñez will be seen in the final months of 2003. Work is not for sale.

Galeria Alejandro Sales

C/Julián Romea 16 (93 415 20 54/www.alejandro
sales.com). FGC Gràcia. **Open** *Sept-June* 11am-2pm, 5-8.30pm Tue-Sat. *July* 11am-2pm, 5-8.30pm Tue-Fri. Closed Aug. **No credit cards**. **Map** p338 D3.
Alejandro Sales is a serious young dealer who combines impeccable shows by international blue-chip artists with a solid Spanish stable, which in spring 2003 will include Marina Nuñez. At the same time, work by emerging young creators and some gallery regulars (such as Estrada, also showing in the spring) can be seen in the gallery's smaller room called Blackspace.

Galeria H₂0

C/Verdi 152 (93 415 18 01/www.h2o.es). Metro
Lesseps. **Open** 11am-1pm, 5.30-8pm Tue-Fri; 11am-1pm Sat. Closed Aug. **No credit cards**. **Map** p339 E2.
Architect/designer Joaquim Ruiz Millet and wife Ana Planella publish books and produce design objects (including works by the brilliant Martí Guixé), while running a dynamic gallery out of this charming Gràcia home. Shows feature design, architecture, photography (a Garcia-Alix show is set for May 2003) and contemporary art. You never know what to expect here, and that's what makes it such an artistic wonderland.

The fringe scene

Present-day art activism in Barcelona is typified by a distinctly iconoclastic Catalan style. Some initiatives imitate 1970s models (art parties, performance cabaret, open studios), while others are aligned with anti-globalisation currents. Many galleries are run by collectives and work as mini-cultural centres. Among those worth checking out are the spacious **Centre Civic Can Felipa** (C/Pallars 277, 93 266 44 41) and the huge white basement of **Theredoom Galeria** (C/Marina 65-7; 93 221 13 69/ www.theredoom.com), both in Poblenou. Near the MACBA are the artists' collective **La Xina Art** (C/Doctor Dou, 93 301 67 03) and the free-for-all that is the **Centro Cultural La Santa** (C/Àngels, 93 342 59 46/www.lasanta.org). Occasional projects emerge out of the **22A** group of artists and critics (93 441 84 81/ www.22a.org) and Barcelona Culture Studio (C/Riereta 20 bis, 93 443 30 04) in a Raval loft. In late spring 'Tallers Oberts' sees artists open their studios in Poblenou and the old city, with an information point at the **FAD** (Convent dels Àngels, Plaça dels Àngels 5-6).

Public centres complementing the fringe are **Metrònom** (*see p229*), the CaixaForum's **Mediateca** (*see p105*), and the **CCCB** (*see p90*). The alternative scene also blends into Barcelona's nightlife frontier, where many of the loose ends eventually meet. If you're looking for somewhere to stay and study art, the best and nearest option is **Can Serrat**, a converted farmhouse near Montserrat (93 771 00 37/03 29/www.canserrat.org).

Box 23

C/Ample 23 entl, Barri Gòtic (93 302 38 82). Metro
Drassanes. **Open** 5-8.30pm Wed-Sat. Closed Aug. **No credit cards**. **Map** p345 B4.
Brazilian Edgar Dávila started this tiny gallery with the idea of challenging the conventional exhibition space – as its curtain-lined walls attest. A live-in 'Box Hotel' project will run into 2003 after an excellent first show by Canadian Lind Duvall in late 2002.

Hangar

Passatge del Marqués de Santa Isabel 40, Poblenou
(tel/fax 93 308 40 41/www.hangar.org). Metro
Poblenou. **Open** *Information* 9am-2pm Mon-Fri. Closed Aug. **No credit cards**.
Besides being a multi-disciplinary production centre with studios and facilities for the production of video and Internet art, Hangar has added workshops, video screenings and debates that are open to the public, while offering a regular 'showroom' of residents' work (work is not for sale). Run by the Catalan Visual Artists Association, Hangar also spearheads an open studio project for Poblenou artists in June. Visitors should call first.

Gay & Lesbian

Come as you are; this is laid-back Barcelona.

You're here, you're queer... who cares? Just about nobody in Barcelona, that's for certain. This is a vibrant, open city with an 'anything goes' mindset – do what you like, wear what you like and odds are no one will raise an eyebrow. This is just the place, then, for that sequinned little number you couldn't get the courage up to wear back home. Or you could just stick with Armani – we'll leave it up to you.

This lack of a judgemental population explains why there is not a large gay ghetto here. (For that you need to head down the coast to the resort of **Sitges**, a kind of Fire Island with paella.) Still, there are good hunting grounds. The area of Barcelona bordered by the streets of Diputació and Aragó, Balmes and Villaroel in the Eixample holds a lot of gay bars and restaurants, and is fondly known as the 'Gaixample'. Still, even this is not really a gayhood, because, although it has a certain buzz at night, the strict gridlines and wide streets of the area make it anything but villagey.

Spaniards often live with their parents well past the first flush of youth, so don't be surprised if that Latin lover from a darkened club sweeps you off to the back of a Ford Fiesta. This home-based lifestyle is why there are so many darkrooms and saunas about. Outdoor cruising is a popular evening pastime, and this is particularly so on Montjuïc, near the MNAC (see p108), which theoretically means you could combine a quick fumble with a tour of some of the country's finest Romanesque art.

The following is only a selection, and bear in mind that the gay scene changes more rapidly than any other; bars and clubs come and go at a dizzying pace. It's a good idea to pick up a copy of the free gay map or magazines such as *Nois* or *Shanguide* for the most current listings and events. Websites worth checking out include www.mensual.com; www.freedom-spain.com; www.naciongay.com and www.guiagay.com.

Cafés & bars

Given that the phrase 'gay-friendly' is happily not one you need to think about very much in a town like Barcelona (since virtually every place in the city is gay friendly), the best places are often mixed. **Café de l'Opera** (see p167), **Schilling** (see p169) and **Bar Ra** (see p171), for instance, are justly popular among both the gay and straight communities.

Atame

C/Consell de Cent 257, Eixample (no phone). Metro Universitat. **Open** 6pm-2.30am Mon-Thur; 6pm-3am Fri-Sun. **No credit cards. Map** p342 C5.
A long, spare space that gets busy at weekends, Atame attracts a youngish, male-ish crowd, and has a laid-back atmosphere. Spanish grooves rule, and there's a happy hour on Tuesdays.

Backsy

C/Diputació 161, Eixample (no phone). Metro Universitat. **Open** 11am-2am Mon-Thur, Sun; 11am-3am Fri, Sat. **Credit** AmEx, MC, V. **Map** p342 C5.
A new café-bar that turns the music up after 9pm, until which time you can order sandwiches and pasta salads while contemplating the exotic verdure of the enclosed garden. On Thursdays a babel of non-Spanish speakers meets and mingles.

Café Dietrich

C/Consell de Cent 255, Eixample (93 451 77 07). Metro Universitat. **Open** 10.30pm-2.30am Mon-Thur, Sun; 10.30pm-3am Fri, Sat. **No credit cards. Map** p342 C5.
On weekend nights, this place has as high a proportion of boys per square metre as you're likely to find anywhere. The atmosphere is camp-trendy with the strut-your-stuff crowd in a lighter mood before the serious trawling begins in the clubs. House music is interspersed with short drag acts.

Caligula

C/Consell de Cent 257, Eixample (93 451 48 92). Metro Universitat. **Open** 8pm-3am Mon-Thur, Sun; 10.30pm-3am Fri, Sat. **No credit cards. Map** p342 C5.
The over-the-top oriental decor – lots of red and a big gold Buddah – attracts a more mixed and a quieter crowd than neighbour Dietrich. There are reasonably priced salads and light dishes to be had.

Crazy's Shoes

C/Muntaner 32, Eixample (93 453 66 74). Metro Universitat. **Open** Shop 11am-2pm, 5-9pm Mon-Sat. Bar 10pm-3am Thur-Sat. **No credit cards. Map** p342 C5.
Difficult to classify – a friendly shoe shop where you can get a coffee by day; a quirky bar space at night which, lined with polish and inner soles, is more Almodóvar than many wannabe places. There's a happy hour on Thursdays and a stripper Saturdays.

D-Blanco

C/Villaroel 71, Eixample (93 451 59 86/www.d-blanco.com). Metro Urgell. **Open** 6pm-2am Mon-Thur, Sun; 6pm-3am Fri, Sat. **Credit** AmEx, DC, MC, V. **Map** p342 C5.

The scene's hippest newcomer, with a stylish New York feel. The keynote, as the name says, is white, but as a relief from the snowy rigours of the main bar there is a riotously coloured *salon privée*. Well-heeled twenty- to fortysomethings chow down on elaborate sandwiches and salads until 11.30pm.

The Eagle

Passeig de Sant Joan 152, Eixample (93 207 58 56/ www.eaglespain.com). Metro Verdaguer. **Open** 10pm-2.30am Mon-Thur, Sun; 10pm-3am Fri, Sat. **No credit cards. Map** p339 E4.

The place to go if you're into leather and sex, The Eagle's clientele is of the over-30 and hirsute variety, who may well divest themselves of the leather once inside. A small bar gives off to an enormous backroom equipped with all manner of contraptions. There are sex theme nights to suit many tastes, but they are not for the faint-hearted.

Escandalus

C/Villaroel 86, Eixample (no phone). Metro Urgell **Open** 8pm-3am daily. **No credit cards. Map** p342 C5.

A newly opened bar with tables outside. Inside are glitterballs, chandeliers, leopardskin and red velvet, with cocktails and music to match. A place with potential that could get busier with age.

Ironic Café

C/Consell de Cent 242 bis, Eixample (mobile 627 92 98 53). Metro Universitat. **Open** 6pm-3am daily. **No credit cards. Map** p342 C5.

Recently redecorated in sleek, hi-tech mode, with arty images shimmering across screens lining the walls, this is a relaxed place to sip a cocktail or more prosaic beverage, while taking in the odd performance. Women are also welcome.

New Chaps

Avda Diagonal 365, Eixample (93 215 53 65). Metro Diagonal or Verdaguer. **Open** 9pm-3am Mon-Sat; 7pm-3am Sun. **No credit cards. Map** p338 D4.

A veteran on the scene, New Chaps is true to the butch cowboy implications of its name. Steer horns on the wall, porn on the video, and all sorts of goings-on in the labyrinthine darkroom downstairs. There's rarely a dame to be seen in these parts.

Ouï Café

C/Consell de Cent 247, Eixample (no phone). Metro Universitat. **Open** 5pm-2am Mon-Thur, Sun; 5pm-3am Fri, Sat. **No credit cards. Map** p342 C5.

Go through the curtained portal to a light, airy bar with a young and mainly male crowd. There's also gay soft porn for those the mood.

Punto BCN

C/Muntaner 63-5, Eixample (93 453 61 23). Metro Universitat. **Open** 6pm-2am Mon-Thur, Sun; 6pm-2.30am Fri, Sat. **No credit cards. Map** p342 C5.

A wide space with an Olympic length bar, seating and pool table on the mezzanine, lots of punters, and not much character. One of few places to be packed by 9pm; men come here after work.

Other local clubs with an established gay following include **La Terrrazza** (*see p257*) and **Discothèque** (*see p255*).

Arena Classic

C/Diputació 233, Eixample (93 487 83 42/ www.arenadisco.com). Metro Passeig de Gracia or Universitat. **Open** 12.30am-5am Fri, Sat. **Admission** (incl 1 drink) €5 Fri; €9 Sat. **No credit cards. Map** p342 D5.

There are three discos called Arena offering variations on a well-worn theme. You can switch from one to another freely after getting your hand stamped. The Classic is the more light-hearted with mainly '60s and '70s Spanish tunes, a campy-kitsch atmosphere and a healthy mix of the sexes. Arrive as early as possible to avoid a block-long queue.

Arena Madre

C/Balmes 32, Eixample (93 487 83 42). Metro Passeig de Gracia or Universitat. **Open** 12.30am-5am Tue-Sat; 7pm-5am Sun. **Admission** (incl 1 drink) €5 Tue-Fri, Sun; €9 Sat. **No credit cards. Map** p342 D5.

Large and cavernous, Arena Madre has a spacious dancefloor, a darkroom and pounding house, along with current chart hits. It attracts a younger crowd than Arena Classic, which is practically next door.

Arena VIP

Gran Via de les Corts Catalanes 593, Eixample (93 487 83 42). Metro Universitat. **Open** 12.30am-5am Fri, Sat. **Admission** (incl 1 drink) €5 Fri; €9 Sat. **No credit cards. Map** p342 D5.

This is the most mixed Arena and, again, a youthful venue with lots of space, but heaving nonetheless at weekends. Unofficially the VIP stays open later than the others but it seems to depend on the night. Like the other Arenas, the VIP certainly does its bit for the Spanish retro pop industry.

La Luna

Avda Diagonal 323, Eixample (no phone). Metro Verdaguer. **Open** 10.30pm-3am Mon-Fri; 6am-10.30am, 10.30pm-3am Sat; 6am-10.30am Sun **Admission** €10. **No credit cards. Map** p339 E4.

La Luna is the place of the moment to head to after Metro and Salvation (for both *see p234*). A more relaxed and friendly atmosphere than you might expect from such a hard-drinking crowd.

Martins

Passeig de Gràcia 130, Gràcia (93 218 71 67). Metro Diagonal. **Open** midnight-5am daily. **Admission** (incl 1 drink) €8. **Credit** MC, V. **Map** p338 D3/4.

Martins has had its moments of glory over the last 19 years, but this just isn't one of them. With three floors, a porno lounge, a shop selling accessories – that's cockrings, not handbags – only the punters are missing. It livens up once the crowds from New Chaps turn out, when the action moves to a darkroom with so much history it should be listed.

Stiletto life

A living, breathing, teetering work of art, the legendary Satanassa struts her stuff nightly as queen hostess at Café Miranda (*see p234*), but is also to be seen dancing, singing and draping herself over the bar at Dietrich, Escandalus and Salvation.

How did you end up here, doing this?
I never decided to be a drag queen. I started dressing up and creating a look for when I went out. Different bars and clubs started offering me work, and around the time when *Priscilla, Queen of the Desert* came out the boom happened. In a way the label 'drag queen' is a step forward because we're more accepted – it stops people asking 'Is it a man, is it a woman, is it a transvestite?' Now people just say 'It's a drag queen!'

What's the best thing about Barcelona?
It's a cosmopolitan, European city with a live-and-let-live atmosphere, and a great climate. And it gets lots of gay tourism!

What would you change about Barcelona?
Apart from getting rid of the handful of violent, intolerant fascists you can find in any city, what I'd really change is the way Barcelona has lost, over the last few years, musicals, cabaret, shows and theatre in general. If you want to see a good show or find variety in my line of work then you have to go to Madrid. I'd like to see more cabaret going on in Barcelona.

What's the best thing about your job?
Applause. If you do this job seriously you invest a lot of time and money in it; I've done dance classes, singing classes, learnt a bit about acting and I spend a lot on the clothes and make-up. Even on your day off you're writing out the words of a song or practising a dance routine. So when I hear people applauding, that makes it worth it.

And your worst moment?
A couple of months ago, leaving Salvation at 5.30am and looking for a taxi, someone on a motorbike took my case with outfits for three numbers and CDs with about 40 numbers on them. Quite apart from the money for the wigs and clothes, what really hurt was the music, which is my tool of the trade, and no use to anyone else.

What do you think of the tourists here?
You get all sorts. Obviously there's the tacky beer-swilling type, but on the whole people are appreciative. I find the British and Americans the most respectful, and they know most about music.

What's the weirdest thing that's happened to you?
A friend and I had performed at a party and afterwards we were driving around the mountains. Our car broke down and we ended up climbing down a snow-covered mountain in six-inch heels and leopard-skin. Another time this huge, scary marine had come into Escandalus with his friends, and suddenly his hand was on my arse; he lifted me and carried me on one hand about eight times round the room. I broke my nails and everything.

If you had three wishes…?
Corny but true: tolerance, love, and enough food for everyone.

Where do you get your clothes?
I make them and friends make them, but mostly I work with a designer. The shoes are made to order and these really high ones are around €600 a pair, so breaking a heel is as expensive as it is dangerous.

Metro

C/Sepúlveda 185, Eixample (93 323 52 27). Metro Universitat. **Open** midnight-5am Mon-Thur, Sun; midnight-6am Fri, Sat. **Admission** (incl 1 drink) €9. **Credit** MC, V. **Map** p342 C5.

Another survivor, Metro pulls in men of all age groups, but still has a slightly older feel. There are two areas; the smaller of which has traditional Spanish music (which occasionally leads to some *sevillana* dancing). The larger section has various disco greats and gets very busy, as does the darkroom, which is very dark and very roomy. Enter for adventure but watch your wallet.

Salvation

Ronda Sant Pere 19-21, Eixample (93 318 06 86/ www.matineegroup.com). Metro Urquinaona. **Open** midnight-5am Fri, Sat; 6pm-5am Sun. **Admission** €11. **No credit cards. Map** p342 D5.

This is Muscle Mary heaven, with four bars, two large dancefloors – one house and one disco – and handsome, barebacked clientele and staff. On Sunday night the club becomes La Madame, with a fun-loving gay/straight mix. Other popular events include a regular after-hours weekend party at Souvenir in Viladecans (admission includes coach transport from Salvation or Plaça Espanya). A wild time can be had, but, as ever, be sure to watch your wallet in the darkroom.

Restaurants

In addition to those listed here, there are many mixed restaurants with a gay clientele. **La Veronica** (C/Avinyó 30, Barri Gòtic; 93 412 11 22) and **Venus Delicatessen** (*see p270*) also attract a large gay and lesbian clientele.

La Bodegueta de Muntaner

C/Muntaner 64, Eixample (93 451 51 04). Metro Universitat. **Open** 9pm-midnight Tue-Sun. **Average** €€€. **Credit** MC, V. **Map** p338 C4.

This restaurant offers an enchanting, old-world atmosphere and an excellent Catalan/Mediterranean menu. Although it's open to all, it becomes predominantly gay/lesbian in the evening. Asparagus au gratin and *escalopina* (beef fillet) with roquefort are sure bets. It's a good idea to book; ask for a table looking out on to the enclosed garden.

Café Miranda

C/Casanova 30, Eixample (93 453 52 49). Metro Universitat. **Open** 9pm-midnight Mon-Thur, Sun; 9pm-1am Fri, Sat. **Average** €€ **Credit** DC, MC, V. **Map** p342 C5.

With its elaborate decor, spectacular waiters, drag queens, singers and acrobats, Miranda is quite an institution. When they pause for breath the music is loud and uptempo. At weekends the place is packed with large mixed parties, so booking is essential. People are here primarily for a good time but there is also a reasonably varied menu that changes each season and keeps them coming back.

Castro

C/Casanova 85, Eixample (93 323 67 84). Metro Universitat. **Open** 1-4pm, 9pm-midnight Mon-Fri; 9pm-midnight Sat. **Average** €€. **Set lunch** €7.85 Mon-Fri. **Credit** MC, V. **Map** p338 C4.

If a restaurant can be hardcore, then this is it: a heavy chain curtain welcomes you into the black leather and grey metal interior and unintrusive house music. But fear not, this is not a darkroom, but a dedicatedly gay eaterie with an imaginative menu. Among the delicacies on offer (excluding the gym-toned waiters) are kangaroo steak, duck with fruits of the forest, and beef carpaccio.

La Diva

C/Diputació 172, Eixample (93 454 63 98). Metro Urgell. **Open** 9pm-midnight daily. **Average** €€. **Credit** MC, V. **Map** p342 C5.

Plushly decorated in black velvet and photos of La Callas et al, this cabaret restaurant provides Mediterranean-style food and, from Thursday to Sunday, a singer and drag comedy acts. Drawing a similar crowd to Miranda (*see above*), La Diva is slightly less frenetic but does fill up, so book for weekends.

Services

Saunas

An invigorating sauna may not be a priority for all customers, but you will find enough showers, steam rooms and dry saunas to justify the name, along with bars and porn lounges. On arrival you are supplied with locker-key, towel and flip-flops (a thoughtful detail). Listed here are some of the more popular places.

Sauna Casanova

C/Casanova 57, Eixample (93 323 78 60). Metro Urgell. **Open** 24hrs daily. **Admission** €12 Mon, Wed, Fri-Sun; €9.50 Tue, Thur. **Credit** MC, V. **Map** p342 C5.

This is by far the most popular sauna, attracting a young, pretty, muscled crowd who pound the corridors before making any final decisions.

Sauna Condal

C/Espolsa Sacs 1, Barri Gòtic (93 301 96 80). Metro Urquinaona. **Open** 11am-5am Mon-Thur; 11am Fri-5am Sun. **Admission** €9.50 Mon, Wed; €12 Tue, Thur-Sun. **Credit** MC, V. **Map** p344 B2.

You'll find this place down a small alley off C/Condal. It's a spacious, busy sauna on two floors, much frequented by the after-work crowd.

Thermas

C/Diputació 46, Eixample (93 325 93 46). Metro Rocafort. **Open** noon-2am Mon-Thur; noon Fri-2am Sun. **Admission** €11. **Credit** MC, V. **Map** p341 B5.

This place has a well-equipped set-up and a prettier than average clientele.

Ovlas.

Sex shops

The following establishments all have stock that is chiefly aimed at the gay market, and all have viewing cabins for videos.

Nostromo

C/Diputació 208, Eixample (93 323 3194). Metro Universitat. **Open** 11am-10pm Mon-Fri; noon-10pm Sat, Sun **No credit cards**. **Map** p342 C5.

Sestienda

C/Rauric 11, Barri Gòtic (93 318 86 76/ www.sestienda.com). Metro Liceu. **Open** 10am-8.30pm Mon-Sat. **Credit** MC, V. **Map** p345 A3.

Zeus

C/Riera Alta 20, Raval (93 442 97 95). Metro Sant Antoni. **Open** 10am-9pm Mon-Sat. **Credit** V. **Map** p342 C5.

Shops

Antinous Libreria Café

C/Josep Anselm Clavé 6, Barri Gòtic (93 301 90 70/ www.antinouslibros.com). Metro Drassanes. **Open** 11am-2pm, 5-9pm Mon-Fri; noon-2pm, 5-9pm Sat. **Credit** AmEx, DC, MC, V. **Map** p345 A4.

This spacious and elegant bookshop has an ample stock of gay and lesbian literature, some in English, as well as a large amount of other handy items including videos, postcards and a notice board displaying information on upcoming events and places to stay outside Barcelona. Once exhausted by browsing you can have your well-earned coffee and cake in the teashop at the back.

Complices

C/Cervantes 2, Barri Gòtic (93 412 72 83). Metro Jaume 1. **Open** 10.30am-8.30pm Mon-Fri; noon-8.30pm Sat. **Credit** MC, V. **Map** p345 B3.

Two women run Barcelona's oldest gay bookshop, stocking women's books, magazines and videos on one side; men's on the other. Go downstairs for spicier material and a fair selection of books in English.

M69

C/Muntaner 69, Eixample (93 453 62 69). Metro Universitat. **Open** 10.30am-2pm, 5-8.30pm Mon-Sat. **Credit** MC, V. **Map** p345 B3.

A fashion haven with friendly service. As well as a couple of reasonably priced local labels, the shop carries Paul Smith, Amaya Arzuaga and Evisu along with accessories, pink-tinged books and music.

Nosotr@s

C/Casanova 56, Eixample (no phone). Metro Universitat. **Open** 11am-2pm, 5-9pm Mon-Sat. **Credit** AmEx, DC, MC, V. **Map** p342 C5.

Fancy a Murano glass sculpture of two boys or (at last) girls kissing? Well, as souvenirs go, we suppose it beats a donkey from Benidorm, and this is where you can go to buy one, as well as books, videos and bibelots galore, with or without rainbow flag adornments. In short, all that the aspiringly tasteful lesbo or gay might require is to be found here.

Ovlas

Via Laietana 33, Barri Gòtic (93 268 76 91). Metro Jaume I. **Open** 10.30am-8.30pm Mon-Sat. **Credit** AmEx, MC, V. **Map** p345 B3.

This is a clothing emporium for the young at heart, or at least those with a sense of humour; it stocks a variety of attention-grabbing outer and underwear

Arts & Entertainment

and a good selection of footwear. There's also a bar at which to sip on a cocktail while pondering floral spandex leggings and the like.

Ritual

C/Consell de Cent, 255 Eixample (93 451 9168).
Metro Universitat. **Open** 11am-2pm, 5-8.30pm Mon-Sat. **Credit** MC, V. **Map** p342 C5.
Sandwiched between bars like Dietrich and Atame (*see p231*), this shop could hardly do the sensible thing, so expect to find clothes in which a young man can make his mark when sweeping through the Gaixample night. Choose from Energie, Sixty, Bill Tornade and the shop's own label.

Lesbian Barcelona

You'll find women in many places frequented by gay men in Barcelona, such as **Arena** (*see p232*), **La Luna** (*see p232*) or La Madame at **Salvation** (*see p234*). Regular events and parties are organised by a variety of groups: **Ca La Dona** (*see p319*) and **Casal Lambda** (*see p310*) are good places to get information, as is **Complices** (*see p235*).

Aire

C/Valencia 236, Eixample (no phone/
www.arenadisco.com). Metro Passeig de Gràcia.
Open *Sept-June* 11pm-3am Thur-Sat; 6-10pm Sun. *July, Aug* 6-10pm Tue-Sun. **Admission** (incl 1 drink) €5 Tue-Fri; €6 Sat, Sun. **No credit cards.** **Map** p338 C4.

Part of the Arena group, this red and orange open space of a bar has a pool table and dancefloor. Customers range from virtual schoolgirls to thirtysomething women and a handful of gayboy friends. Very busy at weekends.

Bahía

C/Sèneca 12, Gràcia (no phone). Metro Diagonal.
Open 10pm-3am Mon-Thur, Sun; 6-9am, 10pm-3am Fri, Sat. **No credit cards.** **Map** p338 D3.
This is a friendly and welcoming little bar with a warm interior and a wide variety of music. On Thursdays for €14 you can take part in an informal meal – popular with the international crowd.

Bar Fortuny

C/Pintor Fortuny 31 (93 317 98 92). Metro Liceu.
Open 9pm-1.30am Tue-Sun. **No credit cards.**
Map p337 A2.
The design elements have been kept to a minimum here: one wall is painted in bright Partridge family-style. There are some retro lamps and a large photograph of a bevy of joyful dark-haired naked women. The end result is a bar that is as laidback as its faithful regulars, who spend hours here playing chess and chatting over healthy meals.

D-Mer

C/Plató 13, Sant Gervasi (93 201 62 07/www.d-mer.com). Metro Lesseps/FGC Muntaner. **Open** 11pm-4am Thur-Sat. **Admission** (incl 1 drink) €7. **No credit cards.** **Map** p338 C2.
This is a new and very stylish bar with cool dance music and pretty people on both sides of the bar. The

Join the trendy pack at **D-Mer**.

clientele ranges from trendy young things to women in their forties; and whatever they're up to, they're not swapping cake recipes. At the end of 2002, the promoters opened a more clubby option in the same vein, Disco Mer (C/Rosselló, 208, 93 215 63 91).

Lesfatales

Member's, C/Sèneca 3, Gràcia (no phone). Metro Diagonal. **Open** midnight-4am Fri. **Admission** (incl 1 drink) €6. **No credit cards**. **Map** p338 D3.
There's a mixture of house and techno sounds at this one-nighter club, and live performances as well as stalls selling jewellery and lesbian knick-knacks. As the sexy flyer says, it's 'a party run by girls for girls'.

La Singular

C/Francisco Giner 50, Gràcia (93 237 50 98). Metro Diagonal. **Open** 1-4pm, 8pm-midnight Mon-Fri; 1-4pm, 8pm-1am Sat. Closed end Aug-mid Sept. **Average** €€. **Credit** MC, V. **Map** p338 D3.
A female-run restaurant with good tapas and home-cooked meals at very economical prices. The menu changes daily, so take the chef's recommendation on the best fare of the day.

Trsdimensiones

C/Milà i Fontanals 42, Gràcia (mobile 654 585 221). Metro Joanic. **Open** 7pm-midnight Sun. **No credit cards**. **Map** p339 E3.
On Sunday nights this very laid-back studio-bar becomes a chillout space courtesy of the Lesfatales team, with workshops on different crafts and skills.

¿Y Qué?

C/Topazi 8, Gràcia (93 416 07 33). Metro Fontana. **Open** 6pm-1.30am Mon-Thur; 8pm-2am Fri, Sat. **No credit cards**. **Map** p338 D3.
A highly recommended bar in the laid-back and vaguely hippie style beloved of Gràcia, that serves pizzas, salads and other basic but wholesome fare to a mainly lesbian crowd.

Sitges

An easy half-hour's train ride down the coast is the predominantly gay resort of Sitges. A good deal of its old fishing village charm remains, but at night and especially during summer it comes alive with song, dance and a rowdy camaraderie – stretching across all sexualities and age groups. Its international festivals of film and theatre are renowned, and during the week of Corpus Christi (late May/early June) its streets are covered with vivid carpets of flower petals. The main event here, certainly in the gay calendar, is the local Carnival celebration; a riotous, colourful, week-long affair.

Accommodation

There are few exclusively gay places to stay in Sitges, but pink euros are as welcome as any other. For more options in addition to those listed below, *see p277*. If you're at a loss, Peter and Rico with the **RAS** service (mobile 607 14 94 51, fwww.raservice.com) can help you to find accommodation in both Sitges and Barcelona.

One option is **La Masia Casanova**, which offers luxury suites with a pool, a bar and lots of tranquillity. Book well in advance for the minimum three-day stay (Passatge Casanova 8, 93 818 80 58, rates €90-€120) .

Another option is **Hotel Liberty** – a bright, airy, spacious hotel with modern, comfortable rooms and lush gardens (C/Illa de Cuba 35, 93 811 08 72, www.hotel-liberty-sitges.com, rates €65-€98). Or there's the aptly named **Hotel Romàntic** – one of Sitges' most popular gay-friendly hotels. It's a beautifully restored 19th-century house with a palm-filled patio (C/Sant Isidre 33, 93 894 83 75, rate €85). Another option is **La Renaixença**, which is under the same management. While it is not quite as architecturally or historically distinctive, it does offer attractive gardens and reasonable prices (C/Illa de Cuba 7, 93 894 81 67). Finally, there's the **Hostal Termes** (C/Termes 9, 93 894 23 43, rates €50-€72) which is friendly and central.

Bars & clubs

Sitges' main drag from the centre to the beach, is popularly known as 'Sin Street', and is lined wall-to-wall with terraces where the game of people-watching reaches new heights. In the middle is the always packed **Parrots Pub** (Plaça Indústria 2) which, though one of many possible drinking-and-dancing venues, is a well-used central meeting point. Round the corner is **El Horno** (C/Joan Tarrida Ferratges 6) which attracts a more mature and hairier crowd. **Mediterraneo** (C/Sant Bonaventure 6) is a stylish, spacious spot and a place to see and be seen. **B Side Bar** (C/Sant Gaudenci 7) is a busy new venue with just that little extra: a darkroom. When you feel it's time for a shimmy, choose from **Organic** (C/Bonaire 15) or the busiest club, **Trailer** (C/Angel Vidal 36), which stays open till 5am and pulsates to sounds from many guest DJs.

Restaurants

Good food and a charming terrace can be found at **Flamboyant** (C/Pau Barrabeitg 16, 93 894 58 11, main course €10), while **Ma Maison** (C/Bonnaire 28, 93 894 60 54, main course €12) specialises in couscous and also offers al fresco dining. There's a wide choice at **Can Pagés** (C/Sant Pere 24-26, 93 894 11 95, closed Mon, main course €11), while **Casa Hidalgo** (C/Sant Pau 12, 93 894 38 95, set lunch €18) offers good traditional Spanish food.

Music

Hitting all the right notes.

Classical & Opera

From the soaring acoustics of Gothic squares reverberating with solo classical guitar to the sugar-plum **Palau de la Música** built during the exuberant fanfare of Modernisme, Barcelona might have been built around music. Over the last six years no fewer than four new venues have been built around town (or in the case of the opera house, *re*built): the hi-tech **Auditori**, the phoenix-like **Liceu**, the small **Winterthur** chamber hall and most recently a 600-seat subterranean auditorium attached to the Palau de la Música, due to open in September 2003. Barcelona is still light arias away from, say, Vienna as a musical city, but it has a large and appreciative concert-going public, and dozens of concerts each month, featuring everything on the musical food-chain from touring stars to trembling amateurs. Catalonia even has its own form of folk music, the *sardana*, an irrepressible, chirpy affair full of wind and rhythm that you can, if you wish, hear (and even dance to) every weekend (*see p83* **How to: dance the sardana**).

Much like its audience, classical music in Barcelona clings to the solid and safe, contemplating only occasional flirtations with anything outside the mainstream. They know what they like, and mostly it's Teutonic Goliaths, with the odd Hispanic David slung in for the home supporters. For many, Stravinsky is still a dangerous renegade and Cage is where he should be locked.

Nevertheless there are several cycles of contemporary music, and plenty of interesting contemporary Catalan composers. Of the old guard, Xavier Montsalvatge and the late Frederic Mompou are highly rated, while young upstarts (that is, composers under 50) Albert Guinovart, Joan Guinjoan and Salvador Brotons all enjoy healthy reputations. Carles Santos currently averages a new show every year, showcasing his speciality of magnificent, surreal works that combine all the best excesses. Part opera, part circus, sex show and psychotherapy session, performed with exuberance, energy and wit.

The main musical calendar is strictly seasonal, running from September to June. During this time the city orchestra, the OBC, plays weekly concerts at the Auditori, and the Liceu hosts a different opera each month. Both the Auditori and the Palau de la Música hold several concert cycles of various genres, either programmed by the venues themselves or by independent promoters, of which Ibercamera and Euroconcert are the two most important. Several festivals take place, the foremost of which is the **Música Antiga** (*see p212*) in the spring, while around Christmas and Easter it's difficult to avoid the *Messiah*.

In the summer, the focus of activity moves. Various museums -- including the **Museu Marítim** (*see p101*), the **Fundació Joan Miró** (*see p241*) and the **Museu Barbier-Mueller** (*see p95*) -- hold small, outdoor evening concerts, and there are weekly concerts in several of the city's parks. The more serious musical activity, though, follows its audience and heads up the coast, to major international festivals in the towns of Perelada, Cadaqués, Toroella de Montgrí and Vilabertrán.

INFORMATION AND TICKETS

Apart from the venues themselves, the most thorough source of information is the monthly leaflet *Informatiu Musical*, published by Amics de la Música (93 268 01 22), with details for concerts across all genres. You can pick up a copy at tourist offices (*see p318*), record shops, at the Palau de la Virreina (*see p85*) or at the Generalitat's bookshop almost opposite. The weekly entertainment guide *Guia del Ocio* has a music section, while both *El País* and *La Vanguardia* list forthcoming concerts in their classified ads sections, and usually publish details for each day's more important concerts. Tickets for most major venues can be bought by phone, or over the Internet from the venue itself (check venue listing), or from Tel-entrada or Servi-Caixa (for both, *see p208*).

Venues

L'Auditori

C/Lepant 150, Eixample (93 247 93 00/ www.auditori.com). Metro Marina. **Open** *Information* 9am-3pm, 4-6pm Mon-Fri. *Box office* noon-9pm daily. *Performances* 8pm Mon-Thur; 9pm Fri; 7pm Sat; 11am Sun. **Tickets** varies. **Advance tickets** also from Tel-entrada & Servi-Caixa. **Discounts** (OBC concerts) BC. **Credit** MC, V. **Map** p343 F5.

Nights in red velvet at the **Gran Teatre del Liceu**.

Rafael Moneo's state of the art, 2,300-seat concert hall opened in 1999, providing the city with a much-needed venue. Musically and architecturally, the building is excellent, if a little minimalist for some tastes, though there are still grumblings about its location, particularly from locals used to strolling along to the Palau de la Música and the Liceu. It's true that the Auditori, and the new National Theatre next door, are a little out of the way, but there is a metro nearby and a special bus service to Plaça Catalunya after concerts. Just as well, since there are very few bars or restaurants in the area. Barcelona's main music school and the Museu de la Música are due to move here in 2004, which should liven things up with their respective musical fauna. As well as the OBC's weekly concerts, the Auditori hosts dozens of other performances, covering not just classical music but also jazz, pop and world music.

Gran Teatre del Liceu

La Rambla 51-59, Barri Gòtic (info 93 485 99 00/ box office 93 485 99 13/www.liceubarcelona.com). Metro Liceu. **Open** *Information* 9am-2pm Mon-Fri. *Box office* 2-8.30pm Mon-Fri; 1hr before performance Sat, Sun. Closed 2wks Aug. **Tickets** varies.
Credit AmEx, DC, MC, V. **Map** p345 A3.
Though it was probably not meant as a marketing gimmick, the workman's blowtorch that burnt down the opera house in 1994 acted like a magic wand. The flames devoured a rickety, 19th-century structure with inadequate technical capabilities and a dry programme of tired old operas. In its place has risen

a modern 2,340 seat pleasure palace that on the surface looks almost identical to the original (gold carvings and red plush), but which has increased its backstage area three-fold, and can now receive major international touring productions. There is also a large, subterranean foyer for talks, late-night recitals, children's shows and musical events, and this is soon to be joined by a café and gift shop. Also new are the seat-back subtitles, available in various languages, though so far only the stalls and royal circle have been fitted with them. Everyone else still has to strain their necks and struggle with the Catalan surtitles above the stage.

In addition to opera and concerts, the Liceu receives three or four touring dance companies each season. Nacho Duato is a frequent visitor with his Compañia Nacional de Danza. Nederlands Dans Theater is performing in June 2003, following visits by Ballet Gulbenkian and the Alvin Ailey Dance Theater earlier in the season. This was the venue that Björk chose for her one Spanish concert of 2002.

Palau de la Música Catalana

C/Sant Francesc de Paula 2, Eixample (93 295 72 00/www.palaumusica.org). Metro Urquinaona. **Open** *Box office* 10am-9pm Mon-Sat; 1hr before performance Sun. **Tickets** varies. **Advance tickets** also from Servi-Caixa & Tel-Entrada.
Credit MC, V. **Map** p344 B/C2.
Part wedding cake, part psychotropic vision (and possibly the result of over-indulgence in absinthe), Domenech i Muntaner's sublime Modernista

masterpiece is not to be missed, and there is no better way of appreciating its wild intricacies than during a concert. Acoustically the building has many shortcomings, but the Palau arouses loyalty among both concert-goers and performers alike, many of whom prefer it to the less idiosyncratic Auditori. Commissioned and paid for by the Orfeó Català in 1908, the hall has a narrow auditorium, meaning that most seats are rather far from the stage. Try and avoid the rear half of the upper circle (here called the *segon pis*) if at all possible. The Palau's headline concert cycle Palau 100 brings top names from all over Europe, as do private promoters Euroconcert and Ibercamera, among others. Renovations due to be completed in October 2003 have demolished the ugly church next door to make way for a 600-seat, subterranean chamber hall, a new entrance and a huge tree motif on the extended façade that promises to redefine the word 'kitsch'. Consequently, the Palau is expected to be closed from June to October 2003.

Churches & smaller venues

Various churches around Barcelona, particularly in the Old City, hold occasional concerts. The most beautiful is probably **Santa Maria del Mar** in the Born, with a tall, ghostly interior that exemplifies the Gothic intertwining of music, light and spirituality. Concerts include everything from Renaissance music to gospel singers. At the main cathedral there is a free organ concert every month, usually, but not always, on the second Wednesday of the month. Other churches with regular concerts include **Santa Maria del Pi**, **Sant Felip Neri**, **Santa Anna** and the monastery in **Pedralbes**. In May, keep an eye out for the **Festival de Música Antiga** (*see p212*), when concerts of early music are held in different locations in the Old City.

Auditori Winterthur
Auditori de l'Illa, Avda Diagonal 547, Les Corts-Sants (93 290 11 02). Metro Maria Cristina. **Open** *Information* 8.30am-6.30pm Mon-Thur; 8am-2pm Fri. **Tickets & credit** varies. **Map** p345 B3. This is an intimate, modern venue in the unlikely surrounds of the L'Illa shopping centre, which hosts a dozen or so chamber concerts, including an annual Schubert cycle and a series of song recitals.

Orchestras & ensembles

La Capella Reial de Catalunya, Le Concert des Nations & Hespèrion XXI
Information 93 580 60 69.
Led by the indefatigable and inspirational early music specialist Jordi Savall, these three overlapping groups have the highest international reputation of Barcelona's musicians, playing around 300 concerts a year worldwide, as well as finding time to create a long list of prize-winning recordings. La Capella Reial specialises in Catalan and Spanish Renaissance and baroque music. Le Concert des Nations is a period-instrument ensemble playing orchestral and symphonic work from 1600 to 1850, and Hespèrion XXI plays pre-1800 European music.

Orfeó Català
Information 93 295 72 00/www.palaumusica.org.
The Orfeó Català had its origins in the patriotic and social movements at the end of the 19th century; it was one of 150 choral groups that sprang up in Catalonia at that time. It was sufficiently successful to be able to commission the Palau de la Música, with which it is inseparably identified. Although no longer as pre-eminent as it once was, the Orfeó still stages around 25 performances a year, giving a cappella concerts as well as providing a choir for the OBC and other Catalan orchestras. The group is largely amateur, but includes a small professional nucleus, the Cor de Cambra del Palau de la Música, which gives some 50 performances a year.

Orquestra Simfònica de Barcelona Nacional de Catalunya (OBC)
Information 93 247 93 00/www.obc.es.
These are interesting times for the OBC, which, despite much flak from within and without, has appointed a new artistic director as well as a new

conductor, both under 40. Though they have promised not to meddle with the programming, there are already signs of a change of emphasis and a revitalised programme featuring more adventurous works – no bad thing, given the turgid nature of the last few seasons, though it remains to be seen how the audience will respond. Concerts are held at the Auditori most weekends from October to May, usually on Friday, then repeated on Saturday night and again on Sunday morning (minus formal dress). On a good day, with the right conductor, the OBC are fine. On a bad day, less so. With no fewer than 16 different conductors waving the baton this season, devoted followers could be in for something of a musical rollercoaster ride.

Orquestra Simfònica i Cor del Gran Teatre del Liceu

Information 93 485 99 13/www.liceubarcelona.com.
The Liceu currently offers around ten operas per season, split between dynamic touring productions, new co-productions and occasional revivals. Post-fire, the opera house has become unbelievably popular, and usually sells out well in advance, even though there are now more performances than ever – 150 in the 2002-3 season, compared with 112 two years ago. To help meet demand, at least one performance of each opera is not covered by season tickets, and there's always a full run of a crowd-pleaser from the previous season to end the year (and pull in tourists). In 2002, this was a colourful *Magic Flute* staged by Els Comediants; for July 2003, a production of *Aida* that would make Cecil B. DeMille proud. Highpoints of the upcoming season include an ENO production of Purcell's *The Fairy Queen* and two overlapping Wagners, *Das Rheingold* and *Die Walküre*, both, fittingly, by Deutsche Staastoper Berlin. Plus Calixto Bieito, bad boy of Catalan theatre, is back for those who want him back; his *Don Giovanni* is not covered by season tickets, in an attempt to avoid the outrage that greeted his *Un Ballo in Maschera* two years ago, both here and in Covent Garden.

Orquestra Simfònica del Vallès

Information 93 727 03 00/www.osvalles.com.
Though not quite at the level of the two main city orchestras, this country cousin from the nearby town of Sabadell performs regularly in Barcelona. It can often be found at the Palau de la Música, where it plays a dozen symphonic concerts each season.

Contemporary music

Avuimúsica

Associació Catalana de Compositors, Passeig Colom 6, space 4, Barri Gòtic (93 268 37 19/ www.accompositors.com). Metro Drassanes. **Open** *Information* 9.30am-1.30pm Mon-Fri. **Tickets** €8; €4 concessions. *Book of 7 tickets* €28; €14 concessions. **No credit cards. Map** p344 B4.
This series of 14 small-scale concerts at various venues around town is run by the Association of Catalan Composers. It predominantly features music by association members, much of it being played in public for the first time. A handful of pieces by well-known foreign composers and a couple of modern electronic offerings are usually thrown in as well.

Barcelona 216

Information 93 486 87 81.
A small ensemble with a strong commitment to contemporary music of all types, including serious 'written' compositions and more experimental and avant-garde work. Its activities are as energetic as they are varied, and always worth looking out for.

Festival de Músiques Contemporànies

Information 93 247 93 00/www.auditori.com.
Barcelona's most popular and main-stream contemporary music festival has fluctuated in content over recent years. In 2001 jazz and even flamenco featured quite heavily. In 2002 the programme returned to big-name composers from the late 20th century, performed by groups like The Hilliard Ensemble, Barcelona 216 and the OBC, as well as composer-performers such as Sainkho Namtchylak, the Barry Guy New Orchestra, and Sachiko M and Otomo Yoshihide. Concerts take place at the Auditori, CCCB, Espai and Teatre Lliure.

Fundació Joan Miró

Parc de Montjuïc, Montjuïc (93 329 19 08/ www.bcn.fjmiro.es). Metro Paral.lel, then Funicular de Montjuïc/50, 55 bus. **Open** *Box office* 1hr before performance Thur. **Advance tickets** also from Tel-entrada. **Tickets** €5; €12 for 3 concerts. **Credit** MC, V. **Map** p341 B6.
It may not be the world's best auditorium, but the summer concert series at the Fundació Miró features an interesting selection of improvised music by an array of international musicians. Several of the more light-hearted concerts are held on the roof terrace overlooking the city.

Gràcia Territori Sonor

Information 93 237 37 37/www.gracia-territori.com.
This tirelessly creative collective organises concerts and musical happenings throughout the year, but its main focus is the LEM festival; a hugely diverse cycle covering all types of musical activity, most of it free, and much of it experimental, improvised and/or electronic. Running between October and December, concerts – along with other art forms such as dance, sound installations and poetry – are mostly held in various bars in Gràcia. Larger, more formal events are at L'Espai and CaixaForum.

Metrònom

C/Fusina 9, Born (93 268 42 98). Metro Arc de Triomf or Jaume I. **Concerts** 11pm. **Admission** free. **Map** p345 C3.
Better known as an alternative art space (*see p229*), Metrònom also has a strong commitment to avant-guarde music. It hosts a hugely successful, week-long international festival of avant-garde and

experimental music in January, featuring everything from minimalist weirdos extracting sound from credit cards and wire loops, to extreme noisist types doing things to vinyl that would bring your average DJ out in a cold sweat. A second, shorter festival takes place in June.

Rock, Roots & Jazz

Record sales in Spain are impressively low – around a third of the number sold in the UK, and half of the number sold in France. Catalonia bucks the trend, however, with the highest record sales in Spain, and so top international names are increasingly choosing Barcelona over Madrid as the Spanish stop on their world tours. Combine that with the always strong home-grown music scene and aficionados of all bents should find something to get their bodies moving.

In Barcelona, the local music scene has a strong connection to the region's history. In the 1960s and '70s, ancient Catalan folk songs were revived by singers like Lluis Llach and Jaume Sisa. Today, the popular *mestizo* music scene has a sharp political edge. *Mestizo* music mixes Latin, Caribbean, African and Spanish sounds with urban rhythms and hip hop rhymes in various languages. Top acts include Dusminguet, Ojos de Brujo and part-time Barcelona resident Manu Chao, as well as godfather of Spanish rap, Mucho Muchacho.

Teens here are not immune to the lure of MTV, so you'll see plenty wearing Slipknot T-shirts, while your basic late-20s, early-30s graphic designer types shug ironically to twee folk-pop or kitsch electronica by Juliusmonk and Electrocugat. One of the hottest local bands these days is the retro disco band Fundación Tony Manero, cleverly named after the John Travolta character in *Saturday Night Fever*. But even these disco dollies are turning political, describing their latest album as 'prolet [as in proletarian] disco'.

More traditional forms of music can still be found, of course. And although it should be stressed that the flamenco scene in Catalonia is not what it is elsewhere in Spain, Andalucian immigrants and *gitanos* have stamped, clapped and strummed here for generations. Catalonia has produced a steady string of its own flamenco stars, from the legendary dancer Carmen Amaya to current performers Mayte Martín and Duquende.

Barcelona has had a long love affair with jazz – a politically charged genre that was suppressed by Franco. Many of the jazz greats syncopated their stuff here in legendary underground venues **La Cova del Drac** and

Jamboree (*see p245 and p246*), both of which are still going strong. Today you'll find the new jazz generation performing there.

Barcelona prides itself on hosting wildly eclectic music festivals. There's a day of reggae at the **Sala Apolo** in March, an indie kid's dream in the shape of **Primavera Sound** (May), jazz galore at the **Festival de Jazz de Ciutat Vella** from October to November and country and western line-dancing madness at the **Barcelona Hayride** in December. There are also a number of small-scale festivals grouped under a common cause (anti-racism, smoking dope, wearing black). There are also a series of three-day benders that attract stadium-filling names (*see p246* **The best festivals**)

INFORMATION AND TICKETS

For concert information buy the weekly (out on Thursdays) listings guide *Guía del Ocio* or the Friday newspapers, which usually include listings. Look in bars and music shops for free mags *Metropolitan, La Netro, Nativa, Go, AB, Mondo Sonoro* (all mostly independent pop/rock/electronica) and *Batonga!* (world music). These all have websites, though these are usually triumphs of design over usability. www.atiza.com and www.doctormusic.com have more decipherable information. For festivals there are www.festivales.com and www.whatsonwhen.com.

You can also get information and tickets from **Tel-entrada** and **Servi-Caixa** (*see p208*). Also try specialist record shops, such as those on C/Tallers in the Raval, and in **FNAC** at Plaça Catalunya (*see p185*). FNAC occasionally hosts free preview shows by artists pushing their latest CD.

Rock & pop

As well as the venues listed below, you can also squint at pop-rock superstars performing in one of the sports barns up on Montjuïc, either at the **Palau Sant Jordi** in Montjuïc, or the **Sidecar Factory Club** (*see p251*) or, for hard-edged rock, the **KGB** (*p261*).

Bikini
C/Déu i Mata 105, Les Corts (93 322 08 00/ www.bikinibcn.com). Metro Les Corts. **Open** Gigs 9-10pm. **Admission** Gigs varies. **Credit** AmEx, V. **Map** p337 B3.
Bikini has been a leading light of the Barcelona music scene for almost half a century, but you sense little history here. It was given a makeover a few years ago as part of the development of the L'Illa shopping centre, and is well designed, with metres of accessible bar winding through the three spaces (main venue and two smaller ones), plus quiet chill-out areas. Though most current chart-topping acts

Wednesdays and Saturdays, soul on Thursdays, rock on Fridays and 'erotic opera' for the Sabbath. Who could ask for more?

Magic

Passeig Picasso 40, Born (93 310 72 67/www.magic-club.net). Metro Barceloneta. **Open** 11pm-6am Thur; 11pm-7am Fri, Sat. **Admission** *Gigs* €3-€15. *Disco* (incl 2 drinks) €10. **No credit cards**. **Map** p343 E6.

This L-shaped cellar hard rock/punk venue is suitably cramped, sweaty, smoky and airless. Magic is where Barcelona's youth, who have embraced the resurgence of all things black, noisy and miserable in music, listen to genres such as emo-core (punk with emotional lyrics about girls) and post-rock (starts slow, gets faster, no singing). Old-school rockers aren't left out either, with tributes to Bon Jovi and deceased Who bassist John Entwistle featuring in 2002's programming. Just to throw you though, there's the occasional retro-mod group or acid-jazz DJ thrown into the mix.

Mephisto

C/Roc Boronat 33, Poblenou (93 309 13 15/ www.mephistobcn.com). Metro Llacuna. **Open** *Disco* midnight-5am Thur-Sun. *Gigs* approx 11pm. **Admission** *Disco* (incl 1 drink) €6. *Gigs* €9-€27. **No credit cards**.

A place for those who think Magic is for pussies, Mephisto is an industrial barn bleeding red light. It showcases really, really hard rock, metal and punk. Nashville Pussy, Bruce Dickinson and Backyard Babies have all played here. Lesser-known (and more disturbing) bands that regularly play here include Decapitated, Human Mincer and Dying Fetus. You get the picture. The club also organises trips to rock festivals throughout Europe; most are in metal's spiritual home, Germany. (Note that C/Roc Boronat used to be called C/Lutxana).

Razzmatazz

C/Almogávers 122, Poblenou (93 272 09 10/93 320 82 00/www.salarazzmatazz.com). Metro Bogatell or Marina. **Open** varies. **Admission** varies. **No credit cards**. **Map** p343 F6.

In the warehouse wastelands of Poblenou, this is Barcelona's key non-stadium venue for international artists. It is a particularly good place to find those acts that are mainly of the indie-rock or electronica persuasion. It's one of those pseudo-industrial spaces that have been starkly converted, making a feature of its air-con vents and raw concrete. Very 1989. A nod to comfort, has been given with the provision of ample toilet space, and a gallery overlooking the main hall offers respite from over-enthusiastic dancers. Sala 1 is great for watching big names, such as Oasis or Coldplay, in a relatively intimate space. Upstairs, the even smaller, sweatier Sala 3 plays host to those bands hotly tipped in Razz's Flavour of the Month slot, featuring the *NME*-friendly likes of The Electric Soft Parade and Alpinestars.

Soniquete for flamenco. *See p244.*

now play at Razzmatazz, Bikini's superbly equipped stage still attracts an eclectic range of acts from cabaret circuit troupers like ex-Supreme Sheila Weaver to indie stars the Dandy Warhols, via the mellow grooves of Senegal's Orchestra Baobab.

Luz de Gas

C/Muntaner 246, Eixample (93 209 77 11/ www.luzdegas.com). Bus 6, 7, 15, 27, 32, 33, 34, 58, 64, N8. **Open** *Sept-July* 11pm-4.30am Mon-Thur, Sun; 11pm-5.30am Fri, Sat. *Aug* 11pm-4.30am Mon-Thur; 11pm-5.30am Fri, Sat. **Admission** (incl 1 drink) €15 Mon-Sat; €12 Sun (opera). **Credit** AmEx, DC, MC, V. **Map** p342 C3.

A dressed-up, grown-up crowd queues to get into this lovingly converted old music hall, garnished with chandeliers and classical friezes. They all come to see classic MOR acts like Kool and the Gang, Level 42 and Simple Minds. In between the visits from foreign 'names', though, are the more interesting nightly residencies: blues on Mondays, Dixieland jazz on Tuesdays, cover bands on

Sala Apolo

C/Nou de la Rambla 113, Paral.lel (93 441 40 01/
www.sala-apolo.com). Metro Paral.lel. **Open** varies.
Admission varies. **No credit cards. Map** p342 C6.
The Apolo first opened in 1940 as a dancehall, and
little has changed in its decor since then. Red drapes,
polished wood and globe lights are the backdrop to
occasional concerts by an eclectic range of alternative, leftfield acts. While Brits such as Beth Orton
and Nitin Sawhney have played here, this is also a
good place to discover local and national performers, especially hip hop and *mestizo* groups. The
Apolo is also the hub for countless fringe music
festivals. For clubbing at Apolo, *see p254*, and for
cinema, *see p226*.

Flamenco

In addition to those venues listed here, the
Jazz Sí Club and **Harlem Jazz Club** both
occasionally feature flamenco performances.
(*For both, see p246*.)

Soniquete

C/Milans 5, Barri Gòtic (mobile 639 382 354).
Metro Drassanes or Jaume I. **Open** 9pm-3am
Thur-Sun. **No credit cards. Map** p345 B4.
Hidden off C/Avinyó in the Barri Gotic, Soniquete
offers an opportunity – increasingly rare in
Barcelona – to experience spontaneous 'performances' of flamenco singing, dancing, playing and
clapping. Those who play are mostly Andalucian
immigrants coming in from Terrassa and Sabadell
to what they know to be a space for flamenco as a
genuine form of expression rather than a tourist
entertainment. This means you could spend an
evening here without anyone pulling out a guitar or
exercising their vocal chords, but you'll still hear
some decent *sevillanas* on the sound system. At the
time of writing, a downstairs performance space featuring regular organised shows was about to open.

El Tablao de Carmen

Poble Espanyol, Avda Marqués de Comillas, Montjuïc
(93 325 68 95/www.tablaodecarmen.com). Metro
Espanya/13, 50, 61 bus. **Open** 8pm-2am Tue-Sun.
Show 9.30pm, 11.30pm Tue-Thur, Sun; 9.30pm,
midnight Fri, Sat. **Admission** Poble Espanyol €9;
€6 concessions. El Tablao de Carmen show & 1
drink €28; show & dinner €53. **Discounts** BC.
Credit AmEx, DC, MC, V. **Map** p341 A5.
One of flamenco's greats, the Catalan *gitana* Carmen
Amaya, made her debut on this site in 1929 at the
inauguration of the Poble Espanyol. Named in her
honour, this rather sanitised version of the traditional flamenco *tablao* sits in strange faux
Andalucian surroundings in the Poble Espanyol (if
you book for the show in advance, you don't have to
pay the Poble Espanyol entrance fee). You'll find
both established stars and young new talent, displaying the various styles of flamenco singing, dancing and music, but, because each artist takes it in
turn to demonstrate his or her particular skill, the
show can lose momentum. The emphasis here is on
panache, rather than passion, so you might prefer
your flamenco with a bit more spit and less polish.

Los Tarantos

Plaça Reial 17, Barri Gòtic (93 318 30 67/
www.masimas.com). Metro Liceu. **Open** Flamenco
show 10pm, midnight daily. **Admission** (incl 1
drink) €25; €15.50 concessions. **Credit** MC, V.
Map p345 A3.
This respected flamenco *tablao* has presented many
top stars over the years, including Antonio Gades
and the singer Fosforito. It caters mainly to the
tourist trade, but still avoids the fripperies of some
of the worst of the coach-party venues. The modern,
simple, open space feels a bit school hall with its fold-
away wooden chairs, except that there's a bar and,
this being Barcelona, you have to smoke. Admission
also entitles you to get into Jamboree downstairs (*see
p246*).

Jazz, folk & blues

In summer, one of the best places to hear jazz is
outside. One of the most tranquil outdoor
surroundings for it is **L'Hivernacle** in
the Parc de la Ciutadella. Also, the **Pipa Club**
(*see p248*) in the Plaça Reial holds an autumn
jazz festival in the Scotch Bar at the **Hotel
Ritz** (*see p61*). For Celtic folk music of variable
quality, try Barcelona's ex-pat pubs. The **Quiet
Man** (C/Marqués de Barbera 11, 93 412 12 19)
hosts occasional performances.

La Boîte

Avda Diagonal 477, Eixample (93 319 17 89/
www.masimas.com). Bus 6, 7, 14, 15, 27, 32, 33, 34,
41, 63, 67, 68, N12. **Open** Gigs around 11pm Mon-
Thur; midnight Fri, Sat; 7pm Sun. **Admission** Gigs
€6-€12. **Credit** AmEx, MC, V. **Map** p338 C3.
Barcelona's serious live music scene is somewhat
dominated by the Mas siblings. They took over La
Boîte more than 10 years ago, when it was, in their
words, a 'tacky jet-set' kind of place. Now, this small
subterranean venue still retains a 'tacky jet-set'
entrance and mirror-tiled columns, but it has (thank-
fully) shed the besuited lechers, and replaced them
with head-nodding music-lovers of various ages and
myriad dress-senses. The music here is mostly of a
rock/blues/funk flavour with the odd bit of Catalan
ska or flamenco fusion thrown in, usually performed
by Spanish and American artists. There are new and
untried acts here occasionally as well. For a free taste
of undiscovered talent (possibly), or to strum your
own stuff, try the regular jam sessions (*see p245*
How to: play your funky music).

CAT

Trva de Sant Antoni 6-8, Gràcia (93 218 44 85/
www.tradicionarius.com). Metro Fontana.
Open Sept-June 5pm-midnight daily. Gigs about
10pm Fri. Closed July, Aug. **Admission** €6-€9.
No credit cards. Map p338 D3.

How to play your funky music

If you can't pack a suitcase without slipping in your guitar, zither or euphonium, you haven't wasted your time. There are places where you can share your magic without getting arrested or having cold water chucked at you from a neighbour's balcony.

JAM SESSIONS

La Boîte (*see p244*) has rock, blues and funk jams every Monday, coordinated by various figures from the local music scene such as Alex A, Layla Martín and David Sam. Turn up on the night and sign up on the list by the stage. Layla and David also take on coordinating duties for jams at the **Jazz Sí Club** (*see p246*). Tuesdays are for pop, rock and blues, and Friday is the night for rock. There are jazz jams on Wednesdays – call Joaquín at the club for more information. The bar's run by the local music school, so it's a friendly, tolerant place for those still perfecting their technique, as well as a good place to meet fellow musicians for lunch.

For more serious jazz musicians, the sessions at any of the temples run by the Mas I Mas clan offer an opportunity to show off your virtuoso playing, accompanied by local stars such as saxophonist Llibert Fortuny and guitarist Jordi Farres. At legendary jazz cave **Jamboree** for example (*see p246*), Aurelios Santos coordinates the wildly popular WTF (What the Fuck) jazz jam every Monday. Turn up at 10pm and ask for Aurelios, or email aurelios@masimas.com. If you want to syncopate at the Jazzroom at **La Cova del Drac** (*see p245*) on a Tuesday night, turn up on the night and check in with whoever's coordinating.

OPEN MIC

The only open mic venue in town is the relaxed bar **Kabara** (C/Junta de Comerç 20, mobile 677 058 784), which is open until late every night and offers performers of all bents the chance to display their talents every Wednesday. Just turn up at 8pm and speak to Marlos to sign up for a ten-minute slot. The mic's open from 8.30pm until 10.30pm, though if everyone's having a good time (and they're not too noisy – drums are banned because of trouble with noise and the neighbours) they'll let you play on. The bar hosts concerts on Fridays by performers picked from the Wednesday night Kabaret. In return for performing, the chosen artist gets a percentage of the night's bar takings.

La Boîte.

The Centre Artesà Tradicionàrius promotes traditional Catalan music and culture, hosting music festivals including the Festival Tradicionàrius, a showcase of folk music and dance held between January and April. Concerts, workshops and classes cover indigenous music from the rest of Spain and other countries. It's not all old stuff, however. The centre also takes part in the LEM festival of experimental music known as Sonar (*see p213*), which usually features more bleeps than bagpipes.

La Cova del Drac

C/Vallmajor 33, Zona Alta (93 319 17 89/ www.masimas.com). FGC Muntaner. **Open** *Gigs* 11pm-12.30am Tue-Sat. **Admission** *Gigs* €6 Tue-Thur; €9 Fri, Sat. **Credit** AmEx, MC, V. **Map** p338 C2.

La Cova has a fantastic history as a seminal jazz venue; at its previous site on legendary 'Tuset Street' it was a refuge for bohemians and intellectuals during Franco's rule, but it was also the only major jazz venue in town attracting big American stars. Its own star waned towards the end of the '90s, but it has since been revamped and revitalised by the ubiquitous Mas siblings who've created a classy, if slightly clinical, basement venue and named it Jazzroom. This cellar bar features jazz concerts by mostly Spanish and Latin American musicians, with occasional latin and blues artists spicing up the mix.

DosTrece

C/Carme 40, Raval (93 301 73 06/www.dostrece.net. Metro Liceu. **Open** 11pm-4am Mon; 11pm-3am Tue-Sun. **Admission** (incl 1 drink) €3-€5 Tue, Wed, Sun; €15 Thur; free Fri, Sat. **Credit** AmEx, DC, MC, V. **Map** p344 A2.
This hip-by-numbers restaurant hosts music in its cellar bar – a space easily filled by funky young expats, with American accents dominating the buzz. There's an Argentinean vibe on Tuesdays with tango music, Wednesdays feature yet another jazz jam session of varying quality, and on Thursdays you can hear flamenco or invited artists of various bents. Fridays and Saturdays are DJ nights, then the live vibe returns on Sundays with Brazilian beats.

Harlem Jazz Club

C/Comtessa de Sobradiel 8, Barri Gòtic (93 310 07 55). Metro Jaume I. **Open** 8pm-4am Tue-Thur, Sun; 8pm-5am Fri, Sat. *Gigs* 10.30pm, midnight Tue-Thur, Sun; 11.30pm, 1am Fri, Sat. Closed some wks Aug. **Admission** free (1 drink minimum). **No credit cards. Map** p345 B3.
Squeeze past the narrow bar and the room opens up (slightly) to accommodate a small stage and a laid-back chatty crowd. Jazz and blues often make way for world music, particularly Afro-Caribbean sounds, and flamenco-fusion, as well as rock.

Jamboree

Plaça Reial 17, Barri Gòtic (93 301 75 64/ www.masimas.com). Metro Liceu. **Open** 10.30pm-5am daily. *Gigs* 11pm-12.30am daily. **Admission** *Gigs* €6-€12. **Credit** AmEx, MC, V. **Map** p345 A3.
This cosy, stone-vaulted tavern, another part of the Mas siblings' chain, is one of the principal jazz clubs in Barcelona, if not in the whole of Europe. Old greats like Chet Baker have played here, and the stars of today, such as pianist Bruce Barth and Buena Vista's Jimmy Jenks, maintain Jamboree's heady reputation. Even when the bookings aren't so well known, they're often intriguing and experimental; jazz vs hip-hop sound-offs and poetry jams are all part of Jamboree's extensive repertoire.

Jazz Sí Club

C/Requesens 2, Raval (93 329 00 20/www.taller demusics.com). Metro Sant Antoni. **Open** 9am-11pm Mon-Fri; 6-11pm Sat, Sun. **Admission** free Mon-Wed, Fri, Sun; €3-€5 (incl 1 drink) Thur, Sat. **No credit cards. Map** p342 C5.
The Barcelona contemporary music school, which is situated just opposite, runs this small studio-like bar (a decent café during the day) as a space for students, teachers, and music lovers to meet, practise,

The best **Festivals**

The council website, www.bcn.es, is the best place to hunt down information and reconfirm dates (which are liable to change) on all of these.

Tradicionarius

Start the year in traditional style with a season celebrating Catalonia's musical heritage. Jan-March.

Música Antiga

Renaissance and baroque music, in charming medieval squares. April, May.

Festival de Flamenco de Ciutat Vella

The CCCB's patio is the slightly incongruous venue for a showcase of orthodox and updated flamenco from stars old and new. May.

SONAR

A massive, lost weekend of dance and electronica. June.

Classics al Parcs

Small-scale, outdoor concerts in various city parks. June-July.

BAM

A mixed bag of indie and alternative rock, much of it free, to coincide with the Mercè. Sept.

LEM

From the weird and wonderful to the weird and excruciating. Fun, feisty and free. Oct-Dec.

Festival Internacional de Jazz

Huge autumnal feast featuring every flavour of jazz. Oct-Dec.

Músiques Contemporànies

Contemporary music in all its forms and facets. Nov-Dec.

perform and listen. While they are largely unknowns, there is quality music to be found here. Each night is dedicated to a different musical genre, trad jazz on Mondays, pop/rock/blues jams on Tuesdays, jazz jams on Wednesdays, Cuban music on Thursdays, flamenco on Fridays, rock on Saturdays and rock jams on Sundays. Entrance is either free or there's a small charge that includes a drink, so even if the performance disappoints, it's a good place to start a night out in the Raval.

Nightlife

Put your best stiletto forward; *barcelonins* take their nightlife very seriously.

If there's one thing you need to know about Barcelona nightlife it's this: it starts late and goes on even later. With bars open until 3am, and plenty of them bridging the bar/club divide with music and a dancefloor, crowds don't move to paying nightclubs until well after 2am. If you still haven't had enough when the big clubs close at five or six in the morning, keep your ear to the ground and there's a chance you'll pick up on an after-party that will take you well into the next day.

The feel of the city at night changes as you move through its zones. Down by the seafront, Maremàgnum and Port Olímpic are lined with dockside bars that swarm with tourists in summer, as well as the new superclub **Club Danzatoria** (*see p254*). The labyrinthine backstreets of the Barri Gòtic pulsate with life around C/Escudellers and the Plaça Reial, where many near-perfect late-night bars are tucked into the murky alleyways. Across La Rambla in the Raval and spilling over Avda Paral.lel into Poble Sec, you'll find a few underground bars, some long-established drinking dens with extremely chequered histories and two emblematic city clubs, **La Paloma** (*see p252*) and **Sala Apolo** (*see p254*), in venues rich with vintage atmosphere. Gràcia and the Born have self-contained atmospheres, with nightlife centred around the bars on Gracia's squares and the Passeig del Born.

In the elegant gridwork of the Eixample, tourists are less in evidence, and swish designer bars are spread throughout the district, along with discos and nightclubs. If you want class, aim high: **Otto Zutz** in Gràcia (*see p261*), **Discothèque** and **La Terrrazza** on Montjuïc (*see p255 and p257*) and **Danzatoria** on the slopes of Tibidabo (*see p261*) are all places where altitude corresponds to exclusivity.

Expect bar prices to vary (dramatically) along with the pretensions of the place where you're drinking; a *bar musical* with a defined style, decor and musical policy is a very different proposition from the ordinary bar next door. When you're paying to go into a club, check your ticket for the words *con consumición*, which means you can exchange it for a drink at the bar: worth knowing, as drinks prices in clubs here are steep by just about anybody's standards.

In this section you'll find cheesy discos, Latin ballrooms, tango bars, grungy alternative drinking dens, techno caverns, electro dancehalls and house super-clubs. As far as 'club culture' is concerned, it's a mixed picture. There's a massive scene associated with Spain's home-grown techno, known as *makina*, which has a mainly teenage following and may be of limited interest to outsiders. But internationally recognised electronic artists frequently visit, and others – like Finnish artist Jimi Tenor – have gone so far as adopting Barcelona as their home. One event that has put Barcelona on the map is **Sónar** (*see p213*), whose effects on the city's nightlife extend beyond summertime, as organisers Advanced Music now hold serious parties throughout the year.

Don't miss
Nights out

Monday
Café Royale for soul, funk and grown-up glamour. *See p248.*

Tuesday
Bucaro for ruffling your feathers. *See p258.*

Wednesday
El Cangrejo for class drag acts, sequins and slingbacks. *See p251.*

Thursday
Plataforma (*see p255*) for ear-bleeding drum 'n' bass, or the Powder Room at **Sala Apolo** (*see p254*) for smooth club tunes.

Friday
La Paloma, for old school waltzing followed by one of the city's hottest club nights. *See p252.*

Saturday
... is for super-club chic: **Discothèque** (*see p255*) on winter nights, **La Terrrazza** (*see p257*) under the summer stars.

Sunday
Chilling in style at Twilight, **Danzatoria** (*see p261*) or the Zen Club, **City Hall** (*see p258*).

Arts & Entertainment

INFORMATION

Clubs open (and close) all the time and, with new legislation coming into force in 2003, the nightlife scene is almost certain to become even less stable. In order to have licences renewed any club within 300 metres of a residential building is to have soundproofing installed – which could be the death knell for many smaller venues.

To stay informed of changes and to find out who's playing where and when, look no further than the smorgasbord of flyers obligatory in any fashionable clothes or record shop, or in local bars. Clubs and bars advertise their programmes in the free (Spanish language) magazines *punto H*, *aB* and *go BCN*. The bi-weekly (and bilingual) *Movin' BCN*, available at newsstands, features different clubs every month. On the net, www.clubbingspain.com, maintained by Barcelona residents, posts DJ interviews and weekly club listings in both English and Spanish.

Barri Gòtic

Barcelona Pipa Club

Plaça Reial 3, pral (93 302 47 32/www.bpipaclub. com). Metro Liceu. **Open** 6pm-3am daily. **No credit cards. Map** p345 A3.
With Sherlock Holmes-inspired decor, musty chesterfields, flock wallpaper and collectors' cabinets stuffed with smokers' paraphernalia, the Pipa is one of Barcelona's best loved late-night bars. Catalan celebrities mingle with local bourgeoisie and American Erasmus students. Courses in the art of pipe smoking are offered to serious pundits along with live jazz and gastronomic evenings, but above all it's a great place for a late-night drink. To get in, ring the buzzer next to the sign of the pipe: if there's no answer, it may be that there's just no room.

Café Royale

C/Nou de Zurbano 3 (93 412 14 33). Metro Liceu or Drassanes. **Open** 6pm-2.30am Mon-Thur, Sun; 6pm-3am Fri, Sat. **Admission** €6 after 11pm & Fri, Sat. **Credit** MC, V. **Map** p345 A3.
With its pleasantly scuffed look, mellow orange-velvet curtains and bottomless sofas, this place looks like a lounge club. Early in the week you may find space to relax and listen to the dog-eared library of bossa nova and Latin jazz shelved behind the DJ's cabinet. At weekends, however, it's packed to squeaking point. It's an eclectic unpretentious place with a nice vibe. Which might be why it's where Almodóvar threw his end-of-filming party for *All About My Mother*.

Chez Popof

C/Aroles 5 (93 318 42 26). Metro Liceu. **Open** noon-4am Wed-Sun. **No credit cards. Map** p345 A3.
Presumably at some stage this bar was what it looks like: a rustically appointed cava emporium with a

gruffly appealing Catalan charm. For as long as anyone can remember, though, its sole selling point has been the fact that its wooden doors are ajar when everywhere else is closed: at 4am it's a haze of smoke and broken resolutions, supervised by unsmiling waiters of the old school.

Dot

C/Nou de Sant Francesc 7 (93 302 70 26/ www.dotlightclub.com). Metro Drassanes. **Open** 10pm-2.30am Mon-Thur, Sun; 10pm-3am Fri, Sat. **No credit cards. Map** p345 A4.
Dot is a classic, with the balance just right. There's a tiny bar at the front and then, when you're ready to dance, go through a futuristic portal, behind which a starker dancefloor is kept vibrant by an upfront music policy and vintage movies. One of the first places in town to give DJs a regular weekly slot, it's a stylish segue between a late drink and staying out all night.

Fonfone

C/Escudellers 24 (93 317 14 24/www.fonfone.com). Metro Drassanes. **Open** 10pm-3am daily. **No credit cards. Map** p345 A3.
A deep dark bar barely lit by the multicoloured radioactive glow of its Lego-like brick decorations, Fonfone packs in a mixed crowd for heavy sweating sessions of thumping techno, industrial house and drum 'n' bass. Upstairs, you'll find something akin to a chill-out space, occasionally showcasing the works of local multimedia artists.

Jamboree

Plaça Reial 17 (93 301 75 64/www.masimas.com). Metro Liceu. **Open** 12.30pm-5.30am daily. **Admission** (incl 1 drink) €12. **Credit** V. **Map** p345 A3.
Just as Blue Note precedes Def Jam, an illustrious jazz cellar gives way to beats and rhymes after hours, with B-Boys in baggy basketball vests, bandanas and golf visors showing out in the brick-lined vaults. Downstairs is just about the only dancefloor in Barcelona where you can dance to rap and hip hop all night long: upstairs the glitzier space, Tarantos, programmes smooth R&B grooves; something for the laydeez.

Karma

Plaça Reial 10 (93 302 56 80). Metro Liceu. **Open** midnight-5am Tue-Sat. **Admission** (incl 1 drink) €7. **No credit cards. Map** p345 A3.
Grey-haired ex-hellraisers remember their teenage kicks in this grungy basement venue: Karma has been a staple of the Plaça Reial since the days when decent people didn't go there. Sticking to a rough and ready formula of pop/rock standards and crowd movers, it draws a mixture of local regulars and unfussy visitors.

La Macarena

C/Nou de Sant Francesc 5 (no phone). Metro Liceu. **Open** 11pm-6am daily. **Admission** €5 after 2.30am. **No credit cards. Map** p345 A4.

Say cheese

There's no denying that much of Barcelona's nightlife scene is as cheesy as a wheel of *manchego viejo*, offering '80s-style discos and monster beach bars straight out of Vegas, as well as a mind-boggling array of whacked-out theme bars.

You can't help but wonder sometimes just what they're thinking. Who, for example, thought up vat-sized cocktails served from the scooped out, smoke-spewing porcelain head of a Polynesian god, sucked through a metre-long straw? **Kahiki** (C/Gran Via de les Corts Catalanes 581, 93 323 18 83), that's who. And who thought up a Barbie-pink colour scheme with Austin Powers posters and re-runs of James Bond movies? That'll be Susan at the aptly named **Groovy** (C/Villarroel 82, no phone).

Higher up the hill, 'alternative country' on Wednesday nights at the **Sutton Club** (C/Tuset 13, 93 414 42 17) teaches line-dancing to a herd of Catalan cowboys and girls in a funky multi-tiered space. The half-circle sofas, waiters in dicky bows, marble floors and acres of mirrors may feel strictly ballroom, but don't be fooled by any pretentions to sophistication. Don your ten-gallon hat and be prepared to join in the hoedown as Sam Lardner and the Hurricane Band belt out covers of *Achy Breaky Heart* and *Choo Choo Train*. Yeehaw, indeed.

Down on the seafront the southern belles of **Coyote Ugly (**C/Avda Litoral 24, 93 221 96 84) – styled after the film set – strut up and down on the bar tossing their long tousled locks to ear-bleeding blasts of Pink, J-Lo and Madge. Free shots get the party started, and the dress code is strictly less is more.

The **Baja Beach Club** (Passeig Maritim 34, 93 225 91 00 – pictured) pulls in a very diverse clientele aged 18 to 80, including Barcelona's football team (apparently a regular fixture on Sundays), and the odd A-lister. Leo DiCaprio, David Copperfield and Gwen Stefani are all said to have dropped by. More circus than nightclub, this is the biggest act in Barcelona, with 130 buffed and beautiful staff. Contrary to popular belief, cheekily clad they may be, but naked they are not – although if you're very lucky you may get to lick a worm of whipped cream off the bronzed belly of a nubile young goddess.

Among other exciting stunts, barmen catch ice cubes in tumblers stuck down their pants and breathe fire-balls over glass pyramids of waiting shots, and for just €3 you can spin yourself sick on a gyroscope. Oh, just try to stop us. Meanwhile, the ringmaster fires up a crowd of braying party animals to a bewildering mix of pop favourites, movie theme tunes and the Nou Camp's football anthem.

When the bass kicks in this compact bar the whole place pounds like some tiny chamber of the inner ear. La Macarena is the kind of club where you move in time to avoid being crushed. It's definitely not for the claustrophobic. Electric grooves, elbows, knees and the odd touch of funk are all equally in your face here, making for a frenetic atmosphere. Use the coat-hooks round the dancefloor, but keep an eye on your things.

Malpaso

C/Rauric 20 (93 412 60 05). Metro Liceu. **Open** 10pm-3am daily. **No credit cards. Map** p345 A3.
With its colourful geometry and arty glassed-in installations, Malpaso is very nearly cool, and yet somehow has the earnest feel of the downstairs bar in a savvy youth hostel. Maybe it's the DJ spinning monsters-of-rock classics along with the odd '90s dance track, or maybe it's the noticeboard. Either way, it attracts a mixed bunch, who meet up, drink up and move on.

Sidecar Factory Club

Plaça Reial 7 (93 302 15 86/www.sidecarfactory club.com). Metro Liceu. **Open** 8pm-2.30am Tue-Thur, Sun; 8pm-3am Fri, Sat. **Gigs** 10.30pm Tue, Thur-Sat. Closed Aug. **Admission** (incl 1 drink) €4.
No credit cards. Map p345 A3.
Sidecar has a bar and terrace on the Plaça Reial, and one of the most diverse programming policies of any club in town. The basement space is an important small music venue, as much for local bands as for experimental international groups. It also offers a midweek cinema workshop, a poppy/rocky/indie disco on Fridays and Saturdays and a drum 'n' bass open mic session on Sunday nights.

So_da

C/Avinyó 24 (no phone). Metro Liceu. **Open** 9pm-2.30am daily. **No credit cards. Map** p345 B3.
Posh clothes shop by day, deeply cool bar by night. Once the high-fashion wares are safely locked up in the great white wardrobes near the entrance, and the tubular curtains of the changing room are twisted up out of the way, the projected films start rolling, and ta-dah! There are DJs on decks set on a trestle table in the corner. On Fridays expect smooth Brazilian sounds; other nights vary.

Raval

Aurora

C/Aurora 7 (93 442 30 44). Metro Paral.lel. **Open** 8pm-3am daily. **No credit cards.**
Map p342 C6.
Since the Rambla del Raval opened up, it's been easier to find this idiosyncratic little bar, but stylewise it's still way off the beaten track, with murals and fittings that have been following their own weird course of evolution for years. The many arty/creative/unkempt regulars can make for a cliquey feel, but it's basically friendly, with seats in the cosy loft space upstairs.

Beautiful International Bar

C/Arc del Teatre 15 (93 318 92 23). Metro Drassanes. **Open** 7pm-3am Tue-Sun. **No credit cards. Map** p345 A4.
This is very much a locals' joint, with a tiny dancefloor out back for early-hours smooching to Spanish folk songs. The most distinctive, and unfortunate, feature is a sparkling black mural of the twin towers – and a monstrous bust of Marilyn Monroe winking at you from behind the bar. Good stiff drinks, friendly staff and a toilet flush that has been known to give the odd electric shock are also to be found.

Benidorm

C/Joaquín Costa 39 (93 317 80 52). Metro Universitat. **Open** 7pm-2.30am Mon-Thur, Sun; 7pm-3am Fri, Sat. **No credit cards. Map** p342 C5.
One of the ringleaders of new, cool Raval, this is a lively, smoky little place, and a kitsch paradise of brothel-red walls, crystal lanterns and '80s disco paraphernalia. It boasts the world's smallest toilet, dancefloor and chill-out room. There's hip hop on the first Thursday of every month, sounds from the '70s on indeterminate Fridays and varied electro-grooves the rest of the time.

El Cangrejo

C/Montserrat 9 (93 301 29 78). Metro Drassanes. **Open** 9pm-4am Tue-Sun. **No credit cards. Map** p345 A3.
The original Barcelona drag cabaret, this place attracts a mixed bag of old timers, honeymooners, gay couples and other appreciative revellers. Tuesday and Wednesday feature DJ sessions, but otherwise the act consists largely of mimed, golden-oldie Spanish ballads interspersed with raconteurs whose outrageous get-ups successfully combine early Divine and Prince. You'd have to go a long way to find a more sequin-spangled line up, and if you can imagine being sandwiched between a lemon meringue pie and a paella, you'll get some idea of what the decor is like.

Colours Under Water

C/Sant Climent 11 (no phone). Metro Sant Antoni. **Open** 6pm-3am Thur-Sat. **No credit cards. Map** p342 C6.
On a tiny backstreet at the edge of the Raval, this is a classic 'cultural association' run by a small collective as a meeting place, hang-out and centre for activities that include weekly yoga classes. At the weekends occasional live concerts are followed by parties that pack out the low-ceilinged space: things can get wild, but are always friendly.

La Concha

C/Guàrdia 14 (93 302 41 18). Metro Drassanes. **Open** 4pm-4.30am daily. **Gigs** midnight-2am Sun. **No credit cards. Map** p345 A3.
The sequins, slingbacks, pathos and paunches of the Raval's surviving drag cabaret scene live at on El Cangrejo (*see above*) and occasionally make an appearance here, amid the myriad faces – from '60s sex kitten to kohl-eyed diva – of Spanish screen and

drag icon Sara Montiel, which fill the walls from ceiling to floor. The cobwebs have been dusted off and the wilted flowers replaced to attract a gay-friendly but very mixed new crowd. There's even dancing on the chequered tiles to raï and flamenco, along with the occasional local band playing a gig.

Kentucky

C/Arc del Teatre 11 (93 318 28 78). Metro Drassanes. **Open** *Sept-July* 10pm-3am Tue-Thur; 10pm-4.30am Fri, Sat. Closed Aug. **No credit cards. Map** p345 A4.

One-time pick-up bar, haunt of wayward US sailors and lowlifes of the old Barrio Chino, haven of lost souls and chancers steering by the wrong star. What epic lock-ins have unrolled behind that rattling shutter? What tales could be told of Kentucky? If only, if only, anyone could remember any of it…

London Bar

C/Nou de la Rambla 34 (93 318 52 61). Metro Liceu. **Open** 7.30pm-4.30am Tue-Thur, Sun; 7pm-5am Fri, Sat. Closed 2wks end Aug. **Credit** AmEx, MC, V. **Map** p345 A3.

The London Bar hasn't changed its extravagant look (nothing like an English pub) since it opened in 1910. It's popular among young resident ex-pats and a mixed bunch of party-going *barcelonins*. There are regular live gigs, for which there's no entrance fee, but note that drink prices do go up accordingly.

Marsella

C/Sant Pau 65 (93 442 72 63). Metro Liceu. **Open** 10pm-2am Mon-Thur; 10pm-3am Fri, Sat. **No credit cards. Map** p345 A3.

A well-loved bar that's been in the same family for five generations. It's said that Jean Genet, among other notorious artists and petty thieves, used to come here – attracted, no doubt, by the locally made absinthe, which is still stocked. Dusty, untapped 100-year-old bottles sit in tall glass cabinets, old mirrors line the walls, and assorted chandeliers loom over the cheerful, largely foreign crowd.

Merry Ant

C/Peu de la Creu 23, (no phone). Metro Sant Antoni. **Open** 8pm-2.30am Tue-Sun. **No credit cards. Map** p342 C5.

The bizarre and slightly unhinged work of a rebellious carpenter, the Merry Ant functions as both a bar and a 'cultural association'. Local artist Toto sawed, hammered and glued a collection of found objects into a remarkable, Frankenstein-like vision of interior design. An easy-going artsy crowd unwinds here, amid soft red lighting.

Moog

C/Arc del Teatre 3 (93 301 72 82/www.masimas. com). Metro Drassanes. **Open** 11.30pm-5am daily. **Admission** (incl 1 drink) €12. **Credit** V. **Map** p345 A4.

A compact and businesslike venue, from the door staff to the respectable sound system, Moog has been programming electronic music for six years

with admirable consistency, under the direction of residents Omar and Loe, heads of the Barcelona label Minifunk. There's a bar in the entryway, a scattering of tables, a small dancefloor downstairs and a room upstairs that is enlivened by a mural of Leroy from *Fame*. It's a minimal definition of a club, but it works.

La Paloma

C/Tigre 27 (93 301 68 97/www.softlyclub.com). Metro Universitat. **Open** 6-9.30pm, 11.30pm-5am Thur; 6-9.30pm, 11.30pm-2am, 2.30am-5am Fri, Sat; 11.30pm-5am Sun. **Admission** (incl 1 drink) €6-€8. **No credit cards. Map** p342 C5.

This glamorous, gilded ballroom dates back to 1903, when people knew a thing or two about atmosphere, and it still provides a stunning backdrop for one of the most varied experiences on the circuit – there's traditional dance-hall twirling during the first shift, then, on Fridays and Saturdays, an orchestra plays during the second shift, after which the DJs step up. Late night, Thursday's Bongo Lounge continues loud and clear to a regular crowd, though sometimes the PA system isn't quite up to the demands of modern clubbing. A recent addition is Friday night's 'roots' Barrio Sessions from a handful of Barcelona's most cutting-edge promoters, and, on Saturdays, Tiger Tunes is a trip back to the '80s.

Rita Blue

Plaça Sant Agustí 3 (93 342 40 86/www.margarita blue.com). Metro Liceu. **Open** 1.30pm-2am Mon, Tue, Sun; 1.30pm-3am Wed-Sat. **Credit** V. **Map** p345 A3.

Mexican fusion cooking, bubble-gum cocktails and chilled out clubbing are all in the mix here. Dinner time grooves are funk, soul and house played comfortably low. It's a bit more brash in the steel-floored dungeon downstairs, which serves as extra dining space until midnight when, in true dungeon style, the dining tables are strapped to the walls to make way for the groovers and shakers.

Salsitas

C/Nou de la Rambla 22 (93 318 08 40/ www.octopussy.org). Metro Liceu. **Open** 11pm-3am daily. **Credit** AmEx, DC, MC, V. **Map** p345 A3.

As white and tropical as the inside of a Bounty bar, it is perhaps in spite of and not because of the pillars made over as coconut palms that Salsitas (the bar-restaurant) and Club 22 (the club after midnight) have been riding a tsunami of popularity for so long. The crowd is tanned, toned and trendy. DJs Bass and J Castello keep things swinging with nu-jazz and cocktail music in the second room.

Sant Pere & Born

Astin Bar Club

C/Abaixadors 9 (93 442 96 69/www.nitsa.com/astin). Metro Jaume I. **Open** 11pm-3am Thur-Sat. **Admission** (incl 1 drink) €3. **No credit cards. Map** p345 B3.

Live the high life at winter-only **Discothèque**. *See p255.*

Astin is a functional space, its hard-edged decor as uncompromising as the music. Part of the same anagrammatic family as Nitsa (*see p254* Sala Apolo), this much smaller bar/club caters to the kind of jaded ear that likes to hear Black Sabbath mixed with the Smiths over a Kraftwerk drum sound.

Bass Bar

C/Assaonadors 25 (no phone). Metro Jaume I.
Open 7pm-2.30am Tue-Thur; 7pm-3am Fri-Sun.
No credit cards. Map p345 C3.
Within its tiny confines the Bass Bar occasionally attempts a new look, but the basics stay the same: a battered sofa, a pile of free music rags and a handful of locals working on their dreadlocks. Exhibitions of local artists and collectives adorn the walls, and the music covers everything from Spanish ska to world drumming to Latin. The best bet in the neighbourhood for a late late drink.

Magic

Passeig Picasso 40 (93 310 72 67). Metro Barceloneta. **Open** 11pm-5.30am Thur; 11pm-6.30am Fri, Sat. **Admission** *Gigs* varies. *Disco* (incl 1 drink) €10. **No credit cards. Map** p343 E6.
There's magic in the air – but there's not much air in Magic, an awkward basement club whose big pull is the music: blistering Northern Soul, rare grooves and raucous funk for a crowd of ex- and aspirant mods.

Nao Colón

Avda Marqués de l'Argentera 19 (93 268 76 33). Metro Barceloneta. **Open** midnight-3am Thur-Sat. **Credit** AmEx, DC, MC, V. **Map** p345 C4.
Brushed-steel and teak provide a slick, modern backdrop for the grown-up crowd attracted here by the flash Mediterranean food and bands on Thursdays from 10pm. Expect anything from flamenco fusion to Dixieland to jazz quartets. Then, at midnight, cue the metamorphosis from restaurant to club, as Bamboo kicks in with the organic rhythms of Afro-Brazilian, Latin house and soul, courtesy of resident DJs Tito Rosell and Funky Rodríguez.

República

Estació de França, Avda Marquès de l'Argentera 6 (93 300 50 50/www.republicaclub.com). Metro Barceloneta. **Open** 1.30-7am Fri, Sat. **Admission** (incl 1 drink) €12. **No credit cards. Map** p345 C4.
After a summer break in 2002, República returned to the low-ceilinged, labyrinthine space under the Estació de França. It's popular and pumped up; a dim red glow somewhere off in the far corners is your only guide between the concrete pillars and across the two packed dancefloors. Head left for techno-house, and right for, er, house-techno, with a blissfully tacky pop room in between. Skyfunk currently brings garage, breakbeat, drum 'n' bass and funk once a month.

s:pic

C/Ribera 10, (93 310 15 95). Metro Barceloneta. **Open** 9pm-1am Tue-Thur; 9pm-3am Fri, Sat. **No credit cards. Map** p345 C4.
Another ritzy creation by the Salsita group, though a chill-out space rather than a place to dance. Prepare to be dazzled as you claw your way through the plastic tentacles of the anaemic sea anemone that coats the cylindrical doorframe. Once inside, you'll find another of the Born's formulaic resto-clubs, with steely tables, floral projections and acid-orange walls. Trendy media types hang out in the basement.

Suborn

Passeig Picasso 42 (93 310 11 10). Metro Barceloneta. **Open** 8.30pm-3am Tue-Sun. **Credit** MC, V. **Map** p345 C4.
With tables under the arches looking on to the Ciutadella park, this bar-restaurant metamorphoses into a small club at some unspecified point in the evening, and the raised metal dancefloor fills up to the beats of hectic techno and house. It's friendly, uninhibited and somewhat cramped. The café/club vibe that works so well here has been taken upscale by the unfortunately named s:pic on the same street – with what success is yet to be seen.

Head to **Risco** for a risky, frisky night. *See p260.*

Port Vell & Port Olímpic

Around the right-angled quayside of the Port
Olímpic, you'll find dance bars interspersed
with seafood restaurants, fast-food outlets,
ice-cream parlours, coffee shops and mock-Irish
pubs; with video screens, glittery lights and
go-go girls and boys in abundance, there's little
to choose between them.

El Chiringuito

Bogatell beach (93 221 07 29). Metro Llacuna.
Open *May-Sept* 11pm-3am daily. Closed Oct-Apr.
No credit cards.
Part of the LASAL sessions (which count DJs Mad
Professor, the Herbalizer and Coldcut among its stable of groove mixers), this newcomer to the summer
club scene mixes celebrity DJs with local talent.
Perfect for a spot of moon-bathing, it's a bit of a hike
from the nearest metro, so your best bet is to hop in
a cab and keep your eyes peeled for a laser beam
slashing the night sky.

Club Danzatoria

*Marina Village, C/Ramon Trias Fargas s/n (93 224
04 80/www.clubdanzatoria.com). Metro Ciutadella-
Vila Olímpica.* **Open** midnight-6am Thur-Sat.
Admission (incl 1 drink) €15. **Credit** MC, V.
Map p343 F7.
Between the casino and the seafront, this is the latest
venture by the company that brought you Salsitas
(*see p252*), s:pic (*see p253*) and Danzatoria on the
slopes of Tibidabo (*see p261*). Inside, two spacious
dancefloors sit one above the other, grey steel structures fitted out with basic materials gone sci-fi, like
Barbarella dressed in see-thru household plastics
from the utility cupboard: pillars are coated in coarse
fur and white cushions dot the perimeter. Residents
Javier Navines and Toni Bass deal out house for a
fittingly glam and shiny crowd.

Maremàgnum

Moll d'Espanya. Metro Drassanes. **Map** p343 D7.
A Jekyll and Hyde of a place, limping along during
the day, only to become a monster by night as three
levels of '80s-style bars and clubs flood with cocktail
guzzling hedonists. The row at ground level facing
inland is ablaze with flashing disco balls, bright
lights and neon. The best of the bunch is probably
Mojito, which offers free salsa lessons every night
from 10pm. But you'll be dancing on your own, as
nothing really gets going until after 1am when
gangs of stags and hens turn up. Beware the outra-
geously priced Red Bull cocktails. On the top level,
bizarrely arranged around the rooftop mini-golf
course, are two enormous discos, Starwinds and
Nayandei, as well as a couple of theme pubs.

Montjuïc & Poble Sec

Sala Apolo

*C/Nou de la Rambla 113 (93 441 40 01/
www.nitsa.com/www.maumauunderground.com).
Metro Paral.lel.* **Open** *Nitsa* 12.30-6.30am Fri, Sat.
Powder Room 1-5.30am 2nd & 4th Thur of month.
Admission (incl 1 drink) *Nitsa* €12. *Powder Room*
€9. **No credit cards. Map** p342 C6.
Late nights at Apolo (a stylish old wooden theatre)
are almost synonymous with Nitsa, a club night now
in its ninth year that has lost none of its confronta-
tional electro savvy under the direction of DJ Coco.
Regular visitors to its stage include DJs Dave Clarke
and Andy Weatherall and labels like Rephlex and
Playhouse; the monthly Puticlub night features
unrespectable pop, while residents include such suitably blasé regulars as DJ de Mierda. Challenging
Nitsa's hegemony on Thursday nights, the Powder
Room brings soul, rare groove and breaks: watch
out for deep funk legend Keb Darge at one of
Barcelona's only funk nights.

Barcelona Rouge

*C/Poeta Cabanyes 21 (93 442 49 85). Metro
Paral.lel.* **Open** 11pm-4am Tue-Sat. **No credit
cards. Map** p341 B6.

This is a slightly surreal place that's always packed,
although it seems that few have heard of it. Ring
the buzzer and shift around outside until someone
lets you in – once inside, a long narrow corridor
lined with people from the Planet Gorgeous leads
into a large room strewn with battered sofas and
fuddled oil paintings. The music's lounge, the cocktails hefty and the prices heftier.

Discothèque

*Poble Espanyol, Avda Marquès de Comillas (93 423
12 85/www.nightsungroup.com). Metro Espanya/
50 bus.* **Open** Mid Oct-mid May 1-5.30am Fri, Sat.
Closed Mid May-mid Oct. **Admission** (incl 1 drink)
€12 with flyer, €15 without. **Credit cards** AmEx,
MC, V. **Map** p341 A4.

The towering ceiling, the projections swarming up
the wall, the extravagantly dressed-up dancers on
their tiny crow's nest perches way above the main
floor: Discothèque is all about vertiginous aspiration,

Distrito Diagonal. *See p258.*

and getting on to the guest list for the balcony VIP
bar is the least of it. The winter incarnation of La
Terrrazza (*see p257*), also located in the eerie Poble
Espanyol, its programme includes guest nights for
the biggest name clubs (like Ibizan superclub
Privilege) and DJs (Roger Sanchez, Joey Negro).
Otherwise, it's house on the main floor and lounge
in the smaller room – and if you're fabulous enough
you may make it on to the pages of *Venus*, Nightsun
group's in-house magazine.

Downbeat

C/Elkano 67 (93 441 24 31). Metro Poble Sec.
Open 11pm-3.30am Thur-Sat. **No credit cards.**
Map p341 B6.

Downbeat's back room is tiled halfway up the wall
and smoke-filled halfway down, and pervaded by a
mighty sound from ragga, reggae and dub selectors,
with international acts from reggae promoters
Nyahbingi crew. In the front, tables and benches
and music at conversation-friendly levels make up
a sociable (but also rather smoky) bar area.
Thursday nights are a different proposition: long-
established hip hop collective Stay True brings
beats, rhymes and basslines.

Mau Mau

*C/Fontrodona 33 (mobile 606 860 617). Metro
Paral.lel.* **Open** 11pm-2.30am Thur; 11pm-3am Fri,
Sat; 6.30-11.30pm Sun. **Admission** (membership)
€5. **No credit cards. Map** p342 C6.

It's not easy to find Mau Mau, but it's very easy to
like. Behind the anonymous grey doors (ring the
bell) first timers pay to become members, so make
sure you hang on to your card for next time. Inside,
an enormous warehouse space scintillates with projected light: there are plentiful sofas and a music
policy ranging from deep house to funk to post-rock.
It's one of the most chilled clubs in Barcelona and
particularly recommended for Sunday evenings and
films on Thursday nights. 'Independent as Fuck',
as the flyers state.

Peach

*Avda Paral.lel 37 (93 272 49 80/www.peachclub.
info). Metro Paral.lel.* **Open** midnight-6am Fri, Sat.
Admission (incl 1 drink) €10. **No credit cards.**
Map p342 C6.

Buttercup yellow and unmissable, with its giant
logo gracing a functional-looking warehouse, Peach
functions as a kind of techno annexe to the more
exclusively house-orientated venues run by the
Nightsun group. Inside, white paint, jars of peaches
in syrup and some lamentable Gaudi-themed sculptures complete the decor. The techno soundtrack
features local heavyweights like Angel Molina.

Plataforma Club

*C/Nou de la Rambla 145 (93 218 8115). Metro
Paral.lel.* **Open** midnight-5am Thur. **Admission**
(incl 1 drink) €4.50. **No credit cards.**
Map p345 A3.

One for hardcore drum 'n' bass 'n' jungle junkies. If
a fast, furious and extremely loud underground

scene is your thing, no other place in Barcelona beats it. The love child of DJ collective Dubcelona, Plataforma is also responsible for many of the semi-legal raves that take place outside the city, in Montserrat and in Tarragona. Get information from CD shops around town, such as Tazmaniac (Plaça Vicenç Martorell 2, Raval, 93 301 25 66).

La Terrrazza

Poble Espanyol, Avda Marquès de Comillas (93 423 12 85/www.nightsungroup.com). Metro Espanya. **Open** *End May-mid Oct* midnight-7am Thur-Sun. Closed mid Oct-end May. **Admission** (incl 1 drink) €15. **No credit cards. Map** p341 A4.

If you make it past the critical eye of the door staff, pick your way past the slightly creepy, not-quite-life-size replicas of Spanish squares and alleyways in the Poble Espanyol to the definitive summertime haunt of your fashion-conscious Barcelona hedonist. The club is an open courtyard, with palm trees, a minimal folly of a building, restless go-gos above the DJ cabin, and more posers than podium space. The main terrace sways like a hi-gloss sea of toned flesh, pouts and designer accessories – big-lensed, off-tint shades, soft leather bondage cuffs, pink studded chokers (wear much more and you're overdressed). Resident DJ Sergio Patricio mixes the playlist around house.

Torres de Avila

Poble Espanyol, Avda Marquès de Comillas (93 424 93 09/www.torresdeavila.com). Metro Espanya. **Open** 12.30pm-6.30am Fri; midnight-7pm Sat. **Admission** (incl 1 drink) €15. **No credit cards. Map** p341 A5.

The grand, mock-medieval gatehouse of the Poble Espanyol houses a bar/club that in its time generated excitement and disdain in equal measure: a temple to designer hedonism dreamed up in the late 1980s by Javier Mariscal (the illustrator behind Barcelona's Olympic mascot) and architect Alfredo Arribas. You move between the multiple levels of thumping revival house on hanging steel staircases or in the glass elevator, emerging on the roof terrace in summer for a neat city view.

La Boîte

Avda Diagonal 477 (93 419 59 50/www.masimas. com). Metro Hospital Clinic. **Open** *Disco* 10pm-5am daily. *Gigs* varies. **Admission** (incl 1 drink) *Disco* €12. *Gigs* €18. **No credit cards. Map** p338 C3.

The entrance to this purpose-built music venue and nightclub glows like a lighthouse cabin behind uptown office blocks and car parks off the Plaça Francesc Macià. Behind it you're swallowed up into an underground space with glittering pillars and sinuous lines. The DJ usually follows the concert with highly danceable soul.

La Bolsa

C/Tuset 17 (93 202 26 35). FGC Provença. **Open** 8pm-2.30am Mon-Thur; 8pm-3am Fri; 7pm-3am Sat; 6pm-2.30am Sun. **Credit** MC, V. **Map** p338 C3.

Buy? Sell? Keel over and cry? This may not quite live up to the cut and thrust of high-city living, but it's a boozers' way of playing the stock exchange.

Gusto. *See p260.*

Drink prices fluctuate according to what's selling on the market, so keep an eye on the in-house FTSE Index. DJs play mainly house and Spanish pop on Fridays and Saturdays.

Bucaro

C/Aribau 195 (93 209 65 62). FGC Provença. **Open** 10.30pm-3am Mon-Sat. **Credit** V. **Map** p338 C3.

Looking a tad jaded these days, Bucaro's worn leather sofas and grubby pouffes still manage to pull a crowd of glamour pusses – those floor to ceiling mirrors allow plenty of preening space for Barcelona's peacocks. With the giant skylight looming above the dancefloor coming on like a portal to another world, and a mezzanine for stalking your prey before swooping on to the dancefloor this is a place that knows class when it sees it. Drinks are a couple of euros more expensive if you're sitting down at a table.

City Hall

Rambla de Catalunya 2-4 (93 317 21 77). Metro Catalunya. **Open** 1-7am Thur-Sat; midnight-6am Sun. **Admission** (incl 1 drink) €12 Thur-Sat; €7-€8 Sun. **No credit cards. Map** p344 A1.

You get some idea of just how 'in' this club is as you walk down the mirrored entrance corridor; in, and further in, till you hit the open patios and steps sunk deep into the heart of a super-central city block. After 2am a dressed-up crowd mingles outside in the candlelight. The downstairs dancefloor warms up much later, with monthly residences from Funk d'Void and their home DJs. Finish the weekend with Sunday night's Zen Club garden party.

Distrito Diagonal

Avda Diagonal 442 (mobile 607 113 602/ www.distritodiagonal.com). Metro Diagonal. **Open** 6pm-3.30am Wed, Thur, Sun; 6pm-4.30am Fri, Sat. **No credit cards. Map** p338 D4.

Latin primers

Wouldn't it be nice to wipe the smirk off the podium dancers' faces and show them how it's really done? Or, for that matter, wow the folks back home with your newfound command of Latin rhythms? OK, Rome wasn't built in a day, but Barcelona has opportunities galore to give it a whirl and make a fool of yourself without the risk of bumping into anyone you know.

Caribbean-style *salsotecas* **Agua de Luna** and **Antilla BCN** are kings of the scene, often hosting live, big-name bands from New York, Puerto Rico and Cuba. Discover them at their sensuous best on Wednesday and Thursday nights, when serious *salseros* twirl and shimmy their way across the waxed floors, providing some of the best dancing this side of the Atlantic. Agua de Luna has the most spectacular *rueda de casino* (Cuban wheel – a merry-go-round of stamping feet and gyrating hips that can leave beginners spinning in helpless confusion) in Barcelona, led by the likes of Victor, an ex-Club Tropicana dancer from Havana and sometime backing dancer to Enrique Iglesias.

The rhythmically challenged may do better at Antilla BCN, where the infinitely patient Daniella could probably drag an elegant cha-cha-cha out of an elephant. This is the city's best-known Latin dance school – a good choice if you want to dedicate some time to the art – attracting an energetic, Latin American crowd, smouldering under the neon disco lights and faux palm fronds. Both clubs have sinewy 'taxi-dancers' aplenty,

ready and willing to dance with any lone passengers waiting in 'rank'.

If a night glued to your partner's groin is more your thing, increasing numbers of tango classes are available. Born in the brothels and gambling houses of Buenos Aires at the end of the 19th century, tango was adopted as foreplay to the more serious business of fornication, and predictably enough gained a questionable reputation. Regardless, by the 1920s the dance that had brought together the *candomblé* drum rhythms of former African slaves and the traditional music and dance from the Argentine pampas had become the language of love, making its way out of the *barrios* and into the gilded ballrooms of Europe and New York.

The key to success is adopting the right attitude – it's no good gliding around the dance floor wearing a grin on your face. Keep your back straight, head proud, eyes to the floor, movements deliberate and passionate; accept that you'll be acting out a tale of unrequited love, a jealous feud or some other tormented affair.

You can have a go for free on Tuesday nights at Antilla Barcelona, but nowhere will you find a more authentically Argentine ambience than in the old factory that houses **Tinta Roja** (pictured). It is named after one of the most famous tango songs of all time – you'll find the lyrics pinned up behind the bar, amid walls thickly plastered in the yellowing posters of yesterday's tango stars. It's also, appropriately enough, as warm and snug as

Situated in the Modernista fantasy Casa Comalat, Distrito Diagonal is emerging from obscurity to become one of *the* places to be seen in 2003. It attracts a slightly older crowd, with an easygoing atmosphere bathed in red light, sounds from nu jazz to deep house and plenty of chairs to sink into. Admission to one-off events with international DJs (Sandy Rivera, Dannys Rampling and Morales) cost around €10.

Domèstic

C/Diputació 215 (93 453 16 61). Metro Universitat. **Open** 7pm-2.30am Tue-Thur, Sun; 7pm-3am Fri, Sat. Closed 2wks Aug. **Credit** AmEx, DC, MC, V. **Map** p342 C5.

Yet another of the rash of bar-club-restaurants to hit the city, here with the emphasis on the drinking side, Domèstic has chilled music, bold colours and battered leather sofas that give it a laidback, lived-in feel. Token food is served in the dining room at the front from 9pm to midnight.

La Fira

C/Provença 171 (no phone). Metro Hospital Clínic. **Open** 10pm-3am Tue-Thur; 10.30pm-4.30am Fri, Sat. **No credit cards. Map** p338 C4.

A warehouse-sized space filled with an extraordinary haphazard collection of old funfair detritus: merry-go-round horses, one-armed bandits, crazy mirrors and more. Out of their environment of childhood innocence, they can seem a little macabre; grotesquely smiling clowns' faces leer at the beefcake barmen, the new masters of the big top, as they dish out drinks to a raucous studenty crowd to the sounds of tacky pop.

Fuse

C/Roger de Llúria 40 (93 301 74 99). Metro Passeig de Gràcia. **Open** 11pm-4.30am Thur-Sat. **No credit cards. Map** p342 D5.

'A laboratory of the sensations' – that means they lay on the grub before carting off the tables, as at

a 19th-century boudoir. It's all very Moulin Rouge here, right down to the swinging trapeze hovering above an avant-garde theatre and the freakish mannequins looking down from above. Native choreographers Hugo and Carmen offer weekly classes in the art of seduction.

Agua de Luna

C/Viladomat 211 (93 410 04 40/ www.aguadeluna.com). Metro Rocafort. **Open** 10pm-3am Wed, Thur; 11pm-4am Fri, Sat; 8pm-4am Sun. **Admission** (incl 1 drink) €6 Fri, €9 Sat. **No credit cards. Map** p341 B5.

Free salsa, merengue, rueda and cha-cha-cha classes at 11.30pm Thur.

Antilla BCN

C/Aragó 141 (93 451 45 64/www.antilla salsa.com). Metro Urgell. **Open** 11pm-4am Mon-Thur, Sun; 11pm-5.30am Fri, Sat. **Admission** €10 (incl 1 drink). **No credit cards. Map** p338 C4.

Beginners' salsa classes are 10-11pm Mon, Wed-Fri, for €9. Free tango classes at 11pm on Tue with champions Diego and Pilar.

Tinta Roja

C/Creu dels Molers 17 (93 443 32 43). Metro Poble Sec. **Open** 8pm-1am Tue-Thur, Sun; 8pm-3am Fri, Sat. **Admission** *Before midnight* (incl 1 drink) €8. *After midnight* free. Closed 2wks Aug. **No credit cards. Map** p341 B6.

Live tango, flamenco and jazz Thur-Sat. Tango classes are 9.30-11pm and cost €96 for two months; book ahead.

any parish hall disco – only the menu is fashionably globe-trotting and the changeover actually makes for a pleasurable anticipation as the crowd builds up in the shiny white entry bar. There's a surge into the spacious back room around 1am, where chunky house resounds off fat tapering pillars, and a fashionable but not ridiculous crowd has room to breathe and really dance.

El Otro

C/Valencia 166, Eixample (no phone). Metro Universitat. **Open** 10.30pm-3am Tue-Sat. **No credit cards.** **Map** p338 C4.

With swathes of coloured light spilling out in unexpected directions on to creamy walls, El Otro is a bar that's stylish without committing to any particular fashion. With resident DJs serving up a mixed menu of beats and tunes, frequent exhibitions and occasional concerts, it's a relaxed way to start the night.

The Pop Bar

C/Aribau 103 (93 451 29 58). Metro Hospital Clínic. **Open** 9pm-3.30am Wed-Sun. **Credit** AmEx, DC, MC, V. **Map** p338 C4.

Balls to house, hip hop and the rest of it; instead, here's pure, unadulterated pop and one-hit wonders that you never thought you'd hear again (early Kylie, Rick Astley and Donna Summer). Retro decor is funky brown, orange and white; polka dot toilets, and deep orange, squidgy sofa booths. Two thumbs up for big-screen FashionTV, a welcome change from all those darned projections.

Risco

C/Balmes 49 (93 423 12 85/www.nightsungroup. com). Metro Hospital Clínic. **Open** 11pm-3am Wed-Sun. **Admission** (incl 1 drink) €9. **Credit** MC, V. **Map** p338 D4.

Don't be fooled by the grim entrance under the overhanging concrete portal of a car park: past the door staff, Risco unfolds as a multi-level dancefloor with wall collages, glowing bars and corners dark enough to sulk in. With bar hours, it's basically Nightsun's warm-up club: watch out for big-name DJs, one-off nights and tickets that get you past the queues at Discothèque and Terrrazza, as well as unhinged comedown session Bloody Mary on Sunday night.

Santécafé

C/Comte d'Urgell 171 (93 323 78 32). Metro Hospital Clínic. **Open** 8am-3am Mon-Fri; 5pm-3am Sat, Sun. Closed 2wks Aug. **No credit cards.** **Map** p338 C4.

Look out for the tangerine dream with goldfish tank windows on the corner of Rosselló. Filled with a young, bespectacled crowd from the Jarvis Cocker school of cool, nursing cocktails to the tune of Parisian lounge from the Hotel Costes, funkAfusion, downtempo and deep house.

Gràcia

Gusto

C/Francisco Giner 24 (no phone). Metro Diagonal. **Open** 11.30pm-2.30am Wed, Thur; 11.30pm-3am Fri, Sat. **No credit cards.** **Map** p338 D3.

Everything – and everyone – is sleek and sexy at **Danzatoria**. *See p261.*

A young crowd, a neat little front bar where the DJ plays pre-club electronica, and a turquoise-lit back room that feels weirdly outdoors, although, in fact, it isn't: the sand-strewn floor makes for either an indoor beach or a room-sized ashtray.

Heliogabal

C/Ramon y Cajal 80 (no phone). Metro Joanic. **Open** midnight-5am Thur-Sat. **No credit cards.** **Map** p339 E3.

Gràcia can go a little dead after the bars close, but fear not, hidden behind the red and black shutter is this semi-secret late-night hideout that starts to fill up when other places empty out. Live music and performances after midnight are followed by sociable boozing till sun-up.

Illusion

C/Lepant 408 (93 347 36 00/www.matineegroup. com). Metro Alfons X. **Open** midnight-6am Fri, Sat; 7pm-midnight Sun. **Admission** (incl 1 drink) €6 Fri; €9 Sat; €7.80 Sun. **No credit cards.** **Map** p339 F3.

On Sunday evenings, the cafés along Lepant are full of hyped-up teenagers with tight tops and gelled hair getting clear the story of the weekend so far, before it enters its last mad paroxysm at Illusion. This is the Cathedral Sunday T-Dance Session: a gay/mixed maelstrom with drag performers urging on a thrill-hungry crowd.

KGB

C/Alegre de Dalt 55 (93 210 59 06). Metro Joanic. **Open** 1am-5.30am Fri, Sat. **Admission** (incl 1 drink) €9; (incl 2 drinks) €11. **No credit cards.** **Map** p339 E3.

An echoing underground bunker, dark and more than a little menacing, which has been a fixture for wayward Gràcia youth since the '80s. Although the management has tried other styles, the musical policy always comes back to techno meted out by residents Blueman, Mil Caras and Cesar Gas. If you're up for some hard beats after hours it could hit the spot, but it's not for the faint-hearted.

Mond Bar

C/Plaça del Sol (93 272 09 10/www.mondclub.com). Metro Fontana. **Open** 8.30pm-3am daily. **No credit cards.** **Map** p338 D3.

Over the little footbridge from the main square, this diminutive bar on the Plaça del Sol is Mond Club's little sister, and all week it runs youth-team try-outs for aspiring and usually very good local DJs. The ambience is cliquey and in-the-know, but hospitable, with the emphasis on the offbeat fashion move and the recondite but spot-on musical reference.

Mond Club

Sala Cibeles, C/Còrsega 363 (93 272 09 10/ www.mondclub.com). Metro Diagonal. **Open** 12.30-6am Fri. **Admission** €10. **No credit cards.** **Map** p338 D4.

Most clubs have an agenda, but Mond has a slogan too – 'Pop will make us free' – and entering its third

year of existence it shows no sign of wavering. Resident DJs like Buenavista mix '60s rarities, '80s Spanish chart hits and the latest London indie sensation, always seeking that indefinable factor that defines 'pop'. Packed every week after 3am, it's at its best when celebrity guest DJs (Andy Votel, Jarvis Cocker) grace the stage of Sala Cibeles, the vintage dancehall that hosts the club.

Otto Zutz

C/Lincoln 15 (93 238 07 22/www.ottozutz.com). FGC Gràcia. **Open** midnight-5am Tue-Thur; midnight-6am Fri, Sat. **Admission** (incl 1 drink) €15. **Credit** AmEx, DC, MC, V. **Map** p338 D3.

Otto Zutz has been around a while, so the absolute indifference with which the door staff usher in the desirables and charge the rest is understandable: they've seen them all, from Prince in his heyday, through Bono, who flew in from Florence for a private party, to the Spice Girls in the days when they were five. Besides, it's not as if there's room to waste on people who haven't made an effort. The illusion of space on the downstairs dancefloor is due to that enormous mirror. The soul/funk floor is no bigger, and to get into the VIP room at the top you'll have to summon whatever reserves of inner glamour are left to you after getting in.

Tibidabo & Zona Alta

Atlantic Bar

C/Lluís Muntadas 2 (93 418 71 61). FGC Av Tibidabo/60 bus. **Open** 10.30pm-4.30am Thur-Sat. **Admission** (incl 1 drink) €8. **Credit** MC, V.

Glam has been overruled by cheese at this mansion-club high above the city; expect go-go dancers dripping gold and juggling fire, and taxi dancers shimmying to DJ Juan Diaz's repertoire of pop España, salsa, dance and house. It's at its best in the summertime when the paved terraces and tropical gardens are bedecked with cool, white canopies; if you're truly deserving of red carpet treatment, you may even get to hang in the plunge pool.

Bikini

C/Déu i Mata 105 (93 322 08 00/www.bikinibcn. com). Metro Les Corts/15, 30, 43, 59 bus. **Open** midnight-4.30am Tue-Thur; midnight-5.30am Fri, Sat. **Admission** (incl 1 drink) €9. **Credit** AmEx, V. **Map** p337 B3.

Tucked away at the back of L'Illa shopping centre, Bikini has been through various incarnations since the '50s; the present avatar is a three-room club. The main room has one of the best concert sound systems in town, and after the gig it gets to run through its paces with chart rock and pop; while the Arutanga room plays salsa and Latin, while the Dry Room features a distinctly wet bar with plentiful seating.

Danzatoria

Avda Tibidabo 61 (93 211 62 61). FGC Avda Tibidabo. **Open** 11pm-3am Wed-Sun. **Credit** MC, V.

Arts & Entertainment

Danzatoria (the club formerly known as Partycular) scores big time as the most lavishly sexy in Barcelona; its powder-white VIP reception hall, sleek chrome bars and erotic chill-out zones are peppered with Barcelona's most beautiful assets. After climbing the sweeping staircase to a string of glowing red party rooms, be sure to pause for effect before clattering your best stilettos down the steel staircases leading to cake layers of palm-filled gardens, and with any luck, to some gorgeous-but-shallow creature stretched out on a deckchair with a bucket of iced champagne. Expect to pay €8 and upwards for your favourite tipple.

Mirablau

Plaça Doctor Andreu (93 418 58 79). FGC Av Tibidabo, then Tramvia Blau. **Open** 11am-4.30am Mon-Thur, Sun; 11am-5am Fri, Sat. **Credit** MC, V.
Wander up the hill to the end of Avda Tibidabo after you've been kicked out of Danzatoria (*see above*) and you'll find the doors to one of the city's best views still open. If you've got sufficient reserves of energy left to dance, cheesy Spanish pop music rules the dancefloor till dawn.

Universal

C/Marià Cubi 182 bis-184 (93 201 35 96). FGC Muntaner. **Open** 11pm-4.30am Mon-Sat. **Credit** MC, V. **Map** p338 C3.
The production values of this well-established club on the corner of C/Marià Cubi and C/Santalo are unstinting, but the prices are steep. Multi-angled lights on clustered gantries set up a flattering, cabaret-like semi-darkness on the ground floor, through which you can shimmy to the diagonal bar or try a disembodied boogie. Alternatively, float upstairs to the more laid-back first-floor bar, with its blue-velvet seats, gleaming grand piano, heavy curtains and chandeliers like anchors wrapped in tulle and fairy lights. The usual weekend crowd is moneyed but not oppressively cool, and the music policy is mainstream.

Poblenou

The Loft

C/Pamplona 88 (93 272 0910/www.theloftclub.com). Metro Bogatell or Marina. **Open** 1am-6am Fri, Sat. **Admission** (incl 1 drink) €12. **No credit cards**. **Map** p343 F6.
Razzmatazz has two secondary stages, whose run-down entrance is just around the corner. The Loft occupies both to run a third-storey experiment in electronic urban living. The smaller room Lo-li-ta leans towards electro-hedonism through an ongoing relationship with label Gigolo and groups like Miss Kittin and the Hacker, while the main floor can call on residents DJD!, Mouseup and Sideral. The whole space is spare and post-industrial, with a fire exit that leads to an outside walkway where you can gaze up at the stars or down at Razz Club (*see below*) pounding away next door.

Lokotron

C/Almogàvers 86-88 (no phone). Metro Marina/ 6, 40, 42, 141, N6 bus. **Open** 5pm-midnight Sun. **Admission** (incl 1 drink) €9; (incl 2 drinks) €12. **No credit cards**. **Map** p343 F6.
A dark warehouse teetering on the edge of the railway tracks, this place vibrates to looped techno for a Sunday night crowd in deep denial. You don't have to be loco to dig it, but it helps.

Oven

C/Ramón Turro 126 (93 221 06 02). Metro Poblenou. **Open** 1.30pm-3am Mon-Thur, Sun; 1.30pm-4pm, 9pm-3am Fri, Sat. **Credit** AmEx, MC, V. **Map** p343 F6.
Dropped like a design experiment into the land that time forgot, Oven convinces flocks of glitterati that this post-industrial hinterland is the place for dinner or drinks. It embodies warehouse-chic with acres of space, great sails lit with rainbow colours hanging from the ceiling, deep red sofas, funhouse curved mirrors, and a high priest DJ spinning his stuff before an altar to religious and cartoon deities.

Razz Club

Razzmatazz, C/Almogàvers 122 (93 272 09 10/ www.salarazzmatazz.com). Metro Marina or Bogatell. **Open** 1-5.30am Fri, Sat. **Admission** (incl 1 drink) €10. **No credit cards**. **Map** p343 F6.
On Fridays and Saturdays the cavernous main concert hall of Razzmatazz opens up as a giant indie-flavoured disco, with resident DJ Amable and companions at the decks, as well as occasional celeb invitees (notably Mani from the Stone Roses). Check the website for special parties – often coinciding with a band that's in town. Once inside you can roam freely through two other bars at the front of the building: the Pop Bar, with a select techno-pop playlist; and on the third floor, doom-laden industrial gothic from DJ Akelarre in Templebeat.

Outer limits

Planet

Avda Industria 12, Sant Just Desvern (93 499 03 42/ www.elmirador.org). Bus 63. **Open** midnight-5.30am Fri, Sat. **Admission** (incl 1 drink) €9; (incl 2 drinks) €12. **No credit cards**.
In the suburb/town of Sant Just Desvern on the western edge of metropolitan Barcelona, Planet is a post-industrial, sci-fi fantasy housed in an ex-cement factory, with a crystal-ceilinged, flying saucer-like restaurant 30m (100ft) up the factory's chimney. Designed by Alfredo Arribas, architect of the Torres de Avila (*see p257*), it sits next door to Ricard Bofill's famous Walden Seven building. Music is techno/ house, with a wide range of programming, including concerts by international groups, performances by bizarre circus artists and a bevy of very skilled go-go dancers. At the very top of the chimney, 100m (330ft) up, there's a viewing area from where you can gaze down on the city's twinkling lights.

Sport & Fitness

All hail the mighty Barça.

Estadi Olímpic de Montjuïc.

The excellent climate, coastal location and the legacy of the '92 Olympics combine to give the city many advantages for active sport. On the other hand, with the lack of large green spaces in the central city, most key sporting facilities are located much further afield. And while the sporting calendar features a wide range of top-level events, the sporting public and media have one overriding obsession: el Barça – Futbol Club Barcelona. The club, with its 100,000 paid-up members, dominates not only football but practically all locally important team sports.

Spectator sports

Tickets can often be purchased by credit card with **Servi-Caixa** or **Tel-entrada** (*see p208*). Check www. agendabcn.com for event info.

Major sports venues

Montjuïc venues
Estadi Olímpic de Montjuïc *Passeig Olímpic 17-19 (93 426 20 89). Metro Espanya, then escalators, or Paral.lel, then Funicular de Montjuïc/50 bus.* **Map** p339 A6.

Palau Sant Jordi *Passeig Olímpic 5-7 (93 426 20 89). Metro Espanya, then escalators, or Paral.lel, then Funicular de Montjuïc.* **Map** p341 A6.
Palau dels Esports *C/Joaquim Blume (93 423 15 41). Metro Espanya or Poble Sec.* **Map** p341 B5-6. These jewels in the Olympic crown are now reserved for special events and are underused for sport. However, the Estadi Olímpic is the home of the Espanyol football club (*see p265*) and in 2003 the Palau Sant Jordi is to host both the finals of the basketball Euroleague and the World Swimming Championships (*see p266*). Public transport access to the Estadi Olímpic-Palau Sant Jordi area has been improved but can still be awkward.

Basketball

Although way behind soccer, basketball is the number two team sport, and the Spanish ACB league is probably the strongest national competition in Europe. The season runs from September to early June, with most ACB games played on weekend evenings and European games during the week. In May 2003, the Palau Sant Jordi stages the final play-offs of the Euroleague. Barcelona area ACB teams also include Badalona's DKV Joventut and Basquet Manresa.

How to be a Barça fan

The first rule of being a Barça fan is to call yourself an arse. Yes, Barça fans are widely known, even among themselves, as *culés*, or 'bums'. It's not as bad as it sounds. The name originated from the fans' practice of sitting along the high perimeter wall of the old, open-terraced stadium at Les Corts, offering a unique view to passers-by. The second, and possibly most important rule of being a Barça fan, is to be rabidly *antimadridista* and to celebrate the defeats of 'Franco's team' with as much joy as the victories of your own. Any other team that puts one over on 'the scum' will be adopted as a much loved brother and their shirts sold outside the stadium and worn with pride. Baffled tourists might, therefore, be greeted by the sight of *culés* waving Tenerife flags (plucky Tenerife dramatically denied Real Madrid the Spanish title twice in the 1990s).

A good Barça fan is not known for his *joie de vivre* and should maintain a cynical view throughout triumph and defeat. When the team plays badly it is because there are too many overpaid stars. When the team plays well, it is because there are too many overpaid stars, and so on.

Every Barça fan should attend the stadium equipped with a white handkerchief in case a *pañolada* is called for. This event is a mass waving of handkerchiefs to express dissatisfaction with the team's performance (a distortion of the bullfighting tradition, where the same is done to demand a bull's ear as a prize for a *torero*).

Anyone can qualify to be a Barça fan (it is the club with the most season-ticket holders and fan clubs in the world) and it should be remembered that at least half of *culés* are respectable, middle-aged Catalan ladies –

who, incidentally, are also among the most vocal and foul-mouthed of the team's fans, especially if Madrid are in town.

The true Barça fan is a masochist, deriving as much pleasure from losing as winning. A bad result gives more scope for heated, Sunday afternoon analyses. Catalans use football as a conversational crutch to the same extent that the English talk about the weather. Defeats can always be attributed to machinations by the Spanish government to undermine the Catalan team. All of Madrid's successes should be attributed to the same shadowy conspiracy.

It is optional to learn the words to *el himno*, which is played before every match: *Tot el camp es un clam* ('The whole stadium is as one'), *Som la gent blaugrana* ('We are the blue and purple people'), then after a bit that no one bothers to sing, the stirring chorus: *Tenim un nom que sap totom: Barça, Bar-ça, Baaaar- ça!* ('Everyone knows our name').

FC Barcelona

Palau Blaugrana, Avda Arístides Maillol, Les Corts (93 496 36 75/www.fcbarcelona.com). Metro Maria Cristina or Collblanc. **Ticket office** 9am-1.30pm, 3.30-6pm Mon-Thur; 9am-2.30pm Fri; 2hrs before a game. (Tickets available from 1 day before match). **Tickets** €8-€24. **No credit cards.**

With new Yugoslav coach Pesic, and Balkan giants Fucka and Bodiroga drafted in to beef up the team, fans are hopeful that the Slavic-emboldened Barça basketball team might finally be able to translate its frequent ACB trophies into the much coveted but ever-elusive European triumph. Booking for the 8,000 capacity Palau Blaugrana is advisable.

Bullfighting

Plaza de Toros Monumental

Gran Via de les Corts Catalanes 749, Eixample (93 245 58 04/93 215 95 70). Metro Monumental. **Open** *Bullfights* Apr-Sept 6-7pm Sun. *Museum* Apr-Sept 10.30am-2pm, 4-7pm daily. **Advance tickets** also available from Servi-Caixa. **Admission** *Bullfights* €18-€95. *Museum* €4, €3 concessions. **No credit cards. Map** p343 F5.

This is the only functioning bullring in the city. Fights are held on Sundays in season, but local interest in bullfighting is low, and a card of the most prestigious *toreros* is needed to even half-fill it.

Arts & Entertainment

Football

The beautiful game rules the roost in Spanish sport, and the dominance of **FC Barcelona** is simply overwhelming. It is vested with more than the usual local pride. For decades it has been the single most important symbol of Catalan identity. Along with that spirit come vast resources – the team is loaded. Still, that doesn't mean it wins. In fact, the last trophy won by a team from Barcelona went to the city's other first division club, **RCD Espanyol**, which clinched the Spanish Cup in 2000. Lower division teams in the city include the Gràcia-based **Europa** club and Poblenou's **Jupiter** – entertaining to watch but probably condemned to semi-pro status due to Barça's power.

FC Barcelona

Nou Camp, Avda Aristides Maillol, Les Corts (93 496 36 00/www.fcbarcelona.com). Metro Maria Cristina or Collblanc. **Ticket office** 9am-1.30pm, 3.30-6pm Mon-Thur; 9am-2.30pm Fri; 2hrs before a game. (Tickets available 1 wk before each match). **Tickets** €19-€93. **Advance tickets** (league games only) Servi-Caixa. **Credit** DC, MC, V. **Map** p337 A3.
The 98,000-capacity Nou Camp, the largest stadium in Europe, is majestic even when empty. When it's full and Kluivert, Luis Enrique and company are in good touch, it can be close to football heaven. For all but the biggest games, getting in has been made a little easier by a new scheme that lets members 'rent out' their permanently reserved seats. So now there are several ticket options: firstly, the club usually puts around 4,000 seats on sale a week before the match; phone to find out exactly when and queue an hour or two beforehand at the ticket office at the intersection of Travessera de les Corts and Avda Aristides Mailliol. Next, there's a trickle of rented-out seats, located all over the ground, which become available at the ticket office as and when members decide to free them up. For Spanish league games only, all these official tickets can also be bought through Servi-Caixa. The final, unofficial option is to go to the entrance gates and either try the ticket touts or just ask around if anyone has an extra ticket. Other possibilities for fans include the Barça B team's matches in the 16,000-seat Miniestadi over the road from Nou Camp, and the extremely popular Barça museum and stadium tours. First team training sessions are mostly closed to the public, but if you're deeply devoted you can watch when they use the wire-fenced Masia ground beside the main stadium (usual start time is 10.30am).

RCD Espanyol

Estadi Olímpic de Montjuïc, Passeig Olímpic 17-19, Montjuïc (93 292 77 00/www.rcdespanyol.com). Metro Espanya, then escalators or Paral.lel, then Funicular de Montjuïc/50 bus. **Ticket office** 10am-1.30pm, 5-8pm Fri; 10am-2pm Sat; 10am-match time on match days. **Tickets** €20-€42. **Credit** V. **Map** p341 A6.

The Espanyol club has 25,000 season ticket holders and a 60,000-seat athletics stadium to play in, so getting a ticket is no problem. This middle-of-the-table team has a reputation as an occasional giant killer. A day or two before matches, tickets can be bought at the booths to the right of the stadium entrance and also through Servi-Caixa machines. Free buses for ticket holders run from a stop by Plaça Espanya to the stadium, starting 90 minutes before kick-off.

Other team sports

Handball and roller hockey both have strong followings here, and it's no surprise to learn that the dominant teams are those of **FC Barcelona**, which play in the Palau Blaugrana. In both sports the club has won recent European championships.

Barcelona Dragons

Estadi Olímpic de Montjuïc, Passeig Olímpic 17-19, Montjuïc (93 425 49 49/www.dragons.es). Metro Espanya or Paral.lel, then Funicular de Montjuïc. **Ticket office** match days. **Tickets** €8-€25 per game. **Advance tickets** Caixa de Catalunya or Servi-Caixa. **Credit** (advance tickets) MC, V. **Map** p341 A6.
The city's American football team, the Dragons, has successfully built up a fan base and during their April-June season crowds of 10,000 often turn up for the gridiron game. The players are mostly from the US, and, indeed, the whole six-team European league is funded by the American NFL. After a recent deal with FC Barcelona, the Dragons now play their games in the club's Miniestadi and wear its insignia.

Special events

Barcelona Marathon

Information & entry forms *C/Jonqueres 16, 15°, Born (93 268 01 14/www.redestb.es/marathon_cat). Metro Urquinaona.* **Open** *Office* 5.30-8.30pm Mon-Fri. **Date** 16 March 2003. **Fee** €35-€40. **No credit cards. Map** p344 B1.
Barcelona has redesigned its annual marathon to build up its attractiveness for runners and the public. The course is now entirely urban and flat, with a start and finish next to Plaça Espanya, and a final section skirting along the seafront. It attracts around 4,000 athletes. There is also a half-marathon run as part of the festival of La Mercè in late September, while the city's largest fun-run is the 11km (seven mile) Cursa de El Corte Inglés in May, which attracts around 50,000 participants a year (contact El Corte Inglés, 93 270 17 30/www.elcorteingles.com).

Motor sports

Circuit de Catalunya, Carretera de Parets del Vallès a Granollers, Montmeló, Outer Limits (93 571 97 00/www.circuitcat.com). By car C17 north to Parets del Vallès exit (20km/13 miles). **Times & tickets** vary according to competition; available from Servi-Caixa. **Credit** MC, V.

The Spanish Formula One Grand Prix takes place just outside Barcelona at the Circuit de Catalunya, running from 2-4 May in 2003. There is a long tradition of motorcycle racing in the region, and two-wheeled competitions at the circuit are almost as popular. The biggest of these is the Catalunya Grand Prix in mid June. The track is used by the public, driving their own cars, on 12 weekends a year.

Tennis

Reial Club de Tennis Barcelona-1899, C/Bosch i Gimpera 5-13, Les Corts (93 203 78 52/ www.rctb1899.es). Bus 63, 78. **Open** (members only except during competitions) 8am-10pm daily. **Ticket office** (during competitions) 9am-6pm daily. **Tickets** €19.80-€64. **Credit** AmEx, MC, V.

The big event in Barcelona tennis is the annual Trofeig Comte de Godó, played on clay at the exclusive Reial Club de Tennis in Pedralbes. Part of the men's ATP tour, it attracts many of the world's top players, and invariably almost a full roll-call of the strong 'Spanish Armada' of tennis stars. The 2003 tournament runs from 19-27 April. Tickets available through Servi-Caixa.

World Swimming Championships 2003

Info 93 402 30 60. **Dates** July 13-17 2003.

Barcelona's most important sporting event since the '92 Olympics takes place 13-27 July 2003, when the city stages the quadrennial World Swimming Championships. In the main venue, the Palau Sant Jordi, a 50m pool is to be built specially for the two weeks of competition, while diving and other events will use the existing Montjuïc pools and the Club de Natació Atlètic Barceloneta (*see p268*). Open water events will start and finish at the foot of the Rambla under Columbus' gaze. Barceloneta's beach and portside area is to be another focus with entertainment, terrace restaurants and exhibitions.

Active sports/fitness

The Barcelona Olympics were the stimulus for a great improvement in sporting infrastructure at local level. The 237 municipally run facilities now include a good network of *poliesportius* or sports centres, most of which have a gym with fitness equipment, a hall for indoor sports and a covered swimming pool, as well as more specialised facilities that vary from centre to centre. Charges are low and you don't have to be a resident to use them.

All of Barcelona's beaches have wheelchair ramps and almost all of the city's pools are fully equipped for disabled people. Check with the **Servei d'Informació Esportiva** (*see below*) for details.

Servei d'Informació Esportiva

Avda de l'Estadi 30-40, Montjuïc (information 93 402 30 00). Metro Espanya, then escalators, or Paral.lel, then Funicular de Montjuïc/50 bus.

Piscina Bernat Picornell. *See p268.*

Open *25 Sept-23 June* 8am-2.30pm, 4-6.10pm Mon-Thur; 8am-2.30pm Fri. *24 June-24 Sept* 8am-2.30pm Mon-Thur. **Map** p341 A6.

The Ajuntament's sports information service is based in the Piscina Bernat Picornell building. Call for information on sports facilities (although not all the staff speak English), or consult the Ajuntament's very thorough listings on the Esports section of their website www.bcn.es

Bowling

Bowling Pedralbes

Avda Dr Marañón 11, Les Corts (93 333 03 52). Metro Collblanc. **Open** 10am-2am Mon-Thur; 10am-4am Fri, Sat; 10am-midnight Sun. (Aug from 5pm only). **Rates** (per person per game) €1.50 until 5pm Mon-Fri; €2.50 from 5pm Mon-Thur, until 5pm Sat, Sun; €3.60 from 5pm Fri-Sun. **Credit** MC, V.

This place doesn't just have 14 bowling alleys, it's also got snooker, pool and that favourite Catalan bar sport, *futbolín* (table football). It's cheaper and less busy before 5pm, but if it's full you can leave your name so that you can be paged at the bar when a lane becomes free. Shoe hire available.

Cycling

The city's cycle route network is growing steadily, but visitors still need to be extremely cautious. There are gaps in the network, and regular traffic can be a maelstrom, with little respect for cyclists or cycle lanes. Bikes can be hired and tourist offices sometimes have cycle route maps. The waterfront is a popular area for leisure riding, or try the spectacular Carretera de les Aigües, a flat gravel road which skirts along the side of Collserola mountain (to avoid a killer climb getting up there, take your bike on the FGC to Peu del Funicular station, then take the Funicular de Vallvidrera to the midway stop). For more serious mountain biking, the back of the Collserola hills offers many good forest trails (*see* **A walk in the woods** *p126*).

Probike

C/Villarroel 184, Eixample (93 419 78 89). Metro Hospital Clínic. **Open** 4.30-8.30pm Mon; 10.30am-2pm, 4.30-8.30pm Tue-Sat. **Credit** AmEx, MC, V. **Map** p338 C4.

This impressively large bike shop is a focal point for mountain bikers, with excellent equipment and service departments, as well as maps and information resources. There's also a Probike club that organizes regular excursions ranging from day-trips to a summertime Pyrenees traverse.

Football

Barcelona International Football League

Information 93 218 67 31/649 261 328/ nicksimonsbcn@yahoo.co.uk.

A mixture of locals and foreigners make up this social soccer league.There are currently 17 teams that play matches from September to June, and newcomers are welcome.

Golf

Catalonia has a growing reputation as a golfing holiday destination, and there are some good courses near Barcelona. Visitors may need to book in advance and show proof of a handicap. Courses can be very full at weekends.

Club de Golf Sant Cugat

C/Villa, Sant Cugat del Vallès, Outer Limits (93 674 39 58). By car Túnel de Vallvidrera (C16) to Valldoreix/by train FGC from Plaça Catalunya to Sant Cugat. **Open** *June-Oct* 8am-8.30pm Mon; 7.30am-8.30pm Tue-Fri; 7am-9pm Sat, Sun. *Nov-May* 8am-5.30pm Mon; 7.30am-5.30pm Tue-Fri; 7am-5.30pm Sat, Sun. **Rates** (non-members) €50 Mon; €65 Tue-Fri; €130 Sat, Sun. Club hire €19. **Credit** MC, V.

This tight, attractive course is one of the oldest in Spain, and the easiest to reach from central Barcelona. It is five minutes' walk from the Sant Cugat station. Clubs can be hired and green fees give access to a bar, restaurant and outdoor pool.

Club de Golf Terramar

Camí de la Carrerada, Sitges (93 894 05 80). By car C31 through Sitges, 3km (2 miles) toward Vilanova. By train RENFE from Sants or Passeig de Gràcia, then taxi. **Open** *July-Sept* 8am-10pm daily. *Oct-June* 8am-10pm Mon, Wed-Sun. **Rates** (non-members) €55 Mon-Fri; €80 Sat, Sun. Club hire €20. **Credit** MC.

A few minutes taxi ride from Sitges, this 18-hole course has a relaxed coastal setting. Well equipped for visitors with a pleasant clubhouse and quite reasonable green fees.

Gyms/fitness centres

The busy sport centres run by the city are cheaper and generally more user-friendly than most of the city's private clubs. Phone the **Servei d'Informació Esportiva** (*see p266*) for centres with the right facilities.

Centres de Fitness DiR

C/Casp 34, Eixample (901 30 40 30/93 450 48 18/www.dirfitness.es). Metro Catalunya. **Open** 7am-11pm Mon-Fri; 9am-3pm Sat, Sun. **Rates** €26 for 7 days, then €3.80 per day. **Credit** V. **Map** p344 B1.

This large private chain has ten fitness centres scattered around the city, and among them they offer an excellent range of facilities as well as numerous classes in a wide range of physical activities from spinning to 'mind-body'. Additional installations vary from a huge outdoor pool (at DiR Diagonal) to a squash centre (DiR Campus). A one-week membership is available for the truly dedicated. **Branches**: DiR Campus, Avda Dr Marañón 17, Les Corts (93 448 41 41); DiR Diagonal, C/Ganduxer 25-7 Eixample (93 202 22 02) and throughout the city.

Europolis

Travessera de les Corts 252-254, Zona Alta (93 363 29 92). Metro Les Corts. **Open** 7am-11pm Mon-Fri; 8am-8pm Sat; 9am-3pm Sun. **Rates** *Non-members* €8 per day. *Membership* approx €40 per month plus €65 joining fee. **Credit** MC, V.

Now managed by British fitness chain Holmes Place, the two municipally owned Europolis sports centres are as large and well-equipped as almost any private gym in town. Each has acres of shiny new exercise machines, as well as extensive pool areas, classes, private trainers and weight lifting equipment. Non-members pay a one-day entry fee. **Branch**: Europolis C/Sardenya 549-551, Gràcia (93 210 07 66).

Horse riding

Centre Hípic Sant Jordi

Carretera de Sant Llorenç Savall, Cànoves i Samalús (93 843 40 17). By car C58 or N150 to Sabadell, then B124 to Sant Llorenç Savall (42km/26 miles). **Rates** from €20 per 1½ hrs. **No credit cards**.

A riding establishment in the hills near Montseny specialising in guided cross-country excursions. Options for both beginners and experienced riders, and pony rides for smaller kids. Call ahead to book and get directions to the centre. English is spoken.

Arts & Entertainment

Ice skating

Skating Roger de Flor
C/Roger de Flor 168, Eixample (93 245 28 00/ www.skatingbcn.com). Metro Tetuan. **Open** 10.30am-1.30pm Tue; 10.30am-1.30pm, 5-9pm Wed, Thur; 10.30am-1.30pm, 5pm-midnight Fri, Sat; 10.30am-1.30pm, 5-9pm Sun. **Rates** (incl skates) €9.50; glove hire (gloves compulsory, €1.30). **Credit** MC, V. **Map** p343 E5.
A family-oriented ice rink in the Eixample. Any non-skaters in a group get in free and can hangout in the bar/cafeteria with other ice-aphobes.

Jogging & running

The seafront is the easiest option for an enjoyable jog. If you can handle the initial climb, or use other transport for the ascent, there are some exhilarating runs in Montjuïc, the Park Güell/Carmel hills, and Collserola (such as the Carretera de les Aïgues, *see* **Cycling** *p266*). For information on the Barcelona Marathon and other races, *see p265*.

Sailing

Sailing facilities are concentrated in the Port Olímpic. *See also chapter* **Ports**.

Base Nàutica de la Mar Bella
Avda Litoral, between Platja Bogatell & Platja de Mar Bella, Port Olímpic (93 221 04 32/ www.basenautica.org). Bus 36, 41. **Open** *June-Sept* 10am-8pm daily. *Oct-May* 10am-5pm daily. **Rates** 10hr windsurfing course €120; 16hr catamaran course €150; windsurf hire €15 per hr. **Credit** AmEx, DC, MC, V.
The Base Nàutica hires catamarans, kayaks and windsurf equipment to those who have experience with these craft. There's a proficiency test when you first get on the water (€12, but you only pay if you fail). There are also classes all year round for both beginners and improvers, and storage facilities for members' own small boats.

Swimming

When it's time to take the plunge, Barcelona offers a splashy array of all-weather pools great and small, as well as 25 outdoor pools that open from July to September, and several kilometres of beaches that are clean, safe for swimming, and patrolled by lifeguards in summer. For a full list of facilities and pools, contact the Servei d'Informació Deportiva (*see p266*).

Club de Natació Atlètic Barceloneta
Plaça del Mar, Port Vell (93 221 00 10). Metro Barceloneta, then 17, 39, 64 bus. **Open** *Oct-Apr* 7am-11pm Mon-Sat; 8am-5pm Sun. *May-Sept*

7am-11pm Mon-Sat; 8am-8pm Sun. **Admission** (non-members) €7 per day. **Credit** AmEx, DC, MC, V. **Map** p342 D7.
This beachside swimming complex has one indoor and one outdoor pool, with a third – outdoor, but heated – due for completion in spring 2003. New sauna and gym facilities are also being added to the municipally owned centre.

Piscina Bernat Picornell
Avda de l'Estadi 30-40, Montjuïc (93 423 40 41/ www.picornell.com). Metro Espanya, then escalators, or Paral.lel, then Funicular de Montjuic/50 bus. **Open** *June-Sept* 7am-midnight Mon-Fri; 7am-9pm Sat; 7.30am-8pm Sun. *Oct-May* 7am-midnight Mon-Fri; 7am-9pm Sat; 7.30am-4pm Sun. **Admission** *Oct-May* €8; €4 under-15s. *June-Sept* €4; €3 under-15s. Free under-6s. **No credit cards.** **Map** p341 A6.
The main swimming venue for the '92 Olympic Games, this Montjuïc centre has twin 50m pools, one indoor and one outdoor. Other facilities include a gym and climbing wall. During the Grec festival (*see p214*) it has special night swimming and film projection sessions. Oh, and there are regular naked swimming sessions here for nudists (9-11pm Sat, 4.15-6.15pm Sun).

Poliesportiu Marítim
Passeig Marítim 33 (93 224 04 40/www.claror. org). Metro Ciutadella-Vila Olímpica. **Open** 7am-midnight Mon-Fri; 8am-5pm Sat, Sun. **Admission** (non members) €12 Mon-Fri; €14 Sat, Sun; €30 weekly pass; €90 monthly pass. **Credit** MC, V. **Map** p343 E7.
This new spa-like municipal centre on Barceloneta beach specialises in thalassotherapy, or seawater-based healing. Therefore, it has eight indoor pools, mainly salt water, each with a different temperatures, use and intended effect. Other services include a gym and bike hire.

Tennis

Barcelona Tenís Olímpic
Passeig de la Vall d'Hebron 178-196, Vall d'Hebron (93 427 65 00/www.fctennis.org). Metro Montbau. **Open** 8am-11pm Mon-Fri; 8am-9pm Sat; 8am-7pm Sun. **Rates** (non-members) courts €11.20-€14.60 per hr; floodlights €4.20. **No credit cards.**
This 1992 Olympic tennis facility seems a bit distant from the centre of town, but it has a good metro connection to the centre, and offers 24 tennis courts (mostly clay), as well as paddle courts, racquet hire, and other sports services.

Centre de Tennis Montjuïc
C/Foixarda, Montjuïc (93 325 13 48). Bus 50. **Open** 8am-11pm Mon-Fri; 8am-10pm Sat, Sun. **Rates** €118 per term (3mths). **No credit cards.**
The main attraction here is that good rates are offered to non-members at this pleasant club above the Poble Espanyol. There are seven clay courts and racquet use can be arranged.

Theatre & Dance

Divided between the mainstream and the incomprehensibly exotic, Barcelona is far from Broadway.

The vibrancy of Catalan theatre, less dependent on plot or dialogue than on a festive blend of music, choreography, multimedia sleight-of-hand and slick production values, added to the *barcelonins'* love for light-hearted mega-productions, has sparked a spectacular growth in attendances in recent years. With television actors serving as theatre box-office draws these days, more and more venues are dedicated to unabashed money-making, with musical comedy at the forefront.

The same cannot be said for the much smaller number of venues that programme local contemporary dance, which has more energy and output than venues or audience numbers have been able or willing to absorb, meaning that many dancers leave the city and Catalan dance is often better known outside Spain. The remarkable gusto with which dancers took to contemporary and avant-garde dance after the repressive Franco years was not shared by programmers or audiences, leading to the attitude of self-sufficiency and collaboration that still characterises much contemporary dance in the city.

The tradition of sharing resources goes back to the legendary avant-garde school La Fábrica that operated during the '80s and trained artists such as Cesc Gelabert of Gelabert-Azzopardi, Maria Muñoz of Mal Pelo and Ramón Oller of Metros and is one which continues today with **La Caldera**, an association of local choreographers based in Gràcia and the collective La Porta, both of which programme small-scale and experimental works by local and foreign dancers at spaces such as **Conservas** (C/Sant Pau 58, 93 302 06 30), the **Mercat de les Flors** (*see p270*) and the **CCCB** (*see p90*). In what is slowly becoming a more diverse and stable scene, these groups coexist with established, internationally acclaimed companies such as Lanònima Imperial and Mudances, while younger artists take advantage of the new opportunities opening up, such as Sol Picó's residency at the TNC during the 2002/2003 season (*see p272*).

While contemporary dance is thriving, surprisingly, classical and modern ballet barely exist in the city. There are no major schools, no local companies and no consistent programming anywhere, and this is unlikely to

change in the near future. More surprising still is the range of flamenco shows in a city with little tradition of flamenco dance. Events such as the **Festival de Flamenco de Ciutat Vella** (*see p212*) are an opportunity to see flamenco in its pure state, and some of the best contemporary dancers such as Eva la Hierbabuena and Belén Maya regularly perform in the city. But it is the big shows by artists such as Antonio Canales, Sara Baras and Joaquin Cortés that have won the hearts of Barcelona audiences, and regularly sell out commercial theatres with their accessible, theatrical but quality performances.

VENUES

The winding weekend queues outside the city's large commercial theatres have their counterpoint in a network of modest independent spaces, where a dense, experimental text one week could easily be followed by a rollicking literary cabaret the next. Though these spaces receive some public funding, they remain poor cousins to massive projects such as the Generalitat-sponsored **Teatre Nacional de Catalunya** (*see p270*), and the **Ciutat del Teatre** (Theatre City) on Montjuïc, a rival project run by the Ajuntament. The Ciutat del Teatre brings together three buildings and seven stages around a common square: the innovative Mercat de les Flors space, the Teatre Lliure, and the new Institut del Teatre, the city's most prestigious training ground for the performing arts. A number of local theatre companies and musicians participate in the Ciutat del Teatre, although programming there does not differ greatly from that at the TNC.

SEASONS AND FESTIVALS

The main performing arts season runs from September to June, but the success of the **Festival del Grec** (*see p214*) has resulted in promoters presenting programmes in July and even August. The Grec festival is the best time to catch visiting theatre and dance companies, both Spanish and international. New theatre and dance are showcased at the amateur free-for-all **Marató de l'Espectacle** (*see p213*) and at the high-profile **Sitges Teatre Internacional** (www.sitges.com/teatre), both held in late May-early June. The annual **Dies** de Dansa (*see p214*) offers three days of national and international dance companies in various architecturally significant sites.

TICKETS AND TIMES

Main shows start late, around 9-10.30pm. Many theatres also have earlier (and cheaper) shows at 6-7pm. There are also late shows on weekend nights. Most theatres are closed on Mondays. Advance bookings are best made through the ticket sales operations of **Servi-Caixa** or **Tel-entrada** (*see p208*). Theatre box offices often take cash sales only.

The best place to find information are the *Guia del Ocio*, newspapers and, for Tel-entrada theatres, the *Guia del Teatre*, free at Caixa Catalunya branches.

Associació dels Professionals de Dansa de Catalunya

Via Laietana 52, entl 7, Sant Pere (93 268 24 73/ www.dancespain.com). Metro Urquinaona. **Open** 10am-2pm Mon-Fri. **Map** p3424 B2.
Acts as a clearing-house for the dance companies, with information on who is doing what at any time.

Major venues

Large central theatres such as the **Borràs** (Plaça Urquinaona 9, 93 412 15 82) and **Tivoli** (C/Casp 10-12, 93 412 20 63) are used for large-scale commercial productions, while the **Club Capitol** (La Rambla 138; 93 412 20 38) has been turned into a comedy hall after years as a cinema. The **Monumental** bullring and the **Barcelona Teatre Musical** at the Palau d'Esports (C/Guàrdia Urbana s/n, 93 423 64 63) where a long run of the musical *Gaudí* began in late 2002, are used for mega-shows in the off-season. Ballet and modern dance troupes occasionally appear at the **Liceu** opera house and even the **Teatre Nacional**, while cultural centres such as the **CCCB** (*see p90*) and art gallery **Metrònom** (*see p229*) are often used for contemporary dance.

L'Espai

Travessera de Gràcia 63, Gràcia (93 414 31 33/ http://cultura.gencat.es/espai). FGC Gràcia. **Box office** 6.30-9.30pm Tue-Sat; 5-7pm Sun. **Advance tickets** also from Servi-Caixa. **Tickets** €11-€20; €8.25-€15 concessions. **Credit** AmEx, DC, MC, V. **Map** p338 C3.
This Catalan government showcase for the performing arts combines dance shows (nearly always contemporary) with music. Highlights in 2003 will be new works by Mal Pelo, Cia Corchero Muñoz and the popular contemporary flamenco Increpación Danza company – in one of its increasingly rare performances in its home city. Things heat up in the spring with the popular En Dansa festival, and the autumns are quite good if you're here when the Festival Improvisa is on.

Institut del Teatre

Plaça Margarida Xirgú, Montjuïc (93 227 39 00/ www.diba.es/iteatre). Metro Espanya or Poble Sec/ 55 bus. **Box office** 2hrs before show Mon-Sat; 1hr before show Sun. **Advance tickets** also from Tel-entrada. **Admission** normally free. **No credit cards**. **Map** p341 B6.
Three stages in the spacious new premises of Barcelona's leading theatre and dance school offer intriguing (and often free) shows. Student productions and workshop projects with prestigious visiting directors are often staged. The expanded dance school also means more new choreography from student troupe IT Dansa. The fine collection of Performing Arts Museum is also here.

Mercat de les Flors

Plaça Margarida Xirgú, C/Lleida 59, Montjuïc (93 426 18 75/www.mercatflors.com). Metro Espanya or Poble Sec/55 bus. **Box office** 1hr before show. **Advance tickets** also from Tel-entrada & Palau de la Virreina. **Tickets** €6-€15 **No credit cards**. **Map** p341 B6.
A huge converted flower market with two spaces, the Mercat has long been the city's favoured venue for flexible staging and multidisciplinary performances. As some of its public theatre functions are being usurped by the neighbouring Lliure, it has diversified, adding more dance, world music and new media festivals, as well as occasional cinema.

Teatre Lliure

Plaça Margarida Xirgú, Montjuïc (93 289 27 70/ www.teatrelliure.com). Metro Espanya or Poble Sec/ 55 bus. **Box office** 11am-3pm, 4.30-9pm Mon-Fri; 4.30-9pm Sat; 4-6pm Sun. **Advance tickets** also from Tel-entrada. **Tickets** *Fabià Puigserver* €15 Tue, Wed; €20 Thur-Sun; €15 concessions Thur-Sun. *Espai Lliure* €12 Tue, Wed; €14 Thur-Sun; €10.50 concessions Thur-Sun. **Credit** MC, V. **Map** p341 B6.
Based in the overhauled Palace of Agriculture, built for the 1929 Universal Exhibition, Barcelona's most reputable theatre company presents classic and contemporary drama. Highlights in 2003 include *No To No* by contemporary composer Carles Santos in the spring (first seen at the 2002 Edinburgh Festival), followed by a Rossini opera. The Lliure continues to programme in its intimate space in Gràcia (C/Montseny 47; 93 218 92 51).

Teatre Nacional de Catalunya (TNC)

Plaça de les Arts 1, Eixample (93 306 57 00/ www.tnc.es). Metro Glòries. **Box office** noon-3pm, 4-9pm Mon; noon-9pm Tue-Sat; noon-6pm Sun. **Advance tickets** also from Servi-Caixa. **Tickets** €16.50-€24; concessions €12.50 Tue-Thur; €15 Fri-Sun. **Credit** MC, V. **Map** p341 F5.
Architect Ricard Bofill's Parthenon-like TNC is by far the most imposing theatre building in the city, standing alone on a grand lot near the Plaça de les Glòries. The TNC fills its technically superb halls with solid programming, including translated classics, Catalan and Spanish drama and all genres of dance. In 2003, Catalan versions of Molière and

Kafka will share the space with local authors, while rising choreographer Sol Picó is scheduled to unveil a new piece in late May.

Teatre Poliorama

La Rambla 115, Barri Gòtic (93 317 75 99/www.teatre poliorama.com). Metro Catalunya. **Box office** 5-9.30pm Tue-Thur; 5-10pm Fri, Sat; 5-7pm Sun. **Advance tickets** also from Servi-Caixa. **Tickets** varies. **Credit** MC, V. **Map** p344 A2.

A large comfortable theatre used by commercial producers tresX3 to present musicals and other major productions. Until June 2003 it will host Dagoll Dagom's new terror musical *Poe*, followed by a summer stint with Spain's Color dance company.

Other venues

Other spaces include **Artenbrut** (C/Perill 9-1, 93 457 97 05), **Nou Tantarantana** (C/Flors 22, 93 441 70 22), **Espai Escènic Joan Brossa** (C/Allada Vermell 13, 93 310 13 64/www.espai brossa.com) and **Conservas** (C/Sant Pau 58, 93 302 06 30). In July 2002, Conservas will run its successful four-day In Motion festival, with theatre, dance and film.

Sala Beckett

C/Alegre de Dalt 55 bis, Gràcia (93 284 53 12/ www.teatral.net/beckett). Metro Joanic. **Open** *Information office* 10am-2pm, 4-8pm Mon-Fri. *Box office* from 8pm Wed-Sat. **Advance tickets** also from Tel-entrada. **Tickets** €16; €11 concessions. **Credit** MC, V. **Map** p339 E3.

Founded by the Samuel Beckett-inspired Teatro Fronterizo group, whose guiding light, José Sanchis Sinisterra, is one of Spain's finest contemporary playwrights, this small Gràcia space offers challenging new theatre. Occasionally there are small productions in English.

Theatre companies

Along with those listed below, a few other companies to look for include the intelligently camp **Chanclettes** and the **Compañia Nacional Clásica** for versions of the Spanish masters. *See also p273* **Els Joglars**. James Attridge does a couple shows in English with the **TwelveXTwelve** company; playwright and actor Christopher Hood, known for his television screenplay work in Britain, channels his projects through **Black Custard Theatre**. The **Teatre de la Riereta** (C/Reina Amalia 3; 93 442 98 44) hosts a few English works as well. Information can also be found in the magazine *Barcelona Metropolitan*.

Els Comediants

For more than 30 years, this colourful troupe has enlivened scores of open-air festivals with its unique brand of mime, circus and Mediterranean folklore,

Mercat de les Flors. *See p270.*

all wrapped in vivid costumery. Works performed here are often accessible to international audiences young and old, thanks to its limited use of dialogue. Comediants create a variety of works for traditional stages as well, such as *BI*, a spectacular collaboration with the Chinese National Acrobatics Company, still touring into 2003.

La Cubana

Much loved for its offhand style and disarming humour, La Cubana thrives on a dazzling mix of satire, camp music and audience participation. Cubana director Jordi Milán will present his version of Verdi's *Aida* at the Liceu in July 2003, and it's bound to be unusual. Unfortunately, the company has recently lost some of its best lead actors to lucrative television contracts.

Dagoll Dagom

Under the direction of Joan Lluís Bozzo, this group has fine-tuned Catalan musical theatre, coming up with stellar productions in the old-time Broadway vein. After a Catalan *Pirates of Penzance* and a show exploiting Caribbean clichés (*Cacao*), in late 2002 it opened *Poe*, a terror musical at the Poliorama.

La Fura dels Baus

Sustained rage and a love for visceral epic have kept La Fura dels Baus at the forefront of new Catalan theatre since the mid '80s. The company found fame with the twisted mythology of the 1992 Olympic opening ceremony. La Fura is big business these days. While its 2001 film, *Faust 5.0*, continues to open in world cinemas, for 2003 it is planning a film based on the 2002 porno-cabaret *XXX*, which continues to tour in its theatre incarnation.

Teatre Lliure. *See p270.*

They laid low during 2002, but were back in early 2003 with a playful work, *Coplas del Blanco Miguel*, inspired by Michael Jackson and the poetry of the mundane, followed by Rosa Muñoz's solo *Romance Nº 4*, and Andres Corchero's *Fràgile*.

Mal Pelo

More than any other company, Mal Pelo (meaning 'bad hair') has a particular Catalan sensibility; that curious mixture of the earthy with the poetic and surreal that is often found in the work of Catalan painters and architects. In 2002 Mal Pelo won the Premi Nacional de Dansa for its new work *L'animal a l'esquena* (the animal on your back).

Mudances

Director Àngels Margarit produces highly structured, complex work that involves a creative use of video. Like most of the city's established companies, Mudances is serious about the need to nurture contemporary dance by educating new audiences and future dancers, and often programmes dance workshops and pieces for children. The company will tour the beautiful, whimsical *Origami* during 2003.

La Porta

La Porta is not a company but a showcase for new choreography and experimental dance. In 2003 it will bring overseas artists experimenting with dance and new technologies to the Mercat de les Flors, and continue to programme evenings at smaller venues like the CCCB and Sala Beckett.

Sol Picó

Highly acclaimed for her energy and intensity, Sol and her company explore the fusion of different forms of dance, the use of new technologies and the dancer-audience relationship, making for challenging performances. In 2003 the company will present *La Dona Manca*, or *Barbye Superstar*, a new work developed as part of the TNC residency.

Tricicle

This Catalan mime trio has found enormous success with a simple, clean-cut humour, ensuring packed houses and frequent television work. Carles Sans, Paco Mir, and Joan Gràcia have prepared a new show simply entitled *Sit* (at the Teatre Victoria until mid 2003), which sucks the maximum out of a theme as mundane as resting one's rear.

Dance companies

Other groups worth looking out for include the collective **La Caldera**, established companies **Lanònima Imperial** and **Metros** and newer groups **Projecte Gallina**, **Búbulus**, **Las Malqueridas** and **Transit**, as well as **Nats Nus** and its successful off-shoot **Nats Nens**, which produces contemporary dance for kids.

Gelabert-Azzopardi Companyia de Dansa

www.gelabertazzopardi.com
After more than 30 years working as a dancer and choreographer, Cesc Gelabert's most recent works are an expression of that brief moment in time when mental maturity and physical ability exist in more or less equal measure. The highly acclaimed company formed by Gelabert and partner Lydia Azzopardi spends much of its time touring, but this year it will be producing a new piece, provisionally titled *vuit4dos*, at the Teatre Lliure in June.

Cía. Andrés Corchero-Rosa Muñoz

This is a dancers' dance company, but perhaps a bit difficult for the uninitiated. Andres Corchero and Rosa Muñoz develop poetic and expressive pieces.

Dance schools & workshops

Many of the major companies allow you to join their own classes for short periods, but call to check first. Some, like **Mudances** (93 430 87 63/www.margarit-mudances.com) and **Lanónima Imperial** (www.lanonima.com) also run special workshops. The **Institut del Teatre** runs summer classes but these are often expensive. A good place for contemporary dance classes at almost all levels is **Area Espai de Dansa i Creació** (C/Alegre de Dalt 55, 93 210 78 50), while the very central **El Timbal** (C/Portaferrissa 13, 93 302 73 47) is an acting school that also has drop-in dance classes for students at all different levels and in many different performance styles. A more complete list of dance schools in Barcelona can be found at www.dancespain.com/schools.

Els Joglars

Spain's masters of political satire and social
spoof, Els Joglars, have long revolved around
their charismatic leader, Albert Boadella,
once an *enfant terrible* who was imprisoned
under the Franco regime for his politics.
Increasingly, however, it is the comic genius
Ramon Fontserè – a scruffy 45-year-old actor
who has spent years in relative obscurity –
who is emerging as the Joglars' public face.

Founded by Boadella in 1962, Els Joglars
have lived for 40 years off his biting wit and
fierce creative independence. Reluctant to
accept official subsidies, he has always found
a way to finance the extravagant productions,
which he writes and directs. After *La torna*
in 1977, with Franco dead but the new
democracy as yet unveiled, Boadella was
arrested for insulting the reputation of the
military and the Guardia Civil, and spent two
months in prison. He escaped (a feat which
only enhanced his reputation) and after a
short exile in France returned, only to be
imprisoned again in 1979.

Ramon Fontserè found his place in 1983 as
just another unknown face in the multifarious
company, happy to work in the anonymity of
the collective under Boadella's protective
wing. Els Joglars' rural rehearsal space, is
a sort of Buckminster Fuller-inspired dome
on the outskirts of Vic, far from the capital,
where Fontserè pottered about the woods
hunting for wild mushrooms.

Els Joglars' fortunes began to turn just a
few years ago, when Fontserè took on the
painter Salvador Dalí in *Daaalí* (1999),
which played to a packed house in London's
Barbican. Meanwhile, the genius of the man
who had played Christopher Columbus (in
Columbi Lapsus, 1989); Catalan president
Jordi Pujol (in *Ubu President*, 1980s), and
the eccentric Catalan writer Josep Pla (in *The
Incredible Story of Dr Floit and Mr Pla*,1997)
began to dawn on Spanish theatregoers.
Fontserè's captivating version of the
mad, moustachoed surrealist won him an
unexpected National Theatre prize in 2001.

Emboldened by his lead's interminable
talent, Boadella has now ventured into film.
¡Buen viaje, excelencía! is a painfully sardonic
study of the last days of Franco, his eternal
nemesis. Boadella's witty writing along with
Fontserè's terrifying portrayal of Spain's most
loathsome fascist culminates Els Joglars'
latest act of creative vengeance.

Trips Out of Town

Getting Started	**276**
Around Barcelona	**277**
Tarragona &	
the Costa Daurada	**282**
Girona &	
the Costa Brava	**289**
Vic to the Pyrenees	**296**

Features

Top five Train trips	276
Get into the habit	280
Delta blow	288
How to be king of the castle	292

Getting Started

Your first steps along the road to snow-capped mountains, shady forests and secret coves.

Catalonia is not a big place, but the variety of its scenery is impressive. The Pyrenees running along its northern border are hardly a secret, but few outside the country know about the smaller sierras running parallel to the Mediterranean coastline nor the wetlands to the south, and, while they've heard about the overdeveloped horrors of the Costa Brava, not many travellers have discovered the hidden bays tucked away from the tourist resorts.

Inland, the countryside is dotted with nature reserves, vineyards and villages huddled around Romanesque churches or monasteries. Finding somewhere to stay has become easier since the Generalitat embraced rural tourism. Particularly good are the network of *casa de pagès* – country houses or old farmhouses (*masies*) where you can rent a room or a whole house. For details see the Generalitat's widely available guide *Residències – casa de pagès* (€5).

The Generalitat also has an excellent website – **www.gencat.es/probert** – with particularly good information on walks. For organised walks, try **Spain Step by Step** (93 302 76 29). For information on roads and public transport within Catalonia, visit the Generalitat through **www.mobilitat.org**. The **Palau Robert** tourist centre (*see p318*) should be your first stop for all kinds of information on the region.

By bus

The **Estació d'Autobusos Barcelona-Nord**, C/Ali Bei 80 (**map** p343 E5) is the principal bus station for coach services around Catalonia. General information is on **902 26 06 06**, but each company has its own phoneline.

By road

In July 2001 the Generalitat introduced a new system for naming roads according to the direction in which they run: roads beginning C1 run north–south; C2 run east–west; C3 run parallel to the coast. Thus the A16 and A19 have become the C32; the A18 the C16, and so on. At the time of writing, many maps and guidebooks had been slow to update. Driving in or out of Barcelona, you will come across either the **Ronda de Dalt**, running along the edge of Tibidabo, and the **Ronda Litoral** along the coast. They intersect with several motorways (*autopistes*): the C31 (heading up the coast); the C33/A7 (to Girona and France); the C58 (Sabadell, Manresa); the A2 (Lleida, Madrid), a continuation of Avda Diagonal which connects with the A7 south (Tarragona, Valencia); and the C32 to Sitges. All are toll roads, but where possible, we've given toll-free alternatives. Avoid the automatic ticket dispensers if riding a motorbike – in the 'Manual' lanes you will pay half-price. For more information on tolls, call 902 20 03 20 or see www.autopistas.com.

By train

All **RENFE** (902 24 02 02/www.renfe.es) trains stop at **Barcelona-Sants** station, and some at **Passeig de Gràcia** (Girona, Figueres, the south coast), **Estació de França** (the south coast) or **Plaça Catalunya** (Vic, Puigcerdà). RENFE's local and suburban trains (*rodalies*) are now integrated into the metro and bus fares system. The Catalan Government Railways (**FGC**) also serves destinations from **Plaça d'Espanya** and **Plaça Catalunya**. *See also pp302-3* and RENFE map on p346.

Top five Train trips

Sitges
Wide, sandy beaches; sleepy winding streets and a riotous nightlife. *See p277.*

Girona
A medieval heart, a soaring cathedral and fabulous food. *See p289.*

Tarragona
Once a Roman seat of power and now a tranquil town with impressive ruins. *See p282.*

Puigcerdà
For a day on the slopes or hiking over the hills. *See p299.*

Port Aventura
Do not attempt unless accompanied by a child. *See p220.*

Trips Out of Town

Around Barcelona

Monks and mountains, beefcakes and beaches: it's all just around the corner.

Sitges & Costa de Garraf

Sandwiched between the Mediterranean and the rough, dry peaks of the Garraf mountains, Sitges has long been one of the darlings of Spain's tourist industry. Drawing beach lovers, artsy types and party seekers in near equal numbers, there's a niche here for just about anyone. It's also known as one of Europe's major gay holiday destinations (see p237).

Sitges took its first steps toward becoming the upscale tourist resort it is today when *los americanos* (actually Spaniards who made fortunes in trade routes with Cuba) began building grand summer homes along its coast in the 18th century. Nearly 100 of these mansions are still standing and can be visited on guided tours (call **Agis Sitges**, Plaça Sota Ribes, mobile 619 793 199, for tour times and prices).

Though it gets stiflingly crowded during the summer months, when the otherwise picturesque beaches are dirty and cramped, Sitges has a charm unmatched along the Costa de Garraf. A long seaside promenade, the **Passeig de la Ribera**, passes numerous seafood restaurants and outdoor cafés and is crowned by 'La Punta', the town's 17th-century church, **Sant Bartomeu i Santa Tecla**, perched on a bluff. Near the church is the **Museu Cau Ferrat** (C/Fonollar s/n, 93 894 03 64, admission €3, closed Mon). The museum, which boasts works by El Greco, Picasso, Ramon Casas and others, was once Santiago Rusiñol's home. During Rusiñol's life it was a meeting place for artists such as Picasso and Joan Miró. Across the street is the **Palau Maricel** (C/Fonollar s/n, 93 811 33 11, admission €6, concerts July-Sept Tue-Thur 8pm), a hospital converted into a spectacular Modernista palace. It has an eclectic collection of elaborate marble sculptures, decorative ceramics and medieval and baroque artwork. Unfortunately, for a variety of reasons the Palau is usually closed, but many people discover they can get in to visit it when the doors open for concerts on summer evenings. Also worth a visit is the **Museu Romàntic** in the Casa Llopis (C/Sant Gaudenci 1, 93 894 29 69, admission €3, closed Mon) which portrays the lifestyle of an upper-class Sitges family through various displays of furniture, clocks and antique dolls.

Cultural festivals and special events abound in Sitges, and include the anything-goes carnival; Sitges' loud and colourful *festa major* at the end of August, and the Sitges International Film Festival in October (see p226). Year-round, the centre of Sitges' nightlife is C/Primer de Maig, a short strip lined with bars and clubs that the locals affectionately refer to as the 'Carrer del Pecat' or 'Sin Street.'

Sitges is the most popular destination along the Costa del Garraf, but other towns are well worth a stop too. **Vilanova i la Geltrú**, just south of Sitges, is a busy harbour town with great seafood restaurants. There is a pleasant Rambla through the town centre, along with several beaches and a few museums, including the important **Biblioteca-Museu Balaguer** (Avda Victor Balaguer, 93 815 42 02, admission €2, closed Mon), which contains some El Grecos as well as many artefacts.

The first town north of Sitges on scenic highway C-31 is **Garraf**, a tiny resort with one pretty beach and a few relaxed beach bars. The Gaudí-designed **Celler de Garraf**, a wonderful Modernista building now home to an upmarket restaurant, is on the edge of town. Behind the town, the green **Parc del Garraf** stretches inland, offering an endless variety of trails to hike, bike or explore by car (trail maps are available at the tourist office in Sitges, see p278). Continuing north on the C-31 is **Castelldefels**; it's just 20 kilometres (12 miles) south of Barcelona, and known for its wide, sandy beaches and cheap seafood restaurants.

Where to stay & eat

In Sitges, **El Greco** (Passeig de la Ribera 70, 93 894 29 06, mains €18) is one of the best seafood restaurants. **Bar Restaurante Kansas** (Passeig Maritim, 93 894 02 52, mains €12) is a cheaper yet still good seafood option, with a view over the Mediterranean. **Tribeca** (C/Nou 12, 93 894 56 58, mains €10) is a funky, friendly place, with dishes ranging from moussaka to sushi. For traditional Catalan fare, head to **La Masia** (Passeig de Vilanova 164, 93 894 10 76, mains €12). Order the *embutido* starter – a variety of dried sausages that arrive hanging from the limbs of a shellacked grapevine. **Al Fresco** (C/Pau Barrabeig 4, 93 894 06 00, mains €15) is considered by many to be Sitges' best

Palau Maricel. *See p277*

Sant Bartomeu i Santa Tecla. *See p277.*

restaurant. The ever-changing menu features Mediterranean dishes with an international twist, and the ambience is intimate and artistic.

If you want to stay over in Sitges, the **Celimar** (Passeig de la Ribera 20, 93 811 01 70, rates €80-€125) is a comfortable seafront hotel; some rooms have balconies. Further down and just off the beach is the two-star **Hotel Arcadia** (C/Socias 22-24, 93 894 58 65, rates €35-€65). **Hostal Maricel** (C/Tacó 13, 93 894 36 27, rates incl breakfast €38.50-€55) is a good budget option, as is the **Parellades** (C/Parellades 11, 93 894 08 01, rates €45, closed Oct-Easter). See chapter **Gay & Lesbian** for more accommodation options.

In Castelldefels, there are several cheap seafront paella restaurants to choose from, or you could head to the more upmarket **Nàutic** (Passeig Marítim 374, 93 665 01 74, mains €17). For a luxurious hotel, try the **Gran Hotel Don Jaime** (Avda del Hotel, 22, 93 665 13 00, rates €133.50), which has indoor and outdoor pools.

In Vilanova i la Geltrú, **Peixerot** (Passeig Marítim 56, 93 815 06 25, closed Sun dinner and mid Sept-June, mains €33) gets the pick of the day's fish while there's excellent grilled meat at **Can Pagès** (C/Sant Pere 24, 93 894 11 95, closed lunch Mon-Fri and all of Nov, set menu €12.70). For a pleasant place to stay, the **Hotel César** (C/Isaac Peral 4-8, 93 815 11 25, rates €73-€180) is set in a garden with a heated pool and spa, and a minute's walk from the beach.

Water sports

Many of Sitges' water activities are centred around the Port Esportiu Aiguadolç. The **Centro Náutico Aiguadolç-Vela** (93 811

31 05/www.advela.net) rents sailboats and organises sailing excursions; a one-hour private lesson costs €40 (March-Nov only). The **Yahoo Motor Center** rents jet skis with guides (93 811 30 61, €40 for 15-min ride).

Castelldefels has a large recreational port, where you can rent sea kayaks and all classes of catamaran from the **Catamaran Center** (Port Ginesta, local 324, 93 665 22 11, www.catamaran-center.com). Other options for water sports include the **Windcat House** in Calafell, south of Vilanova i la Geltrú, which runs sailing courses (Passeig Marítim 174, 977 69 30 72, www.windcathouse.com).

Tourist information

Oficina de Turisme de Castelldefels

Plaça de l'Església 1 (93 635 27 27). **Open** *July-Sept* 10am-2pm, 4-8pm daily. *Oct-June* 4-8pm Mon; 10am-2pm, 4-8pm Tue-Fri; 10am-2pm Sat.

Oficina de Turisme de Sitges

C/Sinia Morera 1 (93 894 42 51/www.sitges.org). **Open** *July-Sept* 9am-9pm daily. *Oct-June* 9am-2pm, 4-6.30pm Mon-Fri.
C/Fonollar (93 811 06 11/www.sitges.org). **Open** *July-Sept* 10am-1.30pm, 5-9pm daily. *Oct-June* 10.30am-2pm, 4-7pm Sat; 11-2pm Sun.

Getting there

By bus

Trains are more efficient but finish early; Mon-Bus runs a hourly night service to Plaça Catalunya from Vilanova between 11.59pm and 2.59am, stopping at Sitges train station 13mins later.

By car

C32 to Castelldefels, Garraf, Sitges (41km/25 miles) and Vilanova (extra tunnel toll between Garraf and Sitges), or C31 via a slow, winding drive around the Garraf mountains.

By train

Trains leave at least every 20mins from Sants or Passeig de Gràcia for Platja de Castelldefels (20min journey), Sitges (30mins) and Vilanova (40mins); not all stop at Castelldefels and Garraf. The last train back to Barcelona leaves Vilanova at 9.37pm and Sitges at 10.26pm.

Costa del Maresme

The coast just north of Barcelona is home to a string of pleasant beach towns that make for ideal day trips. Some of the best beaches are in El Masnou, Caldes d'Estrac (also known as Caldetes), Sant Pol de Mar and Calella.

El Masnou's long beaches are an easy 15-minute train ride from Barcelona, but as you'll find along much of the Costa Maresme, train tracks run right along the beach, somewhat spoiling the otherwise tranquil air. In **Caldetes**, the slightly incongruous Modernista houses are the legacy of wealthy summer visitors who flocked to the hot springs here at the turn of the 20th century. The town's well-conserved park is also worth a visit. **Sant Pol**, where you'll find some of the prettiest beaches in the area, is a mostly unspoilt, though rather gentrified, fishing village. **Calella**, at the northern end of the Costa Maresme, is known for its **Parc Dalmau**, a large and lush garden in the town centre, and for its many examples of Gothic architecture. You can visit the **Museu-Arxiu Municipal** (C/Escoles Pies 36, 93 769 51 02, closed Mon, free) to learn more about the town's history.

Also along the coast is **Canet de Mar**, interesting because it was the home of the influential Modernista architect Domènech i Montaner. His former home is now a museum where visitors can see some of his finest work (Casa Museu, C/Riera Gavarra 2, 93 795 46 15) . Also nearby is his remodelled castle of **Santa Florentina**, complete with the intact remains of its 13th-century entrance towers (call 93 487 70 28 to arrange a visit).

Where to stay & eat

In Caldes d'Estrac, the best mid-price restaurant is probably **Can Suñe** (C/Callao, 93 791 00 51, main courses €14, closed Mon, and Mon-Wed from Oct-Jun). There are also double rooms if you want to stay over (June-Sept only, €36.40). For lunch on the seafront, try the **Voramar** (Passeig de Musclera 10, 93 791 09 44, mains €13, closed Wed and all of Oct). In Sant Pol,

La Casa (C/Riera 13, 93 760 23 73, mains €9.60, closed Mon, Tue and all Nov) is a colourful, stylish restaurant with great *torrades*, or, for something more upmarket, head to the wonderful, Michelin-starred **Sant Pau** (C/Nou 10, 93 760 06 62, mains €33, closed all Mon and Sun dinner). In Canet there are plenty of places to eat along the tree-lined Passeig del Maresme, and you can stay at **Mitus**, a charming, family-run *hostal* (C/Riera de la Torre 20, 93 794 29 03, rates €31-€47).

El Racó de Can Fabes

C/Sant Joan 6, Sant Celoni (93 867 28 51/ www.racocanfabes.com). By car A7 or C35 (60km/ 37 miles)/by train RENFE to Sant Celoni. **Open** 1.30-3.30pm, 8.30-10.30pm Tue-Sat; 1.30-3.30pm Sun. Closed 1st 2wks Feb, last wk June, 1st wk July. **Main courses** €47 (set menu €117). **Credit** AmEx, DC, MC, V.

Charismatic chef Santi Santamaria has long been acclaimed as a leader among European chefs, and is one of only three in Spain to be awarded three Michelin stars. Seasonal specialities at his surprisingly relaxed restaurant include prawn ravioli with wild mushroom oil and hot and cold mackerel with cream of caviar. Desserts are superb and there's a fine range of cheeses.

Getting there

By car

NII to El Masnou (10km/6 miles), Caldes d'Estrac (36km/22 miles), Canet de Mar (42km/26 miles), Sant Pol (48km/30 miles) and Calella (52km/32 miles).

By train

RENFE trains leave every 30mins from Sants or Plaça Catalunya for El Masnou, Caldes d'Estrac, Canet, Sant Pol and Calella. Journey approx 45mins-1hr.

Inland

Gaudí's most famous works are in Barcelona, but many fine examples of his and other Modernista architecture are found outside the city as well. Just west of Barcelona next to Santa Coloma de Cervelló, the **Colònia Güell** (93 630 58 07, open daily, admission €4, guided tours €5-€8) was another of Eusebi Güell's ideas for a Utopian garden city for the workers, this time built around a textile factory. Like the Park Güell, it was never finished, but is still worth a visit for Gaudí's extraordinary crypt.

Scattered throughout **Terrassa**, an industrial town a 25-minute train ride from Barcelona, are Modernista factories, homes and markets; one of the best is the outlandish **Masia Freixa**, a striking residence with slender arches and a rolling rooftop. Also interesting are the Visigothic-Romanesque

Get into the habit

Montserrat monastery.

The monastery at Montserrat is certainly the most emblematic in Catalonia, but glorious examples of Romanesque and Gothic churches, cathedrals and monasteries are to be found dotted all over the region. If you really want to get a taste of the monastic life, you can stay in one for a few days. Some monasteries only accept those on spiritual retreat, but many operate guest services for those needing a few days of peace, a quiet place to study or simply a base from which to explore the surrounding countryside. Make sure to call ahead to reserve a room and to find out the specific requirements of each monastery or convent; some may require that you're present at meals or services, while others have a strict curfew.

In Barcelona itself, a good option is **Casal Bellesguard** (Bellesguard, 93 211 82 40, rates €24 per person, full board), a quiet convent with views of the sea that requires silence within its walls. The monastery at **Montserrat** operates a small hotel and cheaper guest quarters (*see p281*), while just down the mountain, away from the bustle of tourists, is **Sant Benet de Montserrat**, a Benedictine convent that is not for tourists but welcomes those looking for a place to spend a day or two of reflection (Ctra de Montserrat km 10, 93 835 00 78, rates €15 per person, full board).

Around 50km (30 miles) west of Barcelona, near Sant Sadurní, is **Font Santa** (Santuario de la Font Santa, 93 891 41 43, rates €25 per person, full board). The guest quarters are simple, but the atmosphere is simply unbeatable, with the jagged rocks of the majestic Pyrenees and ruggedly beautiful Montserrat in the background. There are even ruins of an ancient castle on the site. An hour's drive away is the glorious monastery at **Poblet** (*see p286*), with guest quarters for men only inside the cloister with the monks (977 87 00 89, payment by donation).

A more upscale option, north of Barcelona, is **Sant Marçal**, a 10th-century monastery now used exclusively as a hotel, where spirituality has surrendered quietly to creature comforts (Ctra Santa Fe, Serra de Montseny, 93 847 30 43, €138 per person full board) .

GETTING THERE

Casal Bellesguard: Train FGC from Plaça Catalunya to Av Tibidabo.
Montserrat: *see p281*.
Font Santa: By car A-7 south to Sant Sadurni, then 3km (2 miles) towards Sant Pau d'Ordal.
Poblet: *see p286*.
Sant Marçal: from Barcelona take the A-7 north to Sant Celoni, then take the Ctra Santa Fe (28km/17 miles).

churches, **Santa Maria**, **Sant Miquel** and **Sant Pere**. Otherwise, don't expect much charm; Terrassa once won a Japanese award for being the world's ugliest city. Nearby is the archrival town **Sabadell**, which was another centre of Catalonia's industrial revolution. The best it has to offer the casual visitor is the **Parc Tauli**, a pretty place for a stroll.

Closer to Barcelona are the towns around Collserola park. **Sant Cugat** is known mainly for being the most expensive suburb around, but it has a pretty Romanesque monastery. The **Casa Lluch**, a tiled Modernista creation, is also interesting; see it on the Arrabassada road back to Barcelona. Nearby **Les Planes** has a *merendero* – an area with tables and outdoor grills – for shady picnics. There's a nice walk (or cycle) from Les Planes toward **El Papiol**, a town with a medieval castle and the remains of an Iberian settlement. **La Floresta**, another suburb near the park, is good for short, easy walks in the sunshine.

Where to eat

Braseria La Bolera (Rambla de Celler 43, 93 674 16 75, closed Sun dinner and 3 wks August, mains €7) in Sant Cugat is good for grilled meat. In Terrassa, **Casa Toni** (Ctra de Castellar 124, 93 786 47 08, set lunch €7.40-€11.80) offers a fine range of wines.

Getting there

By car

To Colònia Güell: A2 to Sant Boi exit, then turn towards Sant Vicenç dels Horts (3 miles/5km). To Les Planes, La Floresta and Sant Cugat: C16 via Túnel de

Vallvidrera (exit 8 off Ronda de Dalt). To El Papiol: A2, then follow signs north from Molins de Rei (2.5 miles/3km). To Terrassa: C58 or C16.

By train

FGC trains go from Plaça Espanya to Colònia Güell, and from Plaça Catalunya to Terrassa, Sant Cugat, Les Planes and La Floresta. Journey takes 10-25mins.

Montserrat

Montserrat, a huge sandstone mass that rises abruptly from the low hills of the Catalan countryside, is geologically distinct from the terrain that surrounds it; the mountain's strange bulbous peaks making a dramatic setting for the spiritual heart of Catalonia. The Benedictine monastery of Montserrat sits atop these spectacular mountains surrounded by hermitages and tiny chapels. One of Catalonia's top tourist attractions (and, accordingly, it is unbearably crowded in summer), the monastary is accessible only by painfully circuitous roads with breathtaking views or, more spectacularly still, by mountain cable car. In the Middle Ages, this was an important place of pilgrimage. In those years it grew rich and powerful, while its remote position helping to ensure its political independence. During the Franco era, it became a bastion of non-violent Catalan nationalism.

Today, the **monastery** itself (open 8am-8pm) is not particularly interesting, and the cafeterias and souvenir shops strike an ugly commercial note. The exterior is beautiful, however, and the views around the mountain and the nature reserve are spectacular.

The monastery's prize possession is *La Moreneta,* or the 'Black Virgin', a small Romanesque figure, which, according to lore was discovered in a nearby mountain cave by young shepherds in the 12th century. It is the patron saint of Catalonia, and Montserrat is a popular name for Catalan women. Queues of people still wait to climb the steps and touch the statue of the virgin (8.30-10.30am, noon-6.30pm) inside the 16th-century **basilica** (7.30am-7.30pm), and pray for a miracle. The basilica is most crowded at 1pm, when the monastery's celebrated boys' choir sings mass. Better times to hear them are later, as they also sing at 7pm and at noon on Sundays. The **museum** houses liturgical gold and silverware, archaeological finds, gifts presented to the virgin, works by Dali, Monet, Picasso, Caravaggio and El Greco. There's a good audiovisual display, which offers an interesting overview of the day-to-day life of the 80 or so monks living there (mid Sept-May 9am-6pm, June-mid Sept 9am-7.45pm, admission €2).

After a brief tour of the monastery, many people head for the nearby hills, as the views

and walks are spectacular. As well as **Santa Cova**, the cave where the virgin was discovered (a 20-minute walk or a funicular trip from the monastery), there are 13 hermitages, the most accessible of them being **Sant Joan**, reached by funicular from the monastery or a 20-minute walk with superb views. The tourist office has details of longer walks including a circuit of all the hermitages and the (relatively easy) trek to the peak of **Sant Jeroni**, at 1,235 metres (4,053 feet). Climbing is also popular.

Where to stay & eat

There are several overpriced restaurants on Montserrat, and the best deals are to be had at the newly renovated café beside the gift shops. Local dishes and sandwiches are good and surprisingly well-priced. Even so, picnics are the most popular option here, and the mountain provides an abundance of quiet, scenic spots. The monastery operates a small hotel, **Hotel Abat Cisneros** (rates €40-€76), and cheaper apartments, **Celdes Abat Marcet** (rates €23-€38, minimum 2-day stay), nearby (for both; 93 877 77 01, www.abadiamontserrat.net). Ask for information about campsites on the mountain at the tourist office.

Tourist information

Oficina de Turisme de Montserrat

Plaça de la Creu, Montserrat (93 877 77 77/ www.abadiamontserrat.net). **Open** *Apr-Oct* 9am-7pm daily. *Nov-Mar* 9am-6pm daily.

Getting there

By bus

A Julià-Via (93 490 40 00) bus leaves at 9.15am from Sants bus station and returns at 6pm daily; journey time is approx 80mins. Julià-Via also run guided tours to Montserrat.

By car

Take the NII to exit km 59, or the A2 to the Martorell exit, then the C55 towards Monistrol (60km/37 miles). The road to the monastery is steep with sharp bends and tends to get extremely crowded and slow, especially at weekends.

By train

FGC trains from Plaça Espanya every hour daily from 8.36am to the Aeri de Montserrat (journey time approx 1hr); then a cable car (leaving every 15mins) to the monastery. Last cable car is 6.45pm and last train leaves Aeri de Montserrat at 9pm. Return fare (including cable car) is €11.60. 'Tot Montserrat' is a ticket (€34) available from Plaça Catalunya and Plaça Espanya stations, which includes funicular, train and cable car fares, along with museum entry and lunch.

Trips Out of Town

Tarragona & the Costa Daurada

Wine, women and plainsong.

Tarragona

Tarragona was once a mighty Roman metropolis and capital of over half the Iberian peninsula, and much of its former glory is still evident today. A good introduction is a stroll along the **Passeig Arqueològic** (Avda Catalunya, entrance at Portal del Roser, 977 24 57 96). The path follows the old Roman ramparts, and commands a great view of Tarragona's hinterland and the sea. The walls support three solid towers, two of which were rebuilt in medieval times. Inside the walls, in the **Plaça del Rei**, you will find the ancient **Pretori** (praetorium), now called **Castell del Rei** (977 24 19 52), which has been used as a palace and government office and is rumoured to have been the birthplace of Pontius Pilate. From here you can walk to the ruins of the **Circ Romans**, the first-century Roman circus. Excavations suggest that chariot races were once held here. The **Museu Nacional Arqueològic**, home to an important collection of Roman artefacts and some stunning mosaics, is nearby. Tickets for this also allow entry to the **Museu i Necròpolis Paleocristians** (Avda Ramón y Cajal 80, 977 21 11 75, closed Mon), located on the site of an early Christian cemetery. Thousands of graves have been uncovered interesting if morbid finds include beautifully decorated sarcophagi.

To see all parts of the **Catedral de Santa María**, not to mention some wonderful religious art and archaelogical finds, you will need a ticket for the **Museu Diocesà** (Pla de la Seu, 977 23 86 85, closed Sun, admission €2.40).The majestic cathedral was built on the site of a Roman temple to Jupiter, and is Catalonia's largest. The cloister, built in the 12th and 13th centuries, is glorious, and has some intriguing details including the famous 'Procession of the Rats' relief.

Leading from the old town towards the sea, the **Passeig de las Palmeres** runs to the 'Balcó del Mediterrani' from where you can look down and imagine the gladiator fights in the Roman **amphitheatre** (Parc del Miracle, 977 24 25 79). The Passeig de las Palmeres also

takes you to the bustling pedestrian street of the **Rambla Nova**, from where you can follow C/Canyelles to the **Fòrum** (C/Lleida, 977 24 25 01) to visit the remains of the juridical basilica and Roman houses. Three kilometres north of the city (but an unpleasant walk along a busy main road – take bus No.5 from the top of the Rambla Nova) is the most spectacular of Tarragona's historic relics: the **Pont del Diable** (Devil's Bridge), a Roman aqueduct built in the first century.

Entry to the Passeig Arqueològic; the praetorium and circus; the amphiteatre, and the Fòrum costs €1.90 (60¢ concessions, free under-16s) each one, although entry is free to holders of **Port Aventura** tickets (*see p220*). Opening hours are the same for all: Easter-mid Oct 9am-9pm Tue-Sat; 9am-7pm Sun; mid Oct-Easter 9am-5pm Tue-Sat; 9am-3pm Sun.

Museu Nacional Arqueològic de Tarragona
Plaça del Rei 5 (977 23 62 09/www.mnat.es). **Open** *June-Sept* 10am-8pm Tue-Sat; 10am-2pm Sun. *Oct-May* 10am-1.30pm, 4-7pm Tue-Sat; 10am-2pm Sun. **Admission** (incl entrance to Museu i Necròpolis Paleocristians) €2.40; €1.20 concessions; free under-18s, over-65s. **No credit cards**.

Where to eat

The fishing neighbourhood of El Serrallo is home to the best seafood restaurants: try the paella at **Cal Martì** (C/Sant Pere 12, 977 21 23 84, closed Sun dinner and Mon, closed Sept, mains €14). **La Puda** (Moll Pescadors 25, 977 21 15 11, mains €16.40), opposite the site of the fish auctions, is another place to find exceptionally fresh fish. A good, cheap option in the centre of town is the **Bufet el Tiberi** (C/Martì d'Ardenya 5, 977 23 54 03, closed Sun dinner, Mon, buffet €12.80), while just below the cathedral is the friendly **La Cuca Fera** (Plaça Santiago Rusinyol 5, 977 24 20 07, closed Mon and Nov, set lunch €9.70). In the old town, **Palau del Baró** serves huge portions of seriously Catalan fare in colourful, elegant dining rooms. (C/Santa Anna 3, 977 24 14 64, closed Sun dinner Nov-Feb, mains €12.50.)

Trips Out of Town

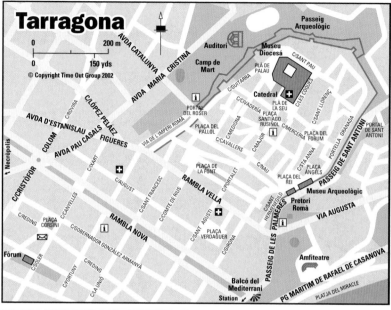

Where to stay

Of the more upmarket hotels, the **Hotel Ciutat de Tarragona** (Plaça Imperial Tarraco 5, 977 25 09 99/www.hotelciutatdetarragona.com, rates €73-€118) is good value. The **Lauria** (Rambla Nova 20, 977 23 67 12, rates €57.80-€68.50) is also good value, has a pool and gives hefty discounts at weekends out of season. Other mid-range hotels include the **Astari** (Via Augusta 95, 977 23 69 00, rates €60.70-€84.40), which has a pool, and the central **Hotel Urbis** (C/Reding 20 bis, 977 24 01 16, rates €62-€91.80). You'll find cheaper digs at the **Pensión Forum** (Plaça de la Font 37, 977 23 17 18, rates €32-€38) and the nearby **Pensión La Noria** (Plaça de la Font 53, 977 23 87 17, rates €29-€37), with little to choose between them.

Tourist information

Oficina de Turisme de Tarragona
C/Fortuny 4 (977 23 34 15). **Open** 9am-2pm, 4-6.30pm Mon-Fri; 9am-2pm Sat.

Getting there

By car
Take the A2, then A7 via Vilafranca (Tarragona 98km/60 miles); or the toll-free N340 (Molins de Rei exit from A2).

By train
RENFE from Sants or Passeig de Gràcia. Trains hourly from about 6am-9.30pm. Journey time to Tarragona is 1hr 6mins.

The Wine Country

Vilafranca del Penedès is famed for two things; its *casteller* team (*see p211*) and its place at the heart of rolling vineyards and wineries. The town itself is worth a visit, with some handsome medieval buildings and the elegant 14th-century **Basílica de Santa Maria**. Vilafranca's wine museum, the **Museu del Vi** (Plaça Jaume I 1-3, 93 890 05 82, closed Mon, admission €3) has old wooden presses and wine jugs, some dating back to the fourth century.

While Vilafranca itself is very easy to navigate on foot, a car is almost essential to explore the surrounding wine region. Penedès' largest winemaker, **Torres**, runs tours at its cellars outside town (not to be confused with its offices opposite the train station). Miguel Torres has long been one of Spain's most influential winemakers, responsible for introducing modern winemaking practices to the region. Torres' free tours include the obligatory visits to the cellars, bottling area and fermentation tanks, and a recent addition is a train ride through a virtual reality tunnel that shows how the weather and soil create aromas in wine.

Jean León, another pioneering brand, recently inaugurated its visitors' centre near Torrelavit, in a modern building with breathtaking views of a valley filled with vineyards.

Some six miles away is Sant Sadurní d'Anoia, the capital of Penedès' cava industry and Vilafranca's major rival. More than 90 per cent of Spain's cava, a sparkling wine traditionally made with local parellada, macabeo and xarel.lo grapes , is made in this tiny town. **Codorníu**, one of the largest producers, offers a wonderful tour to its Modernista headquarters, designed at the end of the 19th century by Puig i Cadafalch. A train takes visitors through part of the 16 miles (26 kilometres) of underground cellars. **Freixenet**, another mega-producer, is nearby.

The **Priorat** area, south of here, has gained fame in the past decade for making full-bodied (and pricey) red wines. Monks were producing wine in the Priorat as long ago as the 11th century, but the area had been all but abandoned when young winemaker **Alvaro Palacios** set up a tiny vineyard here in the late 1980s. He battled against steep hills and a sceptical wine industry, but within a few years he was winning international acclaim. Now the region is one of Spain's most popular among wine buyers.

The small **Alella** district, just east of Barcelona, is best known for whites. More important is **Terra Alta**, near the Priorat in Tarragona, with Gandesa as its capital. It is renowned for its heavy reds. The newly created *denominación de origen,* Montsant, with Falset as its capital, is growing in popularity. Look out for the splendidly weird **Cooperativa Agrícola** in Gandesa, and the **Bodega Cooperativa** in Falset, designed by Gaudí's disciple César Martinell. The **Celler Capçanes**, also in DO Montsant, makes one of the world's top kosher wines.

Many towns have festivals to celebrate the grape harvest (*verema*). In Vilafranca they take place on the first Sunday in October, and Sant Sadurní is usually held a week later. Torres hosts an annual harvest festival in September in Sitges (*see p277*) featuring a grape crushing competition. For more details, ask at the Palau Robert tourist office in Barcelona (*see p319*) or local tourist offices.

Wineries

Can Suriol del Castell

Castell Grabuac, Ctra de Vilafranca a Font Rubí (BV2127) km 6, Font Rubí (93 897 84 26/ www.suriol.com). **Open** by appointment.
A limited quantity of very fine cava is made at this vineyard, centred at a historic *masia*.

Caves Codorníu

Avda Codorníu, Sant Sadurní d'Anoia (93 818 32 32/www.codorniu.es). **Open** 9am-5pm Mon-Fri; 9am-1pm Sat, Sun. **Admission** free Mon-Fri; €2 (incl free champagne glass) Sat, Sun.
Tour includes a short film, a mini-train ride through the cellars and a tasting.

Caves Freixenet

C/Joan Sala 2, Sant Sadurní d'Anoia (93 891 70 00/www.freixenet.es). **Tours** 10am, 11.30am, 3.30pm, 5pm Mon-Thur; 10am, 11.30am Fri. **Admission** free.
The cellars are directly opposite the station.

Jean León

Pago Jean León, Torrelavit (93 899 55 12/ www.jeanleon.com). **Open** 10am-5pm Tue-Sat. **Admission** €3.
Price includes a video, a tour through the museum and winery and a tasting of two wines.

Scala Dei

Rambla de la Cartoixa, Scala Dei (977 82 70 27). **Open** by appointment. **Admission** free.
Housed in a 12th-century monastery. Great reds, in particular the Cartoixa Scala Dei.

Torres

Finca El Maset, Pacs del Penedes (93 817 74 87/ www.torres.es). **Open** 9am-5pm Mon-Fri; 9am-6pm Sat; 9am-1pm Sun. Tours hourly. **Admission** free.

Where to stay & eat

In Vilafranca, the wine bar and store **Inzolia** (C/Palma 21, 93 818 19 38) is the best place to try local fine wines. **El Purgatori** (Plaça Campanar, 93 892 12 63, open dinner only, mains €8) specialises in strong cheeses and local dried sausages, situated in a picturesque corner behind the basilica. **Taverna Ongi Etorriak** (C/Sant Bernat 4, 93 890 43 54, tapas average €3.50) is a Basque bar with a wide variety of *pintxos* and a great wine list, many available by the glass. Try **La Fabrica** (C/Hermenegild Clascar 4, 93 817 15 38, mains €10) for finer dining, with an emphasis on Asian flavours. A good traditional restaurant in the region is **Sol i Vi**, a restaurant with a nice hotel between Vilafranca and Sant Sadurní (93 899 32 04, Ctra. Sant Sadurní a Vilafranca, mains €15, rates €60). Another lodging option is the three-star **Hotel Pere III** (93 890 31 00, Plaça del Penedès, rates €58-€64), in the centre of Vilafranca. In Torrelavit is **Masia Can Cardús** (93 899 50 18, rates €36), a working farm and vineyard with rooms to rent.

Tourist information

Falset C/San Marcel 2 (977 83 10 23); **Sant Sadurní d'Anoia** C/Hospital 26 (93 891 31 88); **Vilafranca del Penedès** C/Cort 14 (93 892 03 58).

Getting there

Alella

By bus Barcelona Bus (93 232 04 59) from Plaça
Urquinaona. **By car** NII north to Montgat, then left
turn to Alella (15km/9 miles).

Alt Penedès

By car A2, then A7 to Sant Sadurní (44km/27 miles)
and Vilafranca (55km/34 miles), or A2, then toll-free
N340 from Molins de Rei, which is much slower. **By
train** RENFE from Sants or Plaça Catalunya; trains
leave hourly 6am-10pm (journey time 45mins), then
taxi for Torres, Jean León and Codorníu.

Falset, Scala Dei & Gandesa

By car A2, then A7 to Reus, and right on to N420 for
Falset (143km/89 miles) and Gandesa (181km/112
miles). For Scala Dei take T710 from Falset, then turn
right at La Vilella Baixa. **By train** RENFE from
Sants or Passeig de Gràcia to Marçà-Falset. Six trains
daily (journey time 2hrs). For Gandesa continue to
Mora d'Ebre (20mins) and catch a local bus.

Costa Daurada

One of the more attractive towns on the coast
is **Altafulla**, just a few minutes north of
Tarragona on the train. The town is split into
two parts; Altafulla Playa hugs the sea with
a modern but elegant esplanade of low-rise
houses and the stately **Tamarit castle**
overlooking a sandy bay, while Altafulla
Pueblo, a jumble of narrow cobbled streets
with a medieval feel, is a ten-minute walk
inland. Local folklore has it that the old town
has been home to a coven of witches for
centuries. Further south along the coast
towards the rather unlovely resort of **Salou**
is the **Port Aventura** theme park (*see p220*).

Where to stay & eat

In Altafulla the **Hotel San Martín** (C/Mar 7,
977 65 03 07/www.hotelsanmartin, rates €51-
€76) has a pool, and is the only hotel open year-
round. The **Faristol** (C/Sant Marti 5, 977 65
00 77, closed Mon-Thur Oct-May, rates incl
breakfast €60), up in the old town, is a hotel,
bar and restaurant in an 18th-century house run
by an Anglo-Catalan couple, with a pleasant
outdoor terrace. The restaurant is particularly
good (mains €11). To rent rooms in the old
town, ask at **El Corral** bar (977 65 04 86) or the
Faristol. Another good, cheap eating option is
La Chunga (C/Mar 9, 977 652 281, mains €8).

Tourist information

Oficina de Turisme de Altafulla

Plaça dels Vents (977 65 07 52). **Open** *mid June-mid
Sept* 11am-1pm Mon, Tue, Thur-Sun.

Tarragona.
See p282.

Getting there

By car

Take the A2, then A7 via Vilafranca; or the toll-free
N340 (Molins de Rei exit from A2).

By train

RENFE from Sants or Passeig de Gràcia to Altafulla
(1hr 15mins). Trains run hourly approx 6am-9.20pm.

The Cistercian Route

Inland from Tarragona are some of the most
striking landscapes in Catalonia, the sweeping
hills dotted with tiny villages clustered around
Romanesque churches, and, on the whole,
blissfully empty of tourists. The three main
architectural gems of the area are the Cistercian

monasteries: **Poblet, Santes Creus** and **Vallbona de les Monges**. A signposted path, the GR175, runs between them and the trail has become known as **La Ruta del Cister** (the Cistercian Route). Not for the unfit, the distances covered add up to over 62 miles (100km), although there are plenty of places to stay en route. Maps are available from all tourist offices in the area.

All three monasteries are also easily accessible by car from **Montblanc**, 112 kilometres (70 miles) due west of Barcelona, and a beautiful town in its own right. In the Middle Ages, Montblanc was one of Catalonia's most powerful centres, with an important Jewish community, a past that is reflected in its **C/Jueus** (Jews' Street), the magnificent 13th-century town walls (two-thirds of which are still intact), the churches of **Santa Maria la Major**, **Sant Miquel** and **Sant Francesc**, the **Palau Reial** (royal palace) and the **Palau del Castlà** (chamberlain's palace).

The great monasteries of the region enjoyed a uniquely close relationship with the Catalan-Aragonese monarchs, and were all built partly to house royal tombs. **Poblet**, a few kilometres west of Montblanc, was founded in 1151 to be a royal residence as well as a monastery. Its founder, Ramon Berenguer IV, is credited with creating the joint Catalan-Aragonese monarchy, and gave generous grants of land to the Cistercian order. The remarkable complex includes a 14th-century **Gothic royal palace**, the 15th-century **chapel of Sant Jordi** and the main **church**, housing the tombs of most of the Count-Kings of Barcelona. The monastery can be visited only on a guided tour.

Santes Creus, founded in 1158 and perhaps still more beautiful than Poblet, grew into a small village when families moved into abandoned monks' residences in the 1800s. Fortified walls shelter the **Palau de l'Abat** (abbot's palace), a monumental fountain, a 12th-century church and a superb Gothic cloister and chapterhouse. Visits to Santes Creus include an audio-visual presentation, though only one a day is in English; call ahead to confirm the time.

Vallbona de les Monges, the third of these Cistercian houses, was, unlike the others, a convent of nuns. It was particularly favoured by Catalan-Aragonese queens, including Violant of Hungary (wife of Jaume I), who was buried here. It has a fine part-Romanesque cloister, but is less grand than the other two.

Note that all three monasteries still house religious communities.

Monestir de Poblet

977 87 02 54. **Open** (last entry 15 mins earlier) *Mar-Sept* 10am-12.30pm, 3-6pm daily. *Oct-Feb* 10am-12.30pm, 3-5.30pm daily. **Admission** €4.20; €2.40 concessions. **No credit cards.**

Monestir de Santa Maria de Vallbona

973 33 02 66. **Open** *June-Sept* 10.30am-1.30pm, 4.30-6.30pm Tue-Sat; noon-1.30pm, 4.30-6.30pm Sun. *Oct-May* 10.30am-1.30pm, 3.30-5.30pm Tue-Sat; noon-1.30pm, 4.30-5.30pm Sun. **Admission** €2.50; €2 concessions. **No credit cards.**

Monestir de Santes Creus

977 63 83 29. **Open** *Mid Mar-mid Sept* 10am-1.30pm, 3-7pm Tue-Sun. *Mid Sept-mid Jan* 10am-1.30pm, 3-5.30pm Tue-Sun. *Mid Jan-mid Mar* 10am-1.30pm, 3-6pm Tue-Sun. **Admission** €3.60; €2.40 concessions. Free Tue. **No credit cards.**

Where to stay & eat

In Montblanc, one of the nicest places to stay and to eat is the **Fonda dels Àngels** (Plaça dels Àngels 1, 977 86 01 73, closed dinner Sun and 3wks Sept, mains €14, rates €37). Alternatively, the **Fonda Colom** (C/Civaderia 5, 977 86 01 53, set lunch €12) is a friendly old inn behind the Plaça Major. If these are both full, try the **Hotel Ducal** (Francesc Macià 11, 977 86 00 25, rates €39-€45).

In L'Espluga de Francolí, on the way to Poblet, the **Hostal del Senglar** (Plaça Montserrat Canals, 977 87 01 21, rates €50-€59) is a great-value country hotel with gardens, a pool and a good restaurant (mains €12). Santes Creus has the very reasonable **Hostal Grau** (C/Pere El Gran 3, 977 63 83 11, closed mid Oct-June, rates €38). Good Catalan food can also be had at the restaurant here (closed Mon and mid Dec-mid Jan, mains €12) or at the **Restaurant Catalunya** (C/Arbreda 2, 977 63 84 32, closed Wed, set lunch €10) further down the hill.

Tourist information

Oficina de Turisme de Montblanc

Antiga Esglesia de Sant Francesc (977 86 17 33). **Open** 10am-1.30pm, 3-6.30pm Mon-Sat; 10am-2pm Sun.

Getting there

By bus

Hispano Igualadina (93 488 15 63) runs a daily service to Montblanc from Sants station. There are more buses running from Valls and Tarragona.

By car

For **Montblanc**, take the A2, then A7, then back on the A2 to exit 9; or take the toll-free N340 to El Vendrell, then the C51 for Valls, and the N240 for Montblanc (112km/70 miles). For **Poblet**, take the N240 west from Montblanc and turn left in L'Espluga

Monestir de Poblet.
p286.

de Francolí. For **Vallbona de les Monges**, take the C14 north from Montblanc towards Tàrrega and turn left on to a signposted side road. For **Santes Creus**, turn off the C51 or A2 before Valls, following signs to Vila-rodona.

By train
RENFE trains leave from Sants or Passeig de Gràcia to Montblanc. There are 5 trains a day. Journey takes about 2hrs.

Tortosa & the Ebre Delta

About an hour further down the coast from Tarragona the railway dips inland to **Tortosa**, a little-visited town with a rich history evident in the fabric of its buildings. A magnificent Gothic **cathedral**, built on the site of a Roman temple, is surrounded by narrow medieval alleyways, and traces of the town's **Jewish** and **Arab quarters** can still be seen (and are clearly signposted). Interesting Modernista buildings around town include the colourful, Mudejar-inspired pavilions of the former slaughterhouse (**Escorxador**), on the bank of the Ebre river.

East of here is the extraordinary **Parc Natural del Delta de l'Ebre** nature reserve jutting out into the sea (*see p288,* **Delta blow**). The town of **Deltebre** is the base for most park services. From there it's easy to make day trips to the bird sanctuaries, especially the remote headland of **Punta de la Banya**. The delta's flatness makes it an ideal place for walking or cycling (for bicycle hire, check at the tourist

office in Deltebre). Small boats offer trips along the river from the north bank about eight kilometres (five miles) east of Deltebre.

Where to stay & eat

In Tortosa there is surprisingly little accommodation, with only one *pensión* – the **Hostal Virgínia** (Avda Generalitat 133, 977 44 41 86, closed mid Dec-mid Jan, rates €27-30). The town's parador, **Castell de la Suda** (977 44 44 50, rates €90.60-€101), built on the site of a Moorish fortress with panoramic views, is worth splashing out for and is also a good place to eat (mains €14).

On the eastern edge of the Ebre delta is a wide, sweeping beach, Platja dels Eucaliptus, where you'll find the **Mediterrani Blau** (977 47 90 46, closed Oct-Mar, €3.20 per person & per tent). In Deltebre the **Hotel Rull** is large but friendly, and organises free 'safaris' for guests on Saturdays (Avda Esportiva 155, 977 48 77 28, rates €57-€87, mains €11). You can also stay and eat at **El Buitre** (Ctra de Riumar, 977 48 05 28, rates €30, mains €15), or the ecologically friendly **Delta Hotel** (Avda del Canal, Camí de la Illeta, 977 48 00 46/www.dsi.es/delta-hotel, rates €58-€79). Local specialities include a variety of dishes made with rice grown in the delta, duck, frogs' legs and the curious *chapadillo* (sun-dried eels). Try them all at **Galatxo,** at the mouth of the river (Desembocadura Riu Ebre, 977 26 75 03, mains €13).

Tourist information

Centre d'Informació
Delta de l'Ebre

C/Doctor Marti Buera 22, Deltebre (977 48 96 79/www.ebre.com/delta). **Open** *May-Sept* 10am-2pm, 3-7pm Mon-Fri; 10am-1pm, 3.30-7pm Sat; 10am-1pm Sun. *Oct-Apr* 10am-2pm, 3-6pm Mon-Fri; 10am-1pm, 3.30-6pm Sat; 10am-1pm Sun.

Getting there

By car

Take the A2, then A7 via Vilafranca; or the toll-free N340 (Molins de Rei exit from A2).

By train & bus

RENFE from Sants or Passeig de Gràcia every 2hrs to L'Aldea-Amposta (2hrs 30mins), then 3 buses daily (HIFE 977 44 03 00) to Deltebre.

Delta blow

Fluttering from balconies, sprayed on to walls and printed on carrier bags all over southern Catalonia you'll see a white knotted pipe on a blue background. This has become the emblem of the locals' campaign to halt the government's cynical *Plan Hidrológico Nacional* (National Water Plan), a scheme to divert water from the northern Ebro (Ebre in Catalan) river to irrigate the south-east, expected to cost in the region of 25 billion euros. Dozens of dams would be built, destroying entire villages in Aragón and Navarra, damaging the environment and, according to the opponents of the scheme, serving little purpose other than to create jobs for corporate friends of the government, including big construction companies and property developers hoping to create yet more second homes along the Mediterranean coastline. The south-east is already intensively cultivated, they say, and what Spain simply needs is to conserve more carefully the adequate water supplies it already has – improving out-of-date irrigation techniques and building desalination plants.

With two canals planned near Tortosa, one to channel water up to Barcelona and the other to take it to Valencia, Almeria and Murcia, the scheme could sound the death knell for the Delta de l'Ebre, an ecologically

remarkable 125-square mile (320-square kilometre) protected area. The towns of the Delta are nothing special, but the immense, flat expanse of wetlands, canals, dunes and productive rice fields is eerily beautiful.

It's also a popular birdwatching destination, and home to nearly 300 of the 600 bird species found in Europe. The area is a vital breeding ground for birds during the winter migratory season. The flocks of flamingos here make a spectacular sight, and the wetlands are crowded with herons, egrets, great crested grebes, spoonbills, marsh harriers and a variety of ducks. Even non-birdwatchers could hardly fail to be enthused by the evocatively named whiskered tern, moustached warbler, lesser short-toed lark and the red-necked nightjar.

If the government's scheme goes ahead, all of this may well be lost, along with the livelihoods of the rice farmers and fishermen in the area. The one glimmer of hope lies in Brussels – a third of the funding would need to come from the EU and it is there the ecologists have set their sights. Many of the environmental big hitters – Greenpeace and the Worldwide Fund for Nature among them – have joined forces with thousands of smaller local groups and have been vociferous in their opposition, but the future remains uncertain.

Girona & the Costa Brava

Ditch the crowds and find the hidden beauty lingering on the *costa*.

Girona

A handsome, prosperous city whose years of historical and economic success have given it a beautifully preserved medieval heart, Girona is split neatly into old and new by the River Onyar, lined by gaily coloured houses and spanned by handsome bridges – one of them, the iron **Pont de les Peixateries**, designed by Eiffel. Running down the east side of the river is the riverside **Rambla**, a good place to start a wander, with a helpful tourist office to get you on your way. This elegant promenade is the social hub of the city and has a string of lively cafés, bars and galleries.

Beyond the Rambla is the heart of the old city, which counts among its treasures a vast Gothic and Romanesque **cathedral** built

between the 11th and 15th centuries. On the site of an ancient mosque, it dominates the city skyline, and has a graceful Romanesque cloister, a soaring Gothic nave (the world's widest), a Renaissance façade and a five-storey tower: an eclectic mix of styles creating an impressive whole. The cathedral museum houses the vast and unmissable 11th-century **'Tapestry of the Creation'**, as well as the **'Beatus'**, an illuminated manuscript from 975.

At its feet lies the labyrinthine **Call**, the medieval Jewish quarter. Before the Jews were expelled in 1492, Girona was home to one of Spain's largest Jewish communities. The excellent Jewish museum in the **Centre Bonastruc ça Porta** (C/Sant Llorenç, 972 21 67 61) – built on the site of a 15th-century synagogue – tells their story. Heading north

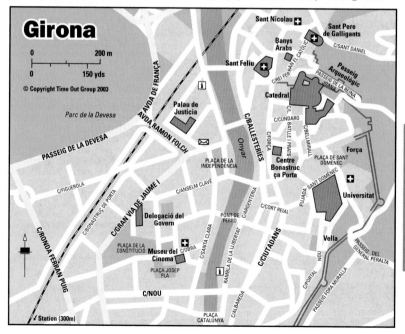

Trips Out of Town

from here, the **Banys Àrabs** (C/Ferran el Catòlic, 972 21 32 62) is actually a Christian creation, a 12th-century bathhouse with a *mudéjar* blend of Romanesque and Moorish .

Nearby is the monastery of **Sant Pere de Galligants**: one of the finest examples of Romanesque architecture in Catalonia, with fabulous carvings in its chapel and cloister. It houses the **Museu Arqueològic** (C/Santa Llúcia 1, 972 20 26 32), which has interesting collections of Roman household objects and 14th-century Jewish tombstones. From here take a stroll along the **Passeig Arqueològic**, the remains of the old city walls. The walk passes through fragrant landscaped gardens and provides panoramic views of the city.

Where to stay & eat

Bland but comfortable, the **Hotel Carlemany** (Plaça Miquel Santaló, 972 21 12 12, rates €112) is Girona's upmarket option, but **Hotel Peninsular** (C/Nou 3 and Avda Sant Francesc 6, 972 20 38 00, rates €56-€60) is better value. The **Apartments Historic Barri Vell** has fully equipped apartments with kitchens, and the added attraction of original fourth-century stone walls downstairs (C/Bellmirall 4A, 972 22 35 83, rates €60). **Pensión Bellmirall** (C/Bellmirall 3, 972 20 40 09, rates incl breakfast €56) is a pretty *hostal* with a small garden.

La Crêperie Bretonne is a fantasy in Gallic retro, specialising in Breton crêpes, cider and towering salads (C/Cort Reial 14, 972 22 35 83, mains €6). Halfway up a medieval flight of steps nearby is another francophile's delight, **Le Bistrot** (Pujada Sant Domènec 4, 972 21 88 03, mains €10). For more typically Catalan fare, with the occasional Jewish dish (and even kosher wine), is **El Pou del Call** (C/Força 14, 972 22 37 74, mains €11). Over the river in the Plaça de l'Independència, meanwhile, is Girona's oldest and possibly best value restaurant, **Casa Marieta** (Plaça de la Independència 5, 972 20 10 16, mains €8).

Tourist information

Oficina de Turisme de Girona
Rambla Llibertat 1 (972 22 65 75). **Open** 8am-8pm Mon-Fri; 8am-2pm, 4-8pm Sat; 9am-2pm Sun.

Getting there

By bus
Barcelona Bus (93 232 04 59), approx 5 buses daily from Estació del Nord.

By car
A7 or toll-free NII.

By train
RENFE from Sants or Passeig de Gràcia (1hr 15mins). Trains leave hourly approx 6am-9.15pm.

From Girona to the coast

Heading seawards from Girona, the C66 takes you to **Púbol**, and the magnificently absurd **Castell de Púbol**, a 12th-century castle Dalí bought and transformed into a home for his wife and muse, Gala. Here she entertained a string of young men, while Dalí himself was not allowed to visit without an appointment. Gala's tomb lies in the castle, overlooked by a stuffed giraffe. Beyond Púbol, a pretty enough village in itself, is **Peratallada**, a walled medieval town surrounded by a moat and charming out of season. The village is well known for its food – succulent *galtes* (pigs' cheeks) are a local speciality. Around here are dotted several other well-preserved medieval villages, many within walking distance. Heading west from Peratallada, a left turn takes you to pretty **Vulpellac**, or turn right to **Ullastret**, which has fascinating ruins of an Iberian settlement from the third century BC and the small **Museu d'Arqueologia** (Puig de Sant Andreu, 972 17 90 58, closed Mon).

Further towards the coast is the medieval village of **Pals**, with fine views and superb buildings, but now seemingly filled with second homes. From here **Begur** is the gateway to the coast: a pretty old town set below the remains of a 14th-century castle, with magnificent views. From there it's a steep three-kilometre (two-mile) walk down to the coast.

Where to stay & eat

In Peratallada, the luxury option is the 11th-century **Castell de Peratallada** (Plaça del Castell 1, 972 63 40 21, rates incl breakfast €120-€240), or try the charming **Ca l'Aliu** (C/Roca 6, 972 63 40 61, rates incl breakfast €49-€52). The **Hostal Mirall una** (Plaça de l'Oli 2, 972 63 43 04, rates incl breakfast €110-€120) is a tranquil, elegant place filled with antiques. Pals has the **Barris** (C/Enginyer Algarra 51, 972 63 67 02, rates €36). In Begur, try the **Hotel Rosa** in the centre of town (C/Pi i Ralló 19, 972 62 30 15/www.hotel-rosa.com, closed Nov-Feb, rates incl breakfast €51-€73).

Peratallada has a surprising number of decent restaurants; the **Restaurant Bonay** is one of the better options (Placa de les Voltes 13, 972 63 40 34/www.bonay.com, closed Dec-Jan, mains €13). In Begur **Els Patis de Begur** specialises in paellas, and is one of few places in town that is open over the winter (C/Pi i Rallo 9, 972 62 37 41, closed Mon, mains €15). In Pals

Girona.

Restaurant Sa Punta, set by a pool, serves excellent Mediterranean dishes (Urbanizacion Sa Punta, 972 66 73 76, mains €21).

Castell de Púbol

Info: Teatre-Museu Dalí (972 67 75 00/www.salvadordali.org). **Open** *15 Mar-14 June, 16 Sept-1 Nov* 10.30am-5.30pm Tue-Sun. *15 June-15 Sept* 10.30am-7.30pm daily. Closed 2 Nov-14 Mar. **Admission** €5.50; €4 concessions. **No credit cards.**

Tourist information

Oficina de Turisme de Begur

Plaça de l'Església 8 (972 62 45 20). **Open** *Apr-June* 9am-2.30pm, 5-8pm Mon-Fri; 10am-2pm, 5-8pm Sat; 10am-2pm Sun. *July-Sept* 9am-9pm daily. *Oct-Apr* 9am-2.30pm Mon-Fri; 10am-2pm Sat, Sun.

Oficina de Turisme de Pals

Plaça Major 7 (972 63 73 80). **Open** *June-Sept* 10am-2pm, 4-8pm daily. *Oct-May* 10am-2pm, 4-8pm Mon-Fri; 10am-2pm Sun.

Getting there

By bus

Barcelona Bus (93 232 04 59) to Girona from Estació del Nord. Sarfa (902 302 025) has 9 daily buses to Palafrugell (some continue to Begur), and regular buses to La Bisbal, which stop at Púbol.

By car

A7 or toll-free NII to Girona. For Peratallada, Pals and Begur take exit 6 from A7 or leave NII after Girona and take C66.

Costa Brava

Visitors often wrongly assume that the Costa Brava is the touristy cluster of **Calella, Lloret de Mar** and **Tossa del Mar** around the local hub of **Blanes**. This is not the Costa Brava proper; the 'wild' or 'rugged' coast – a name coined by journalist Ferran Agullo in the early 1900s – referred to an area 50 kilometres (30 miles) north in the Baix Empordà. With the exception of the unlovely resort of **Roses** the area has largely escaped mass tourism: there being no big sandy beaches and limited public transport. This does not mean the area is undiscovered, however.

The first town of interest is **Sant Feliu de Guíxols**, for centuries the principal port for Girona. It has stunning Modernista buildings along the **Passeig Marítim**, a handful of fine Gothic buildings and a spectacular collection of ancient ceramics in the local museum. The curved sandy beach gets crowded, but offers respite from an otherwise rocky coast.

From here the best way to explore the coastline is to walk along the **Camí de Ronda** path as it curls its way along the coast. Tourist offices have maps. A less-visited beach lies three kilometres (two miles) north at **Sant Pol**. Heading north about 20 kilometres (12 miles), you arrive at the main inlets on the peninsula. The northern ones (**Sa Riera, Sa Tuna, Aiguablava**) are most accessible from Begur.

Tamariu, Llafranc and **Calella de Palafrugell** are charming towns set in small

Trips Out of Town

How to be king of the castle

The idea of a chain of state-run hotels may not sound terribly sexy, but the *paradores nacionales* are actually among the loveliest places to stay in Spain. The scheme was dreamt up in the 1920s by a creative tourism minister who also happened, coincidentally, to be an aristocrat, as a way of saving the country's castles, palaces and monasteries from rack and ruin. Instead they were to be turned into elegantly furnished hotels with the further intention of bringing tourism to beautiful but little visited natural settings.

Of Spain's 86 *paradores*, Catalonia has seven, four within easy reach of Barcelona. The town of Tortosa has the **Castell de la Suda**, built on the site of what was first a Roman, then a Moorish fortress, with a massive internal well (*suda*) fed by the Ebre river. The castle was later converted into a royal palace and the parador retains a regal feel. It has wonderful views over the Ebre delta and Beseit mountains and overlooks the town's magnificent Gothic cathedral. The closest parador to Barcelona is set in a medieval castle in **Cardona** (Ducs de Cardona, 93 869 12 75, rates €100-€117). The old castle spans centuries, and its ninth-century walls enclose a second-century tower and an 11th-century Romanesque church,

along with moats and a lush garden. Cardona is certainly not Catalonia's prettiest town, but the parador's vaulted ceilings, thick stone walls and antique furniture transport you back to another era in a way that makes modern hotels seem bland and ordinary.

Two relatively modern paradors are the sparkling white structure on a headland in **Aiguablava** (*see p291*) and the parador just outside **Vic** (*see p296*), in a stunning location set in the Guilleries mountains above the Sau reservoir. It's also famous for its regional cooking, including its hearty stews and, of course, its versions of the celebrated local sausages. Up in the foothills of the Pyrenees, the parador at **La Seu d'Urgell** (C/Sant Domènec 6, 973 35 20 00, rates €90-€117) is built around the lovely, plant-filled cloister of a rambling 14th-century monastery.

The really good news is that there are excellent deals to be had. Most *paradores* offer a 20 per cent discount on a double room with half-board for a minimum of two nights, and the *'Tarjeta de Cinco Noches'* is worth investigating (a card entitling you to five – not necessarily consecutive – nights to be taken at any point during the calendar year in one or more *paradores*, for €370. See the website, www.parador.es, for details.)

bays, with some excellent restaurants. All three are best reached from Palafrugell, with regular buses. You can hire a boat to explore further, by calling Paco Heredia (972 30 13 10/www.giro nautic.com). Just south of Begur, a narrow road takes you to **Fornells** and **Aiguablava**, both in a larger bay. Aiguablava has a beautiful white sandy beach, a small yacht harbour, an old, luxurious hotel and a squat, rather ugly modern parador set high in the cliff.

The northernmost cove of the peninsula, **Sa Riera**, has one of the largest sandy beaches, and a popular nudist beach, the **Illa Roja**, between Sa Riera and **La Platja del Racó**. From Sa Riera a road leads south to **Sa Tuna**, a picturesque fishing village with a sweet stony beach. A 40-minute walk from there along a coastal path takes you northwards through **Aiguafreda**, a small wooded cove, toward a spectacular building cut into the promontory beyond. Steps lead down to swimming pools cut into the precipitous cliff-face.

Further up the coast is the small resort town of **L'Estartit**, a water-sports centre situated opposite the islands known as the **Illes Medes** (Catalonia's only underwater nature reserve and a popular scuba-diving spot). Glass-bottomed boats leave L'Estartit regularly from June to September, and according to demand in April, May and October, to tour its rare coral deposits.

Where to eat

In Sant Feliu de Guíxols try the **Nàutic** in the Club Nàutic sailing club, for great views and superb seafood (Port Esportiu, 972 32 06 63, closed Mon and 2wks Nov, set lunch €10.50). In Tamariu, there's more good seafood at the **Royal** on the beachfront (Passeig de Mar 9, 972 62 00 41, mains €14), while in Calella is the excellent **Tragamar** (Platja de Canadell s/n, 972 61 43 36, mains €11), a branch of the restaurant Tragaluz in Barcelona. In Aiguablava, the **Hotel Aiguablava** has an excellent restaurant (Platja de Fornells, 972 62 20 58, closed Nov-Feb, mains €18).

Where to stay

In Sant Feliu de Guíxols, the small, friendly **Hotel Plaça** is close to the beach (Plaça Mercat 22, 972 32 51 55, rates €64-€93). The **Casa Rovira** is a rambling, bohemian *hostal* (C/Sant Amanç 106, 972 32 12 02/48 57, closed mid Oct-mid May, rates €46.80-€53.50). North of Sant Feliu, in S'Agaró, is the nearest luxury option, the **Hostal de la Gavina** (Plaça de la Rosaleda, 972 32 11 00, closed Nov-Easter, rates €177-€267), an antique-filled five-star.

Llafranc has the **Hotel Llafranc** (Passeig de Cipsela 16, 972 30 02 08, rates incl breakfast €79-€123), or try the friendly **Hotel Casamar** (C/Nero 3-11, 972 30 01 04, closed Feb, rates incl breakfast €71.50-€88.50). Tamariu has the relaxed **Hotel Tamariu** (Passeig de Mar 2, 972 62 00 31, closed Nov-Mar, rates incl breakfast €80-€110). In Aiguablava, there's the useful parador, **Platja d'Aiguablava** (972 62 21 62, rates €83.80-€132.90) or the stately **Hotel Aiguablava** (*see above*, rates incl breakfast €138-€183). Sa Tuna has the useful **Hostal Sa Tuna** (Platja Sa Tuna, 972 62 21 98, closed Nov-mid Mar, rates incl breakfast €96), with five rooms in a perfect spot by the sea. In Sa Riera is the **Hotel Sa Riera** (Platja de Sa Riera, 972 62 30 00, rates incl breakfast €97.40-€113.60). In L'Estartit is the **Santa Clara** (Passeig Marítim 18, 972 75 17 67, rates incl breakfast €41-€48).

Tourist information

Oficina de Turisme de L'Estartit
Passeig Marítim (972 75 19 10). **Open** *May* 9am-1pm, 4-7pm Mon-Fri; 10am-2pm Sat; 10am-2pm Sun. *June, Sept* 9.30am-2pm, 4-8pm Mon-Sat; 10am-2pm Sun. *July, Aug* 9.30am-2pm, 4-9pm Mon-Sat; 10am-2pm Sun. *Oct-Apr* 9am-1pm, 3-6pm Mon-Fri; 10am-2pm Sat.

Oficina de Turisme de Palafrugell
C/Carrilet 2 (972 30 02 28). **Open** *May-June, Sept* 10am-1pm, 5-8pm Mon-Sat; 10am-1pm Sun. *July, Aug* 9am-9pm Mon-Sat; 10am-1pm Sun. *Oct-Apr* 10am-1pm, 4-7pm Mon-Sat; 10am-1pm Sun.

Oficina de Turisme de Sant Feliu de Guíxols
Plaça Monestir (972 82 00 51). **Open** *Mid June-mid Sept* 10am-2pm, 4-8pm daily. *Mid Sept-mid June* 10am-1pm, 4-7pm Mon-Sat; 10am-2pm Sun.

Getting there

By bus
Sarfa (902 302 025) has 15 buses daily to Sant Feliu from Estació del Nord (journey time 1hr20mins), and 9 to Palafrugell (2hrs); some continue to Begur. Change in Palafrugell or Torroella for L'Estartit.

By car
A7 north to exit 9 on to C35/C65 for Sant Feliu de Guíxols, then C31 for Palafrugell (123km/76 miles); or A7 exit 6 for Palafrugell and Begur via La Bisbal.

Figueres to France

Figueres, while not the *comarca*'s most elegant town, has a lively feel and one of the area's gems, the **Teatre-Museu Dalí**. The museum was designed by Dalí in a former

Cadaqués.

theatre, and contains some of his finest paintings as well as the man himself – he is entombed here. Also worth visiting is the **Museu de l'Empordà** (Rambla 2, 972 50 23 05) on the Rambla, for an overview of the area's art and history, and the **Museu del Joguet**, a toy museum with toys once belonging to Dalí and Miró (C/Sant Pere 1, 972 50 45 85).

Between Figueres and the deep blue sea is the **Aiguamolls de l'Empordà**, a nature reserve and birdwatcher's paradise in the wetlands at the mouth of the Fluvià river. More than 300 species have been recorded, including the stone curlew, kingfisher, moustached warbler and bee-eater. In spring, when icy northern winds make the Pyrenees impassable for birds, more than 100 species have been seen here in a single day. It's home to many types of fish and amphibians – and mosquitoes.

On the coast itself, **Roses** is the area's largest tourist town. A fairly unattractive place, it has a glut of hotels, discos and (often overpriced) restaurants. It's possible that its only redeeming features are a 16th-century citadel, and legendary restaurant **El Bulli**. From Roses the road climbs up through spectacular switchbacks with fabulous views to **Cadaqués**, which sits in splendid isolation at the end of the **Cap de Creus** peninsula. Picasso painted some of his best cubist works here, and Dalí and his surrealist circle later flocked here. In later years the town became the favourite summer resort of Barcelona's cultural elite. Its attraction comes from the fact that, in the tourist-boom, high-rise hotel-building was barred here, so it has kept its narrow streets

and whitewashed houses. The village's cultural season includes a summer classical music festival. Thanks to its chic rating, Cadaqués is relatively expensive, though, so be prepared. The peninsula around it is an extraordinary mass of rock lined by tiny coves.

It's a short walk from here to **Port Lligat**, a tiny bay dominated by Dalí's favourite house, the strange and fascinating **Casa-Museu de Port Lligat**, with two giant cracked heads on the wall before the azure sea. Only eight people are allowed in at a time, so booking is essential. Beyond it a road continues to **Cap de Creus**, with its lighthouse, nature reserve and unique, pock-marked rock formations used as a location in many science-fiction movies. Nearby on the cape's north side, **Port de la Selva** has never received the accolades showered on Cadaqués, yet is also unspoilt, quieter and closer to the magnificent Romanesque monastery of **Sant Pere de Rodes**, often lost in clouds on the mountain above the town.

Alternatively, south of Figueres are the well-preserved remains of the ancient city of **Empúries**, which was founded in 600 BC by the Phoenicians, recolonised by the Greeks and finally by the Romans in AD 2. Ruins from all three periods, as well as the layout of the original Greek harbour, are clearly visible. It's a picturesque and atmospheric ancient site right at the edge of the beach.

Casa-Museu de Port Lligat

972 25 10 15/*www.salvador-dali.org*. **Open** *15 Mar-14 June, 16 Sept-6 Jan* 10.30am-5.30pm Tue-Sun. *15 June-15 Sept* 10.30am-8.30pm Tue-Sun. Closed 7 Jan-14 Mar. **Admission** €8; €5 concessions. **Credit** MC, V.

Sant Pere de Rodes

972 38 75 59. **Open** *June-Sept* 10am-8pm Tue-Sun. *Oct-May* 10am-5.30pm Tue-Sun. **Admission** €3.60; €2.40 concessions; free Tue. **No credit cards**.

Teatre-Museu Dalí

Plaça Gala-Salvador Dalí 5, Figueres (972 67 75 00/www.salvador-dali.org). **Open** *July-Sept* 9am-7.45pm Tue-Sun. *Oct-May* 10.30am-5.45pm Tue-Sun. *June* 10.30am-5.45pm daily. **Admission** €9; €6.50 concessions. **No credit cards**.

Where to stay & eat

In Figueres the **Hotel Duran** has a kind of comfortable, battered elegance (C/Lasauca 5, 972 50 12 50, rates €59-€63, mains €20). Dalí was once a regular in its restaurant, which serves excellent game and seafood. For clean and well-equipped, if unexciting, rooms, try **La Barretina** (C/Lasauca 13, 972 67 34 25, rates €38) or the **Hostal Bon Repòs** (C/Villalonga 43, 972 50 92 02, rates €25). The **President** offers good, solid Catalan fare and excellent seafood (Ronda Firal 33, 972 50 17 00, closed Mon, set lunch €13). Off the C31 to L'Escala, at Siurana, is **El Molí** (972 52 51 39, rates incl breakfast €48), a beautifully restored *masia* with six rooms to rent. Near Roses is the extraordinary restaurant **El Bulli** (*see p164*), for those who can afford it.

In Cadaqués there are few hotels, and many are closed in winter. Try the friendly *pensión*-restaurant **Fonda Cala d'Or** (C/Sa Fitora 1, 972 25 81 49, rates €25) or the **Hostal Marina** (C/Riera 3, 972 25 81 99, closed Jan-Easter, rates €48). **Playa Sol** (Platja Pianc 3, 972 25 81 00, closed Dec-Feb, rates incl breakfast €88-€156) has sea views, while the **Misty** (C/Nova Port Lligat, 972 25 89 62, closed Jan-mid Mar, rates €47-€72) has a pool.

Good places to eat include the pretty **Es Balconet** (C/Sant Antoni 2, 972 25 88 14, mains €13.50) for great paella up a winding street from the bay, and **Ix!**, just off the tourist drag with tables overlooking the sea and a good-value *menú* (C/Horta Sanés 1, 972 25 87 33, mains €13). **Casa Anita** is a long-running, very popular, family-owned place with excellent seafood and long queues (C/Miguel Roset, 972 25 84 71/www.casa-anita.com, closed Mon and Feb & Mon, mains €12).

At Cap de Creus, the **Restaurant Cap de Creus** serves an eclectic range from seafood to curry, and has stunning views over the easternmost tip of Spain (972 19 90 05, mains €14). Near Empúries, if you have a car, the best place to stay is the village of Sant Martí d'Empúries, which has the well situated **Riomar** (Platja del Riuet, 972 77 03 62, closed mid Oct-Easter, rates incl breakfast €60-€90).

Tourist information

Oficina de Turisme de Cadaqués

C/Cotxe 2A (972 25 83 15). **Open** *June-Sept* 10am-1pm, 4-7pm Mon-Sat; 10am-1pm Sun. *Oct-May* 10am-1pm, 4-7pm Mon-Sat.

Oficina de Turisme de L'Escala

Plaça de les Escoles 1 (972 77 06 03). **Open** *mid June-mid Sept* 9am-8.30pm daily. *Mid Sept-mid June* 9am-1pm, 4-7pm Mon-Fri; 10am-2pm Sat.

Oficina de Turisme de Figueres

Plaça del Sol (972 50 31 55). **Open** *Mar-June, Oct* 9am-6pm Mon-Fri; 10am-1.30pm, 3.30-6.30pm Sat. *July-Sept* 9am-8pm Mon-Sat; 10am-3pm Sun. *Nov-Feb* 9am-6pm Mon-Fri.

Getting there

By bus

Barcelona Bus (93 232 04 59) has several buses daily to Figueres from Estació del Nord (2hrs 30mins). Sarfa (902 302 025) has 2 buses daily to Roses and Cadaqués (2hrs15mins), and services to Roses, Port de la Selva, Cadaqués and L'Escala from Figueres.

By car

A7 or NII to Figueres (120km/74 miles). For Roses and Cadaqués, take the C260 from Figueres.

By train

RENFE from Sants or Passeig de Gràcia to Figueres (journey 2hrs). Trains leave every hour.

Teatre-Museu Dalí. *See p293.*

Vic to the Pyrenees

Climb every mountain, ford every stream and then tuck into huge portions of fabulous food.

Vic, Rupit & Les Guilleries

Known mainly for its charcuterie, the market town of **Vic** first began life as the capital of the Ausetian tribe, went on to become a Roman city, and later fell briefly to the Moors, who lost it to the evidently hirsute Wilfred the Hairy in the ninth century. Since then it has remained an administrative, artistic and religious centre, with an extraordinary number of churches. The town sees few tourists, but has many buildings of historic importance; the **Temple Romà** (Roman temple) was only discovered in 1882, when the 12th-century walls that surrounded it were knocked down. Since then it has been sympathetically restored and now houses an art gallery. The **Catedral de Sant Pere** contains Romanesque, Gothic and neo-classical elements, along with a set of sombre 20th-century murals by Josep Lluís Sert. The **Museu Episcopal** (Plaça del Bisbe Oliva 3, 93 886 93 60) is simply unmissable, with its magnificent 12th-century murals and an equally fascinating collection of Romanesque sculpture and art.

Vic is surrounded by the spectacular mountain nature reserves and ideal walking territory of **Montseny**, **Les Guilleries** and **Collsacabra**. The area is full of interesting villages, and can be recommended to anyone with limited time who seeks a taste of the Catalan countryside at its best. The most rewarding route is up the C153 road towards Olot into **Les Guilleries**, stopping at **Rupit**, an extraordinarily beautiful and ancient village built against the side of a medieval castle, with a precarious hanging bridge crossing a gorge. **Tavertet** is an equally picturesque village nearby, perched on the edge of a gorge with sweeping views, but less touristed than Rupit.

Where to stay & eat

There is relatively little accommodation in Vic; its only *pensión* is **Hostal Osona** (C/Remei 3, 93 883 28 45, rates €26). The most comfortable places to stay are located outside the town; notably, at the **Parador de Vic** in a fabulous location overlooking the Ter gorge (Paraje el Bac de Sau, 93 812 23 23, rates €93-€103) – take the C153 north and follow the signs (around 14km). **Can Pamplona** is cheaper, however

(Crta de Vic a Puigcerdà 10, 93 883 31 12, rates €77-€90). In Tavérnoles, just off the C153 from Vic, **Mas Banús** (93 812 20 91) is a giant old *masia*. Self-contained accommodation for six for the weekend costs €251. In Rupit, *hostal* **Estrella** also has a huge restaurant that has been turning out great food for 50 years (Plaça Bisbe Font 1, 93 852 20 05, closed Jan, rates incl breakfast €90, set lunch €14).

Vic has some excellent restaurants. The best is probably **Jordi Parramon** (C/Cardona 7, 93 886 38 15, closed Mon & dinner except Fri, Sat, mains €20), with a short but exquisite list of dishes. The stylish **Basset**, which serves wonderful fish and game dishes, has more typical fare (C/Sant Sadurní 4, 93 889 02 12, closed Sun, set menus €11-€15), as does **Ca l'U** (Plaça Santa Teresa 4-5, 93 889 03 45, closed Wed dinner and all day Mon, Tue, Sun, set lunch €11). The small, colourful **La Creperia** is the budget option, with cheap crêpes, waffles and salads (Plaça Sant Felip Neri 9, 93 886 37 81, mains €4).

Tourist information

Oficina de Turisme de Vic
Plaça Major 1 (93 886 20 91). **Open** 9am-8pm Mon-Fri; 9am-2pm, 4-7pm Sat; 10am-1pm Sun.

Getting there

By bus
Empresa Sagalès (93 231 27 56) from the Fabra i Puig bus station (near metro of same name) to Vic. For Rupit, take a local bus from Vic.

By car
Take the C17, signed for Puigcerdà, to Vic (65km/ 40 miles). For Rupit, take the C153 out of Vic (signposted to Olot).

By train
RENFE from Sants or Plaça Catalunya to Vic. Trains leave about every 90mins. Journey time is 1hr 20mins.

Besalú & Olot

Besalú is a storybook medieval village, with a wonderfully preserved 12th-century fortified bridge spanning the Fluvià River to mark its entrance. Inside the city walls, winding streets

Besalú is storybook beautiful. *See p296.*

lead to two sunny main squares and shops selling local sausages and produce. The old Jewish *call* and the *mikveh* (the only remaining Jewish baths in Spain) are both of particular historical interest (get the bathhouse key from the tourist office). Plan to stay in town until twilight, when daytrippers from the Costa Brava have gone and the softly lit streets are at their most romantic.

From here the N260 runs west to Olot (on the way look for the odd structure built entirely out of twigs just outside **Argelaguer**), with a spectacular view of **Castellfollit de la Roca**, a village perched on the edge of a precipitous crag. The village is prettier from below than within, but the old part makes for a nice stroll, and, if all else fails, there's always the sausage museum (Museu de l'Embotit, Ctra de Girona 10, 972 29 44 63, admission free).

Olot, the largest town in the area, is known mainly for the 30-odd inactive volcanoes and numerous lava slips that surround it to form the **Parc Natural de la Zona Volcànica de la Garrotxa**. Just south of town on the road to Vic is the **Casal dels Volcans**, (Ctra Santa Coloma 43, 972 26 67 62, closed Tue, admission €1.80, 90¢ concessions) an information centre and museum where you can pick up maps for hiking in the area. Olot itself was destroyed in an earthquake in 1427, but has some impressive 18th-century and Modernista buildings. It was home to a school of landscape painters through

the 20th century; the local **Museu de la Garrotxa** (C/Hospice 8, 972 27 91 30, closed Tue & Sun afternoon, admission €1.80, 90¢ concessions) has works by them and by Ramon Casas and Santiago Rusiñol.

Off the G1524 heading toward Banyoles is a delightful beech forest, the **Fageda d'en Jordà,** immortalised by Catalan poet Joan Maragall, and the pretty if heavily touristed village and castle of **Santa Pau**.

Where to stay & eat

In Besalú, a 19th-century riverside inn, **Fonda Siqués** (Avda Lluís Companys 6-8, 972 59 01 10, rates incl breakfast €40-€66) offers clean but drab rooms and is located above a charming restaurant (closed Sun dinner, Mon Oct-May & Jan, set lunch €9 Mon-Fri). For nicer, though still simple, rooms, try **Els Jardins de la Martana** (C/Pont 2, 972 59 00 09, rates €90). A couple of miles north of the town, in Beuda, is a pretty *masia* with a pool, **Mas Salvanera** (972 59 09 75/www.salvanera.com, rates incl breakfast €113). In Olot, **La Perla** is a large hotel with a good restaurant (Avda Santa Coloma 97, 972 26 23 26, rates €57), while **La Vila** *pensión* is modern and very central (C/Sant Roc 1, 972 26 98 07, rates incl breakfast €36).

Restaurants in Besalú include the **Pont Vell** for traditional cooking with a twist and a great view over the medieval bridge (C/Pont Vell 24,

Trips Out of Town

Gorgeous views are all around **Ripoll**.

972 59 10 27, mains €12). Another riverside view is to be had at **Cúria Reial** for good traditional cooking (Plaça de la Llibertat 15, 972 59 02 63, closed Mon dinner, Tue & Feb, mains €16). In Olot, **Can Guix** (C/Mulleres 3-5, 972 26 10 40, closed Sun, 2wks July-Aug, mains €6) has authentic, cheap local dishes, while north of town is the **Restaurant Les Cols** set in a picturesque *masia* with a sunny terrace. While you're there, try the house speciality of cabbage leaves stuffed with duck liver (Crta de la Canya, 972 26 92 09, closed Mon, Tue dinner, Sun, 2wks July-Aug, mains €18).

Just south of Olot, in La Pinya, is **Mas Garganta** (972 27 12 89/www.turisme rural.net/garganta, rates €59 per person, half-board) – an 18th-century *masia* with magnificent views. It runs walking tours with two *masies* nearby, so you can stay in one place and walk without bags to the next.

Tourist information

Oficina de Turisme de Olot

C/Bisbe Lorenzana 15 (972 26 01 41). **Open** 10am-2pm, 5-7pm Mon-Fri; 10am-2pm Sun.

Getting there

By bus

TEISA (972 20 48 68) to Besalú and Olot from the corner of C/Pau Claris and C/Consell de Cent.

By car

For Besalú, take the C66 from Girona, then N260 for Olot.

Ripoll to the Vall de Núria

Known as the 'Cradle of Catalonia', the area around **Ripoll**, north of Vic, was the original fiefdom of Wilfred the Hairy before he became Count of Barcelona. He is buried in the unique monastery of **Santa Maria de Ripoll**, which he founded in 879. The church has a superb 12th-century stone portal; its carvings are among the finest examples of Romanesque art in Catalonia. The monastery museum, **Museu Etnogràfic** (information 972 70 31 44) will be closed for renovations until 2004, but ongoing exhibitions of its displays tracing the customs and history of the area are to be held in the basement of the town hall. Wilfred also founded the monastery and town of **Sant Joan de les Abadesses**, ten kilometres (six miles) east up the C26 road. It is worth a visit for its Gothic bridge as well as the 12th-century monastery. Sadly, neither town holds many other charms.

From Sant Joan the road leads towards **Camprodon**, on the River Ter, site of a fine Romanesque church, and from there a local road veers left up the main Ter valley to the mountain village of **Setcases**, a famous beauty spot now taken over by holiday homes. By now you are into the Pyrenees; the valley road comes to an end at **Vallter 2000** (972 13 60 75), the easternmost ski station As with all ski resorts in the area, the best way to visit is to book a package, from any Barcelona travel agent.

Ribes de Freser, the next town on the N152 north of Ripoll, is an attractive base from which to travel to the pretty if slightly gentrified villages of **Campelles** and **Queralbs**. Ribes is also the starting point for the *cremallera*, the old, narrow-gauge cog railway that runs via Queralbs along the Freser river and up to the sanctuary of **Núria**, with its incredible views. Many choose to walk back to Queralbs (around 2hrs), following a path through dramatic rock formations, pines and crashing waterfalls.

Núria itself nestles by a lake on a plateau at over 2,000 metres (6,500 feet), and is home to the second most famous of Catalonia's patron virgins: a wooden statue of the Madonna that was carved in the 12th century, when Núria was a refuge and place of pilgrimage. The mostly 19th-century monastery that surrounds the virgin's shrine is not especially attractive, but its location is spectacular. Here you can bury your head in a pot to gain fertility, or ring a bell to cure headaches, but most choose simply to hike, ski, row boats or ride horses (you can get maps and information from the local tourist office).

Where to stay & eat

In Ripoll, the cheap sleeping option is **Ca la Paula** (C/Pireneos 6, 972 70 00 11, closed 2wks Oct, rates €36), but **La Trobada** is more comfortable if you can afford it (Passeig Honorat Vilamanya 4, 972 70 23 53, rates €53). If you're hungry, **El Racó del Francés** (Plà d'Ordina 11, 972 70 18 94, closed dinner Mon-Fri, lunch Sat, 3wks Aug, set lunch €15) serves French dishes. In Sant Joan de les Abadesses, the best beds and decently priced local food are to be had at **Janpere** (C/Mestre Andreu 3, 972 72 00 77, rates €42, restaurant closed Mon, set lunches €9-€16).

In Ribes de Freser, the family-run **Hotel Els Caçadors** has good food and comfortable rooms (C/Balandrau 24-6, 972 72 77 22, rates

€34-€39, mains €15). If it's full, try **Hostal Porta de Núria** (C/Nostra Senyora de Gràcia 3, 972 72 71 37, closed May, rates incl breakfast €53). In Queralbs, try the **Calamari Hostal l'Avet** (C/Major 5, 972 72 73 77, closed Mon-Thur, rates €39). The one good place to eat in Queralbs is **De la Plaça**, which has regional specialities (Plaça de la Vila 2, 972 72 70 37, closed Tue, set menu €12.60).

In Núria, there's the three-star **Hotel Vall de Núria** (C/Santuari Mare de Dèu de Núria, 972 73 20 20, closed Nov, rates per person €52-€77 half-board). You are required to stay for a minimum of two nights.

Tourist information

Oficina de Turisme de Núria

Estaciò de Montanya del Vall de Núria (972 73 20 20/www.valldenuria.com). **Open** *July-Sept* 8.20am-8pm daily. *Oct-June* 8.20am-6.15pm daily.

Oficina de Turisme de Ribes de Freser

Plaça del Ayuntamiento 3 (972 72 77 28). **Open** *Sept-July* 10am-2pm, 5-8pm Tue-Sat; 10am-1pm Sun. *Aug* 10am-2pm, 5-8pm Mon-Sat; 11am-1pm Sun.

Getting there

By bus

TEISA (972 20 48 68) from the corner of C/Pau Claris and C/Consell de Cent to Ripoll, Sant Joan de les Abadesses and Camprodon.

By car

Take the C17 direct to Ripoll (104km/65 miles). For Sant Joan de les Abadesses and Camprodon, take the C26 out of Ripoll.

By train

RENFE from Sants or Plaça Catalunya, approx 1 train every 2hrs (journey time to Ripoll 2hrs). For Queralbs and Núria, change to the *cremallera* train in Ribes de Freser.

Berga & Puigcerdà

Some 43 kilometres (27 miles) west of Ripoll on the C26 is **Berga**, capital of the district of **Berguedà**. Just north from there the giant cliffs of the **Serra del Cadí**, one of the ranges of the 'Pre-Pyrenees' or Pyrenees foothills, loom above the town. Berga also has a medieval castle, **Sant Ferran**, with a suitably storybook air, a charming old centre and a Jewish quarter that dates back to the 13th century.

It's famous for the frenzied festival of **La Patum**, held in May, and for the annual mushroom-hunting competition in the **Pla de Puigventós** on the first Sunday in October. Great baskets of different wild mushrooms

Trips Out of Town

(*bolets*) are weighed in before an enthusiastic public. Anyone interested in participating should contact the tourist office.

Heading north along the C16, uphill into the Cadí, you'll come to the small town of **Bagà**, with partially preserved medieval walls around a pretty old quarter and a central square with Romanesque porticos. It marks the beginning of the **Parc Natural del Cadí-Moixeró**, a gigantic mountain park that covers 410 square kilometres (159 square miles) and contains several ancient villages. Rugged and austerely beautiful, the Cadí is rich in wildlife, and can feel more like the American West than the Mediterranean. Chamois, roe and red deer roam the slopes while golden eagles swoop above. All of its villages have medieval architecture, and many offer stunning views. Picasso stayed and painted in the village of **Gósol** in 1906.

Above Bagà the C16 road enters the Túnel del Cadí to emerge into the wide, fertile plateau of the **Cerdanya**. Described by writer Josep Pla as a 'huge casserole', the Cerdanya has an obvious geographical unity, but since a treaty signed in 1659, the French and Spanish frontier has run right across its middle; one Spanish village, **Llívia**, is stranded in French territory. Its **Museu Municipal** (972 89 63 13) contains one of the oldest pharmacies in Europe, with a fascinating collection of ceramics and utensils. Just north of Llívia and also worth a visit is **Dorres**, a laid-back town with wonderful views and sulphur springs.

The snow-capped peaks that ring the valley are laced with ski resorts, including **La Molina** (972 89 20 31) and **Masella** (972 14 40 00). The capital of the area (on the Spanish side), **Puigcerdà**, is a sizeable town heavily touristed by Catalans and French, where discos and après-ski bars mingle with remnants of things medieval. It's a good base (and a memorable train journey from Barcelona) for exploring the area by ski or on foot. The tourist office has maps and itineraries. Other places of interest in the Cerdanya are the cross-country ski centre of **Lles**, which has a Romanesque church, and **Bellver de Cerdanya**, a hilltop village on the edge of the Cadí-Moixeró that was the unlikely scene of a battle during the Civil War. The village has a helpful park information centre.

Where to stay & eat

In Berga, try either the **Estel Hotel** (C/Sant Fruitos 39, 93 821 34 63, rates €44) or the **Queralt Hotel** (Plaça de la Creu 4, 93 821 06 11, rates €43) in the medieval centre. Just north of Berga is **Sant Marc**, which is good for solid country cooking like roasted guinea hen with cauliflower dumplings (Ctra de Queralt, 93 821

04 45, mains €10). In Llívia, **Can Ventura** is a wonderfully atmospheric inn filled with antiques (Plaça Major 1, 972 89 61 78, mains €16). Puigcerdà has plenty of hotels in the town centre, including the small and charming **Avet Blau** (Plaça Santa Maria 14, 972 88 25 52, rates incl breakfast €77-€96). The **Belvedere** is a good deal and has a small garden and terrace (C/Carmelites 6-8, 972 88 03 56, rates €34-€70). A bit more upmarket, the **Hotel del Lago** is a modern pink mansion near the lake (Avda Dr Piguillem 7, 972 88 10 00/www.hotellago.com, rates €74-€80). Cheap, very friendly and dead central is another *hostal*-restaurant, **Cerdanya** (C/Ramon Cosp 7, 972 88 00 10, rates €36-€50, set lunch €10). Or there's excellent regional food, moderately priced, at **Casa Clemente** (Avda Dr Piguillem 6, 972 88 11 66, closed Mon and 1st 2wks July, set lunches €12-€18). Among other things, fantastic pizzas from a huge wood-fired oven are to be had at **El Pati de la Tieta** (C/Ferrers 20, 972 88 01 56, closed Mon-Wed, closed mid June-mid July, mains €13), which is located in a pretty old house with a terrace. Or, if you head a little further out to Bolvir, the sumptuous **Torre del Remei** (C/Camí Reial, 972 14 01 82, rates €203-€321) also has one of the best (and most expensive) restaurants in the area (main courses €68).

Tourist information

Oficina de Turisme de Berga
C/Àngels 7 (93 821 13 84). **Open** 9am-2pm Mon-Thur; 9am-2pm, 5-8pm Fri; 10am-2pm, 5-8pm Sat.

Oficina de Turisme de Puigcerdà
C/Querol, baixos (972 88 05 42). **Open** *Mid June-mid Sept* 9am-2pm, 3-8pm Mon-Sat; 10am-2pm Sun. *Mid Sept-mid June* 9am-1pm Mon; 9am-1pm, 4-7pm Tue-Fri; 10am-1.30pm, 4.30-8pm Sat.

Getting there

By bus
Alsina Graëlls (93 265 68 66) runs 5 buses daily to Berga from the corner of C/Balmes and C/Pelai; journey time is about 2hrs. Same company has daily buses to Puigcerdà from Estació del Nord; journey time is 3hrs.

By car
Take the C16 to Berga (118km/73 miles) and Bagà. From Bagà continue on the C16 through Túnel de Cadí (toll), after which take the N260 east for Puigcerdà or west for Lles and Bellver. A scenic alternative is the C17 and N152 through Vic and Ripoll.

By train
RENFE from Sants or Plaça Catalunya to Puigcerdà. About 1 train every 2hrs; journey takes about 3hrs.

Directory

Getting Around	**302**
Resources A-Z	**307**
Catalan Vocabulary	**321**
Spanish Vocabulary	**322**
Further Reference	**323**
Index	**324**

Features

Fare exchange	303
Stepping out	305
Travel advice	306
Emergencies	309
Average monthly climate	320

Directory

Getting Around

A compact city, Barcelona is best explored on foot, with the help of efficient metro (underground) and bus systems for longer journeys. Bicycles are great for moving about the Old City and port, although in the high season crowds can make them a nuisance. Motorbikes can be handy in traffic, while a car is usually more of a liability (parking space is very scarce), and only comes into its own for trips out of town. For transport outside Barcelona, *see p276.*

Arriving & leaving

By air

Barcelona's airport is just south of the city. Each airline is allocated to one of the two main terminals (A or B) for all arrivals and departures. Both terminals have tourist information desks, cash machines and exchange offices (open 7am-8pm Mon-Fri). For airport info, call 93 298 38 38 (press 1, then 3 for an English-speaking operator). Updated flight info can be found at www.aena.es/ae/bcn/home page.htm.

Aerobús
This bus service runs from each airport terminal to Plaça Catalunya (with stops at Plaça Espanya and Sants). Buses to the airport go from Plaça Catalunya (in front of the Corte Inglés), stopping along the way at Sants railway station and Plaça Espanya. Buses run every 12mins, leaving the airport from 6am to midnight Mon-Fri (6.30am-midnight Sat, Sun); and from Plaça Catalunya, 5.30am-11.15pm Mon-Fri (6am-11.20pm Sat, Sun). The trip takes about 30mins; a single ticket costs €3.30. One local bus, the 106, also runs between the airport (starting at 10.15pm) and Plaça Espanya; it takes

longer, but runs later (last departure from the airport 3.20am; from Plaça Espanya 3.50am).

Airport trains
An overhead walkway starting between terminals A and B leads to the airport train station. Trains stop at Sants, Plaça Catalunya, Arc de Triomf and Clot-Aragó, all of which are also metro stops. Trains leave the airport at 13 and 43 minutes past each hour, 6.13am-10.43pm Mon-Fri. Trains to the airport leave Plaça Catalunya at 11 and 41 minutes past the hour, 5.38am-10.11pm Mon-Fri (5mins later from Sants). Weekend times vary slightly, but there are still trains every 30mins. The journey takes 20-25mins and costs €2.16 one way. Be aware that tickets are only valid for 2hrs after purchase.

Taxis from the airport
The taxi fare to central Barcelona should be about €14-€19 (depending on traffic), including a €2 airport supplement. Fares are about 20% higher after 10pm and at weekends. There is an 80¢ supplement for each large piece of luggage placed in the car boot. Ignore any cab drivers who approach you inside the airport; use the ranks outside the terminal.

Airlines
The appropriate terminal is shown in brackets.
Air Europa (B) 902 401 501/ www.air-europa.com
British Airways (B) 902 111 333/ www.british-airways.com
easyJet (A) 902 299 992/ www.easyjet.com
Iberia (B) 902 400 500/ www.iberia.com
Virgin Express (A) 900 467 612/ www.virgin-express.com

By bus

Most long-distance coaches (national and international) stop or terminate at **Estació d'Autobusos Barcelona-Nord** at C/Ali Bei 80, next to Arc de Triomf rail and metro station; general information 902 26 06 06). The **Estació d'Autobusos Barcelona-**

Sants, by Sants rail station and Sants-Estació metro stop, is only a secondary stop for many coaches, but some international Eurolines services (information 93 490 40 00) stop only at Sants.

By car

Approaching Barcelona from almost all directions, the most direct car access to the Old City area is the Ronda Litoral (the coastal half of the ring road), taking exit 21 (Paral.lel) if you're coming from the south, or exit 22 (Via Laietana) from the north. Motorways also feed into Avda Diagonal, Avda Meridiana and Gran Via, which provide straightforward connections with the city centre. Tolls are charged on most of the main approach routes, payable in cash (the lane marked 'manual'; motorbikes are charged half) or by credit card ('automatic').

By sea

Balearic Islands ferries dock at the **Moll de Barcelona** quay, at the bottom of Avda Paral.lel; **Trasmediterránea** (902 45 46 45/www.trasmediterranea.es) is the main operator. There is also a ferry three times a week between Barcelona and Genoa in Italy, from the **Moll de Ponent**, a few hundred metres further south (Grimaldi Lines; for information, phone its agent Condeminas on 93 443 98 98). Cruise ships use several berths around the harbour; when cruisers are in port, a PortBus shuttle service transports passengers on shore leave to the foot of the Rambla.

By train

The **Barcelona-Sants** station is the stop or terminus for most long-distance trains run by the Spanish state railways **RENFE**. It's about three kilometres (two miles) from the centre, but has a metro stop (Sants-Estació) on line 3 (green, the most direct for the centre) and line 5 (blue). Some international services from France do not go to Sants, but terminate at the 1920s **Estació de França** in the Born, the Barceloneta metro (line 4, yellow). Other trains stop between the two at **Passeig de Gràcia**, which can be the handiest for the city centre and also has a metro stop on lines 3 and 4.

RENFE

902 24 02 02/www.renfe.es.
Open 5.30am-11.30pm daily.
Credit AmEx, DC, MC, V.
Some English-speaking operators. RENFE tickets can be bought or reserved by phone and delivered to an address or hotel for a small extra fee. For information on non-Spanish European trains, call 93 490 11 22 (open 7am-11pm daily).

Maps

Metro and central area street maps are included at the back of this guide. Tourist offices have a fairly detailed street map, and the Ajuntament tourist offices also have a better map for €1.20. Metro maps are available free at all metro stations (ask for *'una guía del metro'*) and city transport information offices

(*see below*), which also have free bus maps. Metro and bus maps indicate access points for the disabled. There is an excellent interactive street map at www.bcn.es/guia.

Public transport

The metro is generally the quickest, cheapest and most convenient way of getting around the city, although buses operate all night and cover some 'holes' in the underground network. Public transport, although now highly integrated, is still run by different organisations. Local buses and the metro are run by the city transport authority (TMB). Two underground train lines (from Plaça Catalunya to Reina Elisenda,

Fare exchange

With a standard fare of €1.05 for any urban-area journey, the ticket system on Barcelona public transport sounds straightforward. It is, but after just a few rides it becomes more convenient and cheaper to use a multi-journey ticket or *targeta*. The basic ten-trip *targeta* is the T-10 (*Te-Deu* in Catalan). It cuts the cost per trip by more than 40 per cent, and can be shared by any number of people, so long as one trip is cancelled on the card for each person travelling.

The T-10, along with the other 'integrated' *targetes* listed below, lets you on to any of the four main transport systems (local RENFE and FGC trains, the metro and buses), and you can transfer between them for free for 75 minutes after the initial validation. In most cases, when transferring you have to insert your card into a machine a second time, but another unit will not be deducted. A single ticket does not allow free transfers.

A T-10 can be bought in newsagents, lottery shops, bakeries and Servi-Caixa cashpoints as well as on the metro and train systems, but you can't buy one on a bus. There are also more expensive versions of all *targetes* used for travelling to the outer zones of the metropolitan region, but the prices listed below will get you anywhere in Barcelona city's urban area.

Integrated *targetes*

All are available at metro and FGC ticket counters, and some at ticket vending machines and Servi-Caixas (currently the T-10, T-50/30).
T-10 Valid for ten trips; can be shared by two or more people. €5.80.
T-Familiar Gives 70 trips in any 30-day period; can be shared. €35.60.
T-50/30 Gives 50 trips in any 30-day period; for one person only. €24.30.
T-Día Unlimited travel for one person only, for one day. €4.40.
T-Mes Unlimited travel for one person only, for any 30-day period. €37.65.
T-Trimestre Travel for one person only, for three months. €103.60.

Other *targetes*

2,3 & 5 Dies Unlimited travel for one person for three (or five) days on the metro, buses and FGC trains. Also sold at tourist offices. €8, €11.30 and €17.30.
Aerobús + Bus + Metro Unlimited travel for one person on the metro and buses (not FGC), including a return trip to the airport. Three-day (€13.80) or five-day (€18) pass. Sold on board the Aerobús.
Barcelona Card A tourist discount scheme with travelcard. *See p73.*

Les Planes or Avda Tibidabo; and from Plaça Espanya to Cornellà) connect with the metro, but are run by Catalan government railways, the Ferrocarrils de la Generalitat de Catalunya (FGC), which also has suburban services.

For details of the Barcelona Card, which gives unlimited travel on public transport, and guided tours, *see p73.*

FGC information

Vestibule, Plaça Catalunya FGC station (93 205 15 15/www.fgc.net). **Open** 7am-9pm Mon-Fri. **Map** p344 A1.
Branches: FGC Provença (open 9am-7pm Mon-Fri, closed August); FGC Plaça Espanya (open 9am-2pm, 4-7pm Mon-Fri).

TMB information

Main vestibule, Metro Universitat, Eixample (93 318 70 74/ www.tmb.net). **Open** 8am-8pm Mon-Fri. **Map** p344 A1.
Branches: Vestibule, Metro Sants Estació (both 7am-9pm Mon-Fri; 10am-2pm, 3-6pm Sat, Sun); vestibule, Metro Diagonal, Universitat (8am-8pm Mon-Fri).

Metro & FGC

The five metro lines are identified by a number and a colour on maps and station signs. At interchanges, lines in a particular direction are indicated by the names of the stations at the end of the line, so you should know which they are when changing between lines. On FGC lines, note that some suburban trains do not stop at all stations.

All metro lines operate from 5am to midnight Monday to Thursday; 5am to 2am Friday and Saturday; 6am to midnight Sunday. The FGC has roughly similar hours.

Buses

City bus stops are easy to find: many routes originate in or pass through Plaça Catalunya, Plaça Universitat and Plaça Urquinaona. Because of the many one-way streets, buses often do not follow exactly the same route in both directions, but run along parallel streets. It can be very difficult to recognise your stop as you approach, as the stops are not labelled and street signs are not easy to locate.

Most bus routes operate between 6am and 10.30pm, Monday to Saturday, although many begin earlier and finish later. Usually there is a bus at least every 10 to 15 minutes, but they are less frequent before 8am, after 9pm and on Saturdays. On Sundays, buses are less frequent still on most routes, and a few do not run at all. You board buses at the front, and get off through the middle or rear doors. Only single tickets can be bought on board; if you have a *targeta* (*see p303* **Fare exchange**), insert it into the machine just behind the driver as you board.

Useful routes

Buses that connect Plaça Catalunya with popular parts of town include:
22 via Gràcia to the Tramvia Blau on Tibidabo and the Pedralbes monastery
24 goes up Passeig de Gràcia and is the best way to get to Park Güell
41, 66 and **67** go to the Plaça Francesc Macià area, which is not served by the metro
41 also goes to Ciutadella and the Vila Olímpica
45 stops in Plaça Urquinaona and goes down to the beach near Port Olímpic.
Three good crosstown routes:
50 goes from north-east Barcelona past Sagrada Família, along Gran Via and then climbs Montjuïc from Plaça Espanya to Miramar
64 goes from Barceloneta beach, past Colom, Avda Paral.lel, Plaça Universitat to Sarrià and Pedralbes
7 runs the length of Avda Diagonal, from the Zona Universitària to Diagonal-Mar, but deviates in the centre (along Passeig de Gràcia and Gran Via to Glòries).

Night buses

There are 16 urban night bus (Nitbus) routes, most of which run from 10.30pm-4.30am nightly, with buses every 20-30mins. Most pass through Plaça Catalunya. Fares and *targetes* are as for daytime buses. Plaça Catalunya is also the terminus for all-night bus services linking Barcelona with more distant parts of its metropolitan area.

TombBus

A special shoppers' bus service (the spooky-sounding name actually means 'round trip') that runs only between Plaça Catalunya and Plaça Pius XII on the Diagonal (7.30am-9.30pm Mon-Fri; 9.30am-9.20pm Sat). Normal *targetes* are not valid on the bus, and single tickets cost €1.20.

Local trains

For trips into the suburbs and surrounding towns, there are (as well as buses) regional rail lines run by the **FGC** and **RENFE**. From **FGC Plaça Catalunya** (the same station as for the Sarrià and Tibidabo lines), trains go to Sabadell, Terrassa and other towns beyond Tibidabo, and from **FGC Plaça Espanya**, to Hospitalet and Montserrat. All trains on the RENFE local network (signed 'Rodalies/ Cercanías' at mainline stations) stop at Sants, but many lines also converge on Plaça Catalunya (for Vic and the Pyrenees, Manresa, the Penedès and Costa del Maresme) or Passeig de Gràcia (for the southern coastal line to Sitges and the Girona-Figueres line north). Ticket prices vary according to zones. For a map of local RENFE lines, *see p346.*

Taxis

Barcelona's 10,500 black and yellow taxis are among its most distinctive symbols, and are usually easy to find. Taxis can be hailed on the street when they show a green light on the roof, and a sign saying 'Lliure/Libre' (free) behind the windscreen. There are also ranks at railway and bus stations, main squares and other locations throughout the city. Fares are reasonable.

FARES

Current official rates and supplements are shown inside each cab (in English). The current minimum fare is €1.80, which is what the meter should register when you set off. The basic rates apply 6am to 10pm Monday to Friday; at all other times (including midweek public holidays), the rate is about 20% higher. There are also supplements for luggage and for animals (€1), and a waiting charge. Taxi drivers are not required to carry more than €12 in change, and few accept payment by credit card.

RECEIPTS & COMPLAINTS

To get a receipt, ask for '*un rebut/un recibo*'. It should include the fare, the taxi number, the driver's NIF (tax) number, the licence plate, driver's signature and the date; if you have a complaint of any kind about a cab driver, insist on all these, and the more details the better (time, route). Call transport information on 010 to explain your complaint, and follow their instructions.

RADIO CABS

The companies listed below take bookings 24 hours daily. Only some operators speak English, but if you are not at a specific address give the name of a street corner (ie Provença/ Muntaner), or a street and a bar or restaurant where you can wait. Note that phone cabs start the meter as soon as a call is answered.

Barnataxi 93 357 77 55
Fono-Taxi 93 300 11 00
Ràdio Taxi 93 225 00 00
Ràdio Taxi '033' 933 033 033
Servi-Taxi 933 300 300
Taxi Groc 93 322 22 22
Taxi Miramar 93 433 10 20

Driving

Driving in Barcelona can be wearing and is rarely a time-efficient form of transport. There's seldom enough driving space, let alone parking space. It's only out in the country that a car becomes an asset. If you do drive while here, bear these points in mind:

● Tourists can drive in Spain with a valid driving licence from most other countries. An

Stepping out

The best way to let Barcelona seduce you is to get out for a stroll. With lively streets, short distances and a labyrinthine old town that is largely pedestrian only, most of the city's delights are best discovered on foot. But just make sure you get off on the right step:

● Take a map with you, then try not to look at it – ask for directions instead.

● Be alert and on your guard against street theft (*see p316* **Safety**).

● Don't expect cars to stop for you at pedestrian crossings, even if you have a green signal.

● In summer, time your urban exploration to avoid the hottest part of the day (2-5pm or so).

Walking times

This is how long popular walks should take, at an easy walking speed; allow extra for stops and diversions.

● La Rambla, from Plaça Catalunya to Colom: 20 minutes.

● Around the harbour, from the Rambla (Colom end) to Barceloneta beach: 25 minutes.

● Along the beach, from Barceloneta to the Port Olímpic: 25 minutes.

● From Plaça Catalunya to La Pedrera, up Passeig de Gràcia: 15 minutes.

● From La Pedrera to the Sagrada Família, along C/Provença: 20 minutes.

● Up Montjuïc, from Plaça Espanya via the escalators to the stadium: 20 minutes.

international driving licence or EU photo licence can be useful as a translation/credibility aid.

● Keep your driving licence, vehicle registration and insurance documents with you at all times.

● It is compulsory to wear seat belts and carry warning triangles, spares (tyre, bulbs, fanbelt) and tools to fit them.

● The speed limit is 50kmph in towns, 90kmph on most highways and 120kmph on motorways – although it is true that most drivers ignore these maximums.

● Legal alcohol limits for drivers are low, similar to those in most EU countries.

● Children under 12 may not travel in the front of a car except in a child car seat.

● Do not leave anything of value, including car radios, in your car, nor bags or coats in

view. Foreign number plates can attract thieves.

● Be on your guard against thefts at motorway rest areas, or thieves who may try to make you stop and get out, perhaps by indicating you have a flat tyre. Keep your car doors and boot locked when travelling.

Car & motorbike hire

Car hire is relatively pricey, but it's a competitive market so shop around. The key is to check carefully what's included: ideally, you want unlimited mileage, 16 per cent VAT (IVA) included and, especially, full insurance cover, rather than the third-party minimum (*seguro obligatorio*). You will need a credit card, or a large cash deposit. Most companies have a minimum age limit and require you to

Travel advice

For up-to-date information for travelling to a specific country – including the latest news on safety and security, health issues, local laws and customs – contact your home country government's department of foreign affairs. Most have websites packed with useful advice for would-be travellers.

Australia
www.dfat.gov.au/travel

Canada
www.voyage.gc.ca

New Zealand
www.mft.govt.nz/travel

Republic of Ireland
www.irlgov.ie/iveagh

UK
www.fco.gov.uk/travel

USA
www.state.gov/travel

---

have had a licence for at least a year. Larger companies often advertise special offers on their websites.

EasyCar
Passeig Lluís Companys, 2nd level of underground car park (no phone/ www.easycar.com). Metro Arc de Triomf. **Open** 7am-11pm daily. **Credit** MC, V. **Map** p343 E6.
Online-only booking and payment. Basic rates for its Mercedes A-Class hatchbacks are low (for example, two days for €64.90), but check the conditions carefully – such as only 100km of free mileage per day, and possible supplements for insurance or late return. There's also a new Sants Estació branch (open 7am-11pm), which rents primarily Toyota Yaris cars.

Europcar
Plaça de Joan Peiró, Sants (93 491 48 22/www.europcar.com). Metro Sants Estació. **Open** 7.30am-10.30pm Mon-Fri; 8am-1pm Sat. **Credit** AmEx, DC, MC, V. **Map** p341 A4.
A large international agency with several offices in Barcelona. Prices change daily – phone for details. Airport branch: 93 298 33 00.

Vanguard
C/Viladomat 297, Eixample (93 439 38 80/93 322 79 51/www.vanguard rent.com). Metro Hospital Clínic. **Open** 8am-2pm, 4-8pm Mon-Fri; 9am-1pm Sat, Sun. **Credit** AmEx, DC, MC, V. **Map** p341 B4.
Scooter and motorcycle hire, as well as cars at good rates. Prices range from a Honda (50cc) for €83.66 to a Yamaha (600cc) for €261. You must be 19 to hire a small bike and have had a licence a year; 25 and three years for larger bikes.

Parking

Parking is not easy; the municipal police readily give out tickets or tow away cars. Don't park in front of doors with the sign 'Gual Permanent', indicating an entry with 24-hour right of access. In some parts of the Old City, access is limited to residents for much of the day.

Pay & display areas
Many streets in the centre of the city and the Eixample are pay-and-display areas (*zones blaves*, blue zones), with parking spaces marked in blue on the street. Parking restrictions apply 9am-2pm, 4-8pm Mon-Sat, when you can park for up to 2hrs; in the centre, the rate is €1.70/hr, less in other districts. If you overstay by no more than an hour, you can cancel the fine by paying an additional €3; to do so, press *Anul.lar denúncia* on the ticket machine, insert €3 and take the receipt that comes out. Most machines accept credit cards (MC, V), but do not give change.

Car parks
Car parks (*parkings*) are signalled by a white 'P' on a blue sign. The main parking companies – private SABA and public SMASSA – both charge around €1.65/hr. You are especially advised to use a car park if you have foreign plates. The car parks below are central and open 24hrs daily:
SABA: Plaça Catalunya, Plaça Urquinaona, Arc de Triomf, Avda Catedral, Passeig de Gràcia, C/Diputació-C/Pau Claris.
SMASSA: Plaça dels Àngels-MACBA, Moll de la Fusta, Avda Francesc Cambó, Avda Paral.lel.

Metro-Park
Plaça de les Glòries, Eixample (93 265 10 47). Metro Glòries. **Open** 5am-1.30am Mon-Sat. **Credit** AmEx, DC, MC, V. **Map** p343 F5.
Park-and-ride facility recommended for anyone coming in to Barcelona with a car for the day. The €4.50 ticket gives unlimited travel for one day on the metro and city buses (but not the FGC). The car park is at the junction of three traffic arteries (the Diagonal, Meridiana and Gran Via), a short metro ride from the centre.

Towing away
Information 93 428 45 95. **Credit** AmEx, DC, MC, V.
If the Municipal Police have towed away your car, they will leave a triangular sticker on the pavement. Call the number on the sticker or the 24hr one above to be told which pound it has gone to. Staff do not usually speak English. It will cost €100 to recover the vehicle during the first 4hrs after it was towed, plus €1.60 for each hr after that, plus (probably) a parking fine.

Petrol

Most *gasolineres* (petrol stations) have unleaded fuel (*sense plom/sin plomo*), regular (*super*) and diesel (*gas-oil*).

Cycling

Recreational bike-riding in Barcelona is on the increase, and there is an incomplete but growing network of bike lanes (*carrils bici*) along major avenues and the seafront. Mass bicycle commuting is a long way off still, for in weekday traffic cyclists still face daunting risks – and tourists are not advised to try it, unless they're experts at home. Rollerblading is also popular. Tourist offices (*see p318*) have route details.

Al punt de trobada
C/Badajoz 24, Poblenou (93 225 05 85/bicipuntrobada@hotmail. com). Metro Llacuna. **Open** *Apr-Sept* 9am-3pm, 5-9pm daily. *Oct-Mar* 9am-2pm, 4-8pm Mon-Sat; 9am-5pm Sun. **Credit** AmEx, MC, V.
A bike-hire place close to the beach. Mountain bikes and Rollerblades cost €3.60/hr, €10.80/half-day and €16/day. There are also tandems, baby seats, bike tours and a variety of other services.

Resources A-Z

Addresses

Most apartment addresses consist of a street name followed by a street number, floor level and flat number, in that order. So, to go to C/València 246, 2n 3a, find number 246; go up to the second floor and find the door marked as 3 or 3a (the letter after the number merely shows that it's an ordinal number – like '3rd' in English). Ground-floor flats are usually called *baixos* or *bajos* (often abbreviated 'bxs/bjos'); one floor up, the *entresol/entresuelo* ('entl'), and the next is often the *principal* ('pral'). Confusingly, numbered floors start here, first, second, up to the *àtic/ático* at the top.

Age restrictions

In Spain, you have to be 18 to drive a car or to have sex and 16 to smoke.

Business

Anyone wanting to set up shop in Barcelona needs to be aware of the intricacies of local, Spanish and EU regulations. It's a waste of time trying to deal with this system single-handed. A visit to the **Cambra de Comerç** (*see p308*) is a must; some consulates can also refer you to various professionals, and a *gestoria* (*see below*) will save you time and frustration.

Admin services

The *gestoria* is a very Spanish institution, the main function of which is to lighten the weight of local bureaucracy by dealing with it for you. A combination of book-keeper, lawyer and business adviser, a good *gestor* can be very helpful in handling paperwork and advising on various shortcuts, although local *gestoria* employees rarely speak English.

LEC

Travessera de Gràcia 96, 2° 2ª, Gràcia (93 415 02 50). Bus 27, 31, 32. **Open** 9am-2pm, 4-7pm Mon-Fri. Closed Aug. **Map** p338 D3.
Offers business, social security, fiscal and general advice about financial procedures in Barcelona. Some English is spoken.

Tutzo Assessors

C/Aribau 226, Eixample (93 209 67 88/tutzoass@fononegocio.com). Bus 31, 58, 64. **Open** 8.30am-2pm, 4-7pm Mon-Fri. Closed 3wks Aug, Fri pm July, Aug. **Map** p338 C3.
Lawyers and economists as well as a *gestoria*. There are some English speakers.

Conventions & conferences

Barcelona Convention Bureau

Rambla Catalunya 123, Pral, Eixample (93 368 97 00/www.barcelonaturisme.com). Metro Diagonal. **Open** Sept-June 9am-2.30pm, 4-7pm Mon-Thur; 9am-3pm Fri. July, Aug 8am-3pm Mon-Fri. **Map** p338 D4.
Specialised arm of the city tourist authority that assists organisations and individuals holding conferences or similar events in the city.

Fira de Barcelona

Avda Reina Maria Cristina, Montjuïc (93 233 20 00/www.firabcn.es). Metro Espanya. **Open** Mid Sept-mid June 9am-2pm, 4-6pm Mon-Fri. Mid June-mid Sept 9am-2pm Mon-Fri. **Map** p341 A5.
The Barcelona 'trade fair' is one of the largest permanent exhibition complexes in Europe. In addition to the main area at Plaça Espanya, it includes a huge site, Montjuïc-2, towards the airport, and administers the Palau de Congressos conference hall in the Plaça Espanya site, which can be let separately.

Courier services

Estació d'Autobusos Barcelona-Nord

C/Alí Bei 80, Eixample (93 232 43 29). Metro Arc de Triomf. **Open** 7am-9.30pm Mon-Fri; 7am-12.45pm Sat. **No credit cards**. **Map** p343 E5.
An inexpensive service available at the bus station for sending parcels on scheduled buses to towns within Spain.

Missatgers Trèvol

C/Antonio Ricardos 14, La Sagrera (93 498 80 70/www.trevol.com). Metro Sagrera. **Open** 8.30am-7pm Mon-Fri. **No credit cards**.
Cycle couriers who also have vans and motorbikes. Delivering a package (weighing up to 6kg/13lb) by bike within the central area costs €2.95, plus tax, unless you have an account with them.

UPS

Avda Diagonal 511, Eixample (freephone 900 10 24 10/fax 93 322 28 02/www.ups.com). Metro Maria Cristina. **Open** 8am-8.30pm Mon-Fri. **Credit** AmEx, MC, V. **Map** p337 C3.
Next-day delivery to many destinations, both Spanish and international. Call at least three hours before required pick-up time. Parcels dropped off at the depot before 7.30pm leave the same day.

Office & computer services

Centro de Negocios

C/Pau Claris 97, 4° 1ª, Eixample (93 304 38 58/www.centro-negocios. com). Metro Passeig de Gràcia. **Open** Sept-July 8am-9pm Mon-Fri. Aug 9am-3pm Mon-Fri. **Map** p342 D5.
Office space, desk space in shared offices, mailboxes, meeting rooms, secretarial services and a wide range of administrative services for hire.

GeoMac

606 30 89 32/geomac@terra.es. **Open** by appt. **No credit cards**.
Experienced American computer technician George Cowdery offers maintenance and trouble-shooting for Macs and networks.

Microrent

C/Rosselló 35, Eixample (93 363 32 50/fax 93 322 13 57/www.microrent.es). Metro Sants Estació or Entença. **Open** 9am-6pm Mon-Fri. **No credit cards**. **Map** p341 B4.
Computer equipment of all kinds for rent: PCs, Macs, laptops, peripherals, faxes and photocopiers.

Directory

Picking Pack Megaservice

C/Consell de Cent 276, Eixample (93 505 45 05/www.pickingpack.es). Metro Universitat. **Open** 9am-8pm Mon-Fri; 9am-2pm Sat. **Credit** AmEx, MC, V. **Map** p342 D5.
A range of computers, internet access, fax, design, printing, mail-outs and so on.

Translators

DUUAL

C/Ciutat 7, 2º 4ª, Barri Gòtic (93 302 29 85/fax 93 412 40 66/ www.duual.com). Metro Jaume I. **Open** *Oct-May* 9am-2pm, 4-7pm Mon-Thur; 9am-2pm Fri. *June-Sept* 8.30am-3pm Mon-Fri. Closed 3wks Aug. **No credit cards. Map** p345 B3.
Services in many languages and excellent desktop publishing facilities. Good rates.

Teodora Gambetta

C/Escorial 29-31, escala C, àtic 2ª, Gràcia (tel/fax 93 219 22 25/ teogam@menta.net). Metro Joanic. **Open** by appointment only. **Map** p339 E3.
Translation of foreign-language documents by legally certified translators (*traductores jurados*); from or into English, French or Spanish. Rates can be substantially higher than for conventional translators, so check in advance.

Useful organisations

Ajuntament de Barcelona

Plaça Sant Miquel 4-5, Barri Gòtic (93 402 70 00/www.bcn.es). Metro Jaume I. **Open** *Sept-June* 8.30am-5.30pm Mon-Fri. *July, Aug* 8.15am-2.15pm Mon-Fri. **Map** p345 B3.
The City Council. Permits for new businesses are issued by the ten municipal districts.

Borsa de Valors de Barcelona

Passeig de Gràcia 19, Eixample (93 401 35 55/www.borsabcn.es). Metro Passeig de Gràcia. **Open** *Information* 9am-6pm Mon-Fri. *Library* 9am-noon Mon-Fri. **Map** p342 D5.
The Stock Exchange.

British Society of Catalunya

Mailing address: Lloyds TSB Bank, Rambla Catalunya 123 (tel/fax 93 688 08 66). Metro Diagonal. **Map** p338 C2.

An informal group for expats that has been organising walks, drinks and other events for over 20 years. €9 annual membership includes an invitation to a Queen's birthday party organised every year.

Cambra de Comerç, Indústria i Navegació de Barcelona

Avda Diagonal 452-4, Eixample (902 448 448/www.cambrabcn.es). Metro Diagonal/FGC Provença. **Open** 9am-5pm Mon-Thur; 9am-2pm Fri. **Map** p338 D4.
The most important institution for business people, the Chamber of Commerce offers a wealth of information and advice.

Generalitat de Catalunya

General information 012/business development 93 476 72 00/new businesses 902 20 15 20/ www.gencat.net.
The Catalan government provides a range of consultancy services.

Complaints

If you have a complaint that can't be cleared up on the spot, ask for an official complaint form (*hoja de reclamación/full de reclamació*), which many businesses and all shops are required to have available (in English). Fill out the form, and leave the pink copy with the business. Take your copy, along with any receipts, guarantees and so on, to an official consumer office.

Oficina Municipal d'Informació al Consumidor

Ronda de Sant Pau 43, Barri Gòtic (93 402 78 41/www.omic.bcn.es). Metro Paral.lel. **Open** *Mid Sept-mid June* 9am-2pm, 4-6pm Mon-Thur; 9am-2pm Fri. *Mid June-mid Sept* 9am-2pm Mon-Fri. **Map** p345 A/B3.
Municipally run official centre for consumer advice and complaints follow-up. You can file complaints in English through the website.

Telèfon de Consulta del Consumidor

901 30 03 03. **Open** *Sept-June* 9am-6pm Mon-Fri. *July* 9am-5pm Mon-Fri. *Aug* 9am-3pm Mon-Fri.
A phone line run by the Generalitat for consumer advice. Can provide addresses of other consumer offices in Catalonia.

Consulates

A full list of consulates in Barcelona is in the phone book under '*Consolats/Consulados*'. Outside office hours most consulates have answerphone messages that give an emergency contact number.

Australian Consulate

Gran Via Carles III 98, Zona Alta (93 330 94 96/fax 93 411 09 04/ www.embaustralia.es). Metro Maria Cristina or Les Corts. **Open** 10am-noon Mon-Fri. Closed Aug. **Map** p344-5 A2/3.

British Consulate

Avda Diagonal 477, Eixample (93 366 62 00/fax 93 366 62 21/ www.ukinspain.com). Metro Hospital Clínic. **Open** *End Sept-mid June* 9.30am-1.30pm, 4-5pm Mon-Fri. *Mid June-mid Sept* 9am-2pm Mon-Fri. **Map** p338 C3.

Canadian Consulate

C/Elisenda de Pinós 10, Zona Alta (93 204 27 00/fax 93 204 27 01/ www.canada-es.org). FGC Reina Elisenda. **Open** 10am-1pm Mon-Fri. **Map** p338 D4.

Irish Consulate

Gran Via Carles III 94, Zona Alta (93 491 50 21/fax 93 411 29 21). Metro Maria Cristina or Les Corts. **Open** 10am-1pm Mon-Fri. **Map** p337 A3.

New Zealand Consulate

Travessera de Gràcia 64, 2º, Gràcia (93 209 03 99/fax 93 202 08 90). Metro Passeig de Gràcia/22, 24, 28 bus. **Open** *Sept-June* 9am-1.30pm, 4-6.30pm Mon-Fri. *July, Aug* call for reduced hours. **Map** p338 C3.

US Consulate

Passeig Reina Elisenda 23, Zona Alta (93 280 22 27/fax 93 205 52 06/www.embusa.es). FGC Reina Elisenda. **Open** 9am-12.30pm, 3-5pm Mon-Fri. **Map** p337 A1.

Customs

Customs declarations are not usually necessary if you arrive in Spain from another EU country and are carrying only legal goods for personal use. The amounts given below are guidelines only; if you approach these maximums in several categories, you may still have to explain your personal habits.

● 800 cigarettes, 400 small cigars, 200 normal cigars or 1 kilogram of loose tobacco
● 10 litres of spirits (over 22 per cent alcohol), 20 litres of fortified wine or alcoholic drinks with under 22 per cent alcohol, 90 litres of wine and 110 litres of beer.

Coming from a non-EU country, you can bring:
● 200 cigarettes, 100 small cigars, 50 regular cigars or 250 grams (8.82 ounces) of tobacco
● 1 litre of spirits (over 22 per cent alcohol) or 2 litres of any other alcoholic drink with under 22 per cent alcohol
● 50 grams (1.76 ounces) of perfume.

If you enter from Andorra, some of these limits are a little higher. Visitors can also carry up to €6,000 in cash without having to declare it. Non-EU residents can also reclaim VAT (IVA) paid on some large purchases when they leave Spain; for details *see p181*.

Disabled

Barcelona's transport facilities and access in general for disabled people still leave quite a lot to be desired, despite steady improvements. For wheelchair users, buses and taxis are usually the best public transport options. There is a special transport information phoneline, and transport maps, which you can pick up from transport information offices (*see p304*), indicate wheelchair access points and adapted bus routes.

Access to sights

Newer museums, such as the MACBA, have good access, but the process of converting older buildings is slow and difficult. Phoning ahead to check is always a good idea even if a place claims to be accessible: access might

depend, for example, on getting a lift key in advance. Here are some wheelchair-friendly venues:

Museums & galleries
La Capella
CCCB
Col.lecció Thyssen-Bornemisza (Monestir de Pedralbes)
Col.legi d'Arquitectes
Fundació Joan Miró
Fundacio Antoni Tàpies
MACBA
MNAC
Museu d'Arqueologia de Catalunya
Museu d'Art Modern
Museu de les Arts Decoratives
Museu d'Història de Catalunya
Museu de Zoologia
Palau de la Virreina

Institut Municipal de Persones amb Disminució
Avda Diagonal 233, Eixample (93 413 27 75). Metro Glòries/ 7, 56 bus. **Open** *Mid Sept-mid June* 9am-2pm, 4-6pm Mon-Thur; 9am-2pm Fri. *Mid June-mid Sept* 9am-3pm Mon-Fri. **Map** p343 F5.
The city's organisation for the disabled has info on access to theatres, museums and restaurants.

Transport
Information 93 486 07 52/fax 93 486 07 53. **Open** *Sept-July* 9am-9pm Mon-Fri; 9am-3pm Sat. *Aug* 9am-9pm Mon-Fri.
English speakers are sometimes available; if not, call the 010 information line (*see p319*).

Buses
All the Aerobús airport buses and the open-topped tourist buses are

fully accessible to wheelchair users. Similar fully adapted buses also alternate with standard buses on all night bus routes and most daytime routes. Transport maps and bus stop signs indicate which routes use adapted vehicles.

Metro & FGC
Only Line 2 (which runs from Paral.lel to La Pau) has lifts and ramps at all stations; on Lines 1 and 3, a few stations have lifts. The Montjuïc funicular railway is fully adapted for wheelchairs. FGC stations at Provença, Muntaner and Avda Tibidabo are accessible, as are many FGC stops further out of the centre of the city: Sant Cugat, Sabadell and others.

RENFE trains
Sants, Estació de França, Passeig de Gràcia and Plaça Catalunya stations are accessible to wheelchairs, but trains are not. At Estació de Sants, if you go to the Atenció al Client office ahead of time, help on the platform can be arranged.

Taxis
All taxi drivers are officially required to transport wheelchairs (and guide dogs) for no extra charge, but their cars can be inconveniently small, and in practice the willingness of drivers to co-operate varies widely. Special minibus taxis adapted for wheelchairs can be ordered from the Taxi Amic service.

Taxi Amic
93 420 80 88. **Open** 7.30am-11pm Mon-Fri; 9am-10pm Sat, Sun.
Fares are the same as for regular cabs, but numbers are limited, so call well in advance to request a specific time. There is a late-night service, but taxis must be requested in advance.

Emergencies

Emergency services 112. The operator will connect you to the police, fire or ambulance services, as required.
Ambulance/Ambulància 061. For hospitals and other health services, *see p310*.
Fire Service/Bombers/ Bomberos 080
Policia Nacional (first choice in a police emergency) 091
Guàrdia Urbana (city police; for traffic but also general law and order) 092. For more information on police forces, *see p315*.
Electricity (all companies) 900 77 00 77
Gas/Gas Natural 900 750 750
Water/Aigües de Barcelona 93 265 11 11
All are open 24 hours.

Directory

Drugs

Many people smoke cannabis very openly in Spain, but you should be aware that its possession or consumption in public places is illegal. In private places, the law is contradictory: smoking is OK, but you can still be nabbed for possession. In practice, enforcement is often not the highest of police priorities, but you could theoretically receive a hefty fine and face a lot of inconvenience. Smoking in bars is also prohibited; proprietors are strict on this issue because it could cost them their licence.

Electricity

The standard current in Spain is now 220V. A diminishing number of old buildings still have 125V circuits, and it's advisable to check before using electrical equipment in old, cheap hotels. Plugs are all of the two-round-pin type. The 220V current works fine with British-bought 240V products with a plug adaptor (available at El Corte Inglés, see p182). With US 110V equipment you will also need a current transformer.

Gay & lesbian

Ca la Dona (see p319) is the main centre for women.

Casal Lambda

C/Verdaguer i Callís 10, Barri Gòtic (93 319 55 50/www.lambdaweb.org). Metro Urquinaona. **Open** 6-9pm Mon-Sat. **Map** p344 B2.
Gay cultural organisation that is the focus for a wide range of activities and publishes the magazine *Lambda* three times a year.

Coordinadora Gai-Lesbiana

C/Finlàndia 45, Sants (93 298 00 29/www.cogailes.org). Metro Plaça de Sants. **Open** 6-10pm Mon-Fri. **Map** p341 A4.
This gay umbrella organisation works with the Ajuntament on issues of concern to the gay community.

Front d'Alliberament Gai de Catalunya

C/Verdi 88, Gràcia (93 217 26 69). Metro Fontana. **Open** 5-8pm Mon-Fri. **Map** p339 E3.
FAG is a vocal multi-group that produces the *Barcelona Gai* information bulletin.

Teléfon Rosa

900 60 16 01. **Open** 6-10pm daily.
The phoneline of the Coordinadora Gai-Lesbiana gives help or advice on any gay or lesbian issue.

Health

Visitors can obtain emergency care through the public health service (*Servei Català de la Salut,* often referred to as the '*Seguretat Social/Seguridad Social*'). EU nationals are entitled to free basic medical attention if they have an E111 form (if you can get one sent or faxed within four days, you are exempt from charges). E111 also works for people from countries that have an agreement with Spain, such as Switzerland, Andorra, Chile, Peru, Ecuador, Brazil and Paraguay. For more information call 93 319 31 11.

For non-emergencies, it's usually quicker to use private travel insurance rather than the state system. Similarly, non-EU nationals with private medical insurance can also make use of state health services on a paying basis, but it will usually be simpler to use a private clinic. If you are a resident registered with the Seguretat Social, you will be allocated a doctor and a local clinic. Information on health services is available from the 010 phoneline (see p319).

Accident & emergency

In a medical emergency the best thing to do is go to the casualty department (*Urgències*) of any of the main public hospitals. All listed below are open 24 hours daily. The **Clínic** or the **Perecamps** are the most central. If necessary, make an emergency call to 112 (and you will be put through to the appropriate service) or 061 (ambulance).

Centre d'Urgències Perecamps

Avda Drassanes 17-19, Raval (93 441 06 00). Metro Drassanes or Paral.lel. **Map** p345 A4.
Located near the Rambla, this clinic specialises in primary attention for injuries and less serious emergencies.

Hospital Clínic

C/Villarroel 170, Eixample (93 227 54 00). Metro Hospital Clínic. **Map** p338 C4.
The main central hospital, the Clínic also has a first-aid centre for less serious emergencies two blocks away at C/València 184 (93 227 93 00; 9am-9pm Mon-Fri, 9am-1pm Sat).

Hospital de la Creu Roja de Barcelona

C/Dos de Maig 301, Eixample (93 507 27 00). Metro Hospital de Sant Pau. **Map** p339 F4.

Hospital del Mar

Passeig Marítim 25-9, Barceloneta (93 248 30 00). Metro Ciutadella-Vila Olímpica. **Map** p343 E7.

Hospital de la Santa Creu i Sant Pau

C/Sant Antoni Maria Claret 167, Eixample (93 291 90 00). Metro Hospital de Sant Pau. **Map** p339 F4.

AIDS/HIV

The actual death rate from AIDS is falling in Spain, but the HIV virus continues to spread in many groups, particularly among young heterosexuals. Many local chemists take part in a needle-exchange and condom-distribution programme for intravenous drug users. Antiretroviral drugs for HIV treatment are covered by Social Security in Spain. Free, anonymous blood tests for HIV and other sexually transmitted diseases are given at **CAP Drassanes** (see p311).

Actua

C/Gomis 38, Zona Alta (93 418 50 00/www.interactua.net). Bus 22, 73, 85. **Open** 10am-2pm, 4-7pm Mon-Fri.
Support group for people with HIV.

Directory

AIDS Information Line

900 21 22 22. **Open** *Mid Sept-May* 9am-5.30pm Mon-Fri. *June-mid Sept* 8am-3pm Mon-Fri.

Complementary medicine

Integral: Centre Mèdic i de Salut

Plaça Urquinaona 2, 3º 2ª, Eixample (93 318 30 50/www.integralcentre medic.com). Metro Urquinaona. **Open** *Information* 9am-9pm Mon-Fri (call for an appointment). Closed Aug. **Map** p344 B1.
Acupuncture, homeopathy and many other forms of complementary medicine are offered by a team of 20 professionals at this well-established clinic. Some speak English.

Contraception & abortion

All pharmacies sell condoms (*condons/preservativos*) and other forms of contraception; along with various brands of contraceptive pills, which in Spain can be bought without a prescription. Condom vending machines can also be found in the toilets of many night-time bars, cafés and clubs, and in petrol stations.

Although abortion is legal during the first 12 weeks of pregnancy for those aged 18 or over, it is usually easier to obtain at a private clinic than at a public hospital.

Centre Jove d'Anticoncepció i Sexualitat

C/La Granja 19-21, Gràcia (93 415 10 00/www.centrejove.org). Metro Lesseps. **Open** 10am-7pm Mon, 12am-7pm Tue-Thur. **Map** p339 E2.
A family planning centre aimed at young people (officially, under 23).

Dentists

Not covered by EU reciprocal agreements, so private rates, which can be costly, apply.

Centre Odontològic de Barcelona

C/Calàbria 251, Eixample (93 439 45 00). Metro Entença. **Open** *Sept-July* 9am-8pm Mon-Fri. *Aug* 9am-1pm, 3-8pm Mon-Fri. **Credit** DC, MC, V. **Map** p341 B4.
Well-equipped clinics providing a complete range of dental services. Several of the staff speak English. **Branches**: Institut Odontològic de la Sagrada Família C/Sardenya 319, Eixample (93 457 04 53). Institut Odontològic C/Diputació 238, Eixample (93 342 64 00).

Doctors

A Centre d'Assistència Primària (CAP) is a lower level local health centre where you can normally be seen fairly quickly by a specialist doctor and, if necessary, referred on to a hospital. Alternatively, there is no shortage of decent private healthcare specialists.

CAP Casc Antic

C/Rec Comtal 24, Barri Gòtic (93 310 14 21/93 310 50 98). Metro Arc de Triomf. **Open** 9am-8pm Mon-Fri; 9am-5pm Sat (emergencies only). **Map** p344 C2.

CAP Doctor Lluís Sayé

C/Torres i Amat 8, Raval (93 301 24 82/93 301 27 05/emergencies 93 301 25 32). Metro Universitat. **Open** 9am-5pm Sat (emergencies only). **Map** p344 A1.

CAP Drassanes

Avda Drassanes 17-21, Raval (93 329 44 95). Metro Drassanes or Paral.lel. **Open** 8am-8pm Mon-Fri; 9am-5pm Sat. **Map** p345 A4.

CAP Manso

C/Manso 19, Poble Sec (93 423 30 81). Metro Poble Sec. **Open** 9am-1pm, 3-8pm Mon-Fri; 9am-5pm Sat (emergencies only). **Map** p341 B5.

CAP Vila Olímpica

C/Joan Miró 17, Vila Olímpica (93 221 37 85). Metro Ciutadella-Vila Olímpica. **Open** 8am-8pm Mon-Fri. **Map** p343 F6.

Centre Mèdic Assistencial Catalonia

C/Provença 281, baixos, Eixample (93 215 37 93). Metro Diagonal. **Open** 8am-8pm Mon-Fri. **No credit cards. Map** p338 D4.
Dr Lynd is a British doctor who has been practising in Barcelona for many years. She can be seen at this surgery from 3.30pm to 7.20pm every Wednesday; at other times, leave a message at the office and she will ring you back.

Dr Mary McCarthy

C/Aribau 215, pral 1ª, Eixample (93 200 29 24/mobile 607 220 040). FGC Gràcia/58, 64 bus. **Open** by appointment only. **Credit** MC, V. **Map** p338 C3.
Dr McCarthy is an internal medicine specialist from the USA. She will also treat general patients.

Opticians

See p207.

Pharmacies

Pharmacies (*farmàcies*) are signalled by large green and red crosses, usually in flashing neon. There are plenty about, and most are open from 9am to 1.30pm and 4.30pm to 8pm Monday to Friday, and 9am to 1.30pm on Saturdays. There are around a dozen 24-hour pharmacies around the city, and many more with permanently extended hours; some of the most central are listed below. Other pharmacies open for out-of-hours duty (*guàrdia*) according to a rota.

The full list of all those chemists which stay open late (usually till 10pm) and overnight on any given night is posted daily outside every pharmacy door, and also given in the day's newspapers. Alternatively, you can also call the 010 and 098 information phonelines (*see p319*). At night, duty pharmacies often appear to be closed, and you will have to knock on the shutters to be served.

Farmàcia Alvarez

Passeig de Gràcia 26, Eixample (93 302 11 24). Metro Passeig de Gràcia. **Open** 24hrs daily. **Credit** MC, V. **Map** p342 D5.

Farmàcia Clapés

La Rambla 98, Barri Gòtic (93 301 28 43). Metro Liceu. **Open** 24hrs daily. **Credit** AmEx, MC, V. **Map** p345 A3.

Farmàcia Vilar

Vestíbul, Estació de Sants, Sants (93 490 92 07). Metro Sants Estació. **Open** 7am-10.30pm Mon-Fri; 8am-10.30pm Sat, Sun. **Credit** AmEx, MC, V. **Map** p341 A4.

Directory

Helplines

Alcoholics Anonymous
93 317 77 77. **Open** 10am-1pm, 5-8pm Mon-Fri; answerphone at other times.
Among the local Alcoholics Anonymous groups there are several that have dedicated English-speaking sections.

Telèfon de l'Esperança
93 414 48 48. **Open** 24hrs daily.
The staff at this local helpline service can consult an extensive database to put you in contact with other specialist help groups – from psychiatric to legal. English is occasionally spoken, but not guaranteed. A private foundation.

ID

From the age of 14, Spaniards are legally obliged to carry their DNIs (identity cards). Foreigners are also meant to carry a national ID card or passport, but in practice it's usually OK to carry a photocopy of your passport, or a driving licence.

Insurance

For healthcare and EU nationals, *see p310.* Some non-EU countries have reciprocal healthcare agreements with Spain, but for most travellers it's usually more convenient to have private travel insurance – which will also, of course, cover you in case of theft and flight problems.

Internet

Internet access options will keep on evolving, but the basic choice is between Internet Service Providers (ISPs) that offer free basic access, such as **Eresmas** (902 501 501/ www.eresmas.com), and those that charge perhaps €75 a year for better service – such as Cinet (93 502 03 39/ www.cinet.es). In both cases, you still pay for your internet time in your phone bill, but a *tarifa plana* (flat rate charge) of around €16 a month to cover the phone costs for your off-peak internet use (weekdays 8am-6pm is not included) is offered by phone companies such as **Telefónica** (information 1004) and **Retevision** (015). Broadband is still experiencing teething troubles in Spain.

Internet access

There are now internet centres all over Barcelona. Some libraries (*see below*) provide internet access, and see also **La Idea** (*see p175*). For other computer services, *see p307*.

Change & Transfer
Estació d'Autobusos Barcelona-Nord, C/Ali Bei 80, Eixample (93 232 81 87). Metro Arc de Triomf. **Open** 9am-9pm Mon-Fri, 10am-8pm Sat, Sun. **Credit** AmEx, DC, MC, V. **Map** p343 E5.
Combined internet centre and currency exchange office. The first 30mins costs €1.20.

Ciberopcion
Gran Via de les Corts Catalanes 602, Eixample (93 412 73 08). Metro Universitat. **Open** 9am-1am Mon-Sat; 11am-1am Sun. **No credit cards. Map** p338 D4.
Very cheap and very fast internet connection in a central location, with 150 terminals. It costs 60¢ for each 30min online.

easyEverything
La Rambla 31, Barri Gòtic (93 318 24 35/www.easyeverything.com). Metro Liceu. **Open** 24hrs daily. **No credit cards. Map** p345 A3.
There are 350 terminals here and 250 at Ronda Universitat 35 (93 412 10 58). Prices vary according to demand: €1.20 can get you as much as 3hrs if it's empty, but only about 30mins when it's busy (usually from around noon-9pm). Connection is slow.

Inetcorner
C/Sardenya 306, Eixample (93 244 80 80/www.inetcorner.net). Metro Sagrada Família. **Open** 10am-10pm Mon-Fri; noon-8pm Sun. **No credit cards. Map** p339 F4.
Small centre next to the Sagrada Familia with iMacs. First 20mins cost €1.80, then 5¢ a min.

Left luggage

Aeroport del Prat
Terminal B. **Open** 24hrs daily.
Rates €4 per day.

Estació d'Autobusos Barcelona-Nord
C/Ali Bei 80, Eixample. Metro Arc de Triomf. **Open** 24hrs daily. **Rates** €3, €4.50 per day. **Map** p343 E5.

Estació Marítima (Balearics Ferry Terminal)
Moll de Barcelona, Port Vell. Metro Drassanes. **Open** 8am-11pm daily. **Rates** €3, €4.50 per day. **Map** p342 C7.

Train stations
There are lockers at Sants (open 7am-11pm), Passeig de Gràcia (6.30am-9.30pm) and França (6am-11.45pm daily), but not at the smaller stations. Rates are €3 and €5 per day.

Legal help

Servicio d'Orientació Jurídica
C/València 344, Eixample (93 567 16 44). Metro Verdaguer. **Open** 9am-2pm Mon-Fri. **Map** p339 E4.
Legal consulting service run by the Justice Department, where you can get free legal advice, and those who qualify through low income and savings can be appointed a legal-aid lawyer. Arrive before midday, and be prepared to wait.

Libraries

Barcelona has more than 20 municipal public libraries; among their many services some offer novels in English and free internet access. Call 010 for the address of the nearest or click on to www. bcn.es/icub/biblioteques.

Ateneu Barcelonès
C/Canuda 6, Barri Gòtic (93 343 61 21/www.ateneu-bcn.org). Metro Catalunya. **Open** 9am-10.30pm daily. **Map** p344 B2.
This venerable old cultural and philosophical society has the best private library in the city, open nearly every day of the year, plus a peaceful interior garden patio and a quiet bar. Initial membership costs €120 (payable in instalments), and the subsequent fee is €13.60 per month.

Biblioteca de Catalunya
C/Hospital 56, Raval (93 317 07 78/ www.gencat.es/bc). Metro Liceu. **Open** 9am-8pm Mon-Fri; 9am-2pm Sat. **Map** p344 A2.

The Catalan national collection is housed in the medieval Hospital de la Santa Creu and has a wonderful stock reaching back centuries. Readers' cards are required, but one-day research visits are allowed (take your passport). The library has internet terminals, and the catalogue is online. On the ground floor are the city's most central public libraries, the Biblioteques de Sant Pau i Santa Creu (Sant Pau for adults, Santa Creu for kids).

British Council/ Institut Britànic

C/Amigó 83, Zona Alta (93 241 97 11). FGC Muntaner. **Open** *Oct-June* 9.30am-9pm Mon-Fri; 10.30am-1.30pm Sat. *July, Sept* 9.30am-2pm, 4-8.30pm Mon-Fri. Closed Aug-early Sept. **Map** p338 C2.
UK press, English books, satellite TV and a big multimedia section oriented towards learning English. (Access is free; borrowing costs €55 a year).

Mediateca

CaixaForum, Avda Marquès de Comillas 6-8, Montjuïc (902 22 30 40/www.fundacio.lacaixa.es). Metro Plaça de Espanya. **Open** 10am-8pm Mon-Fri; 10am-3pm Sat. **Map** p341 A5.
A high-tech art, music and media library in the arts centre of Fundació la Caixa. Most materials are open-access; borrowing costs €3, and you will need to provide your ID card or passport.

Lost property

Airport & rail stations

If you lose something at El Prat Airport, report the loss immediately to the Aviación Civil office in the relevant terminal, or call airport information on 93 298 38 38. There is no central lost property depot for the RENFE rail network: if you have mislaid anything on a train, look for the *Atención al Viajero* desk or *Jefe de Estació* office at the nearest main station to where your property has gone astray, or call ahead to the destination station of the train. To get information by phone on lost property at main railway stations, call their information numbers and ask for *Objetos Perdidos*.

Municipal Lost Property Office

Oficina de Troballes, C/Ciutat 9, Barri Gòtic (lost property enquiries 010). Metro Jaume I. **Open** 9am-2pm Mon-Fri. **Map** p345 B3.
All items found on city public transport and taxis, or picked up by the police in the street, should

eventually find their way to this office near the Ajuntament, but do allow a few days. If an item is labelled with the owner's name or a serial number, the 010 phone information service will be able to tell you if it has been handed in. Within 24hrs of the loss you can also try ringing the city transport authority on 93 318 70 74, or, for taxis, the Institut Metropolità del Taxi on 93 223 40 12.

Media

Most of Barcelona's main print and broadcast media are young, like Spain's democracy. But that doesn't mean they're innocent: the twin worlds of journalism and politics tend to collide fairly frequently. The language factor is also important, with Catalan very strong in broadcasting, and gaining ground in print.

Daily newspapers

There are a few slim but informative free daily papers, including *Barcelona@Más, 20 Minutes* and *Metro*, handed out to commuters every weekday morning. Most are a peculiar mixture of articles in Spanish and Catalan. In Catalonia, as in most of Spain, regional, rather than national, dailies lead the market.

Avui

For many years this was the city's only Catalan-language newspaper; though decent, it's predictably pro-Generalitat.

El País

This rigorous, socialist-leaning paper is Spain's only real national daily. Good entertainment and arts supplements, on Friday and Saturday respectively.

El Periódico

Populist, with a tabloid look but fairly solid content. It's a close second in the circulation race, with 40% of its sales from a Catalan-language version.

La Vanguardia

Barcelona's top-selling daily. Traditionally conservative; a lively, well-designed paper, in Spanish, but with a good Catalan-language listings magazine on Fridays.

English language

Foreign newspapers are available at most kiosks on La Rambla and Passeig de Gràcia.

Barcelona Business

A monthly paper combining business news with a general city focus.

Metropolitan

A monthly city magazine aimed at English-speaking Barcelona residents, distributed free in bars and Anglophone hangouts.

Movin' BCN

A well-designed monthly publication in English and Spanish covering concerts, movies, food, theatre, nightlife and cultural events.

b-guided

Quarterly bilingual style magazine for bars, clubs, shops, restaurants and exhibitions; sold at hip venues.

Listings & classifieds

The main newspapers have daily 'what's on' listings, with entertainment supplements on Fridays. For monthly listings, see *Metropolitan* and music/ scene freebies such as *Mondo Sonoro, AB* and *Go* (found in bars and music shops). Of the dailies, *La Vanguardia* has the best classified section, especially on Sundays.

Anuntis

The largest of the classified-ad magazines, *Anuntis* is published on Mondays, Wednesdays and Fridays (phone 902 50 85 08 to place a free ad).

Guía del Ocio

A weekly listings magazine. Its pocket-sized format and availability in any kiosk make it convenient but not always complete.

Television

Spanish TV takes some getting used to: endless ad breaks, unreliable programme start times and, most irritating of all, out-of-sync voices on the mass of dubbed US and British programmes. For undubbed films look for 'VO' in listings or, on 'dual' TVs, the dual symbol at the top of the screen.

Directory

TVE1

The Spanish state broadcaster, 'La Primera', with news that can be heavily pro-government.

TVE2

Also state-run, TVE 2, 'La Dos' offers rather less commercial fare with some good late-night movies.

TV3

Regional Catalan television – entirely in Catalan, with mainstream programming. Often has films in original version or 'dual'.

Canal 33

Also regional and in Catalan, but with documentaries and extra sports programmes.

Antena 3

A private channel with an emphasis on family entertainment and late-night salaciousness.

Tele 5

Also private. A version of *Big Brother* (*Gran Hermano*)has been the biggest drawcard over the past couple of years.

Canal +

A subscriber channel based around movies and sport, although its news and other programmes are shown unscrambled.

BTV

Most innovative of all, but also the hardest to receive in some areas, the Ajuntament's city channel features a lot of student-produced programmes.

City TV

A private channel, cloned from a Toronto city station. Magazine-style programmes and soft porn at night.

Satellite & cable

Digital satellite TV has taken off, with two providers, Via Digital and Canal Satèlite Digital. Cabling of the city is still incomplete: the main provider is Menta.

Radio

Local radio dials – especially FM – are packed, and Catalan has a strong presence. **Catalunya Mùsica** (101.5 FM) is mainly classical. **Rádio 3** (98.7 FM) is a good Spanish station, with rock/roots. On shortwave, the **BBC World Service** can be heard on 15485, 12095, 9410 and 6195 KHz, depending on the time.

Money

Spain's currency is the euro.

Banks & foreign exchange

Banks (*bancos*) and savings banks (*caixes d'estalvis/cajas de ahorros*) readily accept travellers' cheques (you must show your passport), for a commission, but usually refuse to cash any kind of personal cheque except one issued by that bank. Some foreign exchange bureaux (*cambios*) don't charge commission, but these generally offer you a lower rate; it's worth shopping around. Obtaining money through an ATM machine – which are everywhere – with a debit or credit card is often the easiest option despite the fees charged for withdrawals.

BANK HOURS

Banks are normally open from 8.30am to 2pm Monday to Friday. From 1 October to 30 April most branches also open on Saturday mornings from 8.30am to 1pm. Hours vary a little between banks. Savings banks, which offer the same exchange facilities as banks, open from 8am to 2pm Monday to Friday. From October to May many are open late on Thursdays, from 4.30pm to 7.45pm. Savings banks never open on Saturday. All banks are closed on public holidays.

OUT-OF-HOURS SERVICES

Outside normal hours there are foreign exchange offices open at the airport (Terminals A and B, open 7am-11pm daily) and Barcelona-Sants station (open 8am-9.30pm daily). There's a cambio at the Estació d'Autobusos Barcelona-Nord (open 8.30am-10pm Mon-Fri; 9am-5.30pm Sat, Sun), and more in the city centre. Some in the Rambla are open until midnight (and until 3am from July to September). At the airport, Sants and outside some banks there are automatic cash exchange machines that accept notes in major currencies.

American Express

C/Rosselló 261, Eixample (93 255 00 00). Metro Diagonal/FGC Provença. **Open** 9.30am-6pm Mon-Fri; 10am-1pm Sat. **Map** p338 D4.

All the usual AmEx services, an ATM for AmEx cards and 24hr money transfers anywhere in the world (charges paid by the sender). **Branch:** La Rambla 74 (93 301 11 66).

Western Union Money Transfer

Loterías Manuel Martín, La Rambla 41 (93 412 70 41/www.western union.com). Metro Liceu or Drassanes. **Open** 9.30am-11pm Mon-Sat; 10am-11pm Sun. **Map** p345 A3. The quickest, although not the cheapest, way of having money sent from abroad.
Branch: Mail Boxes C/València 214, Eixample (93 454 69 83).

Credit cards

Major credit and charge cards are widely accepted in hotels, shops, and in many other places (including metro ticket machines, and pay-and-display parking machines in the street). With major cards you can also withdraw cash from most bank cash machines, which provide instructions in different languages at the push of a button. Banks also advance cash against a credit card, but prefer you to use the machine. Don't forget that interest will be charged.

Note: you will need photo ID (passport, driving licence or similar) when using a credit/debit card in a shop, but not usually in a restaurant.

Lost/stolen credit cards

All lines have English-speaking staff and are open 24hrs daily. **American Express** 902 37 56 37 **Diners Club** 901 10 10 11 **MasterCard** 900 97 12 31 **Visa** 900 99 12 16

Tax

There are different rates of sales tax (IVA): for hotels and restaurants, the rate is seven per cent; in shops, it's most commonly 16 per cent, but four or seven per cent on many items. IVA is not generally included in listed prices in hotels and restaurants, in which case the expression *mas IVA* (plus sales tax) must be stated after the price. Be careful of this when getting quotes on expensive items. In shops displaying a 'Tax-Free Shopping' sticker, non EU-residents can reclaim tax on large purchases.

Opening times

Most shops open from 9/10am to 1/2pm and then from 4.30/5pm to 8/9pm, Monday to Saturday, but many do not reopen on Saturday afternoons. Markets open earlier, at 7/8am, and most smaller ones are shut by 2/3pm. Major stores, shopping centres and a growing number of shops open all day, from 10am to 9pm Monday to Saturday. Larger shops are also allowed to open for some Sundays and a few holidays, mostly around Christmas.

In summer, staggered holidays have become more common, but many restaurants and shops still close up for all or part of August. Many businesses work a shortened day from June to September, from 8/9am till 3pm. Most (but not all) museums close one day each week, usually Monday. For banking hours, *see p314*.

Police

Barcelona has several police forces. The **Guàrdia Urbana** wear navy and pale blue, and are concerned with traffic and local regulations, but also help to keep general law and order in the city. The **Policía Nacional**, in darker blue uniforms and white shirts (or blue, combat-style gear), patrol the streets as well, and are responsible for dealing with more serious crime. The Catalan government's police, the **Mossos d'Esquadra**, in navy and light blue with red trim, are gradually

expanding their role, and are now responsible for traffic control in Barcelona province, although not in the city itself. A fourth body is the **Guàrdia Civil**, who wear military green uniforms and watch over many Spanish highways, customs posts and some government buildings, but are not often seen within Barcelona.

REPORTING A CRIME

If you are robbed or attacked, report the incident as soon as possible to the nearest police station (*comisaría*). In the centre, the most convenient is probably the Guàrdia Urbana station in the Rambla, which often has English-speaking officers on duty. In other areas, contact the Policía Nacional (the 24-hour operator on 93 290 30 00 can connect you to the closest *comisaría*).

If you report a crime, you will be asked to make an official statement (*denuncia*). It is frankly unlikely that anything you have lost will be recovered, but you need the *denuncia* to make an insurance claim. For emergency phone numbers, *see p309*.

Guàrdia Urbana Ciutat Vella

La Rambla 43, Barri Gòtic (93 344 13 00). Metro Liceu or Drassanes. **Open** 24hrs daily. **Map** p345 A3.

Postal services

Letters and postcards weighing up to 20g cost 25¢ within Spain; 50¢ to the rest of Europe; 75¢ to the rest of the world. If the shape of the envelope is not considered 'standard', you will be charged double. Mail to other European countries generally arrives in three to four days, and to the USA in about a week. Aerograms (*aerogramas*) cost 50¢ for all destinations. It's usually easiest to buy stamps for cards or letters at *estancs* (*see below*); postboxes in

the street are yellow with a white horn insignia. Postal information is on 902 197 197 or at www.correos.es.

Correu Central

Plaça Antonio López, Barri Gòtic (93 486 80 50). Metro Jaume I or Barceloneta. **Open** 8.30am-9.30pm Mon-Sat; reduced service 9am-2pm Sun. **Map** p341 B4.
Take a ticket from the machine and wait your turn. Apart from the typical services, fax sending and receiving is offered at all post offices (more expensive than at fax shops, but with the option of courier delivery in Spain). To send something express, say you want to send it '*urgente*'. Postal Exprés is a reliable way of sending small packages within Spain and guarantees next-day delivery to provincial capitals and 48hr delivery elsewhere. On Sundays, not all services are available and entrance is via a door on the Via Laietana side. Some post offices close in August.
Branches: Ronda Universitat 23, Eixample; C/Aragó 282, Eixample. **Open** *Both* 8.30am-8.30pm Mon-Fri, 9.30am-1pm Sat.

Estancs/Estancos

The tobacco shop, usually known as an *estanc/estanco* and identified by a brown and yellow sign with the words *tabacs* or *tabacos*, is a very important Spanish institution. First and foremost, they supply cigarettes and tobacco, but they are also the main places to buy postage stamps, as well as many official forms demanded by Spanish state bureaucracy. They also sell public transport *targetes* and phonecards.

Poste Restante

Letters sent Poste Restante should be addressed to Lista de Correos, 08070 Barcelona, Spain. Pick-up is from the main post office, and you'll need your passport to collect them.

Queuing

Catalans, like other Spaniards, have a highly developed queuing culture. In small shops and at market stalls, although people may not stand in an orderly line, they are generally very well aware of when it is their turn. Common practice is to ask when you arrive, '¿*Qui es l'últim/la última?*' ('Who's last?'); see who nods back at you, and follow after them. Say

Directory

'jo' ('me') to the next person who asks the same question.

Religion

Anglican: St George's Church
C/Horaci 38, Zona Alta (93 417 88 67/www.st-georges-church.com). FGC Av Tibidabo/22, 64, 75 bus. **Main service** 11am Sun.
A British church with a multicultural congregation, weekly ladies' meeting, bridge and Bible study.

Catholic mass in English: Parròquia Maria Reina
Carretera d'Esplugues 103, Zona Alta (93 203 41 15). Metro Maria Cristina/63, 78 bus. **Mass** 10.30am Sun. **Map** p337 A1.

Jewish Orthodox: Sinagoga de Barcelona & Comunitat Israelita de Barcelona
C/Avenir 24, Zona Alta (93 200 61 48). FGC Gràcia/58, 64 bus. **Prayers** call for times. **Map** p338 C3.
A Sephardic, Orthodox synagogue.

Jewish Reform: Comunitat Jueva Atid de Catalunya
C/Castanyer 27, Zona Alta (93 417 37 04/www.atid.info). FGC El Putxet or Av Tibidabo/17 bus. **Prayers** call for times.
Reform synagogue.

Muslim: Mosque Tarik Bin Ziad
C/Hospital 91, Raval (93 441 91 49). Metro Liceu/14, 38, 59, bus. **Prayers** 2pm Fri. Call for other times.

Safety

Pickpocketing and bag-snatching are rife in Barcelona, and tourists are a prime target. Be particularly careful around the Old City, and especially La Rambla, as well as on public transport and at stations; but thieves go where tourists go, even to quieter areas such as the parks and beaches. Most street robberies are aimed at the unwary, and could be avoided if you take a few simple precautions:

● Avoid giving invitations to thieves: wallets left in easily accessible pockets, or bank notes flashed in public. Bags should be well closed, and pulled to the front. When you stop, only put bags down right beside you, where you can see them constantly and where a passer-by couldn't easily snatch them.
● In busy streets or crowded places, keep an eye out for who's moving around you. If you're at all suspicious of someone, simply move somewhere else.
● Barcelona street thieves tend to use stealth and surprise rather than violence. However, muggings and knife threats do sometimes occur. Avoid deserted streets if you're on your own at night.
● Despite precautions, sometimes you can just be unlucky. It's best not to carry more money and valuables than you have to, and to take out travel insurance.

Smoking

People in Barcelona still smoke, and smoke in banks, shops and so on. Non-smoking areas are rare in restaurants, although smoking bans in cinemas, theatres and on trains are generally respected. Smoking is banned throughout the metro and FGC, but many people take this to mean on trains only, not station platforms. For places to buy tobacco, *see p208*.

Study

Catalonia is ardently Europhile, and its universities lend enthusiastic support to EU student exchange programmes. The vast majority of foreign students in Spain under the EU's Erasmus scheme are enrolled at Catalan universities. The main language used in universities is usually Catalan, although

lecturers (and students) are often relaxed about using Castilian in class for the first few months with non-Catalan speakers. Foreign students, including EU nationals, who stay for more than three months are officially required to have a residence permit.

Centre d'Informació i Assessorament per a Joves (CIAJ)
C/Ferran 32, Barri Gòtic (93 402 78 00/fax 93 402 78 01/www.bcn.es/ciaj). Metro Liceu. **Open** 10am-2pm, 4-8pm Mon-Fri. Closed afternoons Aug. **Map** p345 A/B3.
City council youth info centre, with advice and information on work, study, travel and more. Also small ads, noticeboards and free web terminals (not for email).

Secretaria General de Joventut – Punt d'Informació Juvenil
C/Calabria 147-C/Rocafort 116, Eixample (93 483 83 83/93 483 83 84/www.bcu.cesca.es). Metro Rocafort. **Open** 9am-2pm, 3-5.30pm Mon-Fri. Closed afternoons June-mid Sept. **Map** p341 B5.
Generalitat-run centre hosting a range of services: 'youth information' on travel, work and study and internet access. Other services include **Habitatge Jove** (93 483 83 92/www.habitatge jove.com), an under-35s accommodation service, and travel information centre **Viatgeteca** (93 483 83 81).

Language classes

In bilingual Barcelona, many who come to stay for a while will want (or need) to learn some Catalan, but this is also a hugely popular location for people studying Spanish. For full lists of course options, try the youth information centres listed above.

American-British College
C/Guillem Tell 27, Zona Alta (93 415 57 57/www.ambricol.es). FGC Plaça Molina. **Open** *Oct-May* 9am-9pm Mon-Fri; 10am-1pm Sat. *June-Sept* 9am-9pm Mon-Fri. **Map** p338 D2.
An established school offering reasonably priced intensive Spanish courses. Accommodation can be arranged either with families or in student residences.

Consorci per a la Normalització Lingüística

Central office: C/Mallorca 272, 8ª, Eixample (93 272 31 00/ www.cpnl.org). Metro Passeig de Gràcia or Diagonal. **Open** *Sept-mid June* 9am-2pm, 3-6.30pm Mon-Fri. *Mid June-Aug* 8am-3pm Mon-Fri. **Map** p338 D4.

The official Generalitat organisation for the support of the Catalan language has centres around the city offering Catalan courses at very low prices from beginners' level upwards, with intensive courses in summer, and self-study centres.

Escola Oficial d'Idiomes

Avda Drassanes (93 324 93 30/ www.eoibd.es). Metro Drassanes. **Open** *Information Oct-May* 10.30am-12.30pm Mon, Thur, Fri; 10.30am-12.30pm, 4-7pm Tue, Wed. *June-Sept.* 10.30am-12.30pm Mon, Thur, Fri; 10.30am-12.30pmTue, Wed. **Map** p341 A4.

The 'official school' has semi-intensive three-month courses at all levels in Catalan, Spanish and other languages. It's cheap, and has a good reputation, so demand is high and classes are big. It also has summer courses, a self-study centre and a good library. For some courses, it may be easier to get a place in the Escola Oficial located at Avda del Jordà 18, Vall d'Hebrón (93 418 74 85).

International House

C/Trafalgar 14, Eixample (93 268 45 11/www.ihes.com/bcn). Metro Urquinaona/bus all routes to Plaça Catalunya. **Open** 8am-9pm Mon-Fri; 10am-1.30pm Sat. **Map** p344 C1.

Intensive Spanish courses all year. IH is also a leading Barcelona centre for TEFL teacher training.

Universities

EU programmes: Socrates, Erasmus, Lingua

The Erasmus student exchange scheme and Lingua project (specifically concerned with language learning) are the main parts of the EU's Socrates programme to help students move between member states. Interested students should approach the Erasmus co-ordinator at their home college. Information is available in Britain from the **UK Socrates-Erasmus Council**, R&D Building, The University, Canterbury, Kent CT2 7PD (01227 762712/fax 01227 762711/ www.ukc.ac.uk/erasmus/erasmus).

Universitat Autònoma de Barcelona

Campus de Bellaterra, (93 581 10 00/student information 93 581 11 11/www.uab.es). FGC or RENFE Universidad Autonoma/by car A18 to Cerdanyola del Valles. **Open** *Information* 10am-1.30pm, 3.30-4.30pm Mon-Fri.

A rambling 1960s campus outside the city at Bellaterra, near Sabadell, with frequent FGC train connections.

Universitat de Barcelona

Gran Via de les Corts Catalanes 585, Eixample (student information 93 403 54 17/www.ub.es/siae). Metro Universitat. **Open** *Information* (Pati de Ciències entrance) 9am-2pm, 3:30-6pm. Aug, holidays 9am-2pm. **Map** p342 C-D5.

Barcelona's oldest and biggest university with faculties in the main building on Plaça Universitat, in the Zona Universitària, as well as in other parts of town.

Universitat Pompeu Fabra

Student information 93 542 22 28/ www.upf.es. Information offices: La Rambla 30-32, Barri Gòtic; C/Ramon Trias Fargas 25-7, Vila Olímpica. **Open** *Both* 9am-9pm Mon-Fri.

Founded in 1991, this social sciences-based university has faculties in various parts of central Barcelona, many of them in the Old City.

Universitat Ramon Llull

C/Claravall 1-3, Zona Alta (93 280 61 62/www.url.es). FGC Av Tibidabo/22, 58, 73, 75, 85 bus. **Open** *Information* 9am-2pm, 4-6.30pm Mon-Fri. Closed 2wks Aug.

Private, expensive university bringing together a number of previously separate institutions owned and/or run by the Jesuits, including the ESADE business school (93 280 61 62/www.esade.edu); there is no strong religious presence in teaching.

Telephones

Thanks to competition in the Spanish phone market, prices are coming down and new options are constantly appearing. Former state operator **Telefónica** still has a virtual monopoly on local calls and most calls from public phones, although this is gradually changing. International calls now cost the same whatever the day or hour. Some phone cards and phone centres give cheaper rates than Telefónica.

Dialling & codes

All normal Spanish phone numbers have nine digits, as the area code (93 in Barcelona and its province) must be dialled with all calls, whether they are local or long-distance. Spanish mobile phone numbers always begin with 6. Numbers beginning 900 are freephone lines; other 90 numbers are special-rate services – in general, the higher the third digit, the higher the rate.

International & long-distance calls

To make an international call, dial 00 and then the country code, followed by the area code (omitting the first zero in UK numbers) and number. To call Barcelona from abroad, dial the international code (00 in the UK), then 34 for Spain.

Australia 61
Canada 1
Irish Republic 353
New Zealand 64
United Kingdom 44
USA 1

Public phones

The most common model of payphone accepts coins (from 2¢ up), Telefónica phonecards and credit cards, and has a digital display with instructions in English and other languages.

For the first minute of a daytime local call, you'll be charged around 15¢; to a mobile phone around 50¢; to a 902 number, around 20¢. This type of phone also gives you credit to make further calls without having to reinsert money. Most bars and cafés also have phones for public use, but they often cost 50 per cent more than regular booths.

Post offices, newsstands and *estancs* sell €6 and €12 Telefónica phonecards. Also on sale at newsstands and shops are cards from many other companies, which offer cheaper rates than Telefónica on all but local calls. The cards give you a toll-free number to call; an operator or automatic system then connects you with the number you want and can also tell you how much you have left on the card.

Phone centres

Phone centres (*locutorios*) can also bring down call prices, and avoid the need for change. Most private centres offer international call rates that are cheaper than Telefónica's for all countries. There are many phone centres along Raval side streets, such as C/Sant Pau, or along C/Carders-C/Corders in La Ribera. Many also offer other services such as international money transfer, currency exchange and internet access.

Cambios Sol

Vestibule, Estació de Sants, Sants (93 491 45 37). Metro Sants Estació. **Open** 8.30am-9pm daily. **Map** p341 A4.

Oftelcom

C/Canuda 7, Barri Gòtic (93 342 73 70). Metro Catalunya. **Open** 11am-11pm daily. **Map** p344 B2.

Operator services

Usually, operators will speak Catalan and Spanish only – except for international operators, most of whom speak English.
National directory enquiries 1003
International directory enquiries 025
National operator 1009
International operator *Europe & North Africa* 1008; *rest of world* 1005
Telephone faults service 1002
Telegrams 933 222 000
Time 093
Weather 906 365 365
Wake-up calls 096. You key in the time at which you wish to be woken, in the 24hr clock, in four figures: for example, punch in 0830 if you want to be called at 8.30am.
General information 010. *See p319.*

Mobile phones

An estimated 80 per cent of Spaniards now have a *móvil*. You pay either with a monthly bill or by using pre-paid phones, charged with vouchers available in newsagents or via any cash machine. Call costs vary greatly according to contract options, but it is quite expensive compared to Britain or the US. Many mobile phones from other countries can be used in Spain with a 'roaming' system, but you will probably need to contact your operator to set it up before you leave home. However, this can be expensive and it may well be cheaper to buy or rent a Spanish mobile.

Rent a Phone

C/Numància 212, Eixample (93 280 21 31/www.rphone.es). Metro Maria Cristina. **Open** 9.30am-2pm, 4-7.30pm Mon-Fri. **Credit** AmEx, MC, V. **Map** p337 B2.
Mobile phones and accessories for rent, either for use in Spain or to take to other countries. Daytime Spanish calls are charged at 90¢-€1.20/min.

Time

Local time is one hour ahead of GMT, six hours ahead of US Eastern Standard Time and nine ahead of Pacific Standard Time. So, when it's 6pm in Barcelona, it's 5pm in London and noon in New York. As in the UK, Summer Time in Spain starts in late March and ends in late October.

Tipping

There are no fixed rules, nor any expectation of a set ten per cent or more, and locals tip very little. It is common to leave around five per cent for a waiter in a restaurant, and people may also leave a small tip in a bar. It's also usual to tip hotel porters and toilet attendants. In taxis, the norm is around five per cent, more for longer journeys, or if the driver has helped with bags.

Toilets

Public toilets are not especially common in Barcelona, although most of the main railway stations have clean toilets, and in some places there are pay-on-entry cubicles that cost 15¢. Generally, it's best to pop into a bar or café; proprietors usually don't mind. Major stores or fast food restaurants are, of course, staple standbys.

Tourist information

The city council (Ajuntament) and Catalan government (Generalitat) both run tourist information offices, and the City of Barcelona has its own efficient information service that's also useful to visitors. Information about what's on in the music, theatre, galleries, sport and so on can be found in most local papers as well as listings magazines (*see p313*).

City tourist offices also sell multi-journey transport tickets, tourist bus tickets and the Barcelona Card discount card. The Generalitat and, particularly, the Ajuntament also have useful websites (partly in English).

Oficines d'Informació Turística

Main office: Plaça Catalunya, Eixample (906 30 12 82/from outside Spain 93 368 97 30/ www.bcn.es/www.barcelona turisme.com). Metro Catalunya. **Open** 9am-9pm daily. **Map** p344 B1.
The main office of the city tourist board (*Turisme de Barcelona*) is underground beneath the Corte Inglés side of the square (look for big red signs with 'i' in white). It has information, money exchange, a shop selling souvenirs and books, a hotel booking service and coin-in-a-slot internet access.
Branches: Plaça Sant Jaume (in Ajuntament building, side entrance on C/Ciutat), Barri Gòtic; Barcelona-Sants station; Palau de Congressos (Trade Fair office), Avda Reina Maria Cristina, Montjuïc; A7 (or E15) Motorway, Montseny-Sud service area, km 117.

Temporary office & 'Red Jackets'

Information booth located at Sagrada Família. **Open** *Late June-late Sept* 10am-8pm daily. **Map** p339 F4.
In summer, Turisme de Barcelona opens this temporary booth (no hotel booking service). 'Red Jacket' information officers (in red uniforms) also roam the Barri Gòtic and La Rambla during the summer, ready to field questions in a heroic variety of languages from 10am to 8pm daily.

Palau Robert

Passeig de Gràcia 107, Eixample (93 238 40 00/www.gencat.es). Metro Diagonal. **Open** 10am-7pm Mon-Sat; 10am-2pm Sun. **Map** p338 D4.
The Generalitat's lavishly equipped information centre is at the junction of Passeig de Gràcia and the Diagonal. It has maps and other essentials for the city itself, but the speciality is a huge range of information in different media on other parts of Catalonia. It occasionally hosts interesting exhibitions.
Branches: Airport Terminal A (93 478 47 04); Airport Terminal B (93 478 05 65). 9am-9pm daily.

Centre d'Informació de la Virreina

Palau de la Virreina, La Rambla 99, Barri Gòtic (93 301 77 75). Metro Liceu. **Open** 10am-Mon-Sat; 11am-3pm Sun. *Ticket sales* 11am-8pm Tue-Sat; 11am-2.30pm Sun. **Map** p344 A2.
The information office of the city's culture department, with details of exhibitions, concerts and special events. Also the best place to buy tickets for the Grec summer festival, and some other city-sponsored events. In the same building is the Botiga de la Virreina bookshop, with a wide choice of books on Barcelona, some in English.

010 phoneline

Open 8am-10pm Mon-Sat.
City-run information line aimed mainly at local citizens, but which does an impeccable job of answering all kinds of queries. You may have to wait for an English-speaking operator. From outside Barcelona, call 93 402 70 00.

Visas & immigration

Spain is one of the European Union countries covered by the Schengen agreement, with many shared visa regulations and reduced border controls (with the exception of the UK and Ireland, the Schengen zone now takes in the entire EU, and also extends to Norway and Iceland). To travel to Schengen countries, British and Irish citizens need full passports; most EU nationals need carry only their national identity card. Passports, but not visas, are needed by US, Canadian, Australian and New Zealand citizens for stays of up to three months. Citizens of South Africa and many other countries need visas to enter Spain, obtainable from Spanish consulates and embassies in other countries (or from those of other Schengen countries that you are planning to visit). EU citizens intending to work, study or live long-term in Spain are required to obtain a residency card after arrival; non-EU nationals have a different procedure and should get a special visa in their home country before entering Spain.

Visa requirements are subject to change, so always check the latest information with your country's Spanish embassy in plenty of time.

Water

You can drink Barcelona tap water, though it is heavily chlorinated and tests have recently detected a carcinogenic agent, which may make long-term consumption questionable. In any case, bottled water tastes much better, and if you ask for water in a restaurant you will automatically be served this unless you specifically request otherwise.

When to go

There's no best time to come to Barcelona. The city is at its liveliest for the many *festes* (*see chapter* **By Season**), while the weather ranges from mild to glorious. In August the city is blissfully traffic-free, although many restaurants and so on are closed. Temperatures are rarely extreme, although the high humidity in summer can be quite debilitating.

Climate

Spring is unpredictable, and warm sunny days can alternate with cold winds and showers; May and June temperatures are perfect, and the city's streetlife is at its most vibrant. The real summer heat, sticky and humid, hits during July and August and many locals leave town. Autumn weather is generally warm and fresh, with sporadic downpours. Crisp sunshine is common from December to February. Snow is rare.
See p320 **Average monthly climate.**

Public holidays

On public holidays (*festes/fiestas*), virtually all shops, banks and offices, and many bars and restaurants, are closed. Public transport runs a limited service on Christmas and New Year's Day. When a holiday falls on a Tuesday or Thursday, some people take the intervening day before or after the weekend off as well, in a long weekend called a *pont/puente* (bridge).

Women

The Catalan capital is in many ways a female-friendly city. Sexism can certainly be found – as some shocking cases of domestic violence have recently shown – but women tourists can have a drink in a bar or go out alone without anyone making much of it, and probably feel safer in general than in many other large cities.

Ca La Dona

C/Casp 38, pral, Eixample (93 412 71 61/http://caladona.pangea.org). Metro Catalunya or Urquinaona.

Directory

Open *Office* 10am-2pm, 4-8pm Mon-Thur. Closed Aug. **Map** p344 B1.
Women's centre hosting several political, artistic and social groups, and a good place for info. It also has a magazine with event listings.

Centre Municipal d'Informació i Recursos per a Dones
Av Diagonal 233, 5ª, Eixample (93 413 27 22/93 413 27 23/ www.cird.bcn.es). Metro Glòries or Monumental. **Open** *Oct-June* noon-2pm Mon-Fri, 4-7pm Tue, Thur. *July, Sept* noon-2pm Mon-Fri. Closed Aug. **Map** p343 F5.
The Ajuntament's women's resource centre. Its publications include a monthly events guide, *Agenda Dona*.

Institut Català de la Dona
Head office/library: C/Viladomat 319, entresol, Eixample (93 495 16 00/www.gencat.net/icdona). Metro Entença. **Open** 9am-2pm, 3-5.30pm Mon-Thur; 9am-2pm Fri. **Map** p337 B3.
Information centre: C/Portaferrissa 1-3, Barri Gòtic (93 317 92 91/ icd@correu.gencat.es). Metro Jaume I or Liceu. **Open** 9am-2pm, 4-6pm Mon-Fri. Reduced hours June-Sept. **Map** p344 A2.
The women's affairs department of the Catalan government.

Working

Barcelona attracts ever-growing numbers of foreign residents and working visitors. Not many from developed countries, however, are drawn here by money, for Barcelona can be a difficult place to find well-paid work, although it is still a not-too-painful place to live cheaply. Common recourses for English-speakers are jobs in the tourist sector (which are often seasonal and outside the city), bar work and English-language teaching – still the best chance of finding work quickly.

For a contract in a school, a recognised English-teaching qualification such as TEFL is useful, though not always essential (for courses, *see p317* **International House**). There is never a lack of demand for private classes either, which are generally much better paid. If you are contracted from your country of origin, legal papers should be handled by your employer. Otherwise, the quickest way to deal with the endless form-filling and bureaucracy is to resort to a *gestoria* (*see p307*).

EU CITIZENS
All citizens of the European Union have the right to live, work and study in Spain, but must become legally resident if they stay for more than three months. If you have a job or study course lined up already, you are ready to make an appointment to present your residency application. In Barcelona, you do this at the foreigners' office (*Oficina de Extranjeros*) at the Delegación del Gobierno (*see below*).

NON-EU CITIZENS
While immigration laws have relaxed for EU nationals, they have tightened for people from the rest of the world. First-time applicants officially need a special visa, obtained from a Spanish consulate in your home country, although you can start the bureaucratic ball rolling in Spain if you don't mind making at least one trip home. This, combined with the length of the process, means that good legal advice from a *gestor* (*see p307*) is especially important. There is also a sizeable undeclared, under-the-table labour market in Spain and many people manage to postpone the bureaucratic paper chase, although this can become counterproductive, even if you don't get caught.

Delegación del Gobierno – Oficina de Extranjeros
Avda Marqués de l'Argentera 2, Barceloneta (93 482 05 44/ appointments 93 482 05 60 8am-3pm Mon-Fri/phoneline 8.30am-2.30pm Mon-Fri). Metro Barceloneta. **Open** 9am-2pm Mon-Fri. **Map** p345 C4.
Arrive early, and make sure you're in the right queue before you start. You can expect shorter waits on Fridays.

Average monthly climate

	Max temp (C°/F°)	Min temp (C°/F°)	Rainfall (mm/in)	Rain (days/month)
Jan	13/56	6/43	44/1.7	5
Feb	15/59	7/45	36/1.4	6
Mar	16/61	8/47	48/1.9	6
Apr	18/64	10/50	51/2	7
May	21/70	14/57	57/2.2	7
June	24/76	17/63	38/1.5	5
July	27/81	20/67	22/0.9	3
Aug	29/84	20/67	66/2.6	5
Sept	25/78	18/64	79/3.1	6
Oct	22/71	14/57	94/3.7	6
Nov	17/63	9/49	74/2.9	6
Dec	15/59	7/45	50/2.5	6

Catalan Vocabulary

Over a third of Barcelona residents use Catalan as their predominant everyday language, around 70 per cent speak it fluently, and more than 90 per cent understand it. If you take an interest and learn a few phrases, it is likely to be appreciated.

Catalan phonetics are significantly different from those of Spanish, with a wider range of vowel sounds and soft consonants. Catalans use the familiar (*tu*) rather than the polite (*vosté*) forms of the second person very freely, but for convenience verbs are given here in the polite form.

For food and menu terms, *see chapter* **Restaurants**.

Pronunciation

In Catalan, as in French but unlike in Spanish, words are run together, so *si us plau* (please) is more like *sees-plow*.

à at the end of a word (as in Francesc Macià) is an open **a** rather like **ah**, but very clipped
ç, and **c** before an **i** or an **e**, are like a soft **s**, as in sit; **c** in all other cases is as in cat
e, when unstressed as in *cerveses* (beers), or Jaume I, is a weak sound like centre or comfortable
g before **i** or **e** and **j** are pronounced like the **s** in pleasure; **tg** and **tj** are similar to the **dg** in badge
g after an **i** at the end of a word (Puig) is a hard **ch** sound, as in watch; **g** in all other cases is as in get
h is silent
ll is somewhere between the **y** in yes and the **lli** in million
l.l, the most unusual feature of Catalan spelling, has a slightly stronger stress on a single **l** sound, so para**l.l**el sounds similar to the English para**ll**el
o at the end of a word is like the **u** sound in flu; **ó** at the end of a word is similar to the **o** in tomato; **ò** is like the **o** in hot
r beginning a word and **rr** are heavily rolled; but at the end of many words is almost silent, so *carrer* (street) sounds like carr-ay
s at the beginning and end of words and **ss** between vowels are soft, as in sit; a single **s** between two vowels is

a **z** sound, as in lazy
t after **l** or **n** at the end of a word is almost silent
x at the beginning of a word, or after a consonant or the letter **i**, is like the **sh** in shoe, at other times like the English e**x**pert
y after an **n** at the end of a word or in **nys** is not a vowel but adds a nasal stress and a y-sound to the n

Basics

please *si us plau*; **very good/great/OK** *molt bé*
hello *hola*; **goodbye** *adéu*
open *obert*; **closed** *tancat*
entrance *entrada*; **exit** *sortida*
nothing at all/*zilch res de res* (said with both s silent)
price *preu*; **free** *gratuit/de franc*; **change, exchange** *canvi*
to rent *llogar*; **(for) rent, rental** *(de) lloguer*

More expressions

hello (when answering the phone) *hola, digui'm*
good morning, good day *bon dia*; **good afternoon, good evening** *bona tarda*; **good night** *bona nit*
thank you (very much) *(moltes) gràcies*; **you're welcome** *de res*
do you speak English? *parla anglés?*; **I'm sorry, I don't speak Catalan** *ho sento, no parlo català*
I don't understand *no entenc*
can you say it to me in Spanish, please? *m'ho pot dir en castellà, si us plau?*
how do you say that in Catalan? *com se diu això en català?*
what's your name? *com se diu?*
Sir/Mr *senyor (sr)*; **Madam/Mrs** *senyora (sra)*; **Miss** *senyoreta (srta)*
excuse me/sorry *perdoni/disculpi*; **excuse me, please** *escolti* (literally 'listen to me'); **OK/fine** *val/d'acord*
how much is it? *quant és?*
why? *perqué?*; **when?** *quan?*; **who?** *qui?*; **what?** *qué?*; **where?** *on?*; **how?** *com?*; **where is...?** *on és...?*; **who is it?** *qui és?*; **is/are there any...?** *hi ha...?/n'hi ha de...?*
very *molt*; **and** *i* or *o*; **with** *amb*; **without** *sense*; **enough** *prou*
I would like... *vull...* (literally, 'I want'); **how many would you like?** *quants en vol?*; **I don't want** *no vull*; **I like** *m'agrada*; **I don't like** *no m'agrada*
good *bo/bona*; **bad** *dolent/a*; **well/badly** *bé/malament*; **small** *petit/a*; **big** *gran*; **expensive** *car/a*; **cheap** *barat/a*; **hot** (food, drink) *calent/a*; **cold** *fred/a*
something *alguna cosa*; **nothing**

res; **more** *més*; **less** *menys*; **more or less** *més o menys*
toilet *el bany/els serveis/el lavabo*

Getting around

a ticket *un billet*; **return** *d'anada i tornada*; **card expired** (on metro) *titol esgotat*
left *esquerra*; **right** *dreta*; **here** *aquí*; **there** *allí*; **straight on** *recte*; **at the corner** *a la cantonada*; **as far as** *fins a*; **towards** *cap a*; **near** *a prop*; **far** *lluny*; **is it far?** *és lluny?*

Time

In Catalan, quarter- and half-hours can be referred to as quarters of the next hour (so, 1.30 is two quarters of 2).

now *ara*; **later** *més tard*; **yesterday** *ahir*; **today** *avui*; **tomorrow** *demà*; **tomorrow morning** *demà pel matí*
morning *el matí*; **midday** *migdía*; **afternoon** *la tarda*; **evening** *el vespre*; **night** *la nit*; **late night** (roughly 1-6am) *la matinada*
at what time...? *a quina hora...?*
in an hour *en una hora*
at 2 *a les dues*; **at 8pm** *a les vuit del vespre*; **at 1.30** *a dos quarts de dues/a la una i mitja*; **at 5.15** *a un quart de sis/a las cinc i quart*; **at 22.30** *a vint-i-dos-trenta*

Numbers

0 *zero*; **1** *u, un, una*; **2** *dos, dues*; **3** *tres*; **4** *quatre*; **5** *cinc*; **6** *sis*; **7** *set*; **8** *vuit*; **9** *nou*; **10** *deu*; **11** *onze*; **12** *dotze*; **13** *tretze*; **14** *catorze*; **15** *quinze*; **16** *setze*; **17** *disset*; **18** *divuit*; **19** *dinou*; **20** *vint*; **21** *vint-i-u*; **22** *vint-i-dos, vint-i-dues*; **30** *trenta*; **40** *quaranta*; **50** *cinquanta*; **60** *seixanta*; **70** *setanta*; **80** *vuitanta*; **90** *noranta*; **100** *cent*; **200** *dos-cents, dues-centes*; **1,000** *mil*; **1,000,000** *un milló*

Date & season

Monday *dilluns*; **Tuesday** *dimarts*; **Wednesday** *dimecres*; **Thursday** *dijous*; **Friday** *divendres*; **Saturday** *dissabte*; **Sunday** *diumenge*
January *gener*; **February** *febrer*; **March** *març*; **April** *abril*; **May** *maig*; **June** *juny*; **July** *juliol*; **August** *agost*; **September** *setembre*; **October** *octobre*; **November** *novembre*; **December** *desembre*
spring *primavera*; **summer** *estiu*; **autumn/fall** *tardor*; **winter** *hivern*

Spanish Vocabulary

Spanish is generally referred to as *castellano* (Castilian) rather than *español*. Although many locals prefer to speak Catalan, everyone in the city can speak Spanish, and will switch to it if visitors show signs of linguistic jitters. The Spanish familiar form for 'you' – *tú* – is used very freely, but it's safer to use the more formal *usted* with older people and strangers (verbs below are given in the *usted* form).

For food and menu terms, *see chapter* **Restaurants**.

Spanish pronunciation

c before an **i** or an **e** and **z** are like **th** in **thin**
c in all other cases is as in **cat**
g before an **i** or an **e** and **j** are pronounced with a guttural **h**-sound that doesn't exist in English – like **ch** in Scottish loch, but much harder;
g in all other cases is as in **get**
h at the beginning of a word is normally silent
ll is pronounced almost like a **y**
ñ is like **ny** in can**y**on
a single **r** at the beginning of a word and **rr** elsewhere are heavily rolled

Stress rules

In words ending with a vowel, **n** or **s**, the penultimate syllable is stressed: eg *barato, viven, habitaciones*. In words ending with any other consonant, the last syllable is stressed: eg *exterior, universidad*. An accent marks the stressed syllable in words that depart from these rules: eg *estación, tónica*.

Useful expressions

hello *hola*; hello (when answering the phone) *hola, diga*
good morning, good day *buenos días*; good afternoon, good evening *buenas tardes*; good evening (after dark), good night *buenas noches*
goodbye/see you later *adiós/hasta luego*
please *por favor*; thank you (very much) *(muchas) gracias*; you're welcome *de nada*
do you speak English? *¿habla inglés?*; I **don't speak Spanish** *no hablo castellano*
I don't understand *no entiendo* **can you say that to me in Catalan, please?** *¿me lo puede decir en catalán, por favor?*
what's your name? *¿cómo se llama?* **speak more slowly, please** *hable más despacio, por favor;* **wait a moment** *espere un momento*
Sir/Mr *señor (sr);* **Madam/Mrs** *señora (sra);* **Miss** *señorita (srta)*
excuse me/sorry *perdón;* **excuse me, please** *oiga* (the standard way to attract someone's attention, politely; literally 'hear me')
OK/fine/(to a waiter) **that's enough** *vale*
where is…? *¿dónde está…?*
why? *¿porqué?;* **when?** *¿cuándo?;* **who?** *¿quién?;* **what?** *¿qué?;* **where?** *¿dónde?;* **how?** *¿cómo?* **who is it?** *¿quién es?;* **is/are there any…?** *¿hay…?*
very *muy;* **and** *y;* **or** *o;* **with** *con;* **without** *sin*
open *abierto;* **closed** *cerrado;* **what time does it open/close?** *¿a qué hora abre/cierra?*
pull (on signs) *tirar;* **push** *empujar*
I would like *quiero;* **how many would you like?** *¿cuántos quiere?;* **how much is it** *¿cuánto es?*
I like *me gusta;* **I don't like** *no me gusta*
good *bueno/a;* **bad** *malo/a;* **well/badly** *bien/mal;* **small** *pequeño/a;* **big** *gran, grande;* **expensive** *caro/a;* **cheap** *barato/a;* **hot** (food, drink) *caliente;* **cold** *frío/a;* **something** *algo;* **nothing** *nada* **more/less** *más/menos;* **more or less** *más o menos*
do you have any change? *¿tiene cambio?*
price *precio;* **free** *gratis;* **discount** *descuento;* **bank** *banco;* **to rent** *alquilar;* **(for) rent, rental** *(en) alquiler;* **post office** *correos;* **stamp** *sello;* **postcard** *postal;* **toilet** *los servicios*

Getting around

airport *aeropuerto;* **railway station** *estación de ferrocarril/estación de RENFE* (Spanish railways); **metro station** *estación de metro*
entrance *entrada;* **exit** *salida* **car** *coche;* **bus** *autobús;* **train** *tren;* **a ticket** *un billete;* **return** *de ida y vuelta;* **bus stop** *parada de autobus;* **the next stop** *la próxima parada*
excuse me, do you know the way to…? *¿oiga, señor/señora/etc, sabe cómo llegar a …?*
left *izquierda;* **right** *derecha* **here** *aquí;* **there** *allí;* **straight on recto;* **to the end of the street** *al final de la calle;* **as far as** *hasta;* **towards** *hacia;* **near** *cerca;* **far** *lejos*

Accommodation

do you have a double/single room for tonight/one week? *¿tiene una habitación doble/para una persona/para esta noche/una semana?* **we have a reservation** *tenemos reserva;* **an inside/outside room** *una habitación interior/exterior* **with/without bathroom** *con/sin baño;* **shower** *ducha;* **double bed** *cama de matrimonio;* **with twin beds** *con dos camas;* **breakfast included** *desayuno incluido;* **air-conditioning** *aire acondicionado;* **lift** *ascensor;* **pool** *piscina*

Time

now *ahora;* **later** *más tarde;* **yesterday** *ayer;* **today** *hoy;* **tomorrow** *mañana;* **tomorrow morning** *mañana por la mañana* **morning** *la mañana;* **midday** *mediodía;* **afternoon/evening** *la tarde;* **night** *la noche;* **late night** (roughly 1-6am) *la madrugada*
at what time…? *¿a qué hora…?;* **at 2** *a las dos;* **at 8pm** *a las ocho de la tarde;* **at 1.30** *a la una y media;* **at 5.15** *a las cinco y cuarto;* **in an hour** *en una hora*

Numbers

0 *cero;* 1 *un, uno, una;* 2 *dos;* 3 *tres;* 4 *cuatro;* 5 *cinco;* 6 *seis;* 7 *siete;* 8 *ocho;* 9 *nueve;* 10 *diez;* 11 *once;* 12 *doce;* 13 *trece;* 14 *catorce;* 15 *quince;* 16 *dieciséis;* 17 *diecisiete;* 18 *dieciocho;* 19 *diecinueve;* 20 *veinte;* 21 *veintiuno;* 22 *veintidós;* 30 *treinta;* 40 *cuarenta;* 50 *cincuenta;* 60 *sesenta;* 70 *setenta;* 80 *ochenta;* 90 *noventa;* 100 *cien;* 200 *doscientos;* 1,000 *mil;* 1,000,000 *un millón*

Date & season

Monday *lunes;* **Tuesday** *martes;* **Wednesday** *miércoles;* **Thursday** *jueves;* **Friday** *viernes;* **Saturday** *sábado;* **Sunday** *domingo*
January *enero;* **February** *febrero;* **March** *marzo;* **April** *abril;* **May** *mayo;* **June** *junio;* **July** *julio;* **August** *agosto;* **September** *septiembre;* **October** *octubre;* **November** *noviembre;* **December** *diciembre*
spring *primavera;* **summer** *verano;* **autumn/fall** *otoño;* **winter** *invierno*

Further Reference

Books

Food & drink

Andrews, Colman: *Catalan Cuisine* A mine of information on food and much else (also with usable recipes).
Davidson, Alan: *Tio Pepe Guide to the Seafood of Spain and Portugal* An excellent pocket-sized guide with illustrations of Spain's fishy delights.

Guides & walks

Amelang, J, Gil, X & McDonogh, GW: *Twelve Walks through Barcelona's Past* (Ajuntament de Barcelona) Well-thought-out walks by historical theme. Original, and better informed than many walking guides.
Güell, Xavier: *Gaudí Guide* (Ed. Gustavo Gili) A handy guide, with good background on all the architect's work.
Pomés Leiz, Juliet, & Feriche, Ricardo: *Barcelona Design Guide* (Ed. Gustavo Gili) An eccentrically wide-ranging but engaging listing of everything ever considered 'designer' in BCN.

History, architecture, art & culture

Burns, Jimmy: *Barça: A People's Passion* The first full-scale history in English of one of the world's most overblown football clubs.
Elliott, JH: *The Revolt of the Catalans* Fascinating, detailed account of the Guerra dels Segadors and the Catalan revolt of the 1640s.
Fernández Armesto, Felipe: *Barcelona: A Thousand Years of the City's Past* A solid, straightforward history.
Fraser, Ronald: *Blood of Spain* A vivid oral history of the Spanish Civil War and the tensions that preceded it. It is especially good on the events of July 1936 in Barcelona.
Hooper, John: *The New Spaniards* An incisive and very readable survey of the changes in Spanish society since the death of Franco.
Hughes, Robert: *Barcelona* The most comprehensive single book about Barcelona: tendentious at times, erratic, but beautifully written, and covering every aspect of the city up to the 1992 Olympics.
Kaplan, Temma: *Red City, Blue Period – Social Movements in Picasso's Barcelona* An interesting book, tracing the interplay of avant-garde art and avant-garde politics in 1900s Barcelona.
Orwell, George: *Homage to Catalonia* The classic account of Barcelona in revolution, as written by an often bewildered, but always perceptive observer.
Paz, Abel: *Durruti, The People Armed* Closer to its theme, a biography of the most legendary of Barcelona's anarchist revolutionaries.
Solà-Morales, Ignasi: *Fin de Siècle Architecture in Barcelona* Large-scale and wide-ranging description of the city's Modernista heritage.
Tóibín, Colm: *Homage to Barcelona* Evocative and perceptive journey around the city: good on the booming Barcelona of the 1980s.
van Hensbergen, Gijs: *Gaudí* A thorough account of the life of the architect.
Vázquez Montalbán, Manuel: *Barcelonas* Idiosyncratic but insightful reflections on the city by one of its most prominent modern writers.
Zerbst, Rainer: *Antoni Gaudí* Lavishly illustrated and comprehensive survey.

Literature

Calders, Pere: *The Virgin of the Railway and Other Stories* Ironic, engaging, quirky stories by a Catalan writer who spent many years in exile in Mexico.
Català, Victor: *Solitude* This masterpiece by female novelist Caterina Albert shocked readers in 1905 with its open, modern treatment of female sexuality.
Marsé, Juan: *The Fallen* Classic novel of survival in Barcelona during the long *posguerra* after the Civil War.
Martorell, Joanot, & Martí de Gualba, Joan: *Tirant lo Blanc* The first European prose novel, from 1490, a rambling, bawdy, shaggy-dog story of travels, romances and chivalric adventures.
Mendoza, Eduardo: *City of Marvels* and *Year of the Flood* A sweeping, very entertaining saga of Barcelona between its great Exhibitions in 1888 and 1929; and a more recent novel of passions in the city of the 1950s.
Oliver, Maria Antònia: *Antipodes* and *Study in Lilac* Two adventures of Barcelona's first feminist detective.
Rodoreda, Mercè: *The Time of the Doves* and *My Cristina and Other Stories* A translation of *Plaça del Diamant*, most widely read of all Catalan novels. Plus a collection of similarly bittersweet short tales.
Vázquez Montalbán, Manuel: *The Angst-Ridden Executive* and *An Olympic Death* Two thrillers starring detective and gourmet extraordinaire Pepe Carvalho.

Music

Angel Molina Leading Barcelona DJ with an international reputation and various remix albums released.
Lluís Llach An icon of the 1960s and early '70s protest against the fascist regime combines a melancholic tone with brilliant musicianship. One of the first to experiment with electronic music.
Maria del Mar Bonet Though from Mallorca, del Mar Bonet always sings in Catalan and specialises in her own compositions, North African music and traditional Mallorcan music.
Pep Sala Excellent musician and survivor of the extremely successful Catalan group Sau. Sala now produces his own music, much of which shows a rockabilly and country influence.
Els Pets Kings of Catalan-language pop, led by the highly charismatic Lluís Gavald.
Quimi Portet Former guitarist for (and creative force behind) legendary Spanish pop band Último de la Fila, now just as respected for his mature solo work.
Raimon Has put some of the greatest Catalan language poets, such as Ausiàs March, to music.

Barcelona online

www.barcelonaturisme.com Information from the city's official tourist authority. Painfully slow.
www.bcn.es The city council's information-packed website.
www.catalanencyclopaedia.com Comprehensive English-language reference work covering Catalan history, geography and 'who's who'.
www.diaridebarcelona.com Local online newspaper with good English content.
www.mobilitat.net Generalitat's website on transport in Catalonia.
www.renfe.es Spanish railways' website, with online booking.
www.timeout.com/barcelona The online city guide, with a select monthly agenda.
www.vilaweb.com Catalan web portal and links page; in Catalan.
www.vanguardia.es Online version of Barcelona daily paper *La Vanguardia*.

Note: page numbers in **bold**
indicate sections giving key
information on topic; *italics*
indicate illustrations.

a

abortion 311
absinthe 165, 166, **173**, 180,
    202, 252
accommodation **46-70**
apartments/rental 69-70
    casa de pages 276
    masies 298
    monasteries **280**, 281
    see also hostels; hotels
addresses 307
age restrictions 307
AIDS/HIV 310-311
Aiguablava 292, **293**
Aiguafreda 293
Aiguamolls de l'Empordà 294
airport & airlines 302
Ajuntament de Barcelona 25,
    26, 123, 221
    building 34, 75, 77, **79**
Alcoholics Anonymous 312
Alella 284, 285
Alfonso XIII 20, 21, 127
All Saints Day 217
Almodóvar, Pedro 53, 79, **223**,
    248
Almogàvers 9, 13
Altafulla 285
ambulance 309
Amenábar, Alejandro 224
American-British College 316
American Express 314
American football 265
anarchism 17, 20, 22-23, 24
    bars linked with 166
Antic Hospital de la Santa
    Creu 86-87, *87*, **90**
antiques **183-185**,
    205-206
apartments 69-70
Aquàrium de Barcelona 100,
    219
Aragon 10-11, 13, 14, 15,
    16, 22
architecture **33-38**, 123
    exhibitions 79
    Gothic 13, **34**, 108
    masies 130
    Noucentisme 21, 36
    Romanesque 10, **34**, 108
    20th century **36-38**, 103,
        129, 131
    see also Cerdà, Ildefons;
        Modernisme
Aribau, Bonaventura Carles 17
Arnau, Eusebi 41, 42
art
    avant-garde 20, 21, 227
    contemporary artists &
        galleries 227-230
    food as 153
    fringe 230
    street **128-129**, 130
    see also Modernisme;
        museums & galleries
Art Market 205
Articket 73

Arxiu de la Corona d'Arago
    see Palau del Lloctinent
Ateneu Barcelonès 312
Auditori 38, 221, **238-239**,
    241
Avinyó, C/ 191
Aznar, José Maria 26, 31

b

B-Parade 214
babysitting 220
Badalona 130
Bagà 300
bags 196
Baja Beach Club 249
banks 314
Barcelona, FC 23, **265**
basketball team 264
    fans 264
    museum **122**, 221
    Nou Camp 121, **122**
    shop 207
Barcelona Card 73
Barcelona Head 100, **128**, *129*
Barcelona On-Line 47
Barcelona Teatre Musical 270
Barceloneta 35, **101-103**
    beach 100
    cafés & bars 177-178
    festivals 101-102, **216**
    restaurants 159-163
    Wounded Star 101, 103,
        128
Barri Gòtic 74, **75-85**,
    181, 223
    accommodation 47-53
    cafés & bars 165-170
    galleries **228**, 230
    nightlife 247, **248-251**
    restaurants 135-141
Barrio Chino **10-11**, 20
bars 165-180, **247-262**
    bar musical 247
    the best 247
    best cocktails 165
    champagne 177
    drink specialities 180
    gay 169, 170, **231-232**, 237
    pintxos **165**, 167, 176
    with revolutionary links 166
    in Sitges 277
    themed 249
    see also clubs; tapas
basketball 130, **263-264**
beaches **100**, 277, 279, 291, 293
beauty treatments 203
beer 180
Begur 290, 291
Bellver de Cerdanya 300
Berga 299-300
    La Patum festival 217, 299
Besalú 34, **296-298**
Betlem 35
Biblioteca de Catalunya
    312-313
bicycles 267
    hire 73, 268, **306**
    repairs 208
    see also cycling
birdwatching 222, 288, 294
Boadella, Albert 273

boat trips 100-101
Bohigas, Oriol 37, 38, 103
Boîte, La **244**, 245, *245*
Book and Coin Market 205
bookshops 179, 183, **185-186**
    gay 235
Boqueria, La 35, 84, 86,
    204-205, 219
Born, the **92-98**, 181
    accommodation 57-59
    cafés & bars 173-177
    galleries 228-229
    market 95, **98**
    nightlife 247, **252-253**
    restaurants 145-150
Borràs theatre 270
Bourbons 16, 18, 19, 20, 24
bowling 183, **266**
brandy 180
bread with tomato 157
Bridge of Sighs 75
British Council 313
British Society of Catalunya
    308
Bruno Quadros building 84
bullfighting 264
Bulli, El **164**, 294, 295
buses 302, 304
    disabled access 309
    long-distance 276, 302
    tickets 73, 303
    TombBús 181, 304
    tours 73
    *for out-of-town services see
        individual towns*
business services 307-308

c

cable cars 101, 104, 110
Cadaqués 238, *294*, **294**, 295
Cadi-Moixeró 300
Café de l'Opera 85, **167**, 231
Café Miranda 233, **234**
cafés **165-180**, 231-232
    see also bars; restaurants
caga tió 218
caganer 218
Caixa Forum 104, **105**, *106*
Calatrava tower *105*, 105
Caldera, La 269
Caldetes 279
Calella 279
Calella de Palafrugell
    291, 293
Cambó, Francesc 19, 21
Camí de Ronda 291
Camprodon 299
campsites 70
Can Culleretes 135
Can Negre 40
Can Serra 112
Can Solé 161
Canet de Mar 279
Cap de Creus 294, 295
Capella, La 90
Capella d'en Marcús 34, **92**, 93
capgrossos 187, **216-217**
Cardona 292
Carnival 218
    Sitges 237, 277
cars & driving 302, **305-306**

parking 306
    roads outside Barcelona 276
    *for out-of-town routes see
        individual towns & regions*
Casa Almirall 172
Casa Amatller 43, **117**
Casa Batlló 42, **117**
Casa Calvet 116, **151**
Casa de l'Ardiaca 76
Casa de la Caritat *see* Centre
    de Cultura Contemporània
Casa de les Altures 130
Casa de les Punxes 43, 112,
    115, 117
Casa Jacinta Ruiz 117
Casa Macaya 43
Casa Milà *see* Pedrera, La
Casa Planells 40
Casa Terrades *see*
    Casa de les Punxes
Casa Thomas (BD shop)
    117, 189
Casa Vicens 41, *119*, **119**
Casal Bellesguard 280
Casas, Ramón 19, 41, 42, 95,
    166, 169, 200
    house of 112-113
Castanyada 217
Castell dels Tres Dragons *see*
    Museu de Zoologia
Castelldefels 100, **277**, **278**
Castellfollit de la Roca 297
castells 211
CAT (Centre Artesà
    Tradicionàrius) 245
Catalan language 32
    classes 316-317
    history 9, 13-14, 16, 17,
        19, 20, 22
    poetry festival 212
    vocabulary 321
Catalunya in Miniatura 222
Catamaran Orsom 100
Catedral de Barcelona 34, 75,
    79, 219
Caves Codorniu 43
CCCB *see* Centre de Cultura
    Contemporània
cemeteries 109, 128
Centre d'Art Santa Mònica 85
Centre de Cultura
    Contemporània 38, 87, *90*, **90**,
        270
Centre Jujol-Can Negre 40
ceramics 189
    museum 126-127
Cerdà, Ildefons 17, **35-36**, 37,
    38, 110, 111, **123**, 128-129
Cerdanya, the 300
chamber of commerce 308
chapels *see* churches & chapels
childcare 220-221
children's activities 219-222
    Barcelona Glòries 181-182
    cafés 175, 177
    shops 186-187
    chiringuitos 103
chocolate 170, 179, 180
    182-183, 199
    museum 96
Christmas 217-218
churches and chapels 34, 35
    Anglican (St George's) 316

Capella d'en Marcús 34, **92**, 93
concerts 240
English mass 316
La Mercè 35, **79**
outside Barcelona 279-80, 282, 283, 286, 287, 289, 296, 298-299
Santa Àgata (chapel) 76, **80**
Santa Anna 34, **76**, 240
Sant Antoni 218
Sant Felip Neri 35, **76**, 240
Santa Llúcia (chapel) 34, **79**
Sant Pau del Camp 34, 87, **91**
Santa Maria del Pi 13, 34, **76**, 240
Sants Just i Pastor 76
see also Santa Maria del Mar
cigarettes & cigars 208, 315
cinemas 182, 183, **224**, **226**
children's films 221
workshop 251
Cistercian Route 285-287
Ciutat del Teatre 104, **269**
Civil War 19, **22**, 104, 109, 119
Clos, Joan 26, 29-30, 31
clothes 191-195
accessories **195-199**, 207
children's 186-187
designer bargains 195
gay 235-236
museum 96
second-hand/vintage 183-184, **197**
Club Capitol 270
clubs 247-262
the best 247
gay **232-234**, 237, 251, 261
Latin 258-259
live music 242-246
in Sitges 277
themed 247
CNT *see* Confederación Nacional del Trabajo
cocktails 165
coffee 177
coin market 205
Col·lecció Thyssen-Bornemisza 125-126
Col·legi d'Arquitectes 76, **79**
colleges 316-317
Col·legi de les Teresianes 41, 124
Collsacabra 296
Colmado Quílez **200**, *201*
Colònia Güell 41, 279
Columbus, Christopher 76, 102
monument 99, **101**, **102**
Comediants, Els 271
comedy 270
comics 186
Companys, Lluís 21, 22, 104, 109
computers
games & software 185
services 307-308
Confederación Nacional del Trabajo 18, 19, 20, 22
conference facilities 307
Conservas 269, 271
consulates 308
consumer advice 181, **308**
contraception 311
convents *see* monasteries & convents
Convergència i Unió 25, 26
correfoc 214, **215**, 216

Corte Inglés, El 111, **182**, 192, 202, 206
Corts, Les 121-122
cosmetics 203-204
Costa Brava 291-293
Costa Daurada 285
Costa de Garraf 277
Costa del Maresme 279
Cotxeres, Les 121
courier services 307
Cova del Drac, La 245-246
crafts 187-189
credit cards 314
crime 89, 316
currency exchange **314**, 318
customs & excise 308-309
cycling **266-267**, 277, **306**
tours 73
see also bicycles

Dalí, Salvador 139, 227, 290, 291, 294
Teatre-Museu Dalí 222, 293-294, **295**, 296
dance 239, 269, 270, **272**
festivals 212, 213, 214, 269-270, 271
information 270
Latin dance & lessons 254, 258, 259
line-dancing 249
schools & workshops 272
tango 10, 258-259
see also flamenco; *sardana*
David-Goliath, Goliath-David 128, *129*
decadència 14
de Flor, Roger 8-9
de Llúria, Roger 8
Delta de l'Ebre 287-288
dentists 311
design shops 189-191
Diada Nacional de Catalunya 15, 95, 98, **214**
Diagonal-Mar 30, 37, 38, 72, **129-130**
Dies de Dansa **214**, 269-270
disabled access 309
sports 266
transport 303, **309**
Discothèque 247, **255**
doctors 311
Domènech i Montaner, Lluís 41, **42-43**, 54, 76, 87, 96, 113, 115, 116, 117, 119, 189, 192, 240
home of 279
Dorres 300
drag acts **233**, 234, 251
drassanes 10, 13, 34, 99
see also Museu Marítim
drinks 180
shops 200, 202-203
see also absinthe; cocktails; coffee; wine
drugs 310
dry-cleaners 187

Edifici Fòrum 38
Eixample 11, 18, 35-36, 41, 46, 73, **111-118**
accommodation 60-65
cafés & bars 178-179
galleries 229-230

gay scene 231
nightlife 247, **257-260**
restaurants 151-155
electricity 310
emergencies **309**, 310
emergencies 309
Empúries **294**, 295
Encants, Els 206
Espai, L' 270
Espanyol, RCD 265
Estadi Olímpic de Montjuïc 105, *263*, **263**
estancs/estancos 315
Estartit, L' 293
Eulàlia, Santa **8**, 75, 216
tomb 79
Europorator 47
exhibitions *see* International Exhibition of 1929; Universal Exhibition of 1888

Fàbrica Casaramona 42, 43
Fageda d'en Jordà 297
Falset 43, **284**, **285**
fans 207
fascism 21, 22, 23
Ferdinand & Isabella 14, 76, 102
Feria de Abril 130, **212**
Ferran, C/ 17, 75
Ferrer i Guàrdia, Francesc 20, 109
ferries 302
Festa de la Diversitat 212
Festa dels Tres Tombs 173, **218**
Festival de Flamenco de Ciutat Vella 269
Festival del Grec **214**, 269
festivals 130, 221, **210-218**
in Berga 217, 299-300
in Cadaqués 294
castells 211
film 90, **226**, 271, 277
fires & fireworks 215
gegants & nans 216-217
shop 187
in Sitges 226, 237, 277
theatre & dance 212, 213, 214, 269-270, 271
see also under music, classical; music, rock, roots & jazz
FGC *see* metro & FGC
Figueres 222, **293-294**, **295**
film 223-226
festivals 90, **226**, 271, 277
local industry & directors **223-224**, **225**, 273
locations 53, 79, 121, **223**
Filmoteca de la Generalitat de Catalunya 226
Fira de Barcelona 307
Fira de Santa Llúcia 217-218
fire service 309
fitness centres 267
flamenco 131, **244**, 246, 259 269, 279
clothes 207
festivals 212, 269
local artists 242
records 206-207
Floresta, La 280
flowers 84, 113, **199**, 204
Font de Canaletes 84
Font Màgica de Montjuïc 104, **106**
Font Santa 280

Fontserè, Ramon 273
food
as art 153
markets 204-205
shops 199-203
football 265
Barcelona International Football League 267
table (*futbolín*) 266
see also Barcelona, FC
Fòrum Universal de les Cultures 2004 30, *36*, 37, 38
Fossar de la Pedrera 109
Fossar de les Moreres 95
Franco, Francisco 22, *24*, 24, 37-38, 124, 166
Fundació Antoni Tàpies 112, **115**
Fundació Francisco Godia 115-116
Fundació Joan Miró 37, 104, **106**, *107*
café 178
concerts 238, **241**
Roof sculpture 129
shop 189
funfair 122, 124, **219**
Funicular de Montjuïc 106
Funicular de Tibidabo 122, **124**, 125
furniture 189-191
design 41, 42, 95

Galeria H₂0 153, **230**
Galeria Olímpica 106
galleries
contemporary 227-230
see also museums & galleries
Gandesa 43, **284**, **285**
gardens 104, 105, 106-107, 125
Garraf 277
Garrotxa (Zona Volcànica) 297
gas emergencies 309
Gaudí, Antoni (i Cornet) 40, **41-42**, 76, 91, 95, 97, 111-115, 116, 117, 119, 121, 124, 192
buildings outside Barcelona 277, 279
Espai Gaudí **115**, 187-189
gay & lesbian scene 118, **231-237**
AIDS help 310-311
cafés & bars 169, 170, **231-232**, 237
clubs **232-234**, 251, 261
lesbian venues 236-237
organisations & advice 310
restaurants 141, **234**
services 234-236
in Sitges 231, *237*
gegants 216-217
Generalitat de Catalunya 31, 46, **308**
history 13, 15, 21, 24, 25, 26
Genet, Jean 10, 87, 173, 252
gifts 103, 118, **187-189**, 200, 207
Girona 276, **289-290**, *291*
gloves 207
golf 267
Golondrinas, Las 99, **100-101**
Gràcia 119-121
accommodation 67
cafés & bars 179-180
festivals 119, **210**, **214**

galleries 230
nightlife 247, **260-261**
restaurants 157-159
Gremial dels Velers 35
Güell, Eusebi 41, 87, 91, 121, 279
guidebooks 186, 323
Guilleries, Les 296
Guixé, Martí **153**, 220
gyms **267**, 268

hairdressers 204-205
Halcón Viajes 208
Hallowe'en 217
handball 265
Happy Parc 221
health 202-203, 268, **310-311**
helplines 311, **312**, 319
herbalists 202-203
Hispanos Siete Sulza 58
history 7-27
  key events 27
  early 7-9, 104
  medieval 8-14, 92-93
  Golden Age 13-14, 92
  decline & unrest 14-16
  18th century revival 16
  Carlist Wars 16-17
  Renaixença 17, 18-19, 35, 39
  radicalism & strikes 17, **18-19**, 20, 21, 22, 23
  20th century 19-26
  21st century 26, 29-32
holidays, public 319
Holy Week **210**, 213
Homar, Gaspar 41, 42, 95
home accessories 189-191
horse riding **267**, 299
Horta **130-131**, 180, *162*, 163
Hospital de la Santa Creu i Sant Pau 42, 43, 113, **116**
  see also Antic Hospital de la Santa Creu
Hospitalet de Llobregat, L' 131
hospitals 310
hostels 46, **70**
Hotel Connect 47
Hotel España 42, **54**, *54*, 87
  restaurant 143
hotels 46-70
  apartment hotels 69
  the best 47
  bookings 47
  budget 51-53, 57, 59, 64-65, 67, 68
  expensive 47-50, 59, 60-61, 67-68, 69
  mid-range 50-51, 54-55, 57-60, 61-64, 67, 68, 69
  paradores nacionales 292
  for out-of-town hotels see individual towns & regions

ice skating 268
Ictineo 100, 101
ID 312
IMAX Port Vell 226
Institut d'Estudis Catalans 19
Institut del Teatre **270**, 272
Institut Pere Mata 43
insurance 310, 311
Integral 311

International Exhibition of 1929 20-21, 36, 104, 108, 110
International House 317
internet access 175, 308, **312**, 313
Isabel II 16, 17
Isla de Fantasia 222

J

Jamancia 17
Jamboree 245, **246**
Jardí Botànic 105, **106-107**
Jardins Cinto Verdaguer 105
Jardins de la Tamarita **125**, 222
Jardins de Laribel 104
Jardins del Mirador 105
Jardins Mossèn Costa i Llobera 107
Jaume I **11-13**, 216
  Llibre dels Feits 13
jewellery 191, **195-196**, 197
Jews 8, 14, 76, 104, 109, 286, 289
Joglars, Els 273
Juan Carlos, King 24, *25*
Jujol, Josep Maria **40**, 42, 43, 121

K

Kentucky 227, **252**
key-cutting 187

L

language *see* Catalan language; Spanish language
launderettes 187
leather goods 196
legal advice 307, **312**
lesbians *see* gay & lesbian scene
libraries 90, 103, **312-313**
Liceu, Gran Teatre del 20, 238, *239*, **239**, **241**, 270
lingerie 196-197
listings 224, 238, 242, 248, 270, **313**
literature 13-14, 17, 19, 22, 23, 87, 323
Llafranc 291, 293
Lles 300
Llibreria, C/ 75, 80
Lliga Regionalista 19, 20
Llimona, Josep 41, 95
Llívia 300
Llotja 13, 34, 95
Llull, Ramon 13-14
London Bar 166, **252**
lost property 313
Louis the Pious 9, 76
luggage 196
  left luggage 312

M

MACBA *see* Museu d'Art Contemporani de Barcelona
Macià, Francesc 21
magic shop 207, *208*
makina 17
mancomunitat 20
mantillas 207

Manzana de la Discordia, La 42, 43, **117**
maps 186, 303
Mar Bella 100
Maragall, Pasqual 25, 26, 30, 31
marathon 265
Marató de l'Espectacle **213**, 269
Maremàgnum 38, 99, **183**, *190*, 219
  nightlife 247, **254**
markets 118, **204-206**
  antiques 183, **205-206**
  second-hand clothes 197
  see also Boqueria, La
Marsella 166, **173**, 252
Martorell, Joanot 14
Masella 300
masies 130, 276, 298
Masnou, El 279
Matches **128**, *129*, 130
May Day 212
Medes, Illes 293
Mediateca 313
medieval trades 92-93
Meller, Raquel 110
Mercat de la Born 95, **98**
Mercat de la Concepció 113
Mercat de les Flors 270
Mercat de Sant Antoni **118**, 123
Mercat de Santa Caterina 93
Mercè, La (area) 72, 76
Mercè, La (church) 35, **79**
Mercè, Festes de la 216
metro & FGC 21, **303-304**
  disabled access 309
  tickets 73, 303
Metrònom **229**, 241, 270
Mies van der Rohe, Ludwig 36-37, 104, 108
Mirador del Rei Martí 76
Miramar 105
Miró, Joan 118, 127, 161, 227, 229
  see also Fundació Joan Miró
MNAC *see* Museu Nacional d'Art de Catalunya
mobile phones 318
Modernisme 18, 35-36, 37, **39-43**, 73, 95, 110, 111-113, 118, 119,
  bars 166, 169, 171, 172
  outside Barcelona 279, 280, 284, 287, 291, 297
  Quadrat d'Or 112
  Ruta del Modernisme (discount scheme) 73
  suggested walk 116-117
  trencadís 40, 121
  see also Domènech i Montaner; Gaudí; Puig i Cadafalch
Molina, La 300
monasteries & convents 35, **280**, **285-287**, 290, 294, 298-299
  Convent dels Àngels 87
  desamortización 17
  Pedralbes 125-126
  Sant Agustí **93**, 128
money 314-315
Montblanc 286
Montcada, C/ 13, 35, 92, 93
Montjuïc 21, 22, 25, 38, 72, 73, **104-110**
  cable car 104, **110**
  cafés 178
  castle (Museu Militar) 16, 17, 35, 104, **108**, 109

cemeteries & executions 109
Ciutat del Teatre 104, **269**
funicular 104, **106**
nightlife 254-257
sports venues **263**, 268
Tren Montjuïc 110
Montseny 296
Montserrat 280, **281**
Monument a Colom 99, **101**, **102**
mosque 316
motor sports 265-266
motorbikes
  half-price tolls 276
  hire 306
Muntaner, Ramon 9
Museu Barbier-Mueller d'Art Precolombí **95**, 238
Museu d'Arqueologia de Catalunya 104, **107**
Museu d'Art Contemporani de Barcelona 38, 87, **91**, *91*
  shop 189
Museu d'Art Modern 42, **95**
Museu d'Autòmates del Tibidabo 124
Museu d'Història de Catalunya 100, **103**, *103*
Museu d'Història de la Ciutat 76, **79-81**, 102
  tours 74
Museu de Carrosses Fúnebres 117-118
Museu de Cera 85, **222**
Museu de Ceràmica 126-127
Museu de Geologia 95, 123
Museu de l'Eròtica 85
Museu de la Ciència **127**, *131*
Museu de la Xocolata **96**, 178
Museu de les Arts Decoratives 126-127
Museu de Zoologia 36, 42-43, **96**, 221
Museu del Calçat 79
Museu del Perfum 118
Museu Diocesà 76, **79**
Museu Egipci de Barcelona 118
Museu Etnològic 104, **107**
Museu Frederic Marès 76, **81**
Museu Marítim 87, 99, **101**, 221
  concerts 238
  see also drassanes
Museu Militar 104, **108**, 109
  castle's history 16, 17, 35
Museu Nacional d'Art de Catalunya (Palau Nacional) 10, 36, 104, **108**
Museu Picasso 92, **95-96**
Museu Tèxtil i Indumentària 92, **96**, 189
Museu Verdaguer 126
museums & galleries
  disabled access 309
  discount schemes 73
  applied arts: ceramics and decorative arts 126-127
  archaeology: Ancient Egypt 118; archaeology 104, **107**
  art: Caixa Forum 104, **105**, *106*; Capella, La 90; Centre d'Art Santa Mònica 85; Fundació Antoni Tàpies 112, **115**; Fundació Francisco Godia 115-116; Monestir de Pedralbes 72, **125-126**; Museu Barbier-Mueller d'Art Precolombí **95**, 238; Museu d'Art Modern 42,

Index

95; Museu Picasso 92,
95-96; *private galleries*
227-230; Sala Montcada
97; Tecla Sala Centre
Cultural 131; *see also*
Centre de Cultura
Contemporània; Fundació
Joan Miró; Museu d'Art
Contemporani de
Barcelona; Pedrera, La
children's 221-222
ethnology 104, **107**
local history: Museu
d'Història de Catalunya
100, **103**, *103*; Museu
d'Història de la Ciutat 74,
76, **79-81**, 102
maritime see Museu
Marítim
military see Museu Militar
outside Barcelona 277, 282,
283, 289, 290, 293-294, 296
religion: Museu Diocesà 76,
79; Museu Frederic
Marès 76, **81**
science & nature: geology
95, 123; science **127**,
131; zoology 36, 42-43,
96, 221
sports: FC Barcelona **122**,
221; Olympic Games 106
textiles 92, **96**, 189
unusual: chocolate **96**, 221;
erotica 85; fairground
machines 124; funeral
carriages 117-118;
performing arts 270;
perfume 118; shoes 79;
Verdaguer (poet) 126;
waxworks 85, **222**
music
classical 238-242
children's concerts 221
choral 240
contemporary 241-242
country music 249
early **212**, 238, **240**
festivals 90-91, 212, 213, 214,
216, 238, 241, 246, 294
folk & blues 244-246
jam sessions/open mic 245
jazz 100, 217, 242, **244-246**,
248, 253
orchestras 240-241
recorded 323
rock, roots & jazz **242-246**,
252, 261
shops 206-207
world music 217
see also flamenco
Muslims 8-9, 10, 11, 13, 14

n

nationalism 19, 20, 22, 25, 26
New Year 218
newspapers 313
newsstands 185
Nonell, Isidre 41, 42
Nou Barris 131
Nova Icària 100
Núria 299

o

office services 307-308
Oficines d'Informació Turística
318
Olot **297**, 298

Olympic Games 25, 38, 72, 105
gallery 106
opening hours 181, 314, **315**
restaurants 134-135
opera 239, **241**
opticians 207
Orwell, George 22
Ou Com Balla, L' 76, **213**, *213*

p

Palafrugell 293
Palau Baró de Quadras 112
Palau de la Generalitat 34, 35,
75, **81**
Palau de la Música Catalana
42, *43*, 43, 93, **96-97**, 238,
239-240
Palau de la Virreina 35, 84, **85**
information centre 319
Palau de Mar 100
Palau del Lloctinent 35, 76
Palau dels Esports 263
Palau Güell 41, 42, 85, *86*, 87,
91
Palau Macaya 113
Palau Moja 35
Palau Montaner 117
Palau Nacional *see* Museu
Nacional d'Art de Catalunya
Palau Reial 34, 76
Palau Robert 319
Palau Sant Jordi 38, 105, 242,
263
Paloma, La 252
Pals 290-291
Papiol, El 280
Paral.lel, Avda 110
Parc de Cervantes 125
Parc de Collserola 126
Parc de l'Espanya Industrial
121, 222
Parc de l'Estació del Nord 118
Parc de la Ciutadella 16, 18, 25,
35, 41, **97**, *97*, 222
L'Hivernacle 175, 244
Tamborinada fair 222
Park de la Creueta del Coll 125,
127, 129
Parc de les Aigües 130
Parc de les Aus 222
Parc de les Tres Xemeneies
110
Parc del Castell de l'Oreneta
222
Parc del Guinardó 130
Parc del Laberint **130-131**,
222
Parc Joan Miró (Parc de
l'Escorxador) **118**, 121
Park Güell 40, 42, 72, *74*,
119, *120*, **121**, 222
parks 125, 129, 130, **222**
concerts 214
Parròquia Maria Reina 316
Partido Popular 26, 31
Passeig de Colom 79, 128
Passeig de Gràcia 18, 111, **192**
Pati Llimona 80, **81**
pâtisseries 199
Pavelló Barcelona (Pavelló
Mies van der Rohe) 21, 36-
37, 104, **108**
Pavelló de la República 37, *38*,
130, **131**
Pavellons de la Finca Güell
124, *127*
Pedralbes 124
Monestir de 72, **125-126**

Palau Reial de 124, 125,
126-127
Pedrera, La 40, 42, **113-115**
Espai Gaudí **115**, 187-189
Penedès 138, 216, **283-285**
Peratallada 290
Perelada 238
perfumes 203-204
museum 118
pharmacies 311
Modernista 116, 117
Philip V 15, 16, *16*, 123
phonecards 315, 317-318
photography
exhibitions 230
shops & processing 207
Picasso, Pablo 19, 76, 127, 166,
169, 227, 228, 294, 300
Museu Picasso 92, **95-96**
pickpockets 85, **89**
pintxos **165**, 167, 176
Plaça Catalunya 19, 11, 22, 24,
111
Plaça d'Espanya 19, 21, 104
Plaça de l'Àngel 75, 92
Plaça dei Rei 76
Plaça dels Països Catalans 38,
121, 129
Plaça George Orwell 76-79
Plaça Reial 17, 35, 41, *75*, 76
Plaça Rovira I Trias 119, **123**
Plaça Sant Jaume 17, 75
Plaça Sant Just 76
Plaça Traginers 81
Placídia, Gala 8
Plan de Estabilización 24
Planes, Les 280
Plaza de Toros Monumental
264, 270
Poble Espanyol 104, **108-110**,
219
Poble Sec 110
accommodation 59-60
cafés & bars 178
nightlife 247, **254-257**
restaurants 163
Poblenou 17, 30-31, 37, 73,
128-129, 163
Hangar project 230
nightlife 262
Poblet, Monestir de 280, **286**,
287
poetry
festival 212
readings 171
police 309, **315**
Pont de Calatrava 129
Porcioles, José María de 24
Port Aventura **220**, 276
Port de la Selva 294
Port Lligat 294
Port Olímpic 72, **103**
nightlife 247, **254**
Port Vell 26, 72, **99-101**
nightlife **254**
Porta d'Europa 99
ports & shoreline
accommodation 49
cafés & bars 177-178
restaurants 159-163
Porxos d'en Xifré 35
postal services 315
Prat de la Riba, Enric 19, 25
Primo de Rivera, Miguel 20, 21,
79
Priorat 284
Púbol, Castell de 290, 291
Puig i Cadafalch, Josep 21, 41,
42, **43**, 95, 104, 112, 113,
117, 166, 284

Puigcerdà 300
Pujol, Jordi 25, 26, *26*, 31
Pulgcerdà 276

q

Quatre Gats, Els 76, 166, *166*,
169
queuing 315
Queviures Murrià 117, **200**

r

Racó de Can Fabes, El 279
radio 314
Radio Nacional de España
21
railways 17, 302, **303-304**
disabled access 309
long distance 276, 303
narrow-gauge 299
tickets 303
top five trips 276
*for out-of-town services see
individual towns &
regions*
Rambla, La 16, 17, 35, **83-85**,
219
accommodation 47-53
nightlife 247, **251-252**
Rambla del Mar 99, *99*
Rambla del Raval 89
Ramon Berenguer IV 10-11,
286
Raval 17, 19-20, 26, 29, 72,
86-91, 181, 222
accommodation 54-57
Barrio Chino **10-11**, 20
cafés & bars 170-173
galleries 228
restaurants 141-145
Razzmatazz 243
Reapers' War 14-15
'red jackets' 319
Refugi Antiaeri 110
republicanism 21, 22
restaurants 126, **134-164**
Basque 157, 158, 167
the best 137
Catalan specialites 157, **160**
gay 234
international: African 150;
Asian 150, 159, 163;
Cuban 150; English/Irish
141; Filipino 145;
Indian/Pakistani 141, 145,
159; Italian 139, 150, 159,
161, 163; Japanese 141,
145, 159, 164; Lebanese
154; Mediterranean 141,
143, 150, 153; Mexican
159; Moroccan 141, 147;
South American 141, 145,
150, 154; Thai 155
llesqueries 157
menu glossaries 154-155,
160
seafood 103, 147, 157, 160-
161, 163, 277, 278, 282,
293
top out of town restaurants
164, 279, 295
vegetarian 141, 145, 150,155,
159
*see also specific towns &
regions*
Reus 43
Ribera, La 10, 13, 16, 34, 72, 92

Ribes de Freser 299
Ripoll 34, *298*, **298-299**
roads 276
Rodoreda, Mercè 32, 119
roller hockey 265
Roman remains 34, 76, **80-83**
  roads 75, 80, 121
  Temple Roma (Vic) 296
  see also Empúries;
    Tarragona
Roses 164, 222, **294**
Rovira i Trias, Antoni 119,
  123
Rubió i Bellver, Joan 43, 117,
  118
running 265, 268
Rupit 296
Rusiñol, Santiago 19, 41, 42,
  95, 161, 166, 169, 277

Sa Riera 293
Sa Tuna 293
Sabadell 280
  orchestra 241
Sagrada Familia temple 41-42,
  112-113
sailing **268**, 278
Sala Apolo 226, **244**, 254
Sala Beckett 271
Sala Montcada 97
Sala Parés 76, **228**
Saló de Tinell 13, 34, 76, **102**
Sant Adrià del Besòs 130
Sant Agustí (convent) **93**, 128
Sant Andreu 131
Sant Cugat 280
Sant Felip Neri 35, **76**, 240
Sant Feliu de Guixols **291**, 293
Sant Joan (festival) **213**, 215
Sant Joan de les Abadesses 34,
  299
Sant Joan Despí 40
Sant Jordi (festival) 81, **210**
Sant Marçal 280
Sant Medir de Gràcia, Festes
  de 210
Sant Pau del Camp 34, 87, **91**
  accommodation 57-59
  cafés & bars 173-177
  nightlife 252-253
  restaurants 145-150
Sant Pere de Rodes
  (monastery)
  34, 294, **295**
Sant Pol 291
Sant Pol de Mar 279
Sant Ponç (festival) 212
Sant Sadurní d'Anoia 284
Santa Anna, 34, **76**, 240
Santa Maria de Vallbona,
  Monestir de 286
Santa Maria del Mar 13, 15,
  34, 34-35, 95, **98**
  concerts 240
Santa Maria del Pi 13, 34, 76
  concerts 240
Santa Pau 297
Santes Creus, Monestir de 286
Santos, Carles 238
Sants 17, **121-122**, 129
  accommodation 67-68
  festival 214
  restaurants 163
sardana **83**, 215, 238
Sarrià 124
Satanassa 233

saunas, gay 234
Scala Dei 284, 285
Schilling **169**, 231
sculpture, public **128-129**,
  130
Segadors, Guerra dels 14-15
serenos 23
Serra del Cadí 299
Sert, Josep Lluís 37, 131
Servei d'Informació Esportiva
  266
Servi-Caixa 208
Setcases 299
Setmana Tràgica 20
Seu d'Urgell, La 292
sex shops 235
shawls 197, 207
shipbuilding 10, 13
shoes 191, 193, **197-199**
  museum 79
  repairs 187
  shops 181-208
  areas 181, 192, 197
  the best 196, 206
  centres 181-183
  gay 235-236
  see also specific products
Sidecar Factory Club 242, **251**
sights, best 74
Sitges 100, 276, **277-279**
  Festival Internacional de
    Cinema de Catalunya 226
  gay scene 231, **237**
  golf course 267
  Teatre Internacional 269
ski resorts 299, 300
smoking restrictions 316
snooker & pool 266
Socialist Party 24-25, 26
Sónar **213**, 247
Spanish language
  classes 316-317
  vocabulary 322
sports 263-268
  active 266-268
  shops 207-208
  spectator 263-266
  Year of Sport 31
  see also specific sports
statistics 31
stock exchange 308
street art **128-129**, 130
strikes 17, **18-19**, 20, 110,
  121
Suárez, Adolfo 24
supermarkets 202
swimming 99, 102, 105, 266,
  266, **268**
swimwear 196-197
synagogues 316
Shlomo Ben Adret 76, **83**

Tamariu 291, 293
tango 10, 258-259
tapas 79, **165**
  patatas bravas 165, 180
Tàpies, Antoni 23, **115**, 227,
  230
targetes 303
Tarradellas, Josep 24
Tarragona 7, 276, **282-283**,
  285
  castells 211
  Teatre Metropol 40
  theatre festivals 212, 213, 214
Tavertet 296
taxes 314-315

hotels 46-47, 314-315
  sales 181, 314
taxis 302, **304-305**, 309
Teatre Grec 104, 214, 269
Teatre Joventut 131
Teatre Lliure **270**, *272*
Teatre Nacional de Catalunya
  270
Teatre Poliorama 22, **271**
Tecla Sala Centre Cultural 131
Telefèric de Montjuïc 104, **110**
Tel-entrada 208
telephones 317-318
television 313-314
Temple Roma d'Augusti 80, **83**
tennis 268
Trofeig Comte de Godó 266
Terra Alta 284
Terrassa 34, 43, **279-280**
Terrazza, La 110, 247, **257**
textiles 197
  museum 92, **96**, 189
theatre **269-272**
  festivals 269-270, 271
  Els Joglars 273
theme parks 220, 222
Tibidabo 22, 38, 73, *122*,
  122-124
  bars & clubs 180, 261-262
  funfair 122, 124, **219**
  restaurants 163-164
ticket agents 185, **208**, 242
time, local 318
tipping 318
Tivoli theatre 270
TNC *see* Teatre Nacional de
  Catalunya
tobacco 208, 315
toilets 318
Toroella de Montgri 238
Torre Agbar 38
Torre Bellesguard (Torre
  Figueres) 124, *125*
Torre de Collserola 38, *122*,
  122, **124**
Torre de la Creu 40
Torre de les Aigües 111
Torrelavit 284
Torres de Avila 110, **257**
Torres winery 138, **283**, 284
Tortosa **287-288**, 292
tourist information 318-319
  websites 276, 306, 323
tours 73-74
Tramvia Blau 125, **127-128**
Transbordador Aeri 101
translators 308
transport 302-306
  disabled access 309
  long-distance 276, 302
tickets 73, 303
  see also specific methods
travel services **208**,
  306
trencadis **40**, 42
TUI Viajes 47
Túnel, El 166
Turó Parc 125

underwear 196-197
Universal Exhibition of 1888
  18, 36, 42, 96, 97, 102
Universal Studios 220
universities 317
University of Barcelona 87,
  317
Úrculo, Eduardo 103

Vall d'Hebron 38, 128, **130**
Vallter 2000 299
Velòdrom 38, 128, **130**
Viajes Zeppelin 208
Vic 292, **296**
views 79, 101, 103, 112, 122,
  124, 161, 177
vigilantes 23
Vila Olímpica 37, 38, **103**, 128
Vilabertrán 238
Vilafranca del Penedès 283-285
Vilanova i la Geltrú 277, 278
Vinçon 113, **191**, 192, 229
Violant of Hungary 216, 286
Virreina, La *see* Palau de la
  Virreina
visas **319**, 320
Vistabella 40

walking 305
  hiking gear 208
  information 276
  maps 186
  tours 74
  trails & areas 277, 281, 291,
    296, 297, 299
  walks, suggested
    medieval trades 92-93
    Modernisme 116-117
    Parc de Collserola 126
    Roman remains 80-81
walls, city 8, 13, 16, 34, 72,
  73, **80-81**, 87, 169
  demolition of 17, 35, 111
War of the Spanish Succession
  15, 95, 98
water
  drinking 319
  emergencies 309
water parks 222
water sports 268, 278
waxworks 85, **222**
weather 319, 320
Western Union 314
Wilfred the Hairy (Guifré el
  Pilós) 9, 14, 296, 298-299
wine 138, 180
  festival 216
  shops 202-203
  vineyards & wineries
    283-285
Winterthur, Auditori 238, **240**
women 13
  services for 319-320
work 320
World Swimming
  Championships 99, 105, **266**

yoga 251
youth information 316

Zona Alta 124-128
  accommodation 69
  bars & clubs 180, 261-262
  galleries 230
  restaurants 163-164
Zona Franca 73
Zoo de Barcelona **219-220**, *221*

HOTELS

Acropolis Guest House 67
Actual, Hotel 63
Alimara, Hotel 69
Aneto, Hotel 54
Arts, Hotel 59
Astoria, Hotel 61
Atenea Aparthotel 69
Banys Orientals 57, 57
Barcelona House, Hotel 50
Bertran, Aparthotel 69
Caledonian, Hotel 60
Catalonia Albinoni, Hotel 47
Catalonia Barcelona Plaza,
  Hotel 67
Catalonia Còrcega 67
Catalonia Princesa, Hotel 57
Ciudad Contal, Hostal 63
Claris, Hotel 60
Colón, Hotel 49
Condes de Barcelona, Hotel 60
Confort, Hotel 67, 67
Cortés, Hotel 50
Eden, Hostal 64
España, Hotel 54, 54
Fontanella, Hostal 64
Francia, Pensión 59
Gat Raval, Hostal 54
Gaudí, Hotel 54
Ginebra, Hotel 63
Girona, Hostal 64, 64
Goya, Hostal 65
Gran Via, Hotel 63
Grand Marina Hotel 59
Grau, Hosteria 57
Guillermo Tell, Hotel 69
Hedy Holiday, Hostal 70
Hesperia Metropol, Hotel 69
Hilton Barcelona 60
Hispanos Siete Suiza 58, 58
Husa Internacional 51
Inglaterra, Hotel 60
Itaca Alberg-Hostel 70
Jardi, Hostal 50
Kabul, Albergue 70
Laietana Palace, Hotel 49
Lausanne, Hostal 51
Majestic, Hotel 61
Maldà, Hostal 51
Mare de Déu de Montserrat,
  Alberg 68, 70
Mari-Luz, Pensión-Hostal 53
Meridien Barcelona, Le, Hotel 49
Mesón Castilla, Hotel 55
Noya, Hostal 51
Nuevo Triunfo, Hotel 59
Oliva, Hostal-Residencia 65, 65
Onix, Hotel 68
Opera, Hostal 57
Oriente, Hotel 49
Orleans, Hostal 57
Palermo, Hostal 51
Paral.lel, Hotel 60
Parisien, Hostal 50, 51
Pelayo, Hotel 63
Peninsular, Hotel 55, 55
Pensió 2000 59
Plaza, Hostal 63
Podium, Hotel 61
Principal, Hotel 55
Ramblas, Hotel 51
Ramos, Hostal-Residencia 54
Regente, Hotel 61
Rembrandt, Hostal 53
Rey Don Jaime I, Hostal 50
Ribagorza, Hostal de 65
Ritz Hotel 61
Rivoli Ramblas, Hotel 49
Rondas, Pensión 65
San Remo, Hostal 65

Sant Agusti, Hotel 55
Sant'Àngelo, Hotel 63
Sants, Pensión 68
Segre, Pensión 53, 53
Splendid, Hotel 64
Suizo, Hotel 51
Terrassa, La, Hostal 57
Toledano, Hotel 53
Triunfo, Hotel 58
Urquinaona, Hotel 59
Via Augusta, Hotel 69
Victòria, Residencia 53
Vitoria, Pensión 53

RESTAURANTS

Abac 145
Agua 159
Agut 135
Al Diwan 154
Al Passatore 150
Alboroque 151
Alkimia 151
Ample 24 135
Asador de Burgos, El 151
Ateneu Gastronomic 135
Atzavara 155
Balsa, La 163, 164
Bar Salvador 146
Bestial 161
Biblioteca 141
Botafumeiro 157
Brasserie Flo 146
Bulli, El 164
Bunga Raya 150
Ca l'Estevet 142
Ca l'Isidre 142
Café de l'Acadèmia 135
Cafeti, El 141
Cal Pep 146
Can Culleretes 135
Can Majó 159
Can Maño 161
Can Solé 161
Cantina Machito 159
Casa Calvet 151
Casa de la Rioja, La 142
Casa Delfin 146
Casa Leopoldo 142, 142-143
Cata 1.81 151
Celler de Macondo, El 150
Comerç 24 146
Comme Bio 150
Coses de Menjar 147
Cova d'en Vidalet 157
dZI 163
Econòmic, L' 147
Elche 163
Elisabets 142
Envalira 157
Espai Sucre 146, 147
Figaro 159
Fil Manila 145
Fragua, La 142
Gaig 162, 163
Gardunya, La 143
Gavina, La 159
Golfo di Napoli, Il 163
Govinda 141
Gran Café, El 137
Habana Vieja 150
Hortet, L' 145
Hotel España 143
Illa de Gràcia, L'
Jean Luc Figueras 158
Juicy Jones 141
Ken 164
Lahore 159
Laurak 158
Little Italy 150
Locanda, La 139

Lupino 143
Mama Café 143
Mastroqué 137
Mercè Vins 137
Mesón David 143
Mesón Jesús 137
Mundial Bar 147
Neichel 164
Octubre 158
Ot 158, 158
Paraguayo, El 141
Parra, La 163
Passadis del Pep 147
Pebre Blau, El 147
Pelmong 141
Pescadors, Els 163
Pla 137
Pla de la Garsa 149
Pla dels Àngels 143
Polenta 141
Pou Dols 137, 139
Pucca 149, 149
Punjab Restaurante 145
Quinze Nits, Les 139
Reina, La 149
Rodizio, El 154
Roig Robi 158
Ruccula 161
Sagarra 145
Salón, La 149
Santa Maria 149
Semproniana 153
Senyor Parellada 150
Sésamo 145
Set Portes 161
Shunka 141
Silenus 145
SoNaMu 159
Sukur 141
Suquet de l'Almirall 161
Taxidermista 139
Teranga 150
Thai Gardens 155
Tomaquera, La 145
Torre de Altamar 161
Tragaluz 151, 153
Umita 145
Venta, La 164
Verònica, La 141
Vivanda 164
Windsor 153
Xiringuitó Escribà 161

CAFÉS & BARS

Arc Café 165
Ascensor, L' 165
Bagel Shop, The 166
Baignoire, La 179
Bar Bodega Fortuny 170
Bar Celta 166
Bar del Pi 166
Bar Kasparo 170
Bar Mendizábal 170
Bar Muy Buenas 170, 171
Bar Pastis 171
Bar Pinotxo 166
Bar Primavera 178
Bar Ra 171
Bar 68 171
Bar Tomás 180
Barcelona de Vins i Esperits,
  La 178
Bilbao-Berria 167
Bliss 167
Boadas 171
Bodega Manolo 179
Bodegueta, La 178
Bosc de les Fades, El 167
Buenas Migas 171
Café de l'Opera 167

Café del Sol 179
Café d'Estiu 167
Café La Cereria 167
Café Que Pone Muebles
  Navarro, El 172
Café Torino 179
Café Zurich 167
Can Ganassa 177
Can Paixano 177
Casa Alfonso 178
Casa Almirall 172
Casa de Molinero 167
Casa Quimet 179
Cerveceria Catalana 178
Circulo Maldà 167
Clansman, The 173
Confiteria, La 172
Dry Martini 178, 179
Escribà 172
Espai Barroc 175
Esquinica, La 180
Estrella de Plata, La 175
Euskal Extea 172, 175
Flash Flash 179
Fronda, La 179
Fundació Joan Miró 178
Ginger 167, 169
Glaciar 169
Granja, La 169
Granja M Viader 172
Hivernacle, L' 175
Horiginal 172
Idea, La 175
Iposa 173
Jai-ca 177
Laie Libreria Cafè 179
Leticia 169
London Bar 166, 252
Luz de Gas – Port Vell 177
Marsella 166, 252
Merbeyé 180
Miramelindo 175
Miranda del Museu, La 177
Morera, La 175
Mos 179
Mudanzas 176
Nus, El 176
Origens 99,9% 176
Palma, La 169
Pilé 43 169
Portalón, El 169
Quatre Gats, Els 166, 169
Quimet i Quimet 178
Rabipelao 169
Ribborn 176
Ruta dels Elefants, La 173
Salambó 180
Schilling 169
Shanghai 169
Sol Soler 180
Stinger 179
Suau 176
Sureny 180
Tèxtil Cafè 176
Tinaja, La 176
Tres Tombs, Els 173
Túnel, El 166
Txirimiri 176
Va de Vi 175, 176
Valor Chocolateria 179
Vaso de Oro, El 177
Venus Delicatessen 170
Vinateria del Call, La 170
Vinissim 170, 170
Vinya del Senyor, La 176
Xaloc 170
Xampanyet, El 176
Xocoa 170

Advertisers' Index

Please refer to the relevant pages for
addresses and telephone numbers

EasyJet	IFC

In Context

Museu Marítim	4
Lonacar	4
Barcelona Bus Turístic	6
University of Barcelona	12
The Fastnet	28
Enforex	28
The Golden Wheels	28
Europerator	28

Accommodation

Barcelona-on-line	48
Visit Barcelona	48
Hotel Prestige	52
Urban Flats	52
Europerator	52
Backpackers	56
Petit Hotel	56
Oh-Barcelona.com	56
House Family B&B	56
HotelConnect	62
B-Home	62
Europerator	62
Tourism Barcelona	66
Acropolis Guest House	66

Sightseeing

Generalitat de Catalunya	78
MACBA/Articket	82
International House	88
Kingsbrook	94
TB Tours	94
Palau de la Música Catalana	94
BCN Rent A Car	114
Icono Serveis	114
BBIGG Internet Café	114

Eat, Drink, Shop Opener

Salsitas	132

Restaurants

Taxidermista	136
Lombardo	140
Dos Trece	144
Fresc Co	144
Travel Bar	148
Sagardi	148
Vilsdvin L'Antiga Taverna	152
Tablao de Carmen	152
Windsor	156
Octubre	156
Barcelonia	156
Little Italy	156

Cafés & Bars

Organic	168
George & Dragon	168
P. Flaherty Irish Pub	174
The Clansman	174
Freud B'Art	174
Mamacafé	174

Shops & Services

Heron City	184
La Roca Village	188
Oxford House	194
Anthony Llobet Salon	194
Kaveh Abadani	194
Noténom	198

Nightlife

Barcelona Metropolitan	250
La Paloma	250
Gran Casino Barcelona	256

Trips Out of Town

Time Out City Guides	274

Maps

Art Escudellers	340
Pizza Marzano	IBC

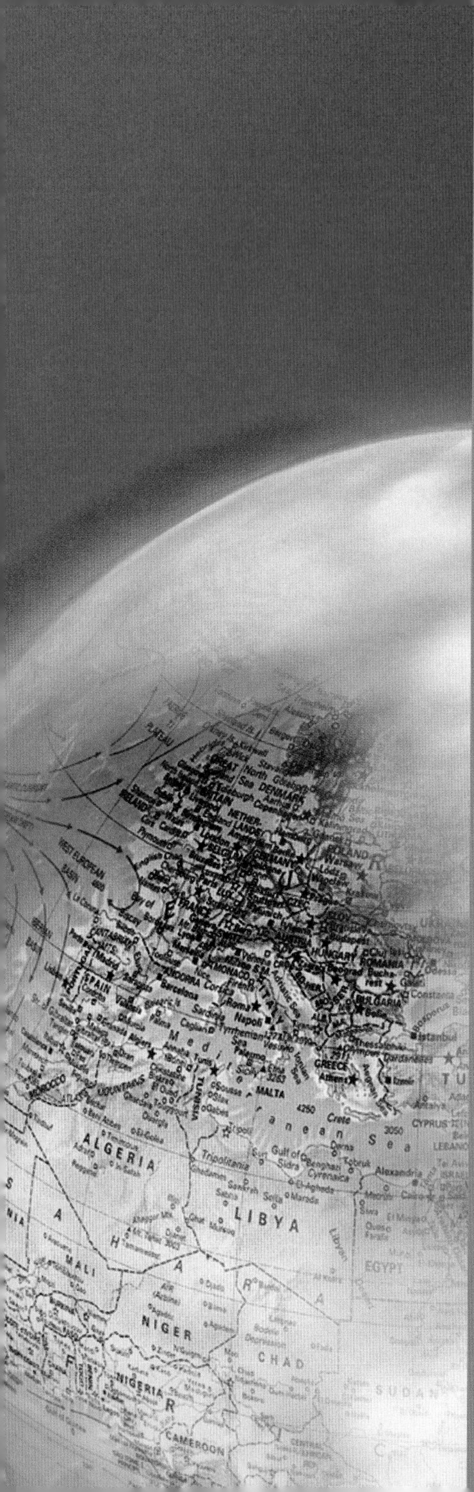

Place of interest and/or entertainment	
Hospital or college	
Pedestrianised zone	
Railway station	
Metro station, FGC station	
Area name	BARRI GÒTIC

Maps

Trips Out of Town 332
Around Barcelona 333
Street Index 334
Street Maps 337
RENFE Local Trains 346
Metro 347
Barcelona Areas 348

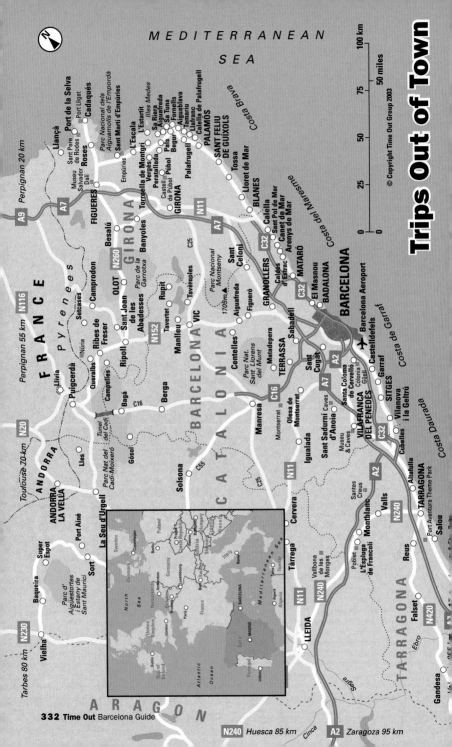

Trips Out of Town

MEDITERRANEAN SEA

FRANCE

Perpignan 20 km

Perpignan 55 km

Toulouse 70 km

Tarbes 80 km

ANDORRA

Pyrenees

CATALONIA

BARCELONA

Costa del Maresme

Costa Brava

Costa de Garraf

Costa Daurada

ARAGON

N240 *Huesca 85 km*   A2 *Zaragoza 95 km*

© Copyright Time Out Group 2003

100 km

50 miles

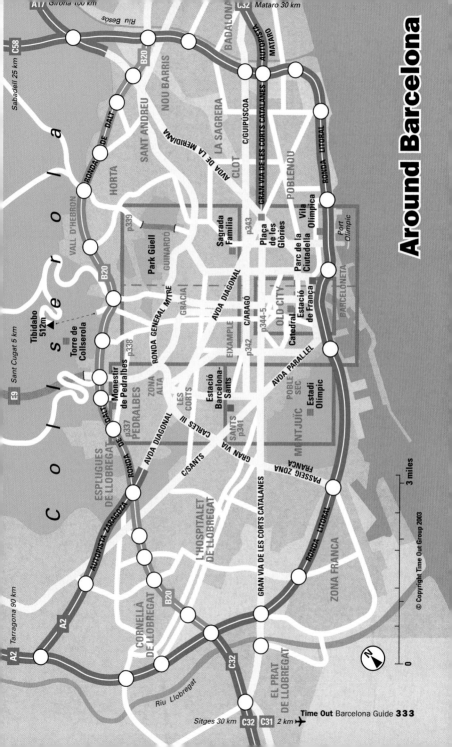

Around Barcelona

© Copyright Time Out Group 2003

Street Index

26 de Gener, C. - p341 A4

Abaixadors, C. - p345 B3
Adrià, C. - p338 C2
Aglà, C. - p345 A3
Agullers, C. - p345 B4
Agustina Saragossa, C. - p337 B3
Álaba, C. - p343 F5-6
Alacant, C. - p338 C2
Albareda, C. - p342 C6
Albert Llanas, C. - p339 F2
Albigesos, C. - p339 E2
Alcolea, C. - p337 A4
Alegre de Dalt - p339 E2-3
Alfons el Savi, Plaça - p339 F3
Alfons XII, C. d' - p338 D3
Alí Bei, C. - p343 E5/ p344 C1
Alió, Passatge - p339 E4
Allada-Vermell, C. - p345 C3
Almeria, C. - p341 A4
Almirall Aixada, C. - p342 D7
Almirall Cervera, C. - p342 D7
Almogàvers, C. - p343 E6-F6
Alt de Gironella, C. - p337 B2
Amadeu Vives, C. - p342 D5/p344 C2
Amargós, C. - p344 B2
Amigó, C. - p338 C3
Ample, C - p342 D6/ p345 B4
Amunt, Passeig - p339 E3
Andrea Dòria, C. - p343 E7
Àngel Baixeras, C. - p345 B4
Àngel Guimerà - p337 B2
Àngel, Plaça - p342 D6/ p345 B3
Àngels, C. - p344 A2
Àngels, Plaça - p342 C5/p344 A1
Anglesola, C. - p337 B3
Anglí, C. - p337 B1
Annibal, C. - p341 B6
Antequera, C. - p339 E2
Antic de Sant Joan, C. - p345 C3
Antoni de Capmany, C. - p341 A4
Antonio López, Plaça - p342 D6/p345 B4
Antoni Maura, Plaça - p342 D6/p344 B2
Aragó, C. - p341-338 B4-F4
Arai, C. - p345 B3
Arc del Teatre, C. - p342 C6/p345 A4
Arc de Sant Agustí, C. - p345 A3
Arc de Sant Ramon del Call, C. - p345 B3
Arcs, C. - p344 B2
Arenes de St Pere, C. - p344 C2
Argenter, C. L' - p344 C2
Argenteria, C. - p345 B3
Aribau, C. - p338-342 C3-C5
Arlet, C. - p345 B3
Armada, Plaça - p342 C7
Aroles, C. - p345 A3
Arquitecte Sert, C. - p343 F7
Artos, Plaça - p337 B2
Ases, C. - p345 C4
Assaonadors, C. - p345 C3
Astúries, C. - p338 D3
Ataülf, C. - p345 B3-4
Atenes, C. - p338 C2

Augusta, Via - p337-338 B1-D3
Aurora, C. - p342 C6
Ausiàs Marc, C. - p343 E5/p344 C1
Avellà, C. - p344 B2
Avenir, C. - p338 C3
Àvila, C. - p343 F5-6
Avinyó, C. - p342 D6/ p345 B3-4

Bacardí, Passatge - p345 A3
Bailèn, C. - p339-343 E3-5
Balboa, C. - p343 E7
Balcells, C. - p339 E2
Ballester, C. - p338 D2
Balmes, C. - p338 C2-D4/ p344 A1
Baluard, C. - p343 E7
Banca, Passatge de la - p345 A4
Banyoles, C. - p339 E3
Banys Nous, C. - p345 B3
Banys Vells, C. - p345 C3
Barceloneta, Plaça - p342 D7
Baró de S. Lluís, C. - p339 F2
Barra de Ferro, C. - p345 C3
Basea, C. - p345 B3
Basses de Sant Pere, C. - p344 C2
Beates, C. - p344 B2
Beethoven, C. - p337 B3
Béjar, C. - p341 A4-5
Bellafila, C. - p345 B3
Benet Mateu, C. - p337 B2
Bergara, C. - p344 B1
Berlín, C. - p337 A3-B3
Bertran, C. - p338 C2
Bertrellans, C. - p344 B2
Bisbe, C. - p345 B3
Bisbe Català, C. - p337 A1
Bismarck, C. - p339 F2
Blai, C. - p341 B6
Blanco, C. - p337 A4
Blanqueria, C. - p345 C3
Blasco de Garay, C. - p341 B6
Blesa, C. - p341 B6
Bòbila, C. - p341 B6
Bogatell, Avda - p343 F6
Bolívar, C. - p338 D2
Bolívia, C. - p343 F5
Bon Pastor, C. - p338 C3
Bonaire, C. - p345 C4
Bonanova, Passeig - p337 B1
Bonaplata, C. - p337 B1
Bonavista, C. - p338 D3
Bonet i Moixi, Plaça - p341 A4
Bonsuccés, C. - p344 A2
Bonsuccés, Plaça - p344 A2
Boquer, C. - p345 C3
Boqueria, C. - p342 D6/ p345 A3
Boqueria, Plaça - p345 A3
Bordeta, Ctra la - p341 A5
Bordeus, C. - p337 B3
Bori i Fontestà, C. - p337 B3
Bòria, C. - p345 B3
Born, Passeig del - p342 D6/p345 C3
Borrell i Soler, C. - p337 A1
Bosch i Gimpera, C. - p337 A1
Bot, C. - p344 A2
Boters, C. - p344 B2
Bou de Sant Pere, C. - p344 C2
Brasil, C. - p337 A3

Brosolí, C. - p345 C4
Bruc, C. - p338-342 D4-5/ p344 C1
Brugada, Plaça - p343 E7
Bruniquer, C. - p339 E3
Brusi, C. - p338 C2-3
Buenaventura Muñoz, C. - p343 E6
Buenos Aires, C. - p338 C3
Buigas, C. - p337 B2
Burgos, C. - p341 A4

Caballero, C. - p337 A3
Cabanes, C. - p342 C6
Caçador, Baixada - p345 B3
Cadena, C. - p342 C6
Calàbria, C. - p341 B4-5
Calaf, C. - p338 C3
Calatrava, C. - p337 B1-2
Calders, C. - p345 C3
Call, C. - p345 B3
Calvet, C. - p338 C3
Camèlies, C. - p339 E2-F2
Camp, C. - p338 C2
Campions, Plaça - p343 F7
Camprodon, C. - p339 E4
Can Toda, Riera - p339 E2
Can Valero, C. de - p341 A7
Canuda, C. - p342 D5/ p344 B2
Canvis Nous, C. - p345 B3
Canvis Vells, C. - p345 C4
Capellans, C. dels - p344 B2
Capità Arenas, C. - p337 B2
Caponata, C. - p337 A1
Carabassa, C. - p345 B4
Caramelles, Plaça - p342 C5
Caravel.la La Niña, C. - p337 B2
Cardenal Casañas - p345 A3
Cardenal Vives i Tutó, C. - p337 A1
Cardener, C. - p339 E2
Carders, C. - p345 C3
Cardona, Plaça - p338 C3
Carles Pi i Sunyer, Plaça - p344 B2
Carme, C. - p342 C6/ p344 A2
Carme, Plaça - p337 B3
Carmel, Crta - p339 E2-F2
Carolines, C. - p338 D3
Carretes, C. - p342 C6
Cartagena, C. - p339-343 F3-5
Casanova, C. - p338-342 C3-5
Cascades, Passeig - p341 A6
Casp, C. - p342-343 D5-E5/ p344 B1-C1
Castell, Avda - p341 B7
Castella, Plaça de - p342 C5/p344 A1
Castillejos, C. - p339-343 F3-5
Catedral, Avda - p344 B2
Cavallers, C. - p337 A1
Cecs Boqueria, C. - p345 A3
Cecs Sant Cugat, C. - p345 C3
Centre, Plaça - p337 A3
Cera, C. - p342 C6
Cerdanyola, C. - p337 A4
Cervantes, C. - p345 B3
Cid, C. - p342 C6
Cigne, C. - p338 D3

Circumval.lació, Passeig - p343 E6
Cirera, C. - p345 C4
Cirici Pellicer, Plaça - p337 A1
Ciutat, C. - p345 B3
Claudi Güell, Passeig - p337 A2
Clos de S. Francesc, C. - p337 B1
Còdols, C. - p342 D6/ p345 A4
Coll del Portell, Avda - p339 E2
Colom, C. - p345 A3
Colom, Passeig - p342 D6/p345 A4-B4
Colomines, C. - p345 C3
Comas, Plaça - p337 A3
Comerç, C. - p343 E6/ p345 C3-4
Cometa, C. - p345 B3
Comercial, C. - p345 C3
Comercial, Plaça - p345 C3
Comtal, C. - p342 D5/ p344 B2
Comte Borrell, C. - p338-342 C4-6
Comte d'Urgell, C. - p338-342 C3-5
Comtes, C. - p345 B3
Comtes de Bell-lloc, C. - p337 A3
Comtessa de Sobradiel, C. - p345 B3
Concepció, Ptge de la - p338 D4
Concòrdia, C. - p341 B6
Concòrdia, Plaça - p337 A3
Consellers, C. - p345 B4
Consell de Cent, C. - p341-343 A4-F4
Consolat de Mar, C. - p345 B4
Copèrnic, C. - p338 C2
Copons, C. - p344 B2
Corders, C. - p345 C3
Corral, C. - p341 A5
Correu Vell, C. - p345 B4
Còrsega, C. - p337-339 B4-F4
Cortines, C. - p343 E6/ p344 C2
Costa, C. - p338 D2
Cotoners, C. - p345 B3
Crèdit, Passatge - p345 B3
Cremat Gran, C. - p345 C3
Cremat Xic, C. - p345 C3
Creu Coberta, C. - p341 A5
Creu dels Molers, C. - p341 B6
Cros, C. - p341 A4
Cucurulla, C. - p344 B2
Cucurulla, Plaça - p344 B2

Dagueria, C. - p345 B3
Dalmàcia, C. - p337 B1
Dalmases, C. - p337 B1
Dalt, Travessera de - p339 E2
Dénia, C. - p338 C3
Descartes, C. - p338 C2
Deu i Mata, C. - p337 A3-B3
Diagonal, Avda - p337-343 A2-F5
Diamant, Plaça - p338 D3
Diputació, C. - p341-343 B5-F5
Doctor A. Pi Sunyer - p337 B1
Doctor Aiguader, C. - p343 E7/p345 C4
Doctor Bové, C. - p339 F2
Doctor Carulla, C. -

p337 B1
Doctor Dou, C. - p344 A2
Doctor Farreras i Valentí, C. - p337 A1
Doctor Ferran, C. - p337 A2
Doctor Fleming, C. - p337 B2
Doctor Font i Quer, C. del - p341 A6-B6
Doctor Ignasi Barraquer, Plaça - p337 B3
Doctor J. Pou, C. - p344 B2
Doctor Letamendi, Plaça - p338 C4
Doctor Roux, C. - p337 B1-2
Doctor Trueta, C. - p343 F6
Domingo, Ptge - p338 D4
Dominguez, C. - p337 A1
Dormitori Sant Francesc, Passatge - p345 A4
Dos de Maig, C. - p339-343 F4-F5
Drassanes, Avda - p342 C6
Duc de la Victòria, C. - p344 B2
Duc de la Victòria, Plaça - p344 B2
Duc de Medinaceli, Plaça - p345 A4
Dulcet, C. - p337 A1
Duran i Bas, C. - p344 B2

Eduardo Conde, C. - p337 A2
Eguilaz, Plaça - p337 B2
Elisa, C. - p338 D2
Elisabets, C. - p344 A2
Elkano, C. - p341 B6
Enamorats, C. - p339 F4
Encarnació, C. - p339 E3-F3
Enric Bargés, C. - p337 A4
Enric Giménez, C. - p337 A1
Enric Granados, C. - p338-342 C4-5
Ensenyança, C. - p338 D3
Entença, C. - p337-341 B3-5
Equador, C. - p337 B3-4
Ermengarda, C. - p341 A4
Escipió, C. - p338 D2
Escoles Pies, C. - p337 B2
Escorial, C. - p339 E2-3
Escudellers, C. - p342 D6/p345 A3-B3
Escudellers, Ptge - p345 A4
Escudellers Blancs, C. - p345 A3
Escullera, Passeig - p342 D7
Espanya, Plaça d' - p341 A5
Esparteria, C. - p345 C4
Esplugues, C. de - p337 A1
Est, C. - p342 C6
Estadi, Avda - p341 A6
Estruc, C. - p344 B1
Eugeni d'Ors, C. - p337 A3
Europa, C. - p337 A3
Eusebi Güell, Plaça - p337 A1
Evarist Arnús, C. - p337 A3
Exposició, Passeig - p341 B6

Farga, Plaça la - p341 A4
Ferlandina, C. - p342 C5
Fernando Primo de Rivera, C. - p337 A2
Ferran Agulló, C. -

p338 C3
Ferran Puig, C. - p338 D2
Ferran, C. - p342 D6/ p345 A3-B3
Figols, C. - p337 A3
Finlàndia, C. - p341 A4
Flassaders, C. - p345 C3
Flor de Lliri, C. - p345 C3
Flor, C. - p344 B2
Floridablanca, C. - p341 B5
Floristes de la Rambla, C. - p344 A2
Flors, C. - p342 C6
Flos i Calcat - p337 A2
Fonollar, C. - p344 C2
Font Castellana, Plaça - p339 F2
Font Florida, C. - p341 A5
Font Honrada, C. - p341 B5
Font, Plaça - p343 E7
Fontanella, C. - p342 D5/ p344 B1
Fontanelles, Ptge - p337 B1
Fontcoberta, C. - p337 B2
Fontrodona, C. - p342 C6
Formatgeria, C. - p345 C3
Fossar de les Moreres - p345 C3
Fra Eloi de Bianya, Plaça - p337 A1
França, C. - p339 F2
França Xica, C. - p341 B6
Francesc Alegre, C. - p339 F2
Francesc Cambó, Avda - p344 B2
Francesc Carbonell, C. - p337 A2
Francesc Macià, Plaça - p338 C3
Francisco Giner, C. - p338 D3
Freixa, C. - p338 C2
Freixures, C. - p344-3 C2-3
Freneria, C. - p345 B3
Fruita, C. - p345 B3
Fusina, C. - p345 C3
Fusteria, C. - p345 B4

Gal.la Placídia, Plaça - p338 D3
Galileu, C. - p337 A3-4
Gall, Plaça - p338 C4
Gandesa, C. - p337 A3
Ganduxer, C. - p337-8 B3-C2
Gardunya, Plaça - p342 C6/p344 A2
Gaudí, Avda - p339 F4
Gaudí, Plaça - p339 F4
Gavà, C. - p341 A5
Gayarre, C. - p341 A4
Gegants, C. - p345 B3
Gelabert, C. - p337 B3
General Álvarez de Castro - p344 C2
General Castaños, C. - p345 C4
George Orwell, Plaça - p345 B3
Gignàs, C. - p345 B4
Ginebra, C. - p343 E7
Giralt el pellisser, C. - p344 C2
Gíriti, C. - p345 B3
Girona, C. - p339-343 E4/ p344 C1
Gironella, Plaça p337 B2
Gleva, C. - p338 D2
Glòria, Baixada - p339 E2
Glòries, Plaça de les - p343 F5
Gombau, C. - p344 C2
Gràcia, Passeig de - p338-342 D3-5/p344 B1
Gràcia, Travessera de - p338-9 C3-F3
Gran de Gràcia, C. - p338 D3
Gran Via Carles III - p337 A2-3
Gran Via de les Corts Catalanes - p341-343 A5-F5
Gran Vista, C. - p339 F2
Granada del Penedès -

p338 D3
Granja, C. - p339 E2
Grassot, C. - p339 E4
Gravina, C. - p344 A1
Groc, C. - p345 B4
Grunyí, C. - p345 C3
Guadiana, C. - p341 A4
Guàrdia C. - p342 C6/ p345 A3
Guillem Tell. C. - p338 D2
Guitard, C. - p337 A3-4

Hercegovina, C. - p338 C2
Hèrcules, C. - p345 B3
Heures, C. - p345 A3
Homer, C. - p338 D2
Hort de la Vila, C. - p337 B1
Hort Velluters, Passagte - p344 C2
Hospital Militar, Avda - p338 D2
Hospital, C. - p342 C6/ p344-5 A2-3
Hostafrancs, C. - p341 A5
Hostal d'en Sol, C. - p345 B4

Icària, Avda - p343 F6-7
Indíbil, C. - p341 A5
Indústria, C. - p339 E3-F3
Iradier, C. - p337 B1
Isabel II, Passeig - p343 D6/p345 B4

Jacinto Benavente, C. - p337 B2
Jaume Giralt, C. - p344 C2
Jaume I, C. - p342 D6/ p345 B3
Jerusalem, C. - p344 A2
Jiménez i Iglesias, C. - p337 A2
Joan Carles I, Plaça - p338 D4
Joan Corrades, Plaça - p341 A5
Joan d'Austria, C. - p343 F6
Joan de Borbó, Passeig - p342 D7/p345 C4
Joan Gamper, C. de - p337 B3
Joan Güell, C. - p337 A3
Joan Llongueras, Plaça - p338 C3
Joan Massana, C. - p345 B4
Joan Miró, C. - p343 F6
Joan Peiró, Plaça - p341 A4
Joan XXIII, Avda - p337 A2
Joanic, Plaça - p339 E3
Joanot Martorell, C. - p341 A4
Joaquim Blume, C. - p341 B5
Joaquim Pena, Plaça - p337 B2
Joaquim Xirau, Plaça - p342 D6/p345 A4
Joaquín Costa, C. - p342 C5
Jocs Florals, C. - p341 A4
Johann Sebastian Bach, C. - p338 C2
John Lennon, Plaça - p339 E3
Jonqueres, C. - p344 B1-2
Jordi Girona, C. - p337 A2
Josep Anselm Clavé, C. - p342 D6/p345 A4
Josep Carner, Passeig - p342 C7
Josep Ciurano, C. - p339 F3
Josep Llovera, Passatge - p338 C3
Josep Maria Folch i Torres, Plaça - p342 C6
Josep Serrano, C. - p339 F2
Josep Tarradellas, C. - p337 B4
Jovellanos, C. - p344 A1
Julián Romea, C. - p338 D3
Junta de Comerç - p345 A3

Lafont, C. - p342 C6
Laforja, C. - p338 C3-D3
Laietana, Via - p342 D5-6/

p344-5 B2-3
Lamote de Grignon, C. - p337 A2
Lancaster, C. - p345 A3
Larrard, C. - p339 E2
Lázaro Cárdenas, C. - p337 B2
Legalitat, C. - p339 E3
Leiva, C. - p341 A4-5
Lepant, C. - p339-343 F3-5
Les Corts, C. - p337 A3
Les Corts,Travessera de - p337 A3-B3
Lesseps, Plaça - p338 D2
Lincoln, C. - p338 D3
Litoral, Avda - p343 F7
Llana, Plaça - p345 C3
Llançà, C. - p341 B4-5
Llàstics, C. - p344 C2
Llauder, C. - p342 D6/ p345 B4
Lledó, C. - p345 B3
Lleialtat, C. - p342 C6
Lleida, C. - p341 B5
Lleona, C. - p345 A3
Llibertat, C. - p338 D3
Llibertat, Plaça - p338 D3
Llibreteria, C. - p345 B3
Llorens i Barba, C. - p339 F3
Lluçà, C. - p337 A3
Lluís Companys, Passeig - p343 E6
Lluís Millet, Plaça - p344 B2
Llull, C. - p343 F6
Lluna, C. - p342 C5
Londres, C. - p337-8 B3-C3
Loreto, C. - p337 B3
Luis Antúnez, C. - p338 D3

Madoz, Passatge - p345 A3
Madrazo, C. - p338 C3-D3
Madrid, Avda - p337 A3
Magalhães, C. - p341 B6
Magdalenes, C. - p344 B2
Maignon, C. - p338 D2
Major de Sarrià - p337 B1
Malcuinat, C. - p345 C4
Mallorca, C. - p341-339 A4-F4
Mandri, C. - p338 C2
Mañé i Flaquer, Plaça - p338 D2
Manila, C. - p337 A2
Manresa, C. - p345 B3
Manso, C. - p341 B5
Manuel Faila, C. - p337 A2
Manuel Girona, Passeig - p337 A2
Manuel Ribé, Placeta - p345 B3
Manufactures, Pgte de les - p344 C2
Maquinista, C. - p343 E7
Marc Aureli, C. - p338 C2
Marcús, Placeta - p345 C3
Mare de Déu de Montserrat, Avda - p339 F2
Mare de Déu del Coll, C. - p338 D2
Mare de Déu del Pilar, C. - p344 C2
Mare de Déu de la Salut - p339 E2
Margarit, C. - p341 B6
Margenat, C. - p337 B1
Maria Auxiliadora, C. - p337 B2
Maria Barrientos, C. - p337 A2
Marià Cubí, C. - p338 C3-D3
Marianao, C. - p339 E2
Marina, C. - p339-343 F3-7
Marítim Nova Icària, Passeig - p343 F7
Marítim Port Olímpic, Passeig - p343 F7
Marítim, Passeig - p343 E7
Marlet, C. - p345 B3
Marquès de Barberà, C. - p342 C6/p345 A3
Marquès de Campo Sagrado, C. - p341 B6
Marquès de Comillas, Avda - p341 A5
Marquès de l'Argentera,

Avda - p343 E6/p345 C4
Marquès de Mulhacén, C. - p337 A1
Marquès de Sentmenat, C. - p337 B3
Marquesa, C. - p343 E6/ p345 C4
Marquet, C. - p345 B4
Marquilles, Plaça - p344 C2
Martí i Julià, C. - p337 B2
Martí, C. - p339 E3
Mas Casanovas, C. - p339 F3
Maspons, C. - p338 D3
Massanet, C. - p345 B3
Maternitat, C. - p337 A3
Mejía Lequerica, C. - p337 A3
Melcior de Palau, C. - p337 A3-4
Méndez Núñez, C. - p344 C2
Mercader, Passatge - p338 D4
Mercaders, C. - p344-5 B2
Mercantil, Passeig - p345 C3
Mercè, C. - p345 B4
Mercè, Plaça - p342 D6/ p345 B4
Mercedes, C. - p339 E2
Meridiana, Avda - p343 F5
Mestre Nicolau - p338 C3
Mestres Casals i Martorell - p344 C2
Metges, C. - p344 C2
Mèxic, C. - p341 A5
Migdia, Passeig del - p341 A6-7
Milà i Fontanals, C. - p339 E3
Milans, Plaça - p345 B4
Mineria, C. - p338 D4
Minerva, C. - p338 D3
Miquel Àngel, C. - p337 A3
Miracle, C. - p337 A4
Mirador Palau Nacional - p341 A6
Mirallers, C. - p345 C3
Miramar, Avda - p341 B6
Miramar, Ctra - p341 B7
Miramar, Plaça - p341 B6
Misser Ferrer, C. - p344 B2
Mistral, Avda - p341 B5
Modolell, C. - p338 C2
Moianès, C. - p341 A5
Moles, C. - p344 B1-2
Molina, Plaça - p338 D2
Moll, C. - p339 E2
Moll Barcelona - p342 C7
Moll Barceloneta - p342 D7
Moll d'Espanya - p342 D7/ p345 B4
Moll de la Fusta - p342 C7/ p345 B4
Moll Gregal - p343 F7
Moll Marina - p343 F7
Moll Mestral - p343 F7
Moll Sant Bertran - p342 C7
Mònec, C. - p344 C2
Monistrol, C. - p339 E3
Montalegre, C. - p342 C5/ p344 A1
Montanyans, Avda - p341 A5
Montanyans, C. - p344 C2
Montcada, Placeta de - p345 C3
Monterols, C. - p337 B1
Montjuïc del Carme, C. - p344 A2
Montjuïc, Carretera - p337 B7
Montjuïc, Passeig - p342 C7
Montnegre, C. - p337 B3
Montmany, C. - p339 E3
Montseny, C. - p338 D3
Montserrat, C. - p345 A4
Montsió, C. - p344 B2
Morales, C. - p337 B3
Morera, C. - p344 A2
Mosques, C. - p345 C4
Mossèn J. Verdaguer, Plaça - p339 E4
Mozart, C. - p338 D3
Muntades, C. - p341 A4
Muntaner, C. -

p338-342 C2-5
Nàpols, C. - p339-343 E3-6
Narcís Oller, Plaça - p338 D3
Nau Santa Maria, C. - p337 B2
Nau, C. - p345 B3
Navas, Plaça - p341 B6
Negrevernís, C. - p337 B1
Nemesi Ponsati, Plaça de - p341 A6
Nena Casas, C. - p337 B2
Niça, C. - p339 F3
Nicaragua, C. - p337 B3-4
Noguera Pallaresa, C. - p341 A4
Nord, Plaça - p339 E3
Notariat, C. - p344 A2
Nou de la Rambla, C. - p341-342 B6-C6/ p345 A3
Nou de Sant Francesc, C. - p345 A4
Nou de Zurbano, C. - p345 A3
Nova, Plaça - p344 B2
Novell, C. - p337 A3
Numància, C. - p337 B2-4

Obradors, C. - p345 A3
Ocells, C. - p344 C2
Oli, C. - p345 B3
Oliana, C. - p338 C3
Olímpic, Passeig - p341 A6
Olles, Plaça - p345 C4
Olot, C. - p339 E2
Olzinelles, C. - p341 A4
Om, C. - p342 C6
Or, C. - p338 D3
Orient, Plaça - p337 B3
Ortigosa, C. - p344 C2
Osca, Plaça - p341 A5
Osi, C. - p337 A2-B1

Pablo Neruda, Plaça - p339 F4
Pacia, C. - p342 C6
Padilla, C. - p339-343 F3-5
Pàdua, C. - p338 D2
Països Catalans, Plaça - p341 A4
Palau, C. - p345 B3
Palau, Passatge - p345 C4
Palau, Pla de - p342 D6/ p345 C4
Palaudàries, C. - p342 C6
Palla, C. - p344-5 B2-C3
Pallars, C. - p343 F6
Palma de Sant Just, C. - p345 B3
Pamplona, C. - p343 F5
Panses, C. - p345 C4
Paradís, C. - p345 B3
Paral.lel, Avda - p341-342 B5-C6
Parc Montjuïc - p341 B6
Parc, C. - p345 A4
Pare Laínez, C. - p339 E3
París, C. - p337-8 B3-C3
Parlament, C. - p341 B6
Patriarca, Passatge - p344 B2
Pau Alcover, C. - p337 B1
Pau Casals, Avda - p338 C3
Pau Claris, C. - p338-342 D4-5/ p344 B1
Pau Vila, Plaça de - p342 D7/p345 C4
Pau, Passatge - p345 A4
Pearson, Avda - p337 A1
Pedralbes, Avda - p337 A1-2
Pedralbes, Plaça - p337 A1
Pedro i Pons, C. - p337 A2
Pedró, Plaça - p342 C6
Pelai, C. - p342 D5/ p344 A1
Penedides, C. - p345 A3
Pere IV, C. - p343 F6
Pere Costa, C. - p339 F3
Pere Gallifa, C. - p345 B3
Pere Serafí, C. - p338 D3
Pérez Galdós, C. - p338 D2
Perill, C. - p338 D4
Perla, C. - p339 E3

Pes de la Palla, Plaça - p342 C5
Pescateria, C. - p345 C4
Petritxol, C. - p344 A2
Petxina, C. - p344 A2
Peu de la Creu, C. - p342 C5
Pi i Margall, C. - p339 E3-F3
Pi, C. - p344 B2
Pi, Plaça - p344 A2
Pi, Placeta - p345 A3
Picasso, Passeig - p343 E6
Pierre de Coubertin, C. de - p341 A6
Pietat, C. - p345 B3
Pintor Fortuny, C. - p342 C5/p344 A2
Piquer, C. - p342 C6
Pius XII, Plaça - p337 A2
Plata, C. - p345 B4
Plató, C. - p338 C2
Plegamans, C. - p345 C4
Poeta Boscà, Plaça - p343 E7
Poeta Cabanyes, C. - p341 B6
Polònia, C. - p339 F2
Pomaret, C. - p337 B1
Pompeu Fabra, Avda - p339 F2
Pons i Clerch, Plaça - p345 C3
Portaferrissa, C. - p342 D6/p344 A2
Portal de l'Àngel, Avda - p342 D5/p344 B1-2
Portal de la Pau, Plaça - p342 C7/p345 A4
Portal de Santa Madrona, C. - p342 C6
Portal Nou, C. - p343 E6/ p344 C2
Pou Dolç, C. - p345 B3
Pou Figuera, C. - p344 C2
Praga, C. - p339 F2
Prat de la Riba, Plaça - p337 B2
Prats de Molló, C. - p338 C2
Premià, C. - p341 A4
Príncep d'Astúries, Avda - p338 D3
Princesa, C. - p343 D6/ p345 C3
Provença, C. - p341-339 B4-F4
Providència, C. - p339 E3
Puigxuriguer, C. - p342 C7
Puigmartí, C. - p338 D3
Pujades, C. - p343 F6
Pujades, Passeig - p343 E6
Putget, C. - p338 D2

Quintana, C. - p345 A3

Radas, C. - p341 B6
Rafael Batlle, C. - p337 B2
Rafael Benet, Plaça - p337 B1
Raimon Casellas, Plaça - p339 F2
Rambla Catalunya - p338-342 D4-5/ p344 B1
Rambla del Raval - p342 C6
Rambla Mercedes - p339 E2
Rambla Prat - p338 D3
Rambla, La - p342 D5-6/ p344-5 A2-4
Ramelleres, C. - p344 A1
Ramiro de Maeztu, C. - p339 E2
Ramon Amadeu, Placeta - p344 B2
Ramon Berenguer el Gran, Plaça - p345 B3
Ramon Trias Fargas, C. - p343 F6-7
Ramon Turró, C. - p343 F6
Ramón y Cajal, C. - p339 E3
Raset, C. - p338 C2
Raspall, Plaça - p338 D3
Rauric, C. - p345 A3
Ravella, C. - p338 C2

Rec Comtal, C. - p344 C2
Rec, C. - p343 E6/ p345 C3-4
Rector Triadó, C. - p341 A4
Rector Ubach, C. - p338 C3
Regomir, C. - p345 B3
Regomir, Plaça - p345 B3
Rei, Plaça de - p345 B3
Reial, Plaça - p342 D6/ p345 A3
Reig i Bonet, C. - p339 E3
Reina Amàlia, C. - p342 C6
Reina Cristina, C. - p342 D6/p345 C4
Reina Elisenda de Montcada, Passeig - p337 A1-B1
Reina Maria Cristina, Avda - p341 A5
Reina Maria Cristina, Plaça - p337 A2
Reina Victòria, C. - p338 C2
República Argentina, Avda - p338 D2
Requesens, C. - p342 C5
Rera Palau, C. - p345 C4
Revolució Setembre 1868, Plaça - p338 D3
Ribera, C. - p345 C4
Ribes, C. - p343 E5-F5
Ricart, C. - p341 B5
Riego, C. - p341 A4
Riera Alta, C. - p342 C5
Riera Baixa, C. - p342 C6
Riera Sant Miquel, C. - p338 D3
Rierta, C. - p342 C6
Ríos Rosas, C. - p338 D2
Ripoll, C. - p344 A2
Rita Bonnat, C. - p337 B3
Rius i Taulet, Avda - p341 A5
Rius i Taulet, Plaça - p337 B1
Rivadeneyra, C. - p344 B1
Robador, C. - p342 C6
Robrenyo, C. - p337 A3-B4
Roca, C. - p344 A2
Rocafort, C. - p341 B4-5
Roger de Flor, C. - p339-343 E4-6
Roger de Llúria, C. - p338-342 D4-5/ p344 C1
Roig, C. - p342 C6
Roma, Avda - p341-338 B4-C4
Romans, C. - p339 E3
Ronda del Mig - p338-9 C2-F3
Ronda General Mitre - p338 B2-D2
Ronda Guinardó - p339 E2
Ronda Litoral - p342-3 C7-F7/ p345 A4-C4
Ronda Sant Antoni - p342 C5
Ronda Sant Pau - p342 C6
Ronda Sant Pere - p342-3 D5-E5/ p344 B1-C1
Ronda Universitat - p342 D5/p344 A1
Ros de Olano, C. - p338 D3
Rosa Sensat, C. - p343 F6
Rosa, C. - p345 B4
Rosalía de Castro, C. - p339 F3
Rosari, C. - p337 B2
Roser, C. - p341 B6
Rosés, C. - p337 A3
Rosés, Plaça - p337 B3
Rosic, C. - p345 C4
Rosselló, C. - p337-9 B4-F4
Rossend Arús, C. - p341 A4
Rovira i Trias, Plaça - p339 E3
Rovira, Túnel de la - p339 F2
Rull, C. - p345 A3

Sabateret, C. - p345 C3
Sabino de Arana, C. - p337 A2
Sagrada Família, Plaça - p339 E4
Sagristans, C. - p344 B2

Sagués, C. - p338 C3
Salou, C. - p341 A4
Salvà, C. - p341 B6
Salvador Espriu, C. - p343 F7
Sancho de Ávila, C. - p343 F5
Sanllehy, Plaça - p339 F2
Sant Agustí Vell, Plaça - p344 C2
Sant Agustí, Plaça - p345 A3
Sant Antoni, C. - p341 A4
Sant Antoni Abat, C. - p342 C5
Sant Antoni Maria Claret, C. - p339 E3-F3
Sant Antoni dels Sombrerers, C. - p345 C3
Sant Benet, Ptge - p344 C2
Sant Bonaventura, Cró - p344 B2
Sant Carles, C. - p343 E7
Sant Crist, C. - p341 A4
Sant Climent, C. - p342 C6
Sant Cugat, C. - p339 E2
Sant Cugat, Plaça - p343 E6/p345 C3
Sant Domènec, C. - p338 D3
Sant Domènec del Call, C. - p345 B3
Sant Elies, C. - p338 C2
Sant Eusebi, C. - p338 C3-D3
Sant Felip Neri, Plaça - p345 B3
Sant Francesc, Placeta - p345 A3
Sant Fructuós, C. - p341 A5
Sant Gaietà, Plaça - p337 B1
Sant Germà, C. - p341 A5
Sant Gil, C. - p342 C5
Sant Gregori Taumaturg, Plaça - p337 B3
Sant Honorat, C. - p345 B3
Sant Iu, Plaça - p345 B3
Sant Jacint, C. - p345 C3
Sant Jaume, Plaça - p342 D6/p345 B3
Sant Jeroni, C. - p342 C6
Sant Joan Bosco, Passeig - p337 B2
Sant Joan, Passeig - p339-343 E4-5
Sant Joaquim, C. - p338 D3
Sant Joaquim, Plaça - p338 D2
Sant Josep Oriol, Plaça - p345 A3
Sant Just, Plaça - p342 D6/p345 B3
Sant Lluís, C. - p339 E3
Sant Magí, C. - p338 D2
Sant Marc, C. - p338 D3
Sant Medir, C. - p341 A4
Sant Miquel, Baixada - p345 B3
Sant Miquel, Plaça - p345 B3
Sant Miquel, Plaçeta - p338 D3
Sant Pau, C. - p342 C6/ p345 A3
Sant Pere, C. - p344 C2
Sant Pere, Plaça - p343 E6/p344 C2
Sant Pere Màrtir, C. - p338 D3
Sant Pere Més Alt, C. - p342 D5/p344 C2
Sant Pere Més Baix, C. - p342 D6/p344 B2-C2
Sant Pere Mitjà, C. - p342 D6/p344 C2
Sant Rafael, C. - p342 C6
Sant Ramon, C. - p342 C6
Sant Roc, C. - p341 A5
Sant Salvador, C. - p339 E2
Sant Sever, C. - p345 B3
Sant Vicenç, C. - p342 C5
Sant Vicenç de Sarrià, Plaça - p337 B1
Santa Amèlia, C. - p337 A2

Santa Anna, C. - p342 D5/ p344 B2
Santa Carolina, C. - p339 F3
Santa Caterina, C. - p345 A4
Santa Caterina, Plaça - p338 C3
Santa Elena, C. - p342 C6
Santa Eugenia, C. - p338 D3
Santa Eulàlia, C. - p339 E4
Santa Eulàlia, Baixada - p345 B3
Santa Fe de Nou Mèxic - p337 B2
Santa Llúcia, C. - p345 B3
Santa Madrona, C. - p342 C6
Santa Madrona, Passeig - p341 A6
Santa Maria, C. - p345 C3
Santa Maria, Plaça - p345 C3
Santa Mònica, C. - p345 A4
Santa Perpètua, C. - p338 D2
Santa Teresa, C. - p338 D4
Santaló, C. - p338 C2-3
Santjoanistes, C - p338 D2
Sants, C. - p341 A4
Santuari de Sant Josep de la Muntanya, Avda - p339 E2
Saragossa, C. - p338 D2
Sardana, Plaça - p341 B7
Sardenya, C. - p339-343 F3-6
Sarrià, Avda - p337 B2-3
Sarrià, Plaça - p337 B1
Seca, C. - p345 C4
Secretari Coloma, C. - p339 E3
Semoleres, C. - p345 C3
Sèneca, C. - p338 D3
Septimania, C. - p338 D2
Sepúlveda, C. - p341-342 B5-C5
Sèquia, C. - p344 C2
Serra Xic, C. - p344 C2
Serra, C. - p345 B4
Sert, Passatge - p344 C2
Seu, Plaça de la - p344 B2
Sicília, C. - p339-343 E3-5
Sidé, C. - p345 C3
Sils, C. - p345 A4
Simó Oller, C. - p345 B4
Siracusa, C. - p338 D3
Sitges, C. - p344 A2
Sol, Plaça - p338 D3
Sombrerers, C. - p345 C3
Sor Eulalia d'Anzizu, C. - p337 A1
Sortidor, Plaça - p341 B6
Sostres, C. - p339 E2
Sota Muralla, Passeig - p345 B4
Sots-tinent Navarro, C. - p345 B3

Tallers, C. - p342 C5-D5/ p344 A1
Tamarit, C. - p341 B5
Tànger, C. - p343 F5
Tantarantana, C. - p345 C3
Tàpies, C. - p342 C6
Tapineria, C. - p345 B3
Tapioles, C. - p341 B6
Taquígraf Garriga - p337 A3-B3
Taquígraf Martí, C. - p337 A3
Taquígraf Serra, C. - p337 B3
Tarongers, C. dels - p341 B6
Tarongeta, C. - p345 B3
Tarragona, C. - p341 B5
Tarròs, C. - p345 C3
Tavern, C. - p338 C2-3
Taxdirt, C. - p339 E3
Teatre, Plaça de - p345 A4
Tècnica, Avda - p341 A6
Templers, C. - p345 B3
Tenerife, C. - p339 F2
Tenor Masini, C. - p337 A3

Terol, C. - p338 D3
Tetuan, Plaça - p343 E5
Tigre, C. - p342 C5
Til.lers, Passeig - p337 A2
Tinent Coronel Valenzuela, - p337 A1-2
Tiradors, C. - p345 C3
Tomàs Mieres, C. - p344 B2
Tordera, C. - p338 D3
Torre, Plaça - p338 D2
Torrent d'en Vidalet, C. - p339 E3
Torrent de l'Olla, C. - p338 D2-3
Torrent de les Flors - p339 E3
Torres i Amat - p344 A1
Torres, C. - p338 D3
Torrijos, C. - p339 E3
Tous, C. - p339 F3
Trafalgar, C. - p342-3 D5-E5/ p344 C1-2
Traginers, Plaça - p342 D6/p345 B3
Trajà, C. - p341 A5
Trelawny, C. - p343 E7
Tres Pins, Cami - p341 A6
Tres Torres, C. - p337 B2
Trilla, Plaça - p338 D3
Trinitat, C. - p345 A3
Trinquet, C. - p337 A1
Tuset, C. - p338 C3

Unió, C. - p342 C6/ p345 A3
Urquinaona, Plaça - p344 B1

València, C. - p341-339 B4-F4
Valldonzella, C. - p342 C5/ p344 A1
Valldoreix, C. - p339 E2
Vallespir, C. - p337 A3-4
Vallhonrat, C. - p341 B5
Vallirana, C. - p338 D2
Vallmayor, C. - p338 C2
Valseca, C. - p339 F2
Veguer, C. - p345 B3
Ventura Gassol, Plaça - p338 D2
Verdaguer i Callís, C. - p344 B2
Verdi, C. - p339 D3-E2
Vergós, C. - p337 B2
Verònica, Plaça - p345 B3
Vic, C. - p338 D3
Vicenç Martorell, Plaça - p344 A2
Vico, C. - p338 C2
Victor Balaguer, Plaça - p345 B3
Victòria, C. - p344 C2
Vidre, C. - p345 A3
Vidrieria, C. - p345 C3
Vigatans, C. - p345 B3
Vila de Madrid, Plaça - p344 B2
Vila i Vilà, C. - p342 C6-7
Viladecols, Baixada - p344 B2
Viladomat, C. - p337-341 B3-5
Vilamarí, C. - p341 B4-5
Vilamur, C. - p337 A3
Vilanova, Avda - p343 E5
Vilardell, C. - p341 A4
Villarroel, C. - p338-342 C3-5
Violant d'Hongria, Reina d'Aragó, C. - p337 A3
Viriat, C. - p337 A4
Virreina, Passatge - p344 A2
Virreina, Plaça - p339 E3
Vivers, C. - p341 A6

Wagner, Plaça - p337 B3
Watt, C. - p341 A4
Wellington, C. - p343 E6

Xuclà, C. - p342 D5/ p344 A2

Zamora, C. - p343 F6

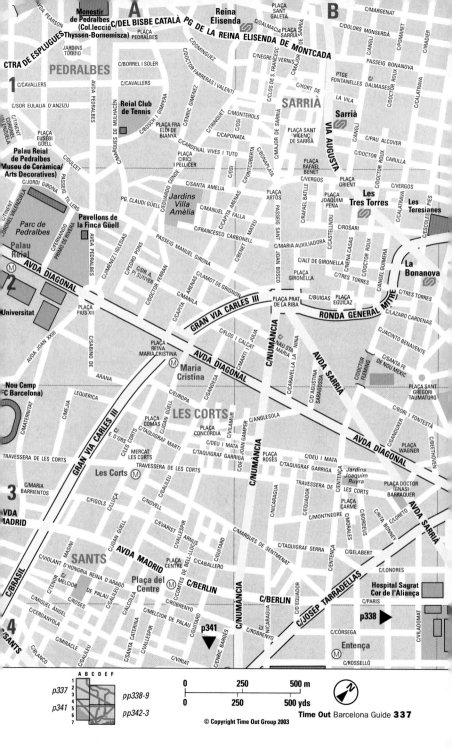

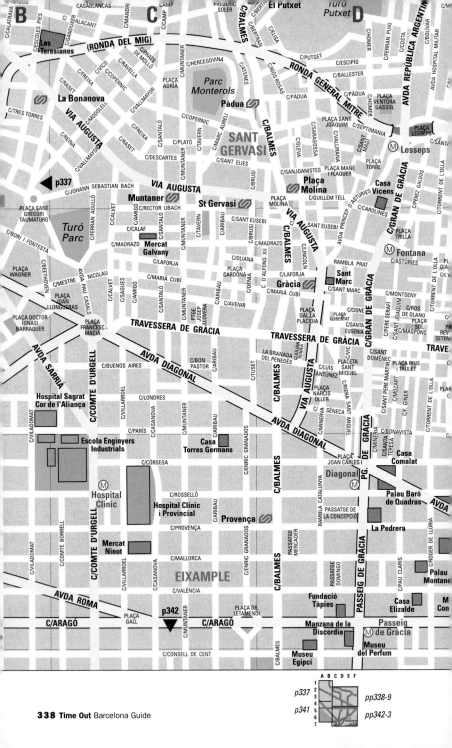

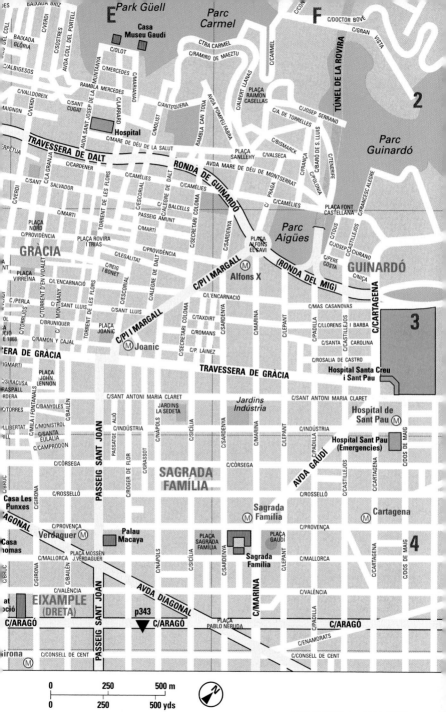

© Copyright Time Out Group 2003

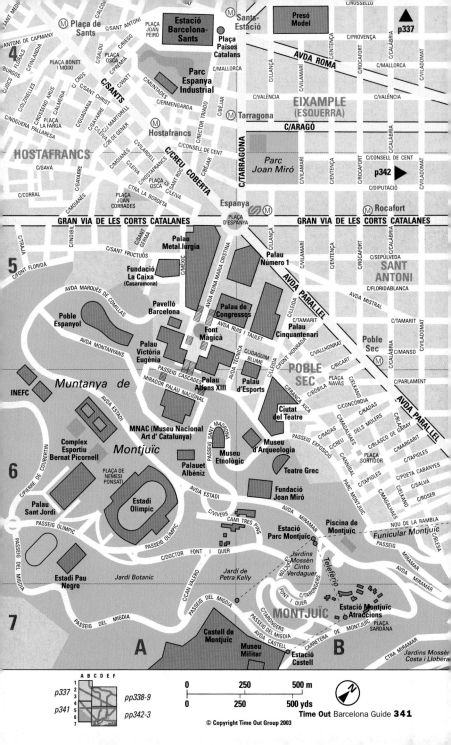

© Copyright Time Out Group 2003

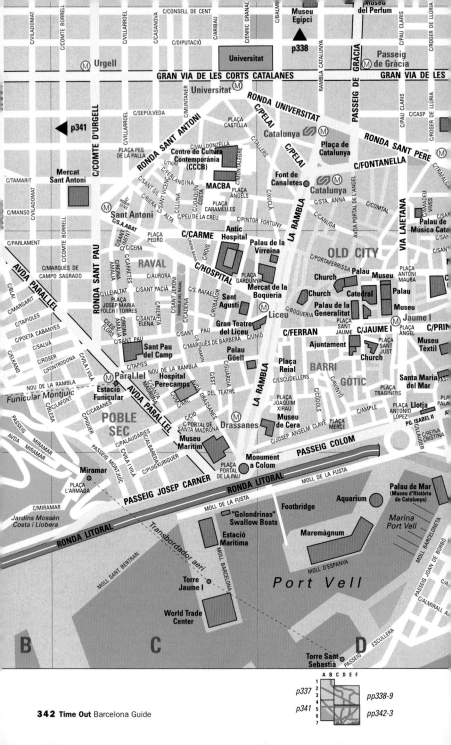

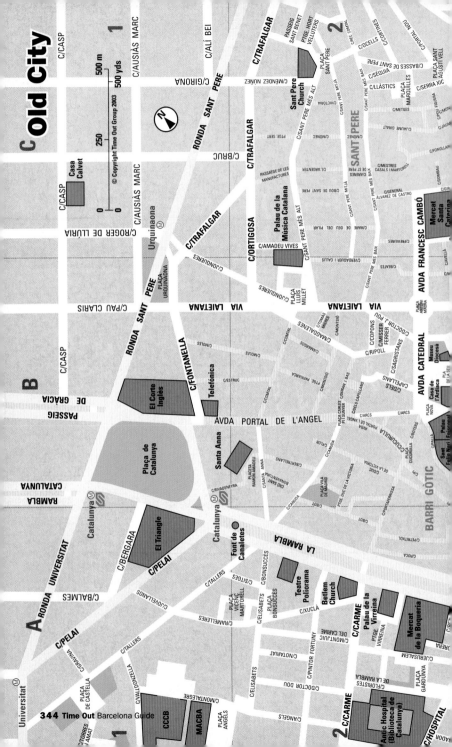

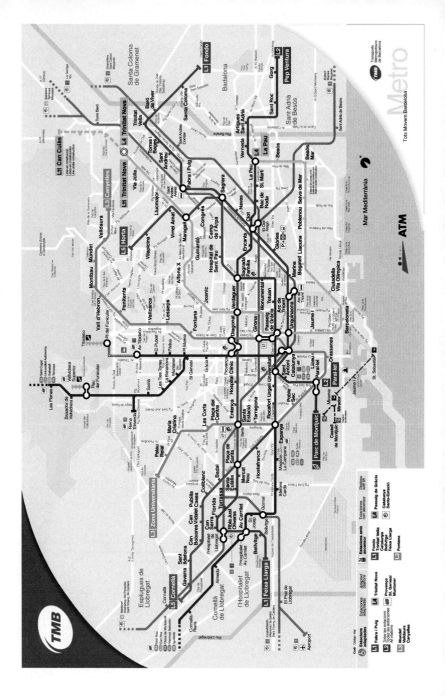

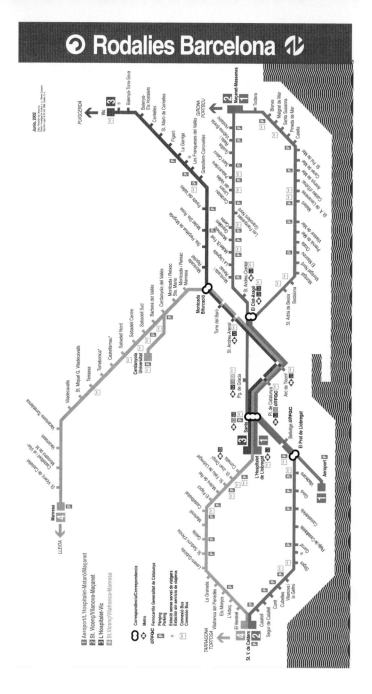

⊙ Rodalies Barcelona ⚞

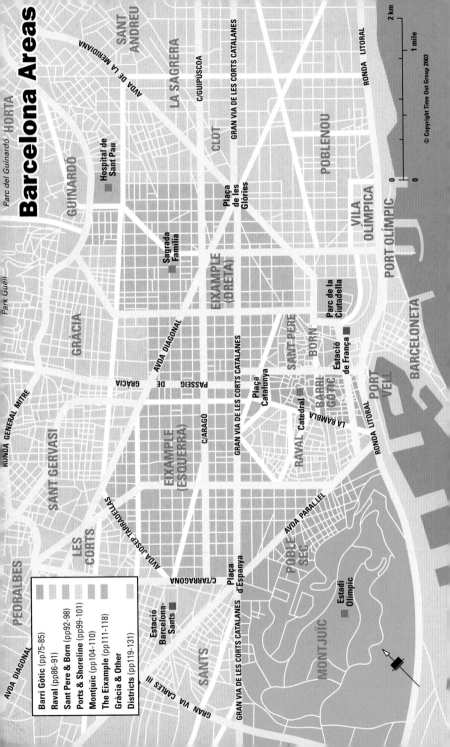